Archaeological Fantasies

MW00534452

Did aliens build the pyramids? Do all the world's civilizations owe a debt of gratitude to a single supercivilization in ancient times? Was Egypt the home of magicians? Is there a fantastic body of ancient wisdom awaiting discovery, which will help to solve the world's problems? These and other scenarios are thrown up by purveyors of what is often dubbed "alternative," "fringe," or "popular" archaeology and ancient history. In reality, such work is properly called pseudoarchaeology, since it is a muddled imitation of the real thing.

In this collection of stimulating and engaging essays, a diverse group of scholars, scientists, and writers consider the phenomenon of pseudoarchaeology from a variety of perspectives. They contemplate what differentiates it from real archaeology; its defining characteristics; the reasons for its popular appeal and how television documentaries contribute to its popularity; how nationalist agendas can warp genuine archaeology into a pseudo-version; and the links between pseudoarchaeology and other brands of false history and pseudoscience. Case studies include surveys of esoteric Egypt and the supposedly mystical Maya, Nazi pseudoarchaeology, and ancient pseudohistory in modern India.

Garrett G. Fagan is Associate Professor of Classics and Ancient Mediterranean Studies and History at The Pennsylvania State University.

Archaeological Fantasies

How pseudoarchaeology misrepresents
the past and misleads the public

Edited by Garrett G. Fagan

Routledge
Taylor & Francis Group

LONDON AND NEW YORK

First published 2006
by Routledge
2 Park Square, Milton Park, Abingdon, Oxon, OX14 4RN

Simultaneously published in the USA and Canada
by Routledge
270 Madison Ave, New York, NY 10016

Routledge is an imprint of the Taylor & Francis Group

© 2006 Garrett G. Fagan for selection and editorial matter.
Individual contributors © for their contributions.

Typeset in Garamond
by Taylor & Francis Books
Printed and bound by CPI Group (UK) Ltd,
Croydon, CR0 4YY

British Library Cataloguing-in-Publication Data
A catalogue record for this book is available from the British Library.

Library of Congress Cataloging-in-Publication Data
Fagan, Garrett G., 1963–
    Archaeological Fantasies : how pseudoarchaeology misrepresents
the past and misleads the public / Garrett G. Fagan.
        p. cm.
    Includes bibliographical references and index.
    ISBN 0-415-30593-4 (pbk. : alk. paper) -- ISBN 0-415-30592-6
(hardback : alk. paper)
1. Pseudoarchaeology. I. Title.
    CC175.F345 2005
    930' .01--dc22

ISBN10: 0-415-30593-4 ISBN13: 978-0-415-30593-8 (pbk)
ISBN10: 0-415-30592-6 ISBN13: 978-0-415-30592-1 (hbk)

Taylor & Francis Group is the Academic Division of T&F Informa plc.

Contents

List of illustrations

Tables

Contributors

Bettina Arnold is Associate Professor of Anthropology and co-director of the Center for Celtic Studies at the University of Wisconsin-Milwaukee. Her research focuses on pre-Roman Iron Age Europe, mortuary ritual and gender in the context of a long-term investigation of the mortuary and social landscapes associated with the early Iron Age Heuneburg hill fort in southwest Germany (see *http://www.uwm.edu/~barnold/arch/*). An additional research focus involves the history of archaeology, especially the symbiosis between archaeology and politics and the role played by archaeological research in the construction of nationalist narratives.

Garrett G. Fagan is Associate Professor of Classics and Ancient Mediterranean Studies and History at Penn State University. He was educated at Trinity College, Dublin, and McMaster University, Canada. His main research interest lies in Roman history, on which he has published a book – *Bathing in Public in the Roman World* (1999) – and numerous scholarly articles. He became interested in the phenomenon of pseudoarchaeology in 1999 and has published articles, organized conference panels, and taught undergraduate courses on the topic.

Kenneth L. Feder is Professor of Anthropology at Central Connecticut State University. He is the founder and director of the Farmington River Archaeological Project and has conducted several major excavations in north-central Connecticut. Feder is a fellow of the Committee for the Scientific Investigation of Claims of the Paranormal (CSICOP) and has contributed a number of articles on "alternative archaeology" to the *Skeptical Inquirer*. Feder is the author of several books, including: *A Village of Outcasts: Historical Archaeology and Documentary Research at the Lighthouse Site* (1994); *Frauds, Myths, and Mysteries: Science and Pseudoscience in Archaeology* (4th edn, 2002); and *The Past in Perspective: An Introduction to Human Prehistory* (3rd edn, 2004).

Nic Flemming studied natural sciences at Cambridge. In 1958, he mapped a submerged Greek city off the coast of Libya and has been using coastal and submarine archaeological data ever since to measure changes in sea level over the last 20,000 years. This work requires the continuous application of analysis to separate archaeological artefacts from geological features. The author has worked extensively in organizations to promote the development of new marine technology and the creation of new techniques for operational ocean forecasting, and he has served on many committees and panels of UN agencies. He has authored or co-authored dozens of articles in major scientific journals (including *Nature*), and his monographs include *Cities in the Sea* (1971) and *Scientific Diving: A General Code of Practice* (2nd edn, 1996).

Christopher Hale is a television producer and writer educated at Sussex University and the Slade School of Fine Art in London. In 1999, he made "Atlantis Reborn" for the BBC's science series *Horizon*, which challenged the ideas of "alternative" writers like Graham Hancock. Prior to this, he had made numerous documentaries, such as "Search for the Sons of Abraham" and "Before Babel." He published a non-fiction book on pseudo-history in 2003, *Himmler's Crusade* (Bantam), an account of the SS-sponsored German Tibet expedition, 1938–39.

Paul Jordan read archaeology and anthropology at Cambridge. He has researched, directed, and produced archaeological and historical documentaries for the BBC and commercial television in Britain for over 25 years, including a series on Egypt and biblical archaeology. He began writing books in the 1970s and has several in print, including the recent *Riddles of the Sphinx* (1998), *Early Man* (1999), *Neanderthal* (2000), and *The Atlantis Syndrome* (2001).

Peter Kosso is Professor of Philosophy at Northern Arizona University. His research interests lie in the fields of philosophy of science and epistemology. He is the author of *Observability and Observation in Physical Science* (1989); *Reading the Book of Nature* (1992); *Appearance and Reality: An Introduction to the Philosophy of Physics* (1997); and *Knowing the Past: Philosophical Issues of History and Archaeology* (2001).

Mary R. Lefkowitz is Andrew W. Mellon Professor in the Humanities at Wellesley College and author of *Not Out of Africa: How Afrocentrism Became an Excuse to Teach Myth as History* (1996), which discusses the origins and aims of the theory that Greek philosophy and culture derived from ancient Egypt. Her articles about the *Black Athena* controversy have appeared in *The New Republic* and *The Times Literary Supplement*, and she is co-editor (with Guy MacLean Rogers) of *Black Athena Revisited* (1996).

Norman Levitt is Professor of Mathematics at Rutgers University. Educated at Harvard and Princeton, his professional interests lie in the fields of geometric topology and related questions in algebraic topology. He is also very interested in anti-science and irrationality in the modern age and has published several books and edited volumes on the topic, including (with P.R. Gross) *Higher Superstition: The Academic Left and Its Quarrels with Science* (1994); (edited with P.R. Gross and M.W. Lewis) *The*

Flight from Science and Reason (1997); and *Prometheus Bedeviled: Science and the Contradictions of Contemporary Culture* (1999).

Katherine Reece is the owner and moderator of the website *In the Hall of Ma'at*. Now a happily retired accountant, Ms. Reece is fulfilling a life's ambition by studying archaeology.

Colin Renfrew is Disney Professor of Archaeology at Cambridge University and one of the leading prehistoric archaeologists in the world. His published output over more than three decades has been tremendous; his major books include *The Emergence of Civilisation: The Cyclades and the Aegean in the Third Millennium* BC (1972); *Before Civilisation: The Radiocarbon Revolution and Prehistoric Europe* (1973); *Archaeology and Language: The Puzzle of the Indo-European Origins* (1987); (with P. Bahn) *Archaeology: Theories, Methods and Practice* (3rd edn, 2000); and *Loot, Legitimacy and Ownership* (2000).

Alan D. Sokal is Professor of Physics at New York University. His main research interests are in statistical mechanics and quantum field theory. He is co-author (with Roberto Fernández and Jürg Fröhlich) of *Random Walks, Critical Phenomena, and Triviality in Quantum Field Theory* (1992) and co-author (with Jean Bricmont) of *Fashionable Nonsense: Postmodern Intellectuals' Abuse of Science* (1998).

David Webster is Professor of Anthropology at Penn State University. He has spent many field seasons in Mexico, Honduras, and Guatemala at major Classic Maya centers such as Becán, Copán, Piedras Negras, and Tikal. Webster's main interests are the evolution of complex societies, ancient warfare, Mesoamerican urbanism, and settlement and household archaeology. Aside from numerous articles in scholarly journals, his major recent books include (with Anncorinne Freter and Nancy Gonlin) *Copan: The Rise and Fall of a Classic Maya Kingdom* (2000); and *The Fall of the Ancient Maya* (2002).

Michael Witzel is Wales Professor of Sanskrit at Harvard University and was educated at Tübingen and Erlangen University in Germany. Before coming to Harvard, he taught at Tübingen and the University of Leiden, and he was director of the Nepal German Manuscript Preservation Project and Nepal Research Centre, Kathmandu (1972–77). Aside from dozens of scholarly articles, his major books include *On Magical Thought in the Veda* (1979); *Early Sources for South Asian Substrate Languages* (1999); *Das alte Indien: Von den Anfaengen bis zum 6. Jahrhundert* (2002); and *The Ancient Indo-Aryans: The Textual and Linguistic Evidence* (forthcoming).

Foreword

Colin Renfrew

Archaeology is the means by which we learn about the origins and development of humankind. For the vast period before the existence of written records, it is our *only* means of learning about our shared origins. It is thus of enormous importance for the understanding of what we are as human beings, of where we came from, and of our place in the modern world. It is a matter of deep concern that in the twenty-first century, as much as in the twentieth (or indeed the nineteenth), archaeology is being misused and its findings misrepresented, on the one hand by the forces of bigotry and on the other by those of crass commercialism.

Archaeological Fantasies is a highly important book in that it illustrates graphically both those pernicious processes and seeks to analyse the roots of this wanton abuse of our shared cultural heritage. It indicates with disquieting clarity that "pseudoarchaeology" – the misrepresentation of the past misusing the material evidence of that past – is not merely the pastime of cranks and nerds preoccupied with UFOs and crop circles. It remains a weapon of misrepresentation used by religious and ethnic fundamentalists for unworthy political ends in a manner that one would hope had perished with the downfall of the Nazis at the end of the Second World War. But in the supposedly sophisticated Western world of today it is inflicted upon an ill-informed public by disturbingly corrupt media, particularly by the intellectually limited world of a television preoccupied by rating wars, which sacrifices the opportunity of saying something valid and informative about our past for short-term financial gain.

The nub of the problem is firmly grasped in N.C. Flemming's clear contribution, "The attraction of non-rational archaeological hypotheses," in which he stresses that "Pseudoarchaeology, like any pseudoscience, is always aimed at the non-expert and the non-professional interested in the discipline concerned." Various polemical tricks make this possible. One is to emphasize that the academic world is self-regarding, set in its ways and resistant to radical new ideas – all of which is often true! Often, it takes quite a long time for new ideas to break in and overcome that resistance and so achieve what philosopher of science Thomas Kuhn has termed a "paradigm shift." Indeed, I would regard the fairly recent rejection of "The mystique of the ancient Maya," as well described here by David Webster, as a shift of that kind within the field of serious scholarship rather than a rejection of pseudoarchaeology. It took a while for the preconceptions of one generation of archaeologists, including such then well-respected specialists as the late Eric Thompson, to be overcome by the new ideas of a younger generation, to which David Webster himself belongs. But that does not, I think, mean that the older generation was practising pseudoarchaeology as defined by Flemming. They were simply slow to see the force of the new interpretations of the data. And the decipherment of the Maya glyphs has now convincingly proved that the older generation was wrong. That is not unusual in science, or indeed in archaeology (as the revolutionary effect of the radiocarbon-dating revolution on our understanding of prehistoric Europe clearly shows). But it does not make the conclusions of that older generation pseudoscience.

Similarly, academic frauds like the celebrated Piltdown hoax are not really pseudoscience in this sense, precisely because they are intended to fool the experts. They are fakes, and thus indubitably false, but they are not part of the same genre. The recent Kamitakamori scandal in Japan, where a hitherto distinguished and well-respected scholar, Shinichi Fujimura, was found salting a palaeolithic site with his own choice of artefacts, is a recent case in point.[1] Pseudoarchaeology may well at times involve or give recognition to frauds and fakes, but it is not really defined by the use of deliberate fraud, even if intellectual dishonesty is common enough. Sometimes, as in the case of some dowsers or ley-line hunters, self-delusion is quite sufficient. (Ley-line hunters are enthusiasts, particularly in Britain, who seek to show that prehistoric monuments, church towers, and even more recent structures are situated along alignments that have deep antiquity and still deeper, if obscure, meaning.)

Bettina Arnold, in her powerful contribution "Pseudoarchaeology and nationalism: essentializing difference," illustrates how the National Socialists in Germany, before and during the Second World War, misused archaeological evidence to build up a Nazi myth of national identity. Disquietingly, she is able to indicate some similar practices in the contemporary "Celtic" revival and to recognize them in the way the film *Braveheart* has been used by politicians of the Scottish National Party for nationalist and ultimately chauvinist ends. Interestingly, she is able to suggest that the slipshod and misleading view of the discipline of archaeology purveyed in Steven Spielberg's *Indiana Jones* trilogy lends credence to the view that archaeologists are motivated by the greed of the looter or by the passion of the nationalist seeking potent symbolic evidence (e.g. the Holy Grail, the Ark of the Covenant) to support some chauvinist myth. As she well puts it:

> The *Indiana Jones* trilogy exploits the profession of archaeology and German National Socialism with equal enthusiasm and with a disregard for accuracy or consequences. None of this would matter much if the average citizen were in a position to distinguish between Hollywood

constructions and archaeological evidence and practice, or if archaeologists were better at communicating with the public. Unfortunately this dual failure has real life consequences, as the recent scandalous handling of the looting of the Baghdad Museum in the aftermath of the US military takeover of that city has clearly shown.

I find most disquieting of all the powerful exposé by Michael Witzel of some current trends in Indian nationalism in "Rama's realm: Indocentric rewriting of early South Asian archaeology and history." The pressure to be oldest is commonly felt even in quite respectable academic archaeology – claims of the oldest city, or the oldest writing, or the oldest metallurgy are relatively common. But this turns into something much more sinister when it is used in an overt attempt to reshape national identity, sometimes for explicit political ends. What is even more disquieting is that among the straight pseudoarchaeologists, often amateurs who put together such a bricolage of misrepresentations to fabricate their synthesis, there are also serious professional scholars. This is the dangerous dividing line where pseudoarchaeology, in the sense set out here by Flemming and Fagan, becomes a nationalist doctrine, as happened in Nazi Germany, sweeping up even serious scholars and carrying them along. Witzel clearly shows how this is happening in some parts of the academic community in contemporary India. That this is no trivial matter is seen in the archaeological arguments that have surrounded the destruction in 1992 of the mosque at Ayodhya, in Uttar Pradesh, by fundamentalists (Renfrew and Bahn 2000: 537). I was personally present at the World Archaeological Conference in New Delhi in 1994, where pressure was exerted by one Indian faction to prevent any discussion of that discreditable episode and where the meetings ended in fisticuffs.

The bigotry of nationalism and of fundamentalism is one powerful force that still encourages pseudoarchaeology. Whether or not the same can be said of postmodernism, as Alan D. Sokal argues here in his powerful paper "Pseudoscience and postmodernism: antagonists or fellow travelers" is, I think, open to question. I am no admirer of the relativist stance of *soi-disant* "post-processual" archaeology myself. Indeed, I laid down the challenge to "post-processualists" to indicate, given their relativist position, how they would reject the pseudoarchaeological fantasies of ley-line hunters (Renfrew 1989), a challenge that they have not taken up. At the same time, however, the leading interpretative archaeologists, however soft their epistemology, have not, so far as I know, dabbled in pseudoarchaeology. Neither Michael Shanks nor Chris Tilley, to name two "post-processual" polemicists, is an advocate of lost Atlantis; nor is either Ian Hodder or Julian Thomas an enthusiast for the vanished continent of Mu. Sokal does not offer specifically archaeological cases in his paper: many of his examples come from nursing, where they may well be relevant. So that, although I am sceptical of the doctrine of "multi-vocality" as advanced by Hodder, and am more impatient than he is of the Mother Goddess devotees who make the pilgrimage to his excavations at

Çatalhöyük, I would not (so far) accuse him of purveying pseudoarchaeology. His work is indeed expounded at an expert level and is thus certainly not pseudoscience as defined by Flemming and Fagan.

Where I do take umbrage is at those popularizers who betray their craft. Flemming's dictum, that pseudoscience is aimed at the non-expert, is not a criticism of popularization, which is by definition aimed at the non-expert. But popularization sets out to convey and make clear and understandable what is indeed already a shared understanding among experts. Good popularization does not lack expertise. What does seem stranger is that books by fantasists like Erich von Däniken and Graham Hancock, dealing with flying saucers and lost continents and of evidently dubious content, sell fast to the general public, even though they are reviewed and rejected by competent specialists. What I find even more extraordinary is that television companies will make what they present as serious documentaries dealing with such pernicious stuff. I do not for a moment believe that the commissioning editors of such companies are taken in by such pseudoarchaeology. They know that it lacks serious content. I can only conclude that the decision to put on seemingly serious programmes with so little real substance is a cynically commercial one, calculatingly seeking high audience ratings (and hence the interest of advertisers) while quite clearly aware that what they are offering is little more than fiction disguised as science.

The contribution here by Christopher Hale, "The Atlantean box," is a very illuminating examination of the painful dilemma in which a serious television director finds himself when working with a controller of programmes with fewer ethical scruples than his own. Why is it that archaeology so often falls victim to the approach of populist pseudoscience? The case of British television in recent years is a particularly painful one. Indeed, there are still successful and popular programmes that deal entertainingly and informatively with recent discoveries, such as the British Broadcasting Corporation's *Timewatch*, or *Time Team*, from Independent Television's Channel 4. But the consistently high standards set in earlier years by a series such as *Chronicle* have been undermined with presentations like the three-part series *Underworld: Flooded Kingdoms of the Ice Age*, shown in the UK on Channel 4 and in the United States on The Learning Channel. This was itself a "sequel" to the previous and equally ill-conceived series *Quest for the Lost Civilisation*, both made by journalist Graham Hancock. Hale and other authors here adequately show up Hancock's disregard for the key facts and his lack of self-criticism. While it is possible that writers like von Däniken and Hancock may actually believe what they write – although I myself suspect, in the words of Flemming "that they are motivated by money and fame to say things that they know are not true" – it is inconceivable that a commissioning editor of a TV channel could contemplate them without suspicion. It is hardly conceivable that the commissioning editor would fail to take some competent advice before committing the channel to the production of such stuff. To commission them without advice would be irresponsible.

What is even more distressing is the episode, with which Hale himself was involved, of the attempt by the highly respected BBC science series *Horizon* to deal with the pseudoarchaeology offered, in this case, by Channel 4 in the Hancock series *Quest for the Lost Civilisation*. He shows graphically how, under the commercial pressure of a deal with the US Discovery Channel, "*Horizon* now had to be a narrative series. Stories were everything. Producers were required to absorb the lessons of Hollywood, and specifically to learn the arcane mysteries of 'three-act structures.'" Hale's paper is the story of how this distinguished BBC series lost its integrity and of how the legitimate aim of debunking the pseudoscience of Hancock's three-part series on Channel 4 sold out to an ethic not far removed from that of the entertainment-dressed-as-scholarship that it was seeking to debunk. He tells how the original objectives were sacrificed, and matters became so confused that he and his colleagues suffered the indignity and the irony of appearing before the Broadcasting Standards Commission to face a complaint from Hancock himself! But the painful truth here is that this was a battle between the amateurs, at least as far as archaeology was concerned, between the fantasist and amateur archaeologist Hancock and the filmmaker Hale, apparently operating without serious archaeological guidance.

What deeply angers me about this tale of the encounter between ineptitude and charlatanism is that the real potential and importance of archaeology as the key to an understanding of the human past has been entirely lost. Why should archaeology be treated in this frivolous and self-serving way, which in other scientific fields would result in a torrent of criticism? Human origins, including the origins of civilization, are a serious matter. For it is only from their serious study that we can hope to achieve a proper understanding of what we are – of what we are as human beings, and as what we are as participants in one cultural tradition that may be different from other cultural traditions. How do these differences arise? What is their significance? What do they tell us about the place of humankind in the world and of our own place in humankind? These are the big questions. And the power of archaeology to answer them is obscured as much by the compromises and trivialization of downmarket TV commercialization as it is by the bigotry of religious or nationalist sects who make it their business to destroy the monuments of other faiths and other traditions. Archaeology invites us to look seriously again at our own values. Pseudoarchaeology subverts and distorts any such aspiration.

These are some of the issues that make this such an important book. Attentive readers may find in it several contradictions and points of contention, but they also will find in it a commitment to rational thought and a refreshing optimism that good archaeology is of real importance in the contemporary world in offering us valid insights into the human past.

Note

1. See http://www.umass.edu/wsp/methodology/antiquity/japan/kam.html.

Preface

This book started out as a workshop on pseudoarchaeology held at the 2002 annual meeting of the Archaeological Institute of America. The workshop generated much interesting discussion, and all but one of the original panelists have contributed chapters to this book: myself, Ken Feder, Nic Flemming, and Chris Hale. Only my colleague Don Redford was unable to participate in this book due to other pressing commitments.

I have been involved in dealing with pseudoarchaeology since teaching a course at Penn State in 1999 entitled "Ancient mysteries: fact and fiction about our human past." The idea of the course, offered as a seminar to incoming freshmen, was to teach the students how ancient history was done by scrutinizing how it ought *not* to be done. So we read von Däniken, Plato (on Atlantis), Hancock, etc. and asked the hard questions. Here were a series of proposals about the past. What made them wrong? Indeed, what gave us the right to declare them wrong? What methodological mistakes were these writers making and, by implication, what might a good methodology for investigating antiquity look like? In the course of these investigations, the students learned to think critically, not to accept what they read on the basis of it being in print, appealingly written, or credited to a person with a string of letters after his or her name. They checked the evidence and looked for internal inconsistencies, logical fallacies, and wild leaps of faith.

Toward the end of this course, I was led to confront the pseudoarchaeologists directly on the Internet. It quickly became evident that arguing with them and their more fanatical supporters was pointless. Logic, coherence, consistency, and plausibility almost wholly evaded them (never mind the interpretative complexities thrown up by the ancient data themselves). People who openly admitted to not having read a word written by a trained Egyptologist were pronouncing how academic Egyptology was all wrong, even sinister. In the most ridiculous moment out of many ridiculous moments, one person who could not read Greek offered a mistranslation of a Greek passage pertaining to the pyramids at Giza; when confronted with a correct translation by a trained classicist (one that demolished his point), he declared Greek grammar to be a matter of opinion! Not all the denizens of these sites were as deluded as that non-Hellenist; some even had coherent positions of a sort, but they were consistently founded on ridiculous assumptions or unexamined articles of faith, e.g., that experts could not be trusted because ... they were experts; that engineering can only be done one way; that significant numbers "discovered" in the proportions of ancient monuments must have been put there by the builders; and so on. The focus was nearly always on what was possible, not what was demonstrable or reasonably inferable from the available evidence. Silly scenarios *might* one day be vindicated, if the appropriate evidence showed up. Who was I to say it wouldn't? Time and time again the discussion veered away from specific bones of contention into an analysis of my motives for questioning the claims in the first place.

The whole experience became farcical. After several frustrating months of this, I was led to think more deeply about pseudoarchaeology: What *was* it, exactly? What were its various manifestations? What demarcated pseudoarchaeology from real archaeology? Why did people find palpable nonsense so appealing? What was the relationship of pseudoarchaeology to other brands of fringe thinking? How could it be countered, since reasoned argument clearly had little or no effect on its followers? Hence my proposal of a workshop discussion on the topic for the 2002 AIA meeting, and hence this book.

Many people have contributed, directly or indirectly, to this project and I'd like formally to thank them all here. (My apologies go to any whom I omit due to error.) First, my thanks to the various contributors, most of whom agreed to join this project after the workshop had been staged. It was always my intention that people from a variety of backgrounds should contribute chapters so that a range of perspectives could be offered on this many-sided phenomenon. Thus, along with professional archaeologists or ancient historians such as myself, Mary Lefkowitz, Nic Flemming, Ken Feder, or David Webster, we have an Indologist (Michael Witzel), a philosopher (Peter Kosso), a physicist (Alan D. Sokal), a mathematician (Norm Levitt), two television producers and writers (Paul Jordan and Chris Hale), and a webmaster (Katherine Reece). As icing on this multi-layered cake, Lord Colin Renfrew very kindly agreed to write the foreword.

Given such varied input, this collection of essays is less a rebuttal of specific pseudoarchaeological claims – excellent examples of which are already on the market (see Feder 2002b; Sprague de Camp 1963, 1970; Steibing 1984; Williams 1991) – as it is a phenomenonological contemplation. Furthermore, given the diversity of the contributors' backgrounds, there will be places where emphases or conclusions vary between chapters. I have not edited the content of the chapters to make them conform to some imagined orthodoxy: diversity of opinion is to be welcomed, not suppressed. But all the contributors, from so many backgrounds, share the conviction that pseudoarchaeology (and its allies in the pseudosciences) is a problem to be confronted rather than ignored. If this book convinces others that this is the case and advances our understanding of what pseudoarchaeology is even a little, then it will have served its purpose more than amply.

I owe a deep debt of gratitude to the Alexander von Humboldt Foundation for the generous support during a wonderful year in Cologne, during which much of the final editing of this volume was completed (among other projects). I would like also to thank Richard Stoneman at Routledge, who approached me after the 2002 workshop about doing this volume, as well as Celia Tedd and Matt Gibbons at the Routledge offices for all their help as it progressed. To all those colleagues and friends with whom I have discussed pseudoarchaeology and pseudoscience over the years, I offer my profound thanks. Some of the names that come to mind most readily are (in no particular order) Simon Weber-Brown, Pete Moroney, Matthew Trundle, Matthew Restall, Greg Egighian, Phil Baldi, John Wall, Mikey Brass, Anthony Sakovich, Paul Heinrich, Don Holeman, and Katherine Reece. I also thank my wife Katherine, to whom my own modest efforts in this project are dedicated.

Finally, some thanks must go to the pseudoarchaeologists themselves, without whose futile efforts none of this would be necessary.

Part I

The phenomenon

Introduction

The epistemology of archaeology

Peter Kosso

Knowledge welcomes challenges. If we claim to know something, rather than simply believe it or think it or wish it, we must be willing to confront potentially challenging evidence and alternative ideas. This is not merely a politeness but a prerequisite to the distinction between knowledge and opinion, and it is true for new, hypothetical ideas as well as for well-established, widely believed ideas.

The responsibility for accepting a challenge comes with the right to claim knowledge. But this does not mean that theorizing in science, archaeology, or history is a free-for-all of skepticism where nothing can be known because everything can be challenged. There are definite standards of appropriate challenge and standards for evaluating how well a challenge has been met. We can tell what counts as good evidence and how evidence supports or undermines a theory. And we can assess the relevance between different ideas to see if they are compatible or contradictory, supportive or refuting. In other words, we can tell and we can agree to what extent the appropriate challenges to a theory have been met and hence to what extent we are justified in believing the theory.

The purpose of this introductory chapter is to demonstrate that these standards of justification exist and to clarify what they are. With a focus on archaeology and the use of material evidence to know what happened in the human past, we will see that there are ways to distinguish plausible from implausible theories. Some descriptions of the human past are more likely than others to be accurate. Assessing the likelihood of accuracy is the topic of this chapter.

There are two parts to the chapter. The first is a general account of the epistemology of the human past, that is, an outline of how archaeological knowledge is possible and how it works. This starts with a description of the inherent difficulties in knowing what happened, when, and why. And it continues with a look at how those difficulties can be overcome using material and in some cases textual evidence. The key is an understanding of the criteria of credible, meaningful evidence and of the procedures and standards of acceptability of a theory about the past. The second part of the chapter is a brief application of the epistemology to the specific case of the pyramids at

Giza. Who built the pyramids, when, how, and for what purpose? It is not so much the answers to these questions that are the concern here as it is the reasons for believing the answers. Why is one account of the ancient Egyptian pyramids more justified, more likely to be accurate, than the others? This is the question we will answer.

The epistemology of archaeology

Epistemology is the systematic study of knowledge. The key concern is to distinguish knowledge, on the one hand, from mere belief, opinion, dogma, and wishful thinking, on the other. This distinction is described under the concept of justification, the good reason for believing something to be true. Justification of a belief, the modern rendition of Plato's epistemic requirement of a *logos*, is about meeting the standards of evidence and reason that indicate likelihood of accuracy (Plato *Theaetetus* 201d). Meeting the standards of justification never guarantees the truth, the accuracy of a belief. Humans are not that good at knowing. Justification is not foolproof, and it comes in degrees. Beliefs, descriptive claims about aspects of the world, can be more or less justified. I know, for example, that the table before me has four legs. This is a highly justified claim. I also know that this same table is made of atoms and they in turn are made of quarks and electrons. This claim has some justification (it is not pure guesswork) but less justification than the claim about the number of legs.

The business of epistemology is to show that there is a correlation between being more justified and being more likely to be true. Justification is therefore most useful as a comparative rather than absolute tool. When given a choice between conflicting descriptions of the same thing, the reasonable thing to do is to endorse the more justified.

Justification comes in degrees, but truth does not. A proposition, a descriptive claim about some aspect of the world, is either true or false. This table either has four legs, or it does not. But justification for the claim comes in degrees. In fact, I have more justification for the truth of this claim than you do, since I can see the four legs directly, while you are relying on the good faith of my testimony. Maybe one of the legs broke off years ago, and I have propped that corner up on a stack of books. The amount of justification for a claim will depend on the amount and quality of evidence, and on the compatibility of the claim with other things in one's network of understanding (for example, your general understanding of the concept of a table, the tendency of people like me to salvage broken furniture, and so on).

More justification is better, since it raises the likelihood of accuracy. But it is certainly possible for a well-justified belief to be false. Based on the evidence of dark clouds, the sound of thunder, and the fact of a thunder shower every afternoon for the past week, I am very justified in believing that it is about to rain on me. The belief is justified but false if the storm happens to miss me this time. It is the task of the systematic disciplines, the natural sciences, studies of the past such as history and archaeology, and the like, to refine carefully the content of justification, the evidence and the network of theoretical beliefs, to bring justification into ever closer correlation with truth.

There is no certainty in science, in archaeology, or in life. Any claim that transcends immediate experience or basic logic is at risk of being wrong. You anticipate that first sip of orange juice in the morning, knowing that it will be both tasty and healthy. But even this is to some small degree uncertain, since all your evidence is of previous encounters with orange juice, not this one. It is conceivable, though very unlikely, that something has changed, in orange juice or in your own body, that will affect how your body interacts with the drink. We live with this degree of uncertainty in our daily lives, and we still claim to know that orange juice is safe and good to drink.

The point about uncertainty and knowledge and orange juice is to preempt a common fallacy, which is a fallacy to argue (or assume) that since there is no certainty, there is no reason to believe anything. The most common form of this fallacy is the argument (or assumption) that since no descriptive claim about the world is justified with certainty, then all descriptive claims are alike in the sense that any one is as justified as any other. This often then cascades into an opportunity to endorse one's own wishful thinking or to indulge in imagination or even political expediency. If all ideas are equal, then why not believe mine? But not all ideas are equal. There is more reason to believe some than others, even if none is perfectly justified to the point of certainty. I suppose, for example, that the idea of bacteria causing disease is somewhat uncertain. Few people actually see these things in action destroying cells. But I will have my surgery in sterile conditions rather than in the garage. The degrees of justification are important.

Knowing that we must attend to the degrees of justification of beliefs, we now need to understand what makes a belief more justified, particularly in the case of archaeology.

The challenges to knowledge

Consider the challenges to justifying the everyday knowledge of our present surroundings, for that will put the challenge of archaeology into helpful perspective. What we see, the evidence of the world around us, is a series of episodic images of the surfaces of things, images that change as we move around and change our own perspective. But what we claim to know is a world of enduring, three-dimensional objects that exist independent of us and our way of looking at them. There is an informational gap between the appearance of things and the reality we know, and somehow we manage to cross the gap by using the evidence (the appearances) and our ability to reason.

The situation is similar, although perhaps more challenging, in science. Here the knowledge claims are more ambitious in that they stray further from what is immediately observed. Things like black holes, curved space–time, and the long process of biological evolution are not only unobserved, they are largely unobservable (although evolutionary microbial adaptation is observable). The theoretical descriptions are based on observations and evidence, or it would not be science. But it is important to note that the observations themselves are influenced by theory. Scientific evidence, after all, is neither haphazard nor uninterpreted, and some prior conceptual under-standing of nature will inform decisions about what to observe, which observations are credible, what the observation means, and how what is observed is causally (and hence informationally) linked to what is not observed. Theory is necessary to turn mindless sensations into meaningful evidence. This is a warning against a pure or naive empiricism as a model of scientific method. Observations are not foundational in the sense of being of indu-bitable epistemic authority. Justification does not flow just one way, from evidence to theory. The epistemic relation is reciprocal in that (revisable) theoretical information is used to make the most of observation, which is in turn used to suggest and test theories.

The predicament is the same for knowledge of the human past, where the people and events of interest are unobservable. What we do observe is evidence in textual and physical remains. Each of these forms of evidence has its strengths and its weaknesses. Textual evidence, the currency of history, ranges from something as candid and mundane as a shopping list to more self-conscious and remarkable records such as treaties and historical narra-tives. It has the potential to be explicit and precise, telling us just what people were doing and what was on their minds. But historical evidence is intentional in a way that archaeological evidence is not. Writers in the past could choose what they wanted to disclose and how it should sound. This makes the written record vulnerable to a subjectivity under the influence of the people in the past, people with ideas and values that we might not understand. Material evidence, the stuff of archaeology, is less at risk of this complication, since it is largely unintended. Archaeology often amounts to digging through rubbish and wreckage, what remains of daily life, not because it was chosen for posterity but because certain conditions have left it intact. Thus archaeology can offer a more candid image of the past, but it is generally less clear and less explicit than the textual record. Material evidence requires more interpretation. It usually takes an expert, that is, someone with sufficient background knowledge to call on, to tell us what a particular object is, how old it is, how it was used, and so on. Archaeological finds give up information about the past only if we have some contextual information to add into the interpretative process.

Interpretation of evidence is key in both history and archaeology. What we find, that is, what can be observed, must be described in terms intelli-gible to us. We have to describe the past in our own terms, with our own conceptual categories, so we risk importing some of our own values. This means that we risk imposing ourselves on the past, seeing and describing it as our own world in different circumstances. It presents a challenge to distinguish between discovery and invention, between finding out what really happened and making things up in a way that accommodates our own sensibilities.

The subjective component of using our own concepts and background knowledge to interpret the past is unavoidable. But the goal is to understand the past on its own terms, to get information from the past itself. This is an aspect of what Thomas Kuhn called the "essential tension," the need to impose some old information on evidence in order to get new information out (Kuhn 1977). It is an essential part of the challenge to discovering things about nature or the human past.

It is important to be realistic about the challenges to knowledge in archaeology. We should neither underestimate nor exaggerate them. Evaluating archaeological claims is not as easy as a directive to get some evidence, and if there is none then your claim is false or if there is any at all then your claim is true. It is more challenging, and more complicated, than this. Evidence comes in degrees of indirectness, and hence degrees of authority. Evidence must be interpreted. And we need to understand how evidence meets theory, that is, what it is to confirm or falsify a theory.

But it is not impossible to meet the challenges, to deal with the essential tension, and to use evidence to distinguish the more from the less justified archaeological claims. There are many cases where we can clearly tell that the requirements of justification are being met. The claim that there was a Nazi Holocaust is clearly justified. The claim that there were New World civilizations before the arrival of Europeans is clearly justified. And so on. But then there are cases where we still struggle for justification, for example in determining how long human beings have been in the Americas. A good strategy for epistemology is to examine the successful cases to distill the methods and standards of appraisal at work there, and then apply those to the troublesome cases.

All of this talk about justification as an indication of a match between what we say happened and the facts of what really happened presumes that there are definitive facts. We do not create facts about the past by virtue of producing descriptions, any more than we create events in the present simply by describing them. There are facts about much of what happens in the present, and we have thoughts, motives, and values regarding what happens. To suppose less of people in the past would be a kind of arrogance.

The facts of the past are independent of us. The goal is to create descriptions that match, and to be able to tell when we have got one that matches. Different situations differ in degree of difficulty, from the account of basic physical events to the understanding of motives and values. The degree of difficulty changes from case to case, but the basic method of justification remains the same. It is that basic method, the way that archaeology can assess the credibility of claims about the past, that we turn to next.

Meeting the challenges

Evidence is the key. Evidence is what separates fiction from non-fiction, make-believe from theory. But the relation between evidence and theory is rich and complex, and to understand method in archaeology we need to know about both the nature of evidence and its use.

Archaeological evidence is not foundational in the sense of being self-sufficient in information or credibility. Evidence itself must be justified and interpreted. Consider the most basic kinds of observations in archaeology, things like potsherds, worked stone, and wall foundations. Even these descriptions, using these terms, rely on the expertise of archaeologists, and this imports their background knowledge into the interpretative process. An expert sees a sherd rather than a lump of ceramic, or sees the stone as worked rather than naturally broken. To see these objects as evidence of activities in the past requires a context, including claims about activities in the past. And these contextual claims, the background knowledge, must be supported by evidence, which must be interpreted and justified with the help of some background knowledge. There is no end to it, no foundation. The relation between evidence and theory is incorrigibly one of reciprocity, and the structure of justification is one of coherence.

Even information as basic as dating an artefact involves this coherence structure. In some cases, such as radiometric dating and dendrochronology, the background knowledge is supplied by the physical sciences. These highlight the epistemic value in having an independent source of support for the evidence. In cases of historical archaeology, dating of the physical remains can sometimes be helped by association with textual evidence. And in still other archaeological cases, dating of the evidence is by comparison with other objects, comparanda, that have been otherwise dated. Meaningful comparisons depend on classifications of types of artefact into identifiable categories, and this is done using terms and concepts based on current theories. In all these ways, dating archaeological evidence is done under the influence of some theoretical background that is itself continually reassessed as new evidence is found in new contexts.

Describing the evidence for what it is is similarly influenced. Labeling something as an amphora fragment, for example, rather than a lump of hard, powdery red stuff, requires some background knowledge, some expertise. This particular amphora fragment might be used as evidence for a theory about trade or about agriculture, but first we need to know the basics of what an amphora looks like and even something about the deposition and preservation of this one. This supporting information, which links the fragment in hand to the object of interest, is what Lewis Binford calls the "middle-range theory" (Binford 1977: 7). It is the information that traces the causal chain from, in this case, the amphora and its use in the past to the sherd and its recovery in the present.

Here is an example of this important part of archaeological method, this middle-range theory. Survey archaeologists in Greece interpret a concentration of potsherds as evidence of a site of human activity, but what can be said of a tenuous but fairly uniform scatter of sherds found in areas between these sites? With the middle-range understanding that ancient Greeks often mixed broken pottery in with the manure from domestic animals and then spread the manure as fertilizer on cultivated land, the off-site sherds become evidence of cultivation. And knowing how much land was under cultivation then functions as evidence for claims about the socio-economic situation of ancient Greece. None of this is certain, and the middle-range analysis is much more complex than simply sherds mean cultivation. But it is a good case of using theory to enrich the informational content of data, and this is characteristic of the empirical base of archaeology.

An important constraint on middle-range theories is independence. They should be justified on independent grounds, by appeal to evidence other than the evidence to which they give meaning and credibility. The former evidence will rely on other middle-range theories, indicating that the essence of justification is broad coherence between ideas, including theoretical descriptions of aspects of the past and more immediate descriptions of objects found in the present. Justification is not an isolated relation between a theory and its evidence. Nor is it unidirectional, from evidence to theory. Justification goes both ways; a theory gains justification from evidence and, typically, will also be used to help to justify some other evidence. And this usefulness, success as a middle-range theory, contributes to the justification of a theory, since it enhances the overall coherence of our network of beliefs about the past. Justification is a holistic phenomenon.

All of this is also true in the physical sciences. Observation is not evidence without some theoretical support. In physics, for example, the sketchy tracks through a particle detector are not evidence for or against any theory unless they can be identified as tracks of this or that particular particle, and this requires a theoretical understanding of how the detector works and how the tracks are formed. And those theories, drawn from chemistry and electrodynamics, are supported by their own independent evidence. And that evidence is influenced by theoretical background knowledge, and so on. This networking is the basic structure of scientific method, and it is coherence in the network that is its justification.

The important point about archaeology is this: descriptive claims about the past must be supported by evidence, but the evidence is always indirect to some extent. It is both physically and informationally removed from the activities of interest. So what we do observe, the immediate data, serve as evidence only with some theoretical support to make the link to the past.

To say that a theory is supported by some particular evidence is to say that the theory explains or predicts the evidence. The evidence is what one would expect to find if what the theory says happened actually happened. Successfully explaining or predicting some evidence is by no means certain proof that the theory is true, since there are always alternative explanations for what is observed and always alternative theories that make the same predictions. A false theory can make true predictions. After all, the tooth-fairy theory fully explains the appearance of the nickel the last time you lost a tooth and will successfully predict the next nickel with the next tooth. Furthermore, predicting some evidence that does not appear is not certain disproof of a theory. A true theory can make a false prediction. This is largely because of the complexity in interpreting the evidence and the potential ambiguity in determining what any particular observation means. The middle-range theories involved could be wrong. If evidence conflicts with theory, perhaps the theory is true but the evidence is misunderstood.

Evidence, either for or against a theory, is never decisive. Even outright lack of evidence is not in itself a conclusive reason to reject a theory when there is good reason for the expected evidence to be missing. In archaeology, evidence can be lost to looting, natural degradation or displacement, or other confounding factors. Evidence is still necessary, and a theory with a record of failed predictions and unexplained missing evidence is a failure. But a single anomaly, in the sense of missing or contrary evidence, is usually not in itself reason to reject a theory. The exception to this is where there is no plausible explanation for why the evidence is missing. A theory describing a huge ancient city of stone buildings predicts literally tons of sturdy and stationary debris. If they are not to be found, the theory is not to be believed. A civilization that lasts for thousands of years with the techno-logical wherewithal to construct huge monuments of stone will not simply disappear without a trace. Such a theory, as we will encounter in an alterna-tive to the accepted account of the pyramids at Giza, lacks justification entirely.

Again, the situation is similar to the one in the physical sciences. Evidence, taken one at a time, neither confirms nor disconfirms a theory. Here is a quick example. The spectrum of electromagnetic radiation emitted by the Sun is good evidence for the theory that the source of the Sun's energy is nuclear fusion taking place at its core. The fusion would explain the details of the spectrum. But this evidence is not decisive, and it is important to know that for a long time there was some important missing evidence as well. The theory predicts the production of particles called neutrinos and their detection here on Earth, but these neutrinos were not detected, despite decades of careful attempts (Bahcall 1990). This missing evidence, even though its absence was not explained, did not force the abandonment of the fusion theory. Nor should it have, since contrary or missing evidence is ambiguous as to which of the many theories involved is inaccurate. Revised middle-range theories and new techniques of detection have finally revealed the predicted neutrinos (Schwarzschild 2002).

The point about the role of evidence in archaeology is this: it would be too simplistic to evaluate a description of the past by saying that if there is evidence on the theory's behalf then it is justified and if there is no evidence then it is not justified and should be rejected. This is the naive empiricism I warned against earlier. It is too simplistic for two kinds of reason. First, evidence comes in degrees of directness and credibility, so different evidence will have different degrees of authority over theory. The degrees are based on the links between the evidence and other ideas in our web of understanding. Second, testing a theory can never be left to a single piece of evidence. Justification comes from links to a large variety of evidence, each in turn linked to independent theories, and so on. Justification is a spread-out property of the web.

Historian E.H. Carr (1961: 37) described this situation as an essential reciprocity between theory and evidence. It may seem like a circular relation of theory justifying evidence and evidence justifying theory, but it is a harmless circle. It is unavoidable and even necessary, as we use what we already know to enhance the meaning and assess the reliability of the new things we discover.

The circularity is a form of what is elsewhere called the hermeneutic circle, and hermeneutics is a helpful model for the structure of justification in archaeology. Hermeneutics is about code breaking as a way of translating an unfamiliar language. Individual symbols on the page must be understood as a means to knowing the larger meaning of the text. We have to know the letters and words individually in order to find the plot and the message. And we first get an idea of the meaning of individual symbols by seeing how they are situated in the larger text. Syntactic patterns are noted, and hypothesized meanings must function together to generate a text that makes sense. In other words, our preliminary understanding of the large-scale meanings influences the interpretation of the small-scale symbols. And the understanding of the large-scale is built up from meaningful individual symbols. In this way, there is a reciprocity between the global, abstract interpretation of the content of the text and the more localized and specific assignments of meanings to the marks on the page.

This is hermeneutics, and it works. It works because of two important constraints. First, any assignment of meaning, either to individual symbols or to the larger ideas of the text, is revisable. And, second, the developing translation of the text must be coherent. It must make sense. It must be generally free of contradictions, and there must be connections between one part of the text and others. What it says here ought to explain or at least be related to what it says there. If the text is not making sense, then revision is called for, although it is usually unclear exactly what aspect of the translation needs to be revised. And even if things are making sense and the picture is coherent, we must keep reading. This is the hermeneutic version of always being open to new challenges. The best way to justify the accuracy of a hypothesized translation is to apply it to new examples of the language to see if those make sense. And the hermeneutic justification is at its best when the coherence is far and wide. That is, the understanding of the big picture is supported by many different parts of the text and not just a single passage. This is the independence in the justification process that was required of middle-range theory.

These same conditions apply to the hermeneutic model of archaeological method. All claims about the past and even about the evidence are, to varying degrees, revisable. This is knowledge welcoming challenge. But the willingness to revise is not wishy-washy, because there are constraining data, observations of the material remains. These are analogous to the individual marks on a page to be translated by hermeneutic methods. Descriptions of the past, our theories of what happened, are analogous to the larger message of the text. The hermeneutic reciprocity between individual symbol and global meaning shows up in archaeology as reciprocity between evidence and theory. The goal, and the criterion of justification, is far-reaching coherence. The evidence and theories must make sense in terms of fitting into an extensive network of evidential and theoretical claims.

There are different kinds of link in the network, different components of coherence. A theory could explain or predict specific evidence. This is what we mean in saying that a theory is tested and (to some extent) confirmed by evidence. A theory could be used to give meaning and credibility to specific evidence. This is using a theory as a middle-range theory. Or a theory could relate more directly to another theory, as different parts of a translated text should be relevant to one another. All of these links contribute to justification in the form of far-reaching coherence.

There is also the requirement to continue to confront new evidence, to keep reading. By exposing ideas on what happened in the past to unforeseen challenges in the present, theories are less likely to harbor inaccuracies. It is not a stagnant or complacent coherence that indicates accuracy; it is a dynamic coherence, coherence maintained through ongoing empirical challenges, that is the hallmark of justification.

When a theory makes a prediction that contrasts with what is actually observed, or when the description of one aspect of the past contradicts the description of another, the coherence of the network is reduced and something must be revised. But what? Which part of the description is more likely to be inaccurate? Is it the theory or the observation that needs to be questioned and revised? These kinds of question are answered by noting that in any network of ideas, some ideas are more deeply entrenched and hence less vulnerable than others to rejection or revision. No claim in the system is foundational in the sense of being immune from doubt, rejection, or revision. But some carry more weight than others. They have more epistemic authority by virtue of having more links into the network. To change or discard a well-connected idea would have far-reaching impact, since many of those ideas connected to it would have to be revised as well. Tampering with the well entrenched tends to decrease rather than increase overall coherence, hence defeating the purpose of the revision.

The relative weight of a claim is not based on a sociological entrenchment. It is not about how many people endorse the claim, or how long the claim has been believed. Rather, it is an epistemic entrenchment. It is about how many other ideas and observations in our network are linked to this one. How many things does this theory explain? How many things contribute to explaining this theory? And so on. Theories used as middle-range theories tend to have a lot of this kind of weight, since they have two kinds of link in the network. They are tested by evidence, and they are used to give meaning to other evidence.

A quick example will illustrate the usefulness of this idea of epistemic weight. There is a great deal of evidence and theory put together over decades of research about the rise of agriculture in Eurasia and the Americas. These fit coherently with ideas about continent-specific cultural innovations, including the development of writing. All of this is broadly coherent and hence well justified. The suggestion that a lost continent of Atlantis is the source of all civilization renders it all incoherent. The resulting system of beliefs is a significant loss of coherence, since it leaves unanswered, that is, unconnected, the central question of the ultimate source of Atlantis' civilization.

The variable weighting of ideas within the coherent network is also helpful in dealing with anomalies, that is, failed explanations or the absence of evidence where it was expected. If the theory is otherwise well connected, well entrenched, it is reasonable to retain it despite the anomaly. Only if more anomalies accumulate for the same theory will they collectively come up with the epistemic authority to force a revision or rejection of the theory. But if the theory itself is peripheral in the web, if it is only sparsely connected to other ideas, then a single anomaly is important. In this case, the evidence must be taken seriously, and rejection of the theory may well be warranted.

Again, we are warned against naive or isolated empiricism or falsificationism as a model of method in archaeology. Justification comes in degrees, measured by embeddedness in our existing web of understanding. Having evidence for a theory comes in degrees, not just in the amount of evidence but in the directness and embeddedness of its interpretation. Evidence can be found to support almost any claim; what counts is how much strain the interpretation of that evidence puts on the coherence of the rest of our network of beliefs. Furthermore, almost any credible theory has some confounding or missing evidence, and it would be misleading and unreasonable to cite a single anomaly as cause to abandon an otherwise well-supported idea. In archaeology as in the physical sciences, justification cannot be isolated to single cases of evidence.

In sum, the epistemology of archaeology, the model of how archaeological claims about the past are justified, works like this. Theory, description of the past, requires evidence, both as motivation and subsequent testing. And evidence requires theory to make it meaningful and credible. This is the essential reciprocity. It is necessary bootstrapping, but it is not defeatingly circular as long as we insist on independence between the theory supporting a bit of evidence and the theory it is evidence for. The standard of acceptance of ideas, the measure of justification, is participation in a broadly coherent network of theories and evidential claims, a coherence that persists even as more observations are added. This is the dynamic nature of coherence. When there is a conflict between a theory and some evidence, sometimes it is the theory that must be revised, and sometimes it is the evidence that must be reinterpreted or rejected outright. The ruling is influenced by the epistemic weight of the competing claims, since that is a reflection of the overall coherence in the larger network.

It is important to acknowledge the complication and potential ambiguity in justifying archaeological knowledge. Denying or ignoring the difficulties risks defending our own claims too simply, or, perhaps worse, rejecting what we do not agree with too casually.

An example: the pyramids at Giza

The preceding model of justification in archaeology has been very general and abstract, and its clarity and plausibility may have suffered for it. So let us apply it to a real example, the pyramids at Giza in Egypt. Answers to the most basic questions are not without some controversy. Who built the pyramids, when, how, and why? Recall that our interest here is not in the content of the conclusions but in how they are reached.

The pyramids offer a good case to demonstrate the important epistemological aspects of archaeology. One reason is that there is significant uncertainty about them. Some of the most basic and important questions are without good answers. It is not that there are no hypotheses, for example as to how the pyramids were built. But of several hypotheses, none stands out as being significantly more justified, that is, better linked into a coherent system of beliefs, than the others. We will want to resist filling this void with our own favorite fantasy.

Even for the descriptive claims that are justified, and are clearly more justified than their alternatives, there is no certainty. None of the answers to the important questions is beyond all doubt whatsoever. Nothing interesting ever is. And again, we should resist exploiting the uncertainty in what is said about the pyramids to make room for our own wishful thinking.

We will see in the case of the pyramids that the only way to understand and to justify the claims made about the past is in the larger context. They must be regarded and evaluated as a big group rather than individually or in isolated pairs of one idea and one bit of evidence. It would be misleading, for example, to try to understand and justify claims about just one of the pyramids, or even about just the three large pyramids at Giza. The necessary context is much broader. Each pyramid is situated in a surrounding complex of burials, buildings, and sometimes boats, and interpreting one of the pyramids alone would be like translating a single line of text without putting it into its larger literary context. There are other Egyptian pyramids, and what we say about the three at Giza must make sense, must be coherent, with what we say about the others. And there is the general social and cultural context of Egypt at the time of the pyramids. Claims about the nature of Egyptian society, technology, government, religion, and so on are all relevant to understanding the pyramids. What is theorized about the pyramids must be coherent with the way in which other aspects of Egyptian civilization are described.

No theory or evidence is justified in isolation, but this does not imply that justification demands the consideration of all possible data. Some details are irrelevant, and it can be a difficult and potentially question-begging decision whether or not to take a particular aspect of the situation seriously. For example, all three of the pyramids at Giza have been measured with great precision. We know their dimensions, their orientations, their slopes, and so on. Several theories have been proposed that explain the design principles of the pyramids, why they were built, based on impressive numerical correlations in the dimensions. Roger Herz-Fischler surveys several such theories specific to the largest of the pyramids at Giza. These include the Pi-theory, which purports to show that the pyramid builders must have known the value of π, since "the circumference of a circle with radius equal to the height is [very nearly] equal to the perimeter of the base of the pyramid" (Herz-Fischler 2000: 67). Herz-Fischler describes fifteen such proposals for the design plan of the Great Pyramid, all of which highlight correlations in dimensional details that Egyptologists regard as unimportant. This shows an important aspect of archaeology and science, that the selection of data is influenced by the theories that one already believes. And sometimes this can degrade the objectivity of the process, if selecting evidence is self-serving. But in this case, Herz-Fischler uses an independent means of evaluating the relevance of these data. He provides a statistical analysis of the proposed correlations and shows that none of the fifteen stands out as being more significant than any of the others (ibid.: 29).

Again, the moral of this story is that justification of a theory is not to be found in an isolated, narrow look at a single aspect of a single pyramid. It must be based on extensive coherence in a broad context. We will see that the generally accepted account of the building of the pyramids is well justified in this holistic way. With conscious reference to modern physics, I will call this account the standard model.

The standard model of the three main pyramids at Giza describes them as being three tombs. The largest, the Great Pyramid, was built to be a tomb for the pharaoh Khufu. The slightly smaller pyramid that is associated with the sphinx was built as a tomb for the pharaoh Khafre, one of Khufu's sons. And the smallest of the three pyramids is the tomb of Menkaure. Each pyramid was built during the reign of the pharaoh, although there is no way to tell if they were done exactly on time. The standard model puts the dates of the three pharaohs at roughly 2550–2528 BC, 2520–2494 BC, and 2490–2472 BC, respectively. This precision is probably unwarranted, and the exact dates are still a topic of discussion and revision, but it is clear that the pyramids were built roughly 4,500 years ago and each took roughly a generation to construct.

This answers the question of when the pyramids were built. To describe them as tombs answers why, although more details on the motives are elusive. Why did they choose the particular pyramid shape in which to entomb the pharaoh? What does the pyramid mean to the Egyptians? These remain important outstanding questions and are the subject of ongoing debate.

Who built the pyramids? According to the standard model, they were built by mortal Egyptians, the minions of the pharaohs. How did they do it? What sort of social organization, technology, and labor schedule did they use to accomplish this enormous task? The Great Pyramid of Khufu is usually estimated to be made of 2.3 million blocks of limestone and granite (this total has recently been revised upward to nearly four million; see Sakovich 2002), weighing up to 80 tons apiece. These had to be quarried, delivered, shaped, lifted (eventually up to the peak at 146 meters), and carefully placed. All this was done without the use of iron tools or wheeled carts, and done in a period of about twenty years. How was it done? The candid answer is that we do not really know. The details of construction are not clearly or securely understood. This is not to say that there are no good ideas on the methods of construction or no tested hypotheses. There are. A huge nearby quarry has been found, and there is reason to believe that ramps were used to haul wooden sledges on rollers to raise the blocks into positions. But the description of how the pyramids were built is still a work in progress within the standard model.

Most important for understanding the epistemology of archaeology is understanding the reasons for believing that the standard model is accurate. Given the imprecision of the dates and the incompleteness in describing the methods, what justification is there for endorsing the model at all?

There are many pieces of evidence in support of the standard model. None is singularly sufficient for justifying the account of the pyramids, and none stands on its own in the sense of being free of some theoretical interpretation. That is the way it is with evidence. It is only by considering the whole, coherent, far-reaching network of claims into which the model fits that we appreciate its justification.

Each of the three pyramids has an interior chamber that contained a sarcophagus. This would seem to be decisive for the ascription as tombs, except that none of the sarcophagi contained bones when it was discovered. (Well, bones of a bull were found in the sarcophagus of the Khafre pyramid, and human bones dating to the Christian era in that of Menkaure.) So there is work to be done to show that each of the stone boxes is in fact a sarcophagus, placed in the pyramid at the time it was built rather than added later. How, in other words, are these data, these stone boxes, evidence of the pyramids being built for the purpose of being tombs for the pharaohs?

The boxes are identified as sarcophagi because they resemble boxes from elsewhere in Egypt found in clear contexts as burials. Some of these held bodies of Egyptians; some were in other Egyptian pyramids; and some were in situations with textual references to death and burial. In other words, there are similar objects in Egypt, some found in pyramids, that are independently interpreted to be sarcophagi. This use of comparanda, comparable objects with independent middle-range theories to give them meaning, is a standard of archaeological method. It is not that the standard model identifies the pyramids as tombs, uses this as the reason to call the boxes sarcophagi, and then cites the sarcophagi as the proof that the pyramids are tombs. This circularity is prevented by insisting that the interpretations, of pyramids and sarcophagi, fit into a much broader picture that includes other pyramids, other contexts, and, importantly, other kinds of data.

Another noteworthy detail is that the sarcophagus in the interior chamber of the Great Pyramid is too big to fit through the passageway leading to the outside. The sarcophagus had to have been put in place during construction of the pyramid, indicating that the pyramid was not only *used* as a tomb, but was indeed *built* as a tomb.

Now consider the evidence of the Giza pyramids in the larger context of other Egyptian pyramids. Although the Giza pyramids are the largest and most famous, there is a line of development starting with *mastabas* and developing into step pyramids. Some of these other pyramids were discovered with entombed bodies in the interior chambers. Some were inscribed with so-called Pyramid Texts. These texts are on interior walls of pyramids, and although they are difficult to interpret, they are generally about "the ruler and his life in the beyond" (Verner 1997: 41). Furthermore, the texts are written to be read in a direction starting at the interior of the pyramid and moving to the outside, as if to guide the entombed king in his passage to the next world.

A few individual pyramids have distinctive features that support the general interpretation of pyramids as tombs and even suggest clues about the methods of construction. Papyri have been found near the pyramid of Neferirkare, for example, describing activities associated with the pyramid. These temple archives list religious duties and festivals, equipment of worship, and even some architectural details of the temple. The point is that the textual evidence associated with this one pyramid, together with the similarity between this pyramid and others, helps us to understand and justify statements about Egyptian pyramids generally.

There are similar clues about construction techniques. The use of ramps, for example, is described in the Anastasi papyrus. It even includes specific dimensions of ramps. And there are physical remains of ramps still in place on the Red Pyramid. Since it is likely that different pyramids, with different sizes and shapes, required somewhat different building methods, generalization might be unwarranted. But the textual reference to ramps and the few remains make the theory of ramps at the Giza pyramids at least worth pursuing.

Each of the pyramids at Giza fits into its own broad context of smaller satellite pyramids and surrounding buildings. It is important to consider the evidence of the pyramid complex and not just the pyramid itself. Each of the pyramids at Giza is within a necropolis. They are surrounded by lesser pyramids, tombs, and *mastabas* that function as burials of the king's family and associates. Some of these sites are inscribed, and in some cases with reference to the king for whom the large pyramid is a tomb. A good example of this is in the Queen's pyramids around the Great Pyramid of Khufu, in particular in the chamber of Hetepheres.

Recent excavations at Giza have revealed settlements of the many workers who built the pyramids. There are houses for the work crews, as well as bakeries and cemeteries with inscribed titles such as "overseer of the side of the pyramid," "overseer of masonry," and "director for the king's work" (Hawass 1997: 41). The numbers of workers estimated to have lived in the settlements is commensurate with estimates of the number of people at work on the pyramid at any time. This is a good example of testing a hypothesis by what philosophers of science call the hypothetico-deductive method. A prediction is rendered, namely that if there were so many men at work on the pyramids then there would have to be material remains of their housing and life support, and then one looks to see if the prediction is true. In this case it is. This does not mean that the hypothesis is surely true, but it is some addition to the justification, some part of the reason to believe it to be true.

One last piece of evidence in favor of the standard model is worth mentioning. Some Egyptologists claim it to be decisive proof that the Great Pyramid was built to be a tomb for the pharaoh Khufu. This is the graffiti in a relieving chamber above the king's burial chamber, which gives names of some work crews and names Khufu himself. The key is that the relieving chamber has no entrance. It is a space above the burial chamber that deflects the enormous weight away from the ceiling, an artefact of engineering never meant to be entered. It was originally accessible only during the construction of the pyramid. And here is a series of so-called builders' marks and the cartouche of Khufu. According to Mark Lehner, the graffiti and the fact that no one had been in the chamber between the time the pyramid was built and 1837, when an explorer blasted his way in, "clinches the ascription of this pyramid to the 4th-dynasty Pharaoh, Khufu" (Lehner 1997: 53). Indeed, some quarry marks are even found on the sides of blocks; they could not have been put there after the pyramid was built. It is tempting to regard the graffiti as singularly decisive for the standard model, but a more realistic evaluation is that it is neither decisive nor singular. The standard model does not depend on this single piece of evidence, convincing as it is. These graffiti do not have to bear the full burden of proof, since they fit wonderfully with both the standard model and with other pieces of evidence. There are workers' graffiti on some of the other pyramids, for example, thus enhancing the credibility of them all.

Like any scientific description of events that cannot be observed, the standard model of the pyramids at Giza has some anomalies, some recalcitrant evidence and even parts of the theory that do not quite fit. Radiometric dating of mortar in the Great Pyramid is one example. The dates are roughly 400 years earlier than the reign of Khufu. This is an important problem, and it cannot be ignored or minimized. It does not force the rejection of the standard model, but some part of the theoretical network must be revised. It is unlikely, and unreasonable, to revise the account of radioactive decay and techniques of radiometric dating, since these ideas are so extensively and coherently connected in theoretical systems of both physics and archaeology. Perhaps, instead, the evidence suggests a recalibration of the dates of the pharaohs. Or perhaps, much more profound changes to the standard model are in order, to the extent that the pyramids were not built during the lifetime of the pharaoh and hence were not built as his tomb. A third possibility for fitting the radiometric dates coherently into the model is to reassess the middle-range theory describing the making and use of mortar. If the mortar incorporates older organic material, the mortar itself could be much newer than the radiometric dates indicate. The important point here is that the evidence is both important and at odds with the standard model. It is also ambiguous, in that the evidence alone does not tell us what part of the model, or what other participating theories, need to be rejected or revised.

Another anomaly for the standard model of the pyramids at Giza is that none of the three sarcophagi were discovered to have bones of a pharaoh, and none of the three pyramids held a statue of a pharaoh. However, this missing evidence is plausibly explained by looting. The pyramids are highly visible and irresistible targets for treasure hunters, and, over 4,000 years, anything of value or interest that is movable has been removed. All that remains are the multi-ton stones, although even some of those have been taken for use elsewhere. This is typical in archaeology. Much of the most informative evidence is in the mundane, the objects of no value to robbers and collectors. The workers' settlements associated with the pyramids, for example, are of lower profile and lesser value to looters, but they will probably be high-yielding and very interesting sources of archaeological evidence.

And, finally, there is an important drawback to the standard model in that it cannot yet describe how the pyramids were constructed. There are convincing and clear answers to the questions of who, why, and when (roughly), but not how. Were ramps used on the huge pyramids at Giza? If so, the ramps themselves would have to have been enormous and so long as to extend beyond the quarry. There should be tons of debris from the mud-brick ramps. The debris is not there, and its absence cannot be blamed on looting. Perhaps the ramps wrapped around the pyramid in a way that required less material. Perhaps, but this is largely speculative and without evidential support. In its current state, the standard model is without a clear mechanism for building the pyramids.

This gap in the description of the pyramids is one reason I like to call it the standard model, to make an explicit analogy with physics. Physicists refer to the current description of elementary particles and processes as the standard model. It talks about forces, fields, particles, masses, charges, and so on (see Weinberg 1992). Many aspects of the standard model in physics are well justified in the sense of theoretical and evidential coherence. But some important details are still unclear. For example, there is no detailed evidence for a fundamental process called symmetry breaking, which is theorized as the source of mass. Mass is not an unimportant detail in understanding matter and interactions, yet this unfinished business in the standard model is not reason to scrap the whole thing. Like the standard model of the pyramids, there is a large network of interrelated, coherent ideas and claims, both theoretical and observational. That is what gives the model its justification. No single anomaly or uncertainty should force its undoing.

Justification is most useful as a comparative tool, so it is appropriate to ask how the justification of the standard model of the pyramids compares with alternatives. Consider the theory proposed and defended by Graham Hancock and Robert Bauval in *The Message of the Sphinx* (Hancock and Bauval 1997). This is a good comparison, since it is the confluence of two streams of "alternative" ideas that are well publicized and highly detailed.

The alternative model is this. The entire pyramid complex at Giza is an "astronomical theme park" (ibid.: 78), begun around 10,500 BC. The pyramids were not built as tombs but as models of stars, in particular, the stars in Orion's belt (for details of this so-called Orion correlation theory, see Chapter 10). The pyramids were begun in 10,500 BC but were finished only in 2,500 BC. They were then used as tombs. The pyramid complex is a message from a lost civilization, with the pattern of stars as its telltale date, since only in 10,500 BC would the stars in the sky match the pattern on the ground.

Two main lines of evidence are cited in support of this proposition, the astronomical alignment and the technological impossibility for Egyptian civilization, as we know it to have been in 2,500 BC, to have built the pyramids. Both of these are given as reasons to push the starting date of the pyramids back by 8,000 years to an otherwise hidden civilization, although neither gives any reason for adding the extra interpretative step that the monuments are a message to the future.

Consider the evidence on its merits. There are narrow shafts in the Great Pyramid that angle up from the King's Chamber and the Queen's Chamber on the north and south sides. These point to important stars, or to where the stars were located in the sky in 2,500 BC. This indicates a stellar orientation of the pyramid. Furthermore, the three pyramids are said to be an exact reproduction of the stars in the belt of Orion, an important constellation to the Egyptians. The position of Orion was most appropriate for this match in 10,500 BC, thus allegedly dating the layout of the pyramid complex. There is a problem though. Orion's belt shows two big stars and a little one, with a subtle bend to the north. The line linking the two bigger pyramids, Khufu and Khafre, to the smaller one, Menkaure, has a bend to the south. The pyramids are not an image of Orion's belt; they are backwards (Krupp 2003). Justification in archaeology depends on coherence of theory and evidence in a broad network of ideas, and the most basic component of coherence is logical consistency. But here is a case of evidence that is outright inconsistent. The diagonal shafts in the pyramids orient the monuments north on the ground to north in the sky, but the alleged match to Orion's belt requires that we flip things over to align north to south.

Then there is the argument that construction projects so enormous and so precise as the pyramids could not have been designed and completed by Egyptians in 2,500 BC, and certainly not in the twenty or thirty years described by the standard model. Here is a clear case of exploiting some uncertainty to make room for a radical alternative theory. Radiocarbon dating of the mortar in the Great Pyramid may challenge traditional dating by a few hundred years, but it is no reason at all to move the date back by *eight thousand years*. And questions about the building techniques may force some revisions in the web of understanding of ancient Egypt and the standard model, but they do not warrant positing an entire new civilization. This would require far-reaching and profound revisions in the web, unwarranted by any anomalies we see today.

The most glaring deficiency in the justification of the Hancock–Bauval model is basic: there is no evidence for the hypothesized civilization other than the pyramid complex itself. There is no reason at all why evidence of 8,000 years of "continuous transmission of advanced scientific and engineering knowledge ... and thus the continuous presence in Egypt" (Hancock and Bauval 1997: 248) should be completely absent. The evidence at Giza is all we have to motivate the theory of the astronomical message from a lost civilization. The theory is used to interpret this evidence, which is in turn the main evidence cited in support of the theory. This is circularity of reasoning at its most insular and self-serving. It lacks the most important ingredients of justification, extensive links to other ideas and independent evidence. It is isolated in its own small web of ideas. It is at odds with the wider understanding of the history of Egypt, including the pyramids at places other than Giza and the archaeological and textual evidence of Egyptian culture. The result is intractable dissonance rather than coherence in the larger web of understanding.

Given the evidence available and the standards of comparing justification, the standard model is the responsible choice. In this case, it is simply a matter of following the advice of the eighteenth-century Scottish philosopher David Hume: "A wise man, therefore, proportions his belief to the evidence" (Hume 1993 [1777]: 73).

The case of the pyramids at Giza, together with the analogy with the standard model of particle physics, displays the important aspects of epistemology of archaeology and science. No single piece of evidence confirms the model or any other description of the past. No single piece of evidence (or missing evidence) falsifies it either. No part of the model is above questioning, revision, or rejection. But some aspects are more secure than others, and this is measured by the security of connection with a coherent network of beliefs. When in doubt, suspect the loosely connected and peripheral ideas. Justification is rooted in the overall coherence between beliefs.

1 Diagnosing pseudoarchaeology

Garrett G. Fagan

Our ancestors were not terribly smart. They had progressed hardly at all before the spacemen arrived. Educating (and mating with) the dim proto-humans, the extraterrestrials forged a new race, modern humanity, and conferred on them the gifts of high culture. They built huge monuments using their advanced technology, monuments that even modern engineers could not hope to mimic. In the art and architecture of the ancients, as well as in myths and stories of "gods" from the sky told around the world, the evidence of early human encounters with the extraterrestrials lies buried, if only one has the will to look.[1]

Just as Plato tells it, Atlantis was a real place. Precisely where it was is beside the point – there are plenty of options – but it did exist and it stands at the root of every ancient civilization. And Atlantis was even more fabulous than Plato lets on, a veritable wonderland of technological achievement, spiritual enlightenment, and psychic capabilities. Unfortunately, the renowned achievements of Atlantis got corrupted in transmission, so only vestiges of its glory remain for us to identify. Blinkered archaeological orthodoxy refuses to contemplate such marvellous possibilities and dismisses them as wishful thinking. However, a group of pioneering thinkers from various walks of life – including a US congressman, several clairvoyants, an amateur tour-guide, journalists, and even a few bona fide professors – have worked on the Atlantis problem, keeping the hope alive that one day, perhaps soon, it will be located once and for all.[2]

In the ancient past, long before the accepted start of recorded history, there was a nameless civilization of fantastic sophistication. It knew of astronomy, of advanced mathematics, of geography, and of high spiritual matters. Its inhabitants were able navigators, who roamed the seas freely, mapping the lands they encountered. At that time, Antarctica was located further north, outside the Antarctic circle, and was home to the great, spiritual civilization. But then a change. The entire surface of the Earth suddenly shifted over its core, forcing Antarctica to the pole, where it began to freeze. There were floods and cataclysms worldwide. The great civilization vanished from the face of the Earth. But some survivors escaped and fanned out across the globe in their ships, bringing the light of high culture to the otherwise benighted populations of the planet. Over the following eight millennia or more they operated as a secret brotherhood of astronomer-priests in locations such as Bolivia, Egypt, and Cambodia. Manipulating matters behind the scenes, they encoded memories of their Lost Civilization in art, architecture, and myth. Yet shamefully, academic archaeologists refuse to recognize the scattered clues to our forgotten Ice Age heritage.[3]

These three scenarios represent just the tip of the iceberg of pseudoarchaeo-logical claims about human antiquity (and they are by no means the wildest). While woefully unsophisticated, fringe notions like these have been doing the rounds for almost a century and a quarter, and their popu-larity shows no sign of abating. Despite great advances in archaeology's investigative methods and modes of analysis – all grounded in vast quanti-ties of verifiable evidence – a self-styled "alternative" movement presents a nexus of often mutually exclusive and outrageous narratives as if they were viable substitutes for real knowledge about the past. In what follows, I address two basic and related questions: What is pseudoarchaeology? And what are its defining characteristics?

The issue of boundaries

In order to identify *pseudo*archaeology, we need to understand what archae-ology is. Put simply, archaeology is the recovery, analysis, and interpretation of the physical remains of past human activity. The discipline therefore has two halves. The first is the collection of data, or field archaeology, and that is an almost wholly pragmatic business. Its methods have evolved from the slash-and-hack practices of amateur pioneers to the careful and codified methods of modern professionals. In addition, advances in science have provided the archaeologist with new, non-invasive investigative tools such as ground-penetrating radar, magnetometry, and satellite imaging. Once unearthed, as much information as possible is extracted from archaeological material through such processes as radiocarbon and thermoluminescence analysis (for dating), or neutron activation analysis and X-ray fluorescence spectrometry (to determine chemical composition). Old practices are constantly being refined and new methods developed. A variety of archaeo-logical manuals, handbooks, and encyclopaedias are at hand to explain the procedures of data collection and analysis.[4]

The second half of archaeology is to make sense of the evidence uncovered in the field. As an analytical and interpretative endeavor, it is difficult and multifaceted – and highly contentious. Apart from differing assessments of particular modes of analysis (for instance, the application of statistics or geographical information systems to data), theoretical debates rage among professionals about how archaeological materials are to be approached, what meaning(s) they carry, what conclusions can reasonably be reached from examining them, and what questions ought to be asked in the first place. Strategies of inquiry informed by fields such as philosophy, biology, psychology, sociology, anthropology, and even postcolonial studies are employed by different interpretative camps within the discipline. While this is not the place to review these various camps, the plain truth is that genuine archaeology is really an assemblage of often distinct "archaeologies," each with its own personnel, publication outlets, and professional meetings. Thus we have *processual archaeology*, which sees itself as reconstructing the past objectively through a scientific process; *post-processual* or *interpretative archaeology*, which views the past as a series of competing modern interpretations firmly rooted in current concerns; *cognitive archaeology*, which focuses on the mental universes of past cultures in such realms as cosmology, religion, ideology, or art; *symbolic archaeology*, which investigates what cultural meanings were communicated by physical remains; and so on.[5] Recently, a case has been made for *analytic meta-archaeology*, a subdiscipline that stands at the intersection of archaeology, philosophy, history, and sociology (Wylie 2002). Debates between these theoretical camps can be sharp and confrontational, as can only be expected in a discipline that seeks to address all aspects of the human societies it studies. Since theory informs the deployment of evidence (see the Introduction to this volume), proponents can sometimes feel that all is at stake when confronting opponents who adhere to very different theoretical positions.

The theoretical debates (which tend to be sharper in anthropological circles than in the more traditional, text-oriented fields such as Egyptology or classical archaeology) make defining archaeological intepretative method in a straightforward manner singularly difficult. We have to dig below the strata of specific methodological disagreements to find those shared underlying characteristics that act as boundary markers between archaeology and pseudoarchaeology. Two are crucial. All camps are united in recognizing the absolute centrality of the data collected by the pragmatic wing of the discipline, and they respect the data's power to threaten or butcher their theoretical sacred cows. Wylie's attitude is typical:

> What you find, archaeologically, has everything to do with what you look for, with the questions you ask and the conceptual resources you bring to bear in attempting to answer them. And yet, you almost never find all or only what you expect. As often as not, the process of inquiry forces you to rethink your questions, to envision possibilities that are very different from any of the prospective answers you might have entertained at the outset. As enigmatic and fragmentary as it is, the archaeological record has infinite capacity to surprise, to subvert even our most confident presuppositions about what must have been the case and why ...
>
> (Wylie 2002: xiv)

A basic characteristic of genuine archaeology, of whatever theoretical bent, is the maintenance of this conceptual flexibility – a willingness to re-examine favored conclusions in the face of surprising discoveries or countervailing evidence, and to change those conclusions accordingly. It is not unreasonable to brand such an intellectual stance broadly "scientific" insofar as it accepts the capacity of the data to reshape interpretations.[6] It is unsurprising that competing archaeological interpretations are rarely resolved definitively in the way that competing models can be resolved by experiment and observation in the natural sciences. Human activity is so complex and archaeological data so scarce that it may take decades of analysis and debate for consensus to emerge, and that consensus will often draw on verified elements of what were formerly competing models. In this sense, archaeology looks less "scientific" and more humanistic. But throughout, an openness to revise conclusions in the face of compelling evidence characterizes the entire interpretative process as conducted by professionals.

It goes without saying that the openness to new data does not equate with credulity. New evidence or arguments have to be thoroughly scrutinized to secure their validity and explanatory power, and longstanding, well-entrenched positions will take considerable effort and particularly compelling data to overturn – archaeological interpretations are not blown like chaff on the wind of every anomaly that shows up. A skeptical approach to new material is entirely appropriate. Challenges to established knowledge have to demonstrate their cogency before they convince people. But once critical evidence is verified and its implications realized, it is incumbent on genuine archaeologists to reassess their positions in the light of new findings.

The second boundary marker between archaeology and pseudoarchaeology is respect for context. While early pioneers in the field consigned unspectacular finds like drab pottery shards to the discard heap, modern archaeology is almost obsessed with such mundanities. The reason is an overwhelming concern for context, since context is absolutely critical to interpretation. Individual objects or assemblages carry very different meanings if found in different contexts (Hodder 1987: 11–23). A spearpoint, for instance, reveals one thing when it is found in an elite burial assemblage and quite another when it is found embedded in the spinal column of a skeleton lying amid a field of arrowheads and spearpoints near the gates of a fort. In the one instance, it demonstrates the use of weapons as status symbols and ceremonial objects; in the other, it tells a rather different story. Likewise, a stratigraphically sealed cache of Egyptian pot fragments found in the Sinai would be interesting; the same cache found in New Hampshire would be sensational. Context conveys meaning.

The centrality of context to archaeological interpretation cannot be overstated. Indeed, the codified techniques of excavation exist primarily to establish as firmly as possible the context of newly revealed evidence, from its stratigraphy (to help to deduce chronology and determine proximate and remote associations) to the recovery of minutiae like shreds of animal bones or pollen grains (to establish characteristics of the ancient environment, ecology, and climate). Furthermore, any given site will yield many objects in many separate contexts, all of which relate to each other in complex ways, and the entire site will itself sit within even wider geographical, chronological, cultural, and historical contexts. In this way, archaeological contexts are nested things, linked to each other by a web of observable associations. Since all of these contexts pertain to masses of physical data, it is statistically inevitable that two or more sites will turn up comparable artefacts or features (town walls with towers, elevated temples, burial grounds, etc.).

But it is consideration of context that establishes the historical relatedness of these comparanda – or not. This is why gross cross-cultural comparisons narrowly focused on specific items (or anomalies) are generally eschewed by professionals, since such an approach ignores or downgrades the interpretative centrality of context for each example. To put it another way, context places limits on the scope of analysis and demands constant attention from the judicious interpreter. So when archaeologists argue that such-and-such an object is being interpreted "without context" or that a proposed lost culture stands "out of context" they are not seeking to evade a difficulty by playing word games. Rather, they are adhering to one of the most basic tenets of archaeological interpretation: to really understand an object's significance, explore its context.

In sum, interpretation in genuine archaeology is distinguished from that in pseudoarchaeology by a conceptual flexibility in treating the evidence and by an overwhelming concern for context as a guide to interpretation.

Defining characteristics of pseudoarchaeology

Pseudoarchaeology is predominantly an interpretative endeavor. Psychic visions and dowsing notwithstanding, its practitioners do not normally uncover new data or direct excavations. Pseudoarchaeological interpretation differs from that of genuine archaeology in eschewing both of the fundamental characteristics established above. First, its practitioners adopt an inflexible stance toward the evidence, which is to be shoehorned into their pet conclusions at all costs. Second, pseudoarchaeologists are practically contemptuous of context. It is not unusual for entire monuments, artistic motifs, or myth cycles to be compared with each other (usually in a literal-minded fashion) and far-reaching conclusions reached without any regard for their respective contexts. As a result, pseudoarchaeology is essentially simplistic, despite its surface veneer of complexity. These traits make it more than just another brand of archaeological interpretation, to be considered no more or less valid than the various schools of archaeological theory mentioned above. Pseudoarchaeology is a different animal altogether.

In the online introduction to his 2002 book *Underworld: Flooded Kingdoms of the Ice Age*, journalist Graham Hancock has this to say:

> The central claim of my 1995 book *Fingerprints of the Gods* is not that there was but that there could have been a lost civilisation, which flourished and was destroyed in remote antiquity. And I wrote the book, quite deliberately, not as a work of science but as a work of advocacy. I felt that the possibility of a lost civilisation had not been adequately explored or tested by mainstream scholarship. I set myself the task of rehabilitating it by gathering together, and passionately championing, all the best evidence and arguments in its favour.
>
> (Hancock 2002c: 1)

Contrast this attitude toward the evidence with that of Alison Wylie's, quoted above (p. 25). Hancock's stated approach contravenes both of the fundamental characteristics of genuine interpretation in archaeology. Despite the cautious wording, it is clear that Hancock had reached his conclusion in advance and that, in forcing whatever evidence he could find into the mold, he could do nothing other than trample roughshod over concern for context when dealing with specifics. In *Fingerprints of the Gods,* the historical contexts of particular artefacts (such as Renaissance maps), specific monuments (such as the Sphinx in Egypt), entire cities (such as Tiwanaku in Bolivia), or whole cultures (such as the Olmec in Central America) are ignored as they are dragged kicking and screaming into the service of Hancock's preordained conclusion. Devotion to that conclusion necessarily entails a refusal to revise it in the face of the evidence, since the conclusion has not been reached on the basis of evidence but vice versa: the evidence has been dragooned into the service of the conclusion. Such are the fingerprints of pseudoarchaeology.[7]

Thus far, I have focused on what might be considered "fringe" ideas about submerged supercultures or spacemen building pyramids. But it follows that when archaeology is pursued specifically in the service of an ideology that limits (if not actively predetermines) what conclusions are allowable – such as religious belief, nationalist or political ideology, or race consciousness – it has, in fact, devolved into the realm of pseudoarchaeology. Precisely as with the fringe mavericks, practitioners operating under such conditions must adopt the mental inflexibility and an unwillingness to consider context that characterize pseudoarchaeology. The cultural superiority of the ancient Aryans was an unquestioned given for the Nazi archaeologist, evidence of the Earth's existence prior to 10,000 years ago is an impossibility for the young-Earth Christian creationist, while for Hindu fundamentalists it is inconceivable that *Homo sapiens* is only 100,000 years old. Such people could never share Wylie's openness to the revising power of data considered in context. (Open espousal of a guiding ideology ought to be carefully distinguished from the subtle, often unconscious cultural influences that affect all interpreters. These influences are compensated for, to a degree, by the publication, dissemination, and criticism of ideas among a wide circle of peers, each operating within their own cultural milieu. In this way, it is hoped, no one set of cultural assumptions can dominate the agenda.) Archaeology conducted under the anti-intellectual constraints of rigid ideologies is more fully explored elsewhere in this volume (see Chapters 7–9), but its "methods" find echo in the matters discussed in the rest of this chapter.

A final point before moving on: the attitudinal definition of pseudoarchaeology offered here – in essence, the adoption of a closed conceptual stance toward the evidence and an unconcern for context – requires that a choice be made. The pseudoarchaeologist can only be defined as such when he or she *willfully* ignores countervailing data instead of rethinking their position in the face of it, or when contextual considerations are *deliberately* bypassed or left unexplored for fear of destroying a preferred conclusion. Both of these failings must also be applied *systematically*. Thus it would be unjust to condemn as pseudoarchaeologists pioneers in the field, such as Heinrich Schliemann (1822–90), because they were motivated by a romantic vision and paid less attention to context than modern practitioners do. The discipline at that time was crude in its methods, lacked a codified practice in its field activities, and was marked by relatively unsophisticated interpretative approaches. However, the same cannot be said in the case of those who ought to have known better, such as the eminent Mayanist Sir Eric Thompson (1898–1975). Convinced (incorrectly) that Maya glyphs were metaphorical and mystical signs with no phonetic value, he deployed his towering influence and gift for invective to retard the decipherment of the Mayan writing system for a generation. In his publications, Thompson appears to have actually suppressed evidence that pointed to a phonetic value for the glyphs. Nor did he pay attention to wider contextual clues indicating that the Maya were not a unique cultural phenomenon, as he preferred to think of them (Coe 1999: 123–66). In doing so, a case could be made that this much-honored figure crossed the line into pseudoarchaeology. Thompson had closed his mind to new evidence, apparently acted deliberately to suppress countervailing evidence, and downplayed local and wider contexts, all to keep his favored conclusions intact. In each instance, he had a choice – and he made the wrong one. It is also very important to note that, despite his best efforts, Thompson's views on Mayan glyphs ultimately lost out. Linguists and epigraphers pursuing a phonetic interpretation of the signs presented a more compelling case, and it was the strength of their arguments, not Thompson's prestige or polemics, that carried the day. Genuine archaeology is self-correcting.

Pseudoarchaeology is not therefore restricted to maverick, unprofessional writers with very strange ideas about antiquity. It is a trap than can ensnare professionally trained academics when their egos, ideologies, or other personal beliefs get in the way of their commitment to honest inquiry. However, academics have the advantage of operating in the university environment, where a culture of criticism and, in most cases, self-criticism will (eventually) reveal distortions or obfuscations employed in the service of unjustifiably favored conclusions – just as it did in the case of Eric Thompson (see Chapter 6).[8] It is noteworthy that truly fringe mavericks almost wholly lack a capacity for self-criticism and very rarely criticize each other, even when they cleave to mutually exclusive and even diametrically opposed reconstructions of the past (as when Hindu and Christian fundamentalists support each other in opposing Darwinian evolution). In addition, they present their ideas directly to the public, for whom it is harder to detect distortions and obfuscations in material that will already be pretty arcane – how many people on the street can discourse comfortably about recent developments in Andean archaeology, or comparative mythology, or limestone geology, or whatever other discipline pseudoarchaeology ransacks for its propositions? A closer study of the "methods" of the pseudoarchaeologists reveals how these distortions are perpetrated and helps to refine our diagnosis of the genre (see also Fagan 2002).

Flawed methods

The diagnostic characteristics of pseudoarchaeology, as manifest in its methods, can be divided into two categories: characteristics of attitude and characteristics of procedure. Between them, they constitute the flawed methods that buttress the unconvincing scenarios thrown up by its practitioners. Given its extent and longevity, it would be impossible to substantiate these individual features with comprehensive references to most, or even many, examples of the genre. Therefore, I largely limit my references to two exemplars, one by journalist Graham Hancock (1995, reissued 2001), the other by science professor Robert Schoch (2003). Hancock's central contention has been summarized above, in the chapter's third paragraph. Schoch believes in a single source for all of the world's pyramids, which he locates in Indonesia on the (predictably) sunken landmass of Sundaland. Rather like the survivors of Hancock's nameless Lost Civilization, Schoch's Sundalanders fanned out around the globe after a natural catastrophe (a cometary impact, in this instance) to bring knowledge of pyramids to the planet. Hancock's book was a blockbuster in the genre, and Schoch's appeared very recently; the differences in their respective intellectual backgrounds also recommends these authors for selection, since the similarity in their mode of presentation says much about the requirements of the genre. However, the characteristics identified below by no means apply to these two books alone. They can be found in pseudoarchaeological works of varying fantastical content.

Characteristics of attitude

1. *Dogged adherence to outdated theoretical models.* Since their scenarios run counter to current archaeological paradigms, pseudoarchaeologists are forced to plunder outdated scholarship for their "theoretical" models, such as they are. In this way, they embrace as central features of their scenarios notions like (hyper)diffusionism (that all the world's civilizations spread from a single source) or catastrophism (that cataclysmic natural events generate historical change). They are not above resorting to entirely disproven ideas. Earth crustal displacement (ECD) was a geological model championed by C.H. Hapgood (1958, 1966, 1970), who held that the weight of the polar icecaps sporadically caused the Earth's crust to be dragged over its internal core, moving poles and continents around in terrific catastrophes (and destroying early civilizations in the process). ECD was rendered untenable by the verification of continental drift through plate tectonics in the late 1960s (an extremely slow process with movement of about 1–2 cm per

year), yet ECD is invoked in several recent "alternative" works, notably by Graham Hancock.[9] A distinct advantage of catastrophism lies in its ability to generate more dramatic narratives than the apparently mundane archaeological hypotheses offered to explain the appearance of civilization by independent invention or its disappearance by gradual and impersonal forces (climate change, shifting demographics, environmental degradation, etc.). And pseudoarchaeology is constantly in search of the most appealing story (see #4).

The mode of deployment of such models in pseudoarchaeology matters more than their mere existence. Diffusionism in itself is not inherently implausible; indeed, it is verifiable in many instances where traits (like languages) have been transferred between cultures, and continue to be. Likewise, natural catastrophes do happen, and they do cause massive damage, although they hardly erase all traces of entire civilizations – quite the opposite, in fact (see the archaeologically fortunate results of the volcanic eruptions of Vesuvius or Thera). What is different in pseudoarchaeological presentations is that these localized processes are moved from the particular to the general, so that they become overarching models to be applied in all-or-nothing dramatic narratives. The enthusiastic catastrophist Robert Schoch, for instance, rather like Immanuel Velikovsky (1950, 1952) before him, believes that many instances of historical change were caused by cometary impacts: Chinese dynasties collapsed, crusades were initiated and migrations sparked when comets hit the planet, or threatened to (Schoch 2003: 191–236). Schoch invokes demonstrated instances of diffusionism, such as the spread of Indo-European languages across the western Eurasia landmass, to support a far broader and more unlikely global dispersal of pyramids across the Pacific and Atlantic oceans (ibid.: 76–81, 273–74). This is neither believable diffusionism nor convincing catastrophism. Its insidious feature is that it begins with demonstrated or uncontested phenomena and extends them into crass implausibilities. Readers are easily carried along unless they are informed and very alert to the subtle shifts as the presentation unfolds.

2. *Disparaging academia.* Suspicion of scholars is a longstanding feature of the genre that goes back to Augustus le Plongeon (1825–1908) and his imaginings about the lost continent of Mu (Jordan 2001: 58). It often manifests itself as sarcastic contempt for what such writers call "academic" or "orthodox" or "conventional" archaeology. Egyptology is a favorite whipping boy. "If you think of Egyptologists at all," writes tour guide and "alternative" speculator John Anthony West (1993: 240), "the chances are you conjure up a bunch of harmless pedants, supervising remote desert digs or sequestered away in libraries, up to their elbows in old papyrus." Hancock's language is also virulent, as he disparages the "astigmatic archaeologist sieving his way through the dust of the ages" (Hancock 1995: 354). Even Robert Schoch, himself an academic, is not immune. He declares at one

point that experimental archaeologist Thor Heyerdahl was not "the kind to remain hanging around libraries, blowing dust off old books and drafting hypotheses" (Schoch 2003: 179).[10] This jaundiced view of academia resonates with popular stereotypes of scatty professors ruminating over irrelevancies and finds echo in the words of the genre's readers and supporters (the Internet offers countless examples). Among them, it is not unusual to find it accepted as a matter of uncontested fact that universities are closed clubs, where novices advance by regurgitating the tired "opinions" of their instructors, where no one is willing to countenance being wrong, and where faculty are afraid to question the tenets of "orthodoxy" for fear of being fired. Extreme versions hint at dark conspiracies seeking to keep from the public the terrible truth about prehistory (whatever that may be). Since, in this world view, academics are scared rigid by the pioneering work of "alternative" writers, the opposition of university-trained critics is interpreted as proof that the pseudoarchaeological speculators are on to something.[11] The circularity of the caricature is impeccable.

This whole nexus of combative attitudes is encapsulated in the view of academia as a religion that passes its dogma down from teacher to student and ruthlessly stamps out opposition by inquisitorial means, especially when challenged from without. In an "Open Letter" posted to Graham Hancock's website in November 2000, retired engineer Robert Bauval, Hancock's occasional collaborator, had this to say:

> For decades the scientific and academic community has had an open field and held the floor on all issues related to the history of mankind. Archaeologists, Egyptologists, philologists, chemists, anthropologists, physicists and many more other-ists than I care to enumerate, have arrived at an established view about the past and have set out their rules and their methods to investigate it. They have formed a massive and global network through universities, museums, institutes, societies and foundations. And this immense powerhouse and clearing-house of knowledge has presented their [*sic*] dogma of history to the general public totally unhindered and unchallenged from the outside ... It was high time that some of the "established" views be challenged, but not in the dark halls of academia and the jargon-loaded verbiage of peer-reviewed journals, but in the wide open air, under the eyes of the public ... On a more sinister note: now this "church of science" has formed a network of watchdog organisations such as CSICOP and The Skeptical Society [*sic*] (to name but a few) in order to act as the gatekeepers of the truth (as they see it), ready to come down like the proverbial ton of bricks on all those whom they perceive as "frauds," "charlatans," and "pseudo-scientists" – in short, heretics.[12]

(Bauval 2000)

Many political advantages flow from adopting this stance. All good stories benefit from a villain, and pseudoarchaeologists like to position themselves as the powerless and heroic underdogs tackling a faceless and arrogant establishment. Their ideas gain a certain romantic cachet thereby (see Chapter 4). The reconstruction of the past pieced together by decades of meticulous archaeology and grounded in masses of physical evidence can be dismissed without exposition as "opinion" or "dogma," and dramatic alternatives suggested. Academic critiques of "alternative" scenarios can be diverted into an examination of the critic's motives, and by definition those motives cannot be anything other than mean-spirited, closed-minded, and authoritarian. University credentials in archaeology thus become the basis for suspicion of a critic: expertise is the *prima facie* reason for rejecting expert analysis. As the underdog, the speculator can combine the roles of martyr and liberator, oppressed for their beliefs but struggling gamely to break the chains of "orthodox" thinking. Von Däniken's call to arms is typical: "It is no longer possible to block the roads to the past with dogmas" (von Däniken 1968a: 67). The air of both self-pity and indignant righteousness that hangs about these works stems from this manufactured political confrontation with academia.

This is not to suggest that there have been no scandals in the history of universities, or that powerful personalities have never sought to suppress notions they see as challenging their ideas (see above on Eric Thompson). But such tactics work only for a time. In reality, universities exist to embrace constant questioning and criticism, and champions of new paradigm-shifting discoveries are not held under house arrest or subject to inquisitorial orders of silence. Quite the opposite: if revolutionary theories stand the test of scrutiny and criticism, their authors rocket to the tops of their professions. In such an atmosphere, new and justified discoveries cannot be systematically suppressed indefinitely: someone, somewhere will make use of them, if for no other reason than to advance their own careers. People do not win Nobel prizes in science for rehashing established knowledge. Far from paying a terrible price, overthrowers of scholarly "orthodoxy" earn terrific rewards. Indeed, the very claim of "orthodoxy" in the case of archaeology is especially absurd, as it reduces an active scholarly community marked by major divergences of opinion on scores of issues to an imagined monolithic "church" seeking to preserve its privileged position by suppressing dissent. It is a mirage, conjured before the eyes of their readership in order to give the pseudoarchaeologists a political advantage when confronting their critics.

3. *Appeal to academic authority.* In a startling *volte-face*, pseudoarchaeologists often gleefully parade support for their ideas from people with academic credentials and affiliations, wherever they can be found. It seems irrelevant to them that such a raw appeal to authority contravenes their favored picture of universities as churches of doctrine, or that the trumpeted credentials and

affiliations are nearly always in areas well outside the subjects being addressed. For example, Hancock several times reminds us that ECD was ringingly endorsed by Albert Einstein in a 1953 letter to Charles Hapgood (Hancock 1995: 9, 10, 11, 468, 471; Einstein even gets his own index entry). However, Einstein was not a geologist, and he died before the process of plate tectonics, which preclude ECD, had been appreciated. Similarly, Schoch is careful to cite the academic affiliations of people he invokes as supporting some part of his diffusionist scenario.[13] In this way, the pseudoarchaeologists hail specific scholars' qualifications when it suits them while denigrating the credentials of hundreds of professional archaeologists, whose work they rubbish. Nobody said that pseudoarchaeology had to be consistent.

Characteristics of procedure

4. *Huge claims*. Pseudoarchaeologists do not publish books or host television programs arguing that the Late Minoan IIIA1 period needs to be down-dated by a decade or two, or that certain classes of ancient pots might have served some arcane symbolic function. Rather, as the opening paragraphs of this chapter attest, their claims are spectacular and history-altering. Once more, the mode of presentation is what matters. Without far-reaching claims put forward and verified, knowledge of the past would not have advanced in the ways it has over the past century. However, it is in the matter of verification that the epoch-making claims of pseudoarchaeology have failed over this same period. There comes a time when an unverified claim that repeatedly fails testing stops being a viable possibility and starts being an article of faith. This is demonstrably the case with most pseudoarchaeological scenarios about lost continents, alien civilizers, or secret brotherhoods of priestly puppetmasters pulling the strings of history. None of these ideas has yielded an iota of verifiable evidence, despite over a century of questing for it. As a result, pseudoarchaeological "evidence" has to be manufactured from whatever sources are to hand (see #6 and #8).

5. *Selective and/or distorted presentation*. Pseudoarchaeological scenarios are characterized by a systematically selective presentation of the evidence, ancient and modern. This is often combined with serious misrepresentation of known facts, making such work at best dubious, at worst deceitful. Items from the ancient past that seem to suit their claims are offered up, and the rest are ignored. A quote from an occasional academic paper or a maverick work is cited as support for specific claims, without indication that the paper is outdated, or that the author retracted the claim later, or that the quote has been misunderstood or cited out of context. Speculators will often assert that mysteries remain unsolved when in fact they have long been solved (e.g., the claim that Egyptian civilization appeared overnight, fully-

formed; see Chapter 5), or they will present as mysterious and ill-understood sites or artefacts that have been extensively studied. While our knowledge of the ancient past will always be patchy due to the nature of the evidence for it, the depth of pseudoarchaeological misrepresentation extends far beyond what is justified by this fact.

Two examples from Hancock (1995) will suffice as illustrations. One of the first claims encountered in *Fingerprints of the Gods* is that Antarctica was ice-free very recently and that it is depicted as such in early Renaissance maps, maps that are then projected back into the deep past by a presumed process of transmission.[14] "The best recent evidence," writes Hancock, "suggests that Queen Maud Land [on Antarctica], and the neighbouring regions shown on the map [drawn by Turkish admiral Piri Reis in 1513], passed through a long ice-free period which may not have come completely to an end until about six thousand years ago" (Hancock 1995: 4). Endnote 2 of *Fingerprints* substantiates this extraordinary claim by referring the reader to Charles Hapgood's 1966 book, *Maps of the Ancient Sea Kings*. The extensive studies of the Antarctic icecap conducted by American, Russian, and international teams of scientists over the preceding decades – which reveal the ice to be hundreds of thousands of years old and which were available to Hancock when he was writing *Fingerprints* – go entirely unmentioned (Denton *et al.* 1991). Instead, a maverick book published almost thirty years earlier is presented to readers as "the best recent evidence" available to Hancock in the early 1990s for the age of the Antarctic ice. But the reader would have to check his notes and do some independent research to discover this fact.

Elsewhere, Hancock discusses the ancient Bolivian city of Tiwanaku (also spelled "Tiahuanaco"), which he presents as tremendously mysterious and suggests may date to 17,000 years ago (Hancock 1995: 62–92). In a 1999 interview with a BBC production team, Hancock states: "I think what's important to stress about Tiahuanaco is that this is a mysterious site about which very little is known. Minimal archaeology has been done over the years" (Hancock 2001: xxii). In fact, dozens of studies of Tiwanaku had been published in the years preceding Hancock's pronouncement; the place was carbon-dated by three collections of samples made in the 1950s, 1980s, and 1990s. The results were mutually consistent and indicated that the earliest possible occupation had occurred around 1500 BC; major excavations were conducted and published by Alan Kolata of the University of Chicago (Kolata 1993, 1996a, 1996b). These studies have yielded much information about Tiwanaku, its interaction with the surrounding region, and its wider place in Andean history. But in the interests of constructing a great "mystery" surrounding the site, Hancock denies this state of understanding and presents Tiwanaku as a place "about which very little is known." To a degree, this could be claimed about any archaeological site insofar as there are many aspects of it that will forever elude us. Such is the nature of the beast. But this more limited sense of mystery is clearly not what Hancock wishes his readership to envision about Tiwanaku. A site of profound mystery is more easily glossed with "alternative" possibilities than is a place pretty well understood in general but with many details outstanding.

This sort of selective and distorted presentation of evidence thoroughly pervades works of pseudoarchaeology. Professor Schoch, for instance, twice describes marine biologist turned diffusionist speculator Barry Fell as an "epigrapher" when Fell had no training in reading ancient inscriptions (Schoch 2003: 150, 195), and his epigraphic expertise did not extend to detecting manifest fakes or distinguishing man-made inscriptions from scratches on stone made by ploughs (Feder 2002b: 121–9). Documenting every transgression in such a mode of presentation, even in a single book of the genre, would take hundreds of pages. However, the examples discussed here are entirely typical of what happens when an apparently factual claim in these works is put to the test. Invariably, it is found that quotes are presented out of context, critical countervailing data is withheld, the state of understanding is misrepresented, or critical archaeological information about context is ignored. It is telling for the validity of their case that these are the means by which the pseudoarchaeologists are forced to advance their propositions.

6.   *The "kitchen-sink" mode of argument.* It is typical for pseudoarchaeological works to range widely over numerous fields of human knowledge. Hancock's and Schoch's books derive arguments from the following disciplines at various junctures: general archaeological method and theory; the history of and regional archaeology in the Andes, Mesoamerica, North America, Europe, China, Cambodia, Indonesia, and Polynesia; Egyptology; anthropology; prehistory; art history; ancient epigraphy; comparative global mythology; comparative religion; philology; linguistics; mathematics; astronomy; and geophysics. These are just the fields that I could readily identify; I am sure I have missed others. It is pertinent here to recall Bauval's belief, cited above (p. 32), that academics have "presented their dogma of history to the general public totally unhindered and unchallenged from the outside." The underlying assumption is that the general public is saturated by unchallenged "orthodox" knowledge, and it is the "alternative" movement's job to challenge that saturation. But it is patently absurd to imagine that a general reader could be so well informed about recent developments in so broad a spectrum of specialized fields as to be able to assess the falsity or validity of specific claims pilfered from so many of them. As a result, he or she will be readily convinced by an apparently impressive body of selected "evidence" seemingly drawn from rigorous scholarly disciplines and set in a dramatic narrative. This is what I call the "kitchen-sink" mode of argument, and it seems designed to overwhelm the reader by sheer weight of data rather than the quality of its particulars. For all its apparent catholicism, however, pseu-

doarchaeology again and again visits a canonical suite of "mysterious" sites (the Nazca lines, Macchu Picchu, Teotihuacán, Easter Island, etc.) and reviews the same "mysterious" myths (flood myth, *Popol Vuh*, etc.) so that the kitchen-sink mode of argument also shares many features with the recycling plant.

7. *Vague definitions.* The genre is unconcerned to define clearly what it is looking for. Key terms like "civilization," resident in the subtitles of many pseudoarchaeology books, are either undefined or so loosely characterized as to be useless. This adds, at the outset, whole strata of vagueness and imprecision to the speculators' efforts. While problematic for those who expect intellectual rigor in their history, vagueness offers major advantages to the pseudoarchaeologist, since it allows great scope for forging links where they are unlikely to exist. Professor Schoch embarks on an almost 300-page quest for the origins of pyramids but offers only the slimmest definition of what constitutes a "pyramid" in the first place: (1) a spirituality, and (2) an "architecture of mass" marked by "little or no interior space" (Schoch 2003: 21–3). The profound imprecision of this definition allows him to include in the category "pyramid" not only the familiar structures of the Egyptians, Maya, or Aztecs but also such non-pyramidal monuments as the round tumulus-and-passage grave at Newgrange in Ireland (*c.* 3500 BC), the round mound of Silbury Hill in England (perhaps *c.* 2000 BC), the earthen mounds/platforms of the Mississippi valley (*c.* 700 BC–AD 800), Javanese Buddhist temple complexes (eighth century AD), and the vast Khmer monumental assemblages at Angkor in Cambodia (tenth–thirteenth centuries AD). It is hard to imagine structures so different in every category of analysis: style, scale, location, form, function, construction materials and techniques, cultural context, and chronology.[15] But, for Professor Schoch, they are all "pyramids," and he is free to compare and link them at will, in whole or in part. (Note, by the way, the supreme disregard for context displayed by such comparisons.)

8. *Superficiality, sloppiness, and grossness of comparison.* The pseudoarchaeological penchant for making connections is as impressive as it is pointless. In a series of protracted investigations, Hancock trawls through obscure myth after obscure myth to "show" that geographically disparate cultures share common mythic imagery and motifs – and so also a common source (Hancock 1995: 93–272). Often, tales are read as accurate accounts of historical events, so that mythic fables of floods or golden ages become euhemeristic records of once-real conditions. Professor Schoch posits a "mythic link" underlying all the pyramids on the planet, a link based on spirituality and stories of the sun and sky gods and serpents and water (Schoch 2003: 54–81). The attraction of myth and religion to the pseudoarchaeologist is not hard to comprehend. These fields present a smorgasbord of potentially linkable categories: motifs and images, words

and phrases, characters and personalities, numbers and symbols, rituals and practices. Armed with a ruthlessly selective approach to the evidence and divested of any requirement to consider issues of context, the pseudoarchaeologist is free to run riot through world myth cycles and religious traditions and to make as many apparent connections as the imagination can conjure up. Their proposed connections are marked by superficiality (no regard for context or nuance) and sloppiness, the latter chiefly manifested in slippage of compared categories. Thus an image here can be linked to a mythic character there, which in turn is reminiscent of a ritual found somewhere else, and all three locations are thereby connected. In fact, this same sloppiness marks their treatment of all categories of evidence. Aside from myths, buildings and artefacts are fair game (see Professor Schoch's comparison of hugely divergent monuments as "pyramids"), as are iconography and artistic styles. In each instance, slippage of compared categories, superficiality of analysis, and grossness of comparison are the order of the day.

9.   *Obsession with esoterica.* The conviction that matters of deep importance are masquerading as mundanities infuses the genre. Thus pseudoarchaeologists love to go around "decoding" ancient messages from all manner of material. Myths and legends are very useful in this connection, as are writing systems, iconographies, site plans, and building dimensions; even the number of statues in the ranks and columns of the famous Chinese terracotta army can be "decoded" (Cotterell and Gilbert 1995; Cotterell 1997, 1999, 2003). Almost any evidence from the past can be presented as harboring esoteric information if only one has the will to see it. By "decoding" modern cityscapes – which include such mysterious features as ancient Egyptian obelisks (in Paris or Rome) and the glass pyramid at the Louvre – it has recently been claimed that devotees of a secret religion have been working clandestinely for the past 2,000 years to shape world events (Hancock and Bauval 2004). Ingenuity, patience, and complete conviction are the essential tools of such endeavors. Reality need not impinge.

An excellent example of commitment to esoterica is the so-called Orion correlation theory (OCT), discussed in more detail elsewhere in this volume (see the Introduction and Chapter 10). The unspectacular observation that the three main pyramids at Giza resemble the three belt stars of the constellation Orion was worked up into a grand scheme that pointed back to a date of 10,500 BC (10,450 BC in earlier manifestations) and suggested matters of deep spiritual importance. The original OCT argued for a wider pyramid map of Orion that included monuments beyond Giza, and there was much talk of exact, faultless, and unbelievable mathematical precision in the star-to-pyramid alignments that bespoke a profound astronomical knowledge on the part of the elusive Giza master planners (Hancock 1995: 356). The subsequent history of the OCT is complicated (see Chapter 10), but it is a story of steady retreat. An implied eleventh-millennium BC construction date for the pyramids (ibid.: 304–6) was retracted when it was shown to be logically impossible;[16] the "wider plan" OCT was retracted when the non-Giza pyramids were shown not to match up with stars in Orion; and claims of faultless mathematical precision in the correlations have mutated into the markedly vaguer claim that the OCT was "a grand symbolic statement that was supposed to be understood on a spiritual and intuitive level."[17] Although the "facts" of the OCT have sustained severe damage, the overall scheme remains in place as a monument to its proponents' unshakable commitment to esotericism. Hancock, in fact, has used the OCT as a model for proposing monumental star maps in Mesoamerica and Cambodia (Hancock 1995, 1998a), but, strangely, his subsequent work (Hancock 2002a) makes little use of this formerly core characteristic of his Lost Civilization.

In a similar manner, symbolist interpretations of Egyptian hieroglyphs, rendered meaningless by the actual decipherment of the writing system nearly two centuries ago, persist even today (West 1993: 129–46). Devotion to esotericism also stands behind the tedious number-crunching that marks many of these works, as supposedly significant numbers are extracted from the proportions of monuments or from site plans or from the contents of myths by means of tortured arithmetic (Hancock 1995: 227–72, 336–38, 429–41; Jordan 2001: 238). The numbers thus "discovered" can be correlated across categories to forge all sorts of links. Unsurprisingly, the Great Pyramid is a frequent victim of such numerological somersaults, an esoteric tradition that goes back to the movements of Freemasonry and Rosicrucianism (see Chapter 5). It is an added bonus for this procedure that the modern age of computers and technology assigns a particular authority to numbers. Pseudoarchaeological numerical "discoveries" may thus appear to be self-evidently valid and so quite above historical justification.

The obsession with esoterica also explains the pseudoarchaeological love affair with anomalies. Again and again, inexplicable "mysteries" and anomalous artefacts are paraded before the reader as evidence both for the ignorance of "orthodox" archaeology (which has trouble explaining them) and for the possibility that hidden landscapes lie behind the familiar façade of history. Given the misleading presentation of evidence in such works, all claimed anomalies ought to be checked thoroughly. Certainly, there are unsolved problems in archaeology, but the degree of mystery is often significantly inflated in pseudoarchaeological works. A classic example is the huge animal figures and complex patterns inscribed on the surface of the Nazca Plain in Peru. Since we have very little evidence from the culture that created them – their construction dates are fixed by ceramic analysis to between *c*. 200 BC and AD 600 – the intended function of the lines remains a matter of uncertainty to archaeology, although several plausible hypotheses have been advanced to explain them (Aveni 1990). For "alternative" archaeologists, however, the Nazca lines are landing sites for spaceships or encoded messages from lost Atlantis. Ignoring clues from the local context, the lines are treated as if they defy all rational analysis (which they do not), and wild speculations are offered up as reasonable explanations. To establish pre-Columbian transatlantic and transpacific visits to the Americas stretching back into the last Ice Age but ongoing through the Phoenicians, Africans, Celts, Hebrews, Romans, Polynesians, and Chinese, Professor Schoch collects a body of data that is a riot of odd finds and superficial correlations heaped on top each other, far too varied and zany to be surveyed here (Schoch 2003: 82–165). Conspicuously absent is precisely the sort of archaeological deposit that would be expected if transoceanic contact was indeed as frequent and as varied as Professor Schoch proposes, namely assemblages of firmly dated pre-Columbian Old World objects in New World contexts (or vice versa). This is the sort of evidence turned up by archaeology in other instances of cultural contact, which includes even the very brief Norse sojourn in Newfoundland around AD 1000. Since Professor Schoch cannot point to any such finds, he has to rely instead on stray oddities and uncontextualized anomalies that supposedly point to vast hidden histories.

10. *A farrago of failings.* A host of lesser vices characterizes the genre, most generated by the attitudes and procedures just reviewed. It would be impossible to catalogue them all here, but a sample will illustrate the problem. Logical fallacies abound, especially the inversion of the burden of proof and the appeal to authority (see #3). If specific claims go unaddressed by critics or are not "conclusively disproved," to use a popular comeback, they are considered valid (Hancock 2001: xli–xlii). But the burden of proof rests not on the critic but on the claimant. Likewise, the modern writers' mere ability to chart patterns is presented as evidence for their speculations, when not a shred of actual evidence exists to suggest that, for instance, the pyramid builders set out to "mirror" starry Orion with terrestrial monuments, let alone "encode" the date 10,500 BC (or 10,450 BC) in them. Mystery-mongering is rampant, even to the point of making unsubstantiated allegations backed by dubious authority. Hancock spends three pages suggesting that quarry marks on the stones in the Great Pyramid, marks that effectively prove that the pyramid was built by the pharaoh Khufu, were forged by Englishman Howard Vyse in 1837. He cites a book by spacemen-built-the-pyramids proponent Zecharia Sitchin in support (Hancock 1995: 302–4). This is really grasping at straws, especially since Hancock more or less admits the "conventional" dating of the pyramids to 2500 BC a few pages later (ibid.: 335). If so, why bring up the specious allegations against Vyse, if not in the interests of raw mystery-mongering? Consistency is another casualty of pseudoarchaeological speculations. We are asked to accept that Tiwanaku – at 12,600 feet (3,850 m) above sea level one of the most elevated archaeological sites in the world – is a city of Hancock's Lost Civilization (see #5). But this

clashes with the proposition that the evidence for this same civilization was submerged by a sea-level rise of just 400 feet at the end of the last Ice Age (Hancock 2002a).

While all good writing uses rhetorical skill in its presentation, pseudoarchaeological works employ a battery of rhetorical strategies not in the service of a coherent argument but as a replacement for it. Suggestions are raised as possibilities in one place and resurrected later as established facts. Rhetorical questions are a favorite means of planting odd notions in the reader's head or shrouding well-studied sites in fogs of mystery: "Can it be coincidence that ... ?"; "Is it inconceivable that ... ?"; "Can it be ruled out that ... ?" False analogies and weak arguments from "common sense" are constantly resorted to (specific examples are cited in Chapter 10).

Another feature of the genre is the invocation of supposedly "hard" sciences in support of arguments that those sciences are largely unfit to substantiate. This procedure may be considered a combination of an appeal to authority (#3) and mispresentation of known facts (#5). Thus the authority of mathematics is summoned to validate numerological speculations marked by arbitrary and preposterous calculations (see #9). Likewise, the astronomical fact of precession is called on to demonstrate the star map "redating'" of the ancient monuments at Giza or Tiwanaku or Angkor to excessively ancient eras. But the essential monument-to-star connection is not firmly established for ancient times; its raw identification in the mind of the speculator is deemed its own justification, regardless of whether it fails to apply to other monuments of the same type or if a pitiless selectivity is required to make the "correlations" fit. Recently, the Great Sphinx at Giza has been redated to very early epochs on the basis of one geologist's opinion that it was weathered predominantly by rainwater and not by wind and sand (West 1993: 221–32; Schoch 1999: 33–51, 2003: 278–98). Since Egypt has been arid at least since 5000 BC, the argument goes, the Sphinx must predate the Egyptians and the traditional date of *c.* 2500 BC. This, too, is an attempt to coopt the authority of a "hard" science (geology) in support of "alternative" historical claims. In fact, geology is singularly unsuited as an archaeological dating tool, since its chronological depth vastly exceeds that of human history, and the rate at which rocks erode is subject to too many variables for it to be used as a "clock" to date relatively recent man-made monuments. Several other explanations for the erosion patterns on the Sphinx and its enclosure are available that accommodate the traditional, archaeologically established date and historical context of the monument. In contrast, a pre-Egyptian Sphinx lacks any archaeological context whatsoever – itself a crushing observation (Jordan 1998). The "precipitation-induced-erosion" proposal is thus unnecessary and is yet another example of modern speculation being offered up as if it were hard fact.

11. *Expectation of a reward at quest's end.* The purpose of all this speculative effort is the expectation that some great benefit will emerge at quest's end.

Unfortunately, the pay-off is usually couched in distressingly vague terms, with dark intimations of imminent disaster or the happier prospect of recovering lost ancient wisdom. Hancock, for instance, suggests that his beloved Lost Civilization left star maps of monuments and encoded information in myths and folk tales as a testament to their existence and a warning to future generations of what can happen when Earth crustal displacement takes place (Hancock 1995: 487–505). What exactly we are supposed to do in preparation for ECD is not made clear – correlate terrestrial monuments with stars, it seems. The ancient-wisdom motif makes an appearance in strikingly religious passages about the Lost Civilization's "science of immortality" and vague hints of great spiritual discoveries that may emerge from his inquiries (Hancock 1998a). Professor Schoch's quest ends on an equally gloomy but no more precise note: pyramids teach us about cometary impacts and their effects on people – although civilization can be snuffed out in an instant, pyramids stand as reminders of its existence for future generations (Schoch 2003: 270–7). Once more, it is not immediately obvious how pyramid-derived knowledge about cometary impacts might be of use to us in the here and now. But failing that, discovering the true origins of pyramids "offers the prospect of better knowing who we are" (ibid.: 84), which is at least comforting. Such notions as these open interesting windows onto the writers' psychology – but that is a subject well outside the scope of the current chapter.

Conclusion

The diagnosis of pseudoarchaeology through analysis of its methods is not a zero-sum game. Not all pseudoarchaeological works employ all the procedures surveyed above; nor does identification of one or two of the features automatically brand a work as pseudoarchaeological. Rather, a preponderance of methodological characteristics is required to assign a work to the genre. More importantly, some of the features charted above overlap with genuine archaeological methods; it is the *mode of deployment* in pseudoarchaeology that matters. For instance, some selectivity in presentation is forced on any historian or archaeologist – publishing every single piece of pertinent evidence is neither practical nor desirable. Archaeologists therefore seek to present a representative sample of their data when publishing their findings, with special attention paid to the most information-laden items (e.g., coins, pottery, inscriptions, or carbon-datable organic material). To this extent, their work is selective in presentation. However, this situation differs from the relentless and ruthless selectivity of the pseudoarchaeologist, who seeks to suppress or ignore any data that may undermine the favored conclusion and who thus presents an unrepresentative sample of data to the reader. In a similar way, the pseudoarchaeologists' reliance on multiple disciplines (see #6) does not generate a genuinely interdisciplinary picture of the past (which can be done well; see Diamond 1997). Rather, pseudoarchaeologists raid a wide range of fields for specifics, which are then assembled under conditions of intense selectivity (#5) and unconcern for context. Such a procedure can only produce a jerry-built scaffold of possibilities reflecting what the speculator thinks the past should look like, rather than a solidly evidenced reconstruction of what it may actually have looked like. And while esoterica certainly existed in antiquity (magical papyri or apocalyptic literature, for instance), their existence hardly justifies "decoding" vague ancient wisdom from rows of statues or from the proportions of (selected) buildings. In all of these instances, as in many others, pseudoarchaeology begins with a known quantity and stretches it into the unlikely to conclude the implausible. What is conceivable trumps what is demonstrable.

It must be remembered that these procedures appear in combination, in a storm of uncontextualized, exaggerated claims and unlikelihoods, distortions and selections, all masked by rhetorical tricks and flourishes. The pseudoarchaeologists' insistence that their claims stand as valid until categorically disproved adds another level of absurdity to their efforts. The "methods" of pseudoarchaeologists, while superficially resembling aspects of real inquiry, are in fact gross corruptions of genuine investigative procedure.

In the final analysis, the claims of pseudoarchaeology are best judged by their results. Thereby is the genre's ultimate characteristic revealed: the zealous pursuit of investigative dead-ends. When, for instance, it is asserted that familiar ancient civilizations are actually inheritances from earlier but lost civilizations, the question that appears to be addressed – "Where does civilization come from?" – is not answered but deferred. For the next obvious question is: "So where did those earlier civilizations come from?" But this question cannot be answered or even approached, since the supposed evidence adduced for the prodigious protocivilizations is either esoteric and untestable (numerological "encodings" or literal interpretations of myths) or hidden and inaccessible (under the Antarctic icecap, under the sea, wholly destroyed by cyclical catastrophes, or in outer space). Ultimately, the pseudoarchaeologists' response to the very important question "Where did civilization come from?" is to say "From civilization."[18] That does not get us very far.

History documents the futility of pseudoarchaeological efforts. The hunt for lost supercivilizations has been on at least since Donnelly's case for a historical Atlantis was published in 1882 (although antecedents can be traced back into the sixteenth century). In the decades since, dozens of locations for wondrous lost protocultures in the remote past have been postulated covering most corners of the planet, millions of pages have been printed, dozens of scenarios proposed and still not a single site – not a settlement, a burial, a potsherd, or a hairpin – to show for it. Over this same period, archaeology has been ongoing across the globe and innumerable sites have been explored, on land and under water. Many millions of archaeological strata have been uncovered and documented, and artefacts by the tens of millions have been unearthed, catalogued, stored, and displayed. Analysis of this huge mass of material has extended our historical perception back into the deepest recesses of the past. Yet the museum cases for Atlantean objects remain permanently empty. That emptiness is the most telling testament to the effectiveness of pseudoarchaeology's investigative methods: they are signposts on the road to nowhere.

Notes

1. This is Erich von Däniken's reconstruction of antiquity, first proposed almost forty years ago (von Däniken 1968a) and restated in a flood of sequels (1968b, 1970, 1971, 1973a, 1973b, 1976, 1977, 1996, 1998a, 1998b, 2000).
2. For a comprehensive overview of the claims bandied about concerning Atlantis and other lost continents, see Jordan 2001.
3. Such are the essential propositions of Graham Hancock's *Fingerprints of the Gods* (1995 [2001]). Hancock's other books (1998a, 1998b, 2002a; Bauval and Hancock 1996) reiterate some of these central tenets of the lost civilization belief system but abandon others (such as Earth crustal displacement; see below). The "new" idea of a great proto-civilization lost on a sunken landmass has a heritage traceable to Ignatius Donnelly (1970 [1882]) and Helena Blavatsky (1888 [1971]). It has recently been championed in Schoch 2003.
4. E.g., Barker 1994; Barker and Grant 1999; Renfrew and Bahn 2000; Roskams 2001; Darvill 2002.
5. For some recent surveys, see Kelley and Hanen 1988; Hodder 1992, 1999; Hodder *et al.* 1995; Hodder and Hutson 2003; Preucel and Hodder 1996; Whitley 1998.
6. Extreme post-processualists and relativists, who would deny the existence of an objective past independent of interpretation, would disagree, but they are few and far between and hardly a dominant force in the discipline. Note that Whitley (1998: 10), when summarizing the extreme relativistic view, does not cite a single actual practitioner. It is true that Shanks and Hodder (1995: 20) state that a genuine commitment to post-processualist (or interpretative) archaeology "means treating, at the outset, objectivity and 'falsity,' science and 'pseudo-science' as equal (many scientific ideas begin as cranky ideas)." Such statements are music to the ears of the pseudoarchaeologist.
7. In the introduction to the revised edition of *Fingerprints* (2001), Hancock claims that his ideas are constantly evolving and changing in light of new discoveries (xvii–xviii). The claim is disingenuous. All that has changed in *Underworld* is the sort of "evidence" presented and the details of the arguments offered to buttress the unassailable conclusion. The willingness to reissue *Fingerprints* without altering a word of the original text demonstrates this amply. Hancock may now distance himself from aspects of his 1995 presentation (see note 9 below), but he is comfortable with the original text, since the preordained conclusion stands beyond the reach of the evidence cited to buttress it. See also the comments of Bettina Arnold in Chapter 7.
8. I recognize that proponents of a "social-constructivist" view of science and scholarship will take issue with this characterization of academic procedure, but we have not the space here to enter this wider debate.
9. While ECD was critical to his original 1995 scenario, Hancock has since distanced himself from it (preferring rapid sea-level rise as the civilization-killing event). Characteristically, he does not abjure ECD entirely – a fudge that fails to acknowledge its fundamental flaws (Hancock 2001: xxxvii–xxxix). ECD also plays a major role in Flem-Ath 1995.
10. While perhaps not as vitriolic as other examples of the genre, Professor Schoch's book does not shy away from innuendo about the world of ancient scholarship. We read, for instance, that scholars go about "assuming" (11, 167, 171) and "asserting" (201) to reach

their conclusions; that they cleave to independent inventionism for ideological rather than scientific reasons; that (unspecified) ideology leads them to ignore evidence of diffusion (81); that graduate schools create narrow specialists unwilling to debate with those outside their specific archaeological foci; and that archaeologists defend the cultures they study to deny a political advantage to rivals studying other cultures (82–3). It is even laughably declared (167) that modern academics downplay the role of the sea as a medium of cultural contact in ancient times because the Romans were landlubbers, and modern scholarship traces its roots back to the Romans. In short, the scholarly positions of historians are repeatedly presented as resting on political, arbitrary, or authoritarian bases.

11. Such opinions as these can be elicited in a few moments by going to the message boards of any number of "alternative" history websites and posting a provocative note in defense of the standard scenarios. Here is a typical attitude from one visitor to the website *In the Hall of Ma'at* (http://www.thehallofmaat.com): "Reflect back on your academic experience. ... Mimic the gatekeepers [of orthodoxy] really well and you might enter the club with a fellowship or better. At least they will pass on your degree. And if you stay to witness this gatekeeping operation you quickly learn that you don't STRAY outside of the bounds of conventionality or tenure will be hard to find indeed. The lesson is not lost. It would be interesting to see how many thesis [*sic*] regurgitate known knowledge rather than striking new ground (like Atlantis)."

12. Note the "us-and-them" way in which the issues are framed. An even more enthusiastic promulgator of the church metaphor is John Anthony West, promoter of astrology and proponent of Egyptian symbolism (on which, see Chapter 5). West believes that Egyptian civilization was inherited from Atlantis. As a denier of evolution, he rails against a straw man – the "Church of Progress" – that he believes dominates modern science and society; see West (1993: 233–42) and his website at http://www.jawest.com. A more subtle method is that of Professor Schoch (2003: 90), who expressly parallels contemporary anthropology's theory of a migration from Siberia into the Americas with Pope Julius II's declaration in 1512 that the peoples of the Americas must be displanted Babylonians, which agreed with Biblical orthodoxy. The equivalence renders both positions raw belief enforced by fiat.

13. Some examples (with page references in Schoch 2003): M. Gimbutas, UCLA (151); J. Needham, Cambridge University (153); M. Xu, Central Oklahoma University (157); Paul Sullivan and Asaf Raza, La Trobe University (171); Richard Fullagar, Australian Museum (171); Arysio Nunes dos Santos, Escola de Engenharia da Universidade Federal de Minas Gerais (244); Stephen Oppenheimer, Chinese University of Hong Kong (246); and Alexander and Edith Tollmann, University of Vienna (265). Pseudoarchaeologists are not above gross misrepresentation of their academic supporters' positions in order to make them fit; see the case of Professor J. Kirschvink discussed by Christopher Hale in Chapter 10.

14. This latter claim has been demolished by McIntosh 2000.

15. The supposed "mystery" of why pyramid-like monuments appear independently in different parts of the globe was solved decades ago by L. Sprague de Camp (1963: 56): in the absence of steel, concrete, or vaults, attempts to build high monuments will lead to a pyramid-like structure; children with building blocks are capable of finding this out quite by themselves. The really interesting archaeological/historical question here is "Why do early civilizations feel the need to build large monuments?" It is not seriously addressed by pseudoarchaeologists. (Professor Schoch's appeal to "spirituality" is too vague to get us very far, since notions of what constitutes the spiritual differ so markedly between cultures.) Monuments, rather, are just an assumed part of "civilization."

16. A sub-characteristic of the genre is a certain tentativeness in advancing its scenarios, so that any given claim can be jettisoned as an innocent "suggestion" or "possibility" when shown to be baseless; see Hancock's cautious wording, p. 27.

17. The story can be traced on the websites of Robert Bauval, Graham Hancock, and the BBC program *Horizon* ("Atlantis Reborn Again," available in transcripts). For a summary with bibliography, see Wall 2002. For Hancock's "Position statement on the antiquity and meaning of the Giza monuments," see Hancock 2001: xxxiv–xxxviii. For criticism of the OCT, see Malek 1994; Legon 1995.
18. And the even more interesting question "What *is* civilization?" is not even addressed; see Chapter 10.

2 The attraction of non-rational archaeological hypotheses

The individual and sociological factors

N.C. Flemming

Introduction

The public seems to have an insatiable appetite for wild archaeological theories, even at a time when genuine archaeological information is more widely available than ever and is more exciting than ever. In practice, many non-experts are able to distinguish sharply between archaeology and pseudoarchaeology, but why do so many people fall for obviously unproven and unverifiable propositions, and why is a sector of the media industry so enthusiastic in promoting this junk? The reasons are powerful but not obvious, and in this chapter I investigate the nature of attraction to fringe archaeology. Throughout, pseudoarchaeology is viewed as standing on a continuum with pseudoscience, and examples are drawn from both genres (see also Chapters 11 and 12).

Pseudoarchaeology, like any pseudoscience, is always aimed at the non-expert and the non-professional interested in the discipline concerned. There are overt and covert reasons for persuading this audience to believe what is being propagated, perhaps political, religious, or commercial, and some of these reasons are explored in other chapters of this book. Three essential elements constitute the phenomenon: (1) a practitioner of the pseudo-activity; (2) a message to be transferred; and (3) a group of recipients or believers. The vehicle of transmission is usually a pseudo-text, which is related in ways yet to be described to a real sector of science and archaeology. The message and the pseudo-text may also be amplified and promoted widely in the modern commercialized media such as television, the Internet, theme parks, and mass promotion of popular book sales.

The practitioner designs the pseudo-product in such a way as to have maximum appeal to the target audience. The subject of this chapter is to try to understand what is implied by that word "appeal." Why do pseudo-subjects have such a strong appeal to a certain audience? What is the practitioner playing on when he/she designs a product to be so seductive? Why does the practitioner not simply present the message as would a politician or scientist presenting a well-thought-out argument? Why do the media so enthusiastically promote pseudoscience and pseudoarchaeology, seldom acknowledging their profound difference from real science and real archaeology? What are the defining tricks and symptoms of a pseudo-presentation (see Chapter 1)? What is the relationship between the pseudo-practitioner and the professional in the disciplines that are being exploited? Why do scientists and archaeologists find it so difficult to refute pseudo-texts and get so angry and frustrated by their inability to do so? Why does the average believer in the pseudo-text find it so difficult to detect the trick and reject it?

Pseudoscience and pseudoarchaeology corrupt the basis of factual knowledge available to the public, and particularly to students. They also corrupt and debase the methodology of establishing empirical evidence for past events (in fields such as geology, archaeology, cosmology, or history), and hence the ability of students or the lay reader to distinguish fact from fantasy or invention. It follows that, in order to combat the slow but apparently remorseless growth of pseudoarchaeology, we must understand its appeal. It is impossible to provide the believer with an antidote if we do not comprehend the nature of the belief and the strength of its attraction.

To achieve this understanding, we will have to calculate when a rational person basing decisions and conduct on evidence and experience may reasonably demand a full empirical proof of a statement, and when he/she is justified in taking statements on trust, that is, in categorizing them as useful and useable but not empirically tested and verified. This is a second-order empiricism, where past experience has shown that the source of the information can be relied upon, even if the information itself has not been checked empirically by the recipient before using it each time.

The puzzle about the flow of "contrarian" pseudo-information is that it claims to be empirically based and founded on scientific and academic methods, even as it contravenes the methods used by the overwhelming majority of scientists and academics. If we can understand the strange and surprising appeal of this kind of statement, and the mechanism by which it appeals, then we can start to disentangle its structure of persuasion and develop an antidote. This is important, because one of the pervasive characteristics of the conflict between archaeology and pseudoarchaeology is the extraordinary sense of helplessness that professionals experience. Their first instinct is to assume that the pseudo-subject is so absurd that no one could possibly be convinced by its arguments. This tempts the critic into an undignified condemnation by invective. On second thoughts, the knowledgeable critic may then attempt to refute the statements in the pseudo-text one by one, but this usually leads to an expenditure of effort that appears almost unending. The critic eventually abandons the task for more creative work, baffled by a cloud of woolly counter-counter-claims hurled back by the believers.

In what follows, we shall proceed from a preliminary definition of pseudo-archaeology to a consideration of why and when people use rational judgments and empirical proofs; a review of the fragility of empirical evidence and the scientific method; a consideration of the psychology of why pseudoscience works; an examination of the motives of pseudo-practitioners; and, finally, a survey of the target audience.

A preliminary definition

The very categories "pseudoarchaeology" and "pseudoscience" are puzzling. Surely the result of empirical enquiry is either demonstrably correct or an unproven but credible hypothesis, or demonstrably wrong? We all make mistakes, theories come and go, dates are revised, stratigraphy is improved, new evidence persuades us to change our mind. This is normal. Science progresses by refining and improving previous approximations to an idealized but testable description of the outside world. Sometimes major discoveries or new theories cause a radical upset and restructuring of previous thought (Kuhn 1996), but this is rare, and it seldom proves that previously accepted ideas were wrong, rather that there are conditions that were not foreseen and that the revised laws apply in this area of new conditions as well as in the old one. Although occasional false dead-end theories are necessarily abandoned, much of the best science and archaeology is a continuous extension of horizons, increasing accuracy, explanation of causality, extending and refining existing laws and accepted facts into new territory, literally or figuratively.[1]

Pseudoscience is not hoaxing, a form of deceptive fraud designed to fool experts. Examples of hoaxing include the Piltdown Man fake human skull and jaw, several famous examples of faked discovery of fossils (usually genuine fossils that the geologist claims to have found in wildly unlikely locations), or phony Chinese dinosaurs made by joining fossils together. In all these cases the perpetrator, a professional scientist, faked data and wrote up the results in the standard academic way in the professional journals. The intention of the fraud was to achieve perfect camouflage by presenting the data as real science. While the villains were seeking to advance their status and fame, they did not appeal to the public but sought to deceive their colleagues.

In contrast, pseudoscience is almost never written in standard academic journals and is designed to be read by, and to mislead, the public and the media. The faker or forger seeks the approval of professionals: the pseudo-writer is delighted, as we shall see, when professionals ridicule his/her work. The pseudo loves the limelight, seeks publicity by whatever means, and often challenges the boffins and nerds to come out of their laboratories and conduct the debate in public.

I have sometimes encountered the suggestion that pseudoscience or pseudo-archaeology performs the valuable function of testing fringe ideas in a speculative and acceptable way, and that the attitudes or beliefs that are now regarded as pseudo will be filtered by time and experience so that some of them will join the complement of recognized academic tenets. This proposal ignores the fact that there are hundreds of speculative ideas floating around in the professional academic world that are clearly labeled as unproven and that are well recognized as good science or good archaeology in waiting. In mathematics, there are conjectures such as the Goldbach conjecture or the Riemann hypothesis, which have been researched but remain unproven for over a century (Sabbagh 2002). In physics, we have string theory, which has been studied by some of the best physicists in the world for more than a decade but has not been proved to represent any part of the objective universe and could still turn out to be an intellectual blind alley (Greene 1999). In geology, the theory of continental drift was held in suspension for forty years until the mechanism of plate tectonics was discovered in the late 1960s. In archaeology (and palaeo-anthropology), theories about human origins, genetics, and migrations are proposed, tested, and often abandoned within a timescale of a few decades. Archaeology now is in a state of rapid growth and change as theories are tested based on new isotope technologies, the decoding of human DNA, linguistics, evolutionary models, cultural models, palaeo-climatology, and new discoveries at sites around the world (Cunliffe *et al.* 2002). Some of the new theories will prosper as they seem to fit the facts, and some will die. This process is not about bad science or sloppy intellectual practices. It is the way academics work. They are quite happy to live with ideas and hypotheses that remain unproven, in limbo, for many years. The correct frame of mind is therefore to suspend judgment until the evidence is convincing. Nor do they think ill of the proponents of abandoned ideas, unless they irrationally promote a pet theory that has been widely recognized as disproved. For example, the late Fred Hoyle, who was greatly respected as an astronomer, attracted humorous criticism for clinging to the idea of continuous creation of matter in the universe long after the Big Bang theory was generally accepted as fitting the facts much better.

Pseudoscience and pseudoarchaeology do not fit into this framework of good theories in waiting. I cannot think of a single example where a "fringe" idea from the world of pseudoscience has been gradually established as proved and has been integrated into the academic textbooks. The only area where this kind of shift may have occurred is in medicine, where cures depending on peculiar skills such as acupuncture and osteopathy have been progressively proved to work on some afflictions by empirical testing and have been accepted into the medical community. Even in these examples, the practitioners tended to work quietly and soberly at their jobs before recognition and did not trumpet excessive claims in the manner of alternative medicine.

Equally, the lack of recognition for pseudo-topics should not be confused with the contemporary reservations about the obsessive determination of some scientists or archaeologists – for example, Marie Curie or Heinrich Schliemann – who pursued convictions toward obscure goals when more normal people would have given up. In both cases, the protagonist was backing a hunch with long odds against them, but they were not working in a way that was counter-factual or denying the established principles of their disciplines.

There are therefore traits about the conduct of pseudoscience and pseudo-archaeology that distinguish them from outright professional frauds, from research into unproven theories, or from scientists who cling to abandoned old theories or mistakes. The next section will attempt to identify some of these traits and how we may detect them.

The use and abuse of rational judgments and empirical proofs

The motto of the Royal Society, founded in 1660, is *nullius in verba*, meaning "on the word of no one." That is, do not believe a story because the speaker sounds convincing, or is important, but check the empirical evidence. This is splendid in principle, but in practice people cannot realistically check every claim put before them. In science and scholarship, conventions and disciplines have been built up so that people working in the same field respect agreed methodologies and tests. A laboratory obtains a high reputation for consistently conducting certain analyses or tests to verifiable accuracy. An archaeologist shows the stratigraphic survey and data-logging methods used on a site. If the report is presented in the standard way, convention says that a third party does not actually have to go to the storeroom or check the field notes and the accuracy of the tape measures before believing the published article.

If there is a big scandal – an accusation of plagiarism or forgery of data – then critics do go back and check the original sources. In my own research (in marine archaeology) I have visited coastal sites described by researchers perhaps 50–100 years earlier and reached quite different conclusions. Before diving equipment was widely used, researchers who saw rectangular stones in the shallow sea usually assumed that such deposits were explicable by a relative change of sea level. Close inspection by divers can reveal whether a structure beneath the water was part of a house, or a fish tank, or a dock, and can thus sometimes show that the structure was originally built in the water, without any subsequent change of level. Divers can identify from its function the depth at which the building was originally constructed, to within an error of 5–10 cm (Flemming 1978, 1998; Flemming and Webb 1986). Since my early research was published in the 1960s and 1970s, some of the sites I worked on have been visited by younger researchers, who write and tell me what they have discovered. This is very gratifying. If they discover something that forces a reassessment of the site, I accept their revision with good grace.

Since I surveyed my first submerged ruins at Apollonia, Libya, in 1958, I have faced continuous questioning about the myth of Atlantis; or whether particular submerged ruins prove or disprove some myth or theory about floods, earthquakes, and other catastrophes; or how one can distinguish genuine archaeological materials under the sea from natural rock formations. Over the decades, I have worked on more than 300 archaeological sites, ranging in age from 1,000 to 45,000 years old, where at least some part of a built structure or artefact was submerged in the sea. I have had to be aware of the popular obsessions with flood myths, local legends, factual data on earthquakes and Ice Age sea-level changes, and sensationalist stories and exaggerations. All my results have been published in refereed international academic journals, or conference proceedings, with occasional writing for the popular market.

This balance of professional standards, ethics, reliability, and checkability in principle, combined with a strong element of trust and convention, is how the scientific, archaeological, and other academic communities work. In addition, the writing style used in professional publications should not be persuasive or hectoring. Fine writing or glowing sentences rich in adjectives and superlatives is strongly discouraged. A deadpan factual presentation with the highest degree of simplicity and clarity compatible with the subject is the ideal. If this were not the case, a bad scientist with a persuasive line of talk could get his/her observations taken seriously for a long time before the errors were detected. Furthermore, it is forbidden in scientific and archaeological circles to publish the same facts more than once in an academic journal, or in different journals. Each journal insists that what is published in its pages is original and has never been published elsewhere. You get one shot to make your case, and you cannot launch a repetitive publicity campaign to sell your ideas. (Some academics do revise papers slightly and re-submit them to other journals, but this gradually diminishes their respect in the community.)

These strict conventions tie the professional hand and foot when compared with the free-ranging pseudo. The pseudo can use language of the most exaggerated and persuasive nature, appear on television, write in newspapers, and publish the same ideas as often as he/she likes. Such activities contribute directly to the goals of the pseudo, which is to persuade the general public and to gain converts (see below). In contrast, for the professional scientist to combat the pseudo, he/she has to abandon their main work to engage in a fruitless and demeaning struggle with wordplay. The purpose of the pseudo in the repeated requests for debate is exactly to produce this situation in public, making the professional look silly, unprepared, and a quitter.

Writers who encourage the popular cause of good science and the rejection of pseudoscience, pseudoarchaeology, and superstition sometimes claim that the average reader/viewer should reject the non-scientific pseudo-writing because it does not stand up to the tests of scientific checkability, proof, and logic.[2] These writers assert that we obviously check things in daily life and imply that pseudo-writings can be detected in the same way. Superficially this is true, but it leaves most people with a helpless feeling of inadequacy, that they are failing to be sensible or purposeful. They find it difficult to see why so much effort is needed to detect pseudo-writing when everyday life seems so much simpler.

They have a good point. The exhortation to check statements for their scientific validity in daily life is indeed wide of the mark. It is obvious that we do not check everything we are told every day in the same way that a food chemist might test for a poison in the laboratory.

Consider Table 2.1, which contains two lists of different ways in which we can encounter information and ideas. All statements or texts of the types in both list 1 and list 2 are treated as acceptable within the social conventions of the day, provided that we know what class of statement we are being given. Usually this is obvious from the context, leaning on the drinks bar, sitting in the theatre, watching a political rally on television, looking up a telephone number, or assembling a bookcase from a flat-pack. We value all the types of expression in list 1 but would not expect any of them to be literally and provably true. They are modes of communication that most of us recognize as having value, often seriously profound or aesthetic value, but they are not empirical or scientific. Thus the advice that we should respect statements that are verifiably true and be suspicious of all others carries no weight at all. There is a grain of truth in it, but it is so small that most people shake their heads and reject the argument. The exhortation does not help us to understand the roots of pseudoarchaeology or pseudoscience. Nor does it work as an antidote or detection system to alert us to danger.

Not only do we accept and value the communications in list 1, but even when we ask for information of the kind in list 2, we tend to believe what we are told, basing our assumption on the respectability of the atlas, directory, manufacturer, and so on. We very seldom perform a scientific test of correctness on a telephone number, or an atlas, or even a book of chemical formulae. Yet this acceptance of authority as the validity of information is exactly counter to the allegedly true spirit of science – *nullius in verba*. We are supposed to doubt and test. But the social structures of responsibility, accuracy, and accountability are such that it is rational most of the time not

Table 2.1 Contrasting logical classes of information

List one	List two
Political manifesto	Train timetable
Classical novel	Cooking recipe
Science fiction	Machinery assembly instructions
Poetry	Scientific textbook
Popular love song	Safety drill instructions
Religious sermon	Road map
Joke	Identity documents
Philosophical argument	Mathematical tables
Autobiography	Chemical formula
Art criticism	Dials and instruments on a machine
Theatrical play	Telephone directory
Advertising slogan	Training manuals
Fairy stories	Dates of major events
Advice from a friend	Two-language dictionary
Journalistic feature	Patent register
Detective thriller	Police forensic record

to express that doubt. (Occasionally a map is wrong, or a price label is incorrect, but not so often as to make us check every time). Life would be impossible if we asked every time for evidence that a train timetable was the true one, or every number in a telephone directory was correct. We do accept authoritative information on the basis of the reputation of the source.

When a document claims to be science or archaeology, whether professional academic literature or derived popular interpretation, it is proclaiming loudly "Check me! I am making the claims of science. The facts that I am giving you should be testable and checkable layer after layer, back as far as you want to go, until we get to the very basis of 'What is knowledge?' Here are the references. Check me! You should be able to check my assertions through the literature, or if you wish, you can perform experiments, or go to the laboratories or companies where they do these things, visit the excavation trenches, and see the processes at work. This is empirical truth to my best ability."

We are invited to check, and given sufficient information so that checks would be easy, even if in general we do not choose to make them. The structure of the argument and the presentation of data is done in such a way as to make checking extremely easy if we wished to do so. To the professional, the ease of checking should be blatantly obvious.

Pseudoscience is laying claim to the same testable authority as real science or real archaeology and uses some of the same jargon as camouflage, but then it makes assertions of the kind that should appear only in list 1. This is why many pseudo-works have the dramatic qualities of a novel, detective story, religious tract, or self-aggrandizing autobiography. The language and plot have the appeal and drama of the genres in list 1, which helps to spread the ideas and has the advantage that the language appeals to non-scientific reviewers who write for the Sunday newspaper magazines.

All the items in list 2 share the characteristic of being blindingly boring as literature or as expressive use of language. Good professional scientific writing is clear, logical, easy to follow, grammatical, well constructed, efficient, maybe even elegant, but it should not be persuasive or enticing. In this writing, jargon is essential to express ideas unambiguously and concisely. There is an obvious dilemma here, a fuzzy boundary, since some scientists write so badly that, even when their experiments are correct, their work is unpublishable. However, I think this is just bad luck and does not invalidate the general point. A scientific truth should stand up because it is verifiably true, not because it reads with the scintillating beauty of Shakespeare or the superficial verbal glitter of Nabokov.

Is the offence in pseudo-texts, then, to combine elements of list 1 and list 2 in an unacceptable way? We can note that there are several legitimate ways of combining genres. For example, valuable work is done using high-tech physics and chemistry to study old master paintings and manuscripts. Interesting research has been conducted on the neurobiology of how humans hear and react to music and art. Formal scholarly biographies of famous archaeologists and scientists combine historical dramatization with a solid understanding of the subject's achievements, which must not be distorted. There is a lighter note in the kind of jokes that you find in specialist science communities.

For example: a hydrogen atom goes into a police station and reports that someone has stolen his electron. The sergeant behind the desk enters the case in his book and then asks "Are you sure?" The hydrogen atom replies: "Yes, I'm positive." This is an absurd fantasy, with no shred of redeeming truth in it. Yet many scientists will laugh at the absurdity, because of the adjacent truth that a hydrogen atom with its single electron missing is electrically positive. But no offence has been caused, no deception, no lie. Everybody knows this is a statement in the category "joke."

More briefly, for mathematicians: $2 + 2 = 5$, provided that 2 is a sufficiently large number. This plays on the fact that some mathematical theorems are known to be true only when the numbers involved are almost unimaginably large. Again, no offence or deception has been caused by this trivial joke (Sabbagh 2002: 213).

Popular science writers and science journalists legitimately use some of the features of list 1. They highlight the human characteristics of the scientists, slip in jokes and ironic asides, point out coincidences, and dramatize competition between research teams, but they do all this in a way that will stand the scrutiny of their professional colleagues. Popularizing books are regularly reviewed in magazines such as *Nature, Science, New Scientist, Scientific American*, or *Science et Vie*, and errors are ruthlessly exposed. The genre and the conventions are understood by the writer, the publisher, the reviewer, and, one hopes, the reader. If a book of this kind has been well reviewed in the professional journals, then it can be trusted as reliable by the general public. In practice, other archaeologists and scientists who are working on closely related sites or experiments will usually be able to judge if a researcher is telling the truth, and if new finds and unlikely discoveries are genuinely possible and significant or are the results of error. They may undertake checks, ask the author for explanations, or try to repeat the work themselves. Academics in nearby fields will tend to take on trust papers published in journals of high academic repute that have strict standards of review and invite changes before publication. Others may try to keep a broad familiarity with topics outside their field by reading magazines such as *Scientific American* or *Archaeology*, where they will trust the repute of professional archaeological journalists.

Umberto Eco, writing on the nature of knowledge and designation of the names of concepts (semiotics and epistemology; Eco 2000) eloquently describes how the conveying of reliable knowledge is always set about with conventions and assumptions, agreed rules that must not be broken. This is quite different from those basic tenets of philosophy and logic that are intended to be true independent of context. When real people are conveying information to one another, there are always unwritten rules about assumptions, what it is honest to say or not say. That is why the pseudoarchaeologist or pseudo-scientist is so reviled by professionals, because, whether the pseudo is aware of it or not, the rules of communication are being broken.

Pseudoscientists are, deliberately or inadvertently, distorting and exploiting the conventions in a way that deceives the reader who is not an expert in the subject. They dazzle and entice the reader with dramatic tricks from list 1. They raise the temperature by creating an appearance of a battle, conflict, suppressed ideas, censorship, and conspiracy in high places. They pick a few scientific facts from the core of a discipline, throw in a few fringe "facts" from marginal scientists or archaeologists who support maverick ideas but are by no means frauds, and then plunge into the wild blue yonder. They claim to be describing a world of true events, things and occurrences that really happened in the verifiable sense that fossil layers can be dated by species, pollen used to indicate climate, or bones dated with carbon-14, but they misquote or select biased sources, blind the amateur reader with unnecessary jargon, misuse jargon, move so quickly from topic to topic that nobody can keep up, and exploit the rules of science against science itself (see Chapter 1).

My analysis of logic and truth here is not meant to replicate serious philosophical analysis. I am trying to describe how people behave and how they react. If this appeal to common sense is regarded as avoiding the tricky philosophical or linguistic bits of the argument, please remember, as Noam Chomsky implies (Chomsky 1972: 19–20), a dog knows perfectly well the difference between a cat and a rabbit, and between a triangle and a circle, without having words for any of them. At this level of discussion, common sense and appeal to simple logic are sufficient.

Each discipline or skill (medicine, archaeology, science, juggling) has its own conventions. When we go to a display of conjuring and juggling we do not expect the artiste to explain afterwards that he/she was able to juggle sixteen billiard balls because he/she can project an anti-gravity field. We respect the incredible skill, artistry, and illusion of a trick, but we do not want to be treated as fools. In each skill or profession there are rules of communication. If you stick to the rules of communication, you can save time and convey more information in a small space, using formulae and symbols. Experts tend to trust text written according to the rules, and this is why there is such condemnation when a scientific fraud is perpetrated by an insider (but fraud is *not* pseudoscience).

The fragility and vulnerability of the scientific method

The established status of science, archaeology, and the other academic disciplines is often assumed to be almost unassailable. There is a tendency, actively encouraged by pseudo-writers, to see academics as the "big battalions," while pseudos represent the "little man," protesting in vain. In this section, I want to show that, in the conflict with pseudoscience and pseudoarchaeology, this is not the case. If academics marshal their ideas and arguments carefully, they can construct strong defenses; but a casual assumption of superiority leaves them open to major damage.

There are three principle reasons for this: (1) a broad weakening of confidence in academic explanations resulting from the growth in relativism and postmodernist deconstruction; (2) the inherent principle of science that its proofs cannot be absolute but are subject to revision; and (3) a deeply felt perception among many people that science and academic methods are crushingly restrictive and pedantic.

Relativism, uncertainty, and doubt

The authority of science and respect for academic integrity have been reduced in recent years by several trends, including partisan controversies about major issues such as global warming, HIV, and genetic engineering, as well as archaeological and historical controversies over educational syllabuses, creationism, racial stereotypes, and evolutionary psychology. There is, in addition, a more pervasive attitude, not based on solid intellectual learning, that the foundations of knowledge have become more relativistic during the twentieth century. I am not questioning here the genuine discoveries and debates about quantum statistics, Heisenberg's uncertainty principle, Gödel's theorem, or philosophical deconstruction of texts, historical relativism, or the social basis of science. But these intellectual studies have diffused into the middlebrow community as, in some cases, a feeling that anything goes. Science becomes purely a social construct. There is no such thing as proof; truth is just the opinion of the majority; multiple conflicting truths may all be valid at the same time. This attitude, which in reality is a cover for sloppy thinking, can be used by pseudos as the first stage of undermining criticism from archaeologists.

I stress that I am not analysing here the validity of these intellectual forces (Penrose 1991) but trying to understand how people behave who often have not studied them and are tempted to use or misuse them at second hand. This attitude is brilliantly dissected by Sokal and Bricmont (2003) and further discussed by Sokal (Chapter 12). At the level of attitudes and behavior, which is the subject of this chapter, refutation of the "all versions of knowledge and truth are equally tenable" is fairly simple. Whatever degree of subversion twentieth-century research and philosophy may have launched against empirical science and the basis of knowledge, it must apply to all versions of the truth at the intellectual level that is relevant. This applies as much to pseudo-theories as to accepted academic ones. That being the case, the discoveries do not favor one or the other version, and we are forced back on to common sense and day-to-day estimates of probability. Is it more likely that one train is late or that the whole printed timetable displayed on every station is wrong? Is it more likely that 20,000 archaeologists are part of a global conspiracy to delude the innocent public or that one enthusiast cannot get his/her facts straight? Do pyramids represent a telekinetic power source of mysterious origins that was transmitted secretly in different cultures around the world 12,000 years ago, or is it just easier for people with no cement to make buildings that are narrower at the top than they are at the bottom?

This counter-argument still leaves the defender of the academic view with a fight on their hands, but at least the fight is on level ground. The appeal to strange discoveries that purport to show that multiple truths apply can be dismissed as irrelevant. Common sense is sufficient for this debate.

Science, archaeology, and self-criticism

Science and the time-dependent disciplines (history, archaeology, geology, cosmology) all use the fundamental technique of error detection, criticism, repeated observation, and revision, which has sustained the accumulation of knowledge through several centuries. This process of speculative search and innovation, followed by self-validation, focusing on errors, followed by correction and revision, is the glory of science. It is laborious, often frustrating, but it works, and knowledge is integrated and cross-connected endlessly with flashes of insight and occasional completeness, which, to the insider, provide profound pleasure.

However, to the untrained mind, the search for errors, the acceptance that the best theory in the world is imperfect or incomplete, and the frequent hesitation of experts to commit themselves with absolute certainty on matters of fact, leaves a baffling impression. Why can't they just say yes or no?

To the pseudo-practitioner, this hesitation and the acceptance of possible non-eliminated errors is an irresistible target. I have observed that a clever debater with well-prepared thrusts and one-line put-downs can make mincemeat of the average academic in minutes on a radio or TV show. The scientist or archaeologist is forced to concede repeatedly that "I could be wrong, of course, it depends on the conditions, nothing is absolutely certain," and before he or she has recovered the lost ground, the show is over. Throughout, the pseudo radiates an almost religious conviction and certainty.

The critic of academia who relishes the freedom of alternative thinking is happy to regard the second law of thermodynamics, or the measurement of the charge on the electron, as easily subject to instant revision on the same scale as the latest speculative theory of the formation of cosmic wormholes or the estimated date for the eruption that destroyed the Bronze Age towns on Santorini (Hardy *et al.* 1990). By skipping quickly from topic to topic and proposing several erroneous grand ideas that the expert has to tackle in sequence, the pseudo makes the expert look like a nit-picking, humorless, narrow-minded pedant, afraid of the vision that awaits the brave person who lets go of such old-fashioned constraints. The pseudo accuses the professional of having a closed mind, having made up their mind without checking the new evidence, and avoiding debate. He/she suggests that every accepted principle of science or archaeology is "only a theory" that needs to be proved and demonstrated afresh. Principles and standards that the professional has accepted for decades now have to be explained and explained again, not because they are in any real doubt but because the pseudo demands genuine empirical proof, now, on this occasion, beyond the personal doubt of this observer. This insistence is made in the name of science. Thus the pseudo reduces the scientific system to paralysis. It is in effect a public request for recapitulation of the five to ten years of study and proof of principles that the professional has mastered but that the pseudo never learned. From the professional's point of view it is a waste of time, since, even if every explanation is given, an audience would never sit through it, and the pseudo would not change his/her mind.

There is no space in this chapter to suggest the detailed tactics for coping with this type of vulnerability, but archaeologists who are challenged to open debate must review with enormous care the lines of evidence that they would use from their own area of expertise to defend the verifiability and proven status of core concepts. Some areas or items of knowledge are much more soundly based than others. The date of the Battle of Hastings, or the signing of the American Constitution, and the half-life of carbon-14 will not be revised by further research (or not much). The date for the eruption on Santorini may be. The charge on the electron and the speed of light in a vacuum are both known to one part in tens of millions. Further research may increase the accuracy to one part in thousands of millions, but the figures will not be doubled or halved. Acceptance of possible error or susceptibility to revision ranges from "Yes, that may be completely changed within five years" to "This is known with an accuracy of one part in so many million, and has been tested millions of times." The academic must make this distinction calmly but very firmly. You must be able to say with conviction that the Chinese did not circumnavigate the globe before the Magellan/Elcano expedition, even if the book on this pseudo-theory (Menzies 2002) were to sell a million copies. Popularity is not proof.

In extreme cases, academics may have to band together to refute anti-intellectual, anti-science campaigns, and a superb example of this is given by the battle against creation science in the USA, which went all the way to the Supreme Court (Shermer 1997: 154–72).

Public distaste for science and academic methods

The third reason for the fragility of science is that its principles repel many people at a psychological level. Science seems to be a prison, a restriction, a straitjacket. It forbids. It proscribes hundreds of impossible and forbidden systems and processes that must never be believed. This is a provocation and a mental prison to many people. Scientists who are caught up in the magic of discovery of what does work, who live with those incredible transitions and reactions that nature does permit, are astonished to find how negatively many people react, because, psychologically, they, the non-expert public, see science as a straitjacket. "Why can't I have perpetual motion, or anti-gravity, or thought transference, or precognition, or levitation, or messages from the dead, or Atlantis, or magic pyramids, or Noah's ark, or go faster than light? Why can't I have people hunting dinosaurs?" It all seems so puritanical and restrictive. The laws of thermodynamics are totally pessimistic: entropy and chaos always increase; knowledge and information are always lost. Life is merely a local decrease of entropy. And we evolved from a common ancestor with the chimpanzee. And the universe will cool down for ever and go dark and utterly lifeless.

To the expert, science works like a motorway, allowing trouble-free traverse through a maze of bogs, pitfalls, traps, and blind-alley diversions, taking you straight to the frontier with the unknown. There you find that science provides you with a range of tools and techniques for penetrating even further into the darkness and mapping out new roads into new worlds.

To the pseudoscience enthusiast, the question is "Why stay on the motorway? What lies on the land between the permitted theories? There are hundreds of questions and possible answers that the expert simply ignores as he/she charges off to that frontier of research that happens to be fashionable, or funded, just now. But what if ...?" Believing in any of the forbidden processes or reactions that have been shown by millions of tests and brilliantly derived theories and proofs to be impossible, or plain wrong, attracts instant opprobrium and condemnation from professionals.

Nevertheless, while scientists, historians, and archaeologists find the rigors of their discipline bracing, creative, stimulating, and beautiful in their complex structure, many people see only the restraints, the limitations, the narrowness created by so many rules, which seem to have developed over centuries of cabal-like esoteric thinking. Why does it take five to ten years for an intelligent teenager to learn enough physics to understand what is really happening at the frontiers of semiconductor research or the reactions of fundamental particles inside a star? Why does it take five to ten years to learn enough about archaeology to tackle genuinely fresh problems? Surely life is simpler than that? Human nature relishes a broad, simple, sweeping answer.

Then along comes a pseudoscientist, who brushes away all the dry rules, breaks out of the restrictive boundaries into an exciting terrain where anything is permitted. The professionals groan with derision, while the pseudos proclaim their great simple truth that ... (fill in the blank). No wonder this leap to freedom looks attractive, especially when combined with the melodrama of conflict, treachery, and self-aggrandizement that is typical of the genre.

Possible lines of defense

The apparent vulnerability of academic research that I have described here leads us to one of the natural lines of defense that the professional can use against the pseudo. It does not always work, but it has a good chance.

A principle of empirical academic statements is that they should be checkable, and that repeating the observation or the experiment would produce the same results or conclusions again and again when performed by different people. It also follows that the more easily a statement can be checked and proved wrong, the more powerful it is as a scientific statement if it survives such tests (Popper 1959: 108–9). Galileo's statement that all objects fall to Earth with the same acceleration is easily checked, and thus is a law of extraordinary power and generality (and it was demonstrated dramatically on the Moon by astronauts using a hammer and a feather).

It is a good habit of all scientists and archaeologists to check their own observations for faults, factual mistakes and errors, wishful thinking, and above all, for alternative explanations. It is one thing to show that event A is always followed by event B, but you cannot prove that A, and only A, actually causes B unless other possible causes have been eliminated and you have shown that B cannot exist unless it has been preceded by A. Preferably, there should be an actual verifiable mechanistic or probabilistic link to show why and how A causes B.

The failure of pseudo-writings to adhere to this principle of self-testing and self-rejection until arguments are necessary and rigorous is a definitive shortcoming in relation to real science and real archaeology. A work is publishable in the real world of science and archaeology when the conclusions presented at the end of the paper have been shown to be the most logical conclusions that follow from the starting information and the data. Referees for journals check that this is so. Pseudo-writings repeatedly rely for their effect on the assertion that "A could be so and, if this is accepted, B could be true also." The alternatives are not checked, and the concepts of greater probability, greatest logical simplicity, or greatest elegance are not even considered. The probability that the first proposition "A" could actually occur (or be wrong) is not estimated. For the scientist or professional archaeologist, the process of checking alternative explanations and eliminating them with evidence is not something that is just done in the back room and then taken on trust. Academic texts need to show overtly and consciously how alternative explanations have been checked and rejected.

The requirement for published self-criticism does not contradict my earlier point that in a developed community the lay person does not need to check all information. In professional publications, the author explains how they have checked alternatives that have been rejected, and the reader analyses the statements. We take the details on trust. Nevertheless, the fact that the process has been described is indicative of skepticism, care, and logic. We should always look for this habit of thinking in serious publications and look to see if it is present in suspected pseudoarchaeological works.

Finally, in the professional world, speculation is permitted at the end of a paper or book, provided that it is clearly labeled as such. Such free-ranging thought, based on previously proven facts, provides guidance for the next line of research.

The psychology of why pseudoscience works

General psychological factors

I suggested previously that human beings in a developed, technically sophisticated society are sensible to accept most information on the basis of authority rather than checking it, and that scientific and academic archaeological information is much more vulnerable to undermining by pseudo-theories than one might expect. The situation is made worse by the psychological bias that actually favors the belief in or adoption of melodramatic pseudo-type information more quickly and instinctively than we adopt scientific or academic proof. I have also suggested that the combination of the jargon and structure of scientific proof (which predisposes us on the basis of experience to accept information as authoritative) with the drama and tension of a novel, fairy story, or thriller is a formula that is very likely to sell like hot cakes. This turns out to be true with more force than one might have expected.

There are three reasons for this situation: (1) the vast "forbidden spaces" left by science in its apparent conquest of the world of knowledge; (2) the evolutionary psychology that predisposes us to react quickly to certain kinds of story; and (3) the pseudos' contrivance of an all-or-nothing religious leap of faith to attract the true converts.

The forbidden spaces

I likened the system of scientific and academic formulae and archaeological techniques to a network of motorways that takes the expert straight to the frontier of knowledge and enables him/her to work there with a set of powerful tools. This pattern of high-speed expressways leaves vast areas of open country in the interstices. If the motorway system represents precisely specified physical laws or established archaeological facts, the open spaces represent all the possible statements that do not comply with the hard rules of science or archaeology. Logically, there are countless millions of statements that are grammatically correct sentences claiming to describe the world but are actually wrong. Whether we say that the Romans discovered Australia, or the human race came from Mars 20,000 years ago, or that humans with a given skin color invented all science/art/mathematics, there is a place for such statements in the wild country between the motorways. Modern academic research has gone through, round, over, and between such statements and disregards them completely as nonsense, but they are still there if you want them. The phrases cannot be banned from the language.

The pseudoarchaeologist works by starting the journey with a short trip along a motorway so that the unconverted reader thinks they are in the authoritative world of academia. Then the reader is led somewhat off the motorway on a minor road of dubious probity, and then, hey presto, suddenly we are in a Disneyland of make-believe could-have-beens and maybes. Every now and then the pseudo-text mentions another piece of established science or archaeology, or travels a little distance on another branch of the motorway to steady the nervous reader, and then plunges back into unprovable assertions dressed up as "alternative archaeology."

From the point of view of the professionals working at the frontier of knowledge, these illogical propositions spring up behind their backs, like a guerrilla uprising in previously pacified terrain. The pseudos are attacking theories and accepted facts that were established decades ago. The professionals have no interest in going back over that ground again. There are far more important things to do, and if we ignore the uprising it will probably go away. Unfortunately, that is not the case. Most pseudo-theories and obsessions rumble on for decades with hardly any change in their core beliefs. Indeed, one of the oddities of pseudoarchaeology is that it is so lacking in truly original or fantastic imagination. The same reworked themes are repeated continuously or in cycles, with none going out of date.

An ironic aspect of the seductive sequence of arguments used by the pseudos is that it is the precise opposite of what popular science writers and good science journalists are trying to do. These important writers try to get the readers attention with everyday information, facts, or stories and then gradually lead them away from the area of hearsay, superstition, and anecdotal explanation towards the rigorous prove-it-or-perish world of science and archaeology. The pseudoarchaeologist is therefore working in exactly the opposite direction to that of the popularizer of serious archaeology (e.g., Johanson and Edey 1981; Pitts and Roberts 1997; Spindler 1994). This is also why writers such as Martin Gardner, Carl Sagan, Michael Shermer and Ken Feder[3] pour unrelenting criticism on pseudo-artistes. Notwithstanding this antithesis, the makers of television science programmes seem to see science popularization and pseudoscience as similar or adjacent activities. This is a terrible mistake. They are logical opposites (see Chapter 10).

Not for nothing does the Dewey Decimal classification system have a section entitled "Popular beliefs." This is the correct library classification for the work of writers such as Spence (1926), Churchward (1931), Velikovsky (1950, 1952), or Hancock (1995, 2002a). I wish bookshops and stationery shops selling magazines used a similar classification. It is anti-educational to have magazines such as *New Scientist* and *Scientific American* overtly grouped with *Bizarre Events*, *UFOs*, and *Fortean Times*.

One of the mysteries of the modern world and the universe as we observe them is the pervasive occurrence of extremely complex systems such as spiral galaxies, viruses, human beings, and advanced civilizations. How did such structured, coherent, complexity arise from a universe that was, presumably, inert, inorganic, and chaotic at the start? Murray Gell-Mann (1994) and Johnson (2001) have written useful books on these themes. The key concept is "emergence," whereby inanimate self-correcting adaptive systems gradually produce structures that have a survival strength greater than that of their chaotic precursors. The difficulty of understanding how long-lived complex systems arise from simple or chaotic ones is a factor that provides a huge target for pseudo oversimplification. Instinctively, we prefer something simpler and more humane.

Many of the occupants of the open spaces are the ancient myths, legends, and fairy stories that exist in every culture. As stories they are splendid, rich in psychological insight, symbolism, and plain good fun. The special appeal of some pseudoarchaeology is achieved by the proposition that some well-known story is actually true and that the evidence can be found by exploration, usually in a remote area. This argument can be used to justify repeating voyages such as that of Jason to discover the Golden Fleece on the Georgian coast of the Black Sea (justifiable journalism) through to claims that Noah's ark has been found on top of Mount Ararat (impossible) or that the Garden of Eden was in northern Iran (improbable), or to search for Atlantis or El Dorado beneath the waters of Lake Titicaca high in the Andes (ridiculous). There is no doubt that the organizers of such trips, and the resulting publications, touch a very sensitive and pleasurable nerve in the reading public. What could be more reassuring at a womb-like foetal level than to find that the stories one heard in infancy, or watched on children's television, are really true?

Granted the power of this search for the literal verification of myths and legends, I have sometimes wondered whether it would be possible to obtain funding to search for the original glass slipper of Cinderella, or the blood-stained key of Blue Beard. I am sure somebody would pay for it.

Pascal Boyer (2001) describes how comparative study of religions in the widest sense (not just the half dozen big monotheistic beliefs) reveals a natural human preference for attributing the cause of troublesome phenomena through sequential explanation or inference. The first and safest supposition is that "someone did it" (ibid.: 164–5, 229). The person may be a presumed enemy, a rival, a powerful priest, or witch using unusual powers. The second supposition is that an inanimate process – storm, flood, drought – caused the problem, but an underlying conspiracy of malefactors is not ruled out. If all else fails, the events are explained by actions or wishes of the gods and spirits themselves (ibid.: 187–9). These ways of thinking, the built-in inference systems, are, in Boyer's view, natural and likely and are most compatible with evolutionary psychology. One does not have to accept the more speculative aspects of this approach to see that these habits of thought might be hard-wired into our psychological make-up. In contrast, the gathering of statistical data, the rejection of unsound evidence, and the construction of testable theories is intuitively the least likely way to solve a problem (ibid.: 369–70). Science and academic analysis do produce fabulously powerful results, but they require hard work, study, and mental discipline. They do not operate spontaneously as untrained mental reflexes. In contrast, the natural ways of the mind make us infinitely susceptible to stories of conspiracy, threat, danger, or risk. They grab us within seconds. Pursuing the same line of reasoning, Noam Chomsky (1972) and Stephen

Pinker (1994) have shown how some information-processing circuits and inference systems are more or less hard-wired into the brain. It is difficult to rid our intellectual efforts of these survival-based macros, even if we know that they are seriously misleading in intellectual terms and produce unverifiable answers.

Thus the "someone did it" attraction leads us to find it plausible that civilization was created by a small number of great individuals with exceptional powers. This gives emotional buttressing to tales of Atlantis, alien visitations, the drowned civilization of Lemuria (Childress 1988), and so on. If someone cannot be blamed for one's circumstances, it is next most attractive to blame some vast natural event or force. Again, we can see the immediate analogues in modern popular beliefs: worlds in collision, great floods, volcanic eruptions, impacting comets, and the gullible readiness to join up events into a single great catastrophe (e.g., Schoch 1999, 2003; Wilson 2002).

Given the psychological attractions of other explanations for the state of the world, who would be happy with an explanation of "random processes leading to complex self-adaptive systems with emergent properties?" And yet that is probably the best modern explanation (Gell-Mann 1994; Johnson 2001). Colin Renfrew's (1972) pioneering work on the emergence of civilization in the Aegean expresses exactly the mindset that is determined to understand how a complex civilization grows indigenously in its locale without the need for the arrival of people from another civilization carrying a secret message.

The mind does not need this capability of understanding complexity in order to survive in the jungle or to escape a saber-toothed tiger. It does not come easily, and we tend to avoid this unsympathetic conclusion if possible. Even when we have a widely accepted emergent process, as in biological evolution of new species, we constantly infer that things evolved for a purpose: the pitcher plant cleverly secretes a digestive enzyme *in order to* kill the insect, the tulip has bright colors *in order to* attract insects, the caterpillar has lurid markings *in order to* make us think it is poisonous. Teleology is infectious.

All cultures and civilizations have developed schools and other training systems whereby accumulated past knowledge, and the means of ordering new knowledge, are transmitted to the younger generation. But it is hard work. Compared with the almost automatic way that we learn our first language, or learn to throw a stone at a target, it is laborious. Some students catch fire almost immediately and see the excitement and potential of the structured discipline. Most of us struggle for years before a subject becomes exciting or rewarding. Pseudoarchaeology makes an appeal that is like a drug mainlined to the synapses. It bypasses reason and appeals to old emotions. The answer is immediate, and dramatically simple. Only believe. But it is presented as science/archaeology, with the added need to provoke a battle of heresy and suppression. Is it surprising that the pseudo-writers have such success?

The great commitment

A final psychological appeal of the pseudo-text is that it forces the reader to make a commitment of belief that is counter-establishment and seems to carry a cost. You cannot simultaneously believe the established archaeology and accept pseudoarchaeology (for example, see Hancock 2002a). After hooking the reader on the melodrama of conspiracy and discrimination, the pseudo presents you with a stark choice: do you believe me? The pseudo does not make millions of dollars by suggesting that geological or archaeo-logical academic texts need a little adjustment to get them into line with his/her new proposals: the proposition is always that previous textbooks must be thrown away or rewritten. Are you with me or against me? Decide now! It looks like a risky strategy for the pseudo, and naturally some readers back off at this point. Nevertheless, it looks brave, and even people who are not converted first time around are left with the impression of a writer who is utterly convinced of his/her own rectitude. For those who are converted, the effect is damaging. Once you have accepted that Atlantis was a superior civilization now lost under the sea, and that as the ocean rose the great leaders escaped the flood and carried wisdom to the four corners of the Earth, you have to go along with all the consequences. The further you are drawn in, the harder it is to admit your mistake and back out without feeling an absolute fool. For this reason, the pseudo-writer knows that it is worth gambling and forcing the punters to take this leap of faith, because it is exactly that which will turn some of them into fanatical preachers of the cause. There is a parallel with religion here. Pascal Boyer (2001: 91–4.) shows how the minor religions (and many of the big ones) contain instinc-tively counter-intuitive propositions that force the convert to make just such a risky leap. Religions do not gain converts by reasoning. People recall viola-tions of intuitive expectation for much longer than day-to-day facts and figures, and these stories gain wide currency.

In summary, pseudo-texts ruthlessly exploit the self-critical caution of science and academic reasoning; they work in the wide open spaces between established ideas; and they attract and seduce the punters with age-old stories of danger and conspiracy, combined with requiring the true convert to make a commitment of faith, against reason (see Chapter 4).

Motives

No book has been written, so far as I know, entitled *Confessions of a Reformed Pseudoarchaeology Millionaire*. In the absence of such inside information, the first and fairest assumption is that the practitioners honestly believe what they preach. Assuming that an engineer, journalist, plumber, or novelist stumbles upon a pseudoarchaeological theory that appeals to them, and assuming that they start to write about it and that the publications start to have a popular appeal, the following factors then come into play:

1. Opposition from professionals and experts stimulates and breeds a conspiracy theory.
2. The media love it and find that the conflict makes a good story.
3. It becomes fun to goad and taunt the experts, who turn out to be very reluctant to fight back in public.
4. The money rolls in.
5. The rejection of authority becomes liberating and exciting.
6. If the pseudo-practitioner plays their cards right, at this point they will attract strong sympathy from the media and public for standing up to censorship, become a hero, and more money rolls in.

If this scenario develops even partially, the protagonist is bound to think "I must be doing something right" and will see no reason to change their views or style of writing. If the success and money are significant, the pseudoarchaeologist has every reason to defend his/her turf. Since the glory of the fight is nine-tenths of the entertainment, the pugnacious, litigious style of pseudoarchaeologists is no surprise; they are prone to threaten legal action if they think they have been defamed, that is, if their ideas are criticized harshly.

One may take a more cynical view and assume that the pseudo-writer knows the difference between archaeology and pseudoarchaeology very well and that they are motivated by money and fame to say things that they know are not true. However, this is not a necessary assumption, and it leads into all sorts of difficult speculation about people convincing themselves or deluding themselves by believing things that are so much to their advantage. That said, one indicator that some pseudo-writers know the dubious nature of their art is the tendency to resort to legal cases or technical appeals and complaints when they have been criticized by academics (see Chapter 10). This is not the normal behavior of researchers, who are usually content to let their work be judged on its merits. Professional scientists and archaeologists receive adverse criticism and either let it stand unanswered on the grounds that their own case is strong enough or reply to it carefully in a subsequent professional paper. Only in the situation of a patent infringement, or claim to prior discovery against all the evidence, is a serious spat likely to break out.

Debates between archaeologists and pseudoarchaeologists are not, from the pseudo point of view, ever meant to be won, or even concluded. The point of the game is to keep it going. As anecdotal evidence for this, I can describe from personal experience a meeting of the Expeditions Panel of the Royal Geographical Society in which we had just completed the interview with a grant applicant who had requested funds to search for the Loch Ness monster using acoustics. As the applicant left the council chamber, other members of the panel looked at me, as the underwater expert, and I said "There is only one way to find the Loch Ness Monster: dam Loch Ness at both ends and pump the water out." The silence that followed was longer than I expected. The discussion resumed after a while, but I realized that the shock that my remark caused was not because of the cost but because the game would then be over. Even intelligent experts in environmental sciences were, at least partially, assuming that the debate between believers and unbelievers would go on for ever.

By analogy, if a diving group found a banal little submerged Bronze Age city off the coast of some Greek island, and if inscriptions, bronze tablets, burials, pottery, and other artefacts proved beyond doubt that it was a market town with the name "Atlantis," most of the believers in the legends would be dismayed and would probably argue *against* the identification. Their belief is about something much bigger, a limitless fantasy, not a real city that really existed at a known place, with a date, a mayor, and local taxes.

The target audience, or keeping the punters happy

I have stated several times that pseudoarchaeology is not a set of serious archaeological principles, ideas, or excavation records designed to gain the confidence and support of professional archaeologists. The aim is to propose a set of alternative principles and alleged records of sites that will attract and hold the interest and belief of the general public and the popular media.

There are many tricks of the trade that hook readers, keep their attention, and persuade them to buy more. The power of these techniques has already been discussed. In the realm of archaeology, there are several special effects that come in useful. Since the evidence on the ground has to be located somewhere, the pseudoarchaeologist often describes data from sites in the most inaccessible and unfamiliar locations: high in the Andes, on small Pacific islands, under the sea, or in outer space. Because of the human factor in archaeology, it is also possible to play on a range of racial, religious, and cult-like beliefs.

I do not have any quantitative data on the typical profile of people who fall for these stories, but, based on several conversations, the gullible punters are not just those with the least education (see Chapters 3 and 4). In my own area of expertise (coastal and submarine archaeology), there have been several sensational pseudo-archaeological books and television films in recent years (Wilson 2002; Hancock 2002a), and many people have been, at least superficially, more or less taken in by them. But I have had conversations with a carpet shop manager, a gardener, and a truck driver that show that they were not convinced for one minute by the arguments or evidence presented. On the other hand, astonishingly, a trained scientist in the area of geology was quite convinced. In the USA, *Scientific American* regularly publishes the percentage belief in different paranormal and pseudo-phenomena and tracks changes over the years. The scores range from 30 to 54 percent of the public accepting many phenomena that most scientists would deny and an increase of 4–10 percent for most paranormal beliefs during the last ten years

(*Scientific American*, September 2001: 21). This probably predisposes about half the population to be credulous or even gullible toward new stories that are condemned out of hand by academic archaeologists. The rapid growth of so-called paranormal television shows confirms the public credulity.

Thus part of the pseudo-trick, at least in the modern world, is to spin up the forces of publicity, television, radio interviews, the cheap popular news-papers, and to run a glitzy website. People are impressed simply by the scale of the publicity, and, if it is well done, by the professionalism of the show. They find it difficult to comprehend that so much money and skill could have been spent by so many technical experts to present a story that is completely untrue. Web bulletin boards and discussion sites are an efficient mechanism for keeping the pseudo-kettle boiling. The pseudo can post statement after statement combating the official archaeological view and presenting selective evidence that few amateurs could refute with personally excavated site data or scholarly reference. Very few professional archaeolo-gists could spare the time to engage in the endless verbal dueling, so the academic fight is left largely to keen amateur archaeologists and a few dedi-cated professionals. (The website *In the Hall of Ma'at* is dedicated to a critical examination of pseudoarchaeology and alternative history; see Chapter 4.)

Conclusion

In this chapter, I have considered why the ideas promulgated by pseudoar-chaeological writers have such appeal, independently of any particular type of archaeology. Each variety of speciality – Noah's flood, finding Noah's ark (termed "arkaeology"), "pyramidiocy," Atlantis, and so on – produces extra details and ornate flourishes. The techniques used by pseudoarchaeological writers are now very well known, and the style is fairly easy to recognize. In this analysis, I have restricted my consideration to those kinds of archaeolog-ical statement that are based directly on material evidence, such as stratigraphic level, radionuclide dating, stable isotope analysis of origin, physical form of structures, and so on. Archaeology quite rightly attempts to deduce from these facts information about societies, population density, food and agriculture, hunting patterns, and, somewhat more speculatively, motives, religious beliefs, social structures, and social conventions in ancient communities. In professional archaeology, the chain of logic from the field data through to social deductions is very clear, and even if the results may be disputed, the methodology is constrained by academic conventions. Pseudoarchaeology makes wildly speculative proposals about this area of knowledge using the same techniques as I have described for the physical phenomena of an excavation. Pseudoarchaeology is aimed at the general reader, and professional archaeologists usually ignore it. Those scientists who choose to write some of their work in a popular style, and the professional science journalists, are the front line of the counterattack against pseudo-thinking, and I wish them every success in the battle.

Notes

1. Examples of theories that achieved wide professional acceptance and were then abandoned as completely wrong include the phlogiston theory of heat, the aether theory of electromagnetic wave transmission, phrenology, various theories of racism and racial superiority, the teleological theory of progress, and the "billiard ball" model of the atom.
2. See, e.g., Dawkins 1998; Evans 1973; Gardner 1957; Gould 2002; Sagan 1996; Shermer 1997.
3. See items in note 2 and Feder 2002b.

3   Skeptics, fence sitters, and true believers

Student acceptance of an improbable prehistory

Kenneth L. Feder

Introduction

My initial foray into the thicket of student preconceptions and misconceptions about archaeology and prehistory occurred almost by accident when I began teaching at Central Connecticut State College (CCSC) in the fall of 1977. I was assigned the task of teaching two courses in my initial semester. The first was a standard introduction to archaeological methods of the sort that I had assisted teaching as a graduate student at the University of Connecticut. That was easy enough. However, the second course I was assigned was another matter entirely. University policy then dictated that all academic departments offer at least one "search" course (e.g., search in psychology; search in economics; search in sociology), and students were required as part of their general education program to take at least two such courses during their attendance at the college.

I have been teaching at Central Connecticut State, first College, and now University (CCSU), for more than twenty-five years, and I still have trouble articulating exactly what the now-abandoned search course program was intended to accomplish. Although the course catalogue briefly described the search course, as a new member of the faculty with just a few years of experience as a graduate assistant, it all seemed quite mysterious. The search course appeared to be intended as a sort of pre-introduction to a field of study aimed at the general cohort of incoming students. The assumption underpinning search courses appeared to be that new students might benefit from gentle exposure to logical thinking, the scientific method in general, and research practices in a specific discipline by focusing on what amounted to "cool topics" in an academic field of study, preferably in a format other than formal lectures. So, for example, a search course in psychology might involve showing students popular movies that dealt with mental illness and discussing the ways in which popular concepts of such illness have changed through time. Similarly, a search course in astronomy might revolve around a series of planetarium programs, or a search course in English could focus on the scripts of popular television shows.

Before my arrival on the scene, members of the anthropology department had tried a number of search course strategies, all of which amounted to a sort of "anthropology lite" that introduced the field in a general way by focusing on a popular topic or topics. I believe that there was an audible sigh of relief from my colleagues in the department when they were informed that the new guy was going to teach the search course that year, and I quickly found out why. Although intriguing in concept, it was extraordinarily difficult in practice to come up with a focus for a search course aimed at students who were understandably naive about the content of our discipline. Anthropology through science fiction, for example, sounds like a great idea for a search course, but with no grounding whatsoever in anthropology, freshmen had a difficult time making the connection between alien cultures and, well, *really* alien cultures. Prior search courses in archaeology had been taught irregularly and had essentially taken the "popular topics" route, a sort of antiquarian travelogue consisting of slideshow visits to interesting ancient places and the presentation of fascinating notions about the human past. The approach had not proved particularly successful.

My initial ideas all seemed (to me anyway) like interesting and different ways of approaching anthropology, but they would never have worked with students without any background in the discipline. So I decided, essentially, to give up trying to devise a fascinating approach that might fulfill the mission of the search course program and instead allow the students themselves to decide the content and approach of the course. I convinced myself that having the students come up with the course syllabus on the first day of class would be an innovative way of fulfilling the search course mandate. My feeling was that if the purpose of the course was to provide new college students with a light, breezy, and painless introduction to how a given discipline explores its database, why not take advantage of the fact that archaeology was something that most students would have a passing familiarity with right from the first day of the semester?

I was not sure what to expect when, on that first day, I entered the classroom. Initially, the students seemed both confused and excited when I informed them that, with my assistance, they would be crafting their own syllabus for the course. After a short period of awkward silence, the floodgates opened and a number of specific topics were suggested by my increasingly eager students. I cannot say that I was surprised by the direction our conversation took concerning the topics that they would like to see covered in a course in archaeology. I had figured that Egyptian pyramids would be high on the list of topics that students might want to "search out." Stonehenge was another obvious choice. And, indeed, students requested that discussions of ancient Egyptian civilization and Stonehenge, as well as the Aztec and Maya, human evolution, and Native American origins be included in the syllabus.

However, what I had not anticipated was a palpable undercurrent in the requests for consideration of an altogether different set of topics. Many of the student suggestions appeared to be fueled by the mysteries that they perceived to be underlying them. They seemed to find Egyptian civilization fascinating, at least in part because they assumed that its origins were shrouded in a mystery so deep that archaeologists had no viable explanation for it (see Chapter 5). It was also my inference that Stonehenge captivated their imaginations because, again, they believed the method of its construction to be intensely mysterious: after all, how would it have been possible for primitive people to have moved those enormous rocks, and what could possibly have been their purpose?

In the prologue of his 1953 novel *The Go-Between*, English novelist L.P. Hartley (1958: 5) maintained that "the past is a foreign country: they do things differently there." To my students, the past was a foreign country where remarkable things were accomplished in mysterious ways that archaeologists were unable to explain and so were interesting to speculate about. Tellingly, however, my admittedly subjective impression was that although many in the class were drawn to discussions of the perceived mysteries of human antiquity, few seemed to be committed to any particular *explanation* for them, prosaic or otherwise. That pattern was one that I found to be true in the subsequent years when I taught the same search course. Students were invariably fascinated by what they perceived to be fundamental mysteries concerning especially the technological and artistic achievements of ancient humans, but it was the rare student who had come to any definitive conclusion regarding the solution of these mysteries. Committed, true believers in any particular explanation for such "mysteries" were hard to find.

For example, virtually all the students I encountered in my first search course had heard of Swiss author Erich von Däniken (this was, after all, the late 1970s, when his popularity in the USA was at its peak), but none was especially devoted to his notion of peripatetic bands of universe-trotting extraterrestrials introducing sophisticated technologies to the primitive denizens of the ancient Earth. Similarly, the majority of these students had heard of the lost continent of Atlantis and were intrigued by the story. Although none of them had read the *Timmeaus* or *Critias* dialogues, where Plato introduces and describes his invented society, the popular television series *The Man From Atlantis*, featuring the actor Patrick Duffy in the role of an amphibious survivor of the destruction of the lost continent, aired in 1977–78. However, it was the rare student indeed who strongly believed that Atlantis had actually existed or that it had been the catalyst for the development of civilization in the ancient Old or New World. That ancient astronauts or lost continents were fascinating and mysterious seemed to be the hook that reeled students in. Whether or not ancient astronauts or Atlanteans were real seemed of secondary importance. It seemed, at least to many of them, that tales of prehistoric ETs or lost continents were the equivalent of Hallowe'en ghost stories – engaging, entertaining and interesting, even if there was every probability that they were not true.

At the same time, it must be admitted, I did not run into very many students in the late 1970s who were strongly skeptical of ancient astronauts, water-breathing Atlanteans, and the like. My subjective impression was that the number of dyed-in-the-wool skeptics about ancient astronauts, Atlantis, or psychic archaeology was small – rarely more than a few in a class of forty students – often mirroring the small number of true believers in such things. In fact, most students seemed to fall somewhere in between, fence sitters who perceived the human past as fraught with mysteries that scientists could not explain or at least had not yet adequately explained but uncertain if extraordinary, reality-bending, or paranormal explanations were necessary. But, wow, wouldn't it be cool if any of it were true?

Quantifying student beliefs

The pattern that I observed of student perception of a mysterious past and student contemplation of speculative explanations for these mysteries but no great certainty if such speculations were valid inspired my plan to examine statistically student perceptions and beliefs concerning human antiquity, particularly as these related to claims about the human past that most archaeologists would find at least unsubstantiated and, to be entirely truthful, often absurd. Such claims made about the human past and unsupported by any archaeological data have been labeled differently by different researchers. Archaeologist Stephen Williams (1991) calls such claims examples of "fantastic archaeology," using that designation in the title of his book: *Fantastic Archaeology: The Wild Side of North American Prehistory*. Archaeologist John Cole (1979, 1982) applied the label "cult archaeology" to claims about ancient astronauts, extreme diffusion, and psychic archaeology. It is reasonably common to hear such claims described as "alternative," "non-mainstream," or simply "pseudoarchaeology." The most colorful appellation comes from the text of a speech given by British prehistorian Glyn Daniel (1979), who, never one to pull a punch, called it "bullshit archaeology." Whatever one's labeling preference, beginning in 1983 I sporadically conducted surveys in my own courses as well as those of my colleagues at CCSU that sought to quantify the level of student awareness of these unsupported, highly conjectural explanations of the human past and the degree of student acceptance of these explanations.

The approach that I took in my surveys was neither innovative nor unique. After posing a series of questions that revealed significant demographic information about those participating in the survey (their age, sex, religion, year in college, major, grade point average), I confronted the participating students with a series of statements, some related specifically to the human past, some related to paranormal and occult topics, and others related to their general world view. Students were asked to rank their level of agreement with each statement using a standard Likert scale (strongly agree, mildly agree, don't know, mildly disagree, strongly disagree). The statements in the survey relating specifically to the human past are provided in Figure 3.1.

1. Aliens from other worlds visited the earth in the prehistoric past and assisted in the development of human technology.

2. There is good evidence for the existence of the Lost Continent of Atlantis.

3. An ancient curse placed on the tomb of the Egyptian pharaoh King Tut actually killed people.

4. Human beings came about through evolution.

5. God created the universe in six actual, 24-hour days.

6. Adam and Eve were the first human beings.

7. The flood of Noah as told in the Bible really happened.

Figure 3.1 Survey questions related to archaeology in surveys administered 1983–2003.

I certainly was not the first nor have I been the only researcher to conduct surveys examining student acceptance of so-called non-mainstream claims about human antiquity. Sociologist William Sims Bainbridge (1978) had conducted a study among his students at the University of Washington, Seattle in 1977/78 that focused, in part, on student acceptance of Erich von Däniken's proposal that technological achievements documented in the archaeological record could be explained as the result of their introduction by extraterrestrial aliens who visited the Earth in antiquity. That study, in fact, was the proximate inspiration for my own surveys that investigated student acceptance of von Däniken's ancient extraterrestrial visitors along with a host of other claims about the human past that clearly fall outside the mainstream of modern archaeology (Feder 1984, 1985/86). Archaeologist Frank Harrold and sociologist Ray Eve (1986) expanded my survey at the University of Texas at Arlington, where they polled their students' opinions about various paranormal, pseudoscientific, and other unsubstantiated phenomena, including those related to the human past. Their results were first presented at a symposium at the annual meeting of the Society for American Archaeology and then published in the *Skeptical Inquirer* (Harrold and Eve 1986).

Discussions between Harrold and Eve, Luanne Hudson at the University of Southern California, and myself led to a coordinated study that involved the administration of an updated questionnaire to students at CCSU, the University of Texas, Texas Christian University, the University of Southern California, and Occidental College (in Los Angeles). The combined sample size was nearly 1,000 students (Feder 1987). Following this, shortly after the tenth anniversary of my initial study, in 1994 I surveyed yet another crop of students at CCSU and published the results (1995). I replicated the study in 1997/98 (Feder 1998). Students at my own university and a sample of archaeologist Patricia Rice's students at West Virginia University were surveyed in 1999, and I surveyed my own students again in 2000. Most recently, in 2003, yet another iteration of the survey was distributed to my own students and administered, graciously, by Garrett Fagan of the Department of Classics and Ancient Mediterranean Studies and History to students at Penn State University.

Other researchers have administered their own versions of my survey instrument at universities in the United States, at Charles Stuart University in Australia (Spennemann 1996), and at the University of Southampton in Great Britain (Richardson 1999). A creationist website has even used a version of the survey instrument, putting it online for anyone to fill out and submit (http://www.tagnet.org/anotherviewpoint/quiz/CreationEvolutionPseudoscience .htm). There are thus abundant quantitative data derived from diverse times and places that allow student beliefs in pseudoarchaeological propositions to be charted in some detail.

Geographical and temporal patterns of consistency and change

Given its wide geographic application, it is not surprising to find regional differences in levels of acceptance of specific cult archaeology or creationist claims. For example, in comparing student agreement levels with topics related to a recent, divine creation of the Earth, Richardson (1999) found that American students are overall less likely to express skepticism (by mildly or strongly disagreeing with statements 5–7 in Figure 3.1) than are their British counterparts. Similarly, my students in Connecticut were overall more likely to express their skepticism about a recent, divine creation of the Earth than were students attending universities in the southern USA (Feder 1987). These results directly reflect the wider context, which sees creationism relatively weak in Europe but much stronger in the traditional "Bible belt" of the United States.

However, in many regards, the statistical breakdown of student responses to statements related to the human past have been shown to be remarkably consistent regardless of where those students come from and where they go to school. The figures also match closely my subjective judgment of student opinions in my first search course in archaeology. In almost every application of the survey, the percentage of students expressing strong agreement with claims about such things as ancient astronauts, Atlantis, the reality of Noah's flood, and the like, although too high to provide archaeologists with great comfort, rarely approaches one-third of the sample and is ordinarily a much smaller proportion. This has been shown to be the case in the American samples as well as those in Australia and Great Britain; as Richardson (1999: 36) found in her application of the survey: "In line with the American survey, British students show little advocacy for strongly expressed statements for support for the 'cult archaeologies'."

Then again, strong skepticism is only sometimes expressed for extreme claims made about the human past. For many of the statements regarding the human past that the students are asked to rate in terms of their level of agreement or disagreement, a sizeable segment, sometimes a plurality, chooses the "don't know," "uncertain," "unsure," or "no opinion" option offered in the particular survey instrument. Perhaps we should laud students who recognize their own ignorance of the archaeological record and have neither embraced extraordinary claims about the human past nor closed their minds to remarkable explanations. However, Richardson (1999: 36) points out that this high proportion of what she labels "fence straddlers" is not necessarily good news for the community of teaching archaeologists: "Given that most of the cult archaeologies have been more than adequately discredited, the 'undecided' option seems far from satisfactory."

A point in a continuum

As noted, the most recent application of the survey involved its administration to students at CCSU and Penn State University, two very different institutions. CCSU has a student population of just over 12,000, while Penn State has over 40,000 at the main University Park campus alone. Central is not highly selective in its enrollment, with approximately 60 percent of those who apply being accepted. Nearly half of its students score between 400 and 499 (on a scale of 200 to 800) on both the mathematics and verbal elements of the Scholastic Aptitude Test (SAT) 1, with a little less than 40 percent scoring between 500 and 599 on each. Penn State is clearly more selective in its enrollment, admitting students who rank higher in their high school graduating class and with somewhat higher SAT 1 scores. Interestingly, even with those differences in our student pools, the results of the survey show a remarkable level of agreement between the Connecticut and Pennsylvania students on the archaeological topics here addressed.

Ancient astronauts

For example, Figure 3.2 presents a simple bar graph breaking down the percentages of students at CCSU and Penn State who strongly agreed, mildly agreed, indicated that they had no opinion, mildly disagreed, or strongly disagreed with the statement: "Aliens from other worlds visited the Earth in the prehistoric past and assisted in the development of human technology" (statement 1 in Figure 3.1). Although the student pools may be different at CCSU and Penn State, the results from the two institutions are so similar that they are very nearly interchangeable.

It is gratifying to report that proportionately very few students at CCSU or Penn State feel strongly that ancient astronauts were responsible for the technological achievements of our species in past millennia; at both institutions, those who strongly agree represent very low (single-digit) percentages of the student sample. At both schools, higher but still single-digit portions of the sample expressed mild agreement concerning the role of ancient astronauts in human antiquity. At the same time and also on a positive note, high percentages – almost 50 percent at CCSU and slightly more than 50 percent at Penn State – are quite skeptical of the ancient astronaut claim, strongly disagreeing with von Däniken's fantasy. Combined with those expressing mild disagreement – close to 20 percent at both CCSU and Penn State – there is a clear picture here of students unsympathetic to the ancient astronaut notion, with nearly three-quarters disagreeing with the claim that ancient astronauts were responsible for human technological development.

Interestingly, this level of skepticism has not always characterized student response to von Däniken's ancient astronauts. When I first examined the results of the 2003 survey, especially those from the students at my institution, it seemed clear that there had been a substantial change in opinion regarding the ancient astronaut hypothesis from the 1983 sample. The combined proportion of those at CCSU who expressed strong or mild agreement with the ancient astronaut scenario dropped from more than 25 percent in 1983 to only about 6 percent in 2003. Moreover, as indicated previously, during that twenty-year period, I surveyed students at CCSU on five separate occasions, providing an interesting longitudinal database for assessing patterns through time in student opinion about ancient astronauts as well as all the other claims made about the human past and included in the survey.

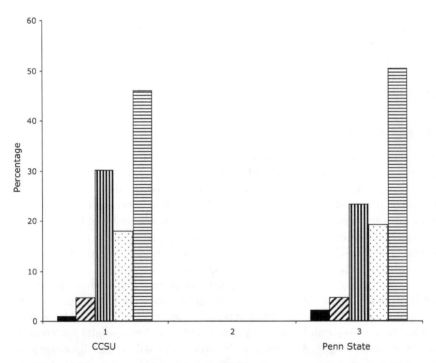

Figure 3.2 Levels of student agreement with ancient astronaut assertion, 2003, at CCSU and Penn State. ■ strong agree; ▨ mild agree; ▥ no opinion; ⬚ mild disagree; ▤ strong disagree

Figure 3.3 presents a line graph depicting the percentage figures for each of the response choices (strongly agree, mildly agree, don't know/no opinion, mildly disagree, strongly disagree) to the ancient astronaut statement for each of the years in which I surveyed students at CCSU. Complete consistency in student opinion over the years would have produced five parallel horizontal lines, and this clearly is not the case. In fact, the graph does not show consistent levels of agreement or disagreement but instead reflects a clear and regular pattern of change through time. A reasonable, subjective impression of this graph is that over the past twenty years there is clearly a general decline in the percentage of those expressing both strong and mild agreement as well as those indicating that they did not know whether the ancient astronaut notion had anything to back it up. The graph also shows a coincident increase over the past twenty years in the percentage of those who disagree either strongly or mildly with the ancient astronaut proposition; the level of strong disagreement alone has more than doubled, from less than 20 to over 45 percent.

A statistical analysis confirms the significance of the subjective impression just suggested. A linear regression was run on each of the five lines presented in the graph. Briefly, there are many ways of drawing a straight line through an *x,y* data set placed on an orthogonal graph. Using a least-squares procedure, linear regression produces a "best-fitting" straight line for such *x,y* data. A best-fitting line produced through the least-squares

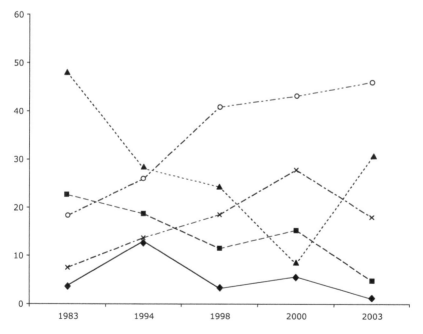

Figure 3.3 Changing levels of student agreement with ancient astronaut assertion at CCSU, 1983–2003. ◆ strong agree; ■ mild agree; ▲ no opinion; ✕ mild disagree; ○ strong disagree

procedure is one in which the sum of the squares of the differences between the *actual* y values (the measurement of the dependent variable) associated with each x (the independent variable) and the y value at each x data point *predicted* by the derived line is the smallest it can be; any other derived line would produce a larger sum of the squared deviations. In many cases, the best-fitting line looks about right; it is pretty close to the line you would draw by eye in order to summarize graphically the distribution of a group of x,y points that might not exhibit a perfectly linear relationship.

In this case, the year of the study was designated the x (independent) variable, with the percentage measured for each year for each response, successively, being designated as the y (dependent) variable. Look at the numerical values for the slopes of the best-fitting lines for mildly disagree and strongly disagree (see Table 3.1). As would be expected, their slopes are positive; in other words, as the value of x increases (reflecting a more recent year date) so does the value of y (reflecting an increase in the percentage of those expressing skepticism about the ancient astronaut hypothesis). The slopes for the best-fitting lines for "don't know/no opinion," "mildly agree," and "strongly agree" were all negative (indicating a decrease through time).

Simply because the regression lines are defined as "best-fitting" does not guarantee that they fit the data well. You can always depict a relationship between two variables as a best-fitting line, but "best fit" does not necessarily mean "good fit." Fortunately, we also have at our disposal a measure of the goodness of the fit between the best-fitting line and the actual data. Called "Pearson's r", this statistical value reflects a measurement of the degree of correlation between the regression line and the actual data points.

The r statistic reveals whether or not two variables "co-vary." It helps to answer the question: "As the value of x changes, does the value of y also change in a regular, consistent, and in this case linear way?" An r close to 1 indicates a very good fit between the best-fitting regression line and the actual data, suggesting that x and y consistently co-vary. An r close to 0 indicates that there is no correlation between the two variables; that the value of one is not predictable from the other; and that when graphed, the xy points do not fit together nicely on a straight line but that y sometimes increases as x increases, sometimes decreases, and sometimes remains the same.

For example, Pearson's r provides me with an objective measure of whether the percentage of students at my institution expressing strong

Table 3.1 Ancient astronauts: regression line slope and Pearson's r

	Slope of line	*Pearson's* r
Strongly agree	−0.137	0.221
Mildly agree	−0.813	0.875
Don't know	−1.426	0.743
Mildly disagree	0.802	0.794
Strongly disagree	1.566	0.956

disagreement with the ancient astronaut hypothesis changed in a consistent, patterned way through time. Did it regularly and predictably increase, decrease, or remain the same, or did it vary unpredictably from year to year? In fact, as noted previously, the percentage of those who strongly disagreed with the ancient astronaut hypothesis increased regularly between 1983 and 2003, and, as expected, Pearson's r for the calculated regression line is very close to 1 ($r = 0.956$). Pearson's r therefore provides mathematical support for my subjective analysis accomplished simply by eyeballing the graph; it certainly looks as if the percentage of those strongly disagreeing with the ancient astronaut hypothesis increased through time. An r of 0.956 strongly confirms this mathematically. Had the percentage of strong disagreers varied unpredictably through time, showing no overall increase or decrease but going up and down, the best-fitting line would not have been a good fit at all, and r would have approached 0, indicating a very weak or no significant correlation between time and strong disagreement with the ancient astronaut hypothesis.

Similarly, Pearson's r calculated for the change between 1983 and 2003 in the percentages of those expressing "mild disagreement" (a regular increase through time), "mild agreement" (a regular decrease over time), and those who chose the "no opinion" option (a regular decrease through time) also shows quite a tight fit between the statistically derived regression lines and the actual data for the pattern of change through time; in each of these cases, the value of r approaches 1.0 (Table 3.1). The relatively low value of r (0.221) for strong agreement is an indication that, although that percentage seems to be consistently declining over time, there is too much up and down – for example, a sharp increase between 1983 and 1994, then a sharp decrease between 1994 and 1998 – for us to conclude that there is a very regular, linear decrease or increase in strong agreement with the ancient astronaut hypothesis over time.

In summary, the initial impression of a linear increase between 1983 and 2003 in the percentage of CCSU students who disagreed (strongly or mildly) with the ancient astronaut hypothesis is borne out by the regression and by Pearson's r, as is the initial impression of a decrease in the percentage of those who had no opinion about the ancient astronaut proposition and at least those expressing mild agreement with the proposal. This would all appear to be good news.

It might seem that at least von Däniken's ancient astronauts are largely passé, and his is one variety of pseudoarchaeology that we need no longer concern ourselves with. Would that it were so. On this issue, our 2003 glass appears to be three-quarters full, but that still leaves it about one-quarter empty; a shockingly high proportion – 30 percent at CCSU and close to 25 percent at Penn State – remain undecided about the thoroughly discredited notion of ancient astronauts and opted for the "no opinion" choice in the survey.

It is distressing to report that von Däniken's proposals may experience a resurrection with the recent opening of what amounts to an ancient astronaut theme park in Interlaken, Switzerland (http://www.mysterypark.ch). The park is in fact von Däniken's brainchild (Powell 2004). The centerpiece is a 41-meter sphere that houses von Däniken's office and a display of his twenty-eight published books. As the website for Mystery Park promises: "With a little bit of luck, you could meet him personally." It is unclear whether a theme park in Switzerland will have any impact on the opinions of American students. However, it is possible that the popularity of ancient-astronaut-oriented science fiction (the film and subsequent television series *Stargate*, for instance) may play a role in revitalizing interest in von Däniken's fantasy.

Atlantis

Students at CCSU and Penn State also exhibit an extraordinary level of agreement in their responses to the statement: "there is good evidence for the existence of the lost continent of Atlantis" (statement 2 in Figure 3.1).

Although the results (Figure 3.4) show a somewhat higher percentage of agreement than was the case for the ancient astronaut statement, still only single-digit percentages of students at both universities express strong agreement with the cult archaeology of Atlantis. At the same time, however, levels of skepticism are lower on this issue, with students expressing strong disagreement at only about the same frequency as those expressing strong agreement. At both institutions, more than one-quarter of the sample

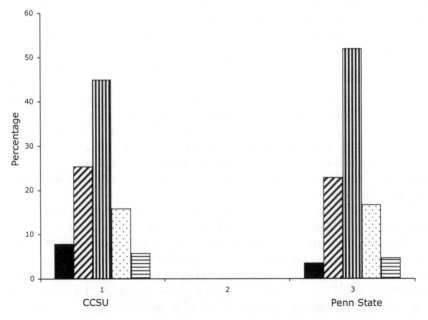

Figure 3.4 Levels of student agreement with Atlantis assertion, 2003, at CCSU and Penn State. ■ strong agree; ▨ mild agree; ⦀ no opinion; ⬚ mild disagree; ☰ strong disagree

expressed mild agreement that there is good evidence for Atlantis, and close to half in the CCSU sample and more than half of the Penn State sample simply do not know if Atlantis existed or not.

The higher level of agreement, at least mild agreement, and the much higher percentage of those opting for the "no opinion" response for the Atlantis statement when compared with the response to the ancient astronaut statement (compare Figures 3.2 and 3.4) is almost certainly a factor in the ebb and flow in popularity of specific elements of cult archaeology, especially in their role as grist for the cable television and science documentary mill. Atlantis is currently a very popular topic for documentary producers, particularly on cable channels in the USA ostensibly devoted to science, while ancient astronauts get very little coverage. For example, Disney's animated feature *Atlantis: The Lost Empire*, released in 2001, inspired a self-serving television pseudo-documentary that was little more than an extended commercial for the film, intercutting clips of the animated movie with interviews with various writers claiming the historical reality of the Atlantis myth (Feder 2002).

Although there are changes between 1983 and 2003 in how my Connecticut students responded to the statement in which the historical reality of Atlantis is claimed, what is consistent is the fact that those admitting that they just do not know along with those expressing mild agreement consistently dominate the sample (Figure 3.5).

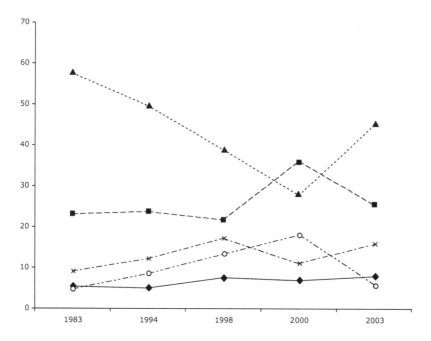

Figure 3.5 Changing levels of student agreement with Atlantis assertion at CCSU, 1983–2003. ◆ strong agree; ■ mild agree; ▲ no opinion; × mild disagree; o strong disagree

Table 3.2 Atlantis: regression line slope and Pearson's *r*

	Slope of line	*Pearson's* r
Strongly agree	0.138	0.779
Mildly agree	0.309	0.392
Don't know	−1.114	0.731
Mildly disagree	0.321	0.701
Strongly disagree	0.347	0.459

At the same time, there have been a number of regular changes through time in student opinions about Atlantis. The percentages of those expressing strong agreement with the reality and significance of Atlantis are consistently low, fluctuate hardly at all, and so produce a nearly perfectly straight horizontal regression line. The negligible slope of the line (0.138; Table 3.2) and its high *r* value (0.779; Table 3.2) bear this out statistically. The percentage of those expressing mild agreement shows some consistency as well, albeit with a spike in 2000. Strong disagreement shows an overall rise until it falls off in 2003, perhaps as a result of the spate of Atlantis documentaries that we have endured in the past few years. Those stating that they did not know or had no opinion shows a dramatic drop-off between 1983 and 2000 but then jumps back up in 2003. The slope of the regression line for "no opinion" is a negative number (−1.114), reflecting this decline through time, and its *r* value is rather high (0.731), reflecting the good fit between the regression line showing a general decrease through time in those responding "don't know/no opinion" and the data points.

King Tut's curse

A cult archaeology claim that currently gets only occasional coverage on television in the USA is the supposed curse on the tomb of Egyptian pharaoh Tutankhamun. In fact, the most recent television treatment of this claim of which I am aware was cable news reports discussing the article by Mark R. Nelson (2002) published in the *British Medical Journal* showing, in case there was any uncertainty about it, no pattern of higher mortality among those who entered Tut's tomb or who were directly involved in removing and analysing artefacts from the burial chamber when compared with other Europeans who were in Egypt at the time of the discovery, excavation, and analysis of the tomb but who were in no way involved in the excavation.

However, as certain as the evidence is for a lack of any curse, students at CCSU and Penn State are not so sure about it (Figure 3.6). Although, again, true believers are few and far between at both institutions, and the combined percentage of those expressing mild and strong disagreement is close to 40 percent at CCSU and nearly 50 percent at Penn State, appallingly high percentages – 40 percent at CCSU and close to that figure

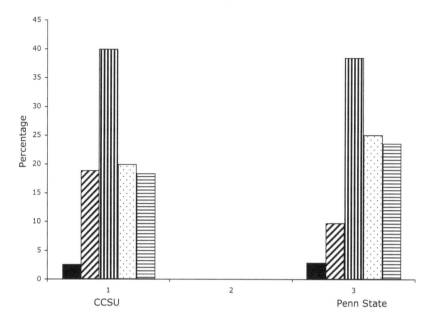

Figure 3.6 Levels of student agreement with Tut's curse assertion, 2003, at CCSU and Penn State. ■ strong agree; ▨ mild agree; ⦀ no opinion; ⬚ mild disagree; ☰ strong disagree

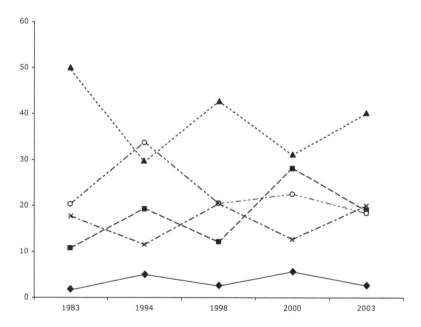

Figure 3.7 Changing levels of student agreement with Tut's curse assertion at CCSU, 1983–2003. ◆ strong agree; ■ mild agree; ▲ no opinion; ✕ mild disagree; ○ strong disagree

Table 3.3 Tut's curse: regression line slope and Pearson's *r*

	Slope of line	Pearson's r
Strongly agree	0.092	0.388
Mildly agree	0.548	0.58
Don't know	−0.577	0.509
Mildly disagree	0.058	0.104
Strongly disagree	−0.137	0.164

at Penn State – simply have no opinion about whether or not a curse on the tomb of Tutankhamun actually killed people.

Student responses to the statement about the validity and deadly efficacy of Tut's curse produce a series of sawtooth patterns reflecting swings in student opinions during the twenty years of data collection at my institution (Figure 3.7). Most clearly reflecting the jumping around of student opinion from year to year are the regression lines for those who mildly and strongly disagree; both produced very low *r* values, indicating that there is no tight, linear fit between time and opinion about Tut's curse (Table 3.3).

Human evolution

Researchers of student opinions related to the human past have previously noted a difference in the character of student responses to those topics that might be labeled general "human antiquity" and those that impinge more directly on religious belief, especially biblical literalism (Harrold and Eve 1987). Most of the remaining statements addressed in this survey – statements 5–7 in Figure 3.1 – are the latter, dealing with issues discussed in the Bible.

The results of the survey as it relates to statements 5–7 should be interpreted in the context of how students responded to statement 4 in Figure 3.1: "Human beings came about through evolution." In the 2003 survey at CCSU and Penn State, and consistently at CCSU since 1983, students expressed a very high level of agreement with this statement (Figure 3.8). In fact, in the 2003 survey, student responses to that statement were nearly identical at both institutions, with very high combined percentages of those who strongly or mildly agreed; 72 percent at CCSU and 68 percent at Penn State were in agreement with the theory of human evolution. At both institutions, the percentage of those opting for the "no opinion" choice concerning whether or not human beings arose through evolution hovered at around 15 percent (a little lower at CCSU, a little higher at Penn State) with only about 10 percent at both schools strongly disagreeing.

A high level of agreement with this general statement regarding human evolution is nothing new at my institution. CCSU student response to the statement "Human beings came about through evolution" has been quite consistent over the course of the last twenty years, especially among those who disagree either strongly or mildly (Figure 3.9). The "mildly disagree"

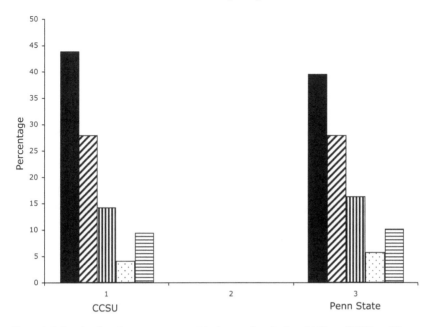

Figure 3.8 Levels of student agreement with theory of evolution, 2003, at CCSU and Penn State. ■ strong agree; ▨ mild agree; ▥ no opinion; ▦ mild disagree; ▤ strong disagree

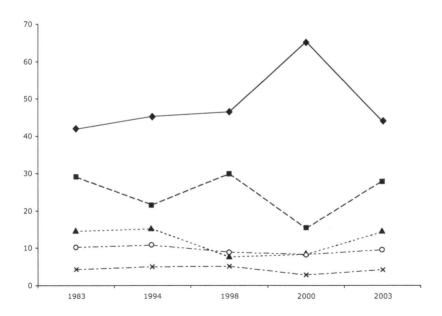

Figure 3.9 Changing levels of student agreement with theory of evolution at CCSU, 1983– 2003. ◆ strong agree; ■ mild agree; ▲ no opinion; ✕ mild disagree; ○ strong disagree

Table 3.4 Human evolution: regression line slope and Pearson's *r*

	Slope of line	*Pearson's* r
Strongly agree	0.538	0.417
Mildly agree	−0.228	0.270
Don't know	−0.202	0.404
Mildly disagree	−0.030	0.241
Strongly disagree	−0.078	0.578

and "strongly disagree" responses are nearly horizontal lines; the slopes of their respective regression lines are close to zero, indicating extraordinary consistency in the percentages of those expressing mild and strong disagreement with the notion of human evolution between 1983 and 2003 (Table 3.4). The "strongly disagree" regression line shows the closest fit to the data, producing an *r* of 0.578. The percentage of those in mild agreement on this issue as well as those answering "don't know/no opinion" are less consistent, showing a slight overall statistical decline, but the level of correlation between the data and the respective regression lines is relatively low. Strong agreement increases more substantially, with a proportionately larger positive regression line slope and relatively high *r* value.

Evolution and biblical literalism

So the good news would seem to be that at least at these two schools located in the northeastern United States, a relatively high percentage of students in the early twenty-first century agree, either mildly or strongly, that human beings evolved. However, what is extraordinarily interesting is that, at the same time, these same students expressed relatively high levels of the "no opinion" response when confronted with statements that reflect a literal interpretation of the Bible.

Specifically, on creationist claims of a literal, six-day creation, the historicity of Adam and Eve, and Noah's flood, surprisingly high percentages responded "no opinion." Beginning with the young-Earth creationist claim of a divine creation of our planet over a period of six, actual, 24-hour days as described in Genesis (Figure 3.10), there are proportionately few true believers (less than 10 percent at both institutions) and a far higher proportion of those strongly skeptical (33 percent at both schools). However, there also are astonishingly high percentages at CCSU and Penn State – 38 and 33 percent, respectively – of those answering "no opinion." The statistics force the conclusion that at least some of those expressing agreement with the concept of human evolution (see Figure 3.8) are not sure that that process did not take place over the course of six, 24-hour days!

There has been little change at my institution over the past twenty years in the percentages of those in strong and mild agreement with the claim that the Earth was created in six literal days, as well as those expressing mild

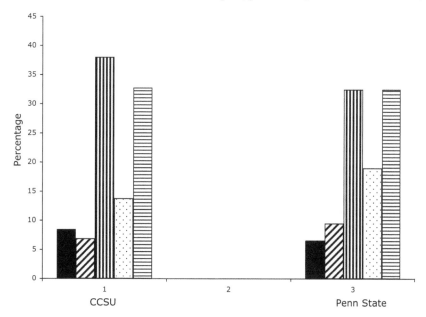

Figure 3.10 Levels of student agreement with claim of a literal six-day creation, 2003, at CCSU and Penn State. ■ strong agree; ▨ mild agree; ▥ no opinion; ▨ mild disagree; ▤ strong disagree

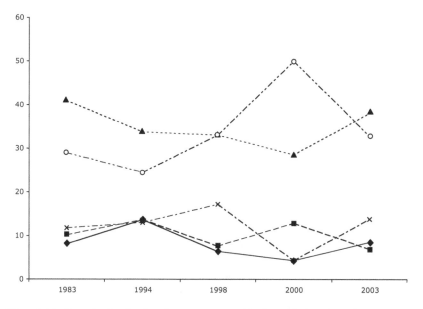

Figure 3.11 Changing levels of student agreement with claim of a literal six-day creation at CCSU, 1983–2003. ◆ strong agree; ■ mild agree; ▲ no opinion; ✕ mild disagree; o strong disagree

Table 3.5 Six-day creation: regression line slope and Pearson's *r*

	Slope of line	Pearson's r
Strongly agree	–0.124	0.262
Mildly agree	–0.113	0.272
Don't know	–0.351	0.544
Mildly disagree	–0.034	0.053
Strongly disagree	0.612	0.466

disagreement. These percentages have remained at a fairly consistent, low level between 1983 and 2003 (Figure 3.11).

As can be seen in Table 3.5, the slopes of their respective regression lines are close to zero, reflecting this consistency; there is no temporal pattern of increase or decrease in the percentages of students selecting one of these responses. At the same time, there is a pattern of slight decline over time in the percentages of those who do not know or have no opinion about human evolution, and an even more substantial increase in the percentage expressing strong disagreement with the idea of a six-day creation.

Although students at CCSU and Penn State were divided in their opinion as to whether or not "Adam and Eve were the first human beings" (statement 6 in Figure 3.1), belief levels were much higher than was the case for a six-day creation (Figure 3.12). The combined proportion of those who either strongly or mildly agreed that Adam and Eve were the first people was a shocking 37 percent (CCSU) and 34 percent (Penn State) of the sample. Skepticism, both strong and mild, was measured at 32 percent (CCSU) and 43 percent (Penn State), while the percentage of those stating that they had no opinion was fully 30 percent at CCSU and nearly 25 percent at Penn State. I suppose I should not be surprised at this, having once had a student approach me after class to inquire, in all sincerity, as to whether the fossil cast of a *Homo habilis* I had shown in class was what Adam and Eve looked like. So, again, the numbers show more than a bit of confusion on the part of the students surveyed. At least some of those who expressed some level of agreement that human beings came about through evolution also either accept that Adam and Eve were the first people or, at least, have no opinion one way or the other.

There does not seem to be any particular pattern through time in students' response to the statement identifying Adam and Eve as the first human beings (Figure 3.13). The graph gives a general impression of a slight increase in those expressing mild agreement; in fact, the regression line for the percentage of those expressing mild agreement or acceptance of Adam and Eve exhibits the largest positive slope (0.294) in the group of evolution/biblical literalism statements. At the same time, there seems to be a slight decline in the percentage of those expressing strong agreement with Adam and Eve, but the slopes of the rest of the regression lines do not indicate any substantial pattern of increase or decrease for any of the other responses, and their *r* values are quite low (Table 3.6).

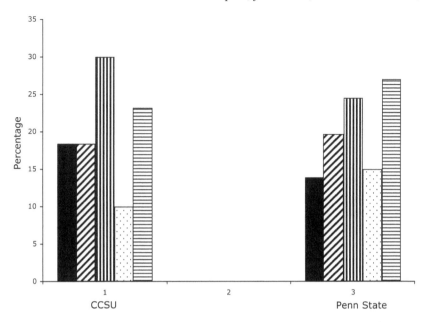

Figure 3.12 Levels of student agreement with claim that Adam and Eve were the first humans, 2003, at CCSU and Penn State. ■ strong agree; ▨ mild agree; ⦀ no opinion; ⦂ mild disagree; ☰ strong disagree

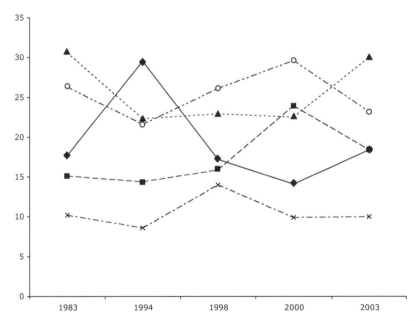

Figure 3.13 Changing levels of student agreement with claim that Adam and Eve were the first humans at CCSU, 1983–2003. ◆ strong agree; ■ mild agree; ▲ no opinion; ✕ mild disagree; ○ strong disagree

Table 3.6 Adam and Eve: regression line slope and Pearson's *r*

	Slope of line	Pearson's r
Strongly agree	−0.150	0.187
Mildly agree	0.294	0.560
Don't know	−0.186	0.323
Mildly disagree	0.039	0.143
Strongly disagree	−0.002	0.005

Finally, regarding the historical claim of a universal deluge, students at CCSU and Penn State were generally less skeptical in their response to the statement "the flood of Noah as told in the Bible really happened" (statement 7 in Figure 3.1) than they were to other Bible-related assertions. As can be seen in Figure 3.14, a remarkably high proportion of students expressed strong or mild agreement with the historical reality of Noah's flood; fully 43 percent of the CCSU students and a remarkable 46 percent of the Penn State students. However, 36 percent of the CCSU sample and 28 percent of the Penn State students stated that they had no opinion on this issue, and at both schools, skeptics, strong and mild, were in the minority.

It is conceivable that the higher level of student acceptance or uncertainty concerning Noah's flood derives from shoddy or at least misleading newspaper reporting of Robert Ballard's underwater archaeology in the Black Sea in 2000, sponsored by the National Geographic Society. Following the work of Ryan and Pitman (1997), Ballard maintained that at least some of the archaeological features he encountered with his remotely operated submarine date to an early post-glacial period when seawater, rising rapidly as the result of glacial melting, may have catastrophically breached the barrier between the Mediterranean and the Black Sea. Newspaper headlines reporting his discoveries and interpretation, with headlines like "New Evidence of Great Flood" and "Found: Possible Pre-Flood Artefacts," were confusing at best, misleading at worst, but no more problematic than the phrasing on the National Geographic Society's own website, which put it this way: "Ballard discovers proof of a flood of biblical proportions" (see http://www.nationalgeographic.com/blacksea/ax/frame.html).

The changes in response percentages through time are all over the place on this issue, and the graphs reflects this in the sawtooth appearance of their temporal distributions (Figure 3.15). Those expressing mild disagreement as well as the percentage of students opting for the "don't know/no opinion" response show this quite clearly, but the strong and mild agreement responses do not exhibit any particular pattern of change through time either. On the other hand, the percentage of those expressing strong disagreement with the reality of the Noahian deluge seems to increase slightly over time. It comes as no surprise, therefore, to find in Table 3.7 that most of the values for correlation between the regression line and the actual data distribution are close to zero. The only strong correlation can be

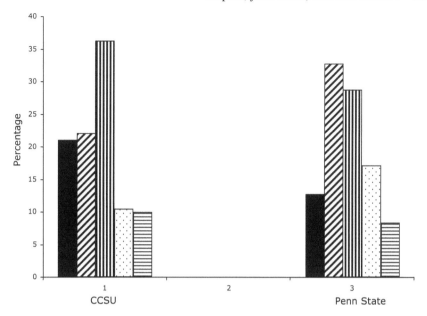

Figure 3.14 Levels of student agreement with historical validity of Noah's flood, 2003, at CCSU and Penn State. ■ strong agree; ▨ mild agree; ⦀ no opinion; ⬚ mild disagree; ☰ strong disagree

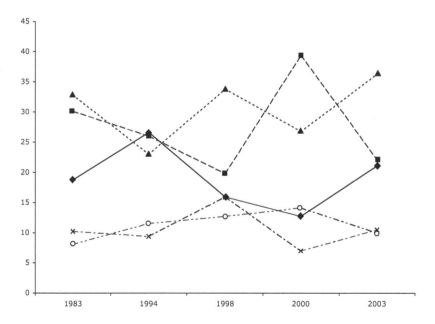

Figure 3.15 Changing levels of student agreement with historical validity of Noah's flood at CCSU, 1983–2003. ◆ strong agree; ■ mild agree; ▲ no opinion; ✕ mild disagree; o strong disagree

Table 3.7 Noah's flood: regression line slope and Pearson's *r*

	Slope of line	Pearson's r
Strongly agree	−0.136	0.190
Mildly agree	−0.156	0.149
Don't know	0.092	0.123
Mildly disagree	0.012	0.028
Strongly disagree	0.198	0.624

found for the distribution of those expressing strong disagreement (r = 0.624).

Conclusions

Based on more than twenty years of surveying student opinions about extreme reconstructions of human antiquity, I believe it is safe to conclude that the sky is not falling. That is very good news. Despite the prevalence of hyperventilated documentaries on television, despite the popularity of the works of writers like Graham Hancock (1995, 2002a) and Robert Bauval (Hancock and Bauval 1996), despite the grand opening of von Däniken's ancient-astronaut-themed Mystery Park, and even despite the existence of the Internet and the ability of anyone to say practically anything about the human past on a website – despite all this, students do not appear to be descending into a swirling vortex of pseudoscientific beliefs about the human past. Rather, they seem to be aware of and interested in claims about ancient astronauts, super-sophisticated civilizations in the distant past, Pharaoh's curses, Noah's flood, and the like, but the majority simply are not intellectually or emotionally committed to such notions. As has consistently been the case among the various student populations sampled in the past twenty years, the proportion of true believers in ancient astronauts, the lost continent of Atlantis, Noah's flood, etc., has been consistently, mercifully, small. To be sure, in most cases the proportion of students who confidently dismiss such claims is small as well, but our biggest challenge and opportunity as teaching archaeologists continues to be the proportionately large segment of our student population that simply is not sure, does not know, has come to no conclusion about such claims, or maybe even could not care less about them.

To those who assert that pseudoscientific claims are better left unaddressed in the archaeology classroom, that it is a mistake even to bring up the assertions of pseudoarchaeology because students are largely unaware of such nonsense, look carefully at the graphs presented in this paper. It is apparent that in mentioning ancient astronauts, Atlantis, Noah's flood, or King Tut's curse, we are dealing with a harvest sprouted from seeds that have already been sown. It is clearly the case in the current iteration, as it has clearly been the case in many of the past applications and versions of the opinion survey, that although most of our students do not feel passionately about any particular pseudoarchaeological claim, they are well aware of many of them, with some agreeing and others disagreeing with their validity.

As just mentioned, in every case dealt with here, a not insignificant portion – and in a number of cases a plurality – of the student sample maintains that it simply does not have enough information to form an opinion about the legitimacy of nonsense promulgated about human antiquity. Their minds, we assume, are open, as they should be. If we elect *not* to address extreme claims, especially those with which our students are already familiar, I would assert that it may be interpreted by many that we *cannot* address them.

The interested and open minds of our students represent fertile ground for the purveyors of fantasies about the human past, but they are equally fertile ground for archaeologists scientifically examining that past. Although certainly the mash of nonsense about human antiquity that students are exposed to in popular media presents teaching archaeologists with a challenge, it also provides us with an opportunity. Pseudoarchaeologists exploit the public's fascination with the past at the same time that they exploit the scientific and historical naivete of that same public. Maybe, in turn, we should exploit pseudoarchaeology. It is important to recognize that a sizeable fraction of our students select archaeology courses to fulfill general education or distribution requirements from a broad list of social or behavioral disciplines precisely because their interest has been sparked by bad television documentaries and worse books. So be it. Let us not ignore what those bad documentaries and worse books claim: let us use them as jumping-off points for explaining the methodology and results of scientific archaeology. This is not a question merely of debunking ancient astronauts, Atlantis, or Pharaoh's curse – at least that is not all that this should be about. It is also about explaining how such claims are assessed, like all others, by testing through the collection, interpretation, and analysis of archaeological data. Explaining these processes, after all, is what many of our courses are supposed to be about.

In the marketplace of ideas, there is clearly a demand for information about the human past. If archaeologists do not supply that demand, others will – and do. Ignoring popular pseudoscience about the human past does not make it go away. The notion of a mysterious, inexplicable, improbable prehistory may ebb and flow in its particulars, but it is always there, and it always will be so long as there is cable television, the Internet, and ancient astronaut theme parks. It is the responsibility of teaching archaeologists to recognize this and to respond by sharing with their students, as well as with the general public, archaeological knowledge and the results of the scientific investigation of our shared human past.

4   Memoirs of a true believer[1]

Katherine Reece

When I was asked to write this chapter I accepted without hesitation, but I must admit that I then had second thoughts. Did I really want to examine why I used to think the way I did? Why I used to insult and belittle archaeologists and historians? Why I used to believe they were hiding critical information from the general public? Did I really want to hold my former thought processes up to the light? That is not a comfortable thing for me to do, least of all in public. There was also the possibility that my words would be taken out of context and thrown back at me by so-called alternative writers, who like to trivialize and insult my efforts.[2] This was (and is) a very real concern for me, considering how much I have seen these same writers twist words with the skill of the best "spin doctors." I also did not want to slur people I know and like but who still support the "alternative" side. However, in the end I decided to view this chapter as a cathartic experience, a chance to examine my past emotional stance of anger towards the academic practitioners of history, and to delve into why I accepted so readily and without question what the "alternative" historians were offering.

Into the quagmire

In *Fingerprints of the Gods*, which has been one of the most popular "alternative" history books of recent times, Graham Hancock refers to archaeologists and Egyptologists in less than flattering terms. They are called "astigmatic" (Hancock 1995: 354), their ideas labeled "superficial" (ibid.: 341), and their research dismissed as "trivializing the mystery" (ibid.: 295). ("Alternative" writers love to pose as the only ones who *really* appreciate mystery and wonder.) Even the late I.E.S. Edwards of the British Museum is taken to task. His theory that ramps were used to construct the pyramids at Giza appears in *Fingerprints* under the rubric "rampant stupidity" (ibid.: 284), despite the physical evidence for the use of ramps at several other pyramid sites. "Alternative" history books frequently assert that archaeologists hide our real history or that they are afraid of the public finding out the truth.

Now just why professionals would want to hide this information away or what is so damaging about it I have never quite known. That detail is never fully explained. However, that is not the point of such suggestions. Rather, the point is to raise the political standing of the "alternative" writer in the eyes of readers and to put those readers in a position of feeling superior to professional scholars, both intellectually and morally. After all, these writers are going to tell us what the self-serving archaeologists will not! They will bring us into their circle and share hidden knowledge with us. It gives the reader a feeling of being included in a great mystery. Through his website, Graham Hancock continually reiterates this position of superiority. When a report in the *Hindustan Times* mistakenly identified Hancock as a marine archaeologist, Hancock stated on the message board of his website: "Given my line of work, and my position on archaeology, I find the label 'archaeologist' offensive and unhelpful when applied to me."[3] I can well imagine that most archaeologists who spend their workdays in detailed research would find the label "archaeologist" offensive when applied to Hancock as well.

When I first began to read "alternative," books I had an inclination to be anti-establishment, as most readers of the genre seem to be; clearly, the writers know their target audience well and exploit this inclination fully. While academics are referred to in insulting ways, with accusations that they are desperate to protect their tenured positions in the hallowed ivory towers, "alternative" historians and researchers are held up as courageous and pioneering. They brave the adversity of the intellectuals and suffer the criticism directed at them from academia. Reading this, who would want to be on the side of the obstructionist old Professor Phuddy Duddy? I certainly did not! I wanted to be on the side of the free thinkers, the open-minded, and the curious. What could be better than to join the "quest" (a favorite word in "alternative" works) for the true and hidden knowledge of human history? In my case at least, such essentially political considerations as these were fundamental to my initial allegiance to "alternative" history.

My introduction to ancient monuments came in the form of Erich von Däniken's *Chariots of the Gods*, which I read as a teenager.[4] A small group of girls in my high school had formed an informal club to exchange books, and that was how it fell into my hands. I was fascinated. It was so utterly different from anything that I had ever been exposed to before that, without actually traveling, I was in culture shock. How could primitive humans have ever built such things? And so long ago! The motives for these incredible feats of engineering could not possibly have been so boring as to please a ruler or honor the gods! I thought, "Just imagine what would happen if someone told us today to build a pyramid for Gerald Ford!" Encouraged to think along such lines by von Däniken, the standard explanations just did not "work" for me. There had to be some sort of higher reason for these mysterious lines or those wonderful pyramids. But what could it be?

What is interesting to me now is how I was so ready to dismiss "conventional" theories that I actually knew nothing about, and how willing I was to accept von Däniken's viewpoints concerning them. Independent resources were scarce, and von Däniken certainly did not present the "standard" scenarios in any detail or review the evidence on which they were based, or outline their chains of reasoning. He just mentioned them, dismissed them, and concentrated on his own proposals. But having gained my political allegiance, he put me in a position of agreeing with him, despite my utter ignorance of what I was agreeing with him about! It seems so silly now, but at the time the process had its own internal logic.

I can still remember the look on my teacher's face. There I was at 17 standing before the class and giving my speech on how the human race was "constructed" by aliens. I discussed the "runways" and "parking areas" in the Peruvian desert at Nazca, the statues and reliefs of ancient astronauts found all over the world, and the amazing construction projects that no local culture could possibly have achieved on its own. Surprisingly enough, no one laughed at me, perhaps since they too would soon be delivering speeches on their topic of choice, and they did not wish to set a bad precedent. But the look on my teacher's face was one of shock. You could almost hear her thoughts as she wondered how she had failed me to the point that I could believe such things. Her only comment, though, was a dismissive and rather loud "Okay!"

Looking back, I think she made a critical mistake in glossing over my "alternative" presentation, but she was quite young and just out of college herself, so she may not have had the confidence to take a step outside "normal" classroom procedure. Nevertheless, I would have preferred had she quietly taken me aside and suggested some books that could have answered some of the questions that I had been told were unanswerable, or pointed me to some analysis that could have shown the dishonesty of von Däniken's apparently decisive "arguments" and "evidence." After all, by this time (the late 1970s), he had already been exposed. But I had no knowledge of that, nor was any presented to me. Books were available on the Nazca lines that would have shown the photographic deception behind von Däniken's "runways" and "parking facilities." Information was available on early Egypt that demolished his claims about that period (i.e., that Egyptian civilization had appeared fully formed, more or less overnight). After all, information concerning the pre-dynastic period of Egypt had been available since the late nineteenth century through the work of William Flinders Petrie. I cannot guarantee that exposure to such "conventional" work would have changed my mind at this early stage, but it may have planted some seeds of doubt.

As it was, I had a lot of interest but very little actual knowledge. I had always been interested in history, but the educational system I was part of did not put a high priority on it. We studied the history of the United States and of my home state of Alabama in particular, and some European history with a heavy concentration on England; we glossed over the pre-Columbian history of the Americas and instead discussed the Spanish conquest and subsequent periods. As for the rest of the world, we learned only the barest hints.

This curriculum was unfulfilling for me; I was curious. I had, on my own, read about Egyptian history to some extent, but it was limited to the eighteenth dynasty and, in particular, Tutankhamun. (This was the late 1970s, and the Tutankhamun exhibit was still making the rounds in North America.) Of the early dynasties and the founding of Egyptian civilization I knew almost nothing. The accomplishments and culture of the Egyptians therefore seemed extremely mysterious to me. I had no knowledge of the long period of evolution that led up to such wonders and to such a complicated and complex cultural system that stood behind them.

This was long before the Internet, and I lived in a small farming community in Alabama. There was not a wide selection of books available to me, and, quite frankly, at that time if a scholarly book had been available I would probably have considered it dull and wondered what the author was leaving out. This was how I had been told academics operated, so I now expected it of them. Rather than reading the alternative books with a healthy dose of skepticism, I would in the future read so-called mainstream books in that manner. The distrust of the academic had been planted in my mind, and it grew freely.

The years after high school were rather hectic ones for me, complete with marriage and children, with little time and money for books. I rarely had the time or the funds to go searching for books about ancient Egypt; family members did give me books from time to time, but these were the very general "coffee table" type of book. They were insufficient to provide any answers or refute in any detail the "alternative" works I had read. I suppose that, due to different marketing schemes, books explaining "mainstream" theories could only be found in faraway bookstores, but *Fingerprints of the Gods* (originally published in 1995) was available in the five feet of bookshelves at the local drugstore. The title was close enough to *Chariots of the Gods* to make me pick it up. After reading the cover blurb, I had to have it.

It was everything *Chariots of the Gods* had been, and so much more.[5] Like *Chariots*, it carried the reader along on a quest for hidden histories, but it was fuller, more detailed and much richer. The author, Graham Hancock, described in riveting terms his travels to exotic places, his emotional responses to the monuments he saw in those places, and the gradual evolution of his radical ideas. His central argument was more believable than von Däniken's as well. Instead of star-skipping aliens, now it was a human (but lost) civilization that had existed long ages ago. It offered a glimpse into a bright past lost in the mists of history, a glorious time in a far-off epoch to contrast with a dreary and worrying present. If only, Hancock urged his readers, we could overcome our species' amnesia and learn the secrets of our true heritage. I was hooked. How phenomenal would it be if we could recapture this lost spiritual knowledge of the ancients! Perhaps, using it, we could live in as peaceful a world as they had. It is an idea that is like balm to a modern soul. How could you not believe? Why would you not *want* to believe?

"Alternative" history capitalizes on such romanticism by making the reader feel included in something special. It is almost as if a knowledgeable guide has taken you by the hand and invited you to come on a journey through time and visit sacred places, to discover hidden truths and to contemplate ill-studied wonders that may hold the answers to humanity's greatest questions. I later came to see that, even though these sorts of books have been in print for well over a century, each new one claims to be putting forth startlingly original and fresh information. Yet, despite their self-presentation as visionaries, their authors are often doing nothing more than reviewing previously published claims and repeating them, even if those claims have long been disproved. In many of these books, when you check the references (if they have references at all) you will find that they refer to the author's previous books or to books written by other "alternative" writers. While this makes tracking down the sources to check specific claims very difficult, it is an excellent way to spread the gospel of "alternative" thinking."

And so through *Fingerprints of the Gods* I was introduced to the work of other "alternative" authors, those free-thinking visionaries out there challenging the accepted wisdom. I was told how very brave they were to be sticking their necks out and taking the heat in the struggle to learn the truth. I learned about Robert Bauval and his Orion correlation theory; I learned about John Anthony West and the new research conducted by him and his academic collaborator, Robert Schoch, on the age of the Sphinx; and I read about "Earth crustal displacement," as championed by the Flem-Aths (who were only aping the work of Charles Hapgood, who was himself influenced by the ideas of Hugh Auchinloss Brown).[6] It was all very exciting. It was also, I see now, a political rather than an intellectual process. The gurus of "alternative" history had invited me to join their party, and I had gratefully accepted.

The fact that the opposition party – the academic community – dismissed out of hand "alternative" claims, such as the proposition of a Sphinx several millennia older than fourth-dynasty Egypt, was good evidence of exactly what "alternative" authors had been telling me all along about how academics worked. West, in fact, claimed that Schoch had presented their ideas at a conference of geologists and had gained the support of over three hundred delegates, yet *still* the tenure-protecting academics in archaeology would not yield. I could not help but think: "What are they hiding, and just who did these academics think they are that they should keep the truth from the people?" I was incensed.

I was very excited the night that I watched the NBC special *Mystery of the Sphinx* (it originally aired in the USA in 1993, but I first saw it a few years later after reading *Fingerprints*). The program presented the new geological findings that the Sphinx was thousands of years older than the stodgy academics wanted to admit. Everything was laid out so clearly, with easily understandable computer graphics and simple explanations. The weathering effects of wind erosion were compared with those of water erosion, and the differences were clear and undeniable. If a layman like myself could see it so easily, why did Egyptologists refuse to consider it? It was obvious viewing the Sphinx from its side that the head was far too small for the body. That, and the fact that it was in much better condition than the body, showed quite clearly that the head had been recarved at some point and that the body showed the best history of the weathering patterns. This was real, hard evidence! Yet the academics still refused see the truth. I watched aghast as pyramid expert Mark Lehner demanded a potsherd as evidence for the ancient pre-Egyptian civilization that had built the Sphinx. A potsherd! Here was the evidence of the Sphinx itself, and he wanted a potsherd? I was incredulous and very disappointed in the Egyptological community that they could not see that wind-generated erosion was not the cause of the Sphinx's weathering patterns. I could not believe that they would not accept the evidence that had convinced all those supportive geologists (none of whom actually appeared on the program, apart from Schoch himself) but instead used only a flaking old inscribed stone to place the Sphinx in the reign of Khafre. I discussed the program with my co-workers the next day and complained about the deceit of Egyptology in keeping such important information from us. Who were they to deny us our true history? How dare they!

Out of the swamp

When I bought a computer and acquired Internet access in 1996, I gleefully began to search for information on the Sphinx and the lost civilization that stood behind the Egyptians, the Olmec and all the others, the civilization that had inspired primitive humans and put us on the path to high culture and enlightenment. There was no shortage of websites devoted to such themes. Finally, one day I found the website of Graham Hancock himself[7] and began posting on its message board. I thought that it might provide me with more information about these long-lost people who had seeded all the world's civilizations. I started out looking for more information about those seafaring teachers, but instead, in the end, my Internet experience made me realize that they were never there to begin with. It happened like this.

I began posting on the Sphinx and, copying my alternative mentors, I spoke of Egyptologists in an insulting manner. My ignorance at the time was profound, since I was not even aware of the actual weathering mechanisms that Egyptologists and (as it turned out) most geologists thought were the cause of the Sphinx's present appearance. However, this did not stop me suggesting that the academics were hiding things from us, or that they were foolish for not accepting the observable evidence of water-induced weathering patterns on the Sphinx, and so on. I did not know that what was truly observable were flakes that fell from the Sphinx every day as the process of salt crystallization literally peeled it away. It turned out that the erosion of the Sphinx was an ongoing process and was not brought about in any single phase millennia ago.

Through my contact with Hancock's message board, I met some very well-informed "mainstream" researchers who pointed out the errors and omissions of fact in *Fingerprints of the Gods* and who informed me about the complexity of the Great Sphinx's geology. They explained that Egyptologists did not think wind-blown sand was the culprit in creating the erosion patterns on the Sphinx. They also explained how the *Mystery of the Sphinx* program had used a straw man argument, setting up a fake position so that it could be knocked down to give the appearance of overturning, through scientific means, a position that was weak and yet widely supported by academics. I learned that three hundred geologists had not supported John Anthony West and Robert Schoch at that conference. Rather, geologists saw a poster presentation at a geological conference and had asked to be kept informed about Schoch's work – a very different thing entirely! I also learned that the builders of the Sphinx discovered a huge flaw in the native lime-stone and had been forced to make the body longer in order to stabilize it, thus creating the impression, when the Sphinx was viewed from the side, that the head was too small for the body.

Ironically, it was through contact with these same "alternative" writers, via the Internet message boards, that caused me to trust the "mainstream" side more and the "alternative" side less. In their books, "alternative" writers often state that they will be attacked for their views. But to me it appeared that it was they who attacked people who dared to question them. Tough questions were avoided, danced around, and the questioner attacked rather than answered. This made me wonder who was truly hiding the truth.

The more I searched and learned about different subjects discussed in the "alternative" books that I had read, the more disappointed I became. My disappointment was not only with the writers whom I had thought were imparting truth and wisdom to me but also – and mainly – with myself for having been led down the proverbial primrose path.

It seemed as if almost everything I had once accepted as fact blew away like a house of cards in a hurricane. The layer of mica in the Pyramid of the Sun at Teotihuacán in Mexico, which had supposedly been tested and shown to have been transported mysteriously from thousands of miles away? It was local and not mysterious at all. The allegedly native myths of "white" gods bringing civilization to Central and South American natives? They turned out to be the product of Spanish manipulation of native myths to serve their own imperialist ends. Lord Pacal at Palenque was not depicted on the lid of his sarcophagus riding a spaceship or operating complex machinery. Rather, he was shown with typical Mayan symbolism passing through to the after-life. Pyramids worldwide were not the same but were instead built differently at different times, served different purposes, had different mean-ings, and had their own distinct evolutionary histories. Tiwanaku in Bolivia was not a city that stood out of time and place but rather fitted exactly into Andean chronology. The pyramids at Giza were not laid out to symbolize the belt of Orion in 10,500 BC; their location was a by-product of the topography of Giza combined with a religious need for each pyramid to have a clear view of the northern sky. And so on.

I began to read scientific journals, papers, and "mainstream" books, which made me realize how much easier it is to do "alternative" history – and to read it. It is much simpler to ask how the ancient Andean people could have constructed massive buildings of stone and imply some mysterious and hidden history with as yet unknown technology than it is to take the time to study their culture, learn their language(s) and review volumes of previously published work on the topic. To understand how the ancient Andean people were actually able to create such wondrous works, you need to understand their system of *mit'a* service (a governmental method of marshalling labor) and to study their labor and textile taxation. This reveals how the authorities reciprocated labor services and how this system worked to the advantage of king and peasant alike (Moseley 2001: 72–8).

I increasingly began to spend my time on the Internet looking for the "mainstream" counterpoints to the "alternative" historians' arguments, but there were only a few such sites out there. Compared with the overwhelming number of sites publicizing "alternative" scenarios, the "mainstream" sites were not making much of an impact. I thought of other people who were reading pseudoarchaeology books, who might want to know the opposing side but lacked the access or the resources to find it.

I wanted to do something. I wanted to help those people who were searching for the truth about history to have an easily accessible "mainstream" counter to these "alternative" claims. So the concept of *The Hall of Ma'at* website was born. *The Hall of Ma'at* is owned by myself and operates with a board of directors: Don Holeman, John Wall, Doug Weller, Paul Heinrich, and myself. One of our primary goals is for the website to become an online "warehouse" of information on a variety of subjects. Part of the problem with refuting alternative history is that it encapsulates such a variety of cultures and civilizations from around the world that a researcher in one discipline alone is ill-equipped to refute the variegated claims of "alternative" historians. Current subjects addressed at *Ma'at* include Afrocentrism, the early history of the Americas, ancient astronauts, Antarctica, the Bermuda Triangle, the development of civilization, dating methods, the lost civilization (which is how writers like Graham Hancock today mask their belief in Atlantis), general methodological problems in "alternative writing," numerology, out-of-place artefacts, and the so-called Orion correlation theory. Since Egypt is so commonly discussed in alternative writings (see Chapter 5), we have an area for Egypt in general and also sections for Giza and the Sphinx. The articles assembled at the site consist of work previously published in journals and magazines such as *Current Anthropology*, *KMT*, *JARCE*, and *Skeptical Inquirer*, but we also have original articles that were written specifically for the website. There is also a section titled "Unforbidden Geology," where a geologist explains how ancient people created such beautiful works of art with simple tools. The site also provides webspace to Jon Bodsworth for his ever-growing collection of images from Egypt (http://www.egyptarchive.co.uk).

The Hall of Ma'at has surpassed all our original expectations for Internet traffic, the willingness of academics and respected publications to have their work electronically "reprinted" at the site, and in educating the interested lay person. We were very pleased to have been featured in the May/June 2003 issue of *Archaeology* magazine. The ire of "alternative" writers, who usually refer to us with schoolboy abuse, is a sure sign that we are on the right track!

Conclusion

That is the story of my intellectual journey. However, it *is* a personal story. I do not think it is safe to lump all believers in "alternative" history in one group or personality type, or to imagine that they all share the same reasoning processes, let alone the same goals and ideas. There are a great variety of "alternative" scenarios, each with its own agenda and set of followers. But two things do seem to unite them: they believe their "alternative" writers, and they are convinced that scientists, historians, and archaeologists do not know everything. This latter point is certainly true, but personally I have never seen *any* professional make the claim that they do.

One complaint I often see made by true believers is that academics do not write for the "common man." From the outside, it seems that very few academics publish outside the scientific journals or university presses. Unfortunately, this creates problems of perception. The impression of exclusive clubbishness is generated. Furthermore, the mass media, to generate interest, usually report that new discoveries "surprise" or "shock" scientists or archaeologists, that textbooks will have to be rewritten because of this or that new find. While revision of past theories in the light of new evidence is a normal part of science, "alternative" writers capitalize on reports like this by emphasizing that the academics have once more been shown up as not knowing everything, their ideas once more shown to be wrong. The political stock of the "alternative" free thinkers rises in the eyes of their followers, while that of the professionals dips ever lower.

A case in point would be the recent "discovery" of Caral, an ancient city in Peru that was highly touted in the media as the earliest urban center yet found in the Americas.[8] Because of my interest in Andean history, I knew that in fact Caral fitted perfectly into what was already known. The excavated and published sites of Aspero, Los Gavilanes, Huaca Prieta, Nanchoc, Kotosh, La Galgada, and Piedra Parada, among others, are as old as or older than Caral.[9] These places had monumental architecture, plant domestication, and class structures. While the media reported that archaeologists were surprised to find an urban settlement this old in the Andes (Caral dates to *c.* 2600 BC), the truth of the matter is that since the 1960s it has been theorized that Caral had been built in *exactly* this timeframe. Robert Feldman,

Paul Kosok, Michael Moseley, Ruth Shady-Solis, Elzieth Zechenter, and others had all discussed this site previously in journals, dissertations, and books, and they had all tentatively dated Caral to this early period.[10] However, none of this professional work made it into the mass media reports of shocking new, history-altering discoveries at Caral. So the notion that Caral has rewritten Andean history and has shown up the ignorance of researchers in the field persists in the public domain and is then spun and passed on to the "alternative" true believers by their gurus.

Today's lay researcher has an advantage that I did not have at the beginning of my search for knowledge: a greater variety of books written by professionals, and the Internet. I still live in a remote area today, but thanks to the plethora of online bookstores I can usually find the books I need and have them delivered to my door. I am deeply grateful that publishing houses have seen the demand for good archaeological books and are attempting to fill that demand. However, in my experience, those who are genuinely interested in more in-depth learning face the real problem of the cost and availability of material. Small university-press print runs result in higher costs per unit, costs that can put specialized professional work outside the budget of the average reader. The situation with the cost of journals is even worse. The result is that those without institutional access to scientific journals have to depend on the mass media to interpret new finds for them, and, as we have just seen, the mass media are not the most reliable source. They seem to prefer to present new discoveries in the flashiest most sensational manner possible, with little or no concern for the truth. My favorite example of this process (although admittedly an extreme one) comes from Kent Weeks' book *The Lost Tomb*, where he writes about speaking to a reporter about his rediscovery of tomb KV5 in the Valley of the Kings in Egypt. While discussing this tomb, Weeks mentions that its pillared hall was one of the largest ever found. The reporter asked Weeks if he found any colored balls. For obvious reasons, Weeks was confused. The reporter then asked if billiard halls were common in ancient Egypt. Weeks tried to correct the reporter, who commented: "Billiard hall? Pillared hall? What difference does it make? Who cares? Besides, it makes a better story" (Weeks 1998: 110–11).

Notes

1. I would like to thank Garrett Fagan for his assistance in writing this chapter. I have no training in the arts of writing, and his assistance regarding grammar and suggestions on where I needed to clarify my points have been greatly appreciated. However, his input in no way influenced the content of my account, which is my personal story.

2. Examples of insults or twisted words:
   http://www.grahamhancock.com/features/maat_methods-p1.htm, where all the discussion focuses on political matters to do with how Hancock is misrepresented, defrauded, slighted, etc. by his critics;
   http://www.grahamhancock.com/phorum/read.php?f=1&i=94711&t=94711 (insults);
   http://www.grahamhancock.com/phorum/read.php?f=1&i=56402&t=56402 (insults).

3. Notice at http://www.grahamhancock.com/phorum/read.php?f=1&i=151580&t=151546.
4. For a summary of the book's contentions, see Chapter 1 by Garrett Fagan.
5. See note 4.
6. See Bauval and Gilbert 1994; Brown 1966; Flem-Ath 1995; Hapgood 1958, 1966, 1970; West 1993.
7. http://www.grahamhancock.com.
8. See, e.g., http://news.bbc.co.uk/1/hi/sci/tech/1298460.stm.
9. Dillehay 1992; Feldman 1980; Grieder *et al.* 1988; Kosok 1965; Sandweiss and Moseley 2001.
10. See Feldman 1980; Moseley 1992; Shady-Solis 1997; Zechenter 1988.

Part II

Five case studies

5   Esoteric Egypt

Paul Jordan

"Esoteric Egypt" here denotes the vision of an ancient Egypt replete with arcane knowledge and significance. This view has been elaborated at odds with scholarly Egyptology by people who believe that they can see a great deal more hidden inside the Egyptian heritage than the scholars do, by virtue of their openness to mystic, symbolist or some other highly complicated avenue of interpretation. How far the ancient Egyptian culture may or may not itself have tended towards esoteric expression needs brief discussion, since that question stands at the start of the long line of esoteric speculations about Egypt that predates the enterprise of Egyptology.

It is true that the state religion of the Egyptians was conducted by initiated priests in the dark seclusion of their temples, away from the sight and participation of the people at large. Some rituals were reserved for kings alone, themselves credited with a semi-divine standing. But the priests were not an exclusive fraternity cut off from the everyday life of the community. Priesthood was a largely hereditary business, with the top ranks assigned to relatives of the king and lower orders handed down from father to son as a secondary profession to be followed on a rotational basis. As the long history of pharaonic Egypt unfolded, the career attractions of the priestly life led to the purchase of positions. It was all conducted with a pragmatism characteristic of Egyptian civilization.

This is not to say that the religion these priests served was not a complex and sometimes profound affair. It was also an evolving system that saw some major innovations during its history of more than 3,000 years; the rise of Amun from Thebes as the prime god of the New Kingdom is a case in point. Amun was indeed the "hidden" god who worked his works invisibly like the wind, but his invisibility did not make him an inherently esoteric proposition. Neither was the resurrection god Osiris, whose cult arose in Middle Kingdom times and maintained its popularity through the rest of Egyptian history: the Osirian rituals were a good deal less esoteric than the Eleusinian mysteries of the Greeks. *The Book of What is in the Underworld*, known as *The Book of the Dead* and in fact a composite from inscriptions and papyri of different (but not early) periods, may be obscure and fantastic, but it is not an esoteric production.

What we know of the religious beliefs of the Egyptians in their own words comes from inscribed texts in temples and tombs and from papyrus writings found mostly in tombs. Among the oldest materials are the Pyramid Texts from late Old Kingdom pyramids (*c.* 2400 BC), while the papyri come more from New Kingdom (*c.* 1570–1070 BC) and later sources. The older texts tend to display obscurities arising from what we may call their primitive origins at the dawn of Egyptian civilization, and the later ones are loaded with the complexities that arrive in mature and back-ward-looking cultures. But however obscure and complex the beliefs they express, the Egyptian texts are *not* esoteric in the sense that they set out to convey by cryptic and symbolic methods a whole lot of deep meaning quite different from their surface meanings, of significance only to a select band of initiates.

The same can be said of the practices of popular magic and superstition in ancient Egypt. There are magical wands and figurines, prophylactic amulets and spells to protect and heal and bring back from the dead in the afterlife. But there is no sign in this material of the esoteric knowledge and deep wisdom of the ages that some people would like to see hidden in the Egyptian legacy. There is not even any sign, until Greek times, of an everyday astrology of planetary influences. The medical writings of the Egyptians are a mixture of practical good sense and magical procedures, not characterized by any real knowledge of anatomy (despite the semi-dissection involved in mummification). Egyptian mathematics really got no further than trial and error and approximation, while their geometry was practical and untheoretical (Wilson 1951). Their astronomy could assist them to highly accurate alignments of monuments but resulted only in garbled star maps on coffins and on tomb and temple ceilings: they only became acquainted with the constellations as we know them today (through classical times back to the Babylonians) in the last few centuries BC.

From the evidence we have from them, the Egyptians were not, then, a noticeably esoterically minded people. But they stand in the front rank of candidates for retrospective esoteric interpretation by some enthusiasts in the world today. How did this situation come about? The answer lies in certain of their cultural traits and in the particular relationship of their civilization with influential successor civilizations that had close dealings with them in the ancient world.

The roots of esoteric Egypt

To begin with, that relationship had an important geographical aspect. Egypt is a very unusual country in its topography, and other ancient cultures could only interact with one end of it, as it were. Away from the Delta region of Lower Egypt, Egyptian civilization stretched along a narrow filament of cultivated land a thousand miles into Africa through mostly bleak desert on both sides. The Bronze Age Canaanites communicated with ancient Egypt in its eastern Delta region; the early Israelites (whatever the precise nature of their experiences at the hands of the Egyptians) likewise encountered Egypt via the eastern Delta; the Cretans and Phoenicians sailed their ships into Delta ports; the Greeks, who were to play such a part in conveying acquaintance with ancient Egypt into Western culture, established their trading relations in the Delta, where by their time the seat of Egyptian power was established; Alexander's successors in Egypt ruled from their great Greek city on the western Delta coast, which the Romans took over, and Jews and Christians congregated there; the Arabs invaded Egypt through the eastern Delta.

For all these peoples, Egypt presented itself as a fairly adjacent and familiar Delta world, full of antique wonders but with an even more wonderful, and mysterious, world stretching beyond it along the fabled Nile, whose sources bubbled up in the totally unknown African interior. Memphis, at the southern apex of the Delta, where only the single stream of the Nile continued into Upper Egypt, was already mysterious enough with its prodigious pyramids and temples of exotic gods.

The Bible would contribute to the picture, but it was really the Greeks who first handled the matter of Egypt in a way that still influences our modern outlook. It is not simply that the Greeks transmitted a certain view of ancient Egypt into later times: the very presence of the Greeks, especially after the establishment of Greek rule under the Ptolemies with a large Greek-speaking population in Lower Egypt, itself influenced the character of latterday Egyptian belief.

The Homeric poems have some references to Egypt, but it was only when the Greeks established a regular trading presence at Naucratis on the most westerly branch of the Nile in the Delta, in the late seventh century BC, that real acquaintance with Egyptian culture began – and then it was with an already very old and arguably decadent version of that culture. Thales, the pioneer natural philosopher, is said to have visited Egypt in the first half of the sixth century and to have introduced the study of geometry from there to the Greek world. Plato's ancestor Solon would have been there at about the same time. The Egypt into which Greek merchants and travelers were venturing was not the aloof and mighty Egypt (centered on Memphis) of the Old Kingdom, terminated 1,500 years before, nor the imperial power of the New Kingdom (centered up-river at Thebes), that had declined several centuries previously. After difficult times, power had now been established at the Delta town of Sais, after which this era is named. It was a backward-looking epoch, when nostalgia for Egypt's past greatness and self-confidence generated a fancied renewal of old Egyptian ways and forms in art, religion, and language.

An example of the anachronistic impulse of Saite times is furnished by the so-called Inventory Stela, found at Giza in 1858. It records, along with a list of temple possessions, the claim that Khufu built his great pyramid beside a pre-existing temple of Isis and the giant carving of the Sphinx that he found already in place at Giza. Enthusiasts for a vast age of the Sphinx and of the Isis doctrine have always made much of the Inventory Stela. But this Saite relic is in fact a badly executed piece of work that any Old Kingdom carver would have been ashamed of, and its language is replete with anachronisms. It is a sort of pious fraud whereby a Saite ruler tries to cloak his "renovations" at Giza in the mantle of Khufu's reputation and at the same time promote the latter-day veneration of Isis.

In the same spirit and at about the same time, the Egyptian priests of Sais began the long process of turning their old ibis-headed god Thoth – messenger and scribe of the gods – into the distinctly more esoteric entity that the Greeks would call Hermes Trismegistos. By the third century BC, identified with the Greek messenger-god and endowed with the "thrice Greatest" epithet, there was a new god and a new set of religious writings to do with him, some of them of an occult and astrological character. Thoth was now the chief god of magic and spell making, whose name was never to be directly spoken; and, in fact, his adherents were not above employing hieroglyphic signs in a freshly devised symbolic fashion in the writings woven around him (which was to set a disastrous precedent for future attempts to translate the hieroglyphs). However, the point is that all this farrago of Thoth and Hermes was a Hellenistic concoction, in Greek, that had very little to do with its Egyptian antecedents: the Hermetic literature is no guide to the beliefs of old Egypt.

Meanwhile, Herodotus had famously visited Egypt in the mid-fifth century BC and written up a good deal of anecdotal and unreliable material about it. However, he did point up the notion of Egypt's vast antiquity and the unique continuity of its long history. Plato in the early fourth century, whether or not he actually visited Egypt himself, made some use of Egypt in his written works and crucially credited the Egyptians with historical records – as shown to his ancestor Solon – that told the story of a long ago war between Athens and Atlantis and the cataclysmic demise of the latter. In general, Plato, following Herodotus and in keeping with his countrymen as a whole, extends to the ancient Egyptian civilization a far greater antiquity than modern Egyptology assigns to it. In the *Laws*, the anonymous Athenian asserts that the Egyptians' art of 10,000 years before was just as good as it is in his day "and I am not talking loosely, I mean literally 10,000 years" (Plato *Laws* 2.65E). This awed and excessive overestimate of the longevity of ancient Egypt is still with us in some quarters. Very likely Plato believed in it, but Egypt's antiquity and general venerability were really artistic devices to color the exposition of his philosophy.

Plato was interested in the Egyptians' Thoth, but he was not interested in learning more of the language that this god was supposed to have personally devised – the language of the very Egyptians themselves, written down in the hieroglyphic signs to be seen on their monuments and in the cursive "longhand" version of the hieroglyphs we call "hieratic" that tended to be used on papyrus (until the even more everyday "demotic" script was developed). This failure of interest in the language and writing of the Egyptians was by no means confined to Plato – nobody in the classical world of the

Greeks and Romans concerned himself to create an account of the Egyptian tongue and the various ways of writing it. If someone had done so and his work had come down to us, much of the mystery-mongering about ancient Egypt might never have got going at all.

As it was, it fell to a full-blooded Egyptian of Ptolemaic times to try to make the history and religious customs of his people accessible to the wider world by writing his *Egyptian Memoirs* in Greek in the first half of the third century BC. Manetho set out his material in a chronological framework of ruling dynasties, which Egyptologists still employ. He was writing late in the day as far as his own country's history was concerned, but he spoke the language and could read the old records, which clearly survived in his time in better shape than we have them now. Unfortunately, Manetho's own work has not survived as such, being known only in excerpts quoted by later writers. We do have writings by first-century BC and first-century AD authors like Diodorus Siculus, Strabo, and Pliny, which take on the casually unreliable approach of Herodotus. Diodorus leaned on Herodotus and also developed the Hermes theme by comparing this god to Moses of the Jews and Zoroaster of the Persians (Hornung 2001). Strabo scoffed at Herodotus but has left us little to improve on him. Pliny has some sensible things to say about the pyramids and the Sphinx, although he gets its measurements wrong (Jordan 1998). The account of the Egyptians' Osiris and Isis cycle of religious beliefs in Plutarch's *De Iside et Osiride* (= *Moralia* 351C–384C) is fatally contaminated with mystical themes from late classical philosophy: it is significant that its title puts Isis before Osiris, at a time (Plutarch was born in the reign of Claudius) when even the resurrectional promise of this god had been eclipsed by his consort's starring role as the mother of all goddesses. It was at about this time that the idea began to gain ground that the striking and frequently beautiful hieroglyphs of ancient Egypt (some of them now to be seen on genuine monuments brought to Rome) were not a mundane means of writing down an everyday spoken language but rather a symbolic apparatus for communicating ineffable mysteries to initiates in the know – highly esoteric, in fact.

Plotinus, a Greek from Egypt who studied in Alexandria early in the third century AD and then went to live in Rome, interpreted the hieroglyphs symbolically in terms of his neo-Platonic philosophy, which centered on the return of the individual soul to the Great Good. Horapollon, another Egyptian Greek, wrote a work in the fifth century devoted to *Hieroglyphica*, but they were all symbols to him too. When this book resurfaced in Florence in 1422 (Greener 1966), it put Renaissance inquiry into the subject on the wrong track for centuries.

Meanwhile, life went on in Roman Egypt in what sounds like one of the most agreeable episodes in all human history. The Romans regarded Egypt as an ideal tourist venue, and the tourism could conduct you through a colourful religious landscape as well as the vivid geographical one around you. In this situation, Hellenistically derived esotericism luxuriated into areas like astrology and alchemy. Indeed, alchemy takes its name (through Arabic) from the Egyptians' own name for their unusual country: "Kemet" – the Black Land (a reference to the rich alluvial mud that made farming possible along the Nile). The art of embalming may have taught the Egyptians a thing or two about chemistry, but there are no ancient Egyptian alchemical texts, only Greek ones.

The esoteric tradition centered on Thoth/Hermes gave birth (around AD 200) to the belief that further sacred texts by Thoth had been buried in the by then lost tomb of Alexander the Great, somewhere in Alexandria (Hornung 2001). Ammianus Marcellinus, a Greek from Antioch who wrote his *History* in Rome at the end of the fourth century, mentions in one of his many digressions that there were underground galleries at Giza built to save the wisdom of the ancients from being lost in a great flood (Ammianus Marcellinus 22.15.28–30). Such notions enlarged the lurking suspicion that wonderful works of ancient wisdom were cached away in certain long-lost but once pivotal locations, which might be rediscovered by people "in the know" who could somehow initiate themselves into the old mysteries by acquiring the necessary arcane knowledge. This, too, is an idea that has never gone away and constitutes a staple element of modern pseudo-Egyptology.

Esoteric Egypt in Christianity and Islam

When Christianity became the compulsory religion of the Roman Empire, the temples at the Siwa Oasis west of the Nile and at Philae in the south were probably the last places where the old religion of Egypt was observed before final closure under Justinian in the sixth century. For the Christians, Egypt had resonance in both the Old Testament and the New. The powerful story of the Israelites' career in Egypt attached to the Egyptians an aura of despotic persecution made all the more sinister by the appellation of "Pharaoh" without a personal name. Moreover, Moses and Aaron strove with Pharaoh's magicians in the Bible, reinforcing the growing reputation of the ancient Egyptians as exponents of magic powers.

In the New Testament, St Matthew's gospel sent Joseph and Mary out of Herod's way into Egypt, and the Coptic Church could claim that the Holy Family's refuge had been the very site of one of its most famous monasteries; legend even suggested that Jesus learned Egyptian magic there (Hornung 2001). Both the Jews and the Christians – especially the Gnostic heretics among them – were impressed with the esoteric potential of Hermes Trismegistos, and strands of Christian and Jewish esotericism were to travel into Europe and be taken into Renaissance speculation about the mysteries of ancient Egypt. In the meantime, the Arab conquest of AD 640–1 took esoteric Egypt into the Islamic orbit. By the time the Arabs came to Egypt, all familiarity with the ancient writings that so visibly covered the walls and columns of temples and tombs was gone. The language that those writings recorded was still in use among the non-Greek-speaking part of the population, in the form of its descendant tongue called Coptic, which was now written with a modified Greek alphabet. But, for the incoming Arabs, the hieroglyphs were an even more complete mystery than they were for the Greeks and Romans and the Copts themselves.

The Arabs were thus well set up to view the ancient Egyptians, whose relics were all around them, as very mysterious and magical people. Stories of fabulous treasure behind magically opened doors, like those of the *Arabian Nights*, go back to robbing expeditions into Egyptian tombs, where the treasure deposited with the dead might still sometimes be found in place behind the "false doors" carved with mysterious hieroglyphs that were a common feature of the ancient Egyptians' burial places. The Arabic accounts of al-Mamun's forced entry into the Great Pyramid in the ninth century AD picture him encouraging his men with the promise of vast treasure inside and, in some versions (Tompkins 1971), disguising the absence of any such reward for their labors by smuggling in an amount of loot sufficient to pay their wages, if no more.

But the accounts also credit al-Mamun himself with a less greedy interest in the Great Pyramid: his intelligence network had told him that the pyramid also contained a secret chamber with charts of the heavens and the Earth of great antiquity and accuracy. His interest in these things would not be surprising, since we know him to have made his Dar-al-Salaam ("City of Peace" – Baghdad) into a great seat of learning with a library and astronomical observatory. He is said to have had terrestrial and celestial maps made as a result of Aristotle's appearing to him in a dream, which reminds us that the Arab world maintained a far greater acquaintance with the Greek heritage than Dark Age Europe did.

In Europe before the Renaissance, the Christian tradition was inclined to spiritual allegory as opposed to straightforward assessment in the interpretation of such classical texts as came to its attention. Besides, it was chiefly interested in the Biblical association of anything to do with the ancient world, including Egypt, and many misassociations were entertained: for example, that the pyramids were in reality the granaries set up by Joseph during his successful years with Pharaoh. This idea was sagely countered by the Patriarch of Antioch in the ninth century, who declared "they are astounding mausolea, built on the tombs of ancient kings" (Greener 1966: 55). A twelfth-century rabbi who traveled by the pyramids was sure they were built by witchcraft, but the otherwise bogus travel book ascribed to Sir John Mandeville of the fourteenth century at least took the view that the pyramids were tombs.

The renaissance of esoteric Egypt

The Renaissance in Europe witnessed the dawning realization that behind the Roman heritage lay an older Greek one that needed to be recovered by reading it up in its original language; and one of the sources for such a re-education of the West lay in the Muslim world's preservation of many Greek works. With the Venetians trading to Alexandria, it became possible, if far from safe (there were so many pirates in the Mediterranean), for merchants and then pilgrims to visit Egypt. The pilgrims went out of Biblical inspiration but could not help bringing back information (and much misinformation) about the antique wonders of Egypt. Very interestingly, in the early sixteenth century the Milanese Girolamo Cardano took his cue from the Renaissance rediscovery of Greece to suggest that behind the science of the Greeks them-selves there lay an older body of knowledge that had to be looked for in Egypt, where it seemed that Pythagoras thought the world's system of measures had first been taken directly from nature itself (Tompkins 1971). Later in the sixteenth century, Johannes Helferich brought back to Europe an account of Giza that mixed circumstantial information with fantasy uncritically culled from the locals (like priests getting into the head of the Sphinx to awe the ancient Egyptian populace) and includes a woodcut of a well-endowed female Sphinx, which Helferich took to be a representation of Isis.

When George Sandys published his *Relation of a Journey Begun in 1610*, he was able to furnish an impressively accurate picture of the Sphinx and pyra-mids at Giza, but he was pessimistic about ever understanding the ancient Egyptians' inscriptions. For him, the hieroglyphics "which consist of signifi-cant figures, are hardly to be interpreted" (Greener 1966: 49). This sobering conclusion did not stop him offering a "translation" of an inscription so fancifully rendered in a woodcut in his book that Egyptologists can make nothing of it, as "Oh you that enter the world, and go out of it; God hateth injustice." He obviously thought that he was dealing with some sort of picture writing, since he claimed that "by a Sphinx the Egyptians in their Hieroglyphicks presented a Harlot" (ibid.: 52).

John Greaves, who would one day be professor of astronomy in Oxford, set out for Egypt in 1638. He was not in search of Isis or any arcane secret of the hieroglyphs but rather of the ancient system of measure and what we would now call geodesy (literally, "Earth division") thought to underlie all latterday metrical units. He did a lot of useful work at the pyramids, although seriously hampered by the general dilapidation at Giza. Greaves concluded that the pyramids themselves were the product of the ancient Egyptian theology that counted on the preservation of the body to preserve the soul: a notably unesoteric conclusion (ibid.).

Greaves left his measuring gear in Egypt, to an Italian who had been sponsored to go there by the Jesuit scholar Athanasius Kircher in a similar search for the supposed ancient and universal units of measure behind cubits and feet and stadia, miles and leagues. For his part, Newton used the data that Greaves brought home to devise a scheme of profane and sacred cubits that expressed the size of his gravity-laden Earth.

It was widely assumed that the pyramids had been built in keeping with some such ancient system: and the notion could not be far away that they also, in particular the Great Pyramid, embodied and enshrined that system as a demonstration for all time. This line of thought would be developed in the nineteenth century into time as well as space, so that the Great Pyramid could be seen as not just a spatial reckoner but a temporal one too, with predictive as well as retrospective force.

Meanwhile, Kircher was as interested in the hieroglyphs as he was in the cubits. The rediscovery of Horapollon's work in Florence in the fifteenth century had revived attempts to understand the ancient Egyptians' writings. The very word used since classical times to name the ancient Egyptians' inscriptional signs, "hieroglyphs," means "holy carvings" in Greek – a concept that predisposed the Renaissance to view them as something more than just a way of writing an old language. Moreover, they were found on the walls of sacred temples and religious monuments, and there is about them, by their very nature as vivid pictorial imagery, something suggestive of symbolic mysteries: even when they have been translated, this air of mystery is apt to cling. Horapollon's symbolist interpretation was readily accepted, and his rather wild "font" of hieroglyphs (which could have been checked against real Egyptian monuments brought to Rome from Egypt) was copied by artists and architects in Renaissance times. Kircher himself published six works on the hieroglyphs between 1643 and 1676. He had the advantage of some familiarity with the Coptic language and guessed (correctly) that the hieroglyphs might have been used to write an earlier form of Coptic, the language in other words of the ancient Egyptians. He even conjectured that the hieroglyphs represented sounds and constituted a real alphabet, in which he went too far since, though many of them have a phonetic value, it is not always a single letter in our sense that they stand for, while others do have a sort of indicative picture meaning (though not esoteric). For all these reasonable conclusions, Kircher persisted in the notion that any rendering of an everyday language that the hieroglyphs might carry was really subordinate to a deeper, symbolic meaning at the same time. Before the Egyptian writings were understood, there was always scope for the symbolic interpretation of the hieroglyphs: since we came into possession of a detailed knowledge of the full range of the Egyptian records, there has been rather less excuse for it.

Kircher's misapprehensions about the hieroglyphs did not hamper him from producing some translations of his own. According to Sir Alan Gardiner (Greener 1966), Kircher managed to persuade a group of signs on a Roman-period obelisk rendering the Greek title "Autocrator" (of the Roman emperors) to really mean "the originator of all moisture and all vegetation is Osiris, whose creative power was brought to this kingdom by the holy Moptha." Sir Alan dryly commented that "the holy Moptha still remains a mystery to Egyptologists." In the eighteenth century, there were several attempts to tie up the Egyptian hieroglyphs with the Chinese signs that were becoming more familiar with trade and exploration. There was a suggestion that China might have been a colony of ancient Egypt: this idea of the cultural colonization of the world, born in the dawn of European empire building, has also never gone away and is a constant feature of what I have called the Atlantis syndrome (Jordan 2001), only Egypt is now itself usually seen as a colony of some pre-existing but vanished super-civilization.

Freemasonry, Rosicrucianism, and the cracking of the code

Eighteenth-century interest in ancient Egypt from the Hermetic standpoint contributed greatly to the development of Freemasonry in Europe, and to the movement called Rosicrucianism, which promoted the idea of a highly secret brotherhood devoted to a body of "ancient wisdom." Here we encounter another strand of pseudoarchaeological esotericism that shows no signs of going away: modern presenters of the Atlantis syndrome make much of such a long-lasting line of brothers in pursuit of some sort of more or less "magical" science. These brothers, especially in the form of a lineage of Egyptian priests unknown to Egyptologists (they had their American and Far Eastern equivalents, too), are credited with preserving the ancient wisdom of Atlantis (or wherever) into Egyptian historical times and beyond. The Rosicrucians claimed Egyptian origins for their order, and Egyptian motifs are prominent in Freemasonry's iconography. Cagliostro founded a specifically Egyptian Masonry in 1784 on a claimed basis of secret knowledge learned in the subterranean vaults of the Egyptian pyramids (Hornung 2001). This "secret knowledge" line of speculation ran on into the musings of Madame Blavatsky and her Theosophy and its offshoots in the late nineteenth and early twentieth centuries: the writings of this school are full of the most bizarre and brazen assertions, meriting no consideration here, and Blavatsky and her successors rather gave over Egypt in favour of Tibet and worlds less real altogether, where we have no need to follow them. But Theosophist ideas have undoubtedly influenced strains of esoteric "Egyptology" in the works of other writers, as we shall see; and while she was on the subject of Egypt, Blavatsky did pioneer the view of the Great Pyramid as a temple of initiation and its stone sarcophagus as a baptismal font upon emerging from which the neophyte was born again and became an adept (Blavatsky 1931).

The results of the intense scrutiny and recording of Egypt's remains by the team of savants that accompanied Napoleon there at the end of the eighteenth century made, when they were published in the early nineteenth century, for the greatest advance in Europe's knowledge of ancient Egypt before the decipherment of the hieroglyphs. Measurement and mapping of the pyramids at Giza further promoted the idea that an ancient system of mensuration might well be enshrined in them, including degrees of arc with implications for latitude and longitude. Moreover, the pyramids were seen to be very accurately aligned on the points of the compass: the scene was set for a century of fantastic metrological speculation at Giza.

Thanks to the discovery of the Rosetta Stone by Napoleon's men, hopeful attention was turned again on the problem of the ancient Egyptians' writings. The Rosetta Stone carried hieroglyphic and demotic inscriptions as well as an easily readable Greek text (it was a summary of religious benefactions by Ptolemy V just after 200 BC). Some people thought that the hieroglyphs would soon be revealed as a symbolically expressed version of the rather mundane meaning of the Greek text; not surprisingly, no progress was made in that direction. However, Thomas Young managed tentative identifications of individual signs in the hieroglyphic text enclosed in oval "cartouches," which evidently "spelled out" the names of Ptolemy and Berenice. Jean-François Champollion thought at first that the hieroglyphs had only been used phonetically to record foreign names like that. His breakthrough came when he recognized, on the basis of his knowledge of Coptic, that a text copied from the monument at Abu Simbel in the far south of Egypt recorded the name of the native Egyptian pharaoh Ramesses (known from Manetho): "Re" still meant "sun" in Coptic, and "mss" meant "son of." This pharaoh was the "son of the Sun God," and the way was open to identifying other hieroglyphs as sounds representing a language directly ancestral to Coptic. The hieratic and demotic scripts demanded much study to tease out their way of rendering the language; the complex interaction of phonetic and ideographic elements in the scripts had to be explored; and the whole grammar of this ancient part-Semitic and part-African language needed to be established. But from the 1830s onwards, the tongue of the ancient Egyptians came to be well understood and the writings of ancient Egypt to be read. The symbolist interpretation of the hieroglyphs was now untenable without the sort of mental gymnastics that Kircher had employed to regard them as both literal and symbolic at the same time.

Pyramidiocy and other esoteric eccentricities

The Great Pyramid at Giza carries no formal inscriptions at all of ancient Egyptian origin – there are workmen's markings on some of the hidden blocks of the weight-relieving chambers above the king's burial chamber that very usefully certify that this pyramid was built for King Khufu (and some have come to light only in recent years, disposing of insinuations of nineteenth-century fraud). Perhaps the very lack of any inscriptions that might have made this pyramid's purpose clear to one and all has always recommended it to the lunatic fringe; that, and the matter of its unequalled interior complexity of passages and chambers, which can be measured to the heart's content to produce masses of figures to manipulate. The exploration and clearing of these passages gathered pace in the first half of the nineteenth century, along with some clearance of debris around the exteriors of the Great Pyramid and its companion pieces at Giza. John Taylor, in his *The Great Pyramid: Why Was It Built? And Who Built It?* (1864) was able to manipulate improved measurements very ambitiously. He determined that the perimeter circle of the Great Pyramid's base divided by twice its height produced a figure close to *pi* at 3.144; he thought that the perimeter might represent the circumference of the Earth, and the height might represent the distance from the Earth's centre to the North Pole. He arrived at his "pyramid inch" by dividing the perimeter of the pyramid by 366 (the number of days in the year rounded up) and concluded that Newton's sacred cubit was twenty-five of these pyramid inches. Happily, the English inch turned out to vary from this old ideal by only one-thousandth part. Taylor fostered the notion that the Great Pyramid was planned and built to pass on the knowledge of the ancients to the future; and that the "Lost Tribes of Israel" were the means by which the English had come by their inch with so little deviation from the original.

Taylor influenced the Astronomer Royal of Scotland, Charles Piazzi Smyth, to venture to Egypt at the end of 1864 with an imposing array of special measuring rods and instruments and even an intriguingly miniature camera that took plates only one inch square (we trust it was a pyramid inch). The object was to verify and refine the ideas that he shared with Taylor and had already aired in *Our Inheritance in the Great Pyramid* (Smyth 1864). Smyth satisfied himself that *pi* was in the height/periphery ratio of the Great Pyramid and speculated that the precise length of the year at 365.24 days was in there too. He was keen to date the Great Pyramid by means of the celestial alignments of the Descending Passage, which leads down from the outside into its deepest depths. He plumped for an alignment of this passage on Alpha Draconis, which was calculated to have been at the north celestial pole at the autumn equinox of 2170 BC. (This approach to pyramid dating, with various shafts in view, has produced several noteworthy theories to date, some useful and some not.) All in all, Smyth was certain that the Great Pyramid had been designed and built with an astounding exactitude, in line with its divine inspiration.

When Piazzi Smyth published his *Life and Work at the Great Pyramid* (1867) it met with detraction, chiefly in light of its espousal of the theme of divine revelation. The year 1867 also saw the published claim of Robert Menzies that the entire interior disposition of the Great Pyramid was a retrospective and prophetic world chronology of Biblical bent, with one pyramid inch to the year (Tompkins 1971). Smyth himself went on to multiply the height of the Great Pyramid (newly ascertained by him) by 10^9 (because he thought that for every 10 of height there were 9 of width in the structure), which came out in English miles at 91,840,000, more or less the distance of the Earth from the Sun. The wonderfulness of this arbitrary calculation still exercises modern writers on Atlantological themes, like Erich von Däniken (1971).

An engineer called William Petrie got caught up in Piazzi Smyth's speculations and longed to measure the Great Pyramid with even better instruments. His son William Flinders Petrie was keen to find out if it all really stood up by determining the still part-obscured basal dimensions of the monument and measuring not just the one pyramid but its companions and indeed the whole surrounding topography. Flinders Petrie satisfied himself as to the claimed extreme accuracy of the Great Pyramid's layout, but he also noticed those signs of slightly botched execution and unfinishedness that always dog the Egyptian monuments (like most things human). He accepted that there were ancient units of measurement to be discerned in the structure, but not the sacred cubit in place of the traditional royal cubit of about 21 inches. His base measurements did not match Smyth's, partly because he differed as to what to measure, and although he thought *pi* was there, he could not see the days of the year. His *The Pyramids and Temples of Gizeh* (Petrie 1883) found him wryly amused to realize that when he had started his work fifteen years before he could little know it would be himself who "would reach the ugly little fact which killed the beautiful theory."

A near contemporary called David Davidson rather reversed Flinders Petrie's progress from entertainer of the esoteric to rational archaeologist by starting skeptical about it all and ending up a believer who thought pyramid study establishes the Bible as the inspired work of God (Davidson 1932). For example, he was able to square Petrie with Smyth by noting Petrie's discovery of the inward curve (and so lengthening) of the sides of the Great Pyramid, thereby restoring the sacred cubit. He came to think that the Great Pyramid demonstrated its builders' acquaintance with the specific gravity of the Earth and Sun, the solar parallax, the precession of the equinoxes, and even the speed of light. Davidson pushed the idea that the monument had been constructed to function as a prompt to future generations to rediscover such knowledge by enshrining all these details in its complex fabric. Such *tours de force* of super-interpretation of the dimensions of the Great Pyramid prompted an American naval officer of the day, who was also an amateur Egyptologist, to remark that "If a suitable unit of measure is found – say versts, hands or cables – an exact equivalent to the distance of Timbuctoo is certain to be found in the roof girder work of the Crystal Palace, or in the number of street lamps in Bond Street, or the specific gravity of mud, or the mean weight of an adult goldfish" (Tompkins 1971: 111).

In the twentieth century, the esoteric came to the fore at the pyramids, with various speculators teasing out the most extraordinary truths from their own private insights into the meaning of its features. Morton Edgar (1924) and others of his ilk elaborated the prophetic chronology business to great lengths: the Great Pyramid's Descending Passage was the Fall of Man; the Ascending Passage was the Christian dispensation; the Grand Gallery was spiritual enlightenment; the "Great Step" at the top of the Grand Gallery led into the "Antechamber of Chaos," which was the Great War; the King's Chamber was 1953 (or at least its south wall was) for what that has turned out to be worth; and human perfection will arrive all round in 2914. Along the way, it will come as no surprise to hear, the Exodus, the Crucifixion, and the Second Coming are flagged up in the Great Pyramid (Rutherford 1957). *The Great Pyramid: Your Personal Guide* (Lemesurier 1987) dates the entrance of the Great Pyramid at 2623 BC, follows the Descending Passage down-ward as the "Path of Rationalistic Materialism," reaches 1914 with the Underground Chamber and 2004 ± 3 as the "Pit of Physical Destruction," ending up in 2569 in the dead end of the short passage leading away from the Underground Chamber; on the other hand, the Ascending Passage rises via the "Path of Physical Ritual" to AD 33, followed by a sudden explosion of "Enlightenment" in the Grand Gallery, itself topped by some sort of "Consciousness Transformer" in 1999 (the book was published in 1987, remember) and an age of "Psychic Reintegration" in the King's Chamber, lasting until 3989, with the relieving chambers above pointing to "Unknown Dimensions of Consciousness." Lemesurier then turns to the Queen's Chamber as presaging "Hyperconsciousness," most likely between 7276 and 8276. As if that were not enough, the Great Pyramid's layout simultaneously sets forth the spiritual progress of the individual life, with initiation conducted through the monument's passages and chambers as the means to achieve the wisdom of a man of 70 while still young, and indeed to tap into all the wisdom of the ages. Lemesurier thinks that the Great Pyramid may also have been a giant theodolite and astronomical observatory. What it absolutely was not, apparently, is what Egyptologists conclude it quite clearly was – a tomb.

Richard Proctor at the end of the nineteenth century thought it both a tomb and an observatory, its Descending Passage serving first to observe the polar region of the night sky and then its Ascending Passage taking over as the pyramid grew under construction – with a mirror of water at the junc-tion of the two passages to allow observation to be maintained. It would have continued very well as the long slot of the Grand Gallery was built up, until the top closure of the King's Chamber turned the pyramid over from observatory to astronomically aligned tomb (Proctor 1883). The Grand Gallery, with its lines of corbeling, would evidently have served as a scale for detecting the phenomenon of precession (which conventional science history attributes to Hipparchus in the second century BC). *The Dawn of Astronomy* (Lockyer 1894) extended ideas like this to all the temples of Egypt (and Stonehenge): Sir Norman Lockyer believed, for example, that the Ptolemaic Temple of Dendera with its late zodiac was really the third build on the site, the original having been erected by King Pepi I in 3233 BC (about a thou-sand years earlier than modern Egyptology would place him). He thought that the Sphinx was a half-lion, half-virgin hybrid that had been carved in the fourth millennium to symbolize the conjunction of the zodiac signs of Leo and Virgo at the summer solstice: it is worth emphasizing that there is nothing to indicate that the ancient Egyptians knew of our zodiacal constel-lations before just a few centuries BC.

The Alsatian René Schwaller, who liked to add de Lubicz to his name and sometimes to be known more timelessly as "Aor," took on Lockyer's ideas of astronomical alignment and precessional observation at the Egyptian monu-ments, working mostly at Luxor and Karnak. He was also influenced by

Theosophy and alchemical speculation. He managed to maintain in the twentieth century Kircher's belief in the simultaneously mundane and symbolic meaning of the hieroglyphs. For him, the ancient Egyptians were endowed with a symbolist sort of consciousness, altogether more harmonious with nature than that of us moderns with our scientifically analytical outlook, which was seamlessly expressed in their language, art, religion, social organization, and "sacred science": *pi* and *phi* (the ratio of the golden section) were everywhere in their works, even in the folds of their pharaohs' loincloths (Schwaller 1998 [1958]; Tompkins 1971). Schwaller died in 1961, but his labors live on in the popularizing zeal of John Anthony West, whose *Serpent in the Sky* (1993) is a study of Schwaller's ideas. West has also published *The Case for Astrology* (1973), and he leads "Magical Egypt Tours": he believes that if you don't see Egypt through symbolist eyes, you don't see it at all.

The idea that the Egyptians knew about the 26,000-year cycle of the precession of the equinoxes has been espoused by various writers – it was even noted among them that the sum of the diagonals of the square base of the Great Pyramid came to 25,826.68 pyramid inches (astonishing precision of measurement!), which was close to the number of years of the cycle (Tompkins 1971). But the people who really put precession on the map of "alternative archaeology" were unlikely candidates for this distinction, being *bona fide* historians of science who published a book called *Hamlet's Mill* (de Santillana and von Dechend 1969) in which the phenomenon of precession (which arises from the Earth's slow rocking on its axis like a spinning top and shifts the field of the stars through time) was chased through the myths and iconography of the whole ancient world, including Egypt. Much has been made of the idea and its alleged evidence by subsequent practitioners of Atlantology, Graham Hancock in particular. The notion suffers from the immediate difficulty that precession is nowhere described as such, let alone explained (it took Newton to do that) in any ancient text that predates what we know of Hipparchus; it is only by cunning interpretation of ancient myths and images, which are ostensibly about something else, that precession can be discerned in them, aided by some pretty esoteric numerological speculation involving the 72 years that mark one degree of shift in the zodiacal system and any number of permutations by multiplication, division, and addition.

Along with precession, the concept of ancient geodesy and the ancient establishment of geodetic markers around the world has developed from its nineteenth-century basis. Tompkins' useful but uncritical *Secrets of the Great Pyramid* includes a long appendix by Livio Catullo Stecchini that develops the idea of the Egyptians' use of their geodetic knowledge to place their cities and temples at points on a system of meridians and latitudes of significance to them. Their primacy in these matters (or that of their Atlantean teachers) saw to it that the rest of the ancient world took up the system. This idea has not gone away either and has been extended by von Däniken and Hancock. Again, the thought seems to be that these marker positions were designed to enshrine and perpetuate the geodetic knowledge of the ancient wisdom, to be rediscovered in later times, Whether they were supposed to serve some esoteric purpose of their own, as ley lines or foci of "Earth energy" or something of the sort, is not always clear. Chiefly, one suspects, it is the fun of poring over maps with a lot of precessional number crunching to guide your ruler that has summoned these markers into pseudo-existence.

Egypt and the Atlantis Syndrome

The dubious credit for inventing the Atlantis Syndrome as we know it goes to the American writer Ignatius Donnelly in the 1880s. He leaned heavily on ancient Egypt to elaborate his speculations, but his intentions were entirely unesoteric. He took Plato at face value about Atlantis, ignoring entirely both his artistry and his philosophical purpose. Donnelly believed there to be sound geological, faunal, floral, linguistic, and cultural evidence to support the view that a seminal ancient civilization – but not one with occult powers or an especially advanced technology – had flourished on a large island in the North Atlantic until flooded over about 11,500 years ago as a result of a natural disaster (with none of Plato's suggestion of divine retribution). Before its demise, Donnelly's Atlantis had seeded the ancient world with colonies in which its brand of universal and essentially Bronze Age culture had thrived. He thought that Egypt was the oldest of the colonies of Atlantis, in which he diverged from Plato. Consequently, to know what that Atlantean culture was like, we may turn to ancient Egypt as the nearest thing available to us (Donnelly 1882).

Donnelly considered that in the mythology of Egypt (and that of Peru, whither the Atlanteans had also extended their empire) might be discerned the original religion of Atlantis, which he took to be Sun worship, and also a record of its history and general cultural legacy. Donnelly was really the first of a long line of myth interpreters who have trawled the world's folktales and more sophisticated mythologies to divine real history and real science in stories that are ostensibly (and frequently grotesquely) at odds with the interpretations they put upon them (Jordan 2001). But without meaning to be esoteric, Donnelly had promoted a method of alternative inquiry into the past that is full of esoteric potential. The idea that myths contain disguised data about history and science opens the way to ingenious interpretation by people who think they are in possession of special insights into them. The next step is to believe that the original devisers of the myths deliberately set out to transmit real knowledge by means of their stories, however unreliable and inevitably misleading it might seem to use the colorful vagaries of mythology in that way. And the next stage is to elevate those myth makers into an elite of priests-cum-astronomers endowed with the high purpose of passing their vast body of profound knowledge down to future ages. To be able to tap into those priests' messages makes the modern myth interpreters feel part of the exclusive elite themselves, and a real esotericism is created (see Chapter 4).

Donnelly in the nineteenth century also contributed an idea to crank Egyptology that has come to the fore in recent years: the belief that Egyptian civilization appeared very suddenly in the world, without any local background development. Donnelly knew nothing of predynastic Egypt for the simple reason that very little of it had then been turned up and recognized. The sparse and unspectacular beginnings of things, both in human cultural processes and in biological evolution, are necessarily harder to track than the striking and profuse examples from established cultures and large biological populations, especially in the early years of their study. When Donnelly was writing, the apparent lack of background development for Old Kingdom Egypt allowed him to conclude that the Egyptian civilization had appeared in full fig overnight – which could only mean that it had been brought to Egypt fully formed from elsewhere, from lost Atlantis, in just the same way that the European powers were planting their version of civilization in their colonies around the world in Donnelly's day. How old Atlantis had come by its own civilization was not something that Donnelly felt compelled to look into.

The early Egyptologists were not immune to the notion of superior invaders as the mainspring of cultural progress (it was in the air of empire), but they discounted Atlantis, preferring to conjecture sometimes about superior races coming in, with a superior intelligence that could develop a superior civilization in due course. The Australian Elliot Smith, professor of anatomy in Cairo and then Manchester and London, was a sort of Donnelly without Atlantis, who thought there had indeed been a seminal ancient civilization to which all the rest of the world's civilizations owed their inspiration: it was Egypt itself, without benefit of any prior example (Daniel 1981). Smith's Manchester School of skewed Egyptology thrived between the world wars and was rivaled by Lord Raglan's variation on the theme, which saw Sumer substituted for Egypt. Both were quite incapable, like Donnelly, of crediting the generality of the human race (except in the one unexplained case of Atlantis, Egypt or Sumer) with any powers of cultural invention at all: their descendants like von Däniken and Hancock show exactly the same incapacity. On a perhaps lower level of intellectual interest, the interwar years also saw the popularization of the "Curse of the Pharaohs" thanks to the discovery of Tutankhamun's tomb. In fact, no royal tomb of ancient Egypt has ever been found with esoteric imprecations against despoilment, although private tombs could run to not very blood-curdling warnings like "Any man who harms this tomb will be judged with me by the great god" (Greener 1966: 7). Still, the "Curse of the Pharaohs" considerably boosted the public's association of the esoteric and sensational with Egyptian culture.

An interwar visionary from Virginia called Edgar Cayce ("the Sleeping Prophet") went one better than paltry curses by actually claiming to have been an Egyptian sort of priest in Atlantean times. Cayce painted a picture of old Atlantis quite at variance with Donnelly's (or, needless to say, Plato's): his version rejoiced in about 10,500 BC in all the high technology of the 1930s (e.g. aircraft, elevators, radio, photography – but not the Internet). Yet all this had not saved the Atlanteans from destruction as a result of meddling (obscurely) with the forces of nature. Cayce believed that Atlantis had split into fragments before vanishing altogether – the piece he called "Poseidia" would, he prophesied, rise again in 1968–69. It did not. Nor did we get the Egyptian Hall of Records, which was supposed to come to light by the Sphinx before the end of the millennium (Cayce 1997). Cayce's prophecies have, incredibly, inspired and funded well-equipped investigations to try to find, among other things, long-rumored underground chambers by the Sphinx, using the latest methods of remote sensing. Where it has been possible to follow up the indications of subterranean anomalies, only natural geological features – fissures and porosities – have been found; but not all have been followed up since the early 1990s, allowing enthusiasts for Cayce's ideas to imagine themselves as victims of professional Egyptological obstruction. For "obstruction," the Egyptian authorities would no doubt read "responsible restriction."

Alleged secret chambers under the Sphinx go hand in hand with repeated efforts to date the Sphinx itself as much earlier than the fourth dynasty of the Old Kingdom of ancient Egypt, around 2500 BC. Very recent attempts have been made, on geological grounds to do with erosion by running water, to date the Sphinx to several thousand years before this date but have been robustly countered with a geological interpretation involving evaporation and flaking that does not conflict with the Egyptological dating (Jordan 1998). Any dating of the Sphinx (and the nearby temples) to a period thousands of years before the beginnings of the ancient Egyptian civilization is itself an exercise in the esoteric, broadly speaking, since no known human group has been archaeologically demonstrated to have existed at the time that was capable of making these things or culturally disposed to want to. You have to fall back on survivors from Atlantis and that secret lineage of astronomer-priests to "explain" how the early Sphinx could have been conceived and created. John Anthony West – in line with his mentor Schwaller – wants to backdate this monument, both as one in the eye for modern science and as part of his conviction, memorialized at his website, that "Egyptian civilization was not a development, it was a legacy." Geologist Robert Schoch, who first made his case for the great age of the Sphinx in the 1990s, now attributes the Giza monuments to the persistent constructional tendencies of the survivors of the comet-induced destruction of what we might call "Atlantis in Indonesia" (Schoch 2003).

Secret chambers meet up with ancient astronomy in recent attempts to bolster Cayce's 10,500 BC dating of Atlantis and its colonies by reconstructing the night skies of that remote epoch and relating them to various monuments and groups of monuments around the world. The pyramid fields at and around Giza in Egypt were for a while the favorite place to make such a match between monuments on the ground and stars in the skies. Robert Bauval and Graham Hancock, together and on their own, have been at the forefront of this line of inquiry in our day (e.g. Hancock and Bauval 1996). Starting with the not very striking "match" between the three stars of Orion's belt and the three pyramids at Giza (neither trio is quite in a straight line, and in both cases two items are more prominent than the third), the theory was elaborated that the rest of Orion was also matched by further pyramids and other monuments arranged beside the Nile just as Orion lies by the Milky Way. The "faultless precision" of the match was talked up. Furthermore, a super-match was advertised for 10,500 BC, when a gaze up at the night sky could be turned down to Earth to find heaven's pattern perfectly mirrored on Earth. It all unraveled very quickly when it was pointed out that many stars had no terrestrial equivalents at all and that what there were in the way of identifications were hopelessly misaligned away from the central three points. Even the match of the Giza pyramids and the belt stars is not as good as was claimed. Hancock and Bauval make little of it all nowadays, sticking only to an idea of a general similarity (in their eyes) between Earth and heaven at Giza in ancient days. Further computer-generated views of the night skies of 10,500 BC, as they would have looked behind the Sphinx before sunrise at the vernal equinox, were supposed to show that the ancient astronomer-priests had left us a powerful indicator of a secret chamber under the rump of the Sphinx, which no doubt we could penetrate forthwith but for the obstruction of the Egyptian author-ities (just as they obstruct attempts, according to the esoterically minded, to find secret chambers in the Great Pyramid by sending little robots up the narrow airshafts of the King's Chamber.)

It should always be remembered that these people also thought there was a giant face and a pyramid field to be seen in photographs of the surface of the planet Mars in the region of Cydonia: a whole scenario of a 20,000-year-old civilization on Mars, destroyed by cometary impact, was contrived (Hancock 1998b). Better photographs demolished the whole fantasy in short order. But the recklessness of the proposition should be noted as a guide to the likely reliability of all speculations about anything whatever from such sources. Its simply never needed hindsight and better photographs to know that faces and pyramids on Mars were balderdash. When Hancock nowadays discerns ancient underwater cities off the Indian coast or anywhere else, the pyramids and face on Mars should give even his most enthusiastic followers pause.

Hancock appears not to be as interested in ancient Egypt as he was; he seems to have exhausted its possibilities for his purpose, which is now to search for evidence of an ancient, lost seafaring civilization of uncommon accomplishment that lay behind the rise of the early civilizations we do know about in the Old and New Worlds. He does try to get something going in his *Underworld* for the Delta coast of Egypt, with fishermen's stories of massive edifices submerged out to sea, but nothing comes of it: one that got away, then (Hancock 2002a). But his earlier work (*Fingerprints of the Gods* and *Heaven's Mirror*) has featured Egypt extensively. In continuity with Donnelly, he makes much of what he takes to be the sudden appearance of the ancient Egyptian civilization, without Donnelly's excuse for doing so: there is none now for imagining that Egyptian civilization "emerged all at once and fully formed" (Hancock 1995: 135).

Conclusion

There is never really anything all that new under the sun of "alternative archaeology" and its Egyptian subsidiary, just ingenious permutations of old hat for the most part, with eager seizures on anything new (or new to the speculators) that seems to throw a spanner in the works of the professional study. All things Egyptian remain a perennial attraction for the public at large (as the television programs show) and for that section of the public that revels in the "ancient mysteries" (as the sales of authors like Hancock demonstrate). It has to be faced that there is just something about the ancient Egyptian heritage of monuments and writings – sunlit but sometimes subterranean, vivid but sometimes obscure, beautiful but sometimes grotesque, everyday but sometimes mysterious – that will always continue to fascinate: and to tickle the palate of everyone with a taste for the esoteric. The themes will remain: the huge antiquity of Egyptian civilization and even some of its existing monuments, beyond the wildest dreams of the Egyptologists; the suddenness of its inception, without local antecedence; its possession from the first of preternatural knowledge, especially in the astronomical sphere; the presence in its midst of an invisible brotherhood of prodigiously wise men bent on transmitting its heritage of knowledge to future generations; its inveterate recourse to abstruse symbolism in myth and number to enshrine that vital knowledge; its bequest of complex constructions with hidden passages and chambers ever awaiting our discovery, full of ancient lore; its being, quite simply, something altogether more mysterious than it plainly appears to be.

6 The mystique of the ancient Maya

David Webster

It is not in my nature to discredit any marvelous story. I am slow to disbelieve, and would rather sustain all such inventions; but it has been my unhappy lot to find marvels fade away as I approach them.

(John Lloyd Stephens)

Introduction

Some years ago, while I was working at the great Classic Maya center of Copán, a distinguished-looking, gray-haired gentleman approached me in a restaurant and asked if I was an archaeologist. I responded "Yes, I'm David Webster from Penn State University." He shook my hand and introduced himself as "Mr so-and-so, a shaman from Pasadena." I was only momentarily taken aback by this unorthodox reply because I long ago learned that the ancient Maya attract all sorts, self-appointed modern shamans among them.

To put this more bluntly, some ancient societies, just like rock bands, attract groupies. While Egypt takes pride of place in this regard, the Classic Maya run a close second. Why should this be so? Why should ancient Egyptians or Maya be so fascinating? Why do they exert such a powerful hold on the imagination of the public, as well of some archaeologists? The most general reason is the commonplace human impulse to appropriate ancient cultures as the repositories of our hopes, or fears, or fantasies. But why the Maya in particular?

There are many answers to this last question, but all of them relate in some way to what the late Gordon Willey, long the dean of Mesoamerican archaeologists, once called the "Maya mystique." Willey coined this label for a set of interpretations, assembled over several decades, that eventually portrayed the Classic Maya (AD 250–900) as one of the world's most accomplished and unique ancient civilizations. This mystique, still beloved by much of the public, has three main origins. One derives from the historical enterprise of Maya archaeology – more specifically the circumstances of the discovery of Maya civilization, the traditional focus of fieldwork, and the decipherment of Classic inscriptions. A second, closely related to the first, emanates from the writings of influential figures in the field, and the third from the conviction that because the Maya were unique they were not easily understood from the perspective of comparative anthropology or history.[1]

What follows is my own conception of the main elements of the mystique, the ways in which they emerged, and the reasons why they were finally rejected. My paper owes a heavy debt to Marshall Becker's (1979, 1984) much earlier, meticulous dissections of the intellectual currents that produced the "vacant ceremonial center" and "peasant–priest" models.

The Maya mystique

Here, somewhat simplified for the purposes of this discussion, are the major elements of the Maya mystique:

1. The Classic Maya were intellectually and aesthetically gifted people whose innovations in writing, art, astronomy, mathematics, and architecture contributed heavily to the cultural foundations of later Mesoamerican civilizations. This reputation early on earned them the sobriquet "Greeks of the New World," and, without question, they left us one of the most flamboyant archaeological records found anywhere in the world.

2. The Maya lacked the kings, nobles, officials, and social classes so conspicuous in other historically documented complex societies. Maya leaders were instead priestly theocrats (variously imagined as benevolent, altruistic leaders or cruel oppressors) whose authority derived from moral example, control of religious ideology and ritual, and esoteric skills. Priests and peasants formed the two basic components of Maya society. Peasants lived in dispersed farmsteads and practiced extensive (swidden) agriculture.

3. Imposing Maya centers were vacant ceremonial places built by pious farmers who congregated there for collective rituals. While a few priests or acolytes might have lived for extended periods in special dormitories, there were no dense resident populations, royal palaces, or complex urban institutions such as were found, say, in the Aztec capital, Tenochtitlán, or in Old World cities such as Rome. Although Maya centers exerted profound cultural and religious influences, they were not political capitals as we normally understand them and certainly not the establishments of royal dynasties.

4. Inscriptions and mathematical symbols carved and painted on monuments at these centers recorded arcane astronomical, calendrical, and ritual information, but nothing that we regard as history, such as the names and titles of rulers and events in their lives. Accompanying images depicted priests, gods, or supernatural animals and plants.

5. Apart from a little raiding for sacrificial victims, or perhaps an occasional internecine political squabble, the Maya lacked serious warfare. From time to time they had to defend themselves against incursions of

"foreigners" (usually visualized as "Mexicans"), but war was not waged for tribute or for territorial aggrandizement, as in virtually all other ancient civilizations.

Closely related to these elements was the apparent abandonment of the great centers in the southern half of the Yucatán peninsula between about AD 790 and 900.[2] Shortly thereafter, most of the surrounding countryside was thought to be deserted as well, the inhabitants having either died or decamped to other regions. Some Mayanists believed that this disaster was caused by the decadence of the old Classic theocratic system, whose leaders eventually became destructively oppressive. Others cited foreign invaders or environmental degradation. While not strictly speaking part of the mystique, this dramatic "Classic Maya collapse" reinforced the uniqueness of ancient Maya culture and shrouded it in mystery (Webster 2002).

To the above list I would add one other idea that emerged in the early 1970s and is still with us in one form or another – that the Maya were accomplished agrarian ecologists who somehow managed to maintain dense populations for centuries on fragile tropical landscapes.[3] This perspective emerged in reaction to the earlier belief that Maya populations subsisted on maize grown using long-fallow swidden agriculture.

Nowhere will one find a statement of the mystique as succinct as I have provided above, and each of its elements has a somewhat separate history. The "peaceful Maya" conception began to take hold well before 1900, during the "exploratory" period of Maya archaeology. The idea of the Maya as the innovative "mother culture" of Mesoamerica followed shortly, stimulated by new understandings of their complex mathematical and calendrical systems. According to Becker, J.E.S. Thompson began to develop the "priest–peasant" political model about 1927. A few years later, he first suggested that Maya rural populations were dispersed around virtually empty vacant centers (Gann and Thompson 1931). These two models converged in the late 1930s and remained highly influential in the popular imagination, and among many archaeologists, for decades.

Whatever their disparate origins, by the 1940s and 1950s all the basic elements of the mystique formed a distinct package of well-established conventional wisdom. In fact, when I first began to study the Maya in college in the early 1960s, most of them were still quite obtrusive in the professional and especially the popular literature, although by then they were under severe assault as new data accumulated.

I personally would place the heyday of the mystique "model" between about 1940 and 1957, an important interlude in the history of Maya studies.[4] By 1940, ambitious, multi-year expeditions to such centers as Quirigua, Piedras Negras, Uaxactún, and Copán had been finished or were winding down. The Second World War discouraged new field operations on this scale, which were traditionally sponsored by big institutions such as Harvard University, the University of Pennsylvania, and (most important of all) the Carnegie Institution of Washington, and they did not revive until about 1956.[5] During this interval of comparatively dormant fieldwork, Maya archaeologists produced many site reports and also some important synthetic works, the most influential of which were Sylvanus G. Morley's *The Ancient Maya* (1946) and J. Eric S. Thompson's *The Rise and Fall of Maya Civilization* (1954). Both were extremely popular (I was assigned the latter as a college text), and both purveyed major elements of the Maya mystique.

Looking back over the literature of the day, it is difficult to say just how firmly individual Mayanists subscribed to the basic propositions of the mystique or whether they simply acquiesced in it given the intellectual climate of the time. As Walter Taylor (1948) asserted in his celebrated critique of American archaeology, many Mayanists were not trained as anthropologists, and their publications tended to be descriptive rather than broadly interpretative.[6] Consider the widely read book *The Maya and their Neighbors* (Hay *et al.* 1940), replete with articles about corbeled arches, Maya observatories, and ceramic sequences but practically devoid of discussions of social or political institutions, economic behavior, or any other organizational features. The Classic Maya in human terms appear only negatively, as a kind of void defined by an exterior encrustation of material cultural traits or intellectual achievements. Where speculation about ancient organization or behavior did occur, it was typically cursory and brief and often consisted of simply attributing ethnohistoric patterns documented for the sixteenth-century Maya to earlier times (e.g., Rivet 1960: 45–50; Morley 1946). Sometimes it is difficult to know exactly what individual Mayanists thought.

As early as 1920, Sylvanus Morley referred to Maya "castes" and "classes" but then surmised that rulers were "probably priestly" (Morley 1920: 29). Conversely, George Brainerd (1954: 74–5) later described the recently discovered Bonampak murals as depicting a complex hierarchy of priests but then went on to vaguely identify the "suggestion ... of a sort of royal family." Moreover, Becker (1979, 1984) notes that the popular writings of some authors, such as Thompson, were quite different from their professional ones, a point to which we will return later.

To be fair, there were voices of dissent, much of it from scholars who were not professional Mayanists. As early as the 1930s, Frenchman Jean Genet identified a glyph related to war and claimed (correctly) that glyphs on the thighs of "vanquished warriors" carved on monuments named the individuals and/or their places of origin (Houston *et al.* 2001). Unfortunately, Genet died young and unheeded. Pedro Armillas (1951) believed that intense forms of Maya warfare had considerable time depth, as indicated by impressive fortifications, and Robert Rands (1952) wrote the first lengthy study of Maya war. Betty Meggers (1954) postulated that Maya civilization developed elsewhere in Mesoamerica and was doomed to failure once transplanted into the inhospitable tropics.[7] Miguel Covarrubias (1957) asserted that hieroglyphic writing had multiple, non-Maya origins, and hence the

Maya were not any sort of "mother culture." Nevertheless, the mystique remained influential and seductive, even to some of the erstwhile skeptics:

> Few other cultures in the world have undergone the endless, painstaking, almost frantic scrutiny that scientists and amateurs have directed toward the famous Maya. Explorers, archaeologists, epigraphists, and astronomers have succumbed to the fascination of a unique and grandiose civilization that arose out of the isolation of the tropical jungles of Middle America, created by unknown artists, architects, and astronomers, who were at the same time priests and rulers.
>
> (ibid.: 204–5)

The discoverers of Maya civilization purveyed this aura of mystery and glamour very early on, although not the idea of uniqueness.

Discovering the ancient Maya

The Spanish who first explored and settled the northern Yucatán in the sixteenth century encountered a thriving indigenous culture that included rulers, nobles, and tax-paying peasants. Many of these people lived in towns with impressive temples and palaces. Priests consulted sacred books, and lords mustered up arrays of fierce warriors who fought each other in frequent inter-polity wars. So pervasive is the romantic idea of the sudden and complete collapse that many people, including some of my own anthropological colleagues, are surprised to hear that a vigorous variant of Maya civilization survived this late.

Equally impressive to the first Spaniards were the ruins scattered so thickly over the landscape. Landa marveled that

> If Yucatán were to gain a name and reputation from the multitude, the grandeur, and the beauty of its buildings, as other regions of the Indies have obtained by gold, silver, and riches, its glory would have spread like that of Peru and New Spain. For it is true that in its buildings and the multitude of them it is the most remarkable of all things which up to this day have been discovered in the Indies; for they are so many in number and so many are the parts of the country where they are found, and so well built are they of cut stone in their fashion, that it fills one with astonishment.
>
> (Landa 1941: 171–2)

No one at the time knew how old these places were, but Landa speculated that people larger and stronger than the Maya of his day must have built them. Here we see the beginning of one element of the mystique – mysterious monumental architecture, and lots of it. About the same time, it became apparent that generally similar buildings could be found hundreds of miles to the south of the Yucatán. Surveying the ruins of Copán in western Honduras in 1576, Diego Garcia de Palacio concluded: "here was formerly the seat of a great power, and a great population, civilized, and considerably advanced in the arts" (Parry and Keith 1984: 547).

Of the many subsequent travelers who visited Mayan ruins, none were more influential than John Lloyd Stephens and his artist companion Frederick Catherwood. Indeed, they almost single-handedly invented the idea of a great ancient civilization in the Central American tropics, although they did not call it "Maya."

Arriving at Copán more than 250 years after Palacio, Stephens described what he saw in words that Mayanists (myself included) still love to quote:

> The city was desolate. No remnant of this race hangs round the ruins, with traditions handed down from father to son and from generation to generation. It lay before us like a shattered bark in the midst of the ocean, her masts gone, her name effaced, her crew perished, and none to tell whence she came, to whom she belonged, how long on her voyage, or what caused her destruction ... all was mystery, impenetrable mystery, and every circumstance increased it.
>
> (Stephens 1949: 81)

With this and similar passages, illustrated with the wonderful drawings of Catherwood, Stephens unwittingly helped to sow the seeds of the Maya mystique.[8] Here were imposing buildings moldering in the forest and monuments carved with strange visages and hieroglyphs. And here was the ultimate mystery – what happened to all the people who once inhabited these places and made these wonderful things? Dramatic notions of the Maya collapse thus long predate the rise of professional and systematic archaeology.

Stephens' romantic effusions mark him as a man of his time, but he was extremely astute in other ways. His travels in Europe, Egypt, and the Near East had acquainted him with the remains of ancient Old World civilizations, and at Copán he recognized something new and unexpected:

> The works of these people, as revealed by the ruins, are different than the works of any other known people; they are of a new order, and entirely and absolutely anomalous: They stand alone ... unless I am wrong, we have a conclusion far more interesting and wonderful than that of connecting the builders of these cities with the Egyptians or any other people. It is the spectacle of a people skilled in architecture, sculpture, and possessing the culture and refinement attendant upon these, not derived from the Old World, but originating and growing here without models or masters, having distinct, separate, and indigenous existence; like the plants and fruits of the soil, indigenous.
>
> (ibid.: 373)

Stephens' conclusion ran counter to the heavily diffusionist opinions of his day. It served to make the Maya even more impressive, but at the same time more exotic, because they could not easily be explained with reference to influences from Egypt or other Old World cultures.

Even more important, Stephens made the uniformitarian assumption that, although independent in its origins, ancient Maya civilization (as we would call it now), possessed kings and nobles, warriors and statesmen, and that the monuments recorded history. Put simply, ancient Maya culture resembled in broad outline its Old World counterparts. It was this common-sense, comparative view that later generations of Mayanists sometimes forgot.

The centers

Contributing heavily to the Maya mystique, as Stephens and Catherwood well knew, was the remoteness of many of its great centers. Portuguese traders and missionaries visited the mysterious temples of Angkor in Cambodia as early as the sixteenth century, and the imposing monuments of Egypt had always been familiar to locals and travelers alike.[9] One of the few places in the world where one could still literally discover "lost cities" by the mid-nineteenth century was the interior of the Maya lowlands.[10] Stephens even entertained the romantic notion that somewhere deep in the unexplored forests there still lurked living Maya kingdoms. A generation later, Alfred Maudslay sent sculptures back to the British Museum from Yaxchilán, a site then so remote that no one even knew whether it was in Mexico or Guatemala. When the Carnegie Institution crew shut down their project at Uaxactún in 1937, they left the site in considerable disarray, thinking that no one was likely ever to go back to such an isolated place.

Frequently unsettled political conditions, not to mention jaguars and snakes, promised both danger and adventure, so exploring Maya ruins made for compelling stories.[11] These tales were packaged for public consumption under such titles as *Mystery Cities* (Gann 1925) and *They Found the Buried Cities* (Wauchope 1965), and these books were widely and avidly read.

Not only were Classic Maya centers romantically remote, but many of the individual buildings were extremely well preserved. One could climb the very staircases used by ancient priests and stand inside the summit temples. Some archaeologists lived for weeks inside intact palace rooms. All around, as Stephens and Catherwood found, stood elaborately carved stelae and altars. This abundant, flamboyant, and accessible archaeological record is in large part a legacy of the Classic collapse and the following demographic decline. No later people dwelt thickly on the Maya landscape to tear apart the old ruins (as so often happened in Egypt) or submerge them beneath their own constructions (as in Mesopotamia).

The forests are mostly gone now, and travelers face only the hazard of intestinal upsets, but the ruins remain. Copán, Tikal, Palenque, and many other sites have been extensively restored and can easily be reached by road, air, or ship. Because they are much more accessible than their counterparts in Egypt or Southeast Asia, the great Maya pyramids and palaces attract thousands of tourists every year. Even the armchair traveler is repeatedly bombarded with images of imposing Maya places. The rebels in the film *Star Wars* strike back from a base hidden beneath the temples at Tikal, and each year brings another spate of beautifully illustrated books. Such accessibility and visibility today powerfully reinforce the lingering Maya mystique.

Archaeologists early on fell under the spell of buildings, and not just in the Maya lowlands:

> It is fair to say that it is the magnitude, number, and artistic elaboration of the monumental structures which have borne the main burden of support for judgments as to the level of sociocultural integration achieved by the "Classical" cultures of Mesoamerica.
>
> (Kaplan 1963: 398)

Kaplan's statement is particularly apt for the Maya because nowhere else did ruins so richly yield up such superb art, and dates and inscriptions to. Moreover, many Classic buildings utilized a kind of false or corbeled arch not apparently found elsewhere in Mesoamerica, a feature eventually singled out as a defining characteristic of Classic Maya culture.

As early as the eighteenth century, fabulous stories began to circulate about the scale of these lost "cities"; in Stephen's day, Palenque was rumored to be three times the area of London (Stephens 1949: 2.253). Such claims were quickly disproved, but the temples and other structures themselves were so numerous and so large that they shaped the perception of Maya urbanism: "In contrast to the modern practice of determining the size of a city by its population, Maya cities have generally been measured by the magnitude and extent of their architectural remains" (Pollock 1965: 382). The apparent "perpetual building" and "ceaseless alteration" of these great structures showed that the priest-rulers were able to muster and organize huge workforces.

Impressive as they were in their own right, some of the great buildings also seemed to have highly sophisticated astronomical alignments. Excavations at Uaxactún's Group E revealed an archetypal "observatory" that commemorated the equinoxes and the summer solstice. Many other "E Groups" recorded elsewhere were apparent testimony to the ancient Maya obsession with solar events.

For all practical purposes, the first seventy years of systematic Maya archaeology consisted of the study of temples, observatories, tombs, ball courts, sweat baths, and other great buildings at the centers of major sites. Scant attention was paid to the smaller structures in the landscapes around them, so little was known (although much was assumed) about the overall distribution and numbers of Maya people.[12] No matter what kind of site was excavated, most efforts focused on the "hard" deposits (buildings and other durable and immovable features) as opposed to the "soft" deposits – the pottery, stone tools, and other more ephemeral remains from which archaeologists commonly derive behavioral inferences today.

Early explorers such as Stephens routinely called Copán, Palenque, and other sites "cities," at least in the sense that they were central places in larger political systems permanently occupied by high-ranking leaders, that they had complex internal social organization, and that their inhabitants did a variety of economic tasks. One way that the "vacant ceremonial center" model emerged from this sensible position is revealed in changing attitudes toward elite residences (see Webster 2001 for a more detailed discussion).

Explorers of Maya centers had little difficulty in recognizing the functions of temples, ball courts, and other structures, and there was also another class of low but impressive multi-roomed buildings that they labeled "houses" or "palaces" (common-sense labels often used by local Indians). When he and his party first reached Palenque in 1840, Stephens exulted that they were able to set up their camp in the palace of a long-dead king. He further speculated that the complex arrangement of rooms included facilities for "public and state occasions," while other chambers served as private royal residential quarters or "chapels." Stephens even guessed that the relief sculptures found in the palace might well depict the very royal people who had lived there.

As systematic archaeology commenced, it became evident that such conclusions were consistent with Cortes' eyewitness description of elite residences during his brief 1519 foray into the Yucatán and Landa's somewhat later accounts of sixteenth-century Maya settlement patterns. Moreover, the ruins of Mayapán, a Yucatecan capital abandoned a generation prior to the arrival of the Spanish, had an extremely urban-looking layout, with thousands of residences crammed within its encircling wall, including many that were obviously lived in by families of rank.

The first generation of professional Mayanists assumed that complex social and political organization was necessary to support Maya cities (Becker 1979: 6). Elaborate residences for kings and nobles were expected features of such "urban" places. Alfred Tozzer (1911) identified the Central Acropolis at Tikal as a residence, and Sylvanus Morley noted that at Copán "There seems to be no reason for doubting that some of the stone buildings were the residences of the rulers, nobles, and higher priests" (Morley 1920: 7).

Unfortunately, the glyphs associated with some famous palaces (e.g., at Palenque) could not be deciphered, and little thought was given to the more mundane archaeological correlates of "palace" structures beyond the assumption that they would yield facilities for cooking, sleeping, and other domestic activities. These features turned out to be difficult to identify when such buildings were extensively excavated, as at Piedras Negras.[13] Archaeologists concluded that "The excavations at Piedras Negras indicate that the ' ... palaces' were not used for domiciliary purposes" (Mason 1938: 307). This assertion coincided almost exactly in time with the larger convergence of the "priest–peasant" and "vacant ceremonial center" models.

Although the label "palace" was retained to describe a kind of Maya building, it was stripped of all its behavioral and comparative connotations. As late as 1956, Michael Coe wrote that "palace" was a misnomer for buildings that were unsuited to domestic use and must instead have served ceremonial purposes: "Structures clearly identifiable as royal residences are absent in the Classic Maya area" (Coe 1956: 387). If priests used the great centers only intermittently for ceremonies, and there were no dynastic rulers or nobles, then there should be no "palaces" in anything like the Old World sense, or "cities" either.

I have attributed the evolution of the vacant ceremonial center model partly to the lack of comparative perspectives, but the anthropological climate of the times also contributed positively to this conception. Many anthropologists believed that swidden agriculture necessitated a dispersed pattern of residences. As Becker (1984) points out, ethnographers also studied several "vacant" ritual-administrative towns in highland Mexico and Guatemala that archaeologists appropriated as living exemplars of the old Classic Maya pattern. In a weird reversal of the normal order of interpretation, at least one ethnographer so fell under the sway of the Classic Maya vacant center model that he extended it, quite without supporting evidence, to mid-twentieth century, highland Indian Guatemalan towns in general (ibid.: 24).

Although anthropology was supposed to be a social science, there was no detailed analysis of the concept of urbanism (such as developed by geographers and sociologists). As late as 1956, Gordon Willey (1956: 110) lamented this lack of definition for any kind of settlements – while providing none of his own. Only much later did George Andrews (1975) systematically try to apply a general definition of urbanism to Maya centers; revealingly, Andrews was an architect.

By the early 1940s, Thompson had firmly rejected the older, complex city model in his popular writings: great Maya sites "were almost certainly religious centers to which the people, who lived in small settlements scattered over the surrounding country, repaired for religious purposes and, possibly to attend markets and courts of justice"(Thompson 1942: 12–13). This rapidly became the prevailing public conception.[14]

The inscriptions

Besides the great ruins, nothing was so impressive as the inscriptions, or more precisely the presence of writing. Writing was seen as both the hallmark of high cultural attainment and the key to understanding just who the ancient Maya were, how they organized themselves, and how they thought about the world. Other kinds of archaeological remains required painstaking on-the-spot excavation, but inscriptions could be copied and studied by people who never set foot on a Maya site. And what a varied lot these early epigraphers were: engineers, businessmen, Spanish priests, English lords, journalists, novelists, doctors, judges, astronomers, and even the odd gold prospector. Nothing is so central to the Maya mystique as the history of the efforts to find the key to the glyphs (Coe 1999; Houston *et al.* 2001).

At this point, a comparison with Egypt is pertinent. The culture of the Nile valley maintained a considerable continuity for thousands of years, right down through New Kingdom times. Its kings figured prominently in the Bible, countless ancient conquerors and tourists visited Egypt, wrote about it, and appropriated both its monuments and its intellectual achievements.[15] Fantastic accounts of Egypt began in antiquity and were endlessly elaborated right down through early Christian, Islamic, and modern times (see Chapter 5). Nevertheless, one set of fortunate circumstances favored a reasonably sensible view among archaeologists: the decipherment of hieroglyphs. Everyone knows about the famous discovery of the Rosetta Stone in 1799, and of the subsequent decipherment of Egyptian writing by Champollion and Young in the early 1820s.

The all-important consequence is this: *ancient Egyptian writing could be understood before the development of systematic Egyptian archaeology.* A decade before Stephens and Catherwood speculated about the glyphs on Copán's stelae and altars, scholars were effectively reading Egyptian inscriptions. As something we could call "professional" archaeology developed in the Nile valley, it was already closely linked to historical accounts of Egypt, coupled with knowledge (however imperfect) of its ancient hieroglyphs – messages directly from the ancient Egyptians. Whether such insights much constrained the wildest ideas of the public is doubtful, give the extremely long tradition of mystification of many things Egyptian. Nor did they inhibit the wild speculations of some professional archaeologists. Rather, my point is that they certainly helped to constrain the most unbridled and fanciful interpretations of Egyptologists.

By contrast, the Classic Maya were anonymous in the traditional written sources available to Euro-American historians. And because Classic inscriptions strongly resisted decipherment (there being no long bilingual inscriptions comparable to that found on the Rosetta Stone), the epigraphic situation was exactly reversed.[16] Why this happened is less important than the fact that *Maya archaeologists carried out eighty years of fieldwork before the principles and content of the inscriptions became clear.* Such insights materialized in the late 1950s and early 1960s, and only since 1980 has there been a flood of effective interpretations. This lag between archaeological and epigraphic data allowed much greater scope for the free reign of imagination and for dubious conclusions *on the part of professionals* than was the case in Egypt.

Not that self-appointed experts were reticent about their presumed ability to read the inscriptions. For pure, unadulterated goofiness along these lines, I heartily recommend Augustus Le Plongeon's (1896) *Queen Móo and the Egyptian Sphinx*, a diffusionist tract that reversed the usual thinking and derived most of the Old World's civilizations from the Maya, as revealed by the inscriptions at Chichén Itzá.[17]

Less dramatic, but much more important, is that by the beginning of the twentieth century epigraphers could understand one major component of Maya inscriptions: mathematical notations (including the use of "place" and "zero"). These in turn provided the key to the ancient calendrical systems and their associated astronomical observations. For the first time, archaeologists were able to put Maya chronology on a reasonably firm footing and thus silence once and for all the many claims of extreme and even absurd antiquity put forward by romantics such as Le Plongeon and others.

What most impressed Mayanists was the Long Count calendar, which began thousands of years in the past and ran in an essentially linear fashion into the future.[18] Internal to the workings of the Long Count were thirteen great *baktún* cycles, each consisting of just over 394 solar years. Because dated monuments could be related to construction episodes, tombs, and ceramic sequences, Maya archaeologists determined that the most conspicuous accomplishments of Classic civilization fell almost entirely within the great ninth cycle, or between AD 435 and 830.[19] Using counts of dated monuments as a barometer of cultural vigor, they more exactly identified the interval from AD 730 to 790 as the pinnacle of Maya achievement. There followed a steady decline in Long Count dates, which in its turn charted the Maya collapse, with the last date occurring early in the tenth cycle (AD 909). Conversely, a handful of late eighth-cycle dates placed the beginnings of Classic Maya civilization at shortly after AD 300, so the early fourth century was envisioned as a kind of threshold for the explosion of Maya genius.

Because all this mathematical and calendrical information formed parts of longer inscriptions, it seemed to promise insights into the other, more obdurate content. An obvious pattern was that most carved monuments were dedicated on "period-ending" dates of recurring minor cycles within the Long Count and other calendars, and were accompanied by frequent references to astronomical events. Such cryptic subject matter, in tandem with the opacity of the accompanying non-calendrical inscriptions, caused influential Mayanists to reject Stephens' sensible assumption that the glyphs recorded history:

> The Maya inscriptions treat primarily of chronology, astronomy – perhaps one might better say astrology – and religious matters. They are in no sense records of personal glorification and self-laudation, like the inscriptions of Egypt, Assyria, and Babylon. They tell no story of kingly conquests, recount no deeds of imperial achievement; they neither praise nor exalt, glorify nor aggrandize, indeed they are so utterly impersonal, so completely non-individualistic, that it is even probable that the name-glyphs of specific men and women were never recorded upon the Maya monuments.
>
> (Morley 1946: 262)

This from Sylvanus Morley, the most eminent Maya scholar who once, like Stephens, was a firm believer in the historical content of the glyphs.[20] And if the glyphs recounted no history, named no kings or nobles, and concerned themselves with esoteric rituals, the "priest-theocrat" dimension of the mystique was powerfully reinforced. Moreover, the hieroglyphs revealed that Maya civilization was highly uniform. Everywhere the glyphs

> ... *tell the same story*. ... Whatever their significance may be, it is the same everywhere, that is to say they must treat of matters common to all, such as a generally accepted astronomy and the common religious philosophy arising therefrom, and not of purely local matters. Throughout the Maya area, the undeciphered glyphs deal with an extremely limited subject matter and are essentially homogeneous.
>
> (Morley 1940: 149; italics in original)

This vision of a unique and highly uniform Classic Maya civilization suggested that the cross-cultural comparisons so central to American anthropology, and earlier so sensible to Stephens, were simply not relevant. With very few exceptions (e.g., Coe 1957) one searches the pre-1960 literature in vain for any sort of comparative perspective.[21] The ancient Maya, it was thought, should be understood in their own terms (or at most through comparisons with later Mesoamerican peoples), not with reference to what was known about the broader human condition.

Morley himself, in chapter 9 of his 1946 book, avoided the strict priest—peasant dichotomy that became so dominant a little later. Lacking clues from the inscriptions, he simply attributed the political and social patterns observed by the Spanish in the sixteenth century to the Classic Maya, asserting that Maya culture is "known to be continuous."[22] Use of this "direct historical approach," as anthropologists call it, is still strong among Mayanists, and many feel that use of wider analogues is inappropriate.

The inscriptions presented still another intellectual pitfall. Not only did the Maya seem unusually precocious and unique in their mathematical and calendrical skills, but prior to the Second World War their dated monuments constituted the only absolute chronological framework available for any region of Mesoamerica.[23] Maya ceramic sequences could be tied to Long Count dates, so when their *ceramic* vessels showed up in distant places (or foreign pottery was found at Maya sites) a web of chronological connections could be extended far beyond the Maya lowlands.

Archaeologists dislike venturing into uncharted chronological waters, and consequently very few concerned themselves with Preclassic or Formative cultures – then considered as dating before about AD 300 – anywhere in Mesoamerica.[24] Morley was surprisingly uninterested in the forebears of his beloved Classic Maya (Brunhouse 1971: 244–5), and this neglect served to strengthen the idea of a sudden, *in situ* blossoming of Classic culture early in the fourth century, centered on a few sites like Uaxactún and Tikal in the northeastern Peten region of Guatemala.

This kind of developmental pigeonholing made for some strange definitions. Morley (1946: 38–9) asserted that two culture traits – (1) writing, along with "chronology" (i.e., sophisticated calendars); and (2) the use of the corbeled vault for stone roofs – constituted the *sine qua non* of Maya civilization. By insisting on this narrow conception, he explicitly and deliberately severed the idea of Maya civilization from the wider and older tradition of Maya culture and language in eastern and southern Mesoamerica. Preclassic Maya were mainly simple farmers, comparatively uninteresting and certainly lacking the cachet of the civilized attainments that flowered so suddenly after AD 300. The few early dated objects that seemed to contradict this view were summarily dismissed. Here a kind of self-fulfilling mindset was at work: avoidance of the chronological *terra incognita* of the Preclassic preserved the comforting image of an explosion of Classic genius and at the same time ensured that little or no contradictory information was forthcoming.

Morley and others realized that not all of the impressive Classic Maya achievements could suddenly have appeared full-blown. He speculated that calendars must have developed for 600–700 years prior to the first preserved dated monuments, although just where remained unknown. Archaeologists also knew that "temples" and "palace-type buildings" existed by the end of the Preclassic (Willey 1956: 108). Still, the main rhetorical assertion was that a kind of critical mass was reached in the early fourth century, and Maya culture thereafter was qualitatively different from what went before.

By the 1940s and 1950s, many archaeologists had accepted an even grander set of evolutionary assumptions: throughout Mesoamerica, a stage of creative, theocratic, and peaceful Classic cultures was sandwiched between an earlier era of simple farming communities and a later set of decadent, cruel, and warlike Postclassic societies, these last including the Aztec and their contemporaries (Steward 1949, 1955; Willey and Philips 1958). Somehow, a wave of decline and barbarism swept over even the brilliant Classic Maya after about AD 900, a phenomenon often attributed to the baleful influences of "foreigners," typically envisioned as "Mexicans." Nothing shows this as well as attitudes about Maya warfare.

The peaceful Maya

Much of my own career has been spent undermining one of the most durable cornerstones of the mystique – the idea that the Classic Maya were a peaceful civilization – so a bit of personal experience is pertinent here.

Just how strongly people cherished their "peaceful Maya" was brought home to me in 1970 while I was completing my PhD fieldwork at the site of Becán.[25] My research centered on an extremely large fortification, consisting of ditches, causeways, and earthworks, that (much to my surprise) turned out to have been built around AD 150–250 instead of at the end of the Classic period, when one might expect a good deal of conflict. A wealthy visitor and amateur Maya enthusiast was greatly impressed by his tour of

Becán's temples and palaces but became visibly agitated when I showed him the earthworks. Somewhere, he despairingly lamented, there must have been a peaceful civilization. As a good (if fledgling) comparative anthropologist, I had no reason to share this fond belief, but I felt a twinge of guilt that my work had so disillusioned him, especially right in the middle of the Vietnam War, when one needed all the mental refuges one could find. His attitude was a classic example (no pun intended) of the widespread propensity to appropriate the past as a kind of emotional Shangri-la.

Years later, I am still puzzled about just how and why this Utopian perspective emerged and so powerfully gripped the imaginations of both Mayanists and the public.[26] The first Maya people encountered by the Spanish in the sixteenth century were impressively warlike, and fortified sites such as Mayapán and Tulum, which just predated the arrival of Europeans, had long been known. Why should the Classic Maya have been any different? Yet, somehow, the "peaceful Maya" assumption began with some of the earliest Maya archaeologists. Alfred Maudslay, who in the 1880s explored imposing ruined sites along the Usumacinta River, saw monuments replete with the military themes that are especially common in this region. However, he claimed that what to us are obvious weapons were instead "ornamental staves." Observing captive figures on a stela at Ixkún, he surmised that they represented the conquest of the "aboriginal inhabitants of the land" or the defeat of foreign invaders who eventually conquered the Maya.[27]

By the first decades of the twentieth century, numerous objects and monuments depicting weapons and captives had been widely published (e.g., Spinden 1912), but their aesthetic and artistic merits were emphasized rather than their broader behavioral implications.[28] Explicit statements of the "peaceful Maya" position followed:

> War scenes are almost entirely absent from the sculpture of the south-eastern cities. There are, however, a few scenes that may represent prisoners being brought in captive, and one or two armed warriors are found sculptured on the monuments of the northwestern area. We may safely conclude, however, that the Mayas were living in peace among themselves and that war was confined to the repulsion of invading hordes descending from Mexico. Militarism or civil war would have put an effective stop to the building operations and artistry that characterize the Great Period of the Old Empire.
>
> (Thompson 1927: 12)

Here we see two conflated ideas – that the achievements of Classic civilization were inconsistent with war, and that where war did exist foreigners were the culprits.

A few archaeologists were puzzled by all of this. J. Alden Mason (1938: 308–9) thought that the docility of the Classic Maya was much overrated. Citing evidence of the smashing and mutilation of monuments, he wondered why war was seldom mentioned as a cause of the collapse. Nevertheless, by 1946 the peaceful Maya idea had become an orthodoxy:

> Old Empire [i.e., Classic period] sculpture is conspicuously lacking in the representation of warlike scenes, battles, strife, and violence. True, bound captives are occasionally portrayed, but the groups in which they appear are suggestive of religious, even astronomical interpretation, and warfare as such is almost certainly not implicated
>
> (Morley 1946: 70)

Such assertions betray the obvious defects of a non-comparative perspective. Two kinds of negative evidence were cited repeatedly to deny the existence of serious forms of ancient conflict: the absence of fortifications at major centers (more apparent than real, as we have since discovered) and the presumed settlement pattern of dispersed rural farmsteads. A little burrowing in the anthropological or historical literature would have revealed many warlike societies with similar settlement features; nor did one have to look far afield. Most capitals and towns in the Basin of Mexico were unfortified, as were surrounding rural communities, even though intense inter-polity conflicts raged there for generations. And however regrettable it may seem, the production of great architecture and art has seldom anywhere in the world been incompatible with war.

Still, so confidently and so often was the "peaceful Maya" view propounded that hardheaded non-Mayanists became convinced. Even Julian Steward, whose comparative anthropological and historical grasp was unsurpassed, opined that the peacefulness of the Maya might make them a true exception to regularities otherwise present in the rise of civilizations elsewhere in both the Old and New World (Steward 1949, 1955).

To be fair to Thompson, Morley, and others, they did grudgingly admit a little fighting to capture sacrificial victims or to repel invaders, and even the occasional internecine conflict. But their general attitude seems to have been that of a respectable family with an insane relative — keep quiet and hope that people do not take much notice. And by the 1940s, Mayanists were very prone to agreeing about much such comforting conventional wisdom.

The sociology of Maya archaeology

Anyone observing a set of national archaeology meetings in the USA today will be astounded at how many Mayanists there are. Whether trained as anthropologists, epigraphers, geographers, art historians, or in the "harder" biological or physical sciences, most have professional credentials. Add in their colleagues from Latin America and Europe and the numbers must reach into many hundreds. Listening to their presentations and watching their interactions will shortly reveal many different perspectives and schools of thought, as well as distinct factions and mutual antipathies. The field today is not only large, it also lacks a common center or any sort of effective hierarchy. No individual, group, or institution enjoys much dominance (although pretensions abound). In short, Mayanists are a contentious and unruly lot, and they tend to interact as equals, especially if they are well established in the profession. All this is a bit messy, but a lot of research gets done, huge amounts of information are generated, and one's work is always evaluated very critically. Eventually, the whole field benefits.

The same observer, magically transported back to the 1940s or early 1950s, would quickly notice that all the active Mayanists would probably fit into a good-sized bus. Moreover, as I have already pointed out, many of these practitioners, although often very talented, were by today's standards amateurs. Comparatively few were trained as anthropologists or held permanent academic or museum posts. Only a handful of public or private institutions funded research, along with some wealthy individual patrons. No huge granting agencies such as the National Science Foundation or the National Endowment for the Humanities existed, and competition for funds and the few formal jobs was fierce. Able and experienced people like John Longyear, who devised the ceramic sequence at Copán, effectively dropped out of the profession when their bids for a handful of available positions were unsuccessful.

Under these circumstances, a handful of powerful Mayanists, both in the USA and abroad, dominated the field. Among these, three stand out, two of whom we have already met. By the mid-1940s, Sylvanus Griswold Morley (professionally educated as an archaeologist) was the pre-eminent Mayanist, famous for his tireless pursuit of inscriptions and for the excavations that he oversaw at Chichén Itzá and other sites. Another rising star was J. Eric S. Thompson, an English veteran of the Coldstream Guards who learned to speak Mayan and who excavated many sites in Belize and the Yucatán. Both men were closely connected with the Carnegie Institution, the premier funder of big Maya projects up to the early 1950s.[29] The third was A.V. Kidder, a close friend of Morley's since college days and chief of the Carnegie Institution's anthropology programs after Morley's death in 1948.

Morley anointed the Maya the "Greeks of the New World" at least as early as 1928 (Ruz 1950: 112), although the "mother culture" dimension of the mystique probably began to form around the turn of the twentieth century as the sophistication of Maya mathematics and calendars became apparent. Few Mayanists by the 1940s were inclined to buck Morley's strongly anti-historical conceptions of Maya inscriptions, his vision of a sudden Classic florescence, or his marginalization of the Preclassic cultures. Thompson succeeded Morley in the role of pre-eminent Mayanist and was an extremely prolific writer. Among many other accomplishments, he compiled important catalogues of glyphs, but he was also highly antagonistic toward the work of Russian epigrapher Yuri Knorozov, who in the 1950s correctly argued for the essential logosyllabic character of the script (Coe 1999). Not only did his opposition retard decipherment, but younger and more insightful scholars in the USA were intimidated by Thompson's undeniable erudition, vast field experience, and professional influence. Tatiana Proskouriakoff might well have published her brilliant 1960 study of the dynastic inscriptions at Piedras Negras sooner and more forcefully had it not been for Thompson's then dominance of the field.[30]

Another element in Thompson's thinking sprang from his personal experience of Maya people. He lived among them and admired them as dignified, sociable, honest, and well ordered in their communal arrangements. Just such personality traits, he imagined, enabled their ancestors to create a great and unique civilization.

Even more significant, as Marshall Becker (1979, 1984) points out, was the tension between Thompson's popular writings, which played up elements of the mystique, and his much more circumspect professional publications. Becker identifies Thompson as the primary architect (beginning as early as 1931) of the vacant ceremonial center model, and Thompson also strongly promoted the "peaceful Maya" perspective and the "peasant rebellion" explanation for the Classic collapse.[31] All these figured prominently in his most widely read book, *The Rise and Fall of Maya Civilization* (Thompson 1954). According to Becker, Thompson, who never held a permanent academic post, was acutely aware of the need to augment his income by playing to his public audience.

Kidder's main contributions were to the archaeology of the highland Maya, but he wielded wider influence because he controlled a major source of funding, and he took his cues concerning lowland Maya civilization heavily from Morley and Thompson.[32] Becker (1984: 45–6) points out how Kidder, in successive introductions (in 1947 and 1950) to the important Carnegie Institution work at Uaxactún, at first championed a complex model of Maya cities and then fell under the sway of the vacant ceremonial center idea (Kidder 1950).

An example of Kidder's influence is shown in the issue of "palace" buildings discussed above. One of Kidder's employees, A.L. Smith, excavated what we now know to be a royal palace, Group A–V at Uaxactún, and seems to have come close to identifying it as such (recall Stephens' much earlier common-sense hunch about Palenque's royal establishment). Faced with Kidder's conviction that such buildings could not have been royal residences, Smith prudently decided instead that "during its last phase A–V served as living quarters for priests or acolytes or high officials and their families, and that religious ceremonies there were for them and not open to the general public" (Smith 1950: 44).

Many other such examples could be given, but the point is that today no individual can possibly dominate the field in this manner, although Gordon Willey (himself for a time an advocate of the vacant ceremonial center perspective) continued the tradition to a degree throughout the 1960s and 1970s.

Demise of the mystique

The influence of the Morley/Thompson/Kidder triumvirate (along with some others) peaked in the early 1950s, just as a mass of accumulating data was about to bring down the Maya mystique. Contributing to its collapse were some specific but unexpected field discoveries, but more significant were the advent of radiocarbon dating, breakthroughs in decipherment, and results of sophisticated settlement and household research.[33]

Mother culture?

The "mother culture" idea became untenable as archaeologists discovered monuments and other objects with Preclassic inscriptions outside the Maya lowlands. By the late 1950s, radiocarbon dating had also revealed that impressive Olmec sites on the Mexican Gulf coast dated to roughly 1200–400 BC. Since the 1960s, archaeologists have documented abundant Preclassic remains throughout Mesoamerica, and it is clear that writing, monumental architecture, art, calendars, and many other supposedly "Classic" traits emerged well before AD 250. All this chronological realignment effectively silenced the champions of Maya precociousness.[34]

Priests and peasants?

In 1952, Mexican archaeologist Alberto Ruz Lhuillier excavated the most famous of all Classic Maya tombs, buried deep beneath the Temple of the Inscriptions at Palenque. This was plainly a royal tomb, and the "temple" had been purposely designed as the mortuary monument for a king (Ruz 1973). Suddenly, Stephens' conviction that he slept in a royal palace at Palenque (just a stone's throw from the Temple of the Inscriptions) looked very sound indeed.

By the late 1950s, epigraphers had identified "emblem glyphs," parts of longer statements that included the names and titles of particular rulers. Suddenly there were kings aplenty. While Maya political leadership, as in all ancient civilizations, was strongly theocentric, it was not theocratic. Other privileged people also emerged from the inscriptions, including royal spouses and other family members, along with a whole series of nobles sporting their own impressive titles. Settlement and household archaeology revealed a continuum of residences that reflects much more complex social organization than that encompassed by the old "priest–peasant" model (Abrams 1994).

Vacant ceremonial centers?

With the realization that the Classic Maya had dynasties of kings and royal palaces, the old vacant ceremonial center conception gradually fell apart. The Palenque palace turns out to have been just the kind of place Stephens imagined it to have been, and scores of similar courtly places are now known, most notably the Central Acropolis at Tikal (Coe 1967; Harrison 1999). These impressive complexes were clearly used over long periods by ruling families and their courts, and the glyphs connected palaces with particular kings and nobles (Webster 1989). Some centers, such as Copán and Palenque, had very dense permanent populations (albeit over small areas). Although predominantly courtly places dominated by the households of kings and nobles (Inomata and Houston 2001), Maya centers clearly fulfilled a complex mix of residential, political and ceremonial functions.

Each big Classic site was increasingly envisioned as a "preindustrial city in function and in most aspects of form except for population density" (Hammond 1975: 58). Mayanists proclaimed, with apparent relief, that the burden of Maya uniqueness could be jettisoned, and "that the 'true city' model brings ancient Maya society into the mainstream of cultural evolution, entailing as it does the institutions of state-level governance, an urban-type economy, and the correlates of a complex class system" (Willey and Hammond 1979: xii).[35] Stephens would have loved this comment.

Ahistorical inscriptions?

The ancient Maya might not have written anything corresponding to our modern notions of history, but their inscriptions emphatically mention kingdoms, along with the names and titles of real people, their births, deaths, wars, rituals, and other events in their lives. From all this, it is possible to assemble a historical record that would have astounded Morley, Thompson, and Kidder (e.g., Martin and Grube 2000).

I often point out to my students a central paradox of archaeology – that we can amass data, form strong opinions about the past, and test them, but that (short of a time machine) we cannot go back to check the reality against our reconstructions. Yet something very much like this happened in the case of the Classic Maya. A widely accepted model of an essentially prehistoric society was suddenly juxtaposed with coherent messages from the ancient people themselves (if not a time machine at least time capsules), and the model was found wanting.

Peaceful Maya?

In 1946, spectacular polychrome wall murals were found at Bonampak, near Palenque. Painted around AD 800, they depict (among other things) scenes of warfare and the subsequent humiliation and mutilation of captives. This was the first big nail in the coffin of the "peaceful Maya" theory. Thereafter the weapons, conflicts, captives, and sacrifices so prominent in Maya art began to seem much more sinister. An apparent system of huge early Classic defensive earthworks was found at Tikal (Puleston and Callender 1967), and shortly thereafter I excavated the even earlier fortifications at Becán

(Webster 1976). Since then many more have been found, and there is direct archaeological evidence that Dos Pilas, Aguateca, and other centers were destroyed by violence. Most revealingly, war and its related rituals turned out to be pervasive themes of the inscriptions (Martin and Grube 2000; Webster 2000).

So abundant and convincing is all this evidence that the Classic Maya are beginning to rival the Aztec in their reputation for bellicosity. The rhetoric has recently reached proportions perhaps more appropriate to the Assyrians: "It may well be that vengeful dynastic vendettas, total destruction of cities and the enslavement of whole populations occurred throughout Maya history" (Martin 2001: 176). With allowances for the hyperbole, this was basically my view of Maya warfare thirty years ago.

The Classic Maya collapse

About all that remains is the Classic Maya collapse, which is not so much a component of the mystique model as the background to it. Recent research has revealed that the collapse was much more varied than previously imagined (Demarest *et al.* 2004). I have elsewhere (Webster 2002) tried to demystify the perennial puzzle of the Maya collapse and will only say here that it was present at the birth of Maya archaeology and that it will probably persist until the end, because both archaeologists and the public prefer simple answers to complex historical processes and the frisson of a good human catastrophe well removed in time.

Conclusion

A fundamental dimension of pseudoarchaeology is the tension between professional and public (or "popular") conceptions of the past. The history of the Maya mystique shows that this dichotomy is not so simple. In the Maya case, professional archaeologists were (and to a degree still are) active participants, wittingly or not, in the origin and perpetuation of a set of very exotic and appealing conceptions about the ancient people they studied. These conceptions spilled over into the popular imagination, where they remain widely believed and valued. We should, however, remember that the founders of systematic Maya archaeology were inventing their discipline not too long ago – about the time my grandparents were born. Many of them were not "professionals" in the modern sense, however skilled and intrepid they were at fieldwork. As professional archaeology matured, there was an inevitable process of self-correction – more fieldwork, better analytical tools, and more sophisticated anthropological and comparative perspectives eventually brought down the old version of the Maya mystique.

If Morley or his contemporaries could be magically whisked from the 1940s to the present, they would find their beloved Classic Maya almost unrecognizable. These people no longer represent some mysterious or exotic

"Other" of the kind that anthropologists have sometimes been accused of creating from their subjects. On the contrary, the research of the last forty years has made the Maya much more comprehensible within the broader comparative perspective intuitively used by Stephens long ago.

Unfortunately, it is almost always easier to develop new, good ideas than to make old, bad ideas go away. Even as evidence accumulated that undermined the mystique, many Mayanists only grudgingly yielded their ground (particularly with regard to warfare), a process that still continues. And the general public remains strongly attracted to many of the old elements of the mystique, not because they are true but because they are comforting and attractive. Like my visitor at Becán many years ago, they resent having their cherished beliefs about the Classic Maya challenged.

The archaeologists who generated these ideas were people of their times, and I am acutely aware that hindsight makes criticism easy. What is clear is that many Mayanists were seduced by their own rhetoric, by their own emotional investments in a particular vision of the past, and by lacunae in their data into creating a mystique that resonated with a wide audience. Whatever their private opinions, archaeologists today are still adept at exploiting the public fascination with the ancient Maya. Every month or so, some new discovery – a rich tomb, an ornate temple, or a new and revealing decipherment – is trumpeted by the press, and there seems to be a never-ending production of films that play up the mystery of this lost people. All this is a legacy of the old mystique, and it is unquestionably very good for Maya archaeologists, who must after all make their reputations and secure funds for their research in a very competitive academic environment. Like Thompson long ago, many of us are a bit Janus-faced, purveying one view professionally and another publicly. Nor are we immune from perpetuating the mystique in new ways.

At the beginning of this paper, I mentioned one such late (in the 1970s) addition to the original mystique: the idea that the ancient Maya were accomplished tropical ecologists. By adopting new staple crops, building agricultural terraces, making drained fields in wetlands, and micromanaging their habitats, they carefully husbanded their natural resources and so were able to maintain highly productive subsistence economies and dense populations on fragile tropical landscapes. Moreover, many of these innovations required great planning and effort and were managed by Maya administrators.

This fondly (and widely) held idea has puzzled me throughout my career, because it does not square with what I know of the demographic fluctuations so common in time and space throughout the lowlands, or with the plain facts of the collapse.[36] Moreover, ethnographers have commonly observed societies that build impressive agro-engineering features using only domestic labor and use them with little or no bureaucratic oversight. Recent research suggests that many such features identified in the Maya lowlands simply do not exist (having been misidentified from remote-sensing images) or that they were built long before populations reached high levels (e.g.,

Pohl and Bloom 1996). Studies of the largest known terrace systems reveal the Maya not as consummate ecologists but as people who had to work ever harder for less and less reward (Murtha 2002). And although the Maya had other dietary options, isotopic studies of bone show that they depended heavily on maize, as all archaeologists originally believed. My prediction is that the "tropical ecologist" idea will eventually run its course.

A *leitmotif* of my analysis has been the frequent lack (or distrust) of comparative anthropological perspectives by archaeologists trying to understand the ancient Maya. What finally put paid to the mystique was not so much the adoption of such perspectives but one of the most important products of Classic Maya culture – the inscriptions. Ultimately, it is the epigraphic messages left *by the Maya themselves* that convinced Mayanists of the existence of kings and nobles, their impressive households, their wars, and many other unexpected things. The irony is that these unique messages were required to open up our minds to the fact that the Maya were not so unique after all.

Notes

1. The Classic Maya continue to be a kind of wild card among ancient cultures in part because of the influence of the Maya mystique; see, for example, Bruce Trigger's (1993) comparative study of ancient civilizations.
2. Prior to the application of radiocarbon dating, the precise correlation between our own calendar and the ancient Maya Long Count remained uncertain. There were two main alternatives, which differed by 260 years; here I use the collapse dates according to the now dominant (and later) correlation.
3. See Harrison and Turner 1978 and Fedick 1996 for pertinent articles.
4. See Black 1990 for an excellent summary. Becker gives the slightly wider range of 1935– 60 for the mystique.
5. An exception is the Carnegie Institution project at Mayapán in the early 1950s. However, Mayapán is a late Postclassic site in the Yucatán and not directly pertinent to the Classic Maya mystique. The year 1956 saw the inception of the massive Tikal project, initiating a whole new and different era of research.
6. Many were not even professionally trained as archaeologists, although much of their fieldwork was technically superb. A good example is Gustavo Stromsvik, a Norwegian sailor who jumped ship in Yucatán, became an archaeological handyman, and eventually restored many of the buildings now visible at Copán. Morley's biography (Brunhouse 1971) wonderfully portrays these pioneering times and characters.
7. In this, Meggers echoes Alfred Maudslay's earlier speculation that the Classic Maya originally founded the great cities of Teotihuacán and Tula in the central Mexican highlands before being driven to the east and south by enemies.
8. It bears remembering that Stephens and Catherwood were gentleman travelers who greatly benefited from publishing popular accounts of their explorations and who can be excused a bit of hyperbole. Their books were bestsellers in their day and are still in print.
9. And many such mysterious places were not very ancient. Angkor had functioned as the center of a major Cambodian kingdom right up until AD 1435.
10. More specifically (to use modern geopolitical terms) in Belize, Guatemala, and the Mexican states of Chiapas, Campeche, and Quintana Roo.
11. These centers also produced carved and painted objects much coveted by both institutions and private collectors, and massive looting continues today.

12. The first systematic settlement surveys were carried out on a modest scale by the Ricketsons at Uaxactún in the early 1930s, and Robert Wauchope later excavated several of the house mounds they found. A handful of similar small structures were excavated by E.H. Thompson (1892) in the early 1890s. Such exceptions aside, settlement and household archaeology remained uncommon until the 1950s, when Gordon Willey and his colleagues systematically surveyed the Belize Valley in 1954–56. Publication of this pioneering effort in 1965 firmly established the method in Maya research.

13. Satterthwaite 1935. What we now know to be a royal throne was found at Piedras Negras in a palace room but was not recognized as such at the time.

14. Franz Termer (1951: 105) claimed that he developed the ceremonial center model completely independently of Thompson.

15. Our own solar calendar, for example, derives from Egypt via Julius Caesar's liaison with Cleopatra's court (Duncan 1998).

16. Landa's misunderstood Maya "alphabet" could be considered a kind of Rosetta Stone, but its significance would have been understood far earlier had it really consisted of a long, bilingual inscription.

17. Even at the time, this widely read book was seen as a bit over the top, and Le Plongeon had to publish it at his own expense.

18. The Long Count interval itself was probably envisioned by the Maya as part of a much longer cycle of creations or worlds. The current "creation" (i.e., the Long Count as archaeologists know it) will end on 21 December 2012 with the completion of the thirteenth *baktún*. Had Classic Maya civilization survived until that date, a new Long Count would presumably have begun. Anticipate all sorts of wackiness among the non-Maya as this date approaches.

19. According to the later, and now dominant, correlation with the Gregorian calendar. This period was called the "Golden Age" by Morley.

20. Morley 1915: 33. Until at least 1940, Morley apparently believed that place names and rulers' names might still be found in the glyphs, and also that the Maya kept historical records of a perishable kind (Morley 1940: 148–9). By 1946, he had taken a more extreme ahistorical position.

21. Thompson did love to make offhand comparisons with mediaeval Europe.

22. A rather strange statement at a time when archaeologists usually viewed Postclassic Maya societies as decadent and influenced in unfortunate ways by "Mexicans."

23. Apart from some late dates preserved in oral and literary traditions of the Aztec and other sixteenth-century peoples.

24. These two terms are synonymous. "Preclassic" is fashionable among Maya archaeologists, while highland archaeologists prefer "Formative." Much of the best early work on Formative cultures was done in the Basin of Mexico and other highland regions far from the Maya lowlands.

25. Becán was discovered in 1941, but most archaeologists dismissed its earthworks as fortifications because this interpretation did not conflict with the "peaceful Maya" concept. Pedro Armillas (1951) presciently identified them as one of the earliest and largest defensive systems in Mesoamerica.

26. Stephen Houston suggests to me that the presumption derived partly from the fact that Morley, Kidder, and others were trained in the American southwest, whose inhabitants also enjoyed a reputation for peacefulness. Maudslay and Maler did not fit this mold, however, and the "peaceful Maya" idea seems to have quite early roots.

27. It is true that military scenes are much more common at some sites than others. Yaxchilán and Piedras Negras, along the southwestern margins of the Maya lowlands, have plenty of them. They are much less abundant and obtrusive at Copán, on the southeastern frontier.

28. A famous object called the Leyden plate much impressed archaeologists because it bore one of the two earliest dates (AD 320) then known. Morley, for one, recognized that a main element of the iconography was a figure standing on a captive, but somehow this

theme, later so characteristic of Maya kingship, did not impress him as having any military implications.

29. Morley was a principal founder and planner of the institution's anthropology and archaeology programs.

30. To give Thompson his due, he readily admitted that Proskouriakoff's (1960) insights were correct.

31. Cyrus Thomas, famous for his investigations of the "mound builders" of the eastern United States, called Copán and Palenque "sacred centers" as early as 1899.

32. See, for example, Kidder *et al.* 1946 for his advocacy of Morley's writing/calendrics/corbeled arch syndrome.

33. One very important discovery was that Classic Maya polities and regions exhibited much more variability than envisioned by Morley, even in the themes of the inscriptions.

34. However, the obvious lesson was lost on Covarrubias and others, who immediately christened the Olmec the "mother culture" in their own turn, thus initiating arguments that continue to this day.

35. Archaeologists still quarrel about whether Maya centers were comparable with cities elsewhere in terms of scale, function, and internal complexity. Some of us feel that Willey and Hammond dragged the Maya a bit too far into the urban "mainstream" (Sanders and Webster 1988; Webster 2002), but this is not the place to pursue these controversies.

36. My own opinion is that we vastly overestimate Classic Maya populations in most parts of the Maya lowlands. The issue of how so many people were supported disappears if this turns out to be the case.

7 Pseudoarchaeology and nationalism

Essentializing difference

Bettina Arnold

Pseudoarchaeology and nationalism in political context

P.T. Barnum may or may not have said "There's a sucker born every minute," but there is not much doubt that whoever said it was right on the money. There is not much doubt either that the sucker phenomenon has been recognized and exploited by the unscrupulous and the fanatical ever since the first sucker drew breath. The real question is not so much who benefits – snake oil salesmen, confidence tricksters, propaganda ministers, or other dealers in flimflam and illusions, who come in many colors – but rather why there should be a sucker born every minute. What is it that leads otherwise apparently sane and rational people to collude in their own deception? It is relatively easy to understand why political systems, particularly nationalist movements and dictatorships, are so often enablers in a process of self-delusion, since expediency is the hallmark of most seekers of power and influence. A more difficult question is what distinguishes the misappropriation and misrepresentation of the deep past, as represented by the archaeological record, its investigation and interpretation, from the other forms of "fringe" enthusiasm available for manipulation by nationalist interests. Moreover, do different forms of nationalism make predictable use of different forms of archaeological and historical interpretation? And are there differences in the exploitation of archaeology compared with pseudoarchaeology in the construction and reification of nationalist meta-narratives?

The cooptation of the archaeological past for political purposes as a topic has become something of a growth industry in academic publishing in the last fifteen years.[1] However, most of these studies have been viewed from the perspective of the political systems that typically benefit from the appropriation and exploitation of the past. The motivations or agendas of the intended audiences for these manipulations tend to be discussed in passing without being subjected to a critical analysis in their own right. Constructing a nationalist view of the past is viewed from the perspective of those in power in most of these case studies when in fact it is a complex interaction between the power structure and the majority population. Popular media, including film and non-academic publications, are also rarely analysed as transmitters of nationalist narratives about the archaeologically and historically documented past, even though they play an important role in the blurring of the line between fact and fiction that makes such narratives so dangerous.

In addition, nationalism cannot be viewed solely as a negative force but must be considered a continuum ranging from the construction of a positive collective self-image to the superior ranking of an "imagined community" (Anderson 1983) at the expense of other groups (Arnold 2002), what Ignatieff has called "authoritarian ethnic nationalism" (1993: 8). At one end of the continuum are citizens peacefully celebrating the anniversary of their nation's creation; at the other, genocide. Nationalism, as Smiles has so cogently put it:

> is the servant of many masters ... dependent on circumstances and ideological persuasion. It can be marshaled for repressive as well as emancipatory ends. The nationalism associated with imperial expansion may share the same beliefs in manifest destiny and cultural aptitudes as the nationalism organized to resist imperial domination. Nationalism, in other words, is effective both as an imperial device to orchestrate national unity and as a more localized politics of resistance to that very imperialism.
>
> (Smiles 1994: 27)

The chimera-like quality of cultural nationalism, the expedient use of the past in the construction of nationalist agendas, and the role of consumer/audience complicity in the production of nationalist pasts, particularly in political systems that make use of pseudoarchaeological "cultural genealogies" (ibid.: 27), will be explored in this essay in two contexts: National Socialist Germany and Celtic nationalism in continental Europe and in the British Isles.

Motives and agendas

Shaping public opinion and attracting public attention are two obvious motivations for various other forms of exaggeration or fabrication masquerading as fact (Boese 2002: 5), with personal gain a close third. Fanaticism is another potent force, in the form of the misguided beliefs of an individual or a group of people who seek approbation and validation in some public form. Public praise of and support for a complex of ideas or beliefs require not only a potent message but also an effective delivery system, which at least partially explains why it is with the emergence of print media that the "imagined communities" known as nations first appear in Europe. Not coincidentally, the systematic study of past human behavior based on material remains, known today as archaeology, developed as a profession almost in parallel with European nationalism.[2]

However, aspiring dictators, drug-addled cult members, and unscrupulous charlatans out to make a fast buck at someone else's expense account for

156   *Bettina Arnold*

a relatively small proportion of the world's population. The motivations of nation-states in search of cultural capital from which to stitch together a collective identity have been extensively studied; archaeology is of obvious utility to such entities – as long as it conforms to their agendas. When it does not, pseudoarchaeology and pseudohistory can be fostered and supported to fill the breach (Arnold 1999). More mysterious is what moves the general public to cooperate with such programs of mass delusion. Michael Shermer (1997: 6) argues that hope

> drives all of us – skeptics and believers alike – to be compelled by unsolved mysteries, to seek spiritual meaning in a physical universe, desire immortality, and wish that our hopes for eternity may be fulfilled. It is what pushes many people to spiritualists, New Age gurus, and tele-vision psychics, who offer a Faustian bargain: eternity in exchange for the willing suspension of disbelief (and usually a contribution to the provider's coffers).

This rather positive assessment of what motivates people to be complicit in their own deception fails to acknowledge a flip-side to hope as a motivator that is an even more potent force in the process of self-delusion: fear. Most people may hope that there is a life after death, but that hope is based in part on the fear that in fact there may not be such a thing. Most people would prefer to believe that their nation, or religious denomination, or other imagined community is superior to the rest, but they rather suspect that it may not be. Anyone who preaches a message that sedates that doubt will find legions of supporters, just as the company of those who tell us only good things about ourselves (not all of which may be true) will generally be preferred to that of those who present us with a less comfortable but more accurate self-image. Recognition of this simple but universal aspect of human psychology – the need to appear greater to oneself and to others than one truly is – is a characteristic of all nationalist regimes, and the manipula-tion of the deep past so that it presents to the members of an imagined community the face it most wants to see is a potent weapon in the creation and maintenance of the nationalist fiction of the superior race or culture.

There is another factor involved in public participation in the construc-tion of a wholly or partially fictitious past that often has the mangling and misrepresentation of archaeology as a corollary, and that is the frequently indifferent if not actually hostile attitude of the average citizen to science and scholarship and the methods by which they are practised. Cole refers to the ambivalent anti-elitism of the general public, consisting of "vilification of the Establishment coupled with an inordinate respect for and envy of it" (1980: 7). Harrold and Eve (1984: 4) make the point that "cult archaeology can often provide [answers] that are more psychologically satisfying to many individuals." Television producer Tom Naughton's attitude toward this issue is quite revealing and makes it clear that the popular media pander directly to what they perceive as the simultaneous aversion of the general public to "scholarship" and their desire for entertainment:

> Television is not about education or providing news and information. Television is about storytelling and holding the largest audience for the longest amount of time. Programmers will do anything they can to accomplish this. Pseudoarchaeology programs are in many ways more fun to watch than programs on archaeology.
>
> (cited in Fagan 2003: 49)

It is not a coincidence that some of the most successful pseudoarchaeologists, Swiss ex-hotel keeper Erich von Däniken being perhaps the most obvious example (Feder 2002b: 204–30), have no formal training, often lack any kind of post-secondary degree, or have a degree in a completely unrelated subject (Radner and Radner 1982: 17–26), as in the case of Barry Fell (1917–94), the retired Harvard marine biology professor who was a proponent of regular pre-Columbian European contact with the New World (Feder 2002b: 106–48). An anti-intellectual orientation, often accompanied by feelings of inferiority and suspicion of what is perceived as academic elitism, is partly responsible for the proliferation of various forms of contemporary "lunatic fringe" preoccupations, including UFOs, the existence of Atlantis, and the construction of the Egyptian pyramids by aliens (for other examples, see Chapter 12). Pseudoarchaeologists like von Däniken and Fell pander to the notion that credentials, degrees or professional training are not only unnecessary, they actually produce an army of scholar clones who are too brainwashed to see the "truth." The popular media, especially television and film, do nothing to dispel this tendency; in fact, they have often been accused of actively pandering to it. This results in a schizophrenic production of "knowledge": what the public is presented with by the popular media versus what is disseminated by scholars and professionals in various fields and disciplines requiring post-secondary education or professional training.

Neil deGrasse Tyson, the astronomy columnist for *Natural History* magazine, coined the term "astro-errors" to describe the inaccuracies related to astronomy and astrophysics that he has documented in Hollywood films. He makes a point of distinguishing between what he calls "bloopers" – "mistakes that the producers or continuity editors happened to miss, but would ordinarily have caught and fixed" – and "astro-errors," which were "willingly introduced and indicate a profound lack of attention to easily verifiable detail" (2002: 26). It would be easy – and entertaining – to compile a dossier of "archaeo-errors" in Hollywood films and television programs, but since that is not the primary purpose of this discussion, I will briefly discuss one particularly egregious misrepresentation of archaeology and archaeologists that happens to combine contemporary manifestations of pseudoarchaeology with the manipulation of the past by German National

Socialist archaeologists, who engaged in their own form of pseudoarchaeology: Steven Spielberg's *Indiana Jones* film trilogy.

Pseudo-Nazi archaeologists: the curse of Indiana Jones

Indy has been more of a bane than a boon to archaeologists. On the one hand, the number of people who assume that archaeologists are people who dig up dinosaur bones has declined significantly since the first film came out in the early 1980s; on the other hand, the number of people who think that archaeologists are people who spend about ten minutes a year in the classroom, ignore international antiquities laws while engaged in looting escapades around the globe, and occasionally shoot, stab, whip, or otherwise dispatch the natives of various non-European countries, has increased exponentially.

Interestingly, the few nuggets of fact buried in the morass of romanticized (infantilized?) and occasionally racist notions of archaeology and its practitioners in the Indy films involve the Nazi use and abuse of archaeology, and the pursuit by Nazi archaeologists of "objects of power," including the Holy Grail, the Ark of the Covenant, and the Spear of Longinus. There can be little doubt that while Steven Spielberg has not been particularly concerned with accurately representing archaeology as a profession, he takes German National Socialism, and particularly the Holocaust, more seriously – although historians are critical of *Schindler's List* for much the same reasons that archaeologists have mixed feelings about Indy and his exploits (Manchel 1995). However, this has not stopped Spielberg from blending invention and fact in such arbitrary ways that the two can be disentangled in his films only with great difficulty.

Part of the problem is that there is no code of ethics in film making comparable to the techniques used by the restorers of old paintings or ancient art. The professional credo of such restoration work is that it must be done in such a way that the restored ("fake") sections can be distinguished from the original ("real") sections in perpetuity. In other words, there is currently no way to ensure that movie "audiences observe the difference between perception and reality" (ibid.: 92) in order to separate the personal vision of the film maker from the historical (or archaeological) sources. This distinction is critical because, as Manchel and others have pointed out, movies "have the ability to affect people's values and attitudes" (ibid.: 96). In the case of *Schindler's List*, that was presumably one of Spielberg's motivations, but damage can be done inadvertently through sins of both omission and commission, as has happened with the portrayal of archaeology in the *Indiana Jones* trilogy. The fact that the Indy films do not claim to represent archaeology accurately in the way that a documentary (at least theoretically) is expected to do is not the issue. The problem lies in the *blending* of fact and fiction, so that where one begins and the other ends cannot be determined by the average viewer. In effect, archaeology as represented in the Indy trilogy is pseudoarchaeology in the dictionary sense of the prefix "pseudo": it is a false and spurious representation of the field, superficially similar but morphologically unlike the real thing. The fact that the film is intended to entertain rather than deceive does not change that.

Ironically, Spielberg's representation of archaeology as an academic discipline is less carefully researched than some of the background information on Nazi pseudoarchaeology. The SS-Ahnenerbe (Ancestor Heritage Society), led by party ideologue Heinrich Himmler, did send archaeologists out on expeditions to search for the Grail, the Ark, and the Spear, among other items (Arnold 1992; Hale 2003). Spielberg, his scriptwriters, and/or the concept developers of the trilogy actually seem to have read some of the available source material on this topic (Manchel 1995: 95). The American archaeologist who is missing at the beginning of the first film (*Raiders of the Lost Ark*) is named Ravenwood, a name too close to that of the author of a questionable work on the Spear of Longinus (Ravenscroft 1973) to be coincidence, for example.

Another "convergence" between reality and fiction is the fact that the *magnum opus* of Otto Rahn, an SS-Ahnenerbe scholar and Himmler protégé, closely parallels two of the Indy films. Rahn was convinced that the Holy Grail was secreted in the vicinity of Montségur in the French Pyrenees, a mountain fastness associated with the Cathars, a sect persecuted by the Catholic Church between AD 1208 and 1229 in the Albigensian Crusade of Pope Innocent III. Rahn believed that the Cathars who guarded the Holy Grail in their castle at Montségur were connected in an unbroken line to Druids who had converted to Manichaeism, a dualist religion that blended elements from Buddhism, Christianity, Gnosticism, Mithraism, and Zoroastrianism. The Cathars held that humans were created by Satan (Sklar 1977: 141–4) and that death was followed by a form of reincarnation, none of which endeared this heretical sect to the Catholic Church. The last heroic stand came in 1244. According to local lore and oral traditions, which Rahn recorded, on the night before the final assault, three Cathars carrying the sacred relics of the faith slipped unnoticed over the wall. They carried away the magical regalia of the Merovingian king Dagobert II as well as a cup reputed to be the Holy Grail. Rahn believed that they had hidden it somewhere in the honeycomb of passages and caves under Montségur and other nearby mountains. He spent years searching for its hiding place.

This mix of Nazis, Arthurian legend, and pseudoarchaeology complete with treasure hunters and remote locations obviously appealed to Spielberg, for whom archaeology in the *Indiana Jones* films was never more than a means to an end, the framework within which to present the crowd-pleasing mix of action adventure and stereotypical clichés that characterizes many of his films. The fact that he returned to the theme of the Nazis and their obsession with pseudoarchaeology and the occult after abandoning it in *Indiana Jones and the Temple of Doom* was obviously motivated by the second film's (relatively) poor box-office showing compared with its predecessor. In *Indiana Jones and the Last Crusade*, when Indy is heard to declare "Nazis. I hate these guys" (Barta 1998: 127), it is to the cheering of audiences and the chinging of cash registers. Clearly, Spielberg was on to something good. Ironically, he had hit upon the same winning combination that the Nazis had discovered before him (ibid.: 128).

The *Indiana Jones* trilogy exploits the profession of archaeology and German National Socialism with equal enthusiasm and with a disregard for accuracy or consequences. None of this would matter much if the average citizen were in a position to distinguish between the Hollywood construc-tions and archaeological evidence and practice, or if archaeologists were better at communicating with the public. Unfortunately, this dual failure has real-life consequences, as the recent scandalous handling of the looting of the Baghdad Museum in the aftermath of the US military takeover of that city has clearly shown. Also, as Tony Barta points out in a recent essay, making a distinction matters, because "the mythic Nazi was from the very beginning the accompaniment of the nastier historical one, and was designed – by the Nazis themselves – to create the cinematic representation of the future" (ibid.: 128).

The fact that the past, particularly the "deep" past based on archaeolog-ical evidence, has been invoked and appropriated by so many nationalist movements and regimes testifies to its political significance as cultural capital. The Nazis recognized this quality as well, and they exploited it as ruthlessly as they made use of other tools that could aid them in the construction of an appropriately glorious vision of themselves. The crucial difference between pseudoarchaeology as practiced by a nationalist regime and scientific archaeology lies in the respective approaches to interpretation: nationalist pseudoarchaeology is not interested in what actually happened in the past, only in how the past can be made to fit *an already existing view of the past*, while scientific archaeology adjusts its interpretations based on new data, *whether those data require the jettisoning of previous interpretations or not*.

Pseudoarchaeology has been both manipulated and endorsed by nation-alist movements partly because of the frequently marginal and disenfranchised character of its discourse and the perceived lack of professional status of its practitioners. Historically, this has led many pseudoarchaeologists to become willing collaborators in nationalist projects, since the legitimacy denied them by the "professional" establishment has frequently (and often cyni-cally) been offered in exchange for the "validation" of a politically useful past. Nazi Germany remains one of the best-documented and most extreme examples of the manipulation and distortion of archaeological evidence for political purposes.

Nazi pseudoarchaeology and the invention of German national identity

German National Socialism was underwritten by a patchwork of pasts, some based on fact, some manufactured, most predating Hitler's rise to power in

1933. In 1990, when I published an article in *Antiquity* that provided a brief summary of the appropriation of the past by German National Socialism (Arnold 1990), there were a scant half-dozen articles on the subject, none written by a German archaeologist. Since then, and especially within the past five years, there has been a veritable explosion of extremely well-researched and critically analysed volumes by German archaeologists on the subject.[3] The basic outline of the appropriation and misuse of the archaeological past by National Socialist ideologues has been presented in numerous contexts and will not be reiterated here. I will instead focus on National Socialist use of pseudoarchaeology, which by association will require some discussion of the obsessions of Heinrich Himmler, Nazi ideologue and enthusiastic supporter of pseudo-research of all kinds.

Germany in the years after the First World War has been described as "a magnet for malign cranks, a vessel into which they might pour their poison" (Meades 1994: 41). The Nazi Party was an equal opportunity organization when it came to some of the more extreme forms of weirdness that flourished during this time, including spiritualism, back-to-nature movements, numerology, astrology, dowsing, and every conceivable form of pseudoscience. In 1935, Himmler, together with Hermann Wirth and six others (Kater 1974: 454), founded the Deutsches Ahnenerbe: Studiengesellschaft für Geistesgeschichte ("Ancestor Heritage Society"); also related was the Externsteine Stiftung ("Externsteine Foundation"), which, under Himmler's patronage, was headed by Julius Andree (ibid.: 80). Eventually, the Ancestor Heritage Society morphed into the notorious SS-Ahnenerbe and supported much of the archaeological research conducted in Germany and other parts of the world.

Ackermann devotes an entire chapter to Himmler as a "protector of pseudo 'scholarly' disciplines" (1970: 40–53), which illustrates the close relationship between Nazi ideology and "fringe" research of all kinds – including the so-called medical research conducted on human subjects, characterized by the same anti-intellectual scientism as other SS-Ahnenerbe activities (Berger 1990: 1435–40). The following quote of Ackermann's illustrates this point particularly well: "In this respect the historiographic illumination of the past was of secondary importance – indeed, the ideological goals forbade the truly scientific exploration of germanic-German history. ... It is therefore significant that National Socialism completely repudiated any absolute and objective research" (1970: 41; translated by author). The anti-intellectual character of the National Socialist program was quite explicit, particularly with respect to the training of young boys and men. Hitler is reported as having said in a conversation with Rauschning about his pedagogical principles: "I don't want an intellectual education. Scholarship spoils the young. ... But they must learn control. I want a violent, dominant, fearless, brutal youth ... one that will shock the world" (ibid.: 124; translated by author). He could have added "biddable and gullible" to the list, since that was clearly a significant part of the re-education program developed by the party, one of the reasons for the proliferation of pseudo-disciplines during the period between the two world wars.

The SS-Ahnenerbe was dedicated to Himmler's belief that the prehistoric and historical record of the Germanic people had to be rectified, "purified" and restored to its original, pre-Christian glory. Links between modern Germans and their ancestors, termed *germanische Erbströme* ("streams of germanic patrimony") by Himmler, had to be retraced and reconnected, and prehistoric archaeology was one way of achieving this goal. A frequently used analogy was that of a chain leading directly back into the past. Every fourth child born to an SS man, for example, received a candlestick with the inscription "You are only a link in the clan's endless chain" (Sklar 1977: 101). Ultimately, all SS activities, including its archaeological and pseudoarchaeological programs, had one goal: securing, purging, and healing German "blood," which Himmler's grotesque notions of "racial hygiene" viewed as tainted and continually threatened by "Jewish–Bolshevik subhumans" (Hüser 1987: 13).

It is this aspect of the SS program that connects the manipulation and misuse of archaeology by Nazi ideologues to the Holocaust. The disciplines of archaeology and history were to be handmaidens to this effort, tolerated only if they supported the state's agenda (Ackermann 1970: 42). Since the evidence frequently did not fit the National Socialist ideologues' view of the past, results were manufactured or exaggerated, while inconvenient discoveries or interpretations were suppressed or denied (Arnold 1990: 469). As a result, by 1938 international scholarly opinion of the regime had rapidly eroded, and professional German scholars, archaeologists among them, many of whom had contacts outside Germany, began to be concerned about the effect of the *Germanomanen*, the "Germano-maniacs" (ibid.: 470), on their disciplinary reputations.

The response of German archaeologists trained before 1933 to attempts by the state to engage in the *Gleichschaltung*, or "ideological mainstreaming," of their profession, is a good example of the complex interaction between the power structure of a totalitarian regime and its members, not all of whom are necessarily in agreement with all aspects of the ideological program. On the one hand, many German archaeologists of the time were active and supportive party members. On the other hand, this did not make them willing to have their research put on a par with the activities of the party's fantasists, whom they vocally despised and gradually worked to remove from positions of influence. While active resistance, along the lines of organizations like the student resistance movement the White Rose (Shirer 1981: 1022–3), did not occur in the archaeological establishment, various covert forms of resistance were practiced, particularly by the archaeologists of the SS-Ahnenerbe, some of whom, like Herbert Jankuhn, Werner Buttler and Hans Schleif, had excellent international reputations. Through intrigues and networking, the exerting of subtle pressure on party officials and publications denouncing the "lunatic fringe" and its activities (the Externsteine in particular spawned a flurry of articles and monographs decrying the unprofessional and pseudoscientific approach to the excavation and interpretation of sites), archaeologists defended their discipline with some success from total cooptation by the *Germanomanen* (Arnold 1990: 470). The outbreak of war in 1939 not coincidentally also had an impact, but by then many of the "lunatic fringe" elements had been removed from their positions.

The independent German–Dutch scholar Hermann Wirth, who was convinced that "civilization" was a curse that could be lifted only by a return to a simpler, more "traditional" way of life as materially documented in the archaeological and historical records, is a good example of a "Germanomaniac" (Kater 1974: 11–16). His early publications, especially *Der Aufgang der Menschheit* ("The Rise of Humankind"), published in 1928, and his "translation" of the so-called "Ura Linda-Chronik," a text that ostensibly documented the history of a Frisian family between the sixth and first century BC, were vilified by Germanists (ibid.: 14) for their dependence on a naive kind of romantic nationalism. The Ura Linda-Chronik turned out to be a skillful forgery, inked on artificially aged Dutch machine-made paper dating to around 1850. Wirth's refusal to accept the scientific evidence for fraud made him a target for the scorn of scholars like Bolko von Richthofen, Gerhard Gloege, Arthur Hübner and K.H. Jakob-Friesen (ibid.: 16). Von Richthofen in fact publicly and in print criticized Wirth for his gullibility, drawing Himmler's ire, who repeatedly admonished him to desist from his defamatory attacks on the Chronicle and on Wirth, finally commenting in a memo: "I will send Mr. von Richthofen a last letter on this subject, but after that my patience will be at an end" (Ackermann 1970: 49). Himmler's defense of Wirth was ultimately to no avail; he remained a marginal figure with respect to academic scholarship, and by 1938 Himmler had distanced himself from his former crony.

Nazi neo-paganism and pseudoarchaeology

A fundamental element of Himmler's ideological program was the confrontation between the nascent, state-organized, neo-pagan belief system and the Christian faith in its various denominations (Ackermann 1970: 40, 62; Höhne 1967: 146-7; Meades 1994: 38), which he and other high-ranking Nazi officials had repudiated because of its dependence on a "semitic" religious tradition that emphasized the brotherhood of all human beings (Ackermann 1970: 41). This anti-Christian attitude is clearly stated in an SS educational pamphlet dating to 1937: "What is Christian is not Germanic; what is Germanic is not Christian! Germanic virtues are manly pride, heroic courage, and loyalty – not meekness, repentance, the misery of sin and an afterlife with prayers and psalms" (ibid.: 56; translated by author).

One of the reasons Himmler was an early champion of Otto Rahn's "research" on the Holy Grail and the persecution of the Cathars was because the Albigenses, as they were known in France, were a non-Christian sect who viewed Lucifer as the Bringer of Light (the literal meaning of his name), in addition to being associated with one of the most potent symbols of power known in Biblical tradition in the form of the Grail. Rahn's second book, entitled *Lucifer's Court Servants: A Tour of Europe's Benevolent Spirits*, was in effect a travel diary describing the locations where pagans and heretics were martyred by the Catholic Church. After Rahn's death in 1939, Himmler had 10,000 additional copies printed and distributed (Ackermann 1970: 58). He took an active interest in "reawakening" the German people to their pre-Christian, pagan past and the persecutions suffered by their ancestors at the hands of the Catholic Church.

Himmler liked to present himself as a reincarnation of Heinrich I, who married a great-granddaughter of Widukind, the Saxon king converted to Christianity together with his people after their defeat by Charlemagne. Heinrich I also reportedly refused to be anointed by the Church when he was crowned in Fritzlar in AD 919 (ibid.: 60), which made him an ideal candidate for Himmler to glorify in his "return to paganism" campaign. In 1936, on the 1,000th anniversary of the death of Heinrich I, Himmler gave a speech in the cathedral of Quedlinburg, where the bones of the king were supposed to have been laid to rest. Himmler admitted in a pamphlet published in honor of the occasion that in fact it was not known what had happened to his remains (ibid.: 61).

One of the hallmarks of Himmler's brand of pseudoarchaeology was not to let the absence of evidence get in the way of the pursuit of his agenda. Less than a year after the anniversary celebration, Himmler announced that SS Obersturmführer Heinz Höhne had been ordered to conduct excavations in the Quedlinburg crypt and had (surprise!) discovered the bones of the great king. Himmler thereupon established a fund in honor of Heinrich I, which was announced in July 1938 to all the towns of central Germany with historical connections to the ruler, and the crypt itself became an official national memorial (Ackermann 1970: 61–2). Every 2 July from that year on, Himmler held a "vigil" in the crypt at midnight to commune with his ancestor and namesake (Höhne 1967: 145).

Party ideologues stressed the association between the introduction of Christianity to the Germanic tribes and the battles against the pagan Saxons waged by Charlemagne, who was crowned Holy Roman Emperor at Aachen in AD 800. As the ruler of the Franks, Charlemagne was linked by Nazi propaganda with the "Romanized" French and thus demonized as "Carl the Saxon Slaughterer" (Ackermann 1970: 56) in reference to the 4,500 Saxon captives he was supposed to have executed in 782 during his campaign in what is now Niedersachsen (Lower Saxony). He was also reputed to have destroyed the most important ritual site of the Saxons, the place where the Irminsul, or World Tree, was worshipped. Hermann Wirth and other members of the Vereinigung der Freunde germanischer Vorgeschichte ("Union of the Friends of Germanic Prehistory") were convinced that this site was identical with the Externsteine, a sandstone formation not far from Detmold where the meetings of the group were regularly held (Halle 2002) (Figure 7.1). The location is picturesque, and there is evidence of its use by anchorites from a nearby Benedictine monastery, but there is no archaeological evidence to support a Germanic occupation of the site. Nevertheless, Himmler assigned SS-Ahnenerbe archaeologist Julius Andree the task of directing excavations at the Externsteine (ibid.; Kater 1974: 80). He dutifully "discovered" that it had indeed been used during the period in question as a solar observatory, and he interpreted enigmatic graffiti on some of the chamber walls as "runes" related to the solstices (Arnold 1990: 470–1).

The juxtaposition of the Christian Charlemagne and the Saxon king Widukind, supposedly forcibly converted during the Saxon campaigns (ibid.: 59), was favored by both Himmler and party ideologue Alfred Rosenberg as a "correction" of the "false history" that had denied the German people the right to acknowledge their glorious pre-Christian past. However, Hitler actually passed an edict forbidding the use of the pejorative term "Carl the Saxon Slaughterer" for Charlemagne, a good example of the many rifts and differences of opinion regarding ideology and policy within the Nazi Party. Hitler saw Charlemagne as the unifier of the German people and the creator of the German Reich; the introduction of Christianity could be forgiven such an inspiring leader (Ackermann 1970: 57). Hitler was never an enthusiastic supporter of Himmler's neo-pagan cult in any case (Arnold 1990: 469).

Figure 7.1 The Externsteine sandstone formation near Detmold, site of pseudoarchaeological investigations by German National Socialist archaeologists (photo: B. Arnold).

From 1935 onward, the SS organization had what has been described as its "spiritual headquarters" (Frischauer 1953: 247) in the Wewelsburg castle in Büren near Paderborn (Figure 7.2), variously referred to in the postwar literature on the Third Reich as Himmler's "Valhalla" (Höhne 1967: 143), his "jewel" (Ackermann 1970: 105), and his "Camelot" (Höhne 1967: 141–2; Hüser 1987: 6). According to an apocryphal tale, Himmler was supposed to have heard a prophecy that the next invasion from the east would be withstood and halted by a lone castle in Westphalia, whereupon he scoured the area looking for a fortress that fitted the bill (Höhne 1967: 143). The castle itself is of interest to those fascinated by the Nazi obsession with the occult, but more significant is the fact that it is located in a region of northern Germany that is occupied by three sites of importance in Nazi pseudoarchaeology: the Externsteine and the Hermann Monument near Detmold in Nordrheinwestfalen, and the Sachsenhain near Verden in Niedersachsen.

The Hermann Monument commemorates the destruction of three Roman legions in AD 9 by a tribal confederacy led by the leader of a German tribal rebellion whom Tacitus refers to as "Arminius," a name that was later Germanized as "Hermann." The erection of the monument in 1875, just four years after the end of the Franco-Prussian war, which marked the birth of the German nation-state, was intended to represent freedom from both the ancient and the recent Mediterranean military threat (Arnold 1998: 242–3; Geary 2002: 22). Pseudoarchaeology was involved in the creation of the Hermann Monument only in the sense that it was erected on what was

Figure 7.2 Wewelsburg Castle, cult site and "spiritual center" of the SS (photo: B. Arnold).

known to be a Celtic Iron Age hill fort, and in fact there is no evidence that local Germanic tribes ever inhabited the summit. Based on recent archaeological discoveries, the battle itself is now thought to have taken place significantly further north and west (Arnold 1998: 242; Wells 2003).

The Sachsenhain is particularly representative of what was referred to during the Nürnberg trials by the German prehistorian Assien Böhmers as "the hoax research characteristic of that time" (Kater 1974: 81–2). Himmler "investigated" the site in 1935 and erected rows and circles of 4,500 megaliths or standing stones, each one supposedly from 4,500 villages in Niedersachsen (Ackermann 1970: 56) intended to commemorate the pagan Saxon captives ostensibly slaughtered at the site. There is absolutely no evidence of any prehistoric activity at this location (in spite of Himmler's erection of megaliths at the site), and the entire Sachsenhain complex has been called "probably the most comprehensive work of ersatz prehistory ever undertaken" (Meades 1994: 36–8). It also exemplifies the anti-Christian and neo-pagan elements of the new "religion" that Himmler hoped to impose on the German people. Solstice ceremonies conducted there for members of the SS paralleled those held at the Externsteine in Horn not far to the south and west of the Sachsenhain. The National Socialist practice of justifying action in the present by reference to the archaeological or historical past is summed up neatly by the following excerpt from a Himmler speech delivered during one of the solstice ceremonies at the Sachsenhain: "Back then 4,500 heads fell that had refused to bend; today heads are being proudly raised that will never bend again!" (cited in Ackermann 1970: 56; translated by author).

Himmler recognized that no society could survive without a belief system. The question was what would replace the Christian faith? An "ancestor-based" tradition that had its roots in the Romantic movements of the previous century was outlined, complete with Germanic names for the days of the week, months, and holidays (Christmas became Jul, for example). One part of this wholesale invention of a religious tradition, which depended in part on the cooptation or construction of archaeological sites to lend it legitimacy (Arnold 1992: 34–6; Lurz 1975), was the so-called Thing-movement. Initiated in 1933, this artificial neo-pagan tradition was based on a bizarre mélange of Scandinavian/Germanic mythology that emphasized solar worship and focused on large, pageant-rich communal gatherings in open-air theaters designed to mimic Greek and Roman theater prototypes. To qualify as a *Thingstätte*, the term coined to describe the open-air theaters/places of worship that were to be the focus of this neo-pagan cult, evidence was required of Germanic occupation of the prospective site. Communities competed with one another for the honor of acquiring such a monument, and by 1935 twelve such cult sites had been dedicated. At one of these locations, the Heiligenberg *oppidum* (Julius Caesar's term for Celtic hill forts) across the river from the city of Heidelberg, there was no archaeological evidence for a Germanic occupation (Figure 7.3). The site was ultimately granted *Thingstätte* status on the basis of fabricated archaeological evidence, and most of the Roman, Celtic, and Bronze Age occupation horizons were destroyed in the construction of the *Thingstätte*, which was used for only one open-air ceremony before the Thing-movement was terminated in 1935 (Arnold 1992: 36). The main reason the movement was abandoned was that popular resistance to the replacement of the Christian faith had proved too strong and threatened other, more important, National Socialist agendas.

Resistance to ideological mainstreaming, including the imposition of a neo-pagan religion based on pseudoarchaeological and pseudohistorical interpretations of the past, occurred at several levels, demonstrating the extent to which the public must be willing to be duped if such manipulations are to be effective:

- *Professionalism.* Within the professions and academic disciplines there was resistance by a handful of individuals who were able to work within the system to maintain what they believed was the scientific rigor of their field of expertise (Arnold 1990: 472–3).
- *Apathy.* Members of the National Socialist military machine and civilian bureaucracy were, like most human beings the world over, more concerned with personal safety, comfort, and leisure than with ideology. Höhne describes the constant complaints on the part of the RuSHA (Rasse und Siedlungshauptamt, or "Central Department of Race and Settlement") regarding the lack of interest in ideology on the part of the reserve troops (Verfügungstruppe) and the general SS (Allgemeine SS),

Figure 7.3 The open-air *Thingstätte* on the summit of the Heiligenberg near Heidelberg (photo: B. Arnold).

whose response to the overblown prose style and convoluted, romanticized wanderings of Himmler and other party ideologues was "a huge
yawn" (Höhne 1967: 146). The "educational evenings" during which
such presentations were made were among the worst attended of the SS
gatherings (ibid.).

* *Resistance.* The general public was also not entirely passive, particularly
  with respect to the replacement of the Christian faith (Protestant or
  Catholic) by a state-conceived and controlled neo-pagan religion. The
  Thing-movement is a good example of the effect of "bottom-up" resistance to state policies involving ideology, even within a totalitarian
  state. This was one area in which Himmler's ideological program
  encountered serious difficulties, even within his handpicked elite, the
  SS. Two-thirds of the general SS remained officially affiliated with a
  Christian faith, but in the SS reserves and in the Death's Head units,
  where participation would have been expected to be greatest, no more
  than 69 percent of members were officially affiliated with Himmler's
  neo-pagan tradition, and these numbers dropped significantly after the
  outbreak of war in 1939 (ibid.: 147–8).

Pseudoarchaeology, pseudohistory, and Celtic nationalism

Celtic nationalism and the appropriation of "Celtic" symbolic capital by
neo-pagan sects may at first glance appear to have little in common with the
abuses of the deep past by National Socialist ideologues. However, both the
Celtic (also referred to as the Gaelic) revival that underwrote nationalist and
separatist agendas in the Celtic-speaking areas of the British Isles[4] as well as
in continental Europe (Diaz Santana 2002; Dietler 1994, 1998; McDonald
1989) and German National Socialism were born out of the Romantic
movement, and they share the appropriation of the archaeological past in the
construction of national identity. The Ura Linda-Chronik has its counterpart
in the poetic output of the invented Scottish bard Ossian, for example,
whose German translation in 1794 "kindled an interest in archaic German
history and references to the prehistoric, heroic past of the German people"
(Smiles 1994: 34) on the continent as well as in Scotland.

Comparing German and Celtic nationalism serves several purposes: (1) it
challenges the tendency to view the German National Socialist exploitation
of the past as historically specific to that particular time and place; (2) by
highlighting the similarities between two case studies that at first glance
seem unlikely candidates for such an analysis, the meta-narratives of pseudoarchaeology and nationalism are exposed; (3) it reveals that archaeologists
are willing to support nationalist agendas, particularly in countries in which
their research has traditionally been underfunded and accorded little respect,
in much the same way that nations that are struggling with inferiority
complexes are vulnerable to manipulation by nascent dictatorial regimes
(Arnold 2004; Galaty 2004); (4) it demonstrates that the two forms of

nationalist exploitation of the past not only have common roots but are also inextricably entangled in their contemporary manifestations.

The selection by National Socialist fantasists of the Externsteine as the spiritual center of the Germanic world (Arnold 1990: 470–1, 1992: 34; Halle 2002) was born of the same Romantic and antiquarian fascination with ruins and archaeological landscapes that characterized most of northern Europe in the eighteenth and nineteenth centuries. In France as in Britain, Neolithic sites like Stonehenge or Carnac were considered symbols of national pride, and faux megaliths, tumuli, and other monuments were erected in the gardens of the rich in a number of European countries during this period (Smiles 1994: 29).

The Externsteine site is still described today as "a powerful spiritual center of our ancestors" on the unofficial Externsteine website (*www.externsteine.de*), even though absolutely no verifiable archaeological evidence for Germanic activity or occupation of the site was uncovered during Julius Andree's excavations at the site under Himmler's patronage (Arnold 1992: 34; Halle 2002). Every *Walpurgisnacht* (the night of 30 April / 1 May), considered by pagans to be the night when witches meet to consort with the devil, a major pagan festival is still held at the site, and the website reflects contemporary neo-pagan beliefs as well as the legacy of National Socialist pseudoarchaeology. Ironically, one of the main attractions at the site is a large bas-relief cut into the cliff that depicts Christ being taken down from the cross, part of the anchorite legacy associated with the nearby monastery of Corvey. Elements of this relief were interpreted by Nazi fantasists as representing the survival of pagan beliefs in spite of Christian domination, a kind of coded message on the part of the local Saxon people, but there is no evidence to support this notion. The same is true for the supposed "runes" inscribed in various places at the site, supposedly representing solar and lunar worship and the solstices.

When comparing German and Celtic nationalist manipulation of the past, it is important to distinguish between Celtic nationalism as constructed by the English and the Celtic nationalism of the minority Celtic-speaking groups in the British Isles. As Kidd and others have pointed out: "the different national contexts of enlightened historiography in Ireland and Scotland led to the emergence of widely divergent constructions of Gaeldom" (1994: 1198). The latter form of Celtic nationalism is at least in part due to feelings of cultural inferiority encouraged by British imperialism, and in its defensive as well as aggressive self-aggrandizing rhetoric it often resembles German nationalism after 1871, when the new German nation-state was seeking legitimacy and respect in post-Napoleonic Europe. Just as Nazi ideologues like Himmler repeatedly sought to emphasize the greatness of prehistoric Germanic culture independent of, or indeed preceding, developments in the Mediterranean and the Middle East (Arnold 1990), an important dimension of Irish cultural patriotism, for example, was to demonstrate that the pre-Christian, "Milesian" Ireland had been a great civilization in its own right. Ireland's claim to fame as the "island of saints and scholars" was due not only to a derivative continental culture imposed by Christian missionaries but also to the Celtic, rather than Latin, roots of its civilization (Kidd 1994: 1203). Claims that this ancient Milesian kingdom of the Gaels, for which no archaeological evidence exists, had once been the equal of the classical civilizations of Greece and Rome (ibid.: 1202) repeat almost verbatim pronouncements made by German nineteenth and early twentieth-century nationalists (and echo the claims of modern Indian nationalists; see Chapter 9). Old English antiquary and poet Geoffrey Keating, for example, developed "an account of a fabulous high civilization in pagan Irish, or Milesian, antiquity to refute the slurs of English commentators" (ibid.: 1199), while eighteenth-century "Catholic myth maker" Charles O'Connor is cited by Kidd as "having made the proud boast: 'All the modern nations of Europe (the [Irish] Scots alone excepted) are indebted to the Greeks and Romans for their letters and learning'" (ibid.: 1202).

The monumental expression of nineteenth-century European nationalism based on archaeological and early historical sources is represented in several European nations in the form of a Celtic or Germanic tribal leader who challenged the hegemony of Rome. In Germany, Arminius, the destroyer of three Roman legions in AD 9, is commemorated by the colossal bronze Hermann Monument; in France, Vercingetorix of the Arverni, who led a tribal rebellion against Julius Caesar in Gaul in 52 BC, is memorialized by a bronze statue; in Belgium, the monumental bronze statue of the Celtic tribal leader Ambiorix celebrates a victory over Caesar in 54 BC; in England, the marble statue at Mansion House in London of the British tribal leader Caractacus represents his resistance to the Claudian invasion in AD 43; and, finally, the monumental bronze statue of Boudicca on the banks of the Thames pays tribute to that queen of the Iceni, who in the first century AD led a campaign against the Romans that destroyed London itself, then a thriving Roman colony (see Table 7.1 and Figure 7.4).

Table 7.1 Monuments to tribal leaders who resisted the Romans

Tribal leader	Date of rebellion	Type of monument	Location of monument	Date of monument
Ambiorix (Eburones)	54 BC	Bronze statue	City square, Tongeren, Belgium	1867
Vercingetorix (Arverni)	52 BC	Bronze statue	Celtic *oppidum* of Alesia (Alise Ste Reine), France	1863–65
Arminius (Cherusci)	AD 9	Bronze statue	Celtic *oppidum* on the Groteburg, Detmold, Germany	1875
Caractacus (Silures)	AD 54	Marble statue	Mansion House, London, England	1856
Boudicea (Iceni)	AD 60/61	Bronze statue	Westminster Bridge, London, England	1871

These monuments share a number of significant features that illustrate the pan-European nature of the nationalist manipulation of the primitive, tribal, essentialist past, part of an invented tradition based on the expedient interpretation of archaeological and textual sources:

- All five monuments commemorate leaders of tribal rebellions against Roman imperialism.
- All five rebellions occurred more or less within a 100-year period of Roman occupation of these territories.
- All five monuments were constructed within a twenty-year period marked by a number of conflicts between the nations erecting them.
- All five monuments are based on very sketchy archaeological and historical evidence. We know next to nothing about the individuals represented, and what we do know comes from hostile (i.e. Roman) sources. The variant spelling of the names (Caractacus/Caratacus; Boudicca/Boudicea/Bodicea; Arminius/Hermann – the second is a nineteenth-century invention, while the first is the kind of name that was given to non-Romans while serving in the Roman army, which

Figure 7.4 Boudicca monument, London (photo: B. Arnold).

Tacitus claims Arminius did – is just one example of the extent of the obscurity that surrounds these national symbols.

- The locations of the monuments are in some cases ironic (the erection of a monument to Boudicca in a city where a destruction horizon known as the "red layer" marks her razing and burning of the original Roman town), in some cases expedient and directly counter to the archaeological evidence (the Hermann monument stands on a Celtic hill fort that has not produced any evidence of Germanic occupation, and recent archaeological investigations place the pivotal battle much further north and west). In other cases, the site is archaeologically associated with the event but culturally ambivalent (for example, the statue of Vercingetorix is located on the site of his eventual defeat by Caesar's invading forces, ushering in the Mediterranean cultural and linguistic traditions that still characterize France today).

- Historical accuracy was not a consideration with respect to costume and accoutrements. Boudicca wears a diaphanous dress that clearly owes more to nineteenth-century English notions of Roman women's clothing than anything an Iron Age woman, let alone a woman warrior, would have worn. The scythes on her chariot's wheels are not documented archaeologically, and although we know quite a bit about Iron Age British horse harnesses, these sources were clearly not consulted by the sculptor. Vercingetorix and Ambiorix sport a mélange of military hardware ranging from the Bronze Age (Vercingetorix' sword) to the mediaeval period, while nothing like Arminius' winged helmet is known from contemporary Germanic contexts. Caractacus is depicted as a heroic nude adorned with some strategically placed classical drapery, a miniature shield, and a battle-axe of mediaeval type.

The "manufactured past" represented by these monuments to Celtic and Germanic tribal leaders is just one manifestation of the cooptation of archaeology and history in the construction of a nationalist cultural identity. There were numerous nineteenth-century "lunatic fringe" organizations in the British Isles that dabbled in one way or another in the (unsystematic) exploration and interpretation of archaeological sites. Stonehenge is probably the best-known manifestation of this phenomenon (Burle 1999; Chippindale 1983), but a more obscure example from Ireland is a bizarre conflation of *Raiders of the Lost Ark*, Freemasonry, and British (English) imperialist attitudes toward the Celtic-speaking minority populations of the Islands. As it happens, Indiana Jones and the Nazis were not the only ones searching for the Ark of the Covenant. Several eighteenth-century sources, among them the writings of Charles Vallancey, make reference to the Hill of Tara in County Meath as the possible final resting place of the Ark. In the late nineteenth century, a London-based group known as the British-Israelites (many of whom were also Freemasons) followed up on these rather obscure hints by mounting a campaign to conduct excavations at the site, starting with the initial proposal to dig on the hill as early as 1875. Since Tara is known to have been the seat of the Irish high kings, and as the spiritual center or heart of Ireland has both historical and symbolic significance for the Irish people, this proposal was opposed by a large number of scholars, literary lights and society figures (including Robert Cochrane, W.B. Yeats, and Maud Gunne; Carew 2003). Opposition to the proposed British-Israelite operation at Tara was due in part to the interest in sites related to the pre-Roman history of the islands that characterized the Celtic/Gaelic revival (Corlett 2003: 42).

British Celtic nationalism in effect combined both Celtic and Germanic cultural patrimony in the construction of a national identity, a particularly striking illustration of the multi-vocality of cultural symbols, especially those derived from the ambiguously polyvalent archaeological record. Initially, the cultural capital represented by images of ancient Britons defending their land against invading Romans provided a powerful morale booster during England's eighteenth-century wars with France, with England's self-proclaimed love of freedom being linked to the Celtic past and the contemporary conflict with France presented as analogous to the earlier struggle against the Romans (Lang 1997: 105). Over time, however, the English turned away from the archaic past as a source for the creation of a national identity, looking instead to their Anglo-Saxon (i.e., "Germanic") heritage. By the mid-nineteenth century, "Saxonism" had replaced the emphasis on Celtic roots, with nationalistic appeals to the Celtic past occur-ring only among the Welsh, Scots, and Irish. This attitude shift has been attributed to England's emergence as an imperial power that was better able to identify with the Roman Empire as well as notions about race that permanently separated "backward" Celts from "advanced" Anglo-Saxons. It is worth pointing out that Hitler's ambivalence about whether or not to attack England was due in part to his belief that the English qualified on the basis of race and cultural affinity as members of the "Germanic" Reich, and that eugenics "experts" in both countries were in regular communication with one another in the post-First World War period.

Our ancestors, ourselves: pseudoarchaeology and nationhood

The archaeologically documented past is an attractive source of symbolic capital precisely because its time depth lends credibility while simultane-ously providing enough ambiguity to support an almost infinite number of interpretations (Arnold 1999, 2002). As Smiles (1994: 38) has put it:

> Such appeals to the archaic past indicate how effective a symbol, because innocuous, the barbarian ancestor could be, redolent of a past so remote as to be either immune from class, religious or party interests or so ambiguous as to allow many different interests to seek confirmation from one and the same source.

This is why the material remains of the Celtic past could be successfully appealed to both by English nationalists and by the Celtic "fringe" attempting to create an identity separate from English domination: "In the rarified world of abstract patriotism Caractacus and Boadicea join Arthur and Alfred not as Celtic chieftains but as patriot heroes, staunch defenders of these islands against the evils that might beset it from outside" (ibid.: 45).

How does Celtic nationalism manifest itself today? For most members of the general public, especially in the United States, the term "Celtic" is automatically associated with Ireland first, followed by Wales, Scotland and Cornwall, and for a much smaller number, Brittany and the Isle of Man. Nationalists in those regions, on the other hand, have begun to use the term "Gaelic nationalism" in order to emphasize language as the primary distinguishing membership criterion for these twenty-first-century imagined communities, intentionally distinguishing themselves not only from the nineteenth-century imperialist British use of the term but also from the continental Celts documented primarily on the basis of archaeological remains. Continental Celtic nationalism, in the meantime, is increasingly becoming associated with the emerging polity of the European Union.[5] Several exhibitions of archaeological finds from across Europe have had "the Celts" as their central theme, at least partly to provide an apparent cultural precedent for the creation of this new socio-political entity. The emphasis in this case has tended to be on a construction of Europe linked by a shared Celtic past, based of necessity on archaeological as well as textual evidence supporting that vision while conveniently ignoring equally compelling evidence for significant temporal and geographical differences. Partly in response to this appropriation of the term "Celtic" by a supra-national entity, it has become *de rigueur* among British archaeologists to question the use of the term "Celtic" in association with the archaeological record of the British Isles (James 1999). Once a cultural symbol loses its essentializing association, it no longer has the qualities necessary to support a nationalist agenda and must be replaced by a new term that emphasizes differences rather than commonalities.

There are parallels between the representation of National Socialist German and Celtic nationalism in popular culture as well. If German National Socialist archaeology as represented by Hollywood has the Indiana Jones trilogy, Celtic nationalism has the blockbuster *Braveheart*, loosely (one could say barely) based on the story of William Wallace as portrayed in the romanticized, nationalistic tearjerker by Jane Porter, *The Scottish Chiefs* (Porter 1866). Interestingly, the parallel between German nationalism and Celtic/Gaelic nationalism is drawn explicitly in a recent critique of the film by Colin McArthur: "Narratives about certain societies – the ante-bellum American South and Nazi Germany spring to mind – seem particularly prone to a mélange of savagery and sentimentality, and narratives about Scotland show something of the same tendency" (1998: 175–6).

The historical accuracy of the film – starring Mel Gibson as the larger-than-life Scottish rebel leader who trounces the English, led by Edward I, at the Battle of Stirling Bridge in 1297, only to be hanged, drawn, and quartered eight years later – is not at issue here. The film does about as good a job of faithfully representing thirteenth-century England and Scotland as *Indiana Jones* does of accurately representing archaeology as a discipline or National Socialist German archaeology as a phenomenon. What is interesting is the response to *Braveheart* in Scotland at a time when calls for a separate parliament were taking on new momentum, since this illustrates the participatory role of the public in the perpetuation and proliferation of pseudo-visions of the past. The expedient use of the past by political systems (it does not matter what kind of past it is, i.e. whether pseudo or backed by archaeological or historical evidence, as long as it supports the political agenda of the moment) is also illustrated particularly neatly by the *Braveheart* phenomenon, as the appropriation of the film by the Scottish National Party (SNP) clearly shows (ibid.: 179). McArthur provides the following excerpt from a speech by the SNP's National Convener, Alex Salmond MP:

> We should be ashamed that it has taken Hollywood to give so many Scots back their history. ... And George [Robertson, Labour MP] and Michael [Forsythe, Conservative Secretary of State for Scotland] should also be worried, because now, as anyone who knows the story and has seen the film will know, the real villains are not the English but the establishment leadership of Scotland who bought and sold their country for personal advancement.
>
> (McArthur 1998: 181)

McArthur's conclusion is telling: "there is a connection between *Braveheart's* debased Romanticism, its post-1789 populist nationalism and xenophobia, and the way it has been appropriated by individuals and institutions in Scotland" (ibid.). Film, fiction, poetry, art, and other media are not in and of themselves "pseudo"-anything. However, they *can* promulgate pseudo-perspectives on persons, things or even concepts (see Chapter 2). In addition, the fact that most nationalist movements make calculated use of the emotional response evoked by such media is proof of their potential vulnerability to manipulation.

The most recent conflation of pseudoarchaeology, neo-paganism, and Celtic Romanticism is the New Age movement, particularly the various neo-pagan traditions that combine many of the elements presented in this essay (Bowman 2002). The anti-establishment attitude of most fringe movements also characterizes this one, with the addition of a Luddite element that emphasizes a distrust of technology and science. It is no coincidence that many neo-pagans are also drawn to various forms of re-enactor groups, including the Society for Creative Anachronism and the denizens of various "Renaissance" festivals in North America and Europe. Living in the past has become a way of life to an unprecedented degree in the West, evolving from a form of upper-class entertainment at the court of Louis the XIV in seventeenth- and eighteenth-century France to a pan-national movement that attracts people from all social classes. As it has been put it in a recent essay:

> In their broadly retrospective and romantic "vision", the exponents of "Celtic Christianity" [and various neo-pagan groups based wholly or in part on a constructed "Celtic" tradition], follow an approach which can be traced through Arnold and Renan and as far back as Macpherson's Ossianic translations of the early 1760s. They also pursue outdated lines of scholarship.
>
> (Meek 2002: 251)

In effect, a "primitivist, alternative culture" has been created "on the Celtic fringe" (ibid.: 252) that is rooted in an earlier scholarly tradition, borrowing freely and indiscriminately from written and archaeological sources and generally unaware of or uninterested in more recent scholarship that has questioned or refuted many of the sources on which the practitioners of these groups rely. Ironically, the marginality of the Celts, which is part of the appeal of this cultural complex for New Age seekers, Christian as well as pagan, is, as Meek points out, "an external and essentially Anglocentric" perspective (ibid.: 253). As in most such invented traditions, the chosen people are described as the first or the only ones to engage in a range of behaviors, including a true symbiosis with nature, an emphasis on simplicity, and a tolerance of religious differences (ibid.: 257–60).

The popular press in most European countries and in the United States has tended to reinforce these assumptions, stressing the piety, simplicity, and moral superiority of these idealized denizens of an imagined Celtic past. A particularly good example is represented by a recent Swiss magazine cover (Figure 7.5), rather ironically titled *Facts* magazine, which shows an artist's conception of a "Celt" of indeterminate gender, although the dagger in the right hand suggests that the individual is intended to be male. The eyes are closed, the arms spread wide in a gesture presumably intended to convey worship; heavy gold bracelets adorn the one wrist that is visible, gold fibulae hold a cloak at the shoulders, and what looks like a gold torque is around the neck. The cover reads: "The Celts: Our Ancestors: Strong, Intelligent, and Pious." The illustration is shown again in the text of the article, but this time more of the scene is visible, and it is clear that the man exhorting the gods is standing in front of a large bonfire or funeral pyre, while an aged individual with beads threaded in his/her hair and wearing an antler headdress is leading?/supervising(?) the proceedings. The article text is typical of the "our ancestors, ourselves" rhetoric that dominates such publications, drawing parallels between life today and life in a reconstructed 2,100-year-old Celtic town, part of a virtual exhibit documenting ongoing excavations in the northern part of the city of Basel in Switzerland. The following description would make most archaeologists cringe:

The only thing missing is the Opel *Astra* [a popular European family car] with a child seat, and the middle class idyll would be complete. The little wooden houses are arranged in tidy rows, low ridges neatly separate the lots, and the fenced in verandas are cozily designed. And there's a dog racing around in the front yard.

(Widmer 2003: 101; translated by author)

Figure 7.5 Cover of the Swiss magazine *Facts* with the headline: "The Celts: Our Ancestors".

Despite periodic disclaimers – the caption of another illustration showing a man and a woman chopping and clearing trees in a downpour states "Hard work: Life back then bore little resemblance to the Celtic kitsch of today" – the article concludes with the sentence "Why go abroad then (to search for the Celts)? Switzerland is a *bona fide* Celtic country" (ibid.: 106).

In a shift that is clearly linked to changing contemporary political config-urations, as continental Europeans have been reclaiming their Celtic pasts, the Celtic-speaking peoples of the British Isles have been rejecting the label, if not the concept. Expedient manipulation of archaeological discoveries and historical records characterizes the reinvention of the Celts in both contexts as well as in North America, in large part apparently motivated by popular interest as much as political advantage: fertile ground, in other words, for producers of pseudoarchaeology and pseudohistory, whose publications litter the New Age sections of most bookstores and who clutter the Internet with spurious sites. What can those of us engaged in serious scholarship do about this, if anything? Engage rather than withdraw, and provide resources and access to information for the interested general public that can be clearly distinguished from the "alternative" sources, on an individual level by presenting public lectures whenever possible, and on a larger scale by making effective use of the Internet, which is increasingly becoming the information source of choice for most people. Pseudoarchaeology may always be traveling with us, but we do not have to let it drive the train.

Notes

1. Among others, Abu el-Haj 2001; Arnold 2002, 2004; Atkinson *et al.* 1996; Ben-Yehuda 1995; Crooke 2000; Diaz-Andreu and Champion 1995; Diaz Santana 2002; Dietler 1994; Galaty 2004; Gathercole and Lowenthal 1989; Graves-Brown *et al.* 1996; Hall 2000; Halle 2002; Härke 2000; Hallote and Joffe 2002; Hamilakis 2002; Haßmann 2002a, 2002b; Jones 1997; Kohl and Fawcett 1995; Kuhnen 2002; Lech 1998; Leube 2002; Meskell 1998; Oestigaard 2002; Reid 2002; Silbermann 1982, 1989; Steuer 2001; Veit 1989.
2. Arnold 1990: 465, 1998: 243; Diaz-Andreu 1996: 48–54; Smiles 1994: 26–45.
3. Among others, Halle 2002; Halle and Schmidt 1999; Haßmann 2002a; Kuhnen 2002; Leube 2002; Steuer 2001; Veit 2002.
4. Belchem 2000; Crooke 2000; Edelstein 1992; Ellis 1998; James 1999; Kidd 1994; Smiles 1994.
5. Arnold 2002: 111; Collis 1996; Dietler 1994: 595–6; Fitzpatrick 1996; James 1999: 11, 19; Shore 1996.

8 Archaeology and the politics of origins

The search for pyramids in Greece

Mary Lefkowitz

If for nothing else, the 1990s will be remembered as a period of resurgent nationalism and ethnic self-assertion. Along with this trend has come a less violent but nonetheless powerful desire to rewrite history in support of new political and social claims (Morris 1996: 172; Howe 1998: 221 n.14). In these attempts to reconstitute the past, there is an insistent effort to claim priority, whether in the process of land acquisition or in the discovery of a cultural advance. As a result, the ancient past has acquired a new relevance.

But in the case of ancient civilizations it is not always easy to discover who was there first or who initiated the great innovations. More often than not, the results of traditional archaeological research are inconclusive, and experts disagree among themselves. Wherever doubts exist, and they are plentiful in the early stages of human history, it is tempting, particularly for amateurs, to develop strategies that help to supplement lost information and construct persuasive narratives. Pseudoarchaeology is one of the most potent of these creative techniques. Its purpose is to set with certainty the priorities that have disappeared over time, to locate the innovators, whether individuals or civilizations, and to seek out and trace the relationships between disparate discoveries and events all over the world.

Pseudoarchaeology has several characteristics that distinguish it from scientific archaeology:

1. Pseudoarchaeology proceeds from the assumption that civilizations, like human beings, have family trees, and that the earlier cultures in effect beget the later. In the case of significant achievements, such as the building of pyramids, it seeks to determine priority with certainty and to proceed from the assumption that every great invention or idea can have occurred only once in human history and is spread or diffused from that one source.
2. Pseudoarchaeologists set out to confirm, rather than to test, a hypothesis. They do not try to account for all the available data but rather to seek out data that support their initial assumptions.
3. Whenever possible, they employ apparently new, previously untested methodologies that appear to give the results they desire.

4. Pseudoarchaeologists are contemptuous or dismissive of traditional methodologies and procedures (unless they conform to their needs).
5. They appeal to the imagination of their readers by suggesting that their findings have a wide application and significance.

For a detailed analysis of pseudoarchaeological "method," see Chapters 1 and 2.

The practice of pseudoarchaeology has its roots in antiquity. According to the fifth-century Greek historian Herodotus, the Egyptians believed that theirs was the oldest civilization. In an attempt to establish their priority, the pharaoh Psammetichus (Psamtek I, 664–610 BC) devised an experiment. He arranged for two infants to be raised in isolation, so that not even the people who fed them spoke to them. After two years, the shepherd who looked after the two children reported that the first intelligible word that they spoke consistently was *bekos*. Psammetichus then inquired which people called something *bekos* and discovered that it was the Phrygian word for bread. As a result of the experiment, Herodotus tells us (at 2.1–4), the Egyptians were compelled to acknowledge that the Phrygians must in fact be older than themselves.

Like many modern researchers, Psammetichus thought that he could answer a complex historical question by a simple experiment, and he did not repeat his experiment in order to see if similar results could be obtained a second or subsequent time. He also assumed that human culture was handed down like real estate or physical property from earlier to later generations. In effect, Psammetichus anticipated by 2,000 years the invention of the hyperdiffusionist model, according to which cultural influence is supposed to proceed in a linear fashion from earlier to later civilizations, so that resemblances between the practices of a later people and those of an earlier people could not possibly be coincidental (Lloyd 1975: 150, 1976: 5). But at least the pharaoh deserves credit for acknowledging that his experiment did not give him the answer that he wanted to hear. A modern pseudoarchaeologist would probably have ignored that experiment in favor of more cooperative data.

The question of priority appears to have been as important for Herodotus himself as it was for Psammetichus, because he chose to use the *bekos* story as a preface for the book that he devotes to a description of Egypt. Because Egypt was an older civilization than that of Greece, Herodotus assumed that many aspects of Greek civilization must inevitably have derived from it. When in the course of his travels he witnessed ritual practices that reminded him of what he had seen in the festivals of Dionysus, he did not suppose that the resemblances could have been purely coincidental but thought that they must have come from Egypt into Greece (2.49). He believed that the names of the Greek gods came from Egypt, because that is "what the Egyptians themselves say" (2.50.1–2). He did not find it remarkable that the Egyptian priests used the same names for the gods as he did, even though in other respects their language was different from his own, because he knew that the

Egyptian civilization was the earlier. So strong was his faith in Egyptian priority that he did not notice that his Egyptian informants were simply using the Greek names that Greek residents in Egypt had already given to the Egyptian gods (Assmann 2000: 32).

The *Black Athena* controversy

Now once again questions have been raised about Egyptian priority, specifically in relation to the civilization of ancient Greece. Were the Greeks the founders of Western civilization, or was it really the Egyptians? The debate about the origins of Greek culture came to the attention of the academic world as a result of the publication of Martin Bernal's *Black Athena* (1987). Bernal argued that classical scholars had tended to downplay or ignore Egyptian and Near Eastern influences on Greek culture because of racial prejudice and cultural arrogance. He cited Herodotus and other ancient Greeks who believed that their religion and some of their laws had derived from those of ancient Egypt and who supposed that some of their important thinkers and philosophers had studied with Egyptian priests. Although he did not say so explicitly, Bernal gave priority to Egypt, rather than to any of the civilizations of the Near East, because he sought to provide the academic credentials for a theory about Egyptian origins that has gained credence for many years among peoples of African descent (Lefkowitz 1996: 20–3). According to this theory, the Greeks had consciously borrowed or had even *stolen* philosophical and scientific knowledge from ancient Egypt. As the author of *Stolen Legacy*, one of the most influential books on the subject states: "the Greeks were not the authors of Greek philosophy, but the Black people of North Africa, the Egyptians" (James 1954: 158).

The "stolen legacy" notion is widely believed in the USA and also in the Francophone world through the writings of Senegalese intellectual Cheikh Anta Diop (Fauvelle-Aymar 2000: 27–46). Bernal and the other proponents of the "stolen legacy" idea did not appear to realize that the notion that Greek philosophy was derived from Egypt has its origins in the mythology behind Masonic initiations, which are in turn based on an anachronistic reconstruction of Egyptian civilization in an eighteenth-century French novel. The author of the novel in question, *Séthos*, was a French priest, Father Jean Terrasson. He described an elaborate Egyptian mystery system whose initiates received philosophical training in what was virtually a university. For a hundred years, *Séthos* was regarded as historically accurate, but after hieroglyphics had been deciphered, it became clear that the Egyptian mystery system portrayed in the novel was fictional (Lefkowitz 1997: 91–154; Hornung 2001: 160–1, 186–7).

Pseudoarchaeology plays a central role in this strange cultural debate, which has more to do with the racial politics of the USA than it does with ancient history (see especially Schmitz 1999: 191–249). To shore up his arguments about the extent of Egyptian influence, Bernal sought to show that the Egyptians had invaded Greece in the third and second millennia BC and that they had left many linguistic and archaeological traces of their occupations behind them. His theories had a remarkable imaginative appeal, because they seemed to offer a means of restoring to Africa, at least intellectually, some of what Europe had taken away from it in the course of the slave trade. It was less apparent at the time when the second volume of *Black Athena* was published (Bernal 1991) how much in common his work had with that of other practitioners of armchair archaeology, such as Sigmund Freud in *Moses and Monotheism* or Immanuel Velikovsky in *Oedipus and Akhenaton*.

Instinctively, perhaps, Bernal drew on some of the strategies employed by pseudoarchaeologists:

- He proceeded from the assumption that ideas and practices flow in one direction only, from the earlier civilization to the later, rather than back and forth, and he had a tendency to interpret influence as a sign of borrowing.

- He had an explicit goal in undertaking his research: "to lessen European cultural arrogance" (Bernal 1987: 73).

- However, unlike Freud and Velikovsky, Bernal did not turn to the world of science to find support for his theories but rather revived methodologies from the past that traditional scholars had long since discarded. Like Herodotus before him, Bernal based his theories on the few myths and mythological genealogies that connected Greece to Egypt and on analogies between Greek and Egyptian words that sounded somewhat alike. But after Egyptian hieroglyphs had been deciphered, and it became possible to read what the ancient Egyptians said about themselves, rather than to see them through Greek eyes, scholars realized that much of what the ancients had seen as connections between ancient Egyptian and Greek civilizations had been based on misunderstanding (Lefkowitz 1996: 14–15). Traditional archaeologists had long since tried to distinguish critically between myth and history, and linguists had already catalogued the relatively few loan words that had made their way in historical times from Egyptian into ancient Greek. Since Egyptian and Greek belong to different language families, they do not otherwise share a common vocabulary (Jasanoff and Nussbaum 1996: 179–80; Jasanoff 1997: 57–68).

- Perhaps because so little factual evidence could be garnered to support his theories, Bernal devoted much of his energy to encouraging his readers to distrust the work of traditional ancient world scholarship. He spoke contemptuously of the connection of Greek to the Indo-European language family as "the Aryan hypothesis," thus indirectly linking it with the racist theories of the Nazis. The characterization was doubly misleading. First, there is no doubt about the existence of an Indo-European language family, even though there will always be some uncertainty about the exact nature of proto-Indo-European, the parent language from which the known languages derived. Second, linguists no longer believe that proto-Indo-European originated in India among the Aryans, or worshippers of the Brahmanic gods in India. Rather, it may first have been spoken somewhere in the area of the Black Sea (Hoenigswald and Woodard 2004: 535).

• Bernal characterized his approach to ancient history as a "paradigm shift" in thought, using, misleadingly, a term that Thomas Kuhn had applied to *scientific* revolutions (Baines 1996: 42). He argued that reconstruction or narrative of ancient history must always be conjectural and based on models. These narratives could be judged on the basis of "competitive plausibility," that is, whatever gave the most credible or acceptable result. Bernal himself did not discuss the obvious limitations of his methodology, which derive from its subjectivity: who determines what is credible or acceptable? What if someone else came along with a different but equally plausible reconstruction? Who would vote on the outcome, and whose vote would count?

Bernal was able to elicit sympathy for his arguments about scholarly prejudice and historical constructions because of his stated motives. Now, however, it seems remarkable that Bernal's attempts at reconstructions should have been taken as seriously as they were, even by students of the ancient world. The notion that facts are in effect only opinions and that history is a form of fiction has now been discredited (see especially Haack 1997: 57–63; Evans 1997: 190–1, 210–20; Fernández-Armesto 1997: 203–29; Williams 2002: 231–58). But at the time it seemed exhilarating and liberating to suppose that scholars had been prevented from seeing the truth by the social prejudices of the time.

No scholars of the ancient world were persuaded by Bernal's theory of Egyptian invasions of Greece in the third millennium BC and during the time of the fifteenth dynasty in Egypt, when the Hyksos overlords were in power (1674–1566 BC). The theory was primarily based on Bernal's notion of "competitive plausibility." Bernal did not in fact conduct any new investigations or excavations but drew on what he could find in books. Many of his arguments relied heavily on myth. For example, he suggested that the elaborate irrigation systems used in Boeotia and Egyptian works on the Nile *might have* inspired the Greek myths about Heracles controlling large bodies of water. Heracles' ancestors had connections with Egypt, through Io, who had settled there, and her great-great-grandson Danaus, who returned from Egypt to Argos in Greece with his fifty daughters.

Bernal seemed to believe that ancient writers, because they were ancient, had an accurate knowledge of their history. So he accepted their accounts at face value. He believed (Bernal 1991: 124–8) the story told by Plutarch in the second century AD about the so-called tomb of Alcmene (Plut. *Mor.* 577F). In the fourth century BC, the Spartans found a bronze inscription at

Thebes "with many remarkable characters, probably very ancient; the appearance of the characters was distinctive and foreign, most like Egyptian characters." Agesilaus, the king of Sparta, sent for Conouphis of Memphis, an Egyptian who was believed in Plutarch's time (second century AD) to have taught the astronomer Eudoxus and to have known Plato and other Greeks (Gwyn Griffiths 1970: 285–7). After studying the inscription for several days, Conouphis said that it dated back to the days of when Proteus was king, and Heracles had learned the script (Plut. *Mor.* 578F–79A).

Unfortunately for Bernal's argument, the tomb and the inscription have disappeared, if they ever existed in the first place (Tritle 1996: 306–7). Conouphis, despite his genuine Egyptian name (Gwyn Griffiths 1970: 285–7), may be a character from historical fiction. The connection of this monument to Alcmene, the mother of Heracles, is certainly fictional, a product of folk tradition of a much later date. There are many other examples of ruined buildings in Greece that have acquired mythic histories that have little or nothing to do with their original time or purpose. The stone where Homer is supposed to have taught his disciples (the so-called *daskalopetra*) on the island of Chios is in fact a ruined shrine of the goddess Cybele, built hundreds of years after the poet's death (Barber 1995: 693). The inhabitants of the village of Pityos in the north of the same island direct visitors to the house of Homer (Haniotis 1971: 173), even though the ruins identified as the poet's house are at most only a few hundred years old.

In order to support his theory of an Egyptian invasion of Greece, Bernal managed to find two examples of that most characteristic of all Egyptian structures, the pyramid: the Menelaion in Laconia and the so-called tomb of Amphion and Zethus in Thebes. The pyramid at the Menelaion in Laconia was, in his opinion, particularly significant, because it was the Spartan "national" shrine. He argued that the presence of a pyramid at that site showed that the Spartans consciously connected their ancestry through Heracles to Egypt. The failure of traditional scholars to point that out, he argued, was a prime example of the flaws in the "Aryan" model of the history of Greece (Bernal 1987: 53–4). Bernal promised to discuss the Menelaion at greater length in chapter VI of volume II of *Black Athena*. In practice, however, he neglected to do so, without explaining why. Had he discovered that the Menelaion, the sanctuary of Helen and Menelaos, was not after all a true Egyptian pyramid? It is in fact only "a sort of small stepped pyramid, built up round a spur of rock," dating at the earliest to the second half of the seventh century BC (Pendlebury 1930: 47). In *Black Athena Writes Back*, Bernal asserts that the Spartans used the pyramid form because they believed in "their Heraklid 'Syrian or Egyptian' descent" (Bernal 2001: 99). That is certainly possible, but in the absence of any explicit ancient evidence about what the Spartan kings may have thought about Heracles, it may make more sense to assume that the pyramid form was chosen in imitation of the great Egyptian pyramid tombs, or simply because terracing was well suited to the top of a hill.

The other structure cited by Bernal as evidence of an Egyptian invasion also turns out not to be a real pyramid. This is the so-called tomb of Amphion and Zethus near Thebes, a prehistoric structure that was identified in historic times with the mythological twin sons of Zeus who were said to have built the walls of Thebes. Greek archaeologist Theodore Spyropoulos excavated this tomb in 1971–3 and identified the structure as a step-pyramid or ziggurat built in the third millennium BC. By that time, the Egyptians had stopped building step-pyramids, but (as Bernal argues) the builders of the tomb may have been following an older fashion. Bernal notes that although most archaeologists have not been persuaded by Spyropoulos' arguments, they may have been motivated by anti-Egyptian sentiments. Why had "Aryanists" classified the tomb as a *kurgan* or type of burial mound found to the north of Greece, in south Russia and the Balkans if not to promote the Indo-European character of Greek culture (Bernal 1991: 124, 128–33)? But in fact the reason why most archaeologists believe that the tomb is an ordinary burial mound similar to those found throughout Greece has less to do with politics than with physical reality. The mound appears to be more pyramidal in shape than it was in antiquity, because the hill has been cut away in modern times. It is much smaller than any Egyptian pyramid, or indeed than any of the Etruscan mound tombs at Cerveteri. Nothing in the structure suggests any parallels with Egyptian burials (Tritle 1996: 321–3).

That there are no Egyptian pyramids in Greece should not surprise anyone who has some knowledge of Egyptian and Greek history and civilization. Why should the Egyptians have chosen to invade Greece, since the Greeks were not troubling them and had no natural resources to offer them? There is no reference to any such invasion in the Egyptians' own extensive records, although there was continuous trade with Greece in both earlier and later periods (Coleman 1996: 281–5). It is possible that the monumental buildings at Mycenae and Tiryns, and in particular the great *tholos* tombs, may have been inspired, directly or indirectly, by the pyramids (Matton 1966: 48–9). But even in those cases there is a marked difference of architectural style and scale, which can be accounted for by differences in religious attitude between the two cultures. The Egyptians believed in an afterlife and so devoted great energy to the preparation of tombs and the preservation of bodies. Their government was highly centralized, and great importance was attached to the welfare of their pharaoh. The Greeks had a more practical attitude toward burial and imagined that only the insubstantial souls of the dead survived the grave. Well into historical times they lived in independent city-states, and until their conquest by Philip of Macedon in the fourth century BC, the Greeks never had a single ruler.

From Egypt to Greece

Nonetheless, as students of ancient art may be surprised to discover, there are in fact remains of structures in Greece that have been called pyramids. I first learned about these buildings not from archaeologists but on a radio talk show in 1997. I was speaking over a telephone hook-up on the Armstrong Williams show with Richard Poe, the author of *Black Spark, White Fire*, a book that argues that Greek civilization was inspired by an African ancient Egypt (Poe 1997). Poe thinks that the Egyptian influences occurred naturally, and that Egyptian ideas were absorbed rather than stolen by the Greeks. When he claimed that a decisive argument in favor of his theory was the presence of pyramids in Argos, I expressed some doubt about his statement. At that point, my connection to the radio station was cut off. Had I questioned Poe's veracity too sharply? I thought I knew what I was talking about. In all my many visits to the city of Argos and the Argolid, I had never seen any pyramids.

I later discovered that Poe most likely had in mind two buildings that receive minimal notice even in the more detailed guidebooks. In fact, until the 1990s, and the renaissance of the debate about Egyptian influence, these structures had been of interest only to archaeologists and military historians. Archaeologists had sought to identify these unusual structures with two build- ings that the second-century AD traveler Pausanias had seen during his visit to the Argolid. On his way from Argos to Epidaurus, "on the right" (that is, south) of the road before one comes to Tiryns, Pausanias says that "there is a building that closely resembles a pyramid (*pyramidi malista eikasmenon*), which has carved upon it shields of the Argolic type" (2. 25.7). He was told that it was the common tomb (*polyandria*) of the soldiers who died in the battle between the legendary brothers Acrisius and Proitus for the throne of Argos (Apollodorus, *The Library*, 2.2.1). If in fact the building had been constructed for that purpose, it would have been erected four generations before the Trojan War, around the end of the fourteenth century BC. The other building that Pausanias saw was of a considerably later date. He was told that the "pyramid" at Kenchreai, to the southwest of Argos, was the common tomb (*polyandria*) of the Argives who were killed in the battle between Sparta and Argos at the Argive city of Hysiai in 669/8 BC (2. 24.7).

In his commentary on Pausanias, Sir James Frazer describes a building "commonly known" as the pyramid at Kenchreai, not far from the Erasinos River, with masonry in a style somewhere between Cyclopean and polygonal (Frazer 1913: II 213). He also saw an "ancient pyramid" with polygonal masonry at Lessa, on the way to Epidauros, but regarded it as a different building from the pyramid decorated with shields that Pausanias had seen near Tiryns (ibid.: II 232–3). Frazer notes that some scholars of his day thought that these pyramids, because they were found in Argos, provided confirmation of the legend that Danaos had come there from Egypt with his daughters. Frazer notes that according to Plutarch (*Pyrrhos* 32.9), Danaos landed with his daughters at a place called Pyramia when he came to the Argolid to escape from Egypt (Frazer 1913: II 214).

So Poe was justified in saying that there had been buildings like pyra- mids in the Argolid, even if there were none specifically in the city of Argos, and even though there is no indication that either of them had been built by Egyptians. In the last few years, Poe has apparently discovered the existence of additional pyramids: "A number of pyramids dot the Greek landscape to this day, structures of great antiquity and mysterious origin" (*www.richardpoe.com*). Why had none of my archaeologist friends ever mentioned them to me in connection with the *Black Athena* controversy, or beforehand? Bernal would almost certainly insist that the reason in both cases was political. In his view, no classicist would wish to acknowledge that there was any connection between Egypt and Greece. But there is another explanation, far less interesting from the point of view of motive but almost certainly the true one: archaeologists had long since discovered that the pyramidal buildings in Greece did not have much in common, either in form or in function, with the pyramids in Egypt.

Let us begin with the two "pyramids" that Pausanias saw in the Argolid. Neither, so far as we know, is still standing. The pyramid that served as a common tomb for the soldiers killed at the Battle of Hysiai was at ancient Kenchreai (see Figures 8.1 and 8.2). That town lies twelve miles southwest of the pyramidal building that stands today at Helleniko near the fountain of Kephalari on the Erasinos River (Pritchett 1980: 67–8; Fracchia 1985: 685; Simpson 1965; Figure 8.2). The pyramid decorated with shields that served as a common tomb for the soldiers killed in the war between Proitus and Acrisius was located somewhere near Tiryns. The ruins of a pyramidal

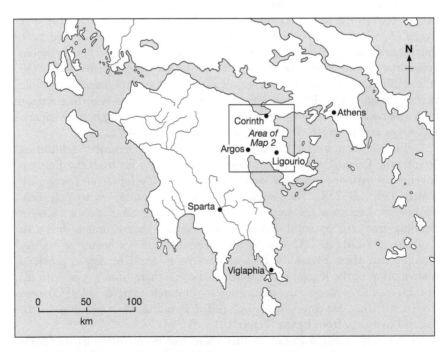

Figure 8.1 Map of Greece (drawn by B. Nelson).

building can still be found not far from Ligourio at the site of ancient Lessa, twenty miles to the east of Tiryns, to the north (that is, to the *lefthand* side) of the ancient road from Argos to Epidauros, but no trace of the buildings that Pausanias saw remains; the artistic merit of the pyramid with shields may have made it particularly vulnerable (Pritchett 1980: 70). So we will never know how closely they resembled any of the pyramids of Egypt.

Pausanias says nothing about the two pyramidal buildings that have survived at Helleniko and Ligourio (Figures 8.3 and 8.4). Aside from their inwardly sloping walls, these two buildings bear no great resemblance, either in size, masonry, or function, to any of the pyramids of Egypt. Egyptian pyramids were tombs for pharaohs and members of their families and courts, but the Argolid buildings could never have been used for burials. They have large central rooms and are much less solid than pyramids that were designed to be used as tombs (Figure 8.5). They are much smaller than the smallest Egyptian pyramids, such as that of the eighth-dynasty

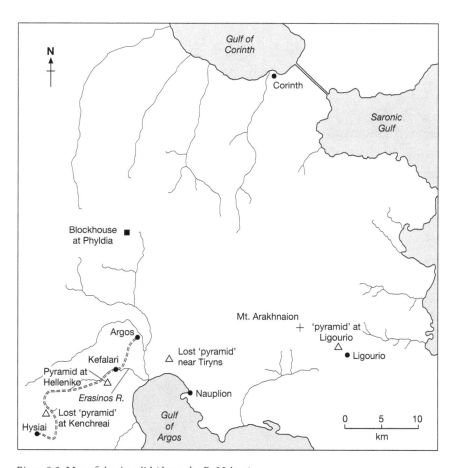

Figure 8.2 Map of the Argolid (drawn by B. Nelson).

pharaoh Ibi, the base of which is 31.5 meters (most pyramids are much larger; Lehner 1997: 17; see Figure 8.6). In fact, the sides of the Helleniko pyramid are so steeply inclined that they would have intersected before they could have formed a structure that resembled a pyramid. The floor plan of the structure is in any case rectangular rather than square (approx. 12.5 ×

Figure 8.3 The "pyramid" at Helleniko (photo: A. Macres).

Figure 8.4 Remains of the "pyramid" at Ligourio (photo: A. Macres).

14 m; McAllister 1976: 445; Tomlinson 1972: 35–6). So the sloping sides could never have come together in a point, as they would on a square pyramid.

Both the Helleniko and Ligourio pyramids were excavated scientifically in August 1937 by archaeologists from the American School of Classical Studies in Athens. The excavators found that both buildings were situated

Figure 8.5 The large central room of the "pyramid" at Helleniko (photo: A. Macres).

in the countryside, in a valley; each had walls roughly 10 meters in length. Each was built with local stones, which were not shaped into uniform rectangular blocks but rather were cut along their sides so as to fit together. Since that "polygonal" style of masonry was commonly used in the fourth century BC, the excavators dated the stone structures to that period. The archaeologists' findings were published in *Hesperia* in 1938 by one of the investigating archaeologists, Louis E. Lord (1875–1957), under the title "The 'Pyramids' of Argolis" (Lord 1938: 481–527).

However, Lord and his colleagues did not find any evidence that the two pyramids, or the structure of similar size without sloping walls in Phyktia near Nemea, could ever have been tombs. No indications of any burial were found in any of the buildings. Their doors fastened from the *inside* (ibid.: 527). No pottery remains excavated from beneath the floors of the "pyramids" dated to a time earlier than the late fifth century BC (Scranton 1938: 528–38). None of the Egyptian objects listed in Pendlebury's catalogue were found in these buildings (Pendlebury 1930). A fragment of an inscription found in the Ligourio pyramid dates from the late fourth century BC (Scranton 1938: 537). In 1941, archaeologists completed the excavation of a pit in the Ligourio pyramid and found no potsherds dating to a time earlier than the fourth century BC (Frantz and Roebuck 1941: 112). Neither building could have been used as a watchtower, because their situations do not offer sweeping views of the surrounding areas. Fragments of pottery, coins, and fragments of inscriptions found in the "pyramids" suggest that the structures were reoccupied in the Hellenistic and Roman periods (Scranton 1938: 528–38).

In August 1939, Lord investigated the remains of three other slightly smaller buildings in the same region, each built using polygonal masonry.

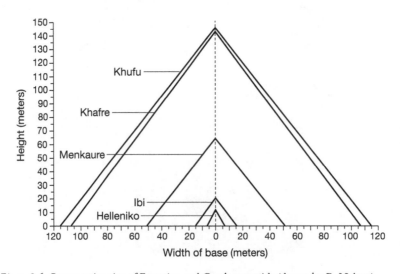

Figure 8.6 Comparative size of Egyptian and Greek pyramids (drawn by B. Nelson).

These he took to be "blockhouses" or stations along ancient roads that had been used as control points during times of invasion or political upheaval (Lord 1941: 93–109). There was considerable chaos in the countryside in the 360s BC and again in 351 (Tomlinson 1972: 143). As a result of his investigation of the buildings in the 1970s, Mark Munn suggested that they had been constructed with sloping walls in order to accommodate ladders or stairs along the offset of the walls, leading to higher stories made of brick and wood (Munn 1983: 333). Although from time to time they may have been used as fortifications, Munn argued that the Argolid buildings might also have been used for storage of water or of large amounts of liquid, such as olive oil, or for storage of dry goods. Circumstantial evidence led him to believe that they were multipurpose farm towers, privately constructed and owned (Munn 1982: 278, 1983: 334–5).

Munn's conclusions were supported by an investigation undertaken in 1982–3 by Helena Fracchia of a "pyramid" near Viglaphia on the coast of southern Laconia (see Figure 8.1). This structure had been identified by Pausanias as the tomb of Kinados, one of Menelaus' steersmen (3.22.10). If that had been its true function, it would date from the twelfth century BC, the time of the Trojan War. However, it is even more likely that the building was associated with local legends about Menelaus, because later generations did not quite know exactly what it was, like the tomb of Alcmene in Thebes or the house of Homer on Chios described above. Fracchia's investigation showed that like the "pyramids" in the Argolid, the Viglaphia building was not a perfect square and was relatively small (17.5 × 16 m); nor had it ever been used as a tomb. Pottery remains dated no earlier than the fourth century BC. Like the Argolid pyramids, it is located on a hill in a valley, without a wide outlook, has a door facing east, and provisions for water storage.

Fracchia also conducted a survey of the pottery remains at the Argolid pyramids and confirmed that they dated from *c.* 350 BC onwards. She found close analogues to the three Greek "pyramids" in the Crimea, where there are pyramidal towers dating to the fourth–third centuries BC on ancient farms (e.g., Dufkova and Pecirka 1970: 145–6). These rural structures may have been used for storage and production, as well as for occasional housing of workers (Fracchia 1985: 683–9). Christos Piteros investigated the buildings at Helleniko and Ligourio again in 1995; he concluded that in both structures the walls of the ground floor inclined inward "for stability reasons" and that each supported a second or third story (now lost) made of mud-dried brick (Piteros 1998: 372). Analogues can still be found in Greece from the Byzantine era (ibid.: 351).

So Poe's assertion about the presence of Egyptian pyramids in Argos proved after all to be misleading. The "pyramids that dot the landscape in Greece" are in fact few and far between, and in any case they are not real pyramids. It is true that none of the so-called pyramids can be dated with precision, because no ancient source mentions them. Archaeologists have used pottery remains and masonry style to determine the probable time of their original construction. In so doing, they have relied on criteria for dating that are based on knowledge accumulated and re-evaluated by many different specialists over many years. Admittedly, however, this method of dating buildings and discovering their probable use is based on analogy rather than absolute certainty.

From Greece to Egypt

Caution on the part of archaeologists can be mistaken for hesitation, and natural reluctance on the part of archaeologists to make final pronouncements can be understood as a sign of uncertainty. The temptation to question supposedly subjective criteria such as style becomes greater when researchers want to use archaeological remains to confirm a particular theory, especially when politics of some kind are involved. The methodology of conventional archaeology is unromantic in the extreme; surely it is much more interesting and exciting to think of the structure at Helleniko as a pyramid than as a multipurpose farm tower.

Here is where parascientific research and pseudoarchaeology come into play, especially when investigators are eager to assign originality to a particular civilization. As we have seen, such archaeology is characterized by its rejection (often on cultural or moral grounds) of traditional methodologies, and a desire to use myth as history, or to assume that history, especially if inconvenient, is no more accurate than myth. Whenever possible, pseudoarchaeologists will come up with new, previously untested, methodologies, and seek to impress their audience with an array of specific technical data.

Inevitably, perhaps, a Hellenocentric theory arose to counter the Afrocentric theory that Bernal and Poe sought to support. According to the new theory, the Greeks invented the pyramid form, which was later adopted and developed by the Egyptians. In 1992, a study of the dating and significance of the Argolid pyramids was undertaken under the auspices of the Academy of Athens, the results of which were later published in their *Proceedings* (Theocaris and Veis 1995). In this article, academician Pericles Theocaris, in collaboration with Georgios Veis, described how they had used thermoluminescence (TL) in surface layers from the stones to determine the dates of the two Argolid pyramids. In the past, the TL method had been employed primarily to distinguish ancient pottery from modern fakes, but the authors suggested that the same technique could be used to date limestone blocks, since they too would have been exposed to sunlight during the course of construction. According to their calculations, the pyramid at Helleniko could be dated to 3240 ±640 BC and the one at Ligourio to 2520 ±680 BC. The article described in detail how the TL experiments had been conducted. A site survey was undertaken as well, using magnetic and electromagnetic measurements. The authors compared the Argolid pyramids with similar buildings in Egypt and Anatolia dating to the third and second millennia BC, using advanced structural techniques; they also mentioned the pyramidal edifices found near Thebes and in Stylidha (Stylis) in Phthiotis.

In support of their argument, the authors reconstructed the ancient road from Argos to Epidaurus so that Pausanias might have seen the Helleniko pyramid on his right, rather than on his left, on his way to Tiryns. That way, it was possible for them to identify the Helleniko pyramid with the pyramid with shields that Pausanias believed to be the tomb of the soldiers killed in the battle between Proitus and Acrisius, the traditional date of which fitted in with their proposed TL dating. The shields on the Ligourio pyramid (which they dated to the second millennium BC) were supposedly an indication of connections with the other civilizations in the eastern Mediterranean that had also begun to use shields at the same time. They remarked on the close relationship between the Egyptians, Hittites, and "proto-Greeks" during that period of history. Detailed measurements undertaken by the authors showed another possible link to Egypt. The axis along which the two Argolid pyramids lie is virtually the same parallel as the azimuth of the dog star, Sirius (Sothis or Sopdet in Egyptian) at the time of its heliacal rising (*c.* 19 July) during the periods of their respective construction (Theocaris and Veis 1995: 232–4). The heliacal rising of Sothis (that is, the time when the star's rising is closest to that of the Sun) was important in the Egyptian calendar because it coincided with the annual inundation of the Nile. The dates of the Sothic cycles (2781–77 and 1321–17 BC) are fundamental in Egyptian chronological records and in establishing the chronology of the Mediterranean region (Shaw and Nicholson 1995: 42, 276).

Two more articles about the TL were published in English-language journals, with further details and rather more conservative conclusions. An article by Theocaris in collaboration with Ioannis Liritzis and Robert Galloway of the University of Edinburgh suggested rather later dates of 2730 ±720 BC for the Helleniko pyramid and 2260 ±710 BC for the Ligourio pyramid. They also used TL to determine the date of a Mycenaean wall and found it to be reasonably accurate (Theocaris *et al.* 1997: 399–405; Hammond 1997a: 18). The TL dating indicated that the Argolid pyramids were roughly coeval with the pyramids in Egypt.

A second article provided further control data by using TL methodology to determine a date for the foundation wall on the western side of the polygonal retaining wall beneath the Temple of Apollo at Delphi. Using scrapings from a piece of marble from an inter-block surface, they arrived at a date of 420 ±300 BC, which corresponds roughly to the known archaeological age of the foundation wall (550 BC). They reached the conservative conclusion that although TL dating had too large a margin of error to be used to date architectural structures precisely, it was still helpful "in differentiating between periods of construction that are far apart, or revising established views based on typology of finds or masonry of the structure"

(Liritzis *et al.* 1997: 479–96). In his summary of the work undertaken by Liritzis and his colleagues, Norman Hammond, writing as the archaeological correspondent of *The Times*, suggested that the TL method had promise: "This newly developed chronicle of sunlight may well illuminate unexpected corners of the past" (Hammond 1997b: 24).

Nonetheless, questions remain about the reliability of the new methodology. In the case of the Argolid buildings, the research appeared to have been undertaken in order to establish an early date for these buildings rather than to determine the reliability of TL dating in general. If Theocaris, Veis, Liritzis, and Galloway had begun by first using TL on buildings of known date to establish a baseline and had then applied their techniques to the unusual buildings in the Argolid, their research might have appeared to be more objective. But as it was, their initial experiment was not blind or double blind, and control data were supplied only later. Why had they picked these particular buildings to examine? Why not also examine the building with polygonal walls at Phyktia, which Lord had investigated along with the two pyramids? Theocaris and Veis indicate in the first paragraph of the academy paper that they chose the structures at Helleniko and Ligourio because they were *pyramids*. As such, they had particular valence in the current controversy about the origins of Greek civilization

There were other problems as well. The TL dating, as the researchers admitted, was only very approximate: a methodology that is accurate within ±200–750 years can only serve as a rough guide. The other pyramidal structures they mention do not support their argument. As we have seen, the so-called tomb of Amphion and Zethus near Thebes is not a pyramid. The only surviving ancient structure at Stylidha in Thessaly is not a pyramid but rather a long wall made of large rectangular and trapezoidal blocks (MacKay 1976: 697). The wall has some inclined stones, but these are upward-slanting "jogs" used to accommodate the rising terrain (Lawrence 1979: 351–2). Since the structure at Helleniko could not have been the pyramid that Pausanias saw near Tiryns, it had no known association with the Mycenaean period and could not have been the tomb for the soldiers slain in the mythical war between the brothers Proitus and Acrisius.

Then there is the question of how the samples for TL dating had been selected. In each case, the stones used in constructing the pyramids might have been recycled from earlier buildings; if such stones were not exposed to light in the course of a later reconstruction, they would endow the newer version of the building with a greater antiquity than it was entitled to. In any case, even if more experiments were undertaken, and the TL dating turned out to be a helpful determinant of date, that still would not prove that the two structures in Argos are pyramids, or that they had any connection with the Egyptians. It is in fact not particularly significant that the Argolid buildings appeared to be oriented in relation to the axes of the azimuth of the star Sirius or Sothis at the time of its heliacal rising. The Egyptians measured time by the rising of Sothis but used sightings of the constellation of Orion (Sah, the consort of the goddess Sothis or Sopdet) for the orientation of pyramids and sun temples, at least in the early part of the third millennium. Orion is the focus of the "air shafts" in the Great Pyramid, perhaps because it is the intended goal of the *ba* or soul of the pharaoh (Shaw and Nicholson 1995: 234). The Egyptian pyramids in general are aligned with the cardinal points of the compass, as determined by sightings of the Great Bear (north) and Orion (south) constellations (ibid.: 42; Lehner 1997: 106, 212). In fact, the Argolid "pyramids" are not so precisely sited; the building at Ligourio lies at an almost 45° angle to the cardinal points of the compass (Lord 1938: 33, 39).

Aside from these questions about the ways in which the researchers made use of the scientific data that they collected, it is possible to discern in their Academy of Athens report (Theocaris and Veis 1995) some affinities with the work of pseudoarchaeologists. Why did they not attempt to make clearer distinctions between myth and history? Why did they disregard the work of prior archaeologists in the late 1930s, which had been verified in the 1980s by the independent investigators Munn and Fracchia? Was it not at least misleading to say that "no other excavation or dating work was undertaken until 1992," when the academy-sponsored researchers began their inquiry (Theocaris *et al.* 1997: 399)? Ignoring the work of previous researchers perhaps does not quite amount to outright contempt for traditional scholarship (#4, page 181), but their research was undertaken to confirm a theory (#2). They employed a novel and previously untested scientific methodology (#3), and they appealed to the imagination of their readers (#5) in supposing that the Argolid pyramids had some meaningful connection with astronomy and religion.

Despite these obvious problems with the research undertaken by Theocaris, Liritzis, and their colleagues, the two long-neglected Argolid pyramids suddenly acquired a political significance. An article about the academy-sponsored project had appeared in a Greek newspaper in 1992, and in 1994 the popular journal *Davlos* ("Torch") published an article about the Helleniko and Ligourio buildings, with photographs, measurements, and diagrams showing how they could be reconstructed as pyramids. The author of the article, Vasileos Katsiadramis, argued that the pyramid near Helleniko had been used as a *heroon*, or shrine for a hero, and that its small size, in contrast to the large size of its Egyptian counterparts, could be explained by the nature of Greek religion, which reserved the greatest honors for god rather than man, in contrast to the tribute paid to human pharaohs by the Egyptians. In its Greek manifestation, the pyramid form was superior to that of its Egyptian counterparts in its restraint and modesty. The tombs, in his opinion, provide silent testimony to true ancient history that had long been ignored (Katsiadramis 1994: 9215–36).

Katsiadramis' article looked scientific, with its lists of measurements and geometrical reconstructions and its citations of ancient sources. More extravagant claims about the priority and importance of Greek pyramids were made in two accompanying articles. The first of these, by Panagiotis Hatziioannou, claimed that twenty-six pyramids are scattered throughout Greece and asserted that the "pyramid" on the peak of Mt Taygetos was comparable to the Great Pyramid of Egypt. He cited the opinion of scholars and academicians that the Greek pyramids antedated the Egyptian pyramids by 1,200 years. He argued that pyramids are geometrical constructions, that Pythagoras invented geometry, and that the first-century BC geographer Strabo explained how to determine the circumference of the Earth by means of an arithmetical formula (2.5.3–4). Hatziioannou offered further "proof" from symbolism and language: the pyramid form has a mystical meaning in Orphism and in the Greek mysteries; the word "pyramid" derives from *pyr* (fire), which means light and fire and sun in ancient Greek; the corresponding Egyptian word is *khouti* or *khoufu* (Hatziioannou 1994: 9216–24).

The other short article cited Pausanias' descriptions of the two pyramids that he saw in the Argolid and provided background information about the feud between Proitus and Acrisius. Its author, Diamantis Koutoulas, also noted that Pausanias' testimony was confirmed by a statement in Diodorus Siculus that the legendary King Minos of Crete built a pyramid as a tomb for himself as well as the famous labyrinth (1.89.3; Koutoulas 1994: 9233).

In fact, none of the arguments produced by these three authors did much to support the case for the priority of the Greek pyramids, at least among archaeologists. Hatziioannou mentioned only in passing the TL study that had been sponsored by the Academy of Athens, since the results had not yet been published. The notion that the top of Mt Taygetos was a pyramid appeared to be a fantasy; the conical shape of the peak is the result of a natural phenomenon (Lazos 1995: 114). In any case, it would have been impossible to build a pyramid on a mountaintop using the technology available during the third or second millennium BC. The three *Davlos* authors approached the ancient sources with a naive confidence in their reliability. They did not doubt that the pyramid tomb of Minos mentioned by Diodorus had actually existed. They did not consult any of the scholarly work that had been done on Diodorus' historical technique and his uncritical approach to local legends. They did not ask whether Acrisius' grandson, the hero Perseus, had literally been the founder of Mycenae. They did not question the veracity of Plato's account of Atlantis, which is almost certainly a complete fiction (Nesselrath 2002: 42). They made no attempt to distinguish myth from history.

Another problem was that the *Davlos* authors (and Theocaris, Liritzis, *et al.*) had ignored the work on the pyramids and similar buildings undertaken by Lord and other scholars. They did not seem to realize that the buildings at Helleniko and Ligourio could not have been the two pyramids mentioned by Pausanias. They also did not take advantage of the available etymological dictionaries. How had Hatziionannou managed not to discover that the word *pyramis* has nothing to do with light? The *y* in the root of the ancient Greek word for fire, *pyr-* is short, not long as in *pyramis*, which is cognate with ancient Greek *pyros* (wheat). The geometrical structure was in fact named after a kind of wheat cake (Chantraine 1984: II 958; Shaw and Nicholson 1995: 233). Khoufu or Khufu, the pharaoh whom the Greeks called Cheops (2551–2528 BC), is the builder of the Great Pyramid (Lehner 1997: 108–9). His name has nothing to do with light; rather, it is an abbreviation of the phrase *Khnum-kuefui* ("Khnum [the ram-god] protects me"; Shaw and Nicholson 1995: 152).

In 1995, historian Christos Lazos published a much more sober and objective discussion of the pyramid question. He reviewed all the reports about the pyramids and provided in appendices excerpts from the articles by Lord and Scranton and those of the Academy of Athens researchers. But while he expressed some real doubts about the theories of the Hellenocentrists, he noted that there was constant communication between the Egyptians and the Greeks, and he suggested that no final determination could be made until new diagnostic measures were discovered (Lazos 1995: 128).

It was certainly true that the chronology of the *Davlos* articles was so shaky that their arguments could equally well have been used to bolster the Afrocentric theory of Egyptian priority. No doubt it was these articles, or some report of them, that were the ultimate source for Poe's statement about pyramids dotting the landscape of Greece (Poe's wife is a Greek-American who has "multitudinous social and professional contacts in the Greek community"; Poe 1997: xx).

When professional archaeologists objected to the earlier dating proposed by the TL researchers, *Davlos* writers responded with contempt, characteristic #4 of the strategies employed by pseudoarchaeologists. Traditional archaeologists, they alleged, were blindly adhering to the dogma of "light from the East." Ancient myths and texts supported the TL dating and the priority of the Greek pyramids; human civilization began not in the Near East, as claimed in the Old Testament, but in Greece (Koubalakis 1996a: 10355, 1996b: 10417–20). When archaeologist G.A. Pikoulas argued against the TL theory of dating (Pikoulas 1996: 60–3), Katsiadramis, the author of the first *Davlos* article about the Argolid pyramids, responded by accusing him of childishness (1996: 10873–81). Katsiadramis presented trajectory calculations to show that such a tower would have been inadequate for defense with the kinds of weapon that were in use during the Hellenistic era. He claimed that Pikoulas' reconstruction of the Helleniko pyramid as the base of a fourth-century tower was reminiscent of a construction with a child's Lego™ blocks. Ridicule can be an effective tool, but I know from my own experience that demonizing an opponent is a device most often employed when better arguments are not available. Poe, for example, claims that my objection to the Afrocentric "stolen legacy" notion derives from adherence to orthodoxy: "how far our universities have drifted from the Greek ideal – the very ideal Lefkowitz purports to defend" (Poe 1997: xiv). Perhaps Katsiadramis was not aware that the remains of such towers still exist in Greece (Lawrence 1979: 189–91; Ober 1985: 130–80). There is a fourth-century tower, with walls that slant inward, still standing on the island of Kea (Kazamiakis 2003: 24–7).

In 1998, archaeologist Christos Piteros published a very careful new report on the Argolid pyramids, with new photographs. He reviewed the articles by Theocaris, Liritzis and their colleagues and concluded that (1) their chronology was unacceptable because it was based on an experimental methodology that had not been sufficiently tested; (2) there was no archaeological record of pyramids in the Argolid in the Mycenaean era; (3) the masonry of the walls of the two structures was not Mycenaean; (4) no Mycenaean pottery was found in the two Argolid "pyramids"; (5) the comparison with Egyptian pyramids was misleading, because of structural differences; and (6) there is no real doubt about the dating of the structures to the fourth century BC. He pointed out that the Helleniko pyramid could not have been the same building that Pausanias saw on his way from Argos to Epidaurus, as the academy researchers had mistakenly supposed (Piteros 1998: 369–71).

Nonetheless, at least as far as I can determine, the arguments and evidence adduced by experienced archaeologists like Piteros has in no way dampened the enthusiasm of the Hellenocentrists. No new evidence from TL dating has been adduced; instead, there seems to be an increased reliance on evidence from mythology, the possible significance of astronomical measurements, and astrology. In 1997 (too late for Piteros to have discussed it in his 1998 article), Liritzis published a popular book about the two Argolid pyramids, based on his earlier work. Once again, he does not try to show why the findings of Lord and other archaeologists should be disregarded, and he again asserts that the sites were not investigated during the period 1938–91, despite the work of Munn and Fracchia. Instead, he defends and develops the Hellenocentric interpretation of the two "pyramids." Again he brings up the argument that the presence of shields on the pyramid at Ligourio help to place it the third millennium BC, but without acknowledging that the Ligourio structure cannot have been the same building near Tiryns that Pausanias saw, which was supposed to have been the tomb of the men killed in the battle between Arcisius and Proitus.

In the book, however, Liritzis makes a new suggestion about the orientation of the two Argolid "pyramids." Using measurements and charts, he argues that the long corridors in the two Argolid buildings are aligned in relation to the belt of the Orion constellation and suggests that this orientation explicitly connects them with the Egyptian pyramids. He claims that this connection is acknowledged in the Greek myths, which preserve a record of the settlement of Argos under Inachus and of his descendants' subsequent settlement in Egypt, and finally of the return of Danaus (the great-grandfather of Proitus and Acrisius) to Argos. Liritzis acknowledges that the Ligourio pyramid is not aligned with the heliacal rising of Orion but rather with the stars in the belt of Orion during the period between the fall equinox and the winter solstice. This new alignment for the Ligourio pyramid makes it conform with the highly eccentric "Orion correlation theory" proposed by Robert Bauval, who argued that the pyramids at Giza were oriented with the stars in Orion's belt (Liritzis 1998: 162). As if in confirmation of the significance of this revised siting for the Ligourio pyramid, Liritzis cites passages from Hesiod to show that for early Greek farmers the setting of Orion (*c.* 4 November) was a good time to plow their fields (*Works and Days* 615; West 1978: 312). But since the setting of the Pleiades and Orion can be seen with the naked eye, there is no reason, either practical or mythological, why they should have sited their buildings in order to track or represent the movements of these stars.

In 2001, Koutoulas published an article about the so-called tomb of Amphion and Zethus, based on Spyropoulos' earlier work, dating it to 2500–2000 BC. The article also suggested that the tomb has a particular astronomical orientation, facing east towards the constellation Taurus. That orientation in itself is significant, Koutoulas argues, because Taurus has a connection with the ancient settlement of Thebes: Zeus took the form of a bull when he abducted Europa, the sister of Kadmus, the founder of Thebes (Koutoulas 2001: 23). This suggestion is a perfect example of strategy #5 of pseudoarchaeology, which encourages readers to make imaginative leaps that enable us to connect everything with something significant, and with the deeper meaning of the universe, while ignoring the much more realistic possibility that the siting of the "tomb of Amphion and Zethus" had no particular significance, either in relation to the stars or to anything else. In the world of pseudoarchaeology, the possibility of meaninglessness or coincidence is unacceptable. The reference to Europa and the bull is in fact irrelevant to the question of the astronomical orientation of the tomb. Rather, it is a conjuring trick that lends to Koutoulas' argument a sense of completeness and solidity, like the many measurements cited in the other Hellenocentric materials, or far-fetched etymologies.

Ultimately, what drives the search to find the builders of the first pyramids is more than a desire to be the first inventor of something great. Behind it also lies suspicion, an envy that does not easily allow that other nationalities or ethnicities might have had the ability to do something remarkable. Similarly, behind the desire to show that philosophy was invented in Egypt we can find a deep resentment of the acclaim that has for so many centuries been lavished on the ancient Greeks by people of European descent. The yearning is so strong that it overrides the absence of evidence. It allows intelligent people to support the "stolen legacy" proposal and encourages them readily to accept speculative "proofs," such as those provided by pseudoarchaeology. As Michael Shermer has said about leading Afrocentrist writer Y.A.A. ben-Jochannan: "He takes a valid point about the influence of ideology on knowledge, stirs in the ignorance or apathy of an audience about historical events, adds a few historical facts and a series of eccentric inferences about the past, and makes pseudohistory" (Shermer 1997: 35).

Hellenocentrists resort to the same tactics. Their desire to show that Greeks invented pyramids is fueled by resentment of the Afrocentrists' attempt to deny the Greeks the credit for the achievements of their ancestors. In this case as well, the desire for priority is so compelling that it encourages the use of speculative dating procedures and reliance on mythologies and even on coincidences.

It should go without saying that both parties would be better served by the search for the truth, wherever it might take them. Does it really matter who invented the pyramid, when undeniably the greatest examples of the genre in the Mediterranean area are to be found in Egypt? On the other hand, why try to insist that the Egyptians invented philosophy or invaded Greece when it is clear from what they wrote that they had other interests? I do not believe that the two pyramidical buildings in the Argolid can tell us anything about either Egypt or Greece that we do not already know from other contexts. I am sure that they would have remained obscure had it not been for the politics of the debate about the origins of the Greek achievement.

If at some time in the future thermoluminescence or some other new dating system, once thoroughly tested, can show that the Argolid "pyramids" should be dated to an earlier period, we should all be prepared to reconsider the question of what these buildings are and why they were constructed. Even if the walls of the Helleniko structure could be assigned with confidence to the middle of the third millennium, a much more accurate method than TL would be needed to show that they predated the construction of the Great Pyramid in Egypt. In any case, we should remember that these are not the pyramid-like buildings that Pausanias saw, and that aside from their inwardly slanting walls there is nothing specific to connect them with Egypt. But until a real reason is found to revise their dating, on the basis of the information now available there is no reason to disregard or dismiss the work of archaeologists since 1937 that identifies the Argolid structures as fourth-century multipurpose farm towers. This determination of their function deprives the "pyramids" of their drama and significance, but, unlike pseudoarchaeology, at least it reflects our best-informed understanding of what happened in the past.

Acknowledgments

My thanks to Professors S. Iakovidis, David Jordan, Joshua Katz, John Morgan, and Mark Munn for essential advice; to Mr I. Kotoulas for his help in obtaining materials needed to write this article; and to Mr D.I. Lambrou, the publisher of *Davlos*, for kindly sending me copies of the articles in his magazine. The photographs were taken by Dr A. Makres, and the maps and chart were designed by Bill Nelson.

9 Rama's realm

Indocentric rewritings of early South Asian archaeology and history[1]

Michael Witzel

Was Ihr den Geist der Zeiten heisst,
  das ist im Grund der Herren eigner Geist.

(Goethe, *Faust*)

Introduction

India is witnessing a wave of indigenously minded revision and rewriting of its archaeology and history that manifests itself at all levels of society: in scholarly publications, in the press, on the Internet, and in government publications, policy statements, and administrative actions. This includes "patriotic" and increasingly nationalistic reinterpretations of the (early) history of the subcontinent, re-evaluations of past attempts to write that history, and fantastic descriptions of lost littoral lands or whole continents, or of great rivers with early advanced civilizations. It is further claimed that all human civilization originated in India in *c*. 10,000 BC, that Indian civilization has enjoyed an unbroken continuity from 7500 BC onward, and that Indo-European-speaking Europe was peopled from the Gangetic plains. This alarming revisionist trend cannot be evaluated properly without briefly reviewing a historical heritage that reaches back 200 years.[2]

Indian nationalism and revisionism

Various kinds of indigenous rewriting of South Asian history have been attempted since the late nineteenth century as a reaction to colonialism. While the early British conquests in Bengal and the neighboring regions in the eighteenth century did not produce many intellectual repercussions, by *c*. 1820 a reaction had set in, exacerbated by the introduction of English as the language of administration over local languages like Persian and Sanskrit. The early movements include societies such as the Calcutta-based Brahmo Samaj (founded in the 1820s) and the Punjab-based Arya Samaj (founded by Dayanand Sarasvati in the 1870s), both of which were largely religious in outlook and aimed at a reform of contemporary Hinduism (Bergunder 2002: 135). Sarasvati, in his *The Light of Truth* (1915), laid the foundation for current irrational claims of "modern science in the Vedas," that is, in the most ancient religious texts of India (composed *c.* 1500–500 BC). Other pioneers included the nationalistically minded monk Vivekananda (Harder 2003: 90; Bergunder 2002: 172), who stressed that the spiritualism of India was the country's unique gift to the whole world and that all of India must unite under Hinduism,[3] and Aurobindo's idiosyncretic, spiritual reinterpretation of the Veda, coupled with a strongly nationalistic view of Indian religion's superiority.[4]

In the 1920s, revisionism intensified as the movement for India's independence from Britain gained momentum. The two most prominent figures in the contemporary formulation of this more politically oriented Hindu nationalism were Golwalkar (1906–73) and Savarkar (1883–1966). They and their teachings are of great importance for the topic under review in this paper.

In *We, or the Nationhood Redefined*, Golwalkar (1939) denies any immigration of the "Aryans" into the subcontinent, as had been advocated by European linguists and historians since the later part of the nineteenth century. By "Aryans," most people in India understood and still understand these to be speakers of the ancient Indo-European languages Vedic, Sanskrit, and Prakrit, and modern Indo-Aryan (IA) languages such as Hindi, Marathi, and Bengali. Sometimes "Aryans" is understood to refer to all Hindus or Indians.[5] Golwalkar (ibid.: 8) stresses that the Hindus have always been the indigenous "children of the soil," terminology clearly reminiscent of contemporary fascism (*Blut und Boden*, see below). Savarkar (1969: 1) offers a religious and cultural definition of Hindu-ness, which he calls *Hindutva*.[6] His goal is an independent Hindu nation-state, inhabited by a homogeneous Hindu population adhering to Hindu religion and culture. No Aryan invasion or immigration into the primordial and perennial Hindu fatherland was ever possible. His definition has different components: territorial, political, nationalistic (Hindu realm, *hindurastra*), ancestral (children of the fatherland[7] with roots in the Hindu or Aryan "race," *jati*), cultural (Sanskrit-based Hindu culture), and religious (followers of Hinduism[8]). In sum, "a Hindu means a person who regards the land of Bharatvarsha (the Indian subcontinent) from the Indus to the seas, as his Fatherland as well as his Holyland" (Savarkar 1969: 1; Michaels 2003: 14). This definition contains factors of inclusion as well as exclusion: non-Hindus, such as Muslims (and Christians), cannot be proper Indians unless they are "Hindu Muslims," that is, Hindu by culture and Muslim by religion. Conversely, all Indian non-Christians and non-Muslims are automatically counted as Hindus, even the aboriginal tribal populations. Unification is thus achieved by exclusion and incorporation: a unified, continual Indian ("Hindu") identity, based on Aryahood and "Aryan" beliefs, is timeless in India and has formed all of its history (Thapar 1992: 23). Many long to regain this primordial age of bliss, the golden age of god Rama's realm (*ram raj*).

These revisionist ideas were more or less at the margin of post-independence India under the internationally and socially oriented Nehru–Gandhi governments. But since about 1980 a remarkable shift has taken place. In many areas, the change has been visible as a shift from the center-left (in India called Marxists) to the political right, marked by religious themes, and generally, a more nationalistic (*Hindutva*) outlook. In the investigation of the Indian past, this was spearheaded by an unlikely figure, Zoroastrian (Parsi) K.D. Sethna (1980), who has been living at the neo-Hindu *ashram* of Aurobindo in Pondicherry since his student days. He is highly regarded by all that see themselves as the "rewriters of history." Some critics (Bergunder 2002; Bryant 2002) have characterized him as a cool, detached writer, distant from the trench warfare of the right and left. However, this is not exactly the case (see below).

The spread of revisionist ideas was furthered by such publishers as the late S.R. Goel[9] (1921–2003), with his heavily subsidized firm Voice of India, and his son, P.K. Goel, with his firm Aditya Prakashan,[10] where most of the revisionists are published. Their books are sold cheap, some via outlets in the USA, especially in Houston. It is important to note that such publications are avidly read by the rich and influential Indian diaspora in the USA and elsewhere, where they have helped to shape a nostalgic and romantic view of a homeland left long ago for brighter and greener shores. In India, too, such views have made steady inroads among professors, teachers, and the general public (Bryant 2001, 2002) in spite of vigorous public dissent on the part of the Indian Historical Congress (IHC) in its annual meetings, e.g. Mahadevan's presidential lecture (Mahadevan 2002).

The revisionists' guild also includes a number of scholars and writers who do not openly espouse the *Hindutva* line. However, as we will see, the Golwalkar–Savarkar tenets have now sunk so deeply into the public, political, and even scholarly discourse that their fundamental principles ("one realm, one people, one culture") appear regularly, even if sometimes in an imperfect and unconscious fashion. Such scholars include the Indo-Europeanist S.S. Misra (1992, 1999; cf. Witzel 2001b), and the archaeologists S.R. Rao (1981) and B.B. Lal[11] (1997, 2002a, 2002b, 2003). In recent times, the latter has come out very clearly in public speeches against the "Aryan invasion."

By the mid-1990s, all this had turned into a "cottage industry" (Witzel 2001a), where a slew of authors copy and refer to each other while churning out one book after another that are often difficult to trace as they are published in obscure outlets. A wide range of authors is represented, from astrologers and bank clerks to professional archaeologists. Almost all are without any professional background in the fields they write about (Bergunder 2002: 169). They all have their own peculiarities, hobby horses, and deficiencies; however, there is not the space here to go into specifics.[12] The matter has come to a head with the recent increase in popular support for nationalistic parties (BJP),[13] which have played the *Hindutva* card and were in power 1998/9–2004. During that period, India witnessed increasing government support for rewriting history in the *Hindutva* mold and using archaeology in the furtherance of this goal (Panikkar 2001). This process included rewriting school textbooks; reordering and redescribing the National Museum in New Delhi; introducing "traditional sciences" such as astrology and "Vedic mathematics" into university curricula; large-scale reshuffles of scholarly boards, with the replacement of "Marxists" by *Hindutva* devotees; support for "imaginative" archaeology (along the Sarasvati, in the Gulf of Cambay, see below); aborting publication of or banning certain books; and a whole slew of other projects that will be discussed later in this paper.

Theory, procedure, and practice in rewriting

In this section, some of the concepts of *Hindutva* are examined as they appear in the works of recent rewriters of history and the *Hindutvavadins*, the followers of *Hindutva*. Our focus is on how the rewriters proceed in their investigations and what their methods are – whether they acknowledged them or not.

Recalling Savarkar's concept of "Fatherland" and the idea that "Aryans" and Hinduism are autochthonous, any type of *ancient* immigration into the subcontinent is refuted "scientifically":[14] if people had indeed moved into India, it was only invaders such as the Greeks, Muslims, and British. In support of the idea of South Asia being an attraction to outsiders, any imaginable reason is brought up, such as India being a country where it was "nice" to live (Misra 1992: 100). Conversely, Afghanistan, too, is regarded as a former Hindu territory,[15] just because some statues of Buddhist or Hindu deities have been found there that clearly belong to the Buddhist mission in Central Asia.

Everything that goes against the unity of "India" – in prehistoric(!) and historical times – is regarded as an effusion of British *divide et impera* politics and their version of history, and all ancient or more recent linguistic and cultural dividing lines are overlooked.[16] In sum, Indian history, as we have it now, is declared a product of colonial Indology (Chakrabarti 1997; Bergunder and Das 2002: 10; Hock 2002). As Frawley (1994: 4) puts it, the persons perpetuating this mistaken interpretation are the academic historians (on the Aryan/Dravidian dividing line) and all those who follow Marxist tenets based on the Aryan immigration theory ("caste instead of class fight").

It is common to all revisionists that they want to proceed "scientifically," marshalling a host of evidence that seems to point in the direction of their aims. The preponderance of such evidence – usually at variance with mainstream results and theories – is then depicted as initiating a Kuhnian "paradigm shift" in the understanding of Indian history (Witzel 2001a: 25, 72, 75). In other words, the rewriters believe that they are at the forefront of scholarship, while scholars in the mainstream are seen as clinging to hold-out positions, which will disappear as soon as their authors die.

Another important point is the debating style of the revisionists. While investigating at length the themes they have selected, they use a traditional scholastic debating style in confronting critics, against whom they wish to "score points." They use the methods of traditional Indian[17] or European debate, such as quoting antiquated and recent "authorities" on an equal footing,[18] confusing the issue by raising irrelevant points, misrepresenting others' views, *ad hominem* attacks, and so on, and then draw the conclusion that they have "won" the debate. However, the revisionists are often limited in their mastery of the subjects they discuss (see below), lack a general perspective, and, most importantly, fail to carry out the required counter-checks that might test the validity of their theories. Nevertheless, they invariably congratulate themselves that they have "won" the argument in question and then draw large-scale, "paradigm-shifting" conclusions from this "victory."

A few examples illustrate their techniques. The revisionists' way of "winning" arguments takes strange forms. They quote, nineteenth-century style, any "authority" they can get hold of to bolster their claims, quite often irrespective of the progress made over intervening centuries. They frequently use outdated statements and juxtapose them with more recent ones to show that a *non*-revisionist view is not tenable. As an illustration, we may use a critical issue for the revisionist view: the first importation of horses from the steppes into South Asia around 1800 BC (Meadow 1998, 2002). Revisionists must champion the presence of horses in South Asia much earlier, since the Veda (*c.* 1500–500 BC), which the revisionists want to date to *before* the Indus civilization (2600–1900 BC), is full of horses, chariots, and horse races, but the Indus civilization was *not*.[19] Specialists in the fields concerned (palaeontology, zoology) would quickly point out that the revisionists' claims are usually spurious and false. A "seventeen-ribbed horse" is mentioned in the oldest Indian text, the Rigveda (RV).[20] The revisionists claim that this was an indigenous descendant of the early *Equus sivalensis*, which developed 2.6 million years ago and had died out by *c.* 10,000 BC. In making this claim, they overlook that to have seventeen pairs of ribs is an individual, not a generic aberration among the domesticated (steppe) horses (*Equus caballus*), which usually have eighteen pairs of ribs (Witzel 2001a: 60, with n. 184).

The revisionists are habitually misinformed and peddle half-truths. Many archaeologists who have claimed to have found horse bones in the Indus civilization are not palaeontologists and can hardly judge the bones they find – if indeed they preserve them at all. The decision about what type of equid (horse, half-ass, or donkey) has been found to rest on a few phalanges, since the half-ass, the indigenous onager of South Asia, has virtually the same skeleton as the horse (Meadow 1998). Revisionist evidence is usually questionable, debatable, or inconclusive. Any four-legged animal must be a horse (Lal 2003), even though it may as well be an onager. For example, they ignore that parts of skeletons can "travel" through archaeological layers:

smaller bones (such as phalanges or teeth) are easily carried through rat holes and thus can appear at levels that may precede the date of the animal in question by hundreds, even thousand of years. Unless reconfirmed by other methods such as carbon-14 dating, such stray finds remain dubious.

However, the rewriters assemble all such "scientifically proven" cases ("archaeology has found horses"), argue from the "preponderance" of opinion (of archaeologists, not palaeontologists), and then criticize those mainstream authors (palaeontologists) who argue against their new "theories" (e.g., Meadow and Patel on horses) as being "isolated," using "incomplete" evidence, or worse, being "colonialists" and even "Hindu haters."[21]

As should be implicit in the foregoing, the revisionists habitually employ special pleading. They leave out all contradictory evidence or, if it is brought to their attention, they spirit it away by creating secondary or tertiary arguments and auxiliary, *ad hoc* assumptions that satisfy only the author in question and his[22] loyal followers but not the scientists to whom they are supposed to be addressed. All such "new data" are then used to insist that we are about to experience a "paradigm shift" (cf. Witzel 2001a: 25, 72, 75).

In sum, revisionist procedure remains *scholastic*, resting on the *auctoritas* of selected scholars and sacred texts, and on sophistic discussion methods, going back to a long tradition of point-by-point rebuttal in pandit-like discussions meant to destroy the adversary (who may quite literally lose his head; Witzel 1987). Nevertheless, revisionist views and theories (such as those of Sethna, examined next) have been accepted as the new "irrefutable" truth by patriotic, nationalistic, and chauvinistic elements and are debated endlessly in the various Internet forums (such as the so-called "Indian Civilization" Yahoo! forum). They are also making constant inroads among otherwise respected specialists (see below).

K.D. Sethna's work

As a case study, we may examine more closely the work of K.D. Sethna, a recent revisionist. Sethna is even classified by some Western scholars as balanced and scholarly, and he is regarded by rewriters and nationalists alike as their great model, a *Bhisma Mahapita* (the revered "grandfather" Bhisma of the Mahabharata). Sethna, by birth a Zoroastrian (Parsi, born 1904), earned a BA and then went on to stay at a religious institution, the Aurobindo *ashram* in Pondicherry. This is his only tertiary qualification. His voluminous books deal with various aspects of prehistoric India and include much material discussed in an outwardly rational fashion, without overt signs of nationalism or chauvinism. However, even a brief glance at his work reveals serious basic flaws.

In his study of cotton (*Karpasa*, 1981), Sethna is surprised to note that this material is not found all over the Vedic texts (roughly, *c*. 1500–500 BC), except in some late Vedic *sutra* texts. He cannot imagine that cotton, which has been found by archaeologists in the Indus (Harappan) civilization, would not be mentioned in the supposedly earlier Vedas. It is, after all, an all-important item of daily use in the hot and humid climate of the subcontinent. He draws a simple conclusion: if cotton is not mentioned in the Vedas, they must be *older* than the first archaeologically attested use of cotton cloth in the Indus civilization (2600–1900 BC). In short, we get the sequence: the Vedas before 2600 BC, then the Indus civilization in *c*. 2600–1900 BC, then the post-Indus civilizations until Candragupta Maurya (321–297 BC), whom Sethna redates to *c*. 900 BC (see below). Sethna's scenario is immediately contradicted by the archaeological situation before 2600 BC.

Before 2600 BC, there were only small *agricultural* communities in South Asia. This changed with the widespread integration caused by the emergence, *c*. 2600 BC, of the primarily agriculture-and trade-oriented Indus civilization. It covered most of Pakistan, northwest India and Gujarat; and it had a network of large cities, which disappeared during the collapse in *c*. 1900 BC. Conversely, the horse-and chariot-rich Vedic texts are characterized by small tribal units of late Bronze Age *pastoralists* roaming around the Punjab (Witzel 2001a) that must be dated *after* 1900 BC, given the invention of the spoked-wheeled chariot around 2000 BC and the importation of the first domesticated horses into South Asia by *c*. 1800 BC.

As is typical of the revisionists' unilateral approach to history (ibid.), Sethna does not ask *why* cotton is not mentioned in the early Vedic texts. This is not difficult to imagine. The Vedic texts deal mostly with ritual, which is always very conservative. In the Rigveda, woolen garments are preferred due to the cold winters of the Punjab and even in Delhi. Sethna has also not checked up on other types of cloth (see Rau 1971). What Vedic people wore "at home" is quite another matter that can only be reconstructed fragmentarily. Every sensible "Aryan" would rather wear cotton than wool in the Indian summer. However, the various types of evidence from the texts are not discussed. Sethna's argument remains unilateral.[23] Worse, his conclusion is based on a typical *ex nihilo* argument: "cotton it is not mentioned, therefore the Vedic people did not yet have it." This procedure has been ridiculed, e.g. in Indo-European studies, as "the Indo-Europeans had only four fingers" as one cannot reconstruct the names of all five fingers. Needless to say, none of these counterpoints is found in the post-Sethna writings of the revisionists.

Sethna's procedure is further exemplified by his elaborate redating of the well-established Maurya (*c*. 321–50 BC) and Gupta (AD 320–*c*. 500) dynasties of northern India (Sethna 2000). In contrast to Vedic dates, this is a case that can easily be counter-checked by sources outside India. Sethna wonders about Candragupta Maurya (*c*. 321–297 BC) and Candragupta Gupta (*c*. AD 320–335) and assumes that it is the Gupta and not the Maurya king that is to be dated to the period of Alexander's successors. This idea is based on a number of quite involved arguments that cannot be replicated here in detail.[24] In Sethna's view, Candragupta Gupta (AD 320–335) reigned around 300 BC, and Candragupta Maurya (321–297 BC) preceded him by 600 years. But Candragupta Maurya's grandson, the famous emperor Asoka (*c.* 268–232 BC), was in contact, according to his own inscriptions, with Western kings called Tulamaya, the *yona-raja* ("Greek king") Antiyoka, Maga, and Alikasudara. These kings have traditionally been taken as Ptolemy of Egypt (285–247 BC), Antiochos of Syria and Iran (260–246 BC), Magas of Cyrene (306–258 BC), and Alexander of Epirus (272–*c.* 260 BC), all successors of Alexander the Great, who had died in 323 BC. All of them, taken together, establish a time bracket of *c.* 285–239 BC, which neatly overlaps with the "traditional" BC date of Asoka (268–232 BC) and which closely follows that of Candragupta (321–297 BC) and his son Bindusara (Greek: Amitrokhates).

However, Sethna is unperturbed. He explains that Tulamaya and the others could be kings that reigned west of the Mauryan empire, or even that they were non-Greek kings or "Iranized" Greek magnates settled in the East. However, this typical *special pleading* by secondary explanation, which spirits away the consistent evidence of the Greek and Indian texts, cannot be maintained; on the contrary, the whole revisionist scenario can easily be discarded even on *intra*-Indian evidence. Asoka's inscriptions are written in early Brahmi and Kharosthi script, and the version at Kandahar (southern Afghanistan) even in Greek and Aramaic. These two local languages were used by Asoka instead of Indian dialects, since Aramaic had been the administrative language of the Persian empire (*c.* 558–330 BC), and, obviously, Greek was that of the immigrants settled by Alexander in various parts of his realm. One must wonder how both languages and scripts could have been used in eastern Iran by Sethna's "early Candragupta Maurya" in *c.* 900 BC, particularly in forms of both language and script that are *centuries later* than those of early Greek and Aramaic attested anywhere else "at 900 BC" – a date, indeed, for which we have no Greek scripts at all. In addition, Brahmi and Kharosthi have been derived, directly and indirectly, from the imperial Persian form of the Aramaic script, current in the sixth to fourth centuries BC. There simply cannot be any Asokan Brahmi and Kharosthi in 900 BC. In addition, Candragupta Gupta's inscriptions (AD 320 onwards) are in a late, post-Brahmi form of the script that simply cannot be dated to 300 BC.

In sum, Sethna argues, like so many of the rewriters, along unilateral lines and completely disregards the extensive surrounding web of evidence and reasoning that contradicts his arguments. His methods are identical to those of the out-and-out fringe writers in archaeology, who argue untenable or even risible positions about the ancient past (see Chapter 1). Nevertheless, Sethna's work has been hailed as "logical" and "scientific" by nationalistic revisionists in India and also by some in the West. Sethna's unilateral constructions obviously clash with the established dates, which are supported by a web of extra-and intra-Indian evidence. However, the matter is endlessly discussed in follow-up books of the rewriters' guild and on nationalistic websites – usually by leaving out the counter-evidence.

The attitude emerging from Sethna's "objective" and "scientific" research is in fact typical of the whole rewriting group. He and his followers use "logical" arguments, but they usually confine themselves to unilateral issues (e.g., "no cotton attested, therefore not yet known"), and they neglect the evidence that would put their arguments into perspective (e.g., the Vedas cannot be before 2600 BC but must be *post* 2000 BC because of chariots and horses, impossible before *c.* 1800 BC). Therefore, one must wonder why such work has been called scientific (Bergunder 2002: 169; Bryant 2002). At best, it represents just the first, exploratory part of an argument – the proposal of "new evidence," but it lacks the necessary secondary step, the discussion of *all* known facts in an attempt to set the new proposition into a web of reasoning. In sum, it remains spurious and unilateral, it is contradicted by established facts, and it falls prey to Occam's razor. In the end, even if Sethna does not say so openly, he is clearly driven by the idea of establishing the "correct history" of an ancient unified Indian realm (the Savarkar–Golwalkar *mantra*), a history that in his view had been distorted, in the nineteenth and twentieth centuries, by British historians and Indologists alike, who insisted on an "Aryan invasion."

The Aryan invasion

The idea is now widespread that Indian history, as we know it, is nothing but the product of colonial (and, more recently, of "Marxist") efforts and that it was sustained by "colonial Indology" (thus the programmatic title of a polemical book by the Cambridge-based Indian archaeologist Chakrabarti, *Colonial Indology: Sociopolitics of the Ancient Indian Past*).[25] According to the revisionists, the whole scholarly field of Indology, which emerged in the late eighteenth and early nineteenth centuries (i.e., before British dominance of most of India was firmly established), is seriously tainted, if not worthy of outright rejection, especially the insistence on an early "Aryan invasion" of India around 1500 BC.[26] It is only to be expected that some British writers wrote from the point of view of empire. Obviously, such writing had to be overcome. Some nationalist Indian writers, before and after independence, had already tried to do so (note especially the voluminous *History of the Indian People* by the Bharatiya Vidya Bhavan [Majumdar 1951]). Historian Romila Thapar (1996), too, insists on the need for revision, but of both colonial and nationalistic historiography. Kulke and Rothermund (1998a, 1998b), Witzel (2003a), and Thapar herself (2002) have now provided such exercises.[27]

Recalling Savarkar's "unity principle," the revisionists observe that the Vedic "Aryan invasion" and that of the British were regarded as similar by some of the (British) historians of the late nineteenth and early twentieth centuries (Hock 2002: 233). In both cases, a "white race" was seen as subduing the local darker-skinned population, and this was used as a prop for British imperialism. That agenda was often neatly reciprocated by the conviction among some in the Indian upper classes (Brahmin and Ksatriya) that they were the "relatives" of the dominant British "Ksatriyas." Though usually misrepresented by the revisionists, present-day Western scholars have no reason to support such old theories or to defend the various turns that nineteenth-and early twentieth-century scholarship took.

The rewriters see their suspicions confirmed by the "Aryan invasion theory" postulating an *external* origin for the leading sections of the "Aryans," as well as for their language, poetry, religion, and social structure. The theory was developed in the latter part of the nineteenth century, when the Hunnic, Germanic and Slavic invasions of Western Europe were being studied and when scholars (notably the Leipzig *Junggrammatiker* school) realized that proto-Indo-European was quite different from Vedic Sanskrit and that it reflected a temperate climate. The deduction was that Sanskrit was not the mother language, just an older sister of other ancient Indo-European tongues such as Greek, and that tropical India could not have been the homeland of the Indo-European languages, as had been assumed earlier.

Curiously, the older "British, colonial" writing of history is often refuted by the revisionists using facets of postcolonial theory.[28] The rewriters tend to use any piece of writing or evidence that seems to sustain their claims, such as the critiques of Inden (1990) and Chakrabarti (1997).[29] Conversely, the rewriters take little notice of advances made in more recent decades. As Thapar (1989, 1992, 1996) points out, the hermeneutic foundations of revisionism are stuck in the categories of the nineteenth century. Max Müller (who died in 1900) and other nineteenth-century persons figure prominently.[30] In fact, the revisionists like to see the world in stark contrast: on the one side, archaeologists, historians, and Indologists, whom they like to denounce as the "5 M's" (Müller, Macauley, Marxists, missionaries, and mullahs), and righteous Hindu rewriters on the other. The current rejection of all earlier ("colonialist") and current ("Marxist") writing of Indian history is most vocal on the various Internet forums ("Indian Civilization, Rediff," etc.[31]), usually characterized by the familiar unilateral, spurious arguments.

The proper evaluation of historical and archaeological data is not helped by the postmodern stance of some writers, who disregard the fact that certain results of the natural sciences, archaeology, and philology are well beyond current fashionable doubt and are not just replaceable hypotheses.[32] The revisionists use such postmodern fashion to their advantage and maintain that traditional humanities do not deal with *facts* but with *opinions*, which can be accepted or discarded at will. They have a new "grand project" in mind that would rewrite Indian history. Recalling the Savarkar–Golwakar principle of the hoary unity of the Hindu realm, people, and religion, they insist that Indian civilization has been "damaged" by centuries of Muslim and British rule while conveniently forgetting that large areas of the subcontinent, such as Nepal, Rajasthan, and much of South India, were never part of Muslim realms or of British India but were governed according to Hindu (or, in the case of Hyderabad, Muslim) predilections.[33] The

Maharaja of Baroda, for example, instituted reforms in the religious field. The case of the continuously independent and very conservative Hindu kingdom of Nepal is especially instructive, but it is never mentioned by the revisionists in this context. Their rejection of colonial history focuses especially on what the revisionists call the "Aryan invasion theory" (AIT).[34]

The AIT of a hundred years ago postulated "light-skinned," IA-speaking, nomadic cattle herders who came through the northwestern passes from Central Asia or Europe, and who enjoyed the military advantage of chariotry and iron weapons. The invaders subdued the "dark skinned," Dravidian-speaking local populations of farmers and hunter-gatherers and imposed their "Aryan" language, religion, and culture on the aboriginals. After the discovery of the Indus civilization in the early 1920s, with its large-scale, well-planned cities and sophisticated technology, this scenario was expanded. Now the "Dravidian" Indus cities were destroyed by Aryan marauders. The last British director-general of Indian archaeology, R.E.M. Wheeler, for example, believed that the Indo-Aryans, with their heroic god Indra as their "leader," destroyed the Indus civilization. He famously said "Indra stands accused" in 1966 (an adage that he actually obtained from his colleague V.S. Agrawal, who served as a local guide in Wheeler's time). This kind of characterization necessitated the identification of the partially walled Indus cities with the Rigvedic *pur*. However, W. Rau (1976) has identified *pur* as rather ramshackle, earthen ring walls reinforced by wood, not unlike those at Sintashta in the Ural "land of towns," one of the possible homeland areas of the Indo-Iranians.[35]

However, archaeologists and philologists now view things differently. A certain amount of continuity of Vedic culture with the Indus civilization and its sister cultures is due to the fact that the Indo-Aryans employed the local populations for such matters as agriculture (Kuiper 1955, 1991) or pottery production.[36] Continuity of local styles is thus to be expected *a priori* (Ratnagar 1999). However, new elements appear as early as in the early post-Indus Cemetery H culture (*c.* 1900 BC onward), where traditional painted pottery appears *together* with a new burial style (cremation or exposure with subsequent burial of the bones in urns) *and* with a new motif painted on urns that seems to reflect Vedic beliefs.[37]

If the so-called "invasion" of IA speakers is not (yet) visible in the archaeology, it must be stressed that such movements rarely leave clear physical traces.[38] (Note, for example, the case of the Huns or Avars; Witzel 2001a.) However, such intrusions by steppe pastoralists are visible in the Bactria–Margiana archaeological complex (BMAC) of 2400–1600 BC) and in the upper Oxus/Zerafshan region. It is just a matter of time before such small camps are also discovered in the northwest of the subcontinent. Such statements are habitually ridiculed by revisionists, as if they could exclude what archaeology might discover.[39] In fact, in the trajectory of the intrusions of steppe people into the late BMAC, by *c.* 1400 BC a reflex of such cultural traits, including the domesticated horse, is visible in the Gandhùra grave culture of the northwestern subcontinent. Clearly, there is a trail of steppe involvement, whether initially IA-speaking or not (cf. the comparable situation in Mesopotamia, 2300–1350 BC).

For the past five decades or so, the best specialists have no longer seen the influx of IA speakers as an "invasion." Linguists first, and archaeologists somewhat later, have stressed that such a scenario is too simple-minded and largely wrong. Evidence for the so-called massacre of the population of Mohenjo-Daro (Wheeler 1966) was actually found in *several* archaeological layers, and the irregular arrangement of skeletons may very well be due to flooding that swept the corpses into a street corner and buried them here and there. Linguists and philologists have pointed to the complex "Indianization" of the IAs and the relatively long period of bilingualism that is visible, even in the extremely hieratic hymns of the Rigveda.[40] Several archaeologists, historians, and philologists have now proposed to re-evaluate the mode of influx of IA speakers into the subcontinent.[41]

The immigration of such fringe groups – visible in Near Eastern *written* sources – turns out to be a combination of various scenarios: there is imperceptible influx of pastoral people, there are clashes with the settled agriculturalists over water and grazing rights, there is cattle raiding, there is a gradual influx into the cities (often by hired soldiers, with palace coups), and there is outright invasion by motley groups of border peoples, who are not necessarily ethnically homogeneous (e.g., in Mesopotamia, the Guti, Lullubi, Kassites, and Mitanni between 2300 and 1450 BC). How many of these scenarios are actually visible in the RV has not been investigated yet; most descriptions remain superficial. A huge amount of spade work would have to be done first (Witzel 1995): all 1,028 hymns of the RV would have to be indexed with multiple indicators, such as location, poets, "kings" (chieftains), individual poetical traits, grammatical peculiarities, loan words, social indicators, details of agriculture and pastoralism, and so on. Thus far, this simply has not been carried out in a comprehensive way, in spite of many detailed studies of one or other of the phenomena.

Whatever the original influx of speakers of IA, whether large or small, the period of acculturation that followed is linguistically traceable (Kuiper 1991, 2000), just as it is in Mesopotamia with Akkadian. Both groups amalgamated, with the local population ultimately "Aryanized" and the IAs in turn "Indianized." In the past few years, genetics (especially the study of the male non-recombinant Y chromosome) has added further hard data to this scenario.[42] "Genetic evidence is often superior to (multivariate) palaeontological evidence as it is more specific than that of distinguishing types reflected in osteology, which are merely based on the adaptation to living conditions. Further, genetic evidence frequently allows us to pinpoint (sub-) branches in the cladistic (family) tree at a particular point in time and space" (Witzel 2001: 9, §7).

Still, some apologists and rewriters are not satisfied. Chakrabarti (1997: 225) thinks, in Irenic fashion, that such types of influx can "hardly be called entirely alien in the subcontinental context." While the speakers of IA have indeed emerged out of the Hindu Kush and the BMAC area, they were certainly as alien in speech, religion, and custom as the average Pathan or Tajik is in India today, if not more.[43]

Archaeology and texts

Some archaeologists insist on the *continuous* "cultural tradition ... Indo-Gangetic ... from the beginning of food production in the seventh millennium BC to the present."[44] Shaffer (1984) loudly protests the "linguistic tyranny" of earlier models. However, this is a much too narrow, purely archaeological view that neglects all spiritual and some material culture, but it is grist to the mills of the revisionists, who quote him with glee (Witzel 2001a: 27, §11.4).

It ought to be noted that even in archaeology, continuous cultural traditions are the *norm* everywhere, and that visible interruptions of such continuity are the *exception*. Even in an actual invasion scenario, sometimes coupled with system collapse, such as that of the later Roman Empire (Wells 1999: 78), many aspects of the previous civilization continue – especially those that are best visible to the archaeologist, such as pottery (Ratnagar 1999). Rather, it is the accidental discovery of *new* materials (e.g., the recent one of graves of the Huns in Hungary), or sometimes that of minute indicators of differences that establish the influx of a new population (e.g., that of the Avars near Naples; see Witzel 2001a). However what is important is to note the Maya-like *system collapse* at the end of the Indus civilization and the partial continuation of its traditions – although not in all regions[45] – on the reduced level of the village. This is quite similar to what happened in Bactria–Margiana *c.* 1600 AD. Only by 1600/1500 BC do steppe nomads from the north make their actual entry into the BMAC, adapt to the BMAC cultural traditions, and spread them all over the Iranian plateau.[46] Slightly later, we witness the first IA words in documents of the Kassite occupiers of Iraq (1677–1162 BC, of unclear ethnicity and isolated language), and in those of their neighbors, the Mitanni (*c.* 1450–1350 BC) in northern Mesopotamia. It is about this time – or for linguistic reasons, even slightly later – that the speakers of Vedic IA must have moved into the Greater Punjab. In all this, linguists refer only to "speakers" of a particular language, not to Indo-European, Indo-Iranian or Indo-Aryan ("Aryan") people, or worse, "races."

If the texts do not help much to distinguish the phenotype of the speakers of IA and their foes, the few skeletons that have been unearthed in the Indus civilization do not help much either.[47] Based on this rather limited evidence, there is, in the view of palaeontologists, no indication of *demographic* discontinuity from 4500 to 800 BC,[48] and an influx of outside populations is not visible. The remnants of the Harappans, including the people of the post-Harappan Cemetery H, are physically very close to each other, while the people of Mohenjo Daro stand somewhat apart (a fact now underlined by genetics; see Mehdi *et al.* 1999). Palaeontologists, and in their wake, archaeologists and revisionists, therefore insist that "Aryan bones" have not been found.[49] This overlooks that we do not know at all whether a massive *invasion* of outsiders took place that would have left a definite mark on the genetic make-up of the local Punjab population. Recent genetic information (Kivisild *et al.* 2003; Basu *et al.* 2003; Cordaux *et al.* 2004) indicates that such influx was relatively small (Witzel 1989: 249, 1995, 1999a 1999b; Allchin 1995). This had already been assumed by those (Witzel 2001a) who have applied Ehret's model (1988), which stresses the *osmosis* manner of cultural transmission. Other variations are the "billiard ball" or Mallory's *Kulturkugel* model. In all these cases, cultural change is effected by transmission from one innovative group to the next, not by invasion. Ehret (ibid.) shows the relative ease with which ethnicity *and* language shift in small societies due to the cultural/economic/military *choices* made by the local population in question (Witzel 2001a: 22, §10). Other sophisticated models have been developed over the past few decades,[50] although not due to revisionist criticism of the older theory but as inconsistencies were noted. Linguists such as Kuiper (1955, 1991), Emeneau (1956), and Southworth (1979), archaeologists such as Allchin (1982, 1995), and historians such as Thapar tried to find new explanations and proposed a new version of the immigration theory, usually stressing both early bilingualism and the mutual interaction of all groups involved.

In this light, it is no longer surprising that palaeontology, based on multivariate analysis of skeletal features, has not found a new wave of immigrants into the subcontinent after 4500 BC. "Aryan" cemeteries (if they existed at all in RV times,[51] beyond the textually attested single graves) were composed, according to later Vedic texts, of grave mounds 3 to 6 meters high; both are unlikely to be found easily in the deep alluvium of the constantly shifting Punjab rivers (Witzel 2001a: 10, 21, 65). However, this scenario can now be refined by genetic investigations – hardly apparent in Kennedy 2000 – which again and again point to an early founding population (visible in female genes: mtDNA M2, and M3) and multiple later additions, as evidenced by the data derived from the study of the non-recombinant male Y chromosome (Cordaux *et al.* 2004). (All this does still not entail "racial" differences; see Cavalli-Sforza *et al.* 1995).

Various fields of the sciences and humanities thus provide increasing evidence for a multilayered settlement of the subcontinent; however, such data are not reflected in the nationalistic and *Hindutva* rewriting of early South Asian history.

Revisionist variations

As has been described above, we can distinguish several types of rewriting, ranging from the legitimate to rehashing outdated accounts of history, to (biased) revisionism, and to plain fantasy, however motivated.[52] In the intensely nationalistic but professional *History of the Indian People* (Majumdar 1951–), the revisionists genuinely try to reconsider the writing of ancient Indian history, which they believe was very much the creation of nineteenth-century British political ideology. Others, the autochthonists, try to show (or simply believe in) an indigenous origin of the "Aryans" in the subcontinent. Various combinations of these two strands are possible.[53] At least three major varieties of revisionism can be identified (Witzel 2001a):

1. A "mild" version insists on the origin of the RV Indo-Aryans in the Punjab and so is the "autochthonous" or indigenous school.[54] Its roots go back all the way to Aurobindo and Dayanand Sarasvati.
2. The more strident and increasingly popular "out of India" school, which believes that the Iranians and even all Indo-Europeans emigrated from the Punjab or the Gangetic plains.[55]
3. The most intense version is what I call the "Devabhasa school" (Witzel 2001a). It derives all languages of the world from Sanskrit, "the language of the gods" (*devabhasa*), and is prominent with traditional pandits.[56] However, writers like Choudhury (1993) derive even the Chinese civilization from India (1990), and the American "pandit" and astrologer David Frawley, a.k.a. Vamadeva Shastri, even sees the origin of all world civilizations in northern India *c.* 10,000–6000 BC.[57]

Indologists and students of South Asia have been exposed to versions 1 and 3 for decades but have habitually neglected them as utterly unscholarly.[58] However, they have paid closer attention to the professionally motivated if sometimes exceedingly nationalistic version of rewriting (Majumdar 1951–), which does not even allow, for example, the entry of a Chinese army into India (*c.* 647 AD) to help the successor to King Harsa.

Over the past twenty years or so, revisionist discussions have intensified. They now increasingly include version 2, the adherents of which attempt to make it the "mainstream" view inside India and with emigrants, the non-resident Indian diaspora outside the subcontinent. All or most of the types of revisionism listed above agree in their refusal to allow the Aryan invasion theory. They also do not allow even a gradual trickling in of IA speakers, the so-called "Aryan migration theory" ("AMT"), which they nevertheless nearly always call an "invasion." Instead, the "Aryans" of the RV are seen as just a section of the many tribes that, in *Hindutva* fashion, have "always" been resident in India (Witzel 2001a: 23 *et seq.* §11). This stance has spawned an ever-growing list of defensive, openly apologetic and, increasingly aggressive tracts. From the revisionist point of view, any immigration or invasion just cannot be right as it is a "colonial" or "Marxist" theory that violates the ancient unity of India. Therefore, revisionists try to disprove any immigration "scientifically" with a long list of imaginative, diversionist, defensive, and apologetic writings. Many of them, like Sethna (see above), use the scientific concept of proof, or the fashionable Kuhnian idea of "paradigm shift" or postcolonial criticism (Nanda 2003). However, the typical lack of a split in their mind between scientific investigation and mythical thinking (Roland 1988; Witzel 2001a; Nanda 2003) allows them to integrate, seamlessly, traditional beliefs with the most recent results of "hard science," which, as they frequently endeavor to show, are already contained in the sacred Vedic texts anyhow.

Thus they assert their belief in what the ancient (mostly religious) texts and traditions supposedly have always maintained: that the Indian era and calendar go back to 3102 BC (18 February, to be precise[59]) or to an even earlier era (*yuga*). Therefore, India must have a long prehistory that was faithfully recorded in the Puranas up to c. AD 320, the beginning of the Gupta realm, (backdated by Sethna to 300 BC). The various data of recorded history and archaeology supposedly fit into this scheme unproblematically to produce the "true" ancient history of the subcontinent.[60] In other words, the revisionists compose scholastic works that try to be "logical" but that both lack a critical-historical approach and thinking "outside the box" of tradition (Witzel 1987). In short, they are exercises untouched by enlightenment (Witzel 2001a: 77, 2003b; Nanda 2003). Their "method" clearly reflects the internalized *Hindutva* credo of Savarkar and Golwalkar, whose main points come up time and again in seemingly endless variation: one undivided Hindu fatherland (*bharatvarsa, punyabhumi, matribhumi*), inhabited by one Hindu "race" (*jati*) that belongs to one culture and follows one religion, eternal Hinduism (*sanatana dharma*).

The Indus script

Unfortunately, the one type of evidence that might clinch the matter of an "Aryan invasion," the decipherment of the so-called Indus script, has remained elusive. A reading as early Dravidian[61] or, as the revisionists usually propose, as Sanskrit would clearly indicate who inhabited the Indus area around 2600–1900 BC. However, in spite of dozens of attempts (Possehl 1996) of a more or less thorough nature, but more often than not plainly amateurish,[62] the Indus signs have not been read. One obvious reason is that the proper materials for a decipherment have not yet been employed, such as a proper sign list, or the use of the thirty-odd loan words from the Indus area that are attested in Mesopotamian sources (Ratnagar 1981), and, especially so, any use of the more than 300 loan words found in the earliest post-Indus text, the RV (Kuiper 1991; Witzel 1999a, 1999b). The language to which these RV words belong must reflect that of the Greater Punjab, and thus of a considerable section of people belonging to the Indus civilization.[63] Recently, however, it has been proposed by Farmer (Harvard Round Tables 2001–3, etc.) that the 400–600 Indus signs and primary combinations of signs are not a script at all but a loose collection, perhaps not even a system, of symbols of unknown meaning. This theory would destroy any possibility of reading them as representing the sounds of a known or unknown language.

Nevertheless, ever since the discovery of the Indus civilization in the early 1920s, many if not most scholars and lay persons have "read" the signs as representing a (proto)Dravidian language (cf. Hock 2002: 234; Witzel 1999a, 1999b, 1999c; Mahadevan 2002). This is a mere extrapolation from the dominant ("colonialist") assumption that the invading Aryans conquered the earlier inhabitants of the subcontinent, the Dravidians. This assumption was initially bolstered by the location of Brahui, a Dravidian language found in nearby Baluchistan, but it has since been shown that this language is a mediaeval import from central India (Elfenbein 1987).

All these difficulties do not deter the revisionists. Many have published curious "decipherments" in which the "Indus–Sarasvati" language predictably turns out to be Sanskrit.[64] Some "decipherments," like that of Rajaram and Jha (2000), are not only absurd, they also involve the faking of evidence (Witzel and Farmer 2000a, 2000b): Rajaram was in possession of a photo of a (broken) seal of the hindquarters of a typical Indus bull, which he nevertheless wanted to turn into a horse to fit his interpretation of the accompanying inscription, which supposedly mentions a "Vedic" horse. As indicated above, revisionists have to find horses in the Indus civilization as the Vedic texts, which supposedly precede it, are full of horses and chariots, while palaeontologists deny their existence in the Indus area and in India before *c.* 1800/1700 BC. However, in his book, Rajaram presents a very blurred ("scanned") version of a full horse, along with an "artist's impression": in both pictures, the horse's neck and head are actually part of the broken off part of the seal. In a subsequent interview (Rajaram 2000), and in many Internet writings, he deflects the criticism and excuses his actions, in spite of the published evidence (Witzel and Farmer 2000b), as an honest scanning mistake. Revisionists, from then onward, have been writing only about the "unjust persecution" of a scanning mistake, not about the flawed "reading" and absurd "interpretation" of the seals (Witzel and Farmer 2000a).

The high number of non-Indo-European and non-Dravidian loan words in the RV alone should have acted as a warning in all such decipherments, but this warning has simply been ignored, is declared linguistic "speculation," or, to a very minor extent so far, is explained away with special pleading using secondary explanations: as poetical coinage, or unrecorded Sanskrit words (Talageri 1993, 2000).

The assertion of the "Aryan" nature of all early Indian civilization, including that of the Indus civilization, by *Hindutva* revisionists did not sit well with some South Indians, who, since the beginning of the twentieth century, have cultivated a separate "Dravidian" identity that was frequently expressed in political terms, especially in Tamil Nadu (Aiyar 1922–3; Bergunder 2002: 154–5; Hock 2002: 235). The South Indian answer to the "Aryan challenge" has been to point out (correctly) that South Indians have old classical texts in ancient Tamil, the Cankam (Sangam) literature which began around the start of our era. However, the Dravidian proponents use traditional legends about three successive academies of Tamil poets to push back their literature deep into the past, to dates that match the North Indian fantasies. Worse, they have a "perfectly logical" scenario: part of their ancient homeland, the *Kumari-Kandam*, extending south from Cape Comorin, consisting of India, Sri Lanka, Madagascar, and much of Indonesia, has been lost to indundations around 6750 and 3300 BC. However, the "lost continent" of Lemuria is a nineteenth-and twentieth-century fiction just like that of Atlantis or Mu. It is not entirely surprising that a Western pseudoarchaeologist, Graham Hancock, recently used these legends in his campaign to prove the existence of a postulated lost civilization.

In the same sub-nationalistic vein, several local "Dravidian" readings of the Indus signs have emerged, adding to those equally unproven ones proposed by Western scholars. However, they are rather sketchy and in many respect as plainly fantastic as the "Aryan" ones. R. Mathivanan (1995) finds the Indus signs 4,000 years after the end of the Indus civilization among the "Dravidians" of some village in the jungles of East India – who actually turn out not to be Dravidians but Austro-Asiatic (Santali) speakers (Pathak and Verma 1993). Curiously, the signs, painted on whitewashed house walls, have not changed in shape in all the 4,000 years of alleged use. In a conversation (summer 2002), he confirmed that the signs are indeed used in only one village. He has since expanded his "readings" on a global etymological scale (Madhivanan 2002). The Dravidian background is further expanded by Aravaanan (1980: 4–5), who traces the "similarities" and "identities" between Dravidian and African languages and cultures: "The Dravidians and the black Africans might have originally belonged to one stalk of race ... once there must have been some kind of land bridging both the African and Dravidian continents in the Indian Ocean. ... They called this lost continent 'Kumari" [i.e. Comores Islands, etc.}. ... Modern geography confirms the legendary theory of 'Lost Lemuria' (Kumari)."[65]

Needless to say, all such South Indian revisions of their own separate early history are regarded by *Hindutva* writers as colonialist-and missionary-inspired "seditionist" writings that are meant to destroy the primeval unity of the Hindu "race," its single culture, and its indivisible religion.

Antiquity frenzy

The hoary "Aryan" civilization is supposed to go back at least to the beginning of the present evil age, the Kaliyuga that began on 18 February 3102 BC or even, according to mediaeval Hinduism, well beyond into the mythical *Dvapara* and *Treta Yugas*. Chief among the "proofs" offered in recent years have been "scientific" calculations of an astronomical nature, based on readings in early texts, for "the heavens do not lie."[66] The date of 3102 BC precedes, according to all serious archaeologists, the emergence of the Indus civilization in *c.* 2600 BC. Furthermore, the date of 3102 as the "start of Indian history" was set only in the sixth century AD, when calculations of the beginning of present age, the Kaliyuga (González Reimann 2002), were made retroactively, in the fashion of Archbishop Ussher. The date of 3102, as well as the "astronomically" derived one for the Mahabharata war of 3067 BC (Achar 2003), is further contradicted by the (habitually neglected) internal evidence of the textual sources themselves. The great epic, the Mahabharata – an ever-changing bardic text[67] – abounds in warriors riding in horse-drawn chariots, while no such chariots existed anywhere in the world in 3100 BC, and horses were not introduced into the Indian subcontinent from the northern steppes until 1800/1700 BC (Meadow 1998, 2002).

Worse, the traditional beginning of "Indian history" in 3102 BC was set only in the sixth century AD, not c. 300 BC, when Megasthenes (via Arrian) reported to have heard of the existence of a traditional list of 163 or 164 kings reaching back to *c.* 6000 BC, not 3102 BC. At that early time, however, any ancient Aryan "royal lineages" (Feuerstein *et al.* 1995) would have ruled over small agricultural villages belonging to a number of disparate regional Neolithic cultures. In many parts of the subcontinent, such in as in Frawley's "cradle of all human civilization," the Ganges valley, these great kings would have governed bands of roaming Mesolithic hunter-gatherers, who persisted around the "eternal city" of Benares down to 2000 BC.

Nevertheless, the revisionists (and some archaeologists, such as Shaffer and Kenoyer) see a clear continuity from the Neolithic village of Mehrgarh (Baluchistan), with early food production at 6500 BC, to the Indus and later civilizations, and indeed up to today.

Against such backgrounds, be they nationalistic (Aryan, Pan-Indian, Sanskritic) or sub-nationalistic (Dravidian, South Indian), all of early Indian history is conveniently rearranged. According to the current "Aryan" view of the antiquity of Sanskrit-speaking people, found all over India, the Vedic civilization (10,000/6000–3200 BC) was followed by the early Indus/ Harappan civilization ("Indus/Sindhu–Sarasvati," 3200–1900 BC).[68] However, archaeologists maintain that the period of the village-based Neolithic between 3300 and 2600 BC had only small-scale settlements and is usually called pre-Harappan. It is followed by the Indus civilization proper (2600–1900 BC), which revisionists increasingly call the Sindhu– Sarasvati civilization because they think, mistakenly, that it was concentrated on the Sarsuti–Ghaggar–Hakra ("Sarasvati") River and that it even had its origins there.

This is a fallacy, a product of the revisionists' lack of proper archaeological background. The dry Hakra River (in Bahawalpur, Pakistan), which runs parallel to the Indus, does indeed display a heavy concentration of Indus sites, but for a good reason: this is a fossil landscape that has not changed over the past 3000–4000 years as the river dried up completely in the second millennium BC, albeit in several stages and with several reversals (Mughal 1997). As a result, the area has never again been used for agriculture or permanent settlements and has, at best, been frequented by pastoralists. Consequently, one still can find millions of Harappan potsherds in plain view on the ground – just as the (supposedly pre-Indus) Vedic texts also have it (Pancavimsa-Brahmana 25). In contrast to the Ghaggar–Hakra riverbed, other areas of the Punjab and Sindh have been covered by several meters of alluvium (even a large part of Mohenjo-Daro is underground). While the original area of the Indus civilization has not yet been identified, it is clear that urbanization has spread, along with agriculture, from west (Baluchistan) to east (Possehl 2002).

Although the revisionists call the Hakra–Ghaggar–Sarsuti River the Sarasvati River, it seems to have had a different, non-Sanskrit local name in Indus times.[69] According to the "Aryan" revisionist view, the Indus civilization was interrupted and its sites were abandoned due to the drying up of this river "at 1900 BC ... as satellite photos (of Yash Pal 1984) show."[70] Apart from the fact that satellite photos do not supply archaeological dates, this view is again based on incomplete data. As Mughal (1997) has shown, the river did not dry up all at once in 1900 BC but in stages, receiving water, on and off, from the glacier-fed Sutlej. However, the Indus sites were abandoned *c.* 1900 BC in *all* areas of this large civilization. A civilization of great cities (Harappa, Mohenjo-daro, Ganweriwala, Rakhigarhi, Dholavira, Kalibangan, etc.) reverted to villages and small towns. This reflects a system collapse, such as that of the lowland Maya (well before the Spanish arrival), or much of Western Europe at the time of the Hunnic and Germanic migrations. Archaeologists have given a large number of reasons for this downfall, from collapse of foreign trade, climate change, depletion of the soil, inundations, and earthquakes to the (discredited) "Aryan invasion" of the cities. To make the (gradual) drying up of the "Sarasvati" River responsible for the collapse in all of Pakistan and neighboring India is unilateral at best and ignorant at worst.

In sum, this is just another example among many of how the rewriters fail. If one would assemble all of the revisionist "evidence," one would have to rewrite not only Indian history but also much of archaeology, historical linguistics, Vedic literature, historical geography, zoology, botany, astronomy, and so on, and allow for a "paradigm shift" in *all* these fields of study, leading to a break-up of the sciences into regional, culturally based belief systems: in other words, the creation of new *mythologies* that include *some* observations of nature and the sciences. Scholarship is not ready for an Indian "Mythus of the twenty-first century" (Witzel 2001a: 75, §32; Nanda 2002, 2003).

Out of India?

As if all these fantastic reconstructions of the past and the resulting, creative "new sciences" were not enough, there is, finally, the inevitable dot on the I. This is the so-called "out of India theory." Indian nationalists, ever since

Aurobindo, could not bear the idea that part of the population, especially that one using the "Aryan" language in which the sacred Vedas were composed, could have entered the subcontinent from the outside, which meant that the Vedas stemmed from "foreigners" (3,500 to an imagined 13,000 years ago). It is not surprising, therefore, that someone finally had the revelation that exactly the opposite should be the case: the "Aryans" emigrated westwards from India to civilize Europe. This anti-colonial counter-myth is summed up by Misra (1992: 103): "the centum people separated and left through the Himalayan passes to Caspian or Pamir and then to Europe etc. The satem speakers left after that, batch by batch. The last batch might have been the Iranians." Indian linguist S.S. Misra (ibid.: 100),[71] American astrologer Frawley (1995), and Belgian *Hindutva* sympathizer Elst (1999: 122, 124) repeat this view; which has been summed up recently by the prolific and assertive Maharastran bank clerk S. Talageri,[72] largely copying Aiyar (1975) and Misra (1992). However, the *emigration* of the Iranians and other Indo-Europeans from the subcontinent is *excluded* by the linguistic evidence at large (Hock 1999). *"Why should we allow special, linguistic pleading just in the case of India?* There is nothing in the development of human language in India that intrinsically differs from the rest of the world. Occam's razor applies" (Witzel 2001a: 56 *et seq.*).

Nevertheless, Talageri has found scriptural evidence in the Puranas (texts of the first millennium AD only) for this emigration. The Puranas speak fleetingly[73] of the 100 sons of a King Pracetas who are *asrita* ("leaning on, adjacent") to the *udicya* ("northern direction"), which in Sanskrit texts means the lands of the Punjab and Gandhara (between Islamabad and Kabul). However, this sentence is interpreted by Talageri and others as a *movement*, an emigration of Indian tribes westward (hence the discussion in Witzel 2001b). This is simply a product of revisionist fantasy, which makes the (temperate climate) Indo-European proto-language and its "people" come from Maharashtra (Talageri's own homeland, 1993) or from the eastern Gangetic plains (Bihar, as per Talageri 2000). The latter idea again relies on some king lists of the Epics and Puranas, which date to millennia after the alleged facts and refer to a different political situation[74] (Witzel 1995, 2001a: 30, §12.2).

There would normally be no need to go deeply into these fantasies, just as Indologists have habitually neglected much of the earlier "reconstructions" of Indian history such as that of Tilak (1903), where the "Aryans" are portrayed as having lived "on the Polar Circle." However, the recent rewriters, including Talageri, are acquiring larger followings in India and among the India diaspora year by year. Interestingly, even a respected Indologist colleague from India (having taught in North America for decades) wanted to push Sethna's theory (see above) at a conference of twenty specialists in the spring of 2003, vehemently insisting that we take Sethna's multifarious "evidences" seriously.

The tone of a recent Indian newspaper article is symptomatic of the problem:

> ours was the oldest civilisation in the world and ... our ancestors, the Vedic Aryans, had travelled from India to various parts of Asia and Europe to spread our knowledge, civilisation, and culture. When this is recorded we would be able to hold our heads higher and be able to take on the future with greater confidence.
>
> (Bala 2004)

Proceeding in this fashion, one can certainly build up a considerable and involved "historical" mosaic that lay persons may find quite impressive and attractive – until they begin to check the background of such claims seriously and notice, in due course, that the new, disjointed revisionist theories fall prey to Occam's razor (Witzel 2001a: 75, §32). After decades, even a century, of revisionist debate, one would have expected better.

Among Indian nationalists and revisionist writers, their beliefs are reinforced by a strong sense of grievance at "a thousand years of foreign domination." It is accompanied by a severe inferiority complex (although infrequently admitted; Roland 1988), resulting in over-compensation: India has the oldest civilization of the world and the oldest texts of humankind (the Rigveda), and it can boast all the important inventions in science and technology (mathematics, medicine, aircraft, rockets, atomic bombs, etc.).[75] There is the accompanying myth, heard from Benares to Madras, that the first editor of the RV, Max Müller, stole such secrets and that "the Germans used it to build airplanes and atomic bombs." This kind of belief is found basically in the emerging middle class but also in an increasing number of highly educated people, especially technologists, all of whom have never been exposed, in critical and historical fashion, to the ancient texts of their own culture. They would rather believe any new (preferably "scientific") account of past glories, if written in English, such as the anachronistic writings on ancient Indian history and Sanskrit texts by a science professor in Louisiana, S. Kak. Typically, such writers publish their heady mixture of misinterpretations of the Sanskrit texts and of modern science, always out of context, in science-oriented journals whose editors must take at face value the general (and unfamiliar) Indian cultural background and, especially, all the Sanskrit texts quoted in the author's (tendentious) translations. After publication, the revisionists claim to have passed peer review.

In sum, instead of a serious and unbiased investigation into India's past, be it prehistory, ancient history or even that of the last one or two centuries, one encounters the prefabricated ideas of Golwalkar and Savarkar, which are fast becoming the *Zeitgeist*, although they are nothing but a new myth. We have had to learn in recent history, to our detriment, that myths can be powerful, whether they are the "Mythus of the twentieth century" (Rosenberg 1935) or now that of Golwalkar–Savarkar's ideas in the twenty-first century.

Ein Volk, ein Reich ...

Those propagating the new *Hindutva* myth speak, time and again, of "one people, one realm, one religion." We have heard that before as well, but with one significant addition: "one leader."

There is no space here to go into details, but it must be underlined that the rewriting of history is just one aspect of the Sarwarkar–Golwalkar program. A closer look would identify a large number of items in which this para-and proto-fascist theory goes together with many of the well-tested practices of fascist regimes of the past.[76]

However, there is one major difference – the lack of overt racism. This is because all Indians belong, as Sarvarkar–Golwakar have decreed, to "one people" (*jati*). Even the Muslims and Christians should just "behave as proper Indians." However, it must not be overlooked that India has had, since early Vedic times, its own "lower races": the fourth class (*varna*), the *sudra,* who have been classified as servants of the three upper (*arya*) classes. Later on, there were others below them still. This fact is denied by revisionists, who find "spiritual" reasons for a system of "division of labor" that was instituted 3,000 years ago in the "first constitution of India," the *Purusasukta* of the Rigveda (10.90).[77] However, it has always been the guiding principle and practice of Hindu caste society that all, even the middle- and lower-caste populations (*sudra*), suppress those under them, notably the "outcasts" (*pariah, harijan, dalit*). Yet, even among the Dalits there is always someone below them to denigrate and exploit, although in contrast to current official policies of *Gleichschaltung*. This spirit is now reinforced, with almost daily atrocities reported and many others going unreported, by the upwardly mobile lower middle-class caste groups. These "Sanskritizers" (Srinivas 1952, 1988) profit from the current *Hindutva* movement, which they use to ameliorate their relatively (low) status (Nanda 2003).

Against this background, the rewriting of Indian history is no longer just an "academic" undertaking but acquires – for one billion Indians at all levels of society – wide-ranging cultural, social, and political significance. It is understandable now why the revisionist *Hindutva* project puts such stress on a "correct" representation of the (Vedic) past and on its propagation at all levels, from school textbooks and the National Museum to official government policies.[78] In all of them, *Hindutva* principles are at work and are increasingly implemented. In the end, the Indus ("Sindhu-Sarasvati"), Vedic, and other early Indian civilizations are seen as emanations from an indivisible, inherent "Indian spirit" going back to a hoary Sanskrit-speaking "Aryan" civilization many millennia ago.[79]

It should no longer surprise that, in this rising tide of nationalist fervor, even *bona fide* scholars,[80] including archaeologist and former director-general of the Archaeological Service of India, B.B. Lal, are taken in. In his most recent book, *The Sarasvati Flows On: The Continuity of Indian Culture* (Lal 2002a), as well as in recent public lectures (starting with Bhopal and Delhi 2003),[81] he has propagated the unity of ancient Indian civilization and the identity of the Indus and the Vedic civilizations in particular. However, his turn toward the religious had already taken place in the 1980s when he was tracing, in archaeology, the route of the Hindu god Rama (as per the epic Ramayana) from Ayodhya southward toward Sri Lanka.

Most recently, this long-term view of "Aryan" civilization has been extended by the "finds" from dredging 20 kilometers west of Hazira on the Gulf of Cambay (Gujarat) carried out by the Indian National Institute of Ocean Technology in 2001 and again between October 2002 and January 2003.[82] A piece of wood, radiocarbon dated to *c.* 7500 BC, has been linked, on the one hand, to "more than 2,000 artefacts," including "stone artefacts, potsherds, hearth pieces, animal bones and human teeth embedded in fluvial sands and silts," and, on the other hand, to sonar scanning, at a depth of 20–40 m, of the seabed of the murky waters of the Gulf, which revealed large rectangular features, "a city" with regular streets (Kathiroli *et al.* 2002).

It did not disturb the oceanographers, some archaeologists or the then government, all of whom loudly proclaimed the discovery of the "oldest city in the world" (2002), that virtually all the rules of archaeology have been skirted in this undertaking: there is no excavation of stratified layers; the piece of wood may date to 7500 BC, but the report speaks of the strong tidal currents in the Gulf, exceeding six knots; typically, no metal objects were found. There is no proof of any connections of the piece of wood with the purported "city"; the "artefacts" are, in part, symmetrical objects that are easily formed by the actions of the sea.[83]

In the present context as well as generally, the *Hindutva* attitude toward history results in consistent simplification and falsification of the past, whether it concerns historical or literary documents or archaeological data. It is coupled with a virtual "antiquity frenzy" that is also seen in other emerging nation-states.[84] This means that all the sins of fervent nationalism are now being repeated in India (with the exception of overt racism), and that they seriously affect many fields of study. Many colleagues have already been intimidated or thrown out of their posts, and actual violence has begun too: in December 2003, a colleague's face was blackened by tarring, and his institute at Pune was looted by a subnational group. Obviously, neutral archaeology and historical study are no longer possible in many areas of India, where they are pressed into the service of official policies, just as occurred in Nazi and Soviet times or as still is the case in present-day China with its *Sandai* "three (earliest) dynasties project."[85] As an outside observer, one can take the neutral stance and wait for this new kind of mass deception to play itself out over the next one or two decades. (Although the recent electoral defeat of the nationalist *Hindutva* forces is not a guarantee of permanent change.) After the atrocities of the twentieth century, staying aloof is not a responsible stance, as Pierre Bourdieu admonishes us (Witzel 2003b).

However, as far as India is concerned, there is one redeeming factor. Indian society has always been a very fractious one, with serious disagreements constantly being played out at all levels. The resulting so-called "tolerance"[86] of other views – now also those in archaeology and history – can be maintained as long as there are free elections, independent publishers, and a free press, and as long as they are not muzzled, as once before in recent times, by a new dictator.[87] Only then, would India be completely *Hindutva-gleichgeschaltet*: *ein Volk, ein Reich, ein Führer*.

Notes

1. The present paper was written before the defeat of the nationalistic BJP/DNA government in May 2004; references to "current" politics therefore apply to the time before this change.
2. Cf. Jaffrelot 1996; van der Veer 1994; Bergunder and Das 2002: 11 *et seq.*; Bergunder 2002; Bryant 2002.
3. A curious sideline was provided by Tilak (1903), who traced the Aryans back to the Arctic Circle, from where they supposedly migrated *c.* 4000–4500 BC; the Europeans are allegedly a branch of this migration.
4. For a summary of older anti-invasion writings, see Ghosh 1951: 220–1.
5. There are various formulations, such as Aryan = Indo-Iranian (the common ancestor language of Iranian and Indo-Aryan tongues like Vedic and Sanskrit, as well as the daughter languages Hindi, Bengali, and so on); or the antiquated use of Aryan = Indo-European; or the late nineteenth- and early twentieth-century use designating an "Aryan race." In India, these linguistic, ethnic, and racial usages are confounded in reference to the "Aryans" (and Indians), see, e.g.: "The Indian race as such is far ahead of Caucasians in mathematics" (Venkataraman 2004; the author is a US-based physician).
6. Lipner 1992: 1, 7, n.7; Bergunder 2002: 165; Michaels 2003: 14. *Hindutva* is a neologism, a mongrel formation with the Sanskrit abstract suffix *–tva* added to the non-Sanskrit (Iranian) noun *Hindu* "Indian" (or *hindū*, as Golwalkar has it), which is derived from the Old Persian word for the River Indus (*Sindhu*): *hindush*, hence Greek *Indos*, Latin *Indus*.
7. But also called "motherland" (*matribhumi*) by him.
8. Which remains undefined and is, in fact, difficult to define; some scholars prefer to speak of a group of religions instead. Even the recent, indigenous Second World Hindu Conference in Allahabad (1979) had a very superficial definition: a Hindu is someone who "recites prayers, reads [the sacred text] Gita, uses [the sacred syllable] Om ... , plants [the sacred plant] Tulsi" (Michaels 2003: 15).
9. See his interview (23 June 2000) at http://www.hindu.org/publications/ramswarup/voiceofindia.html.
10. See Bergunder 2002: 168, who describes S.R. Goel as "one of the most stringent but also most intellectual [persons] of Hindu nationalism." His publishing house Voice of India was founded in 1981. Both Goels assert that they want to publish scientific evidence for the aim of rewriting Indian history, *especially* against the "Aryan invasion theory," which would undermine the *Hindutva* claim that the "Aryans" (and thus their modern descendants) were autochthonous to the Indian subcontinent (see below).
11. Cf. van der Veer 1994: 157–9; this is clearly visible in a Japanese TV interview of the mid-1980s, filmed at his excavations at Srngaverapuram.
12. Some exponents: Choudhury 1993; Elst 1999; Danino 1996; Deo and Kamath 1989, 1993; Feuerstein *et al.* 1995; Frawley 1994, 1995, 1998; Gautier 1996; Gupta 1996; Jha 1996; Kak 1994; Klostermaier 1997, 1998a, 1998b, 2000; Lal 2002a, 2002b, 2003; Misra 1992, 1999; Rajaram 1993, 1995, 1998; Rajaram and Frawley 1997; Rajaram and Jha 2000; Rao 1982; Sethna 1980, 1981, 1989, 1992, 2000; Singh 1995; Talageri 1993, 2000; Waradpande 1993. Among them, Choudhury stands somewhat apart by his *extreme* chauvinism: he derives Chinese civilization from India. Gidwani has written an "Aryan" novel (cf. Witzel 2001a; Bergunder 2002: 169 *et seq.*; Nanda 2003).

13. BJP (Bharatiya Janata Party, 1980), along with the other members of the "family" (*sangh parivar*) of organizations, such as Rashtriya Svayamsevak Sangh (RSS) and Vishva Hindu Parishad (VHP).

14. Thus the overstatement of Bergunder and Das 2002: 10.

15. And often even Southeast Asia; cf. Bergunder and Das 2002: 10.

16. Such as the linguistic line dividing the South Indian Dravidian languages from the North Indian Indo-Aryan languages. Note the clear distinction between the North, Center and South of the subcontinent and its many major and minor (sub)regions.

17. See Caraka Samhita 3.83, Nyayasutra 4.2.50, 1.2.10 (sophistical refutation); the method is used in Patanjali's Mahabhasya (150 BC), and still earlier in some late Vedic (Upanishadic) Brahmodyas (Witzel 1987).

18. They also like to play off old, dated, and incorrect statements of the nineteenth century against more recent ones, typically arguing that if linguists and others differ or contradict themselves, how can the field be viable at all? They overlook that all sciences have disagreements about details.

19. The horse (*Equus caballus*) is found, at best, in the late Indus period and in the western border areas (cf. Kenoyer 1995: 226–7; Kennedy 1995: 46; Ratnagar 1999; Hock 2002: 242–3; but note the refutation by Meadow and Patel 1997; Meadow 1999, 2002. Singh (1995: 65–7) offers the absurd idea (much copied in the Internet forums) that Vedic/ Sanskrit *asva* "horse" (= Latin *equus*) originally designated the ass and was transferred to the horse later (see Misra's linguistic acrobatics, 1992). However, Sethna and Singh see spoked wheels in some Indus signs and on spinning whirls (Sethna 1992: 51, 173; Lal 2003) and a horse figurine (Sethna 1992: 419–20; Lal 2003). Singh also has wheeled toys (1995: 169). The revisionists' "chariots" happen to be oxen or bullock carts (including the not securely dated, post-Indus Daimabad chariot, which has full wheels).

20. The reference to seventeen ribs probably has mythological and ritual significance; see Witzel 2001a.

21. In all these cases, scholars have to reinvent the wheel for the benefit of revisionists (as is the case in disputing creationism). This includes re-exposition of the basics in fields such as comparative linguistics (summaries by Hock 1986; Anttila 1989; Szemerényi 1996; Beekes 1995); comparative epic studies (Parry 1930–32; Lord 1991); South Asian archaeology (Allchin 1995; Kenoyer 1998; Possehl 1999); Indus epigraphy (Possehl 1996); zoology and botany (Meadow and Patel 1997; Meadow 1998, 2002); and the evidence contained in the texts, as established by philology over the past two centuries (Witzel 1997, 2001a: 1–23).

22. Revisionism seems to be an exclusively male prerogative, a power play.

23. The RV also does not discuss tigers and leopards, apparently for cultural reasons (Witzel 2003c, forthcoming) and later Vedic texts hardly discuss everyday pottery (Rau 1983), as this is made by lower-class people (*sudras*). Everyday carpentry and artisanship are also passed over in silence.

24. They include such incidental cases as late first-millennium accounts of earlier Indian eras (notoriously difficult to establish as there was no early *common* Indian era; see Witzel 1991); a reinterpretation of Megasthenes' account of 153 or 154 early Indian kings extending back 6,462 years (thus to *c.* 6750 BC, when only westernmost northern India was in the early stages of village-based Neolithic food production); and the reinterpretation of a royal name given by the Greeks as Xandrames (while Sethna has no knowledge of the method of Greek transcriptions of such names).

25. Chakrabarti 1997; cf. Hock 2002; Bergunder and Das 2002: 10.

26. Erdosy 1995; Witzel 2001a; Bergunder and Das 2002: 1; Nanda 2002, 2003.

27. For South India, see Karashima 1984, 2001, 2002; Stein 1985, 1998.

28. Bergunder 2002: 171; Thapar 1992: 23; Nanda 2002.

29. See the severe critique of Chakrabarti's book by Lamberg-Karlovsky 1997/1998.

30. Müller's intentions are frequently misrepresented by the revisionists: based on two completely isolated and opportunistic quotes from his letters, his image has changed

from a lifelong sympathizer of India – someone who went on record saying, in Victorian Oxford, "I point to India" – that to a Christian missionary in disguise who allegedly spent his whole career preparing for the destruction of Hinduism.

31. Some of which specialize in abuse of the subject and individual Indologists (see websites such as http://www.swordoftruth.com, http://www.hvk.org, and http://www.bharatavani.org).

32. See now especially Nanda 2003. Note the extreme stance of Hock (2002: 247) that the sciences (and humanities) produce only hypotheses, differing in degree of probability; see also Bergunder and Das 2002: 12.

33. Ibid.: 10. It is a curious fact that latter-day people who never directly experienced the deprivations and pain of the colonial regime feel most strongly about its depredations.

34. The arguments against the AIT/AMT are refuted by Hock 1999, 2002; Witzel 1995, 1999a, 2001a.

35. Rau 1957, 1976; cf. Hock 2002: 234, 237; Shaffer 1984; Shaffer and Lichtenstein 1995, 1999; Kennedy 1995; Kenoyer 1998; Witzel 2000; Possehl 2002; Lamberg-Karlovsky 2002.

36. Only sacred vessels are made by Brahmins, and in the most archaic fashion, without the use of a wheel. Such Vedic pottery, always executed in the same traditional manner, if found, is therefore undatable simply by style; see Rau 1983; Witzel 2001a: 64, §24.

37. A small human "soul" is drawn inside the belly of a traditionally painted peacock; see Vats 1940; Witzel 1984, 2001a: 21; Kenoyer 1998: 174 *et seq.*

38. See Ratnagar (1999: 222) on extra-Indian cases; see also Chakrabarti 1997; Dhavalikar 1997; Shaffer and Lichtenstein 1999; Hock 2002: 238.

39. Unexpectedly, new civilizations have turned up, such as the BMAC or, in November 2003, that of Jiroft in southeast Iran.

40. Kuiper 1955: 138–40, 185; 1991, 2000; Southworth 1979, 1990, 1995. See also Hock (1999, 2002: 233) on convergence.

41. Allchin 1995; Southworth 1979, forthcoming; Thapar 1968, 2002; Witzel 1995, 2001a.

42. See, e.g., Cavalli-Sforza *et al.* 1994, 1995; Kivisild *et al.* 1999; Semino 2000; Underhill 2000; Bamshad *et al.* 2001; Basu *et al.* 2003; Cordaux *et al.* 2004.

43. Elst (1999) simply denies that any kind of influx can be anything but an "invasion." This is nothing more than wordplay, as speakers of English understand invasion as influx accompanied by violence or military power, while immigration can but may not coincide with such violence.

44. Shaffer and Lichtenstein 1999: 255–6, 1995; Kenoyer 1998: 26, 180 *et seq.*

45. Note that several regions of the Indus civilization reverted to pre-Indus cultural traits. The Indus traits were nothing but a dominant, giant overlay over regional cultures.

46. Lamberg-Karlovsky (2002) underlines that the later Indo-Iranian movements do not show BMAC traits; see also Witzel 2003c.

47. Note that after the Indus civilization, cremation takes over, which reduces the volume of available evidence. Recently, some "West Asian type" graves have been found in Cutch.

48. Lukacs asserts that no significant population changes took place in the centuries prior to 800 BC; see now Kennedy 1995, 2000. However, there are minor differences between the various areas of the northwestern subcontinent, such as Sarai Khola and Harappa, even between Harappa and Mohenjo Daro.

49. Kennedy 1995: 49–54, 2000. See also Meadow 1998; Meadow and Patel 1997; Shaffer 1984; Shaffer and Lichtenstein 1995, 1999; Sergent 1997.

50. Kuiper 1955, 1991, 2000; Thapar 1968, 2002; Anthony 1995; Witzel 1995, 2001a.

51. RV 10.16.14, etc. speaks of burial, cremation, exposing bodies on trees and of "throwing" dead bodies away.

52. Stung by trenchant criticism, Talageri (2000) tries to "scientifically" distinguish between his "correct" version of rewriting and those of the others.

53. For summaries, see Choudhury 1993; Hock 1999; Bryant 1999; Talageri 2000. Bryant (1999: 294) reports that already in 1994–5 he had found that a majority of Indian scholars had rejected the Aryan invasion/migration completely, or were open to reconsidering it.

54. Waradpande 1993; Kak 1994. See Elst 1999: 119; Talageri 2000: 406; Lal 1997: 281, 2002a, 2002b, 2003.
55. Misra 1992, 1999; Talageri 1993, 2000; Frawley 1994; Elst 1999.
56. The opposite is seen in deriving Sanskrit from Arabic in a book published in Pakistan (Mazhar 1982).
57. Frawley's work features heavily in *Underworld* by Lost Civilization fantasist Graham Hancock (2002a).
58. I have planned to write a paper on the Indian version of a "cargo cult" for thirty years, but now seems to be the right time to do so. See now Prakash 1999; Nanda 2002, 2003.
59. This is attested not before Varahamihira, mid-sixth century AD!
60. This is nothing but a scholastic enterprise by which whatever (seemingly relevant) bits and pieces of "evidence" are entered into the scheme, but, as pointed out in detail in Witzel 2001a, counter-evidence is overlooked, neglected, or discussed away by special pleading.
61. Alekseev *et al.* 1969; Knorosov and Volchok 1973, 1981; Parpola 1994; Parpola and Koskenniemi 1969; Fairservis 1992.
62. Such as Jha, Rajaram and Jha, Mathivanan, Pathak, A. and N.K. Verma.
63. In light of recent studies (Witzel 1995, 1999a, 1999b; Lubotsky 2001), this number has to come down somewhat, as quite a few are earlier loans from the general area of the BMAC; see the lists in Lubotsky 2001 and Witzel 1999a, 1999b, 2003.
64. Rao 1982; Rajaram and Jha 2000; Talageri 2000; Witzel and Farmer 2000a. See also Kalyanaraman's version (2000) of Bronze Age *Mleccha "Prakrits,"* by which he understands, against all linguistic knowledge and definition, the "unrefined" languages that "resulted" in Sanskrit.
65. However, in geologically distant times, 60 million years ago! For a summary of the background to this "mélano-indien" theory, see Sergent 1997: 52–8, who, incredibly, follows earlier French researchers in Senegal espousing this theory.
66. See Kazanas 2002 and cf. Zimmer 2003; see also Kak 1994; Achar 1999, 2003; and refutations by Hock 1999; Plofker 2000; Witzel 1999d, 2001a. Kak's "astronomical code" is precariously based on a combination of RV "brick pilings" of the *still non-existent* Agnicayana ritual and the structure of the *still non-existent* complete RV collection. It is favored by Klostermaier (1998a, 1998b), Elst (1999), and other revisionists.
67. See the theory of Parry (1930–2) and Lord (1991).
68. Tripathi (1988), too, argues that the Vedic civilization is an indigenous phenomenon.
69. Based on later names recorded in the Veda, it seems to have been Visampal / Vipash / Vipazh; Witzel 1999c. For a map of the area in Vedic times, see Witzel 1984. For the post-Indus, Indo-Aryan name of the Sarasvati, note the southern Afghan (Arachosian) River Haraxvaiti, see Witzel 1995: 343, 1999; Hock 2002: 24. The same shift of other river names eastwards, along with the migration of Indo-Aryan speakers, is seen in *Sarayu* (*Haroiiu-m, Haraiva*, River *Herat* in northeast Afghanistan), *Sarayu*, modern *Sarju* in North India (Uttar Pradesh); *Sindhu* from the northern Afghan *Sindes* to the Indian *Sindhu* (Indus); east Afghan *Gomati* (modern *Gomal*), *Gomati*, modern *Gumti* in Uttar Pradesh, and so on.
70. Yet this has been known for more than 100 years; see the early researches by Oldham and Raverty, cf. Witzel 1984, summary in Witzel 2001a.
71. His scenario contains a lot of Indo-European invasions into Europe but no invasion, not even an "immigration" or a meager "trickling" *into* India.
72. Talageri 1993: 196, 212, 334, 344–5, 2000: 328, 263. Note especially Talageri (1993: 408):

> This whole description is based on the most logical and in many respects the *only possible* interpretation of the facts. ... Any further research, and any new material discovered on the subject, can only confirm this description ... there is no possible way in which the location of the Original Homeland in the interior of northern

India, so faithfully recorded in the Puranas and confirmed in the Rigveda, can ever be disproved.

73. In *one* misrepresented passage that is given by Talageri (1993: 368; 2000: 260 *et seq.*) twice in *untranslated* form, which makes it easy to impute any meaning desired. In his case, this is a "first historical emigration ... into the areas to the north of Afghanistan (i.e. into Central Asia and beyond)." See Brahmanda Purana 2.74.11, Brahma Purana 13.152, Harivamsa 1841, Matsya Purana 48.9, Vayu Purana 99.11; cf. also Visnu Purana 4.17.5, Bhagavata Purana 9.23.15 (Kirfel 1927: 522).

74. The RV does not support his theory either: it simply does not know of, or refer to, central and eastern North India (Witzel 2001a; cf. Hock 2002: 239).

75. Prakash 1999; Nanda 2003. This view is echoed in the recent statement by Murli Manohar Joshi (then minister, Union Human Resource Development, Government of India):

> A number of complex scientific problems, if not all, may be solved if the Vedas are properly studied. ... Concepts like molecular state of nature and nanosecond were described in the Vedas thousands of years ago. ... The Vedas are not only about philosophy and "sadhus sitting in caves," but also taught about the importance, creation and preservation of wealth. ... The Vedas address many environmental and economic issues and these linkages need to be studied.
>
> (*The Hindu*, 4 April 2004)

76. *Blut und Boden* (patriotic attachment to one's blood and soil; used by B.B. Lal, 2002b); *Gleichschaltung* (the Nazi method of bringing all independent organizations into line, or incorporating them into party organizations); *Nestbeschmutzung* (soiling one's own nest), etc. See Nanda 2002, 2003, with copious examples and bibliography.

77. As per Indologist Paul Mus, on the *Purusasukta*. Recent (BJP) government policy aimed at getting rid of all castes and thus making people at large more easily manageable: *Volksgenossen* ("people's comrades", fellow countrymen). However, social reality is quite different in the villages where the large majority of Indians live.

78. Such as the councils regulating the writing of school textbooks (National Council of Educational Research and Training, NCERT), of historical research (ICHR), of the national center for the arts (IGNCA), and the National Museum in New Delhi. In 2001, the Ministry of Human Resources Development initiated projects on "Vedic astrology" (in fact, Graeco-Indian astronomy/astrology), on Kauilya's (the Indian Machiavelli) Arthasastra recipes for the military (owl extracts for seeing at night, food to last for 40 days, and the like; see Prakash 1999 and Nanda 2003); and archaeological projects such as digging up "all" sites along the dried-up Sarasvati, from Haryana to Cutch, or the extension of the dredging operation in the Gulf of Cambay.

79. Or, with Thapar (1992: 3), of a unified continuous Indian identity, and Aryahood that (in)formed Indian history.

80. See the review of B.B. Lal (2002) by Tripathi (2002). One may add philologists (such as Klostermaier) and archaeologists (such as Chakrabarti and Lal).

81. According to press reports (see Lal 2003), he listed "four myths: that the Aryans invaded India; that the Harappans were Dravidian-speaking; that the Rigvedic Saraswati was the Helmand of Afghanistan; that the Harappan culture became extinct."

82. Chengappa 2002. The then union minister of HRD and for Science and Technology, Murli Manohar Joshi, announced this on 19 May 2001 and again in 2002 as a "human settlement" off the Gujarat coast that could be "older than any settlement found anywhere in the world, a settlement older than the Sumerian (3500 BC), the Egyptian (3000 BC) and the Harappan civilisations (2500 BC)" (*The Hindu*, 17 January 2002; cf. N. Krishna (2002), who even mentions "a flat rock piece with a sort of script ... the earliest known writing"). But, several radiocarbon dates were reported: 2710 BP (uncalibrated), 7600 BP (uncalibrated), and 7500 BC (9500 BP). Pictures of the finds are on the

Underworld website of G. Hancock (2002b), and in more detail also on the *Marine Archaeology* website of the National Institute of Ocean Technology (NIOT, 2002–4); cf. the detailed (geological) discussion of the objects by the website of P. Heinrich (2002), which reveals similar natural "artefacts" found in Texas or Ontario; the same holds for the "script." Cf. further the discussions in *The Hall of Ma'at*, a forum that debunks pseudoarchaeology. Note also the earlier discovery of God Krishna's capital of *Dvaraka*, on the Gujarat coast (Rao 1999).

83. See *The Hindu*, 17 January 2002; cf. Krishnakumar 2003.
84. See the "antiquity frenzy" website of the Warring States Project of the University of Massachusetts.
85. See preceding note.
86. Chattopadhyaya 1998. See also the work on "inclusivism" by P. Hacker (Oberhammer 1983).
87. Note that this has already been the case once in the recent past, during the two-year "emergency" of Indira Gandhi between 1975 and 1977, when her son, Sanjay, acted as a quasi-dictator, "kept the trains running on time," and so on. Most of the opposition was cowed into silence. But then other forces emerged and were elected, ironically in part those belonging to the recently defeated nationalistic, *Hindutva*-inspired government coalition.

Part III

Pseudoarchaeology in its wider context

10 The Atlantean box

Christopher Hale

Giza, AD 2002

It is dawn on the Giza plateau, Egypt. I am here with a crew to film the sunrise over the Great Pyramid. Although this monument is one of the wonders of the ancient world, the place we have set up our camera is close to some drab concrete buildings and a dilapidated stage set, the remains of a concert. The compacted sand is covered in tripod marks and footprints left by other crews. The cameraman has artfully composed out of our shot the endless vista of pollution-enshrouded Cairo suburbs, which roll like an insistent tide against the edge of the plateau. Today, the sky looks unpromising and dull. The Sun, the Egyptian god Re, seems unwilling to perform for the Discovery Channel. Then at about 6.30am, the heavens suddenly brighten but, disappointingly, without any especially photogenic displays. Only much later, when the Sun rises higher, do a few picturesque beams of light shyly emerge just to the right of Khephren's pyramid and, thankfully, we can roll. We are not making another film about the Giza pyramids but rather a Discovery Channel program about the Graeco-Roman "golden mummies" in the Western Desert.[1] The idea is to contrast these pyramids, built during Egypt's Old Kingdom (third millennium BC), with burial practices characteristic of the much later period of the "golden mummies," by which time the pyramids were already a tourist attraction. But because Graeco-Roman Egyptians, apart from Cleopatra, are less of a draw in terms of "audience recognition," we hope that the Giza pyramids will lend the necessary luster to our production. Few films are commissioned by broadcasters these days without the magic quality of "recognition": that is why "history" in the UK often means the history of the British royal family. The Giza monuments are the stellar performers of the ancient world and, as such, are essential casting in any television history of ancient Egypt.

As we waited for the Sun God to perform, I had become aware that there was another crew at work just a few hundred meters away. It turned out to be a Swiss team with an expensive new high-definition camera. When we asked them what they were up to, it turned out that they were compiling "library footage" for the "Erich von Däniken Mystery Park" that has been opened in Interlaken, Switzerland (McKie 2003). Von Däniken is experiencing something of a revival after his fall from grace in the 1970s, and it seems that he has not changed his mind: people from another planet built the pyramids, a Space Age reworking of older notions that Israelites or any number of superior "dynastic races" generated the great monuments of the past.[2]

Television Babel

These close encounters demonstrate that a multiplicity of zany "theories" swirl around the monuments at Giza, choking the offices of the Egyptian Council of Antiquities with requests for permission to film or conduct research there. At first sight, diversity of ideas might appear to be a virtue – if not an obligation – for television, but at a time when history seems to be enjoying an astonishing renaissance on both British and American television, historians remain divided on the value of the medium for conveying history. Some, like Simon Schama and Niall Ferguson, both of whom have formidable academic reputations, have embraced television and the high-level profile that it can offer.[3] However, the response has been mixed. Although many historians acknowledged that Schama and Ferguson had made history into exciting and sophisticated television, others were much more grudging. They carped that Schama in particular "over-dramatized."[4] But that is why so many watched – and why the television bureaucrats are begging for more.

Yet many historians and archaeologists prefer to remain standing warily on the sidelines of television exposure. These Jeremiahs see a dubious television industry colonized by the forces of reaction disguised as the new and remarkable: an endless pageant of programs telling us, for example, that the pyramids were built by survivors of an ancient catastrophe whose lost civilization is waiting to be discovered beneath the oceans of the world. According to this view, television is in danger of being overwhelmed by what has been called "alternative history," a catch-all genre that refers to a variety of speculative ideas about the past. Demonstrably, most if not all of these programs offer little more than reheated nineteenth-century pseudoscientific speculations, but that has not stopped them being presented as new, original, and unfairly disregarded by the "orthodox" academic community. (Fagan and Hale 2001; Fagan 2003).

Alarm over this situation is understandable. At the time of writing, a glance at the schedules of television stations on both sides of the Atlantic shows that there are many programs promoting pseudoarchaeological ideas in the schedules. But there are also very many, if not *more*, programs that cleave to what "alternative historians" disparagingly call "orthodox history." To be sure, individual programs or series can attract attention and excite considerable, if short-lived comment. A good example is journalist Graham Hancock's series *Underworld*, a three-part "sequel" to his previous series, *Quest for the Lost Civilization*. *Underworld* proposed the existence of great Ice

Age civilizations submerged beneath rising sea levels 12,000 years ago.[5] Hancock has been a highly successful practitioner of speculative history, but *Underworld* has not made many waves. Indeed, Hancock used *Underworld* to deliver a rather self-important public apology for past transgressions. He summarized these on his own website:

> Then [when writing *Fingerprints of the Gods*] my top priority was to cram in and get down on the page anything and everything that I thought might weigh in favor of the lost civilization idea. This was more important to me at that time than taking meticulous care with the quality of every source or being choosy about what leads I followed. I was also too quick to attack weaknesses in the orthodox position while failing to take proper account of orthodox strengths. The result was that my case for a lost civilization was anything but bullet-proof, and *Fingerprints* has come in for a massive amount of criticism – some of it richly deserved. Often, for example, I ignored the official carbon dates for sites I was writing about – just brushed them aside on the grounds that C-14 can't date stone monuments directly – and got on with finding my own way through all the good (and bad) reasons to doubt the orthodox chronology.[6]

The pressure for this apology came not from Hancock's own troubled conscience but from Channel 4 Television in London, the broadcaster that commissioned *Underworld* (and had previously aired another Hancock series based on *Fingerprints of the Gods* and *Heaven's Mirror*, called *Quest for the Lost Civilization*). The commissioning editor knew that Hancock could still bring in viewers but demanded that he signal a disengagement from prior ideas that had become stale and discredited.[7] Far from encouraging this highly successful author to churn out ideas at the level of previous efforts, the channel demanded that Hancock make his arguments more convincing. This is an important point. The broadcasters cannot be viewed as wholly opportunistic: in this case, they pushed a high-profile "alternative" author to make his case more impressive. The fact that the resulting programs were simply a more sophisticated rehash of the same tired ideas reveals all too clearly the limitations of Hancock's reworking of older mythologies. But this example suggests that the problem of pseudoarchaeology on television demands a sophisticated response.

Indeed, the television picture of ancient history – which is most vulnerable to the assault of the "alternative" movement (there seems to be little interest in an "alternative account" of the reign of Queen Elizabeth I, for example) – is heterogeneous, just as it is in academic scholarship. It is simply not the case that television always and strategically recycles discredited speculation. Quite the opposite: *it demands innovation*. Even nonsense can become stale. But at the same time television executives, like movie moguls, will always be attracted to a winning formula and will want to try to repeat its success with "innovative" add-ons. This contradiction was once unwittingly crystallized by a well-known BBC executive, who demanded: "I want it the same, but different." Caught between the desire to discover the next "new thing" and the safety of well-worn formulae, television is often engaged in a Sisyphus-like struggle, pushing the rock of innovation up the hill of repetition only to have it roll back to where it started.

In 2004, many of the alternative Atlantis-themed programs appear to have disappeared from television screens – in the UK at least. But the essential feature of this genre is its cyclical appeal. The idea of 'lost civilizations' is a uniquely rich myth, and it is almost certain that the genre will be reinvented.

In the country of story

The problem runs even deeper, because it is qualitative rather than quantitative. It is not the case that television is being invaded and colonized by ideas that the academic world regards as dubious, although that certainly can happen. It is rather that television provides no forum for proper scientific assessment and review, yet it remains the key point of contact between historical interpretation and a very wide public. To be sure, viewers themselves are not by definition uncritical. Indeed, simply *watching* a program about history or archaeology represents an important choice, especially in the United States and other multi-channel television environments, where an infinite variety of dross floods the airwaves. Despite this, however, there is no equivalent of peer review in television. Something altogether different takes command. Television replaces peer review with the exigencies of *narrative*. Evidence is sacrificed to *story* – and story is, I contend, the very core of history's problem with television. By recognizing the centrality of story to television, we can be much more precise about what is troubling about television programs that cover ancient history. All historians are storytellers, but outside television, the construction of the story is subject to the rules of evidence, and that is precisely what is missing in television culture.

Why is this important? The reason is that an emphasis on narrative has the effect of leveling out the differences between approaches to the past. Here are two talismanic phrases that define what the average, canny commissioning executive is in search of: "remarkable new discoveries" and "quest for ... [fill in as appropriate]." In the offices of the Discovery Channel in Bethesda, Maryland, or of the BBC or Channel 4 in London, these are words of power. In their minds, "amazing new discoveries on the Giza plateau" might be either the genuine discovery of the village that housed the pyramid builders or, just as serviceable, the bogus idea that the three main pyramids were designed 12,000 years ago, since they are a match for the belt stars of the constellation Orion. One idea is founded on scientific excavation, the other is vacuous speculation, but the imperatives of television impose equivalence between the two. In both cases, the story has the same form. There is a quest and a discovery – a classic storyline that feeds many a commissioner's need for output.

This formula "quest for ... " immediately implies the ingredients that will deliver viewers in their millions. A quest traditionally demands a hero, a task and, ideally, subsidiary characters who obstruct the hero's progress. These are the key ingredients in any successful narrative: a hero, something the hero wants, and elements that might prevent him acquiring what he wants. A very modest thought experiment illustrates how story imposes equivalence by proposing an imaginary schedule built around the quest motif. Here might be found, for example, "Quest for the Real Nefertiti." This is a story about a real, documented figure from Egyptian history. We alchemize it into a story by adding a hero – or heroine – who has new information or ideas about who Nefertiti was, what she did or where she was buried.[8] Alternatively, there might be another program: "Quest for Atlantis: The Final Answer." This program also features a lead character who will do the searching and, in this case, claim to have discovered the truth. One program is thus founded on genuinely evidence-based history, the other on specious fantasy. But when we encounter them in the setting of the television schedule, there is no apparent difference. This is the key point. Television commissioning is driven not by evidence but by the search for a story: an unfolding sequence of connected events with a hero or heroine who moves through a beginning, middle, and end – and, necessarily, in that order.[9] In the landscape of television, all becomes one in a generic wilderness of stories.

It is this flattening of the landscape rather than the *frequency* with which "alternative" views are promoted that, in my view, is the most insidious ingredient of ancient history on television. This is not to say that frequency cannot be dismaying in itself – Channel 4 Television in London and, with some irony, the Learning Channel in the United States have in the last three years transmitted six hours of television by Graham Hancock, the leading British exponent of "alternative history," whose success appears to have promoted a dispiriting revival of interest in von Däniken's wholly discredited spacemen-built-the-pyramids fantasies.

Outside the mainstream, the dazzling proliferation of so-called "niche channels" in the United States and parts of Europe could assist the "alternative" movement. And the leading authors – like Graham Hancock and his occasional collaborator, retired engineer Robert Bauval – have made good use of the Internet to promote their own fan base through much-visited message boards on their personal websites. Here fans can offer mutual support and, occasionally, communicate directly with their idols: they are highly effective tools for mobilizing propaganda. The relative absence of "alternative" history from current British channels may be merely a dormant period. Hancock and Bauval have recently published a book in which they argue that the monuments and planning of cities like Rome, Paris, and Washington were and remain the work of an ancient elite "priesthood" (Hancock and Bauval 2004). This unlikely scenario is ripe for "visualization." The new television channels need constant feeding, and a menu of "mysteries" is more alluring than is real history. The History Channel might be a special case, but the mother lode of Civil War shows and the biggest-explosions-in-history style of programming may now be an exhausted seam. The channel is turning to programs with titles such as *Angels: Good or Evil?* This surely is a clear example of how forces outside television, in this case Christian fundamentalism, have real impact on programming. And there is a well-evidenced link between fundamentalism and "alternative history" that may prove highly significant. Writers like Hancock and Bauval are fiercely opposed to skeptical organizations such as CSICOP and the Skeptics Society (which oppose the drive to fundamentalism), and with their colleague John Anthony West they appear to have sympathies with an anti-scientific, creationist tendency.[10]

It is increasingly clear, at least in the United States, that for ancient history to compete at all, it must be dressed up as mystery stories and alchemized into a set of puzzles. History *is* puzzling, challenging, and in many respects mysterious: it demands interpretation and then alert reassessment when new data emerge or old data are revealed to be unreliable. That said, scholarship can indeed be inertial and slow to change. But there is a difference between the two camps that follows directly from the imperative of narrative: "mystery" films promise a final revelation, closure, a destination, an answer. This is something that genuine history can never produce, as it is always open to new interpretation. Hancock and his ilk invariably promise these final solutions. They premise their investigations on the failure of "orthodox archaeology" to look at what they claim is neglected evidence that points to an all-embracing conclusion they believe to be the Truth. The supposed blindness of the "orthodox" historians is the premise for a lightning bolt of revelation. Genuine science draws back from such certainties. Testing hypotheses that fit the available evidence can lead to uncertainties, and to new, sometimes more difficult questions being asked. In contrast, the "alternative" camp promises the bliss of a final revelation, even if it ultimately fails to deliver it (since the ideas lack decisive evidence).

The flattening of the landscape of history, the endless flux of programming that conflates any kind of "theory" of the past as equivalent to any other promotes a dangerously false view of how historians can illuminate the past and challenge certainty. But the answer to the dilemma is not a matter of "policing" the media so that only "orthodox views" are represented – that would be absurd and unworkable and might simply give jealous academics an opportunity to score points against rivals. What must be demanded is not more or less programs of different kinds but an opportunity to understand and question how the past is debated – and why some ideas and not others are more powerful as interpretative tools.

There are established and proven methods for how ideas – "theories" – about the past, or indeed about any phenomenon, can be assessed. The most basic demands of any idea are how much available data it takes into account and how much it explains. For instance, the "orthodox" explanation for the Giza pyramids as royal tombs is rooted in plenty of observable data and is in accordance with the pyramids' immediate and wider context. In contrast, "alternative" proposals about the pyramids are based on no evidence (planned by lost civilizations), negative assertions (no bodies have been found in them), or highly questionable possibilities (the Orion correlation theory) (see the Introduction by Peter Kosso). The most parsimonious explanation for the function of the pyramids is that they were funerary monuments, not "mysterious" symbolic artefacts that require gratuitous explanations.

Television, in its current incarnation, simply does not allow very simple judgments like this to be made. Television homogenizes interpretation and makes even rudimentary reality checking very difficult. Story is all. Unlike a book – even one as fanciful as *Fingerprints of the Gods*, for example – a television program is experienced in real time, embedded inside a schedule and lacking any of the apparatus of scholarship, which is, in any case, regarded as extraneous to the business of storytelling. But a scholarly context can only come from the film itself, and it is in this way that the medium is currently woefully lacking. Without any justification, it is a widely held view that any genuine testing or debate would "spoil the story." Debate is allowed only when it can be regarded as obstructing the onward progress of the hero's new theory and thus making his quest more compelling. "Alternative historians" are masters of exploiting this, as they forever accuse skeptical inquiry of being pettifogging or nit-picking, "blocking" innovative thinking.

Another kind of story

In 1998, some colleagues and I in the BBC's science department[11] proposed a dispassionate examination of the old idea of Atlantis. The proposal was eagerly accepted by the celebrated science strand *Horizon*. For more than three decades, *Horizon* has been making what even the scientific community regards as outstanding programs. It has been referred to as the "Rolls-Royce" of science television. The programs are rigorously researched and produced to a very high standard. But *Horizon* is not immune to the same pressures that act on all television programming. Its editors are under pressure to deliver ever bigger audiences, as well as quality. Traditionally, *Horizon* programs were produced with the PBS station WGBH (Boston) and transmitted in the United States as *Nova*. In exchange, some American-produced programs aired under the *Horizon* banner in the UK. Both the BBC and WGBH shared the same production values, but when the BBC signed a production deal with the US Discovery Channel, this relationship was dissolved. Now *Horizon* would need to conform to models provided by a very different television culture, as the Discovery format now became the gold standard. It meant accelerating the pace of programs and catching the attention of a fickle and impatient audience within the first twenty seconds. "Get on the train" was the maxim issued from Discovery HQ in Bethesda, Maryland. Being a Rolls-Royce now had a downside. As much as it evoked high quality, it also implied a lumbering dinosaur from the past. Change was necessary – and *Horizon* even acquired a catchphrase: "pure science, sheer drama." This meant that complicated motives drove the commissioning of a film about Atlantis. The idea was to "test" a popular idea about the past, but it also reflected the tantalizing thought that the mere mention of the word "Atlantis" would draw in viewers. To be sure, this was not merely cynical. There would be little value in preaching to the converted – or in preaching at all.

The most pressing reason for commissioning the program was topical and, very simply, competitive. Channel 4 Television, which is the independent equivalent of *Horizon*'s home station BBC2, had recently broadcast three hours of lavishly funded speculation by Graham Hancock called *Quest for the Lost Civilization*. As planning for the new *Horizon* began at the end of 1998, however, there was little interest in focusing the film on Hancock himself. But that would soon change, for by now *Horizon* had appointed a new series editor who had an almost evangelical belief in the power of story, and stories need above all a lead character.

This obsession with story was really reinventing the wheel: after all, no decent journalist has ever truly neglected the need to hold an audience with a compelling tale. Inside the *Horizon* office, no one seemed to notice. *Horizon* now had to be a narrative series. Stories were everything. Producers were required to absorb the lessons of Hollywood, and specifically, to learn the arcane mysteries of "three-act structures," "turning points," the "negation of the negation" and other alchemical formulae developed by American scriptwriting guru Robert McKee (McKee 1999). McKee's expensive weekend-long courses are designed to enlighten aspiring Hollywood screenwriters, but now they became obligatory pilgrimages for *Horizon* producers. The results were immediate. With draconian insistence, *Horizon*'s new editor used McKee to transform *Horizon*. A new kind of program began to appear, complete with a lush movie-style soundtrack and breathless narration (now termed "voice-over") using the word "astonishing" at every opportunity. There was some complaining from the science community, which valued the sturdy values of the old *Horizon*, but the old Rolls-Royce had been adapted to a new environment and, as in any evolutionary process, there was no going back. The effect on the "Atlantis" film was profound. Stories needed heroes, and there was only one hero available to us in the kingdom of Atlantis.

So, as the film developed, Graham Hancock crept back onto center stage. After all, he was the most successful new propagator of a contemporary Atlantis, and his success appeared to rival that of Erich von Däniken, who had been the subject of a *Horizon* film twenty years earlier. The forensic, open-minded analysis achieved in this older *Horizon* provided a model for our "Atlantis."[12] Producer Graham Massey – who had also made a *Horizon* episode about the Bermuda Triangle – had scrutinized von Däniken's claims one by one and had coolly examined his evidence, which had impressed millions of readers all over the world. In this case, von Däniken's credibility had slowly crumbled away. He was shown to be frequently wrong and, on occasion, not entirely scrupulous. At this stage, we had no idea whether such an analysis would show Hancock to be right or wrong: what was important was Massey's approach. It was dispassionate, uncondescending, and authoritative. We would soon discover that Massey's films had one tremendous advantage: von Däniken himself unashamedly put forward what he saw as hard evidence for his outlandish claims, which could then be tested and, in every case, found wanting. He claimed, for example, that the Nazca lines in Peru were a "landing strip" for alien spacecraft, an assertion that *Horizon* showed to be impossible by driving a truck onto the soft desert gravels – and getting stuck.

Although Hancock used the very same ancient sites as von Däniken did (recycling is a feature of the genre; see Chapter 1) it soon became all too clear that Hancock was a very different kind of creature. As we looked more closely at his television programs and his books, it was increasingly unclear just *what* he was claiming, and what *evidence* he had to support his vague assertions. Although he traveled to plenty of "mysterious" places and took many pretty photographs, Hancock lacked the apparent coherence of von Däniken. His books and the television program began to look more and more nebulous. What *could* we test? This problem would become increasingly acute, especially after we had interviewed Hancock two months into our research.

We had other problems too. If we were to follow McKee, just what was the "story"? Graham Massey's old films about von Däniken were superb journalism, and they unfolded a gripping journalistic investigation without self-consciousness. That, if you like, was the story. Now that was no longer enough: there had to be drama. Films were to be constructed in acts, always three, for some reason; there had to be "turning points," as defined by McKee – and of course a *protagonist*. Hancock gradually turned into that main character. The drama of his "discoveries" would be explored at the beginning of the film and then tested. Everyone involved undertook this in good faith, as we were required to do by both our own standards as journalists and by the BBC's "producers' guidelines." Here are the core statements in these guidelines:

> A factual program ... will meet its commitment to due impartiality if it is fair, accurate and maintains a proper respect for truth.
>
> A program may choose to explore any subject, at any point on the spectrum of debate, as long as there are good editorial reasons for doing so.
>
> It may choose to test or report one side of a particular argument. However, it must do so with fairness and integrity. It should ensure that opposing views are not misrepresented.[13]

Every possible care was taken to ensure that we adhered to these guidelines. We strongly believed that our approach would give Hancock a proper opportunity to argue his case.

Now that we were indeed making a film "about Hancock" and his co-authors like Robert Bauval, a fresh obstacle became very apparent. One of Hancock's methods is to cast his net of evidence very wide indeed (see Chapter 1). It might be the case that gaping intellectual holes and flimsy evidence can be disguised if you are in Tiwanaku in South America in one paragraph (or shot) then winging your way to Easter Island in the next – closely followed by a temple in Egypt and Stonehenge. It made any critic's task extremely hard – tackle him on one point and scores of other examples would be left unexamined. I recognized an old problem from a film I had made, with the psychologist Nicholas Humphrey, about the paranormal:[14] decapitate one claim and, Hydra-like, the creature puts forth another head. The trap is chasing the tail of proving something wrong rather than demanding better evidence for an unlikely claim. It is a hard trap to avoid – as we discovered.

The only solution was to take core areas that Hancock himself appeared to regard as essential building blocks of his scenario. So we began to focus on:

- The "Orion correlation theory," originated by Robert Bauval but absorbed into Hancock's synthesis: both authors suggested that there was a correlation between the pyramids, if looked at in plan (from above, as it were), and the three belt stars of the constellation Orion; the correlation in turn implied that the ancients had enacted an ancient master plan when laying out the Giza pyramids.
- Claims about cultural connections between the Maya and ancient Egypt, which implied that they derived their culture from a common source, namely, a "lost civilization."
- The claim that South American legends referred to "white-bearded strangers" who brought the seeds of culture from across the Atlantic.
- The assertion, questioned by Bauval,[15] that the plan of the temples in the vicinity of Angkor Wat in Cambodia was a depiction of the constellation Draco.
- Claims that the Sphinx at Giza was carved 12,000 years ago (conventional date: 2500 BC).
- The claim that the Bolivian archaeological site of Tiwanaku could be dated to some time between 17,000 and 10,000 BC (conventional date: 1200 BC–AD 1500).
- The claim that there were underwater ruins off the Japanese coast, which were somehow evidence of a lost civilization. Everything suggested that these were natural submarine geological structures, but Hancock attached huge importance to their status as ancient ruins.

This list would be winnowed down further, but these claims seemed to offer strong points of departure. We also wished to emphasize that Hancock's fundamental premise could be boiled down to this: "orthodox" historians date the emergence of "civilization" to a period some time after 5000 BC.

According to Hancock, this ignores evidence of a much more ancient Ice Age civilization that attached considerable and never explained importance to the date 10,500 BC. Survivors from the cataclysmic destruction of this nameless civilization carried the seeds of culture around the world. As with other diffusionist models, Hancock's "lost civilization" appeared to explain bizarre similarities between widely separated ancient cultures like the Maya and the Egyptians. Hancock himself never seemed to see the obvious circularity of his answer to the question we had put to him. Where did civilization come from? Well, it came from *another* civilization. While the archaeologists whom Hancock despised were struggling to hypothesize connections between climate change, the emergence of farming, and the development of socially hierarchical, monument-building societies all over the ancient world, Hancock's lame solution was that civilizations came from an older civilization! The argument simply chased its own tail. Hancock's "theory" was an extreme form of diffusionism, the old idea that civilizations spread from a common source. However, most diffusionist historians had evidence of these source cultures: it is fundamental to Hancock's proposals that the evidence has somehow and conveniently vanished.

Other writers were offering quite similar ideas, but Hancock was clearly a leader in the field, and his books were highly synthetic (e.g., Hancock 1995, 1998a, 2001). They contained very little original research, and much effort was devoted to harvesting ideas about the past from very diverse sources. Hancock's skill lay in making a pattern from such magpie pickings and, in this sense, he really was a true descendant of Ignatius Donnelly, the nineteenth-century speculator who had recast Plato's Atlantis as an alluring myth for his time, and our own (Donnelly 1882, 1970). Donnelly's mishmash of borrowed ideas from science and history had in turn been reinvented by Hancock. The date of 10,500 BC was an ingredient that did not help his credibility. As our researcher soon discovered, the date had an obsessive significance for an American mystic, active in the 1920s and 1930s, called Edgar Cayce, who was known as the "sleeping prophet." After prolonged periods of slumber, Cayce would make portentous pronouncements about the location of Atlantis, the fate of its written culture (hidden under the Sphinx), and the accomplishments of its people (they could fly). In one of his dreams, Cayce claimed to have discovered that Atlantis had been destroyed in 10,500 BC, and for reasons that they never fully explained both Hancock and Bauval adopted this date as a talismanic moment in history and claimed that the Giza pyramids and other monuments were a kind of back reference to this date.

The next step was to become familiar with the scientific work that had been carried out on the core topics we had selected. And here we encountered a new and surprising problem. Few academics working in these fields wanted to discuss our program, at least in the United Kingdom. The strongest response came from the Egyptian Department at the British Museum, whose head ordered his staff to refuse all contact with 'the *Horizon*

program on Atlantis'. In the United States, there was a similar response
from Egyptologist Mark Lehner, who had carried out important work on the
Giza plateau. Their reasons were interesting. They would not accept that we
were genuinely investigative. Both the British Museum staff and Lehner
referred to a program about the Sphinx that had been made by the BBC
history series *Timewatch*, which had focused on the maverick ideas of John
Anthony West and American academic Robert Schoch, both of whom
claimed that the Sphinx had been carved millennia before the "orthodox
date" (of 2500 BC). Lehner had been interviewed by *Timewatch*, but he felt
that his interview had been misused. He believed that he had been turned
into a "token critic" and not taken seriously. In story terms, he had been
presented as one of the obstacles that must obstruct the path of the hero.
Other contributors to the *Timewatch* program felt the same, and they could
not be persuaded that the *Horizon* film would not follow the same course. If
our film was the same kind of animal, then it did not deserve to be fed.

The *Timewatch* example provides good evidence for the problem of story.
No one is going to make a program simply "about the Sphinx." What will
attract commissions is "new thinking" – and here the "alternative" community has a tremendous advantage. It can offer any number of speculative
ideas that masquerade as novel insights. If the "orthodox community" then
pours cold water on these new ideas, a program maker has the makings of a
story: Davids of originality pitted against the Goliaths of academia.
Everyone will have their part to play. This, indeed, was the essence of
Lehner's gripe. Without knowing it, he had been cast as the dismissive,
narrow-minded skeptic.

With our progress seemingly blocked, we made an interesting discovery.
When we approached American academics (other than Lehner) they were,
with just one or two exceptions, generous with their time and commitment.
I am certain that this reflects the power of creationism in the United States:
these scientists knew that pseudoscience is a threat. The recent history of
creationism showed how irrational, pseudoscientific ideas could have a
destructive impact on education and culture.[16] American academics had also
taken the trouble to study and publish on pseudoarchaeology itself (Feder
2002b; Williams 1991): they could see how Hancock and his followers
fitted into an old cultural phenomenon.

The generosity of the American academics meant that we now had
enough material to make more than one film, so a more general account of
the Atlantis myth went into production as "Atlantis Uncovered," and the
film on Hancock continued in tandem as "Atlantis Reborn." It was a unique
experiment that provided both a context and a close analysis through paired
programs.

By now, it had become imperative to secure and film an interview with
Hancock himself. Hancock had contacts inside the BBC, and when I telephoned him his first, very aggressive, response was "Is this the BBC hatchet
job?" My response was to say that what we were proposing could never be in

any sense a hatchet job – we had done too much research for that – and that it would be fair to him but tough on his ideas. I stated that the film would look at his "theories" in the context of the debate about the emergence of civilization. During this tense call, he reasserted ideas already familiar from his books and television series: that civilization had emerged much earlier than archaeologists were prepared to concede and that we were all afflicted by a collective amnesia that denied the evidence for this highly sophisticated lost culture. Modern humans had, he argued, been around for more than 60,000 years – why should civilization have emerged so late? There were issues raised by Hancock's assertions that could not be explored in the film we were making. For example, his "theory" was rooted in a very conventional view of human development: civilization was the peak of human culture. But while early human societies may not have built pyramids, or developed writing, they were highly sophisticated nonetheless: these were the people, after all, who produced rock and cave art all over the world. There were good reasons why "civilization" (in the form of monument-building hierarchical societies) did not emerge until after the last Ice Age, and it was not an inevitable development anyway.[17]

The "amnesia" argument, frequently trotted out I noticed, was absurd. How could we forget something that had yet to be verified or even found? Amnesia turned out to be just one of Hancock's beefs about academics – or rather "orthodox academics" – whom he believed willfully ignored *possibilities*. Civilizations *might* be a lot older than the current evidence indicated, but academics were woefully unwilling to think about this. It was obvious that Hancock simply did not understand science. Nor did he perceive that a new discovery that showed, for example, that the first civilizations were much older than previously thought would be the royal road to academic fame and fortune. It was a simple case of wish fulfillment eagerly lapped up by the hordes of fans that Hancock had acquired. Most seemed to thrive on the "reactionary academics versus visionary new thinking" story that Hancock was spinning.[18] There *is* intellectual inertia in the scientific and academic world, but the process of rational inquiry embraces the struggle between established views and new approaches, which allows intellectual inertia to be overcome by the application of valid evidence and cogent argument. The history of archaeology as an academic discipline is replete with examples of old ideas overturned by new discoveries. In every case, vapid speculations did not win the day but rigorous argument founded on testable evidence.

This was not going to be the fate of Hancock's ideas, as we discovered at the first interview, which consumed an entire, frustrating day and used up many rolls of tape. Hancock was very proud of what he said in the course of the interview and later printed the full transcripts in a new edition of his book *Fingerprints of the Gods* (Hancock 2001). But the problem for us was that his assertions were vague and timid (lots of "possibly" and "it could be"), and his evidence was for the most part painfully thin. Remarkably, he had no explanation for the purported recurrence of the date 10,500 BC in ancient cultures, and some of his assertions were simply absurd. For example, when I asked him to picture what had happened in Egypt in 10,500 BC when the Atlantean supermen had supposedly arrived, he claimed they had built a "monastery" by the Nile and lived in it for close on 8,000 years. When the indigenous Egyptians were "ready," the Atlantean visitors had emerged to pass on their wisdom.[19] This scenario was not backed by any evidence whatsoever (where was this monastery?) and was, to say the least, far-fetched. How did the Atleanteans live for 8,000 years? Did they not reproduce and thus require the construction of new dwellings? Farm? Build boats and sail the Nile? Throw away rubbish? Did they not die and get buried? Did they not eat? Did they not excrete, or was Atlantean anatomy different?

Hancock's hesitancy and lack of conviction were troubling. We returned to London dismayed. We did not realize that a trap had been set – whether deliberately or not it is impossible to say. Hancock's statements were vague, but they shared one lethal characteristic. All his answers were very long and prolix and often ran over many pages of transcript. I had allowed him to speak at length in the interest of fairness and because I was hoping to hear, at some point, a genuine defense of the ideas that had made him famous and, it was said, very rich. In hindsight, this might have been a mistaken strategy, but it was carried out in good faith.

In the production office, I gloomily pored over Hancock's interview day after day searching for his most convincing, evidenced statements and paring down the flood of words. It was hard work – but we needed Hancock's proposals to be clear and worthy of debate. It would be fatal to make him a straw man. And it was also important to convey the romance of his quest for a lost civilization, since that appeared to fascinate his readers. We now set about making the rest of the film with sequences that would test the ideas that Hancock had proposed. Filming took place in Egypt, Mexico, Bolivia, and the United States. We could not afford to travel to Angkor Wat or Japan, but we knew that these parts of Hancock's ideas could be handled in other ways. We selected key contributors to assess Hancock's ideas. Great care was taken to make the right choice; we were not interested in blunt assertions that the "lost civilization" idea was wrong. We wanted to know if there was hard evidence that supported Hancock's case or demonstrated that it was mistaken. These were not the tactics of anyone hastily cobbling together a "hatchet job" and in the most profound sense were completely fair. We took Hancock very seriously indeed, even if he sometimes sounded unconvinced by himself.

Editing began. It was a long and sometimes painful process. At every stage the film was viewed by the series editor and the BBC's lawyers, and judgments about fairness were continually refined. Despite this, no one realized that a ticking time bomb lay buried in the bulging and much-perused folders of transcripts that had pride of place in the cutting room. Hancock's ideas, despite intricate editing decisions, were so convoluted and poorly argued that it was sometimes unclear, first, how to deal with them, and next, how effectively they had been tested. This led to bitter debate. Was he right? Was he wrong? Was he neither? Was he saying what we thought he was saying? The process began to resemble a wrestling match with poisonous jelly. I was reminded of a famous comment by physicist Wolfgang Pauli, who, when asked to assess a student's proposals, concluded in despair: "they are not even wrong." In other words, the hypothesis was not testable and was therefore of little use. Some of Hancock's "theories" seemed to be "not even wrong." As the film was distilled and refined, some sequences were shed in favor of more concrete ideas. Hancock had frequently stressed the importance of Bauval's "Orion correlation theory," and this would become a decisive battleground when the film was transmitted.

As Paul Jordan has argued in his book *The Atlantis Syndrome*, using *complexity* rather than hard evidence is typical of "alternative historians," and the "Orion correlation theory" demonstrates this axiom very well indeed. It boils down to the three pyramids at Giza and three stars in a constellation. Looked at from above, the pyramids resemble the belt stars of the constellation Orion. Although modern constellations were formulated by the Greeks, some of the stars in the Greek "Orion" appear to have had some religious significance for the Egyptians. Photographs show that the three middle or belt stars of Orion have a kink, with one star seemingly offset on a diagonal and slightly less bright than its companions. (These features of the observed stars are in truth hard to detect.) On the Giza plateau, Menkaure's pyramid is also offset and much smaller than the other two pyramids. According to Robert Bauval and Adrian Gilbert (1994) this was taken as evidence that the pyramid builders had mimicked on the ground the pattern of stars in the sky. Originally, Bauval and Gilbert proposed that other stars in the constellation were also represented by pyramids proximate to Giza, but the "fit" was quickly shown to be so poor that Bauval retracted. As the astronomer Ed Krupp remarked during our interview with him, simply matching two sets of three objects in a line is not especially impressive. As Bauval sought to ballast his idea, he noticed another problem: even if the match was accepted, the stars and the pyramids did not line up very well from ground to sky. They were skewed in a way that implied that the Egyptians had made a very poor job of their sky:ground correlation – or had not intended a correlation at all. In some desperation, Bauval introduced an astonishing theoretical stretch. The slow precessional cycle of the stars in the sky can be seen as a cosmic clock. Each moment in the cycle is the fingerprint of a moment in time. This is simple astronomy – but Bauval now claimed to have discovered a perfect match between pyramids and stars when the stellar clock was "turned back" to 10,500 BC. This was I suspect a rather desperate adjustment to get Bauval out of trouble. But the exploitation of genuine science (precession is both observable and explicable) successfully alchemized the "Orion mystery" into a "theory." Indeed, in his interview Hancock had cheekily described the correlation as a "discovery" – implying that Bauval had unearthed genuine evidence rather than merely suggesting that three objects resembled another three objects.

Because Hancock attached so much importance to the "Orion correlation theory," Bauval had also been interviewed. But his explanation and defense of his ideas were thought to be very difficult to understand. As a result, they were used sparingly, so that we relied on Hancock's much clearer explanations of his friend's ideas. The question was: could an observed resemblance be tested? We discovered that astronomer Ed Krupp, who was head of the Griffith Observatory in Los Angeles, had troubled to investigate whether Bauval could be right and had quickly spotted a logical contradiction in the "Orion correlation theory." His comments later led to intense controversy, so it is worth being clear about what Dr Krupp said.

One ingredient in Bauval's Giza speculations involved the enigmatic "shafts" built into the Great Pyramid at Giza. Astronomers had noted that the shafts appeared to target constellations in the sky: the Pole Star to the north and Orion to the south. Bauval seized on this to buttress his ideas, but it caused him no end of problems. The shafts can only be said to target the constellation when they reach the meridian in their apparent passage through the night sky. The meridian is an imaginary north–south line drawn across the heavens that allows astronomers to map the sky. There is no certainty that the Egyptians used a meridian, but once Bauval had accepted that the shafts in the pyramid were pointing toward a position determined by the meridian, the "Orion correlation" began to look very flimsy. The reason is quite simple. If a north–south orientation suggested by the shafts is accepted, then the proposed alignment of the three pyramids at Giza and the belt stars of Orion becomes inverted. In Krupp's words, to get a real match you either have to turn the sky upside down or turn Egypt upside down. Few observations have caused so much acrimony and debate, and Krupp's point is often misunderstood. The upside-down problem has nothing to do with what the ancient Egyptians believed (although they appear to have been both rigorous and precise) – it is a problem of internal consistency in Bauval's position. For if the Egyptians aligned the shafts to north in the sky, why did they not do the same with the supposed Orion correlation? It was a highly effective and dramatic moment in the film, and it clearly showed that Bauval's idea had not survived a test. Very late in the editing, we also discovered that another astronomer, Tony Fairall, had found that the "match" between the stars and pyramids in 10,500 BC was not as precise as Bauval had claimed.

Other issues were more intractable. One of Hancock's other theoretical buttresses is the idea that the Sphinx was much older than the "orthodox" date of 2500 BC. His evidence came from observations made by Professor Robert Schoch, of Boston University, who claimed that the Sphinx had been water-eroded during a much wetter period in Egyptian history. Since Egypt has dried over time, and the Old Kingdom period when the Sphinx is conventionally thought to have been carved was relatively dry, his conclusion was that the Sphinx had to be much older. Schoch had been brought to Egypt by John Anthony West, a disciple of René Schwaller de Lubicz (a French mystic with fascist sympathies), who believed that the Sphinx was created by a superior civilization long before the Old Kingdom (Schwaller de Lubicz 1998; see also Chapter 5). Although Schoch gave West the answer he wanted, his work was genuinely scientific and has caused no end of problems for Egyptologists, who, at first, found the geological argument hard to refute. But it has become clear that Schoch's argument does not take proper account of the effects of salts in the Giza plateau and, even more than that, erosion is a very inadequate dating tool. Although Egypt had a drier climate during the Old Kingdom, the effects of reduced vegetation and highly destructive flash floods taking place periodically over nearly 5,000 years provides a perfectly adequate explanation for the erosive features of the Sphinx. Then we made an intriguing discovery: Schoch had never claimed that the Sphinx was 12,000 years old. He favored a date that fell somewhere between Hancock's and West's wished-for date and the conventional one. When I interviewed him in Boston, he stated on the record that his work had been misrepresented and that he had little sympathy with ideas about Ice Age lost civilizations (although he appears to have changed his mind since; see Schoch 2003). This was potentially much more devastating than simply showing that he was wrong about the date of the Sphinx. Hancock had massaged Schoch's results, just as he had the work of an American geophysicist, Professor Joe Kirschvink.[20] Rather than tackling the age of the Sphinx directly, we could simply point out that Hancock had got Schoch wrong. Schoch also disagreed with Hancock about the Yonaguni Formation, the mysterious submerged rock structure off the coast of Japan that Hancock believed was an underwater city dating back to 10,500 BC. Schoch believed that it was interesting natural geology, no more, no less. It was at this point that a bitter argument developed between the production team and the *Horizon* series editor. If Schoch was wrong about the Sphinx (although that was no longer our main point), how could he be trusted on Yonaguni? In fact, his *claims* about the Sphinx and his *observations* about Yonaguni are not in contradiction. He is a perfectly competent geologist. But now an extraordinary decision was made to remove any reference to Schoch's work on the Sphinx and use *only* his damning comments on Yonaguni. It was a very serious error, imposed on the film, which would damage our standing when the film was broadcast. Even with the best of intentions, mistakes can be made – and paid for.

In the interests of fairness, *Horizon* had decided that Hancock should be allowed to reply to criticism of his work on a point-by-point basis in a second interview, even though the BBC lawyers had advised that this was unnecessary. Despite the cost, fairness was always a priority. In particular, we wanted Hancock to comment on the point made by Ed Krupp that the "Orion correlation" was upside down. It was important that Hancock provide a reply. We were also certain that he would make a much clearer defense than Bauval himself – and we applied the same logic to astronomer Tony Fairall's conclusions that there was not a precise correlation between the angle of the pyramids on the ground and the stars.

Hancock was much more focused at the second session, as he often is, apparently, when faced with criticism rather than the need to outline his views. He is better at defense than exposition. The problem was that he provided *alternative* responses to the most powerful criticisms of Bauval's work. For example, Krupp's comments were either (1) wrong because Orion looks right in the sky, a point that ignored Bauval's dependence on the meridian; or (2) correct, but this did not in itself undermine the symbolic power of the idea. Another tricky dilemma thus presented itself. Which defense was more appropriate to use? Could the second one be construed as implying the first? We thought so and plumped for that.

By now, unfortunately, the film had become a battlefield, with many different cooks snatching away the spoon and stirring the pot. But at no time did any participant lose sight of the central importance of journalistic fairness. Nor, in the horrors of editing, had we anticipated that anyone would think the film was *funny*. But this is precisely what happened, as press previews heralded a comic battle between reason and Hancock's increasingly desperate attempts to defend his ideas. When the film was broadcast, the reaction from Hancock, Bauval, and their followers was loud, bitter, and angry. E-mails flooded into the BBC, and Hancock telephoned the *Horizon* office the morning after transmission and demanded a copy of the transcripts. It was immediately very clear what was about to happen. He was going to claim misrepresentation. Those vacuous interviews that we had worked so hard to make credible were to be his weapon. Battle was joined very quickly.

Battle for Atlantis

Hancock's first recourse was to approach the BBC's Head of Complaints, a canny gentleman called Fraser Steel whose responsibility, first of all, was to judge whether Hancock – now joined by Bauval – had legitimate grounds for complaint. Since the complaint, even at this early stage, was at least twenty pages in length with ten specific points at issue, the BBC had little alternative but to launch an *internal* investigation to assess whether we had made the film fairly. Then, not long after this first assault, Hancock withdrew his forces and announced his intention of taking the battle to an independent body called the Broadcasting Standards Commission (BSC), now OFCOM. The function of this body according to its website is as follows:

> The Broadcasting Standards Commission is the statutory body for both standards and fairness in broadcasting. It is the only organisation within the regulatory framework of UK broadcasting to cover all television and

radio, both terrestrial and satellite. This includes text, cable and digital services. It has three main tasks, as established by the Broadcasting Act, 1996. These are:

- to produce codes of conduct relating to standards and fairness;
- to consider and adjudicate on complaints;
- to monitor, research and report on standards and fairness in broadcasting.[21]

Hancock and his colleague now redoubled their efforts, and an even longer and more complex complaint was submitted to the BSC. Its main thrust was, as anticipated, the use of the interviews. His comments, Hancock complained, had been taken out of context, distorted, and misused to make him seem dishonest and unable to provide responses to his critics. Both he and Bauval were vitriolic about the use of Ed Krupp's upside-down objection – certainly very damaging to the "Orion correlation theory" – and the way in which their responses to it had been edited.

Sadly, the first reaction inside the BBC was alarm and confusion. Although the film had received more editorial and legal attention than most films – certainly ones made by the science department – some team members appeared to have forgotten the collective responsibility that this process necessarily entailed. Now instead of being trenchantly defended, the film would have to be researched all over again and the arguments justified afresh. Rather than closing the wagons, the wagons sped off in different directions with only the producer left to guard the trail. The staunchest defense came from former series producer John Lynch, who wrote to Hancock as follows:

Neither the producer nor the *Horizon* series itself set out to mug you. Your books have reached a very wide audience, as has your television series. Your ideas are attractive to many people who have limited information on which to make a judgment about our history, for no academic historian, archaeologist or scientist reaches such a wide audience with their description of the evidence that supports the established view of the past. Therefore, in the apparent absence of counter argument, your ideas stand to overturn the existing, academically tested interpretation of history in the minds of many people. As a series interested primarily in science, *Horizon* felt that the influence of your ideas was such that they warranted critical examination and testing by people whose expertise could be relied on in the various fields that you cover. That is a wholly appropriate aim, and that was the sole aim of the program. The production team conducted extensive research, at a very detailed level, and arrived at the conclusion that your ideas do not stand up to critical analysis. I am sorry that you are disappointed by that conclusion, but it is the conclusion that was reached in an objective appraisal.[22]

This was absolutely correct and very well put. But now the true power of the "alternative historians" began to become clear. We had planned a forensic, detailed, and reasoned account of their ideas and, we concluded, they were wrong on most if not all points. We did not, and could not, set out to consider every single assertion made by Hancock in his books and television series, but we made a judicious selection of his most important arguments. Most critics of the film saw precisely these qualities. But it is a dispiriting hindsight that the two complainants made the BBC jump to their tune, not the other way around. They seized the agenda, and the BBC, reeling, sought to counter the attacks on the same grounds established by the complainants. A complaint to the BSC resembles a libel action, and in English law the complainant has most of the advantages. He or she has to prove nothing, while the accused has to demonstrate that their statements were justified.

It was six months, dominated by convoluted and sometimes bitter argument among the BBC team, before we appeared in front of the BSC tribunal. The proceedings took place behind closed doors in a building close to Westminster Abbey. The commission, which had been considering a mass of documents that had accumulated over the past few months, consisted of civil servants and public figures. Not one of them had any expertise in history, archaeology, or astronomy – and seemed not have consulted anyone who had. They had made periodic requests for extra transcripts but nothing else.

When we entered the room, Hancock and Bauval were already present. Hancock refused to acknowledge us, but Bauval was disarmingly polite. He was accompanied by his lawyer, who spoke for him throughout the proceedings; Bauval said not a word. This was distinctly odd. Surely Bauval was present to defend his ideas, not to present a legal case? Hancock had come with his wife and collaborator Santha Faia. She appeared to comfort and calm him at frequent intervals – and he often seemed angry. This was undoubtedly genuine, but what the BSC appeared to face, from the start, were two aggrieved individuals who had, in their view, been egregiously mistreated by a powerful media corporation. This is an important point. The argument was about fairness not about whether ideas were right or wrong – although both matters were inevitably intertwined.

As I have implied, a complaint to the BSC is a cheap – or, as the BBC feared, an experimental – pseudo-libel action. Hancock's complaints were indeed framed in legal terms.[23] In other words, although a BSC complaint is not a legal proceeding, the commission was, in this case, asked to assess whether the program complained about had "lowered the esteem in which the plaintiff is held by right-thinking people," i.e. was libelous. As well as commenting on the treatment of their ideas in the film, Hancock in particular had claimed that we had implied he was devious and dishonest, thus reducing the esteem in which he was held. At the tribunal, he claimed that people in his home village in Devon had crossed the road to avoid meeting him: it sounded absurd and self-pitying, but it was a statement about reputation. If the BSC found in his favor, it would – the BBC feared – be very tempting for Hancock to go to court.

That morning, the BSC efficiently and dispassionately worked its way through the evidence. Time was strictly monitored. But since both Hancock and Bauval had complained about the "upside-down" and "angles" issues concerning the "Orion correlation theory," both could spend a great deal of time discussing this one point. One other especially tricky issue concerned the "wrong angles" noted by astronomer Tony Fairall. Why had we asked Hancock to respond to this and not re-interviewed Bauval? The truth was that, as I have stated already, once again that we did not think Bauval's response would be clear – and we also knew, after discussing the matter with him on the telephone, that he would make the same point we had already (and expensively) recorded with Hancock – that it "didn't matter." The ancient Egyptians who laid out their pyramids with a level of accuracy correct to minutes of a degree would not, according to Bauval, have been especially concerned about a star alignment discrepancy exceeding five degrees. And so it went on. Much of the discussion would have been baffling to an outsider unaware of the arcane world of "alternative" history and the steaming passions that it generates. At the end of several hours, both parties went their separate ways to await the outcome. And it was long in coming.

The delay implied some division or uncertainty inside the BSC. It had to deal not only with rather complex disputation but also with the fact that Hancock and his colleague were aggrieved. Months later, it delivered its judgment. Hancock and Bauval between them had made eight separate complaints. They lost all but one. Now this may appear to be a judgment in the BBC's favor – and the BSC commented at length on the good faith of the program makers: "The Commission considers that the program-makers acted in good faith in their examination of the theories of Mr Hancock and Mr Bauval."[24] But because one point had been upheld, it allowed Hancock and Bauval to wage another Internet war based on their claim that they had "won" completely. It was a most unfortunate result – and I suspect it was a fudge by the BSC. It had to offer *something* to the complainants – and it went for the "upside-down" issue that both complainants had been so angry about. Even before the judgment appeared, we had planned to rebroadcast the film come what may. We knew that now, in the aftermath of the BSC judgment, we could show how little the main argument of the film was affected by simply extending Hancock's reply to Ed Krupp.

The decision to reshow the film was immediately misunderstood. There was no obligation at all for the BBC to do any such thing, and the decision was unprecedented. Nor was it a kind of apology. After transmission of "Atlantis Reborn Again," press comment made it very clear that Hancock had gained nothing from making the complaint – and now he had to endure the key arguments of the film being shown again to an audience of three million. If he claimed victory, it was entirely Pyrrhic.

By now, both versions of the film had acquired considerable notoriety. Everyone involved in their making continued to receive streams of often abusive mail from Hancock's fans, who had been very effectively mobilized through his website. It was pointless to respond. The level of venom from readers and admirers was often astonishing – 400 examples of this poisonous discourse can be read on Hancock's website.

The mainspring of this passion, if the hundreds of letters are parsed, shows how Hancock had very cleverly made himself the spokesperson for a constituency of quasi-New Age enthusiasts who believe that "orthodox science" has too much authority and resent the fact. Time after time, correspondents on web pages delivered vitriolic attacks on "academics" and "scientists." It is worth taking full cognizance of this constituency. Most are educated and intelligent but, somehow, have come to hate the reputed power of science to determine various agendas of debate. At the same time, Hancock has allowed many millions of readers worldwide to develop and possess their own highly individual ideas about the ancient past. He allows his readers to take history back from the historians – at the cost of grossly misrepresenting it. The ideas are Hancock's – but somehow a conjuring trick is performed that allows anyone to "believe." The Hancock website is really the focal point of a cult. Our *Horizon* film thus became a lightning rod for the passion and vitriol that had been simmering among Hancock's fans since the publication of *Fingerprints of the Gods*.

These then are the bare bones of a story. It shows what can happen when television tries to mount a skeptical investigation of popular ideas, in this case about the ancient past. In 1987, the film I had made with Nicholas Humphrey, which attempted to do the same for various paranormal phenomena, had been greeted with almost equal disgust by people who thought they had been robbed of their comforts. There is more in heaven and earth, dear Horatio, but somehow it has been commandeered by the mandarins of science.

There may be another problem embedded in this narrative. How much does the academic world care about the health of a scientific culture? Is it enough for ideas to be circulated among a peer group while other public constituencies are left to rot? I am assuming that archaeology and history are forms of science, or at least that they assess evidence in a scientific way. These values, which are more about method than information or data, must be made more widely available. If they were, there would have been little need for television to take on the task of showing how allegedly novel ideas about the origins of civilization can be rationally examined – and, in this case, found wanting.

Notes

1. *Oasis of the Golden Mummies*, aired on the Discovery Channel in 2002.
2. There is an excellent account of these ideas, as applied to ancient Egypt, in Montserrat 2001 and, in more general terms, in Jordan 2001.

3. Simon Schama's *A History of Britain* was broadcast on the BBC and the History Channel between 2000 and 2002. Niall Ferguson's *Empire: How Britain Made the Modern World* was shown on Channel 4 in 2003. The book is published in the United States as Ferguson 2003.

4. As noted by a *Guardian* journalist: "'the trouble with TV is that it has to get ratings,' says [a historian], 'and if you want ratings, you have to do some marketing. Marketing people know what sells and what they're peddling is a simplified, sensational view. We weren't too happy with some of the trailers for *The Big Dig*, which showed a woman going down into a pit and coming back up waving Excalibur.' It is not the first time academics have found themselves at odds with television. Every time David Starkey and Simon Schama present their historical blockbusters, the academics cringe at their crudely dramatic presentation. It's a curiously ungracious reaction because television is the surest way of reaching new audiences and generating interest for your subject" (Smith 2003).

5. *Underworld: Flooded Kingdoms of the Ice Age*, a three-part series produced by Diverse Productions in London for Channel 4, London, and TLC, Washington. Aired in 2002 and 2003.

6. http://www.grahamhancock.com/underworld/underworld1.php?p = 2.

7. Personal communication, Charles Furneaux, commissioning editor, Channel 4 Television.

8. At the time of writing, I became aware that the Discovery Channel had made and broadcast a film, presented by Egyptologist Joann Fletcher, that claimed to have identified the mummy of Nefertiti. It is a delicious irony that Fletcher's claims, apparently buttressed by some hard science, led to her being banned from visiting Egypt. She had somehow forgotten to inform the Egyptian Supreme Council of Antiquities that she was going to make such a claim in a television program – rather than through a joint academic announcement.

9. The *avant-garde* film director Jean-Luc Godard once said that a film had a beginning, a middle, and an end, but "not necessarily in that order."

10. For evidence of this proposal, see the websites of all three (Hancock, Bauval, West), where creationist ideas proliferate, especially on the message boards.

11. Researchers Julian Hudson and Jacqueline Laughton, producer Jacqueline Smith.

12. *Horizon: The Case of the Ancient Astronauts*, first shown August 1978, produced in association with WGBH Nova.

13. The guidelines are available online at http://www.bbc.co.uk/info/policies/producer_guides/pdf/section3.pdf.

14. *Is There Anybody There?* aired on Channel 4 in 1987.

15. *Horizon* interview, 1998.

16. West rejects Darwinian evolution. In his new book 'Supernature' (2005) Hancock also seems to embrace 'intelligent design' – which is essentially another label for Creationism.

17. This is not the place to go into a detailed theoretical critique of Hancock's and other's ideas about civilization; for an excellent recent account, see Jordan 2001: 207–56.

18. This became apparent after the film was shown, when many hundreds of e-mails arrived at the BBC protesting about the film. These and related documents can be read at http://www.grahamhancock.com/horizon/default.htm.

19. Hancock does not use the name "Atlantis," but his theory perfectly fits what has been called the "Atlantis Syndrome"; see Jordan 2001.

20. Kirschvink *et al.* (1997) had published work that implied there had been global slippage of the Earth's crust – or "true polar wander" – over many millions of years: "Life diversified like crazy about half a billion years ago," says Kirschvink, "and nobody really knows why. It began about 530 million years ago, and was over about 15 million years later. It is one of the outstanding mysteries of the biosphere. The geophysical evidence that we've collected from rocks deposited before, during, and after this event demonstrate that all of the major continents experienced a burst of motion during the same interval of time." It is clear that the "burst" of activity took place over many millions of years, but in his book *Heaven's Mirror*, Hancock misleadingly used Kirschvink's proposal as if it supported the

idea of what he called "crustal displacement" *within the last 20,000 years* to explain the destruction of his lost civilization. In his interview with *Horizon*, Kirschvink described Hancock's misuse of his work as "worse than pseudoscience." In this case, Hancock's blushes were spared: the sequence was removed.

21. http://www.bsc.org.uk.
22. Published at http://www.grahamhancock.com/horizon/lynch-letter.htm.
23. See complaints published on website cited in note 18.
24. BSC adjudication; text on website cited in note 18.

11. The colonization of the past and the pedagogy of the future

Norman Levitt

The Moving Finger writes; and, having writ,
Moves on: nor all thy Piety nor Wit
Shall lure it back to cancel half a Line,
Nor all thy Tears wash out a Word of it.
(Edward Fitzgerald, The Rubáiyát of Omar Khayyám, 1st edn, LI)

Jeweler: This little dhow here is made of rubies. Yes sir, it's rubies!
Bullwinkle: No it isn't – it's mine!
Rocky: Well my gosh! If it's made out of rubies "n—"
Bullwinkle: If you're hesitating for me to finish the line, then you've got a long wait!
Jeweler: And I don't have the guts to say it!
Rocky: OK – If it's made out of rubies, then this must be THE RUBY YACHT OF OMAR KHAYYAM!
Bullwinkle, Jeweler: Ugggh!!
(Jay Ward et al., "The Ruby Yacht of Omar Khayyam," episode I)

I

The first epigraph is well known to anyone even superficially familiar with the standard canon of English verse, the second to those of us with a fond recollection of the early precursors of *The Simpsons* and *South Park*. But what has either to do with archaeology and its counterfeit rivals?

Look first at Fitzgerald's little verse, a graceful statement, it appears, of a melancholy truism. But note that in the context of its history, it subtly subverts the very wisdom it propounds. As we know, Fitzgerald imputes the sentiments of his stanzas to a fictitious "Omar Khayyám" loosely modeled on a genuine historical personage. Fitzgerald's Omar is an appealing figure – gracefully melancholy, quizzically skeptical, gently hedonistic, given to meditating on the transience of all earthly things and the futility of all orthodoxy and dogma. Although he was doubtless inspired by the surviving aphorisms of the historical Omar, Fitzgerald nonetheless conjures a phantom. His poem, enduring as it may be, is in essence a pastiche of loose translation, conflation, and sheer invention. Yet its fictitious "author," no more than an orientalized mouthpiece for Fitzgerald's own high-Victorian

Weltschmerz, enjoys a peculiarly vibrant afterlife. For most Anglophone readers, the make-believe Omar has completely supplanted the minor poet (and fairly important mathematician) of mediaeval Persia to whom history attests.

There is, to be sure, nothing malicious or mercenary in this poetic imposture. Fitzgerald was a retiring sort of fellow who much preferred to hide behind his own creation. But his modesty led to the corruption of history, that is, of our cultural sense of the past. As the wonderfully dreadful pun of the second epigraph makes clear, Fitzgerald's confected Omar has entered the "historical record," the diffuse corpus of this society's common notions of what the past was like and who its inhabitants were. Most people who are sophisticated enough to appreciate the pun are not sophisticated enough to doubt the historical reality of the "Persian" persona who was in fact dreamed up by an Anglo-Irish literary dilettante. They accord Omar a status they would automatically deny to Hamlet or Captain Ahab.

The moral, then, is that Fitzgerald has ironically evaded his own rueful maxim. His Moving Finger, in this instance, has been grossly edited and rudely second-guessed. Its inscriptions have indeed been washed out, altered, and to an extent overwritten. I stress again that nothing especially ominous lurks in this example; indeed, to the extent that the real Omar has been rescued from oblivion for Westerners, Fitzgerald deserves credit. Arguably, there is justice in that. But the example reminds us that the displacement of true history by ersatz history is something that takes place very frequently, in all sorts of contexts for all sorts of reasons. We may assent to the fatalism of Omar's "Moving Finger" stanza – but not really! At some subconscious level, we seem actually to regard history not as something that was irrevocably laid down long ago but as something that may be freshly created in our own day.

The reinvention of history is a recurrent phenomenon in our culture and most probably in all cultures. Many of its manifestations are not only cruder but also far more ominous than Fitzgerald's little *jeu d'esprit*. Nonetheless, it seems to be rooted in the unbreakable habits of human societies. In our attempts to get hold of the past, or rather, of a gratifying image of the past, we mold it forcefully and sometimes violently into an icon of a desired vision, ideology, or faith. As it enters into living human culture, the past is anything but an indelible and ineluctable text. It is constantly subject to revision.

The historical record, at least as it is perceived by our own crowded, noisy, multifarious society, is a fearfully cluttered palimpsest. It is a territory perpetually open to colonization and conquest. Frequently, many parties – ethnic, ideological, or merely devotees of a pet theory – claim the same patch of landscape. Their disagreements grow fierce and clamorous. Often, each of the antagonistic constituencies nurtures the illusion that it has exclusive control of the territory, and that the rival claimants have been subdued or routed. However, little ever gets resolved or reconciled in this endless clash of certitudes. Indeed, the last thing one expects from this process is stability and consensus. It sometimes seems that the best we can hope for is an armed truce, each faction jealously guarding its own fable, convinced that it alone cradles historical gold where all the others dote over dross. One ruefully notes as well that these stalemates do not usually result from the ambiguity, obscurity, or simple unavailability of evidence. Again and again, historical myths take shape and solidify, and are subsequently ratified and embraced by fervent partisans, even in the teeth of internal inconsistency and massive disconfirming evidence.

This volume explores, from varied points of view, the phenomenon of fake archaeology, a particular species of willful historical falsification with its own repertoire of rhetorical gestures, pseudoscientific mummery, hortatory tropes, and logical solecisms. It is usually built around a standard expository form, one that accommodates a thousand different cranks and frauds within the same overall narrative framework. It has its own special constituency: one can be reasonably confident that the folks who pick up a book about Atlantis will also tune in to the cable TV special on the extraterrestrial founders of the Old Kingdom and will lurk at the website dedicated to Viking settlement on the coast of Oregon.

Nonetheless, to treat pseudoarchaeology merely as a phenomenon unto itself is to neglect the contours of the larger cultural landscape of pseudo-science and anti-rationalism of which it is merely one colorful manifestation. A single compost of credulity sustains a highly varied population of intellec-tually noxious weeds. Efforts to root out but a single specialized variety run the risk of neglecting deeper and more universal factors that, left uncon-tested, will sooner or later reanimate the same absurdities. In what follows, I shall try to locate pseudoarchaeology within that dismal landscape. I suggest, first of all, that what might be called the "colonization" of the past is a pervasive cultural habit, one that erupts for many reasons in many situa-tions, but which reposes, finally, on the unspoken and probably unconscious assumption that the past is, indeed, open for colonization; that it is receptive to the impress of one's concerns, conceits, or obsessions; that it is truly malleable and can always be molded nearer to the heart's desire. Those who rework the past in this way never admit and rarely believe that this is what they are doing. The notion looks mad on its face; Fitzgerald's Moving Finger seems the most resistless of the iron laws of reality. But this apparently ineluctable common sense, alas, is merely what we evoke by putting the question in a particularly explicit way. If we concentrate on what people and cultures actually do, rather than how they rationalize what they do, we find that the urge to deal with the past as a plastic medium upon which the templates of ideology, or religion, or chauvinism, or mere whimsy, can be imposed is irresistible.

Pseudoarchaeology, then, is a subfield of a larger and older and often more dangerous practice of contrived pseudohistory. In turn, pseudohistory is merely one manifestation of the sweeping human practice of evading rational inquiry in many areas of life and thought, of denying its conclusions and rejecting its methods. Viewed in this light, pseudoarchaeology does not look like something that can be banished by any kind of quick fix. It will not lose its place among mass delusions simply through a program of education or aggressive popularization of honest archaeology, although those things are quite desirable in their own right. Ridicule will not do the job either. If clear exposition, rational analysis, and patient debunking based on solid principles of inference were as efficacious in the moulding of popular opinion as we might like to think, we would long since have seen the final retreat of astrology, homeopathic "medicine," and slot machines.

What we are seeking, in the most general terms, are the as yet undiscovered principles of a new pedagogy, a pedagogy that will reliably inculcate, in the great majority of citizens, an ability and a willingness to deal with all sorts of matters through honest and methodologically sound inquiry, consistently and relentlessly employing the tools of logic, clear language, and deference to empirical fact. This desirable cast of mind is easy to characterize in a general way, but notoriously hard, as generations of philosophers will attest, to specify in the kind of concrete terms that are indispensable to the success of any such pedagogical project, assuming that it is feasible at all. A program of this kind also requires that we learn how to implant within the mainstream population certain specific skills and habits of thought – for instance, the ready use of statistical and mathematical reasoning – to which many people are instinctively averse. It means ruthlessly diminishing the role of traditional religion, as well as the coarser forms of superstition and wishful thinking, in dictating how we are to think about the world. It means persuading people to discard a host of psychological props that, in the short run, comfort them and seem to make life endurable. It requires that people become habituated to the idea that the pain of occasional disappointment, disenchantment, and disillusionment – inevitable when rational inquiry is given the epistemological authority it deserves – is a justifiable price to pay for such clearsightedness as finite human beings might hope to attain.

Admittedly, there is a large measure of arrogance in holding up a single standard of thought and judgment as the only properly human way to deal with the confusion, uncertainty, and pain of the world. There exists a strong cultural predisposition, which has been gaining strength in Western society in recent decades, to decry clear-eyed rationality as in itself pernicious and oppressive. Our culture swarms with apologists for the instinctive, sub-rational approach to life in one guise or another and for a resigned acceptance of a relativistic notion of truth. Most of the papers in this book testify, directly or indirectly, to the pervasiveness and power of these cultural instincts. What I am talking about, to give it a useful name, is a revival of the Enlightenment ideal of rational humanity, an ideal that retains its strength in principle, no matter how low it might rank in current academic fashion and in the value systems of postmodern savants. What is now clear, it seems to me, is that this ideal is defective not in itself but because we lack any sound idea of how it is to be embedded in the tissue of real life. The solution, if any, lies in a deep pedagogy that has yet to be born but that is well worth trying to envision.

II

An important specimen of pseudohistory haunts politics and public discourse in American life. It serves nicely to illuminate the general problem of pseudohistory, its promulgation, and its enthusiastic cultural reception. For example, 140 years after its nominal end, the Civil War remains the touchstone of popular feeling about American national identity. For historians of the current generation, there is no possible doubt about the cause of the war. The singular term "cause" is here the proper and accurate term; if ever there was an epochal event that may properly be termed monocausal, it was the American Civil War. The war – that is to say, the secession of the southern states and the consequent federal resort to military action to abort that secession – was caused, directly and exclusively, by the South's determination to protect and extend slavery, along with that region's concomitant frustration at the waning of its longstanding ability to control the federal government in the interests of slave owners. The documentary evidence that this is so is enormous (Drew 2001). The most telling items are the official statements of the seceding states themselves, which freely and eagerly justify their radical actions in terms that leave no room to doubt that slavery was the only factor that mattered.[1]

Yet the (very accurate) consensus on this essential point is a comparatively recent development among scholars of American history. For decades, following the abandonment of Reconstruction, Civil War history and historiography were heavily influenced, even dominated, by the "Lost Cause" school. Echoing the postwar apologetics of Confederate leaders like Jefferson Davis and Alexander Stephens, these writers and teachers insisted at every turn that slavery *per se* was at most a minor factor in a movement largely driven by the desire of the South to retain cultural and economic autonomy and to preserve state sovereignty against the incursions of an overbearing federal government. On this view, the South was merely asserting the primacy of the original constitutional compact over the revisionist designs of intrusive northerners.

Obviously, this was in its time a doctrine that served the interests of a white-supremacist system built on segregation and disenfranchisement of blacks. It resonated nicely with a romanticized view of the Old South and an idealized view, amounting to hagiography, of leaders like R.E. Lee and Stonewall Jackson.[2] Curiously, its hegemonic status effectively refuted the old saw that the winners get to write history. In this case, victorious Loyalism was eclipsed by a sanitized and cleverly burnished version of its opposite.[3] Lost Causism long allowed the war to be portrayed as a gallant, if tragic, struggle for the independence of a proud people.

While these views held sway, mere evidence fared very poorly as an arbiter of historical judgment within supposedly scholarly circles. In effect, the American past had been shanghaied by a worldview congenial to regional chauvinism, family pride, sentimentality, and a determination to retain as much as possible of the antebellum ascendancy of southern whites over their former chattels. What occurred was a kind of lumpen-intellectual *coup d'état*, a rather brutal and arrogant, but largely successful, ploy designed to colonize the past as a stronghold against the unwelcome demands of the present. If a point of comparison is needed, the usual kind of academic in-group insularity really will not do. A better analogy is the ascendancy of Lysenkoist theory over Soviet biology during the Stalin period (although Lost Causers stopped short of imprisoning their opponents).

That the Lost Cause doxology prevailed for so long in the American academic world and within the circle of professional historians is embarrassing (to academics) but not especially surprising. This episode demonstrates, if anything, that the methodological and procedural fixations dominating academic routine are but frail guarantees of honest inquiry. They are vulnerable, in the end, to being outmatched by obsessions bent on conscripting groundless myth and occluding clear fact in order to sculpt a sense of the past that serves materially or merely symbolically to grant power and status to a purported scholar – or his nation, clan, or cause.

Myth is a seductive ally. It is generally far more potent than truth if one wishes to gain control of ongoing events. Far more readily than truth, it glorifies dubious crusades, assuages ancient hurts, and provides a measure of belated revenge. Consequently, when feelings run high for whatever reason, the urge to construct, sustain, and defend myth can readily overcome the scruples of scholarly conscience as well as the supposed safeguards of scholarly method.

It is crucial to distinguish this sort of thing from mere scholarly contention, the rise and possible fall of theories and hypotheses as they are contrived, propagated, evaluated, criticized and, often enough, abandoned in favor of rivals new and old. Myth making is different from intellectually responsible advocacy of an idea, no matter how heartfelt the latter may be. True, the distinction can never be absolute or free from ambiguity. But it is real nonetheless, and we are obliged to respect it. On one side of the divide lies true debate – noisy, frequently rude and aggressive, often maddeningly inconclusive. This is the quotidian business of scholars, whether their concerns are historical, literary, or scientific. Although the process is inevitably messy and querulous, facts and logic ultimately have a lot to do with the outcome. One would also like to think that the outcome often embodies truth or at least significantly reflects it. On the other side, however, we find the miasmal reign of dogma, which contemptuously turns its back on fact. It is the realm not only of the "Lost Cause" myth but of Holocaust denial, deification of assorted dictators and tyrants, dehumanization of rival tribes or sects, and remorseless chauvinism in a thousand forms.

Tragically, dogma undoubtedly has had far more effect on opinion and motivation, on the fate of people and nations, on the crucial decisions of politicians and warriors, than honest and accurate scholarly discourse has ever managed to achieve.

We should be alerted and alarmed by the fact that the Lost Cause myth, cited above, retains much of its virulence. Its ideological influence still pervades American popular discourse. In the corners of the Internet where Civil War buffs congregate, magisterially obtuse Lost Causers materialize with dismal regularity, ardently proclaiming the high-mindedness of the secessionist conspiracy while assuring us that slavery and the prerogatives of slave owners were marginal or entirely irrelevant to its aims. Rhetoric of this kind stubbornly persists in the face of reams of contrary evidence. It affords us a grim though valuable lesson on the limitations of mere logic as an instrument for the persuasion of one's fellow rational beings.

On the other hand, we cannot assume that concocting spurious history is always the work of reactionary, malefic, or revanchist forces. At times, myth is foisted upon history merely by the desire to have a shapely and entrancing narrative to dwell upon (all the better if it is edifying as well). Again, the American Civil War furnishes instructive examples. The Battle of Gettysburg, for instance, was an event to which there were about 150,000 surviving direct witnesses, most of them reasonably literate and quite eager to testify to what they had seen. Yet from the very first that bloody event has spun off a constellation of myths (Reardon 1997) that even now persist in popular and, indeed, scholarly narratives, despite being rather easy to dispel, in principle, by direct and incontrovertible evidence: Longstreet insubordinately failed to attack at daybreak on 2 July; Warren discovered Longstreet's massed divisions by ordering gunners to fire a shot into the woods and observing the glint of massed bayonets as the Confederate infantrymen instinctively ducked; and so forth. The corpus of myth concerning Little Round Top that has grown up (or rather, regrown) in recent years is especially instructive: the loss of the hill would have doomed Meade's army to certain defeat (not so![4]); Colonel J.L. Chamberlain saved the day by ordering his outnumbered 20th Maine to execute an enormous "right wheel" bayonet charge when it ran low on ammunition, thereby routing the astonished Confederates (it was a much more confused and adventitious affair than that[5]); Chamberlain was the perfect embodiment of Yankee idealism, a valiant soldier during the war, an impeccable scholar and statesman afterward (in reality, he was a far more troubling and ambiguous character[6]). In contrast to the Lost Cause mythology, the revived celebrity of Chamberlain is largely the work of well-intentioned liberals: Michael Shaara, in his celebrated novel *The Killer Angels* (1974); Ken Burns in his much-honored television series *The Civil War* (whose characterization of Chamberlain was based on Shaara's fictional account, together with considerable wishful thinking); or the theatrical film *Gettysburg*, based directly on Shaara's book.

As Civil War buffs (that is to say, the more sober-sided ones) understand full well, the Chamberlain mythology is well-nigh ineradicable. Like that of Robert E. Lee, it has entered a strange, empyrean realm into which mere facts cannot penetrate. A man whose flaws were quite as telling as his gifts has benefited posthumously from a popular apotheosis far more sincere and, in the minds of most Americans, credible than that awarded to any ancient emperor. Politically, it may be just as well that we now have a Union commander invested with the same saintly aura that has long glorified the slavocrat and oathbreaker Robert Lee. (Grant or Sherman could never have qualified for the role, so thoroughly did the Lost Causers besmirch their reputations.) But the matter offers little cheer to those who think that the past should never be held hostage to wishful thinking and that facts, as best they can be extracted by rational inquiry, should always hold sovereignty over opinion.

To archaeologists besieged by Atlantis enthusiasts or hyperdiffusionists insisting that the Maya learned pyramid building at the feet of Egyptian priests or von Däniken groupies convinced that the Nazca Plain is a space-port, it might seem that highly sanitized portraits of Civil War notables are pretty tame stuff and simply do not traduce the ideal of rational humanity to anywhere near the same degree. However, I think that this is much too complacent. In my view, the same underlying psychological mechanisms are really at work. To be sure, the trappings are far more grotesque in one case. The image of ancient astronauts flitting around Peru is far more abrasive to mere common sense than that of a spotless paragon of Yankee valor and learning, misleading as the latter might be. But in some sense, the latter symbolizes a deeper threat to the ethic of dispassionate inquiry. The vulgar, silly tall tale, even if it can be profitably peddled to the lowbrow market, is not likely to fool many educated people. Erich von Däniken may have sold millions of books, but it is clear that cults like his need the sustenance of a peculiar hothouse culture where intellect, if present, is also warped. Such fads seem to be inherently self-limiting. On the other hand, infinitely more subtle falsifications like the Chamberlain legend – or Fitzgerald's half-inadvertent "Omar" – have far greater power to penetrate serious discourse in the guise of well-established fact. This is not to say that routing bubbleheaded "popular archaeology" is a pointless project. But in undertaking it, we have to be aware that it is only a down payment on a more sweeping and conse-quential obligation to abolish the habit of treating history as just so much pliant raw material for the fabrication of pleasing (from whatever point of view) legend.

Ironically, a major obstruction to this goal lies within the academic world itself, and worse, even within the precincts of academic history. The ascen-dancy of postmodernism as a philosophy, or rather, a cultural mood eager to drape itself in philosophical garments, has bred a widespread denial that accurate knowledge independent of the "knower" can be garnered, or that it will be generally recognizable as such even if produced (see Chapter 12). On this view, "objectivity" has no objective meaning at all – it is merely one faction's favored encomium for the kind of narrative, be it sociological, historical, or scientific, that flatters that faction's ineradicably ideological view of the world. Lost Cause mythology is wrong, not because it is objectively false but because it affronts humane political values (that is to say, those of most people who embrace postmodernism). In contrast, the airbrushed legend of black abolitionist leader Sojourner Truth is beyond correction by the historical record simply because the mythic figure of a formidable and eloquent black woman is too precious to be sacrificed to the spoilsport ethic of Rankean positivism (which is, in any case, hopelessly naive).

It seems, sometimes, that Sojourner Truth's surname is the only instance in the literature of postmodernist historians where those five letters appear without sarcastic quote marks. The notion that we can discern the truth of history, or at least pare away enough error so that truth is roughly outlined, is, on the postmodern view, laughably naive. There is only "narrative," to which it is bad form to attach such adjectives as "true" or "false" or "probable." When one particular narrative prevails, the dirty work is invariably done by "rhetoric," never evidence and logic, which are, in any case, simply sleight-of-language designations for one kind of rhetorical strategy, a strategy that deserves no particular deference. The most magisterial spokesman for this strange mixture of nihilism and sophomoric political enthusiasm has doubtless been the philosopher-historian Hayden White.[7] It is noteworthy that White explicitly rejects the idea that the methods of modern science are in any way epistemologically superior to any other mode of constructing narrative.

This kind of uncompromising anti-objectivism has never dominated professional historians. Nevertheless, in combination with the regnant campus political mood, it has muted claims of objectivity and disinterestedness from scholars of history and has softened the longstanding ethical principle that objectivity and disinterestedness are the guiding stars of the field. More recently, a counter-movement has arisen, recruiting both scholars (some of them disillusioned former votaries of postmodernism) and outside critics of the academic microcosm.[8] But the self-confidence of historians still suffers from the effects of postmodernist disdain. Not many serious philosophers (as opposed to postmodernist rhetoricians who offhandedly appropriate the philosopher's mantle) have ever denied the reality of a factual past, and, although few have asserted that history is completely transparent to our limited arsenal of investigative tools, the idea that putatively objective historical inquiry is by definition a waste of time is not especially popular in philosophy departments. Yet academic fashion is not typically in accord with the sturdiest philosophical perspectives; it has a wayward life of its own, and its postmodern infatuation has left a haze that to this day saps the will of scholars to insist on impersonal canons of knowledge.

Somewhat ironically, the enthusiasms of postmodernism have eroded respect for meticulous historical methodology in quite another way. Certain purportedly historical works have established themselves as paragons of insight whose "factual" accounts of the past, along with their ideological perspectives, are simply beyond serious question. The leading examples are probably the books of Michel Foucault (1977, 1978, 1988). In many fields (although not necessarily university history departments as such), these works are immune from serious criticism. In wide swaths of literary studies, gender studies, art history, cultural studies, and cultural anthropology, Foucault has been virtually deified. His terminology, along with the hypotheses on which it rests, has been enthusiastically adopted. His style and tone are aped by scholars junior and senior. It is taken as axiomatic that Foucault's conclusions are simply true, as well as brilliantly original. The notion that his methods might deserve serious objective evaluation, and that his shortcomings in this regard ought to trigger skepticism about his pronouncements, is a heresy never to be entertained. Yet coolly regarded, Foucault's methods, those of an historical autodidact, are at best superficial, impressionistic, and beholden to the quasi-political doctrines he wishes to preach. He sets forth a few "true life" examples, seen through the unabashedly subjective filter of passionate personal opinion, blithely deeming them sufficient to sustain a thesis of enormous scope and generality. Seizing upon a trivial incident, an odd personal quirk, an obscure document, or an isolated turn of phrase, he categorically proclaims it to embody the very essence of the mentality of an era.[9] By the traditional standards of the historian's craft, this kind of thing hardly gets beyond rank speculation and gossip-mongering. But that has not dimmed Foucault's effulgence in the least.

Quite a few academic celebrities have ascended to stardom (as universities reckon such things) through "historical" work similarly predicated on myopic and tendentious readings of minimal evidence, along with ample resort to politically charged rhetoric. One thinks, for instance, of Haraway's book (1990) on primatology, or Shapin and Schaffer's (1989) on the seventeenth-century dispute over the nature of a physical vacuum.[10] In any case, this genre of work, together with its indulgent reception and its immunity from meaningful scrutiny, constitutes a second wing of the postmodernist assault on the ideal of historical research guided by epistemological rigor rather than the cheerleader ethic.

Bogeyman terms like "positivistic" or, even worse, "scientistic" have been hurled at scholars aiming to restore fact and the logic of empirical inquiry to center stage, so far as historical research goes. Their sense of political decency has been questioned as well. This is especially so when they work in traditional areas like diplomatic and military history, areas that are not easily accommodated by the current enthusiasm for "history from below," that is, history allegedly concerned only with the plight and the struggles of the oppressed and marginalized. But historians seem resilient enough to restore, eventually, some kind of reasonable balance between attention to historical elites and concern for the as yet untold story of the voiceless. Captious doubts about truth and objectivity, which are the legacy of postmodernism, have not permanently demoralized the field. Yet there is no certainty that historians will have enough energy left over from internecine squabbles to reach beyond professional circles. Will they eventually take on the purveyors of pseudohistory and myth, who have been so successful at exploiting mass media? One would like to think so, but that task will require a much-expanded notion of the role of public intellectuals and the extracurricular responsibility of academics.

III

The fact that fake archaeology typically takes on grotesque trappings is, I think, at least partially the consequence of the history of archaeology itself and the way in which its discoveries have made their way into public awareness. Unlike even palaeoanthropology, there has always been something numinous, if not positively spectral, in the stories of ancient civilizations unearthed or ancient writings deciphered. Indiana Jones, as the popular personification of the profession, did not spring up from nowhere (on Indy, see Chapter 7). Archaeology, in the public mind, has a long history of association with the uncanny splendor of an alien past, and therefore its most famous figures have had a shaman-like reputation; they can commune with a world of departed spirits in a way denied to most of us. They have long been credited with bringing to light sumptuous treasures as beautiful as they are strange. Therefore, they share in some degree the aura that invests great artists, of whom, after all, they happen to be the living representatives when the artists in question are those of Uxmal or Mohenjo-Daro. Indeed, so far as this layman can determine by reading semi-popular publications,[11] even the most sober and unpoetic members of the archaeological tribe really seem to enjoy this dashing reputation (see also Chapter 6).

The antiquarianism that matured, finally, into the modern science of archaeology has a long history of preoccupation with the eerie and the mystical. As has been pointed out, in this volume and elsewhere, Egyptology arose as a body of highly speculative storytelling built partly on the errors and misunderstandings of the Graeco-Roman world regarding the more ancient pharaonic civilization. Moreover, eighteenth-century accounts of ancient Egypt, though wildly inaccurate, placed particular stress on mysteries, sacred rites, eldritch lore, and thaumaturgic power. In part, this was the "Egyptology" of *Die Zauberflöte*, that is, the fake Egyptian mummery of European Freemasonry (for more, see Chapter 5). The grotesqueries and historical absurdities of this particular "lore" can be partially forgiven in that the Freemasons were a group with serious philosophical, political, and social aims who used their pseudo-Egyptian ritualism as camouflage for ideas and opinions that might otherwise have brought down the wrath of the authorities. Nonetheless, their mumbo-jumbo heavily influenced what the broader culture expected to find in glimpses of the pre-classical past or in non-Western civilizations. In addition to exotic beauty, Westerners anticipated the emergence of ancient or unconventional wisdom, spiritual revelation, and the recovery of arcane lore and mantic powers long lost. Thus an epochal discovery like the Rosetta Stone lives a double life in popular culture. On the one hand, it constitutes a scientific treasure of enormous value; it is a literal foundation stone of historical philology. Simultaneously, it is seen as a spiritual treasure, the key to ancient secrets promising power (the power that built the pyramids!) or even immortality.

This motif endures in the face that archaeology wittingly or unwittingly shows to the public. A book club advertisement that appears in *Archaeology*,[12] for instance, peddles itself to prospective subscribers by promising readers "Intriguing People ... Faraway Places ... Ancient Mysteries." This is forgivable as sales hype, perhaps, but it clearly plays upon expectations of unearthing the "lost wisdom" of the ancients.

Archaeologists (as opposed to, say, documentary historians – or mathematicians) are glamorized in popular culture, in part because some of the best-known figures in the field went out of their way to cultivate a glamorous image. Heinrich Schliemann, obviously, is the type specimen. Contemporary professionals are rather ambivalent about him (Allen 1999; Traill 1993, 1995). He is a combination of admirable and odious traits: obsessive curiosity about the past, unflagging persistence and determination in pursuing that obsession, credulous faith in unlikely myth, shameless hucksterism in publicizing his discoveries, and, most probably, willingness to exaggerate or even to engage in outright deception in order to enhance his public image and outshine his colleagues. But, so far as public perception is concerned, Schliemann is an unsullied champion of truth. No matter how many correctives to the Schliemann legend are published and promulgated, interested laymen are likely always to perceive him as an unambiguously great man, and, moreover, as the fearless rebel who salvaged the resplendent glamour of the Homeric past from skeptics, debunkers, and the hopelessly unimaginative. This particular genie is irrecoverably out of the bottle.

As a myth in his own right, Schliemann sustains a number of alarming misperceptions. He is, to most people, a nineteenth-century incarnation of the Galilean hero, the lone genius who stands against the received wisdom of the official savants and who ultimately prevails by the force of his brilliance. He embodies the notion that one finds the hidden path into the past, not through patient, incremental steps and meticulously skeptical analysis but through great leaps of intuition springing from a near-mystical communion with the spirit of the ancients. He is not the only such archaeological magus. Sir Arthur Evans plays a similar role in popular understanding of how archaeology "works." The blithe self-confidence of his "restoration" of Knossos may appall professionals (see MacGillivray 2000), but those whom the cruise ships bring to "the Palace of Minos" by the tens of thousands are convinced that they have come directly face to face with the past, unveiled in all its sacred beauty. They thank the spirit of Evans for the experience.

We ought not to wonder, then, at the prosperity of cranks and frauds who contrive to project a similar image. They exploit an attitude already fixed in place, one that is all too eager to approve the notion that imagination, intuition, enthusiasm, devout reverence for the past – all, perhaps, accompanied by the suggestion of preternatural vision or clairvoyant powers – are the key to authentic communion with vanished eras. Indeed, the rise of one particular kind of hokum, "psychic" archaeology, goes further and explicitly aligns pseudoarchaeology with paranormal delusions already massively popular in other contexts. By comparison, the kind of scientific archaeology that stolidly focuses on the mundane, on the laborious classification of potsherds and the meticulous recovery of the genetic signatures of ancient seed stocks, has little traction on a popular imagination that wants only to hear about the arcane wisdom of lost millennia and the mantic powers of the priests of vanished cults. Pseudoarchaeology, shrewdly playing to the thirst for aesthetic delight and the hunger for spiritually rewarding tales from a supposed golden age, easily runs roughshod over killjoy shoptalk about stratigraphy, thermoluminescence, and plant genetics. Decades of trophy-hunting archaeology, largely concerned with rich treasures, masterful art works, and spooky images of strange gods, may embarrass modern-day professionals, but the ghost of such practices lingers, and it has set the stage for the emergence of fakery that panders to desires formerly slaked by the gleaming finds of academics.

It is also important to note the peculiar role of orthodox religious belief in shaping the popular conception of archaeology and the purposes it ought to serve. In the eastern Mediterranean, in particular, there is a long-standing tradition of "biblical archaeology," that is, research tied in some fashion to the corpus of legends and ostensible chronicles that constitutes the core of Judaeo-Christian tradition (Davis 2004). For many years, this work went forward on the assumption that its purpose was to confirm the essential truth of scriptural accounts, rather as Schliemann "proved" the historicity of the Homeric poems. The position of archaeology *vis-à-vis* religion has frequently been one of implied deference to a higher-order spiritual truth.

It hardly needs saying that such an agenda is incompatible with the methods and ethics of science. Nowadays, this misalliance can be seen, thankfully, as the folly of a previous generation. Although it persists in comically degraded form among some mercenary antiquarians and religious fanatics,[13] it has for the most part lost its scholarly cachet. Nonetheless, so far as public image goes, there remains a strong sense that archaeology and religion should be linked. Many laymen think religious texts are vital guideposts for archaeological research. They expect that archaeological results, at least relevant ones, will be testaments to the truth of those texts and thus emblems of faith.[14]

The lingering habit of inappropriate deference to religion, when it inter-sects the study of history, has been reinforced to a modest degree by the epistemological relativism that holds sway in a few areas of academic life. For the most part, this is entangled with special pleading on behalf of favored political or cultural perspectives. The dubious postulate that "other forms of knowing" deserve to rank equally with scientific rationality has bolstered "scholarly" claims for the reliability of what would seem to be very questionable accounts of the past. Examples include the myth of an ancient matriarchy – doted upon by academic feminists (Gimbutas 1991; Stone 1976) – and the dogma, common coin among Afrocentrist professors (Diop 1974; Powell and Frankenstein 1997; van Sertima 1983), that black or supposedly black African cultures deserve to be credited with stunning achievements in mathematics and science. These hypotheses, shaky or outright silly as they may be, are often inseparable from claims that there is a deep spiritual reward to be drawn from contemplating the quasi-sacred histories that they posit. A particularly lamentable example is to be found in the litigation over the Kennewick Man skeleton. Some key testimony on behalf of those who wished the remains to be handed over to tribal groups for reburial came from supposed ethnographers. They argued that picturesque tribal legends connected to recent Native American ritual and religious belief should be accepted (under a convenient interpretation) as compelling evidence about the demography and culture of the Pacific Northwest *c.* 9,400 YB (Benedict 2003; Chatters 2001; Thomas and Colley 2001). *Mutatis mutandis*, when one strips away the sentimentality that calls itself "multiculturalism" and the sophistry of postmodern philosophers, the logic of these arguments simply recapitulates that which subordinated Middle Eastern archaeology to the dictates of conventional Western religion.

These days, it is relatively easy for proponents of popular brands of pseu-doarchaeology to claim for their own cults the special privileges traditionally ceded to biblical religion. It is merely a matter of choosing a new lodestar, mystic revelations concerning the Atlanteans or the vanished Mayan or Druidic priests having supplanted Abrahamic legends and the Gospels. The underlying *topos* remains in place: unearthed relics are but tokens and confirming signs of knowledge imparted through otherworldly channels. To question that knowledge is to disparage the religion of the claimant and, as we know, that is the ultimate *faux pas* of American life.

If the foregoing analysis is correct, archeologists who wish to make the broad public aware of the enormous differences between their subject and the counterfeit versions that throng popular literature and the mass media have a grim and not altogether pleasant task before them. First, they must disown some of the most glamorous legends of their past, precisely those that begat widespread interest in archaeology in the first place. Schliemann and similar intellectual swashbucklers must be cut down to size, not only by scholars speaking to a specialist audience but also as a routine aspect of the overall attempt to interest the public in the ancient past. In time, perhaps even mass-market popularizers, tour guides, and travel brochures might be persuaded to ease up on the deceptive "discovery" myths that have been a standard part of their spiel. The reigning curatorial fascination with objects of singular beauty or numinous reputation must be counterbalanced by emphasizing that our investigation of the past owes as much to people who lived and died in poverty and obscurity as it does to potentates and warrior-chieftains who managed to amass vast troves of grave goods. At the same time, we ought to temper some of our enthusiasm for dramatic displays of idols and icons, those that manage to convey through stagecraft and show-manship the idea that the ancients possessed uncanny powers that we have yet to remaster. Obviously, turning away from the "motel of the mysteries"[15] paradigm will be a painful process, given that it is precisely such theatrically shrewd legend-mongering that brings the big crowds and their cash to exhi-bitions – and museum shops.

On a deeper and riskier level, religion – at least religion based on clear historical claims – must be confronted head-on. So far as I can see from the perspective of a curious amateur, the archaeological and documentary evidence we now have throws cold water on the founding myth of Christianity and flatly disallows the historicity of most Old Testament chronicles, even if we strain to read the latter as a regional history subse-quently encrusted with theological bric-a-brac. Archaeology needs to declare, without equivocation, that there is little it can add by way of confir-matory substance to the image of the historical Jesus, let alone the historical King David or the historical Moses. Research can no more verify these legends than it can endorse the legends of King Arthur or Prester John. This proposition must be conveyed to the public without fudging or embarrass-ment. So, too, the underlying reason for affirming it, namely, the extremely strong probability that familiar biblical legends are, indeed, little more than legends, so far as evidence independent of "revelation" discloses. Frankness like this carries obvious risks. It will certainly draw down the wrath of assorted religious potentates and their flocks. But that is already the day-to-day experience of many physicists and biologists – religion will not leave science alone, even when science tries to leave religion alone (see Hall and Hall 1986). Archaeologists ought to get used to being on the firing line.

The plain fact is that from the point of view of scientific and rational history, there is little to choose between grotesque cults celebrating lost continents or the eldritch powers of Stonehenge, on the one hand, and the religions whose chaplains bless every sitting of the United States Congress, on the other. It is hard to debunk one of these effectively while giving a free pass to its near twin. Consistency requires archaeologists, like all scientists, not to concoct exceptions to logic or well-established scientific principles merely to enable religion to escape the consequences of its built-in absurdi-ties. If we wish to be rid of von Däniken's ancient astronauts, Jacob's angel will have to go out the window too, as well as Potiphar's wife, the lawgiver Moses, and King Solomon the wise. Living up to this precept is particularly difficult for archaeologists precisely because they suffer from a long history of neglecting it or embracing its opposite. Beyond that, taking these ideas seriously probably requires a much larger overall cultural shift, one that restores Enlightenment ideals – long allowed to gather dust – to the center of Western intellectual life.

IV

Pseudoarchaeology is one especially egregious form of counterfeit history. In turn, these impostures, whether willful or inadvertent, are part of a far larger web of "cultural practices." The more general phenomenon lacks a convenient name if only because it is defined – very loosely defined – as the opposite of yet another and much rarer cultural practice – the systematic, rigorous use of logic and evidence to explore all sorts of questions. Rigor entails an ethic that at least aspires to objectivity and strives for disinterestedness, despite the near impossibility of realizing these virtues in pure form. But what term shall we use for the willful rejection of this ethic? "Irrationality" is a little too dismissive, because it suggests utter incoherence. "Pseudoscience" is too narrow, because it implies that accurate thinking is the monopoly of credentialed scientists, which clearly is not the case. Rational inquiry of the kind that has infused the natural sciences, giving them their present intellectual power, is a mode of thought that can be brought to bear on a far more extensive range of questions (Haack 1993).

Nonetheless, I think it is most useful to focus on pseudoscience, in the narrow sense, because it often provides the sharpest contrast between sound methodology, honed over centuries by skeptical scrutiny, on the one hand, and wishful thinking disguised by double-talk on the other. Pseudoscience is pervasive in this society and seems to be the most widespread mode of self-deception. To a certain extent, it is popular because science itself is so demonstrably successful and so omnipresent as a force in our personal and social lives. Pseudoscience does not simply arise because the real item lacks prestige. In theory, today's science is much admired, and its practitioners are well regarded. But many belief systems are built around organized wishful thinking. These understandably envy the prestige of science and wish to find a way of sharing in it.

It is tempting to classify pseudoscientific cults according to the actual risk they pose to the well-being of our society. Enthusiasm for fake medicine, for instance, obviously falls into the "clear and present danger" category. It endangers those who believe in it but also those, like young children of believers, who have no direct say in healthcare decisions. Likewise, crank environmentalism, a more subtle phenomenon, perhaps, but one that has made itself felt in a number of areas, not only has inordinate economic costs but also, ironically, itself poses environmental dangers because it obstructs the discovery and implementation of good solutions to real problems (Rauch 2003) while diverting the limited resources of political environmentalism to "problems" that are minor and often non-existent.[16] Creationist pseudoscience, from its crudest versions to the sophistications (and sophistries) of "intelligent design theory" (Gross and Forrest 2003) is dangerous, first, because it undermines the ability of the public, especially students, to discern the strengths and limitations of real science, but even more because it is the leading edge of a powerful movement whose aims are rigidly theocratic.

On the other hand, enthusiasm for tall tales of UFO abductions or Atlantis might seem to be a benign eccentricity at worst. It is very difficult to see how it directly damages its supposed victim and even more difficult to see how it hurts anyone else. One could well argue that pseudoarchaeology as a whole is very much like that – silly but harmless, and of no serious concern to any but the true believer, in whose life it may play the same role that Scrabble tournaments or collecting Hummel figurines does in someone else's. It may offend the vanity of professional archaeologists, in that their patient explanations are given short shrift; but this does not, on its face, seem to be a grave social pathology.

However, I would argue that pseudoscience in any form is at least potentially dangerous and is usually an indicator of real dangers lurking a bit further beneath the surface. I have already alluded to the reason. Pseudoscience, both in itself and in the easy tolerance it finds among the general population, degrades the public's ability to recognize genuine science and to distinguish it from even clumsy imitations. It dilutes the trust that people ought to have in the competence of orthodox science in that it puts scientists in a position where they are perceived as turf-defending spoilsports and blind dogmatists. As a result, it erodes the willingness of the public to defer to scientific expertise in areas where such competence is relevant to the general welfare. The consequences are potentially rather grim.

The lesson, then, is that archaeologists should not be combating pseudoscience as a tactic to decrease the appeal of pseudoarchaeology. Rather, they should be attacking pseudoarchaeology as one particular front in the general war against irrationalism. The hope is that any single struggle of this kind, whether it involves Nazca lines, the Bermuda Triangle, or perpetual motion machines, will help to alert the general public to the dangers, as well as the flaws, of pseudoscience as such, and will hone its ability to think accurately and efficiently about a wide range of subjects.

It is difficult to find a really questionable belief system that is neither religious nor pseudoscientific in character. (I avoid the term "pseudo-religious" because, short of outright conscious fraud on the part of all concerned – supposed believers as well as leaders – it seems very hard to distinguish pseudo-religion from "real" religion.) Most of the outlandish cults that thrive in our society – Scientology or Christian Science, to take prime examples – claim to be at the same time religious and scientific. Their strategy is a natural one. The religious aspect cloaks these sects in the special legal and cultural immunities awarded to "faith," while the pretend science, borrowing its luster from real science, constitutes a short cut to credibility and the appearance of profundity. Consequently, there is no surprise in the emergence of, say, an alternative health movement that simultaneously draws upon ancient Vedic wisdom and, supposedly, quantum physics. With appropriate variations, this pattern comes up again and again, not least in pseudoarchaeology. The supposed demigods who built the Giza pyramids will typically be represented both as supreme scientists and as bringers of supernatural wisdom. Thus, two culturally pervasive tropes – knowledge as the gift of the gods, knowledge as the fruit of science – are fused into one.

It is terrifying to note that pseudoscientific lunacy grows more intense by the day. For instance, it can now be found in the pages of respectable, indeed pre-eminent journals of scientific medicine. Recent issues of the *British Medical Journal* have carried articles (Leibovici 2001; Olshansky and Dossey 2003) claiming, in all seriousness, that the intercessory prayers of strangers (from a spectrum of religions) can improve the prospects of victims of serious disease – despite the fact that the prayers are offered months *after* the observed clinical result. It is small consolation that the fatal methodological flaws of this work are reasonably easy to spot (Bishop *et al.* 2004). The simple fact that it appears at all shows that yearning for miracles has deeply infiltrated the best established of supposedly scientific establishments. In any case, this bizarre episode reveals how pseudoscientists aspire to link their supposed scientific knowledge to mystic forces ostensibly at work in the universe. One of the *BMJ* articles (Olshansky and Dossey 2003), for instance, is full of solemn nonsense about quantum mechanics, non-locality, superstrings, and Calabi-Yau manifolds. I doubt that the authors have any precise sense of what these words mean. But it is sufficient for their purposes merely to display them. Whether they look on them as scientific terms of art or spiritual mantras, or whether they even know the difference, is far from clear.

Scientists are typically nonplussed that anyone would prefer pseudo-science to the real thing. Good science exhibits the beauty of its inner logic, whereas pseudoscience is a tissue of excuses, evasions, and bad faith. How could one thing ever be confused with the other? What is the appeal of the ersatz? There is a persistent feeling in the scientific community that all that is really needed to disperse the fog of pseudoscience is to administer a healthy dose of "scientific literacy" to the community at large. Provided with the intellectual tools required to begin to investigate science seriously, so it is reasoned, the average person will soon learn to distinguish scientific work and its methods from the claims of charlatans.

This misunderstands the nature of pseudoscience and its appeal on several levels (see Chapter 2). First, I think scientists often underestimate the barriers that prevent laymen from making much progress toward scientific competence. The heavily mathematical fields are especially off-putting to tyros. When someone devotes great effort to mastering science only to find that his aptitudes are not up to the task, it is a frustrating and embittering experience. Moreover, science, even when it is more or less accurately grasped, frequently fails to enthuse the non-scientist as it does an interested scientist. In other words, passion for science is quite a specialized taste, anything but uniformly distributed in the population. This is a disparity not effectively addressed by scientific literacy programs. Even the best of them find it hard to generate enthusiasm where none exists in the first place.

No matter how much bravura showmanship goes into its presentation, authentic science leaves many laymen cold. There is a seemingly universal human tendency to desire narratives that in some fashion assist one to make sense of one's position in life, or to confirm one's value system, or simply to provide reassurance that the world and its events are charged with meaning on a human scale. Scientific narratives, to the extent that they do not stray into assertions unwarranted by the science itself, rarely have these qualities. Indeed, they lack the very element most essential for narratives with general emotional appeal: a teleological view of the world. The rubric of science, as it has evolved over several centuries, does not accommodate stories that attempt to discern an overarching purpose in the order of things or those that plead on behalf of particular ethical and aesthetic value systems. Scientists have discovered the hard way that a seemingly unnatural detachment from these issues is a good way to avoid self-deception. True, scientists are as human as anyone else, and sometimes they find it hard to live up to such abstemious principles. Nonetheless, if ever they are justly criticized for backsliding into teleological language, they will usually rephrase their claims or explain that they are merely resorting to colorful figures of speech.

The most important thing that pseudoscience has going for it, as a general rule, is that it has no interest in casting teleology aside or in maintaining the Humean distinction between "is" and "ought." Pseudoscience draws supporters precisely because in one way or another it offers up narratives that openly seek to flatter the hopes and aspirations of the hearer.[17] Alternative medicine, for instance, typically proffers a view of wellness and illness that suggests that patients are not assemblages of atoms strictly subject to physical law but rather agents who can summon numinous spiritual forces that supersede mere physics. UFO enthusiasts reject the picture offered by orthodox astronomy and cosmology – one in which our species is a purely adventitious phenomenon, a tiny, meaningless wrinkle in a universe unimaginably vast. They revel in the idea that we are in fact creatures intensely interesting to mighty alien intelligences, who go to extravagant lengths to spy on us and plumb our secrets. Creationism prospers not only because traditional biblical literalism retains a strong base but also because even very secular people, who distrust fundamentalism as a general rule, are emotionally unstrung by standard evolutionary theory. They shudder at its relentless insistence that the emergence of life in all its plenitude, and of human life in particular, is merely the luck of the draw, shaped by purposeless random variation and not controlled in any sense by a ruling intelligence.

In the context of history and archaeology, a theme that energizes many tall tales is that we of the present are destined to recover a lost vision or to fulfill a grand design that has been unfolding for centuries (see Chapter 1). Historical scholarship of the hardheaded kind finds it hard to evade the uninspiring precept that life – human life at every scale – is just "one damned thing after another." The broad story of the emergence, rise, decline, and disappearance of cultures, states, and societies may be a fascinating one, but modern thinkers are reluctant to discern in it fulfillment of any overarching purpose or progress toward an innate foreordained end-point. To us, teleological historical theorists like Hegel and Marx seem no less quaint than all the other millenarians who prophesied in vain. We accept that we can learn nothing from the Sumerians or the Olmec about the ineluctable trajectory of civilizations. They once were; now they are not. No deeper lesson is available. Teleology is no more relevant to the modern model of historical narrative than it is to a cladistic study of trilobites or diatoms. It is hardly surprising that a good part of the public finds such resignation unsatisfying or even chilling, and yearns, even at the cost of nurturing absurdities, for narratives that reinfuse history with purpose. This impulse is particularly strong when those narratives also offer sops to ethnic pride, nationalist ambition, and favored political schemes (see Chapters 7–9).

We should also note that pseudoscience is frequently fueled by simple resentment. As I have observed previously, the study of science is often difficult and uncongenial. It is not everyone's cup of tea. As a result, proficiency in science provokes envy and hard feelings as well as admiration. It is natural for the public to feel uneasy when certain kinds of important question fall under the exclusive purview of a small clique whose mode of thought is largely opaque. Pseudoscience plays upon these misgivings. It makes a symbolic kind of redress available to the most resentful laymen. This mechanism is at work in a host of pseudoscientific movements, some of them, like "alternative" medicine, clearly quite foolhardy. It is even more glaringly present in fashionable academic work that makes no secret of its ambition to debunk scientific "elitism" (e.g., Dean 1998; Ross 1991; see also Levitt 1998 for some further remarks on these points).

The overall conclusion to be drawn from this analysis is that counterfeit history, including its archaeological version, does not stand apart from pseudoscience in general. It is popular for the same reasons that other brands of pseudoscience are popular. Consequently, any attempt, no matter how well conceived, to combat the influence of ersatz history and to disillusion its advocates will be of limited effect in the absence of a much broader project aimed at undermining pseudoscience as such. The effort would, so to speak, amputate a limb without much damaging the trunk. That limb will inevitably grow back. Yet we clearly see that a wholesale crusade against pseudoscience is a Utopian idea, given the deep psychological roots and the nurturing cultural subsoil from which such delusions grow. So the news is very discouraging to those of us who harbor a visceral hatred of superstition.

Still, the thought persists that, quixotic as it might turn out to be, no struggle is more worthy of our efforts.

V

Having broached the idea of an extravagantly Utopian program for the reconstruction of our culture's attitude toward knowledge and belief, I might as well amplify the fantasy. My hope is that there is a kernel of practicality buried in what, inevitably, will be masses of futile speculation. What is at issue is a grand, or more likely grandiose, daydream: to reshape our civilization so that its canon of accepted knowledge consistently reposes on a foundation of rational thought bolstered by willingness to defer wherever necessary to empirically ascertainable fact.

I postulate three basic points concerning epistemology and its relation to the well-being of society and culture. I recognize that these points are emphatic to such a degree that many present-day intellectuals will be put off by them. Worse, they are unfashionable! They embody the optimism of the Enlightenment, which has not been wildly popular of late. Traditionalists, especially devout ones, have always despised it. Radical egalitarians have long since abandoned it because it is also a skeptical ethic, skeptical, that is, about all classes and conditions of men, and therefore raises questions that the political left prefers not to deal with. The moderate center is too shell-shocked by recent history to be stirred to optimism by any doctrine. Nonetheless, I am convinced that we must retrieve the Enlightenment's clarity about human affairs and the ideological equilibrium that characterizes the best of Enlightenment thought if there is to be any hope of a systematic struggle against irrationality, obscurantism, and superstition.

These are my postulates:

1. There is indeed a rationally oriented, empirically driven mode of thought that deserves special epistemological warrant.
2. This kind of "rational inquiry" is very likely to be the best instrument we have for dealing with a vast range of human problems, going far beyond the realm of the exact sciences.
3. The ability and inclination to employ this kind of thinking as the "default mode" for dealing with problems and open questions can be inculcated in the vast majority of people.

The first point, although likely to provoke the usual round of philosophical quibbles, is, I think, the easiest to make plausible. The stupendous success of modern science cannot be plausibly explained unless it is accepted.[18] This is not to say that there is a fixed "algorithm" for rational inquiry, or that there are no marginal cases. Still less does it contend that the employment of these methods guarantees a solution to whatever question is at issue. Nonetheless, rationality, in this sense, does exist and is part of the repertoire of human behavior. With reasonable confidence, we can recognize it when it is applied and, just as important, recognize when it is imperfectly applied or altogether absent.

The second point is more a leap of faith. The best evidence we have is the bloody litter of thousands of years of human history, the uncounted cases in point that remorselessly illustrate Gibbon's dictum that "History is indeed little more than the register of the crimes, follies, and misfortunes of mankind."[19] But this is evidence from absence. Exercises in imagining "alternative" history may give us some reason to think that the crimes, follies, and misfortunes of the past might have been avoided by a deeper and more habitual commitment to rationality, but this is at best trifling evidence, and possibly only self-deception. Nonetheless, it is hard to believe that the exclusion of evident irrationality – bias, wishful thinking, willful neglect of blunt facts – would have made the situation any worse.

But it is the last point that is the real leap of faith. It seems fatuous to contend that even a single specimen exists of a human being who is rigorously rational across the entire spectrum of his or her affairs. Folk wisdom suggests that unvarying judiciousness is the ultimate folly. Authors – Aristophanes, Molière, even Voltaire – have had a field day with this theme. We should back down, then, and admit that we are not trying to create a race of paragons of dispassionate judgment under all circumstances – none of *Star Trek*'s Vulcans, thank you – but simply trying to find some way of altering culture and education so that a hell of a lot more people are a hell of a lot less irrational a hell of a lot more of the time. But now we see where the real leap of faith is required.

What we are talking about is pedagogy in the deepest sense, the undiscovered art of bringing forth minds that systematically outdo those of this and earlier generations in avoiding self-deception, gullibility, unwarranted assumptions, and the delusions wrought by the ethic of tribal solidarity. That said, we confront the fact that, of all important bodies of knowledge, pedagogy seems to be the most hollow. It is the one in which we apparently have made the least net progress over thousands of years. There is scant evidence to suggest, for instance, that in practical terms our understanding of pedagogy, broadly conceived, is any deeper than that of Plato or Confucius. On the technical fringes, true, we know a few things that our ancestors did not, mostly concerned with the acquisition, by young children, of basic linguistic and mathematical skills, of a sense of how the world coheres, and of a rudimentary canon of ethical judgment. But there is a larger question that is pretty much unanswerable as things now stand: What, exactly, is involved in gradually transforming a neonatal brain into the functioning mind – with its skills, assumptions, prejudices, blind spots, passions, and overall *Weltanschauung* – of a 25-year-old? It would be idle to pretend that we have even a reliable sketch of the process. We can handle the notorious "nature v. nurture" problem on a general level, but we cannot yet say with any specificity how much of one's "philosophy of life" is due to innate predisposition and how much to the corpus of one's life experience, which includes, but is in no wise limited to, the process of formal education.

Given our presumed preference, hubristic though it be, that minds of one kind rather than another should emerge from two decades or so of maturation, what do we know of how this may be achieved? In sum, we know practically nothing. It is hard to believe that the issues that currently roil school systems, administrators, parent associations, faculties, and education school professors in connection with primary, secondary and higher education have much to do with the case. This is not a matter of ability grouping, state-wide standards, high-stakes testing, SAT scores, early admissions, "diversity," "critical thinking," or, indeed, "scientific literacy." We are asking the same question that Plato asked, and all the cultural detritus of our particular mechanism for "schooling" our youth merely obstructs our ability to ponder it. We have – some of us – an ideal of rationality and possibly even wisdom that we would like to see realized much more fully by many more people. What we do not have is the faintest idea of whether this is really under our control, even theoretically, let alone of how to control it. It simply is not the sort of thing we pay much attention to. Indeed, we seem to ignore it far more than earlier civilizations did.

There is some hope that our expanding knowledge of how cognitive behavior is correlated with the physiology of the brain will shed some light on the problem I have raised and even opened the road to a definitive answer. There has been some – very preliminary – work in this direction (Geake and Cooper 2003). Most of this is tentative and speculative. To the extent that it is concrete, it mostly concerns the repertoire of skills associated with ordinary classroom learning at the elementary level – reading, ciphering, and so forth. It has not yet led to any great insights into the theory of intellect at its highest level of insight and creativity. It has had nothing to say yet about the variety of standpoints from which people look at life and why a given genetic endowment coupled with a given trajectory through childhood and adolescence should produce a fervent theist, say, rather than a sardonic atheist. It is light years away from any such insight. Nonetheless, one looks hopefully at cognitive neuroscience as a possible key to a deep pedagogy simply because it is something new under the Sun and because it takes seriously what has been largely ignored heretofore; that we are physical creatures through and through and that our mental life is at root an aspect of our physical life. That is not a bad starting point, although it is no guarantee, either, that this kind of speculation will not lead to a blind alley.

What I have proposed here will be deeply unnerving to many people. At the same time, its natural constituency is quite small. I am, after all, talking first about a cultural ideal – that of rational inquiry – becoming not only socially favored but positively incarnated, in a literal sense, in the brains and minds of most of the adult population. That ideal is "scientistic" in that it is modeled on the way scientific investigation is carried out when it is done accurately and well. The reasons it is desirable are, in some sense, scientistic as well. They embody the hope that we can extirpate scientifically insupportable modes of belief, along with coarse superstition and pseudoscience. Finally, I have just proposed, at least as a worthwhile possibility, a scientistic "techno-fix."

Various opponents of scientism, religious and adamantly secular, conservative and revolutionary, will be greatly alarmed by this concatenation. The reaction will be even more indignant on the part of those who advocate a more latitudinarian standard of knowledge, those for whom "other ways of knowing" are better keys to political justice and a supposedly richer experiential world than narrow-minded science-based monism affords. As a practical matter, this wide-ranging opposition might be of some importance, but I confess that I am unmoved by it philosophically or ethically. To me, the vision of a human society where people talk sense much more frequently and consistently than they talk nonsense is self-justifying on its face.

If I am right about this, even partially, then the obvious conclusion is that the question of pedagogy, understood as the theory and practice of inducing people to become maximally human, ought to be a central problem for our civilization. It is at least as important as quantum gravity or the unraveling of the great mysteries of genetics.

Notes

1. From South Carolina's 1860 declaration justifying its secession from the Union; it is typical of the official statements of the seceding states:

    The Constitution of the United States, in its fourth Article, provides as follows: "No person held to service or labor in one State, under the laws thereof, escaping into another, shall, in consequence of any law or regulation therein, be discharged from such service or labor, but shall be delivered up, on claim of the party to whom such service or labor may be due."

    This stipulation was so material to the compact, that without it that compact would not have been made. The greater number of the contracting parties held slaves, and they had previously evinced their estimate of the value of such a stipulation by making it a condition in the Ordinance for the government of the territory ceded by Virginia, which now composes the States north of the Ohio River.

    The same article of the Constitution stipulates also for rendition by the several States of fugitives from justice from the other States.

    The General Government, as the common agent, passed laws to carry into effect these stipulations of the States. For many years these laws were executed. But an increasing hostility on the part of the non-slaveholding States to the institution of slavery has led to a disregard of their obligations, and the laws of the General Government have ceased to effect the objects of the Constitution. The States of Maine, New Hampshire, Vermont, Massachusetts, Connecticut, Rhode Island, New York, Pennsylvania, Illinois, Indiana, Michigan, Wisconsin and Iowa, have enacted laws which either nullify the Acts of Congress or render useless any attempt to execute them. In many of these States the fugitive is discharged from service or labor claimed, and in none of them has the State Government complied with the stipulation made in the Constitution. The State of New Jersey, at an early day, passed a law in conformity with her constitutional obligation; but the current of anti-slavery feeling has led her more recently to enact laws which render inoperative the remedies provided by her own law and by the laws of Congress. In the State of New York even the right of transit for a slave has been denied by her tribunals; and the States of Ohio and Iowa have refused to surrender to justice fugitives charged with murder, and with inciting servile insurrection in the State of Virginia. Thus the constituted compact has been deliberately broken and disregarded by the non-slave-holding States, and the consequence follows that South Carolina is released from her obligation.

2. See, for instance, D.S. Freeman's idolatrous four-volume biography (Freeman 1935), which reigned for years as the near-scriptural authority on the life, character, and deeds of the Confederacy's foremost commander. By way of contrast, see Nolan 1991 for a far more jaundiced view.

3. "Almost from the moment the conflict ended, the Lost Cause school towered like a colossus over Civil War history writing" (Owens 2003) It is interesting to note that Owens is a contemporary conservative writer, in that political conservatives have long been partisans of "The Lost Cause."

4. What has become the conventional account insists that if the Confederates had taken Little Round Top, they would have been able to rake Meade's entire left flank with a deadly enfilade from the Rebel guns that would have been emplaced on that hill. The truth of the matter is that, even assuming ideal judgment on the part of Confederate artillerymen, Little Round Top could have accommodated only seven or eight guns in all. Moreover, these would have been easy targets for snipers and the very effective Federal batteries in the area and would almost certainly have been destroyed or driven off in fairly short order.

5. The Alabama Regiment attacking Chamberlain's front was probably, all in all, in worse shape than the 20th Maine from the very first. The fabled charge really evolved *ad hoc* when some of Chamberlain's troops advanced a few paces to retrieve their wounded, which spooked the exhausted Confederates into turning tail; Chamberlain's command to "Charge!" probably came after many of his men had spontaneously begun to do just that. The standard account draws on Chamberlain's operational report, but Chamberlain concocted and postdated this document well after the fact, carefully tailoring it to burnish his reputation.

6. After the war, Chamberlain's political career flourished briefly, but he had a knack for making enemies, and his larger ambitions proved futile. As president of Bowdoin College, he adopted an authoritarian style (in keeping with his innate conservatism) that alienated most of his students and provoked them to outright defiance. After his academic career had ended, he became embroiled in a series of increasingly dubious get-rich schemes, which only succeeded in driving him into poverty. Most disturbing was Chamberlain's support for "reconciliation" with the defeated South on the basis of ending Reconstruction and acquiescing in the disenfranchisement of most freedmen and their forcible reversion to a state of virtual serfdom; see Trulock 1992.

7. White 1973. A much younger historian, Joshua Walker, summarizes White's key points with a rather skeptical eye (Walker 2002).

8. Appleby *et al.* 1994; Evans 1997; Windschuttle 1997. Appleby *et al.* and Windschuttle represent the poles of recent criticism. Windschuttle is conservative outright, culturally as well as politically. Appleby *et al.* are academics who flirted heavily with some post-modern ideas and have abandoned them reluctantly, ruefully, and not altogether dismissively. Evans lies somewhere in between.

9. A characteristic example may be found in Part Three ("Discipline") of Foucault's *Discipline and Punish* (1977). Here, the book tries to show that the emergence of European culture into modernity was accompanied by an overarching trend toward the increased regimentation and invigilation of "the body." On this view, there was a prolif-eration of regulations and formularies prescribing the "proper" way to carry out various activities, which at the same time broke those activities into minute steps whose mastery required submissiveness rather than understanding.

As a paradigmatic case, Foucault offers the example of the regulations for military marching. He offers an early seventeenth-century example that merely recommends a cadenced step for a column of marching men and contrasts it with a late eighteenth-century drill manual, which lists a variety of different marching steps and specifies their exact choreography. "We have passed," writes Foucault, "from a form of injunction that measured or punctuated gestures to a web that constrains them or sustains them through their entire succession" (ibid.: 152). The problem with this is that if one looks in detail at some early seventeenth-century manuals of arms, one finds that soldiers' routines are broken down into discrete elements at least as minutely as in the late eighteenth-century example. Barriffe's *Directions for Muster* (1638), the work on which English drillmasters of the seventeenth century relied, specifies thirty-four discrete stages, each with its own command, for the synchronized loading, priming, and firing of a matchlock musket of the period. The instructions for the deployment of a pike are comparably elaborate.

A few pages later, Foucault ascribes increasingly robotic military discipline to the growing predominance of the rifle as the standard infantry weapon. He dates its "widespread use" to the very beginning of the eighteenth century (the Battle of Steinkirk, 1699). "More accurate, more rapid than the musket, [the rifle] gave greater value to the soldier's skill; more capable of reaching a particular target, it made it possible to exploit fire-power at an individual level" (1977: 163 and note 11). The only trouble with this is that throughout the eighteenth century and well into the nineteenth, the standard weapon for the line-of-battle infantryman was the smooth-bore musket, not the rifle. (Rifles, because of the tight fit of the projectile, could not be loaded rapidly enough.) The Battle of Waterloo (1815) was fought with smooth-bore weapons. The invention of the "mini-ball" in the mid-nineteenth century finally made rifled weapons practical for infantry. But even in the American Civil War, where the "rifle musket" was the most common firearm, many regiments were armed with smooth-bore weapons.

In fact, one could (and should) argue that the rapid improvement of the rifle in the late nineteenth century brought to an end the stand-up, line-of-battle tactics that the elaborate marching techniques that Foucault cites were supposed to facilitate. These were replaced by far different "open order" tactics, which rely much more heavily on individual judgment and initiative – a development whose "social" implications exactly contradict Foucault's claims.

10. Shapin and Schaffer's work has been criticized elsewhere (Gross and Levitt 1998: 63–70; Pinnick 1998). Their book is illustrative of the technique by which a postmodern "classic" is created: take a fairly minor incident; declare it to embody, in their purest form, the ideological and doctrinal concerns of the day; ignore whatever personal quirks or agendas might account for the tone or idiomatic character of the narrow piece of the historical record being scrutinized; proclaim that the incident is a "founding moment" that reveals or even creates an enduring hegemonic motif within a vast civilization over centuries of time; and make sure that your enemies, that is to say "modernists," are castigated for their philosophical naivete and their political obtuseness. Then go on to have your work proclaimed as "path-breaking" by ideological allies or followers who disdain the idea that deep and sweeping claims merit an equally deep and sweeping critique as to method and substance before they are celebrated and canonized. Shapin and Schaffer's *Leviathan and the Air Pump* well illustrates this strategy, which seems to have been pioneered by Foucault's *Birth of the Clinic* and *Discipline and Punish*.

11. *Archaeology* and *Archaeology Odyssey* are the journals I personally subscribe to.

12. The November/December 2003 issue (vol. 56, no. 6) of *Archaeology* is the sample I am using.

13. See, e.g., Silverman and Goren 2003. It is interesting to note that one particularly degenerate relic of "biblical archaeology" is the recurrent search for Noah's ark, which still galvanizes biblical literalists and has a shadowy connection with the space program. In part, this is due to the obsessive quest of the late astronaut James Irwin to find traces of the biblical ark on the slopes of Mount Ararat. NASA pilot-astronauts like Irwin are,

basically, pilots with some training in engineering, not, in most cases, scientists by education or temperament. But the public easily conflates the skills of an astronaut with scientific authority. As reported by Leonard David (2002), civilian groups on the fringe of the space program are still trying to conscript space-age technology to confirm the historical truth of the Noachian narrative. It is noteworthy that among their other "technologies" is "remote viewing," a pseudoscientific imposture long since debunked. Needless to say, remote viewing also figures prominently in some other varieties of pseudoarchaeology.

14. A recent issue (November/December 2003) of the scientifically respectable magazine *Archaeology Odyssey* contains, on its inside front cover, a full-page ad emblazoned with the headline: "Startling New Proof The Exodus Took Place – But not where you think!" The natural inference is that the readership of such magazines still contains a significant number of people who see archaeology as properly subordinate, in some fashion, to faith and its historical assertions. A related example is the ossuary supposedly carved with an inscription reading "James, the brother of Jesus." It is most probably an ancient artefact with a forged inscription added to increase its value (Nickell 2003), but that has not stopped the object from being much touted in venues like *Biblical Archaeology Review* and *Archaeology Odyssey*. Indeed, the editor of both magazines, Hershel Shanks, has written a book to cash in on the public's interest in this "find" and used both magazines to promote it; see Shanks and Witherington 2003. Despite the conclusion of a committee of Israeli archaeologists that the inscription is a modern forgery, its authenticity continues to be defended in the pages of *Biblical Archaeology Review*, mostly by attempting to discredit the committee's damning report; see Lemaire 2003 (note the sidebar advertisement for the Shanks and Witherington book in the online version).

15. David Macauly's *Motel of the Mysteries* (1979), a hilarious send-up of the clichés of "lost civilization" archaeology and its popularizations, is still selling well after almost twenty-five years in print.

16. My list of crank environmentalists includes dogmatic opponents to genetically modified crops, as well as the alarmists who continue to agitate over the supposed dangers of low-frequency radiation. These are justifiably called crank movements, not because the fears around which they grew were groundless from the first but because they have consistently shown themselves to be immune to evidence. To the fervent anti-GM activist, for instance, no scientific evidence can ever be strong enough to exculpate a proposed application of such technology, while no evidence of supposed danger can ever be weak or ill-founded enough to disregard.

17. This assertion is seemingly contradicted by the existence of pseudoscientific movements devoted to provoking fear and anxiety rather than offering a soothing or hopeful vision. Examples are readily found in some aspects of extreme environmentalism (for instance, frantic alarmism over genetically modified crops) or in campaigns against vaccination (Fitzpatrick 2004). In these instances, cultists insist on finding grave dangers where competent scientists find nothing of the kind. At first sight, this hardly seems to be an example of consoling faith. Looking more deeply, however, we see that the real *topos* of this narrative is that of the small but dedicated fellowship of those who see the dark menace lurking beneath the smiling surface and who regard themselves as warriors in a gallant crusade against the odds. It is hardly misleading to call this a flattering self-image.

18. The "social constructivist" school of the sociology of scientific knowledge asserts, when it is being frank, that the success of modern science is basically collective self-delusion, which now prevails in industrial society. This doctrine, it seems to me, merely shows that social constructivism is a delusion.

19. Edward Gibbon, *Decline and Fall of the Roman Empire*, iii.

12 Pseudoscience and postmodernism

Antagonists or fellow travelers?

Alan D. Sokal

> The human understanding is not composed of dry light, but is subject to influence
> from the will and the emotions, a fact that creates fanciful knowledge; man prefers to
> believe what he wants to be true.
>
> (Francis Bacon, *The New Organon*, Aphorism 49)

Introduction

In this essay, I propose to investigate the paradoxical relation between two
broad categories of thought: *pseudoscience* and *postmodernism* (both will be
defined more precisely in a moment). At first glance, pseudoscience and
postmodernism would appear to be opposites: pseudoscience is characterized
by extreme credulity, while postmodernism is characterized by extreme
skepticism. More specifically, adherents of pseudoscience believe in theories
or phenomena that mainstream science rejects as utterly implausible, while
adherents of postmodernism withhold belief in theories that mainstream
science considers to be established beyond any reasonable doubt.[1]

And yet, I will argue, there is, at least in some instances, a curious
convergence between pseudoscience and postmodernism. On the one hand,
advocates of pseudoscience – at least the most sophisticated among them –
sometimes fall back on postmodernist arguments when the reliability or
credibility of their evidence is challenged. (This stratagem is admittedly
second best from their point of view, but at least it manages to avert
outright refutation.) On the other hand, postmodernists' professed skepticism is often deployed selectively, so that a disdain for the knowledge claims
of modern science sometimes coexists with a sympathy for (if not outright
belief in) one or more pseudosciences. The bulk of this essay will be devoted
to illustrating these two complementary moves through examples drawn
from various brands of pseudoscience. In the final section, I will argue that
this is not merely an academic exercise but has serious real-world consequences.

Since the three key terms in this discussion – "science," "pseudoscience,"
and "postmodernism" – have been used with widely varying meanings, it is
incumbent on me before proceeding further, to clarify and delimit, as best I
can, how I intend to use these terms.[2]

Note first that each of these terms has a triple denotation: it can be under-stood as referring to a body of thought, to the arguments or justifications that are offered in support of that body of thought, or to the community of advo-cates of (or adherents to) that body of thought. I shall continue this triple usage, while distinguishing the three aspects whenever necessary.

The word "science," as commonly used, has at least four distinct mean-ings: it denotes an intellectual endeavor aimed at a rational understanding of the natural and social world; it denotes a corpus of currently accepted substantive knowledge; it denotes the community of scientists, with its mores and its social and economic structure; and, finally, it denotes applied science and technology. In this essay, I will be concentrating on the first two aspects, with some secondary references to the sociology of the scientific community; I will not address technology at all. Thus, by *science* I mean, first of all, a world view giving primacy to reason and observation and a method-ology aimed at acquiring accurate knowledge of the natural and social world. This methodology is characterized, above all else, by the *critical spirit*: namely, the commitment to the incessant testing of assertions through observations and/or experiments – the more stringent the tests, the better – and to revising or discarding those theories that fail the test. One corollary of the critical spirit is *fallibilism*: the understanding that all our empirical knowledge is tentative, incomplete, and open to revision in the light of new evidence or cogent new arguments (although the most well-established aspects of scientific knowledge are unlikely to be discarded entirely).

It is important to note that well-tested theories in the mature sciences are supported in general by a powerful web of interlocking evidence coming from a variety of sources; rarely does everything rest on one "crucial experi-ment" (see the Introduction). Moreover, the progress of science tends to link these theories into a unified framework, so that (for instance) biology has to be compatible with chemistry, and chemistry with physics.[3] Philosopher Susan Haack (1993, 1998, 2003) has illuminatingly analogized science to the problem of completing a crossword puzzle, in which any modification of one word will entail changes in interlocking words; in most cases, the required changes will be fairly local, but in some cases it may be necessary to rework large parts of the puzzle.[4,5]

I stress that my use of the term "science" is not limited to the *natural* sciences but also includes investigations aimed at acquiring accurate knowl-edge of factual matters relating to *any* aspect of the world by using rational empirical methods analogous to those employed in the natural sciences.[6] Thus "science" (as I use the term) is routinely practised not only by physi-cists, chemists, and biologists but also by historians, detectives, plumbers, and indeed all human beings in (some aspects of) their daily lives.[7,8] Likewise for the term "pseudoscience": the subject matter can be any aspect of the world. The distinction between science and pseudoscience does not concern the subject matter but rather the quality of the methods employed and the reliability of the knowledge (or purported knowledge) obtained.

More precisely, I shall use the term "pseudoscience" to designate any body of thought (along with its associated justifications and advocates) that

1. makes assertions about real or alleged phenomena and/or real or alleged causal relations that mainstream science justifiably considers to be utterly implausible; and
2. attempts to support these assertions through types of argumentation or evidence that fall far short of the logical and evidentiary standards of mainstream science.

This definition implies, first of all, that pseudoscientists are not postmodernists: they make assertions about the natural or social world that they claim to be *true* in an objective sense. Note also that this definition of pseudoscience involves both sociological and epistemic criteria. On the one hand, the mainstream scientific community must reject the beliefs in question as utterly implausible; in addition, this rejection must be *rationally justified* on the basis of the currently available evidence. Ordinarily, this rejection is based on the fact that

- the evidence adduced in support of the beliefs is spurious, grossly mishandled, or otherwise utterly unconvincing;
- the beliefs in question imply numerous observational consequences that are radically at variance with well-established scientific data; and
- the beliefs in question conflict irremediably with well-tested scientific theories within the domain where there is good reason to believe that those theories are valid.

Most often (though not always), pseudoscience also

3. claims to be scientific and even
3'. claims to relate its assertions to genuine science, particularly cutting-edge scientific discoveries.

In this way, pseudoscience attempts to wrap itself in the mantle of genuine science, with the evident aim of capturing for itself some of the epistemic respect that the general public (hardcore postmodernists excluded) ordinarily accords to "science." Moreover, pseudoscience usually exhibits *some* of the logical and sociological characteristics of genuine science, such as

4. It involves not a single isolated belief, but rather a complex and logically coherent system that "explains" a wide variety of phenomena (or alleged phenomena).
5. Practitioners undergo an extensive process of training and credentialing.[9]

However, what pseudoscience utterly lacks is the critical spirit and the robust empirical support that are characteristic of genuine science. Examples of pseudosciences are astrology, homeopathy, "creation science," Judaism, Christianity, Islam and Hinduism.[10,11]

The fact that one can distinguish (in most cases quite readily) between genuine science and pseudoscience does not mean that it is possible to draw a sharp line between them – much less a line based on rigid "demarcation criteria" such as those proposed by Popper.[12] Rather, one would do better to envisage a continuum (Figure 12.1) with well-established science (e.g. the idea that matter is composed of atoms) at one end, passing via cutting-edge science (e.g. neutrino oscillations) and mainstream but speculative science (e.g. string theory) – and then, much further along the way, through shoddy science (N rays, cold fusion) – and ending, after a long further journey, at pseudoscience. Although there is no precise location along this continuum where a line can be drawn, there is nevertheless a radical difference between the established natural sciences and the pseudosciences as regards both methodology and degree of empirical confirmation.[13,14,15]

The term "postmodernism" is even more diffuse: it has been used to cover an ill-defined galaxy of ideas in fields ranging from art and architecture to the social sciences and philosophy. I propose here to use the term much more narrowly, to denote

> an intellectual current characterized by the more-or-less explicit rejection of the rationalist tradition of the Enlightenment, by theoretical discourses disconnected from any empirical test, and by a cognitive and cultural relativism that regards science as nothing more than a "narration," a "myth" or a social construction among many others.
>
> (Sokal and Bricmont 1998: 1)

Thus, postmodernists reject the idea that assertions about the natural or social world can be objectively (and hence transculturally) true or false; rather, they insist that "truth" is relative to some social or cultural group.[16] Frequently, they redefine the word "truth" to denote mere intersubjective

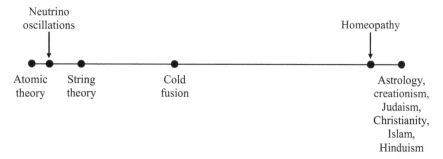

Figure 12.1 A very rough depiction of the continuum from genuine science to pseudoscience, based on the strength of the empirical evidence for or against the given theory and on the soundness of the methodology employed by the theory's advocates. This graph should be interpreted qualitatively, not quantitatively.

agreement (within some specified social group) or practical utility (for some specified goal).[17] Postmodernists therefore tend to reject objectivity even as an ideal toward which to strive (however imperfectly): everything becomes dependent on one's subjective viewpoint, and moral or aesthetic values displace cognitive ones as the criteria for evaluating assertions of alleged fact.

Let me stress that not all the authors whom I term "postmodernist" would identify with that label, since they may use the term in a sense different from mine (which is their right). Conversely, some authors who term themselves "postmodernist" may not be postmodernist in my sense.[18] Finally, it should be noted that there exist many different currents within what I have called postmodernism, which interact only weakly. Thus, some postmodernists (in my definition) rely heavily on Derrida and Heidegger, others more strongly on Foucault, others on constructivist sociology of science (Barnes, Bloor, Collins, Latour, etc.), others on the feminist–constructivist subgroup (Haraway, Harding, Keller, etc.), others on the post-colonial wing (Nandy, Alvares, Shiva, Sardar, etc.).

In order to give a clearer idea of the type of views that I am here calling "postmodernist," it is perhaps useful to provide some examples. Consider the following assertions by prominent figures in the sociology of science:

[T]he validity of theoretical propositions in the sciences is in no way affected by factual evidence.

(Gergen 1988: 37)

The natural world has a small or non-existent role in the construction of scientific knowledge.

(Collins 1981: 3)[19]

For the relativist [such as ourselves] there is no sense attached to the idea that some standards or beliefs are really rational as distinct from merely locally accepted as such.

(Barnes and Bloor 1981: 27; clarification in brackets added by me)

Science legitimates itself by linking its discoveries with power, a connection which *determines* (not merely influences) what counts as reliable knowledge...

(Aronowitz 1988: 204; italics in original)

Assertions like these are in clear contradiction with the view of science I have set forth, i.e., as a fallible but partly successful attempt to obtain an objective (albeit approximate and incomplete) understanding of (some aspects of) the world. These statements exhibit, either explicitly or implicitly, the cognitive relativism and extreme social constructivism that are characteristic of the intellectual current I am calling "postmodernism."

Statements as clear-cut as those just cited are, however, rare in the academic postmodernist literature. More often one finds assertions that are ambiguous but can nevertheless be interpreted (and quite often *are* interpreted) as implying what the foregoing quotations make explicit: that science as I have defined it is an illusion, and that the purported objective knowledge provided by science is largely or entirely a social construction. For example:

> Despite their names, conservation laws are not inevitable facts of nature but constructions that foreground some experiences and marginalize others. ... Almost without exception, conservation laws were formulated, developed, and experimentally tested by men. If conservation laws represent particular emphases and not inevitable facts, then people living in different kinds of bodies and identifying with different gender constructions might well have arrived at different models for [fluid] flow.
>
> (Hayles 1992: 31–2)

> Given their extensive training in sophisticated mathematical techniques, the preponderance of mathematics in particle physicists' accounts of reality is no more hard to explain than the fondness of ethnic groups for their native language. On the view advocated in this chapter, there is no obligation upon anyone framing a view of the world to take account of what twentieth-century science has to say.
>
> (Pickering 1984: 413)

Let me emphasize once again that pseudoscientists are not, at least in the first instance, postmodernists: they make assertions about the natural or social world that they claim to be true in an objective sense; only with great reluctance will they fall back on the comparatively lame assertion that their "point of view" is "just as valid" as that of mainstream science. Indeed, some pseudoscientists are militantly anti-postmodernist. For instance, the leader of a major pseudoscientific cult recently issued an erudite proclamation criticizing

> different forms of agnosticism and relativism which have led philosophical research to lose its way in the shifting sands of widespread scepticism. Recent times have seen the rise to prominence of various doctrines which tend to devalue even the truths which had been judged certain. A legitimate plurality of positions has yielded to an undifferentiated pluralism, based upon the assumption that all positions are equally valid, which is one of today's most widespread symptoms of the lack of confidence in truth. Even certain conceptions of life coming from the East betray this lack of confidence, denying truth its exclusive character and assuming that truth reveals itself equally in different doctrines, even if they contradict one another.
>
> (John Paul II 1998: 10)

Still, some pseudoscientists do employ postmodernist arguments, whether opportunistically or systematically. In the remainder of this essay, I would like to give some examples of that use.

Let me stress in advance that I will not be concerned here with explaining in detail why astrology, homeopathy, and the rest are in fact pseudoscience; that would take me too far afield. Nor will I address, except in passing, the important but difficult problem of understanding the psychological attractions of pseudoscience and the social factors affecting its spread.[20] Rather, my principal aim is to investigate the logical and sociological nexus between pseudoscience and postmodernism.

It goes without saying that none of my case studies should be treated as definitive – quite the contrary. I have no special expertise in any of the fields of study under discussion; I could easily have made mistakes. Moreover, my accounts are in no way claimed to be comprehensive. Rather, my aim is to point the attention of philosophers, sociologists, and historians of science to a phenomenon that deserves a more detailed and rigorous investigation and analysis.

Pseudoscience and postmodernism in nursing

New York Times readers on the morning of 1 April 1998 were treated to a delicious front-page story that was not an April Fool's joke:

> Two years ago, Emily Rosa of Loveland, Colo., designed and carried out an experiment that challenges a leading treatment in alternative medicine. Her study, reported today in The Journal of the American Medical Association, has thrown the field into tumult.
> Emily is 11 years old [9 at the time of the experiment]. She did the experiment for her fourth-grade science fair.
>
> (Kolata 1998: A1)

The technique that Emily tested is called Therapeutic Touch (TT) – a slight misnomer because practitioners do not actually touch the patient. Rather, they move their hands rhythmically over the patient's body, about 2–6 inches (5–15 cm) away, in an effort to "rebalance" the "human energy field" that they believe surrounds the patient.[21]

Emily designed a simple experiment to test whether Therapeutic Touch practitioners can really sense a "human energy field," as they claim. The practitioner and Emily were seated opposite each other at a table, separated by an opaque screen with two cutouts at its base, through which the practitioner placed her hands. A cloth towel was attached to the screen and draped over the practitioner's arms. Before each set of trials, the practitioner was given time to "center" or make any other mental preparations she deemed necessary. Emily then flipped a coin and placed her right hand 3–4 inches (8–10 cm) above one of the practitioner's hands, chosen according to the coin flip. The practitioner was asked to state which of her hands was closer to Emily's hand and was given as much time as she wished in order to decide. In 280 trials involving twenty-one Therapeutic Touch practitioners, they succeeded in choosing the correct hand 44 percent of the time, slightly worse than random guessing.[22]

When I first heard about Emily's experiment, I admired her ingenuity but wondered whether anyone really took Therapeutic Touch seriously. How wrong I was! Therapeutic Touch is taught in more than eighty college and university schools of nursing in at least seventy countries, is practised in at least eighty hospitals across North America, and is promoted by leading American nursing associations.[23] Its inventor claims to have trained more than 47,000 practitioners over a 26-year period, who have gone on to train many more.[24] At least 245 books or dissertations have been published that include "Therapeutic Touch" in the title, subject headings or table of contents.[25] All in all, Therapeutic Touch appears to have become one of the most widely practised "holistic" nursing techniques.

How did a profession based in science come to promote mysticism and quackery? The story is more complex – and more worrisome – than I initially realized.[26]

Pseudoscience in nursing: I

> *Experiential Exercise 5.* This exercise, "The Emperor's Clothes," is designed to test your perception of cues in the healee's energy field. I call the human energy field "the Emperor's Clothes" because, like the emperor's new clothes in the fairy tale of that name, the human energy field is invisible. To a bystander, the healer doing a Therapeutic Touch assessment seems to be attending to something that is invisible or imaginary.
>
> (Krieger 1993: 32)

Therapeutic Touch was invented in the early 1970s by Dolores Krieger, a professor of nursing at New York University, in collaboration with Dora Kunz, a noted clairvoyant and soon-to-be president of the Theosophical Society in America.[27,28] Krieger explains that

> Therapeutic Touch derives from, but is not the same as, the ancient art of the laying-on of hands. ... Therapeutic Touch has no religious base; it is a conscious, intentional act; it is based on research findings; and Therapeutic Touch does not require a declaration of faith from the healee (patient) for it to be effective.
>
> (Krieger 1981: 138)[29]

She notes that

> The term *Therapeutic Touch* may in fact be a misnomer because, in practice, the healer need not make physical contact with the patient (healee). Much of the work done by the person playing the role of healer has as its

primary focus the modulation of the healee's energy field rather than the touch or manipulation of his or her skin.

(Krieger 1993: 11; italics in original)

More precisely,

Illness is an imbalance in an individual's energy field. In Therapeutic Touch, the healer directs and modulates this energy field, using the sense of touch as a telereceptor. ... You as the healer act as a human support system, your own healthy energy field providing the scaffolding to guide the repatterning of the healee's weakened and disrupted energy flow.

(Krieger 1993: 12–13; italics in original)

The Therapeutic Touch process consists of five phases:

1. Centering oneself.
2. Making an assessment of the healee.
3. "Unruffling" the field.
4. The direction and modulation of energy.
5. Recognizing when it is time to stop.

(Krieger 1979: 69)

Krieger is vague about the precise nature of the "human energy field," but she does make clear that it is not merely electromagnetic (Krieger 1987: 7).[30] According to Krieger,

the human energy field [is] a complex of many interpenetrating fields whose properties dynamically interrelate in a pattern we recognize as human nature. This field functions like a transformer. These foci convert energy systems, or prana, into the kind of energies that make our psychophysiological being what it is. The foci or transformers themselves are chakras. Their primary functions are to collect, change and distribute the prana to the organs of our physical bodies. These foci form the matrix of the chemicophysical field and the psychodynamic field in the individual and set the stage for psychosomatic functioning.

(ibid.: 41)

Indeed, energy fields are not limited to humans, as Krieger enjoins the reader to

Take every opportunity to become sensitive to the living energy field. If you are unable to work on people under your present circumstances, assess the energy fields of your pets or other domestic animals, the trees in your neighborhood (particularly if they are coniferous or eucalyptus trees, which radiate an immense energy field relative to their size), or groups of flowers.

(Krieger 1993: 35)

Although the human energy field is as yet unmeasurable by instruments, almost anyone can learn, with sufficient practice, to sense it (Krieger 1979: 3, 57; 1993: 25):

> Most frequently, the cues you pick up in the healee's energy field during the assessment are one or a combination of the following:
> • Temperature differentials, such as a sense of heat or cold.
> • Pressure, or feelings of congestion in the energy flow.
> • Changes in or lack of synchronization in the intrinsic rhythmicity of the healee's energy field.
> • Localized weak electric shocks or tingly feelings as you move the energy centers in the palms of your hands through the healee's energy field.
>
> (Krieger 1993: 46)

Indeed, regular practice of Therapeutic Touch often leads to increased proficiency in the use of other natural human faculties, such as telepathy (Krieger 1979: 70–1; 1987, chapter 5):

> From written accounts in my students' journals, indications of the use of telepathy can be perceived on the average of two-and-a-half weeks from the time they put the healing techniques into consistent practice.
>
> (Krieger 1987: 78)

Healing through Therapeutic Touch occurs by "unruffling" and "rebalancing" the healee's energy field, thereby allowing for the resumption of a more natural energy flow, and by transferring energy in a directed fashion from healer to healee (Krieger 1979: chapter 7; 1993: chapters 3 and 4). One prominent advocate of Therapeutic Touch explains the process as follows:

> In a state of health, the life energy flows freely in, through, and out of the organism in a balanced manner, nourishing all the organs of the body. In disease, the flow of the energy is obstructed, disordered, and/or depleted. Therapeutic Touch practitioners, having learned to attune to the universal field through a conscious intent, direct the life energy into the patients to enhance their vitality. The practitioners also help the patients assimilate the energy by releasing congestion and balancing areas where the flow has become disordered. Drawing upon the universal field, the practitioners do not become drained of their own energy but, on the contrary, are continually replenished.
>
> (Macrae 1988: 4)

Krieger explains the mechanism in greater "scientific" detail, as follows:

> Human beings are open systems. They appear to be a nexus of all fields
> of which life partakes. That is, human beings are the energetic matrices
> of inorganic as well as organic fields, psychodynamic as well as concep-
> tual fields (i.e., electromagnetic is only one interface of the whole
> complex). Human beings are therefore exquisitely sensitive to wave
> phenomena (i.e., energy). I perceive a healer to be an individual whose
> personal health gives him access to an overabundance of *prana* for the
> wellbeing of others. (Prana is a Sanskrit term for what we in the West
> think of as the organization of energy that underlies the life process.)
> Prana is concerned with the intrinsic rhythmicity of energy ...
>
> Using deductive logic I re-examined my previous studies in the life
> sciences. It occurred to me that at the physical level, this projection of
> human energy during the healing act grounds itself in the ill person via
> electron transfer resonance.
>
> (Krieger 1987: 7; italics in original)[31]

As a physicist, I am not impressed.[32]

Pseudoscience in nursing: II

How seriously are Therapeutic Touch and other pseudoscientific "healing
modalities" taken in the nursing profession? I cannot claim to have made a
comprehensive study of this question, but I would like to present briefly
one illustration.

In 1999, the American College of Nurse-Midwives devoted a special issue
of its official organ, the *Journal of Nurse-Midwifery*, to the topic of "complementary and alternative therapies in women's health." An introductory
editorial insisted strongly on the importance of evidence-based practice,
including scientifically sound studies of safety and efficacy (Raisler 1999:
190). Fortunately, a few of the accompanying articles did live up to that
declaration. One article provided a fairly cautious summary of the currently
available evidence concerning the efficacy of complementary and alternative
therapies, underlining the need for randomized and (where possible) double-
blind clinical trials (Murphy *et al.* 1999). Another article provided scientific
information concerning the efficacy and safety of various herbal preparations
claimed to induce labor (McFarlin *et al.* 1999). A third reported a retrospective study aimed at testing whether evening primrose oil is effective in
shortening labor or reducing the incidence of post-date pregnancies (the
results were negative) (Dove and Johnson 1999).

But, the level of most of the remaining articles was abysmally low. Two
articles (Castro 1999; Brennan 1999) presented homeopathic doctrine[33] as
fact, without the slightest critical analysis.[34] While admitting that "the
mechanism to explain *how* homeopathy works has not been discovered"

(Brennan 1999: 292; italics in original), both articles take for granted not only the efficacy of homeopathic remedies beyond the placebo effect but also the validity of homeopathic teachings such as the vital force, the Law of Similars, and the Law of Potentization. A review of a book on "homeopathy for midwives," appearing in the same issue, was equally uncritical (Krov 1999).

Another article discussed the theory and practice of Therapeutic Touch, starting with an uncritical presentation of Kunz's and Krieger's notions of the "human energy field" ("an ovoid of many-colored light interpenetrating and surrounding the physical body, and extending out from it to a distance of about twelve to eighteen inches") and Rogers' theory of Unitary Human Beings ("incorporating Bertalanffy's systems theory with quantum physics") (Fischer and Johnson 1999: 301, 302). To its credit, this article also included discussion of some skeptical studies, including Emily Rosa's famous experiment. The authors "compliment Ms. Rosa for attempting to conduct an experiment to detect energy fields" but assert that "the only reasonable conclusions that can be supported by the data is [*sic*] that a small group of practitioners of TT were unable to detect an energy field around one individual's hand" (ibid.: 304) They went on to cite two "qualitative" studies that took for granted the validity of Therapeutic Touch and reported patients' "experiences" of their own energy fields,[35] but they did not cite any positive evidence that "human energy fields" actually exist or that Therapeutic Touch practitioners can sense them. Nevertheless, they stated unreservedly their belief that

> more definitive proof will come from the investigation of the process of TT, that is, the intentionality involved in the conscious desire to help or heal another. This task, however, may be as elusive as the ability to prove that prayer causes healing. In support of a more spiritual approach to the issue of energy transference, Zefron quoted an anonymous scientist who said, " ... we have come to the conclusion that a vibration of very high intensity and extremely long wave-length with tremendous healing power, caused by spiritual forces operating through the mind of man, is the next thing science expects to discover." It may possibly be the spiritual aspect of this energy exchange that remains so elusive.
>
> (ibid.: 306–7)[36]

Pseudoscience in nursing: III

Tracking down the intellectual precursors of pseudoscience in nursing, one is soon led to the work of Martha E. Rogers (1914–1994), professor of nursing and head of the Division of Nursing at New York University from 1954 through 1975.[37] In her 1970 book *An Introduction to the Theoretical Basis of Nursing*, Rogers single-handedly "created a science that had never existed before," as one of her disciples modestly put it (Phillips 1994a: vii).[38] Here is how the founder of the Science of Unitary Human Beings explained her system in 1986:

Four concepts are postulated to be basic to the proposed system, namely: energy fields, openness, pattern, and four-dimensionality. These concepts are defined consistent with the general language and are given specificity according to the conceptual system under discussion.

Energy fields are postulated to constitute the fundamental unit of both the living and the nonliving. *Field* is a unifying concept. *Energy* signifies the dynamic nature of the field. *Energy fields* are infinite. Two energy fields are identified: the human field and the environmental field. Specifically, human beings and environment *are* energy fields.

(Rogers 1986: 4; italics in original)[39]

After briefly conscripting relativity, quantum theory, probability, evolutionary theory, and space exploration in support of the conclusion that "the closed-system, entropic model of the universe" is no longer tenable, Rogers goes on to explicate the last three of her basic concepts:

In a universe of open systems, causality is not an option. ... Energy fields are open – not a little bit or sometimes, but continuously. The human and environmental fields are integral with one another. Causality is invalid. Change is continuously innovative.

Pattern is defined as the distinguishing characteristic of an energy field perceived as a single wave. ...

Four-dimensionality characterizes the human and environmental fields. It is defined as a nonlinear domain without spatial or temporal attributes. All reality is postulated to be four-dimensional.

(ibid.: 5; italics in original)[40]

An uncharitable reader (such as myself) might object that this pseudoscientific verbiage is perfectly meaningless.[41] But Rogers has an answer:

Definitions increase in clarity and specificity as the conceptual system emerges. The unitary human being (human field) is defined as an irreducible, four-dimensional energy field identified by pattern and manifesting characteristics that are different from those of the parts and cannot be predicted from those of the parts. The environmental field is defined as an irreducible, four-dimensional energy field identified by pattern and manifesting characteristics that are different from those of the parts. Each environmental field is specific to its given human field. Both change continuously, mutually, and creatively. The human and environmental fields are infinite and integral with one another.

(ibid.: 5)[42]

With this clarification in hand, we can push onwards from concepts to principles:

Unifying principles and hypothetical generalizations derive from the conceptual system. The Principles of Homeodynamics are three in number and together postulate the nature and direction of change. These principles are set forth as follows:

PRINCIPLES OF HOMEODYNAMICS

Principle of Resonancy	The continuous change from lower to higher frequency wave patterns in human and environmental fields
Principle of Helicy	The continuous, innovative, probabilistic increasing diversity of human and environmental field patterns characterized by nonrepeating rhythmicities
Principle of Integrality	The continuous mutual human field and environmental field process[43]

(Rogers 1986: 5–6)

In later years, Rogers continued to make improvements to her system, replacing "four-dimensional" with "multidimensional" and finally "pandimensional" while deleting "probability" in favor of "unpredictability."[44]

The Science of Unitary Human Beings makes numerous empirically testable predictions. For example:

> The principle of helicy subsumes within it the principles of reciprocy and synchrony, and postulates further explanatory and predictive dimensions of nursing's theoretical system. The principle of helicy connotes that the life process evolves unidirectionally in sequential stages along a curve which has the same general shape all along but which does not lie in a plane. Encompassed within this principle are the concepts of rhythmicality, negentropic evolutionary emergence, and the unitary nature of the man−environment relationship.
>
> …
>
> The principle of helicy … may be stated in symbolic form thus:

$$H = f\ S\text{-}T_1\ (M_1 \rightleftarrows E_1)i\ f\ S\text{-}T_2\ (M_2 \rightleftarrows E_2)i\text{-}f\ S\text{-}T_n\ (M_n \rightleftarrows E_n)$$

in which	H	stands for helicy
	⟨∞⟩	stands for the spiral of life
	i	stands for innovation and can be read as: "Helicy is

a function of continuous innovative change growing out of the mutual interaction of man and environment along a spiralling longitudinal axis bound in space-time."

(Rogers 1970: 99−101)[45]

Not to mention the following:

> Clairvoyance, for example, is rational in a four-dimensional human field in continuous mutual, simultaneous interaction with a four-dimensional environmental field. So too are such events as psychometry, therapeutic touch, telepathy, and a wide range of other phenomena. Within this conceptual system such behaviors become "normal" rather than "paranormal."
>
> (Rogers 1980: 335)[46]

> Unitary human and environmental rhythms find expression in the rhythmicities of the living–dying process. Just as aging is deemed developmental, so too is dying hypothesized to be developmental. The nature of the dying process and after-death phenomena have gained considerable public and professional interest in recent years. ... A new approach to studying the dying process is provided by the conceptual system herein presented. The nature and continuity of field patterning subsequent to dying, while admittedly a difficult area to study, nonetheless is open to theoretical investigation.
>
> (Rogers 1986: 8)[47]

What is the rational reader to make of the Science of Unitary Human beings? From a logical or empirical point of view, there is only one appropriate word: loony. From a stylistic point of view, Rogers' mumbo-jumbo is perhaps a cut or two above run-of-the-mill New Age fare, but it is vastly inferior to the sophisticated charlatanry produced by virtuosos of the genre such as Jacques Lacan, Julia Kristeva, Gilles Deleuze, Félix Guattari and Paul Virilio.[48]

Despite this, Martha Rogers has attracted around herself a devoted cult of followers, who have edited books with titles like *Explorations of Martha Rogers' Science of Unitary Human Beings*, *Visions of Rogers' Science-Based Nursing*, *Rogers' Scientific Art of Nursing Practice*, and *Patterns of Rogerian Knowing*.[49] Rogers' "visionary" work is kept alive by the Society of Rogerian Scholars, which publishes a thrice-yearly newsletter, the *Rogerian Nursing Science News*, and an annual "scholarly" journal, *Visions: The Journal of Rogerian Nursing Science*.

Most importantly, the influence of Rogers' ideas now extends far beyond her circle of immediate disciples, reaching into the mainstream of the nursing profession. Textbooks on nursing theory often devote a chapter, in utter seriousness, to the Science of Unitary Human Beings.[50] Rogers' work is cited frequently in the academic nursing literature: for instance, *An Introduction to the Theoretical Basis of Nursing* has been cited 289 times since its publication in 1970.[51] Student dissertations extend and apply her system: at least ninety-one dissertations (seventy-four doctoral, seventeen masters) were completed between 1977 and 2002 that had "Martha Rogers" or "Science of Unitary Human Beings" in the title or abstract.[52] And finally, in 1996, a mere two years after her death, Martha Rogers was inducted into the Hall of

Fame of the American Nurses Association, the main professional group for nurses in the United States. Her citation begins and ends as follows:

> Widely known for her discovery of the science of unitary human beings, Martha E. Rogers provided a framework for continued study and research, and influenced the development of a variety of modalities, including therapeutic touch. ...
>
> A proponent of rigorous scientific study, Rogers wrote three books that enriched the learning experience and influenced the direction of nursing research for countless students: *Educational Revolution in Nursing* (1961), *Reveille in Nursing* (1964), and *An Introduction to the Theoretical Basis of Nursing* (1970), the last of which introduced the four Rogerian Principles of Homeodynamics. Following her retirement in 1975, Rogers continued to teach at New York University, was a frequent presenter at scientific conferences throughout the world, and consistently worked to refine her conceptual system. ... She was honored with numerous awards and citations for her sustained contributions to nursing and science.[53]

Postmodernist philosophy in nursing: I

I now propose to analyse the writings of nursing pseudoscientists in an effort to extract their (mostly implicit) epistemological premises. By what means, according to these theorists, can human beings arrive at reliable knowledge of the world? I shall attempt, in particular, to assess the extent to which the advocates of pseudoscience have resorted to postmodernist arguments. (In the next subsection I will focus on nursing theorists whose primary identification is with postmodernism, and assess the extent to which they have endorsed pseudoscience.)

The literature of "complementary and alternative nursing" is replete with contrasts between mainstream scientific medicine – which these authors criticize as mechanistic, reductionist and anti-human – and the evolving "holistic" paradigm.[54] For example:

> Biomedical or Western medicine ... is founded on the philosophical beliefs of René Descartes (1596–1650), that the mind and body are separate, and on Sir Isaac Newton's (1642–1727) principles of physics, that the universe is like a large mechanical clock where everything operates in a linear, sequential form. The mechanistic perspective of medicine views the human body as a series of body parts. It is a reductionistic approach in which the person is converted into increasingly smaller components: systems, organs, cells, and biochemicals. People are reduced to patients, patients are reduced to bodies, and bodies are reduced to machines.
>
> (Fontaine 2000: 4–5)[55]

Of course, this is simplistic, to say the least. For what it's worth, Newtonian physics is perfectly capable of describing complex interactive systems that need not "operate in a linear, sequential form" (whatever that may mean).[56] Scientific reductionism, understood as the view that there are no autonomous principles of chemistry or biology that are not ultimately rooted in physics, in no way entails reductionism *as a methodology* for investigating the world: this may be an appropriate method for studying some phenomena and not for studying others.[57] Finally, science in no way enjoins doctors to ignore the emotional needs of their patients or to treat them as mere "bodies" and "machines." (Insurance companies may do so, however.)

Advocates of "holistic healing" also criticize mainstream science for ignoring alleged good evidence in favor of homeopathy, Therapeutic Touch, telepathy, healing by distant prayer, and other phenomena that are inconsistent with the modern scientific world view. For example:

> When therapies such as acupuncture or homeopathy are observed to result in a physiologic or clinical response that cannot be explained by the biomedical model, many have tried to deny the results rather than modify the scientific model. ... If people limit themselves to the five senses, they will never come to understand human energy fields, electromagnetic fields, thoughts as a form of energy, or the healing power of prayer.
>
> (ibid.: 12)

It is important to note that the foregoing critiques, radical and global though they may be, are aimed at the *content* of modern science, not at its epistemology or methodology. Indeed, advocates of "holistic healing" frequently buttress their case with appeals to scientific evidence of a perfectly traditional kind: experiments, observations, clinical trials, deductions from accepted theories, etc. The quality of this evidence is often ludicrously low, as is the cogency and precision of the reasoning accompanying it; that is why much of this literature can properly be characterized as pseudoscience. But it is not – or at least not yet – postmodernist.

Furthermore, despite the ritual denunciation of soulless modern science, holistic theorists also shamelessly wrap themselves in its mantle:

> Einstein said that all matter is energy, energy and matter are interchangeable, and all matter is connected at the subatomic level. No single entity could be affected without all connecting parts being affected. In this view, the universe is not a giant clock, but a living web. The human body is animated by an integrated energy called the *life force*. The life force sustains the physical body but is also a spiritual entity that is linked to a higher being or infinite source of energy.
>
> (ibid.: 6; italics in original)[58]

(Poor Albert must be turning in his grave.)

> Tibetan Buddhists ... believe that thought is infinitely powerful and actually holds sway over matter. Quantum physics is increasingly lending credence to this notion, in that infinite energy can be an attribute of an infinitely short wave of vibration – that is, energy as ascribed to thought processes helps to make new understandings of mind–body interactions.
>
> (Watson 1999: 106)[59]

The modern-physics-justifies-New-Age-medicine argument is also proferred, in vastly more sophisticated form, by Larry Dossey, executive editor of the journal *Alternative Therapies in Health and Medicine* and author of numerous best-selling books on health and spirituality. Dossey repeatedly invokes quantum mechanics to argue that the mind is "nonlocal" and hence capable of telepathy, prophecy, and healing by prayer-at-a-distance.[60] This idea is picked up by the editors of a handbook on holistic nursing, who assert that

> Era III [nonlocal or transpersonal medicine], the newest and most advanced era, originated in science. Consciousness is said to be nonlocal in that it is not bound to individual bodies. The minds of individuals are spread throughout space and time; they are infinite, immortal, omnipresent, and, ultimately, one.
>
> (Dossey and Guzzetta 2000: 11)[61]

Holistic theorists do, however, also criticize scientific methodology, with the clear aim of "moving the goal post" in studies of alternative treatments. For example, Karen Lee Fontaine asserts that the method of double-blind clinical trials

> is based on the assumption that single factors cause and reverse illness, and that these factors can be studied alone and out of context. Alternative medicine, however, believes that no single factor causes anything nor can a magic substance single-handedly reverse illness. Multiple factors contribute to illness, and multiple interventions work together to promote healing. The double-blind method is incapable of reconciling this degree of complexity and variation.
>
> (Fontaine 2000: 12)

These claims are false. Irrespective of whether the proposed treatment (1) consists of single or multiple interventions, and (2) is standardized or is tailored to the specific patient, it can be compared against a placebo or alternative treatment in a randomized and (in most cases) double-blind study.[62] Fontaine goes on to observe that

Although major alternative medical systems may not have a great deal of quantitative research, they are generally *not* experimental. They rely on well-developed clinical observational skills and experience that is guided by their explanatory models.

(ibid.: 12; italics in original)

But the *inadequacies* of "well-developed clinical observational skills and experience" in providing reliable evidence of statistical causation are precisely what led medical researchers to develop randomized double-blind studies in the first place. Fontaine does not explain how practitioners of alternative medicine manage to escape from these known inadequacies.[63] She concludes by saying that

This text does not offer meticulous documentation for all claims which are made by the various therapies. ... Successful alternative therapies, however, should not be withheld from the public while research is being debated.

(ibid.: 12)

This of course begs the question of whether the therapies at issue *are* in fact successful – an assertion that can be tested only by rigorous research.[64]

These animadversions against double-blind clinical trials constitute blatant special pleading, but they are not *per se* postmodernist. At other moments, however, advocates of pseudoscience do engage in pre-emptive postmodernist rhetoric. Consider the following passage, in which Kuhn's alleged incommensurability of paradigms is implicitly invoked (in a radical form that even Kuhn – at least the later Kuhn – would very likely disavow):

Scientific beliefs rest not just on facts but on paradigms. ... A common yet seemingly almost invisible presumption is that "experts" of conventional medicine are entitled and qualified to pass judgment on the scientific and therapeutic merits of alternative therapies. Since the paradigm is quite different, they are not qualified.

(ibid.: 10)

In other words, each paradigm is entitled to set up its own criteria for judging the scientific merits of proposed theories, and these judgments are declared (by fiat) immune from rational critique by adherents to another paradigm.[65,66]

Some prominent nursing pseudoscientists have endorsed even more explicit forms of postmodernist relativism. A telling example is provided by Dolores Krieger, co-inventor of Therapeutic Touch. Immediately after claiming that Therapeutic Touch "is based on rational theory derived from formal research that requires rigorous replication" – an affirmation that she deems necessary because "science is the reality that Western civilization accepts" – she goes on to emphasize that there is not only one reality, or even specified "alternate" realities, that satisfy all the conditions for reality among the many cultures of our global village, Earth. It is now recognized that the concept of multiple realities is valid; a particular view of reality is dependent only upon the particular facet of human consciousness that is permitted to operate at the time.

(Krieger 1993: 6)[67]

Along similar lines, Jean Watson, distinguished professor of nursing at the University of Colorado Health Sciences Center and former president of the National League for Nursing – and one of the major contemporary theorists of nursing pseudoscience[68] – avers that

The art and science of nursing with its concern with caring-healing and health as a field of study, research and practice within its own paradigm is realizing that in this postmodern time, science, knowledge and even images of nursing, health, environment, person become one among many truth games.

(Watson 1995: 63)

Finally, the grander theorists of nursing pseudoscience – such as Martha Rogers and her successors – have built elaborate systems on a fog of verbiage reminiscent of, though vastly less sophisticated than, that of Deleuze and Guattari.[69] Their method, to the extent that one can be discerned, seems to be to *postulate* an abstract system and then "deduce" its consequences. In principle that procedure could be assimilated to the hypothetico-deductive approach characteristic of modern science, but the trouble is that the starting "principles" are so vague ("Field is a unifying concept. Energy signifies the dynamic nature of the field. Energy fields are infinite") that there is no precise way to distinguish valid from invalid "deductions," much less of deducing falsifiable empirical predictions. The whole exercise becomes, in the end, little more than an elaborate taxonomy of angels, replete with scholastic arguments as to whether those angels are "four-dimensional" or "multidimensional" or "pandimensional." This approach makes contact with another aspect of what I have called postmodernism, namely, theoretical discourses disconnected from any empirical test.

Postmodernist philosophy in nursing: II

Postmodernist ideas originating in literary criticism, continental philosophy, and feminist theory began to be influential among nursing theorists in the early 1990s,[70] when a surprising number of citations to Heidegger, Foucault, Derrida, Rorty, and other "postmodernist" philosophers began to appear.[71]

Theoretical articles on postmodernism in nursing tend to recycle the same arguments and rhetoric as are found in postmodernist writings in the social sciences and literary theory. The argumentation tends to remain on an abstract philosophical or political plane, and it rarely addresses concrete questions of nursing interventions or the methodology by which they should be evaluated.[72] At the level of epistemology, some authors are fairly precise, while others are maddeningly vague:

> Postmodernism is a rejection of the modern, post-Enlightenment concern with the rational and scientific. ... [T]ruth is seen as problematic and not necessarily progressively accessible through scientific exploration or logical reasoning. Complexity and ambiguity are celebrated and inconsistencies, paradoxes and contradictions are not of concern. ... [N]ursing ideas and nursing research are good if the stories they tell allow nurses and people in care to get on with their lives.
>
> (Stevenson and Beech 2001: 144–5, 149)

> Such an ontological and epistemological shift [associated with postmodernism] invites and works with context, connections, relations, multiplicity, ambiguity, openness, indeterminacy, patterning, paradox, process, transcendence and mysteries of the human experience of being-in-the-world ...
>
> (Watson 1995: 61)

Although postmodernist nursing theorists seem in general reluctant to commit themselves concerning specific nursing interventions – particularly those claiming biological effects – a recent debate in the pages of the journal *Nursing Philosophy* brought some of these issues to the fore. An article by health journalist Sarah Glazer, criticizing both Therapeutic Touch and the postmodernist trend in nursing, was answered by Janice L. Thompson on behalf of postmodernism.[73] Thompson repeatedly protested (at least five times in four-and-a-half pages, by my count) that her view is not "antiscientific":

> Like most nurses who have been influenced by advanced study, I have considered the dilemmas of developing truth claims outside the discourses of science. No longer comfortably modern in my professional identity, I don't believe that there is *a* condition for "right reason." There are many. This plural view does not mean that I am nihilistic or antiscientific. It means that I recognize science as one among many way(s) to produce meaning and truth.
>
> (Thompson 2002: 59–60; italics in original)

Glazer responded that

> I do argue that the scientific method is the correct approach for evaluating factual claims about the world (e.g. "Cigarette smoking is a cause of lung cancer," "Energy fields exist that can be sensed by therapeutic

touch practitioners"). Thompson and other nurses of the postmodern persuasion confuse moral with factual issues. Thompson repeatedly insists that she is not "antiscientific." ... But one cannot believe in the scientific method and also believe in "other ways," such as intuition, for evaluating *factual* claims like those of therapeutic touch.

(Glazer 2002: 64; italics in original)

Thompson went on to assert, as did Fontaine, the alleged incommensurability of paradigms, linking it directly with therapeutic touch, shamanic healing, and homeopathy:

As a non-discursive practice, therapeutic touch, like shamanic healing, may elude our current epistemic "paradigms." Precisely for this reason, we should be careful about how and why we judge it. ... [T]o argue for evidence-based practice means we must consider the questions "What evidence?" and "Whose evidence?" These are the very questions that have been and will continue to be highly contested in the ongoing story of therapeutic touch. They are the questions that emerge when allopathic providers encounter the healing practices of homeopathic providers. When western physicians encounter the shamanic practices of folk healers from other cultures. ... They are questions that always emerge when *incommensurable* truth claims meet and the framework for adjudicating these differences eludes us.

(Thompson 2002: 60–1; italics added)

As Glazer observed in her rebuttal:

I find it interesting that Professor Thompson doesn't address the central question of my article, which is why a highly suspect therapy known as therapeutic touch continues to be practised and embraced by nurses. After reading Thompson's critique, I am still not sure whether this is because she finds therapeutic touch to be an embarrassment to the profession or because she believes in it but is unwilling to defend it openly.

(Glazer 2002: 63)

At one point in her essay, however, Thompson descends from the abstract plane and addresses concrete nursing theories; curiously, this is also the only place in the article where her tone shifts from patient rebuttal to indignation. While pleading unfamiliarity with therapeutic touch, Thompson adds that

I am familiar, however, with the work of Martha Rogers and I am offended by the characterization of her offered by an author who appears to have limited knowledge of Professor Rogers' studies. We may disagree with some of the applications that have been made in therapeutic touch, but we should at least acknowledge with respect the commitment of this intellectual who carefully studied the work of her mentors in theoretical physics. She was a widely read and very strong interdisciplinary scholar.

(Thompson 2002: 60)[74]

As Glazer aptly comments: "One does not have to be a physicist to find Rogers' use of physics to justify therapeutic touch laughable" (Glazer 2002: 63). But just for the record, let me state that Rogers does not exhibit the slightest knowledge of physics – not even at the level of the freshman survey course for non-scientists that I frequently teach. Rather, she borrows terms from physics and then throws them around without regard for their meaning.[75]

Concluding remarks

In writing this account of pseudoscience and postmodernism in nursing, I have endeavored to immerse myself in the nursing literature, but my study makes no pretense of being comprehensive. Many questions still await careful quantitative (and of course also qualitative) investigation by sociologists and historians. How widespread is the teaching of pseudoscience in American nursing schools, and the practice of pseudoscience in American hospitals? In what way have these evolved over time? How popular is postmodernist philosophy among professors and students of nursing, both in its "high" form (Heidegger, Derrida, Foucault, etc.) and in its watered-down form (loose talk about social construction and a multiplicity of perspectives)? To what extent, and in what ways, do pseudoscience and postmodernism overlap (both intellectually and sociologically) in the nursing community? To what extent have these trends spread (or developed independently) outside the United States? What are the social and psychological forces underlying the development and spread of pseudoscience and postmodernism within the nursing profession?[76]

Hindu nationalist pseudoscience and postmodernism in India

In an important new book, *Prophets Facing Backward: Postmodern Critiques of Science and Hindu Nationalism in India*, philosopher and sociologist of science Meera Nanda has recounted in dispiriting detail how postmodernist-oriented leftist Indian intellectuals have, since the early 1980s, unwittingly helped pave the way for the rise to power of right-wing Hindu nationalism – a politico-religious doctrine in which pseudoscience, passed off as real science, plays a central role. I propose here to summarize briefly Nanda's story, laying stress on the ideas put forth by "postcolonial" theorists on the one hand and Hindu nationalists on the other, analysing their similarities and differences. Readers interested in a fuller account of the historical and political context are urged to consult Nanda's engrossing book.

Postmodernism in India

In July 1981, a group of Indian scientists and intellectuals published a "Statement on Scientific Temper," in which they lamented the persistence of illiteracy, superstition, and religiously grounded social hierarchies in a country that simultaneously boasted of world-class universities and the world's third-largest scientifically trained workforce. Noting that "the best Indian minds in the pre-independence times insistently propagated the need for the people to think independently and fearlessly, and to question traditional beliefs" – a ferment that led in time to "a critique of the colonial system [and] ... a powerful national movement for our liberation" – the statement regretted that at independence

> No systematic and sustained effort was made to work out, specifically and concretely, what needed to be done to build a society which is animated by a spirit of enquiry rather than passivity and acceptance. The result ... was accommodation, even compromise, with the forces of obscurantism and with the existing inegalitarian social and economic structures.
>
> (Haksar *et al.* 1981: 7)

Three decades later,

> There is a cancerous growth of superstition at all levels. Rituals of the most bizarre kind are frequently performed often with official patronage. Obscurantist social customs are followed even by those whose profession is the pursuit of scientific enquiry. Our entire educational system works in an atmosphere of conformity, non-questioning and obedience to authority.
>
> (ibid.: 7)

The statement's signatories urged the cultivation of rationalist and scientific habits of mind in the service of social justice:

> The spirit of inquiry and the acceptance of the right to question and be questioned are fundamental to Scientific Temper. ... It leads to the realisation that events occur as a result of interplay of understandable and describable natural and social forces and not because someone, however great, so ordained them. ... When the social structure and stratification prevent the application of rational and scientifically proven solutions, the role of Scientific Temper is to lay bare the anatomy of such social barriers.
>
> (ibid.: 8–9)

The idea was not new: decades earlier, Jawaharlal Nehru, the first prime minister of India, had lauded the adventurous and yet critical temper of science, the search for truth and new knowledge, the refusal to accept anything without testing and trial, the capacity to change previous conclusions in the face of new evidence, the reliance on observed fact and not on preconceived theory, [and] the hard discipline of the mind. ... The scientific approach and temper are, or should be, a way of life, a process of thinking, a method of acting and associating with our fellow men.

(Nehru 1946: 523)[77]

The "Statement on Scientific Temper" was an attempt to reclaim Nehru's Enlightenment vision in an unevenly modernizing India.[78]

But, the Statement was immediately subjected to harsh attack from neo-Gandhian intellectuals, using what in later years would be called "postmodernist" arguments. The first shot was fired by Ashis Nandy, who disparaged the statement as "ultra-positivist," "pseudo-empiricis[t]," and "a posthumous child of colonialism" and proceeded to launch a full-scale onslaught against modern science in all its aspects: technological, social, and epistemological (Nandy 1981: 16, 17). Assailing the complicity of scientists in both inter-state warfare and within-state oppression, Nandy observed (correctly) that "science today is big business" and (more dubiously) that "in some [unnamed] countries, more illness is now caused by the modern medical system than by natural causes"; all in all, he asserted, "science today is the main instrument of oppression in the world" (ibid.: 17, 16). But, the problem, according to Nandy, is not merely the misuse of science for oppressive ends; it is the scientific world view itself. In the case of Galileo,

it was the Church which proved itself more open and sought to have plural images of the cosmos. Galileo, like the signatories to the state-ment, thought he knew the truth and he wanted to oust all other concepts of truth. The Church, though it might have gone about it fool-ishly and hamhandedly, objected to that part of the story.

(ibid.: 17)

Asserting that the argument against astrology had already been "so badly mauled by Paul Feyderabend [*sic*] on scientific, normative and methodolog-ical grounds" that the details need not be rehashed, Nandy added that

in a world where arbitrary authorities constantly deny one control over one's fate, a situation created partly by modern science and technology, astrology is for the poor a psychological defence; it is an attempt to find meaning for an oppressive present in a controllable future. ... Everything said, astrology is a myth of the weak; modern science that of the strong.

(ibid.: 17)[79]

The bottom line, said Nandy, is that "We must learn to reject the claim to universality of science. *Science is no less determined by culture and society than any other human effort*" (ibid.: 18; italics in original). Nandy urged the development of a counter-consciousness

> which accepts science as only one of the many imperfect traditions of humankind and which allows the peripheries [of] the world to reclaim their human dignity and reaffirm ... various forms of traditions, religions and myths.
>
> (ibid.: 17)

Over the next decade, Nandy's attack on "Western" science was taken up by a cohort of "postcolonial" Indian intellectuals in books and articles with titles like *Science, Hegemony and Violence* (edited by Nandy), *Science, Development and Violence* (written by Claude Alvares), and "Reductionist science as epistemological violence" (written by Vandana Shiva). These writings make three central claims:

1. *Modern science is fundamentally violent and exploitative*, against both Nature and human beings. This violence does not result merely from the misuse of scientific knowledge through militarist, economically oppressive or ecologically unsound technology, but is inherent in the modern scientific world view itself.
2. *Modern science's claim to universality and objectivity is illusory*. Modern science is, in reality, nothing more or less than the ethno-science of the West; modern scientific "knowledge," far from being objective and universal, is permeated with Western values. Other ways of knowing are equally valid, and in some cases superior.
3. *Each civilization has the right to create its own science*, in conformity with its own traditions.

It is not my purpose here to expound in detail the reasoning leading to these claims, much less to explain why I think this reasoning is grossly deficient.[80] Rather, I would simply like to illustrate, by means of a few quotations of representative passages, these three fundamental themes.

The most innovative aspect of the postcolonial Indian authors on science, compared with Western postmodernists, is the shrill assertion that modern science is inherently violent.[81] For instance, Claude Alvares argues

> that both science and the technology based on it are fundamentally violent forms of handling the world, that violence is intrinsic to science, to its text, to its design and implementation. ... There is no way in which the science of our times can be dissociated from its structure of violence.
>
> (Alvares 1988: 70–1)[82]

Likewise, Ashis Nandy asserts that

> There is a direct correlation between the claims to absolute objectivity, inter-subjectivity, internal consistency, dispassion and value-neutrality, on the one hand, and violence, oppression, authoritarianism, killing uniformity and death of cultures, on the other.
>
> (Nandy 1981: 18)

In fact, Nandy says, "modern science [is] the basic model of domination in our times and ... the ultimate justification for all institutionalized violence" (Nandy 1987b: 122). Vandana Shiva concurs that modern science is intrinsically violent and locates the source of this alleged violence more specifically in scientific reductionism[83]:

> I argue that modern science is violent even in peaceful domains such as, for example, health care and agriculture ... The argument is based on the premise that modern science is quintessentially reductionist. ... In order to prove itself superior to alternative modes of knowledge and be the only legitimate mode of knowing, reductionist science resorts to suppression and falsification of facts and thus commits violence against science itself ...
>
> (Shiva 1988: 232–3)[84]

Secondly, it is argued that modern science's claim to universality and objectivity is illusory. According to Claude Alvares,

> The claim of modern science to a universalism independent of culture (and cultures) is the first instance of its kind. ... For all practical purposes, however, modern science is nothing more and nothing less than western science, a special category of ethno-science. In fact, its too readily assumed universalism has had disastrous consequences for other ethno-sciences.
>
> (Alvares 1992: 150)

Ashis Nandy is even more explicit:

> We must learn to reject the claim to universality of science. *Science is no less determined by culture and society than any other human effort.* ...
>
> *Modern science is one of the many traditions available to humankind. It is also one of the many traditions of science.* Unfortunately, like some of the semitic creeds, it claims to be the only truth outside all traditions. It is time for us to affirm that modern science has the right to praselytise [*sic*] but not to forcibly convert.
>
> (Nandy 1981: 18; italics in original)

Vandana Shiva likewise avers that modern science's "claim to truth" is "fraudulent" and adds that

> The fact–value dichotomy is a creation of modern, reductionist science which, while being an epistemic response to a particular set of values, claims to be independent of values. According to the received view, modern science is the discovery of the properties of nature in accordance with a "scientific method" which generates "objective," "neutral," "universal" knowledge. This view of modern science as a description of reality as it is, unprejudiced by value, can be rejected ... [S]cientific facts are determined by the social world of scientists, not by the natural world.
>
> (Shiva 1988: 233–4, 237)

> If reductionist science has displaced non-reductionist modes of knowing, it has done so not through cognitive competition, but through political support from the state ... The "facts" of reductionist science are socially constructed categories which have the cultural markings of the western bourgeois, patriarchal system which is their context of discovery and justification.
>
> (Shiva 1989: 24, 27)

Finally, the postcolonial theorists seek to create "alternative" sciences on the foundations of traditional religions and values, as well as on the "folk" beliefs of the common people:

> *The common man has not only his traditional or folk science, he has his own philosophy of science.* It might be vague, implicit and non-professional but it is informed with the experience of suffering. Such folk sciences and folk philosophies must be taken seriously. In fact, we can hope to build an indigenous science only when such lost sciences and implicit philosophies are respectfully articulated by contemporary Indian scholars.
>
> (Nandy 1981: 18; italics in original)

The proclaimed strategy is one of syncretism, i.e. incorporating selected elements from modern science while rejecting its world view:

> The critical traditionalism I am talking about does not have to see modern science as alien to it, even though it may see it as alienating. It sees modern science as part of a new cognitive order which can be occasionally used for critical purposes within the earlier traditions. Such traditionalism uncompromisingly criticizes isolation and the over-concern with objectivity, but it never denies the creative possibilities of limited objectivity. ... Such a tradition refuses to give primacy to the needs of pure cognition at the expense of totality of consciousness ...
>
> (Nandy 1987a: 125, 124)

The precise content of the proposed "alternative" science is left vague, as are the criteria for deciding which elements from traditional beliefs and modern science are to be included and which discarded. Nevertheless, the urgency of a new science is stressed:

> The search for alternatives to reductionism is basically a political struggle which cuts across material and intellectual domains. The non-reductionist alternatives that people across the world are building together is a non-violent science that respects the integrity of nature and man and truth and seeks the liberation of the people ...
>
> (Shiva 1988: 255)

> [O]ne day there will have to be post-modern societies and a post-modern consciousness, and those societies and that consciousness may choose to build not so much upon modernity as on the traditions of the non-modern or pre-modern world.
>
> (Nandy 1987a: xvii)[85]

But at the same time that postmodernist Indian intellectuals were singing the praises of "local knowledges" and "pre-modern traditions" against "colonialist Western science," other Indian intellectuals were making this encomium concrete.

Hindu nationalism and Vedic "science"

> [T]he conclusions of modern science are the very conclusions the Vedanta reached ages ago; only, in modern science they are written in the language of matter.
>
> (Swami Vivekananda 1970 [c. 1900], vol. 3: 185)

> Many of the questions arising in Quantum Physics today had been anticipated by Swami Vivekananda.
>
> (N.S. Rajaram 1998: 192)

> [T]he Ṛgveda is a book of particle physics and cosmology.
>
> (Raja Ram Mohan Roy 1998: xiii)

On 23 February 2001, the University Grants Commission (UGC) – the central government body overseeing the funding of higher education in India – announced that

> there is an urgent need to rejuvenate the science of Vedic Astrology in India, to allow this scientific knowledge to reach to the society at large and to provide opportunities to get this important science even exported to the world ... [Accordingly,] the Commission decided to approve in principle [the] setting up of a few departments of Vedic Astrology in

Indian universities ... leading to certificate diploma, under-graduate, post-graduate and Ph.D. degrees.

(Government of India, Department of Education 2001)[86]

The plan provoked a storm of protest from Indian scientists and rationalist intellectuals.[87] But what on earth prompted such a bizarre decision in the first place?

The answer, not surprisingly, is politics: more precisely, the Hindu nationalist politics of the Bharatiya Janata Party (BJP), which governed India between March 1998 and May 2004. The BJP is the political expression of a multifaceted mass movement for *Hindutva*, or "Hindu-ness," "an ultranationalist and chauvinistic movement that seeks to modernize India by recovering the supposedly pristine Vedic-Hindu roots of Indian culture" (Nanda 2003: 4). As part of its program for the Hinduization of Indian education, the BJP rewrote school history textbooks to excise the contributions of Muslims and other non-Hindus, and promoted university-level courses not only in Vedic Astrology (*Jyotir Vigyan*) but also in *karmakanda* (Hindu priestly rituals), *vastu shastra* (sacred architectural rules), "human consciousness and Yogic science," and "Vedic mathematics."[88]

Science plays a central role in Hindu nationalist ideology.[89] As Nanda explains:

> Hindu nationalists are obsessed with science. They are obsessed with science the way creation scientists are obsessed with science. They use the vocabulary of science to claim that the most sacred texts of Hinduism ... are, in fact, scientific treatises, expressing in a uniquely holistic and uniquely Hindu idiom, the findings of modern physics, biology, mathematics, and nearly all other branches of modern natural science.
>
> (Nanda 2003: 65)

At the same time,

> Vedic science is supposed to lead to a better, a more whole natural science that will cure the reductionism and matter–spirit dualism of "Western" science. Vedic science apologists promise to "raise" the lower knowledge (*apāra vidya*) of "mere matter" provided by modern science by integrating it into the "higher knowledge" (*pāra vidya*) of the spirit disclosed by their own traditions.
>
> (ibid.: 66)[90]

In this way, Hindu nationalists seek to legitimate as "scientific" not only such traditional practices as Vedic astrology, *vastu shastra*, and Ayurvedic medicine but also the classical Hindu cosmology in which the human social hierarchy is determined by karma (moral or immoral deeds in previous lives). Furthermore, any aspects of modern science that challenge this cosmology – for instance, the modern understanding of biology, which makes reincarnation unlikely, to put it mildly – are quietly ignored: "Modern science is being absorbed into an elite Brahminical–Vedantic form of Hinduism, without admitting any contradictions between the two, and thus, *without allowing any challenge to the latter's anti-naturalistic, anti-rational, and anti-democratic aspects*" (ibid.: 8; italics in original).

The intellectual method followed by the Hindutva ideologues is straight-forward:

> [A]ny traditional Hindu idea or practice, however obscure and irrational it might have been through its history, gets the honorific of "science" if it bears any resemblance at all, however remote, to an idea that is valued (even for the wrong reasons) in the West. Thus, obscure references in the Vedas get reinterpreted as referring to nuclear physics. By staking a phony priority, modern science gets domesticated; it was always contained in India's "wisdom" anyway.
>
> (ibid.: 72)

The example was set by Swami Vivekananda (1863–1902), one of the founding fathers of modern neo-Hinduism:

> Today we find wonderful discoveries of modern science coming upon us like bolts from the blue, opening our eyes to marvels we never dreamt of. But many of these are only re-discoveries of what had been found ages ago. It was only the other day that modern science ... discovered that what it calls heat, magnetism, electricity, and so forth, are all convertible into one unit force ... But this has been done even in the Samhita ...
>
> (Vivekananda (1970 [1897], vol. 3: 398–9)[91]

After this, he goes on to expound Vedic cosmology:

> The unit from which [gravitation, electricity, magnetism and other forces] spring is called Prana. Again, what is Prana? Prana is Spandana or vibration. When all this universe shall have resolved back into its primal state, what becomes of this infinite force? Do they think that it becomes extinct? Of course not. If it became extinct, what would be the cause of the next wave, because the motion is going in wave forms, rising, falling, rising again, falling again? ... At the end of a cycle, everything becomes finer and finer and is resolved back into the primal state from which it sprang ... And what becomes of all these forces, the Pranas? They are resolved back into the primal Prana, and this Prana becomes almost motionless – not entirely motionless; and that is what is described in the Vedic Sukta: "It vibrated without vibrations" – Ânidavâtam.
>
> (ibid.: 399)

And so on and so forth for pages on end – but without, alas, ever citing anything even vaguely resembling Maxwell's equations of electromagnetism.

Contemporary Hindu-nationalist intellectuals, many of whom are trained scientists and engineers, have brought this art to an even higher level of refinement. For instance, Subhash Kak, a professor of electrical and computer engineering at Louisiana State University and one of the leading intellectual luminaries of the Hindu-nationalist diaspora, claims to find "astronomical codes" in the Rigveda's descriptions of ritual fire altars, using a method that, as Nanda wryly observes, "is breathtakingly ad hoc and reads like numerology 101" (2003: 112)[92] Even more ludicrously, Raja Ram Mohan Roy asserts that "the Vedas are a coded book ... of particle physics and cosmology": thus, verses referring to wild and domestic animals are *really* alluding to fermions and bosons, respectively; passages recounting the destruction of black-skinned people are in fact "about annihilation of anti-matter"; and the phrase "ten-finger form" in the Puruṣa hymn gives us "compelling evidence of [the] universe being considered ten-dimensional in Vedic cosmology," just as in modern superstring theory (Roy 1998: xii–xiii, 115, 56, 30–1).[93] As Nanda comments, this method "eras[es] all distinctions between science and associative thinking, the latter being the hallmark of magic" (Nanda 2003: 115).

But the goal of Hindutva is not simply to claim priority for the invention of modern science; rather, it is to insist that "Western" science is an *inferior* version of the true Vedic science:

> The gist of this argument, as it appears in Hindu nationalist writings on Vedic science, is simple – all that is dangerous and false in modern science comes from the Semitic monotheistic habit of dualistic and "reductionist" thinking, which separates the object from the subject, nature from consciousness, the known from the knower. All that is truly universal and true in modern science comes from the Hindu habit of "holistic" thinking, which has always seen the objects in nature and the human subjects not as separate entities but as different manifestations of the same universal consciousness. For the non-logocentric Hinduism, reality is not objective, but "omnijective," a co-construct of mind and matter together. While Western science treats nature as dead matter, Hindu sciences treat nature as a sacred abode of gods. Thus Hindutva scholars claim that traditions of yoga, transcendental meditation (TM) and Ayurveda are sciences of the future, for they bring matter in alignment with the "cosmic energy" that permeates all matter.
>
> (Nanda 2004)

Of course, if the Rigveda really did contain modern astronomy and elementary-particle physics, one would then be obliged to ask, as Nanda does:

> How did the Vedic sages know all this physics? What was their method? Why don't we find any material evidence of observatories, or

records of observations? Invariably, the answer one gets is that the Vedic sages "intuited," "experientially realized," or "directly perceived ... in a flash" the laws of nature by altering their consciousness through yogic meditation. *By knowing themselves, they came to know the world.*

(Nanda 2003: 115; italics in original)[94]

For instance, one advocate of the convergence of science and Vedanta asserts that

Hindu spiritual doctrines have at the core certain profound insights into the nature of ultimate reality ... Hindu seers were telling us something that is not only meaningful but revelatory about the cosmos and consciousness. ... Their assertions ... [arose] from experiential certitudes resulting from sustained experimentation with the subtlest centers of the inscrutable self. Their words and wisdom are to be taken, therefore, not simply as magnificent mythopoesy but as findings about the translucent aspects of the physical universe ...

(Raman 2002: 89–90)

The method is explained in more detail in another influential Hindutva work:

The Vedic worldview acknowledges that there is an intimate relationship between the cosmic, the terrestrial, and the spiritual, which is expressed in terms of equivalences. The idea of equivalence, which is fundamental to what has been called initiatic science, is that the universe is an interconnected system ... A related idea is that the macrocosm is mirrored in the microcosm ... [and that] the human being is a mirror image of the cosmos. ... By *postulating* interconnections and similarities across Nature, they [the Vedic thinkers] were able to use logic to reach extremely subtle conclusions about diverse aspects of reality.

(Feuerstein *et al.* 1995: 197–8, 227; italics added)[95]

As Nanda points out, reasoning founded on purported but unproved

correspondences and equivalences between different parts of creation is the very essence of magical practices ... [and] was as prevalent in pre-Reformation Europe as it is in India even today. ... In the West, this magical view of the world peaked around the Renaissance, and began to decline with the Protestant Reformation and the rise of the mechanical philosophy in the seventeenth century. It saw a brief revival in theosophy and holistic schools of biology in the nineteenth and early twentieth centuries, especially in Germany. It is now a province of fringe occult groups in the West.

(Nanda 2003: 116)

But the advocates of Hindutva, when they bother to address this criticism at all, insist that this story is Eurocentric and appeal implicitly to the alleged incommensurability of paradigms:

> Western scientific thought ... draws on the traditions of Greek rationalist thinking according to which only what is within the purview of the five senses is taken cognisance of. ... Scientific methods ... follow some kind of closed scientific reasoning which insulates itself against facts that its methods cannot account for. ... How else can they [scientists] dare dismiss Jyotisha [Vedic astrology] which sees a level of existence beyond the purview of the five senses?
>
> (Vasudev 2001)[96]

Another author goes so far as to assert that, in India, any contradiction between science and religion is impossible:

> The idea of *"contradiction"* is an imported one from the West in recent times by the Western-educated, since "Modern Science" arbitrarily imagines that it only has the true knowledge and its methods are the only methods to gain knowledge, smacking of Semitic dogmatism in religion.
>
> (Mukhyananda 1997: 94; italics in original)

What is needed, therefore, is the "decolonization of the Indian mind":

> The Hindu revivalist movement perceives itself as the cultural chapter of India's decolonization. This means that it tries to free the Indians from the colonial condition at the mental and cultural level, to complete the process of political and economic decolonization.
>
> (Elst 2001: 10)[97]

And here we make contact with postmodernism and its critique of the transcultural objectivity of modern science. Indeed, some Hindutva ideologues make explicit use of "postmodernist" rhetoric:

> We must keep in mind that equally valid alternative scientific formulations are possible – just as we have in medical science Allopathy, Homeopathy, Ayurveda, Unani, Acupuncture, etc. It is not justifiable to say that the Western reductionist and mechanistic scientific way of presentation is the only way.
>
> (Mukhyananda 1997: 100)

Others make superficial reference to contemporary philosophy of science in an attempt to make space for "other ways of knowing," such as yogic introspection:

According to the Yogic and Vedic system the scientific method is not entirely scientific; that is, it is not truly objective and cannot give us knowledge of reality. ... The scientific method is based on making an assumption, inventing a theory, and then amassing data or making experiments to prove the theory. Whatever we assume we are bound to find facts to prove it ...

(Frawley 1990: 20)[98]

(If this were true, then scientists would never have to revise their theories.)

[Modern] science ... fails to take into account knowledge that is accessible through introspection and higher states of awareness as cultivated in the spiritual traditions [such as Hinduism]. ... Today we often tend to dismiss their knowledge systems, or worldviews, as mere myth. In doing so, we fail to acknowledge that in our push for objective knowledge we too utilize intellectual modes that are not always strictly rational, as has been shown by philosophers like Michael Polanyi and Paul Feyerabend.

(Feuerstein *et al.* 1995: 195)

(No details of the argument are given; in particular, the authors fail to make the crucial distinction between the context of discovery and the context of justification.[99]) Vedic creationists Michael Cremo and Richard Thompson are even more explicit about their intellectual debts:

We are not sociologists, but our approach in some ways resembles that taken by practitioners of the sociology of scientific knowledge (SSK), such as Steve Woolgar, Trevor Pinch, Michael Mulkay, Harry Collins, Bruno Latour, and Michael Lynch ... [namely that] Scientists' conclusions do not identically correspond to states and processes of an objective natural reality. Instead, such conclusions reflect the real social processes of scientists as much as, more than, or even rather than what goes on in nature.

(Cremo and Thompson 1993: xxiv)[100]

It is worth noting, however, that some advocates of Hindutva are explicitly non-relativist[101] and advocate the Vedas as the foundation for a universal science and religion:

Today we are in need of a philosophy, science, and spirituality that are deep and broad enough to accommodate the emerging global civilization. In releasing our grip on merely local expressions of mind and culture, we inevitably are led back to considering, as did our ancestors, the infinite, eternal, impartite Reality. ... This brings us face to face with the need to create a global spirituality that transcends all parochial religious modes of knowledge and experience. ... The *Vedas* are the earliest available expression of the perennial philosophy, or universal spirituality.

(Feuerstein *et al.* 1995: 274–5; italics in original)

Regardless of their attitude toward postmodernist relativism, all ideologues of Hindutva concur on two key stances, both of which are asserted by fiat: first, that yogic introspection, combined with ratiocination using the method of correspondences and equivalences, provides a valid method for obtaining reliable knowledge of the world; and second, that scientific knowledge, properly interpreted, cannot possibly conflict with Vedantic teachings.[102] In this way, Hindu nationalists aim to "domesticate" modern science, taking what suits them and ignoring or reinterpreting the rest, thereby immunizing the traditional Hindu cosmology from empirical critique. The conclusion is invariably the same: *"Modern Western science is partial science and not total science.* ... [T]he greater the advance in Science, the nearer it is coming to the Vedantic conclusions" (Mukhyananda 1997: 92, 104; italics in original) "[A]ccording to Vedic tradition, science and religion are not only compatible but essentially identical, because both endeavor to know the truth" (Feuerstein *et al.* 1995: 279).[103]

Nanda concludes by pointing out that

There is a deep irony in declaring the rationality found in the three-millennia old Vedic corpus to be at par with how today's natural scientists go about forming and testing hypotheses. If there is one thing that is distinctive about modern science it is that it has learnt to take refutations seriously. Notwithstanding the social interests that promote conformity with the ruling paradigms, and notwithstanding the personal investment of individual scientists in their pet theories, modern science owes its phenomenal success to the institutionalization of skepticism. Paradigms *do* change; old theories and old explanations *are* thrown overboard, however reluctantly and belatedly, when confronted with better evidence, simpler theories, and more comprehensive and consilient explanations.

(Nanda 2003: 121; italics in original)

Pseudoscience, by contrast, is content with recycling "ancient wisdom."

Postmodernism and Hindutva: a comparison

What are the similarities and differences between the ideas advocated by the left-wing "postcolonial" theorists and the right-wing ideologues of Hindutva?

There is one obvious difference: While the advocates of Hindutva are eager to claim modern science as their own, the "postcolonial" intellectuals denounce them for precisely this capitulation to "Western" ways of thinking. But the supposed capitulation is much less far-reaching than it seems: for, as Nanda stresses, Hindu nationalists "claim the Vedas to have presaged all the advances in modern science without admitting that, in fact, modern sciences challenge the metaphysical foundation of the Vedic view of the world" (ibid.: 158). Any findings of modern science that undermine the Vedic metaphysics are either discreetly ignored or else ascribed to Western materialist and monotheistic prejudices. In this way, Hindutva ideologues attempt to have their cake and eat it too.

A second, more subtle, difference concerns their respective attitudes toward the "clash of civilizations." Hindu nationalists believe unabashedly in the existence of an eternal "Hindu world view" or "Hindu mind", which is inherently opposed to the "Western" (or "Judaeo-Christian" or "Semitic") one. Postmodernists, by contrast, are sensitive to anything that smacks of "essentialism"; with some exceptions, they take great care "to define subalternity or marginality not in racial, gender or national identities, but in terms of 'oppositional consciousness' ... [or] the ability to speak" (ibid.: 156).[104] But there is less difference here than meets the eye, for the postcolonial theorists advocate "a *strategic* use of positivist essentialism in a scrupulously visible political interest" (Spivak 1988: 13; italics in original), leading them to an attitude that is in practice not significantly different from that of the Hindu nationalists.[105]

On several key points, the postcolonial theorists and the Hindutva intellectuals are in substantial (although not complete) agreement. First, they agree that political and economic decolonization must be supplemented by a thoroughgoing "decolonization of the mind." The postcolonialists, along with their postmodernist and social-constructivist supporters in the West, insist that modern science, despite its claims to objectivity, is nothing more than the ethno-science of the West, and they urge the development of "alternative sciences" based on the recovery of "local knowledges" and indigenous cultural traditions.[106] The Hindu nationalists concur, and add that decolonization of the Indian mind requires, in particular, "understanding science through Hindu categories. Echoing the postcolonial critiques of epistemic violence, Hindutva ideologues ... see any scientific assessment of the empirical claims made by the Vedic texts as a sign of mental colonialism and Western imperialism" (Nanda 2004). As Nanda points out, "it is the stress on the preservation of cultural difference – rather than its critical examination – that unites the postcolonialists with Hindutva."[107]

Furthermore, the postmodernists and postcolonialists deny the existence of universal standards of rationality and evidence; they insist that *all* sciences are ethno-sciences, and that each ethno-science must be evaluated according to the norms of its own cultural context. This view is, of course, a central tenet of much contemporary "science studies," particularly in its feminist, multiculturalist, and postcolonial wings.[108] Advocates of Hindutva, by contrast, are divided on this question. Some tend toward cultural and intellectual nationalism, while others propound the universal validity of the

Hindu world view. Nearly all accept the validity of modern science as a partial description of the world, but they insist that Vedic science is infinitely superior to modern science, which it both subsumes and surpasses. (The hardcore postmodernists would not agree with this claim to superiority, but the more romantic postcolonials and eco-feminists might, for the reasons to be explained next.)

Finally, many (though not all) postmodernist and feminist critics of modern science lament in particular the disenchantment of nature wrought by the scientific revolution of the seventeenth century, and argue that the "dualist" separation of spirit/God and matter, together with reductionist scientific methodology, are the source of "violence" against both Nature and women.[109] This theme plays a central role in the work of the Indian postcolonial commentators on science, especially Vandana Shiva. Indeed, the feminist, postcolonial and Hindu theorists all coincide in urging that the reductionist world view of "Western" science be replaced by a more "holistic" outlook (although the details invariably remain vague). The Hindutva ideologues simply add that the interconnectedness of all things and the immanence of spirit within matter are central tenets of Vedic metaphysics, which is thus ideally suited to become the foundation of a new holistic science.[110]

It should not be supposed, however, that the Hindu nationalists simply appropriated the theses propounded by the postcolonial theorists. On the contrary, Nanda observes,

> the postcolonial critics of science and modernity ended up rediscovering the case for a uniquely Indian science that was already taken for granted in right-wing circles. ... The right-wingers' relativistic defense of mysticism as science is not based principally on Kuhn and Feyerabend, but rather on more nationalistic principles, which bear the hallmarks of Johann Herder and Oswald Spengler: namely, the idea that each nation has a "cultural soul" and a "destiny" that leave its mark on all intellectual efforts, from music and painting to science. Substitute "paradigm" in place of "culture," and the right-wing was Kuhnian long before Kuhn.[111]

Nanda concludes that

> Each one of the three prongs of the Vedic science project – a critique of dualist science, the idea that standards of rationality are internal to cultures, and that the rationality of modern science is as socially embedded and culturally constructed as that of any other knowledge system – is a part of the central dogma of contemporary science studies, women's studies, and postcolonial studies ... The idea that there is nothing special about modern science that premodern, non-Western sciences need to learn from, and that what counts as reasonable and real

varies with the cultural context, has become a part of the common sense of the postmodern academia. Defenders of Vedic science count upon this widespread and diffused attitude of cultural relativism to garner sympathy for their position.

(Nanda 2003: 122)

Concluding remarks

When all is said and done, the Hindutva ideologues' claim that modern science is contained in the Vedas is about as plausible as the contention of *The Bible Code*, a 1997 best-seller, that future events are encoded in the Old Testament.[112] It would be the stuff of comedy, were the context – destruction of the mosque at Ayodhya by a Hindu mob, repeated pogroms against Muslims and other religious minorities, the potential for nuclear confrontation between India and Pakistan – not so serious. As Nanda observes wearily about the fashion for "Vedic science": "Whatever good they might do for national pride, such claims cannot cover up the fact that Indian people remain mired in a view of the world that is deeply irrational and objectively false" (ibid.: 72).

For lack of both space and competence, I have not dwelt on the historical and political context of Hindu nationalist ideology, but perhaps a few words are in order. Nanda makes a good case that contemporary Hindu nationalism is best viewed as an instance of "reactionary modernism," a term that she borrows from Jeffrey Herf's much-cited study of Nazi Germany's modernity without liberalism, i.e.

> the embrace of modern technology by German thinkers who rejected Enlightenment reason. ... Before and after the Nazi seizure of power, an important current within conservative and subsequently Nazi ideology was a reconciliation between the anti-modernist, romantic, and irrationalist ideas present in German nationalism and the most obvious manifestation of means–ends rationality, that is, modern technology. Reactionary modernism is an ideal typical construct. ... [I]t incorporated modern technology into the cultural system of modern German nationalism, without diminishing the latter's romantic and antirational aspects.

(Herf 1984: 1–2)

In a similar way, Nanda explains, Hindu nationalists seek "dharma and the bomb ... an era when India will have nuclear bombs in its silos and the Vedas in schools" (Nanda 2003: 37; see also pp. 39–42). She further argues that

> the social conditions that led to this phenomenon in the Weimar Republic and the Third Reich – namely, "capitalist industrialization without a successful bourgeois revolution [and] weak traditions of political liberalism and the Enlightenment" – obtain [today] in many parts

of the developing world, including India. In these conditions, the dangers of fascistic nightmares cannot be ignored.

(Nanda 2003: 7; citing in part Herf 1984: 6)

The "postcolonial" intellectuals do not, of course, support the chauvinist and intolerant aspects of Hindu nationalism, and they cannot be held responsible for its rise. But, as Nanda has shown, their denunciations of modern science and defenses of "local knowledges" played directly into the hands of the ideologues of Hindutva, by undermining any principled ground for opposition to Vedic pseudoscience and, more generally, to the Vedic world view. "What reasons can they give against the supposed scientificity of Vedic astrology? Can they hold on[to] their relativist view of all sciences as social constructs and yet challenge the scientisation of the Vedas that is going on in the theories of Vedic physics or Vedic creationism?" (Nanda 2004).

The bottom line is that abstract philosophical debates can have real-life consequences. Nanda tells the following story about the recent craze for *vastu shastra*, the ancient Vedic rules governing the construction of buildings in alignment with the cosmic "life force":

> N.T. Rama Rao, the late chief minister of the southern state of Andhra Pradesh, sought the help of a traditional *Vastu Shastri* to help him out of some political rough weather, and was told that his troubles would vanish if he entered his office from an east-facing gate. But on the east side of his office there was a slum through which his car could not pass. [So he] ordered the slum to be demolished.
>
> (Nanda 1997: 82)

Nanda observes that

> If the Indian left were as active in the people's science movement as it used to be, it would have led an agitation not only against the demolition of people's homes, but also against the superstition that was used to justify it. ... A left movement that was not so busy establishing "respect" for non-Western knowledge would never have allowed the power-wielders to hide behind indigenous "experts."
>
> (ibid.: 82)

This is but a minor example; the crux of the matter is that

> while the Western postmodernists could at least take the hegemony of modern, mostly liberal, ideas for granted, the postcolonial critics were condemning modernity even before it had a chance to take root in the lives of their societies. ...
>
> Under the circumstances of an incomplete modernity that prevail in India, the postmodern-style total critique of modernity amounts to a

grand betrayal of the intellectuals of their vocation. This betrayal is in part responsible for the growth of reactionary modernity that we are witnessing in India under the sway of Hindu nationalist parties. With self-consciously left-wing humanists embracing a nativist and anti-rationalist agenda made respectable by highfaluting postmodern theory, there is hardly any organized resistance left to the Hindu nationalists. This is not to deny that the left and secular intellectuals are carrying out a valiant struggle against the Hindu nationalist policies of cultural indoctrination and ethnic cleansing. But what is missing is the existence of a well-articulated secular worldview which has the power to mobilize popular opinion, and which is not afraid to challenge the purported "wisdom" of popular traditions. ... The new social movements of the secular, left-wing intellectuals in India run the risk of fighting a merely strategic war against the religious right, while losing the battle for the hearts and minds of the masses.

(Nanda 2003: 28)

Some moderate examples

> Whether the accused in a murder trial is or is not guilty depends on the assessment of old-fashioned positivist evidence, if such evidence is available. Any innocent readers who find themselves in the dock will do well to appeal to it. It is the lawyers for the guilty ones who fall back on postmodern lines of defence.
>
> (Hobsbawm 1997: viii)

I would like now to present briefly a few additional instances in which the advocates of shoddy research have resorted to postmodernist arguments (either when the reliability of their evidence was challenged, or else pre-emptively). Unlike the examples analysed in the preceding sections, which dealt with the far end of Figure 12.1 – astrology, Therapeutic Touch and the like – here we will be discussing more-or-less mainstream research in the natural or social sciences that somewhere took a wrong turn. Of course, in science it is no sin to propose a theory that turns out, on closer examination, to be wrong (I myself have done so on countless occasions). The only sin is to cling stubbornly to one's theory when the evidence against it becomes so strong that any fair-minded person would concede the mistake and move on. Alas, this is an ancient and enduring sin, to which even the best scientists are far from immune.[113] What is perhaps novel, however, is the way that postmodernist arguments have lately been invoked, in some circles at least, to rationalize this sin.

Radical environmentalism

Geographer Martin Lewis, in an article entitled "Radical environmental philosophy and the assault on reason," has shown how some exponents of radical environmentalism have turned to postmodernism as a way of rescuing favored theories whose empirical support had become shaky. I would like here to sketch Lewis' argument in abbreviated and admittedly oversimplified form; the reader is referred to the original article for supporting evidence as well as for many important subtleties.

Lewis' critique is concerned with a school of thought that he calls "radical environmental philosophy," or "ecoradicalism" for short. "Most ecoradicals believe that human beings existed for millennia in a state of environmental grace as merely one species among a myriad in a balanced, harmonious global ecosystem" (Lewis 1996: 210). But, the Industrial Revolution shattered this equilibrium, bringing us today to the brink of environmental collapse. "The task for ecophilosophy," Lewis summarizes, "is to explain how such a total rupture could have occurred, and more importantly, to show how balance might be restored in time to save the planet from annihilation. ... The key error is often assumed to lie in the ideological realm, particularly in concepts about nature and the human position within it," (p. 210) though eco-radical theorists differ about the precise location of this central intellectual misstep. "For many radical ecophilosophers, the great error was nothing less than the glorification of reason that began in Europe in the early modern era and that culminated in modern scientific methodology" (p. 211).[114] Others push the pivotal error back to Plato, to the book of Genesis, or even to the Neolithic emergence of agriculture.

Lewis stresses that

> The ecoradical attack on reason and science was initiated within a framework of reasoned debate. Historical evidence was examined, and plausible linkages were hypothesized among developments in philosophy, science, technology, and economics ... Ecophilosophers also sought confirmation of their vision of premodern ecological harmony from the archeological and anthropological record. Moreover, they attempted to ground their entire framework in the science of ecology.
>
> (Lewis 1996: 217)

The trouble, Lewis goes on to note, is that "more careful consideration of the same lines of argument has since discredited the principal concepts of ecoradical philosophy. The roots of modern society are far more entangled and multistranded than they would have it, and the premodern world is now known to have been far less ecologically and socially benign" (pp. 217–18). For instance,

> Torture of animals, male oppression of females, and outright (local) ecological devastation may not have been universal conditions, but they were common enough everywhere. Even if we revert to the upper Paleolithic ... much evidence suggests that human beings at this time were responsible for the extinction of dozens of species of large mammals.
>
> (ibid.: 215)[115]

Finally, "even the science of ecology has failed the Greens, for it now emphasizes continuous flux and patchy distribution patterns, rather than the
stability of coherent ecosystems that once underwrote the vision of harmonious relations between people and nature" (p. 218).

What to do?

> One might imagine that such difficulties with evidence and theory would
> lead to a crisis of confidence and a questioning of assumptions. But
> ecoradical beliefs are often held with a religious vigor; the very existence
> of life on earth is thought to be at stake ... Inasmuch as it is a religious
> world view, this position is impervious to evidence against its key tenets.
>
> (ibid.: 218)

But, Lewis continues,

> environmental philosophy is only partially religious, being in equal
> measure a scholarly pursuit. As scholars, Green thinkers must address
> the evidentiary problems outlined above. It is here that postmodernism
> comes in: as a ready exit from their quandary.
>
> (ibid.: 218)

"The overriding attraction of a postmodern attitude," Lewis points out, is that

> it annuls the inconvenient requirement of empirical confirmation. In
> more extreme versions, the notion of evidence, like the formal rules of
> logic, is regarded merely as a social construct that society's power
> holders use to maintain and justify their positions. Stories of the human
> past invented by an active ecoradical imagination ... can thus be argued
> to have just as much legitimacy as the reconstructions of professional
> archeologists and other "scientists" trapped within the confines of objec-
> tivist discourse. If anything, they have more validity because of their
> moral authority; in the postmodernists' world, ethics are not to be sepa-
> rated from matters of "fact." By the same criteria, the problems implicit
> in the new ecology can simply be ignored. Ecologists are merely
> constructing their own stories about nature, and those currently being
> told in the scientific journals may be regarded as suspect, for they could
> potentially be used to justify a modernist agenda of human-imposed
> environmental change.
>
> (ibid.: 218)

Thus, feminist eco-philosopher Carolyn Merchant avers that

> Science is not a process of discovering ultimate truths of nature, but a
> social construction that changes over time. The assumptions accepted by
> its practitioners are value-laden and reflect their places in both history

and society ... Ecology is likewise a socially constructed science whose basic assumptions and conclusions change in accordance with social priorities and socially accepted metaphors.

(Merchant 1992: 236)

Indeed, geographer David Demeritt goes so far as to urge that "environmental historians and other Green critics should end their search for foundational authority, be it in science or elsewhere, and appeal instead to diverse moral, political, and aesthetic criteria to arbitrate between particular representations of nature in particular situations." Demeritt "does not rule out appropriations from ecological science or other fields of knowledge where they prove useful and convincing" but stresses that "ultimately, environmental narratives are not legitimated in the lofty heights of foundational epistemology but in the more approachable and more contested realm of public discourse" (Demeritt 1994: 22). The net result, as Paul Gross and Norman Levitt point out, is that "in practical terms, this leaves the radical theorist free to accept what flatters his worldview and to reject what does not" (Gross and Levitt 1994: 165).

Lewis cautions that

> it would be a serious error to conclude that postmodernism and ecoradical philosophy share identical concerns, much less that the two movements have somehow merged. Most environmental philosophers strongly mistrust the mainstream Derridean/Foucauldian schools of postmodernism ... Extreme postmodernism is far too relativistic and skeptical for Greens. Whereas poststructuralists condemn the search for the "transcendental signified" as a pointless quest, ecoradicals not only want to isolate the "transcendental signified" in the form of nature, but propose literally to worship it. ... Waving aside the pastiche, superficiality, and cool skepticism of the scholarly *avant garde*, most ecoradicals rather seek a reassertion of religious or quasi-religious values founded upon a spiritualized ecology.

(Lewis 1996: 219)

Their resort to postmodernist reasoning, although frequent enough, is episodic and opportunistic.

Lewis concludes that

> By spreading the message that science is no more reliable than shamanism, and especially by arguing that reason itself is the ultimate source of our environmental crisis, Green philosophers do little to enhance the public's ability to think clearly about the world and its very real problems. Earth-spirit worship may be psychologically beneficial for certain individuals, but at a societal level it is symptomatic of a dangerous tendency toward escapism.

(ibid.: 220)

History

The Swedish historian Arne Jarrick has observed that even postmodernist historians are not consistent relativists: they would reject without difficulty (at least in private) a belief in witches and trolls, or in American creationists' account of the origin of the human species. Furthermore, when they engage in empirical research – as at least the more moderate postmodernists do – they, no less than any other historian, gather evidence and attempt to defend their interpretations with rational arguments. Nevertheless,

> even if most historians in their daily tasks work as if it were possible to get to grips with real circumstances in the past, post-modern rhetoric still contributes to a kind of irresponsibility in thought and work in those situations where it is advantageous to be irresponsible. ... If it is not possible to demonstrate the validity of your own hypothesis, you can always rest on the thought that historical research is nevertheless a form of story, of fiction. If you cannot read something expected from the material, it is always possible to inscribe it there, as, after all, that is what post-modern historians consider that everyone is doing: writing themselves and their time into the text. Perhaps bending the truth a little does not matter, as the truth nevertheless does not exist ...
>
> (Jarrick 2003)

Along the same lines, the British historian Eric Hobsbawm has eloquently decried

> the rise of "postmodernist" intellectual fashions in Western universities, particularly in departments of literature and anthropology, which imply that all "facts" claiming objective existence are simply intellectual constructions. In short, that there is no clear difference between fact and fiction. But there is, and for historians, even for the most militantly antipositivist ones among us, the ability to distinguish between the two is absolutely fundamental.
>
> (Hobsbawm 1993: 63; reprinted in Hobsbawm 1997: 6)

Hobsbawm goes on to show how rigorous historical work can refute the fictions propounded by reactionary nationalists in India, Israel, the Balkans, and elsewhere, and how the postmodernist attitude disarms us in the face of these threats.

Over the past decade, there has been much discussion among theoretically inclined historians of the pros and cons of postmodernist ideas (broadly defined) in historiography.[116] In addition, several historians have published case studies in which they critically analyse the handling of evidence by their postmodernist-oriented colleagues.[117] As I am not a trained historian, I am not competent to take sides on the substantive controversies of historical interpretation being discussed. But if the critics are correct, Jarrick's fears are borne out, and postmodernist rhetoric can indeed serve as a smokescreen for sloppy research and dubious interpretation.

Postmodernists' selective skepticism

> I did not write this work merely with the aim of setting the exegetical record straight. My larger target is those contemporaries who – in repeated acts of wish-fulfillment – have appropriated conclusions from the philosophy of science and put them to work in aid of a variety of social cum political causes for which those conclusions are ill adapted. Feminists, religious apologists (including "creation scientists"), counterculturalists, neoconservatives, and a host of other curious fellow-travelers have claimed to find crucial grist for their mills in, for instance, the avowed incommensurability and underdetermination of scientific theories. The displacement of the idea that facts and evidence matter by the idea that everything boils down to subjective interests and perspectives is – second only to American political campaigns – the most prominent and pernicious manifestation of anti-intellectualism in our time.
>
> (Laudan 1990: x)

It might appear bizarre, at first sight, that postmodernists, who pride themselves on their skepticism toward even the most well-established principles of mainstream science, should sometimes display sympathy for – or even belief in – one or more pseudosciences. After all, many of their skeptical arguments – the theory-ladenness of observation, for instance, or the alleged non-referentiality of language – are *universal* in nature: if valid, they apply to astrology or homeopathy no less than to Maxwell's electromagnetic theory. But on reflection, postmodernists' sympathy for pseudoscience seems less odd. Scientific method, for those who adopt it, serves principally as a *filter* for distinguishing true propositions from false ones, plausible ones from implausible, and more generally for evaluating propositions and theories according to the degree of *rational warrant* that they enjoy in the light of the currently available evidence. Remove or weaken that filter – for example, by denying that there can *ever* be any reasonably objective way to evaluate rational warrant – and you not only let mainstream science flow out; you also let pseudoscience flow in. Furthermore, once cognitive considerations are demoted from their central role in evaluating theories, then social, political, and psychological considerations can move to center stage. In this way, we are led to look favorably on those theories that seem to support our political or personal goals, or whose advocates gain our sympathy in one way or another; we cast a skeptical gaze on theories that we deem politically incorrect (or simply unpleasant) or whose proponents seem unsympathetic.[118] And we deploy the postmodernist arguments – universal though they may logically be – only (or principally) in the case of the latter.

The authors to be considered in this section are not, for the most part, hardcore postmodernists. It would be fairer to call their attitude "postmodernism lite." Still, their strong social constructivism accords reasonably well with my definition of postmodernism as

> an intellectual current characterized by the more-or-less explicit rejection of the rationalist tradition of the Enlightenment, by theoretical discourses disconnected from any empirical test, and by a cognitive and cultural relativism that regards science as nothing more than a "narration," a "myth" or a social construction among many others.

If pressed, these authors might deny claiming that science is *nothing more* than one story among many others; they might even concede that modern science is the best tool yet developed for predicting and controlling the natural world; but they would strenuously avoid conceding that scientific theories might be closer to the *truth* than their non-scientific competitors, or even that they might enjoy a stronger *rational warrant*.[119] Indeed, many of these authors would strenuously deny that transculturally valid evaluations of rational warrant are even possible.

Let me be frank at the outset: my (admittedly incomplete) research turned up many fewer examples of postmodernists expressing unequivocal support for pseudoscience than I expected at first to find. I will therefore have to modify my initial hypothesis as a result of the evidence collected! I propose to begin by presenting the unambiguous cases; next I will present the more equivocal cases; and finally, I will attempt to provide some analysis of the findings.

Postmodernists on pseudoscience: I

Some (admittedly lesser-known) postmodernists have given explicit endorsements of pseudoscience. For instance, Richard E. Palmer, in an article on "postmodernity and hermeneutics," asserts that

> Instances of telepathy or faith healing are incomprehensible within the framework of naturalist assumptions, and it is almost comical to see the absurd lengths to which the empirically minded will go to deny them. ... While it is not feasible here to enter into cases, one may mention a few recent works that ... give a veritable catalog of instances that suggest agencies beyond the ken of naturalism. ... The career of Edgar Cayce, the remarkable psychic, raises many questions about telepathy, perception of illness and great distances, the intuitive prescription of treatment, and so on.
>
> (Palmer 1977: 376)

Palmer adds that "the works of [Erich] von Däniken offer an interesting challenge to the prevailing evolutionary concepts" (ibid.: 377).[120] Likewise,

Gary Lee Downey and Juan Rogers, in an article on "the politics of theorizing in a postmodern academy," propose

> to shift the explicit goals of academic theorizing from producing authoritative, truthful knowledge to producing knowledges that inform popular theorizing in desirable ways. ... [T]his strategy encourages one to view people as doing science in their everyday lives *all the time*. ... Such practices might also include well-established and highly organized forms of alternative science, such as alternative medicines, astrology, parapsychology, and various New Age sciences.
>
> (Downey and Rogers 1995: 275, 276; italics added)

Among well-known postmodernists (in my definition), I have found only two instances of explicit endorsement of pseudoscience. Feminist philosopher Sandra Harding has repeated uncritically a series of assertions from the book *Blacks in Science*, edited by Ivan van Sertima: in so doing, she has swallowed whole some whoppers of Afrocentric pseudoscience along with some genuine facts about African contributions to technology and medicine (van Sertima 1983).[121] For example, Harding states as fact that

> In West Africa between 1200 and 1400, the Dogon reported the rings of Saturn, the moons of Jupiter, and the spiral structure of the Milky Way galaxy ... They also knew that a small star, invisible to the naked eye, had an elliptical orbit around the star Sirius that took fifty years to complete.
>
> (Harding 1991: 223)[122]

These assertions are taken from a pair of articles by Hunter Havelin Adams III (1983a, 1983b), where they are supported by ludicrously weak evidence; indeed, they are easily refuted.[123] As archaeologist Kenneth Feder observes, "The ancient and modern peoples of Africa represent some of the great cultural achievements of humankind and there is no need to exaggerate their intellectual contributions to the world" (2002b: 120).

Along similar lines, Vandana Shiva, in her zeal to discredit "modern Western patriarchal science" and to vindicate both "ancient Indian traditions" and "women's indigenous knowledge,"[124] has endorsed some rather startling superstitions. For instance, she provides the following paean to what might be termed "botanical astrology":

> Sacred seed is perceived as a microcosm of the macrocosm with *navdanya* [nine seeds] symbolizing the Navagraha. The influences of planets and climate are seen as essential to plant productivity. In contrast, HYVs [high-yield varieties] break links with all seasonal climatic and cosmic cycles. ... On the grand scale [biodiversity] involves a relationship between planets and plants, between cosmic harmony and agricultural harmony captured in *navdanya*.
>
> (Mies and Shiva 1993: 169, 171)[125]

In addition, Shiva has endorsed the work of Indian botanist J.C. Bose (1858–1937), who claimed to have established the existence of consciousness in plants (Shiva 1989: 59). Although Bose's theories have long been discredited, it is worth noting that "he remains a hero of the Vedic science tradition," according to Meera Nanda (2003: 107).[126]

Postmodernists on pseudoscience: II

There are numerous instances in which relativist–constructivist sociologists, without explicitly endorsing astrology, telepathy, or other pseudosciences, have criticized the mainstream scientific community for giving short shrift to the alleged good evidence in favor of those theories. For example, Stanley Aronowitz writes that

> Rejected or marginal sciences such as parapsychology, the study of clairvoyance ... are just a few examples of the evidence that the scientific "community" as a site of power determines what counts as legitimate intellectual knowledge, even when the results of the marginalized sciences are obtained by traditional methods.
>
> (Aronowitz 1996: 191)[127]

Along similar lines, Barry Barnes, David Bloor, and John Henry, in their textbook on the sociology of science, write that

> "Astrology ... and homoeopathy ... remain firmly saddled with the label of pseudo-sciences in spite of recent work which seems to some to call for a reassessment (Gauquelin, 1984; Benveniste, 1988)".
>
> Michel Gauquelin's statistical evidence in support of astrology would perhaps be a serious embarrassment to scientists if they were not so good at ignoring it. But one day it could conceivably come to be accommodated as a triumph of the scientific method. Gauquelin's work seems to imply the existence of forces and interactions unrecognized by current scientific theory and yet it is based on methodological principles and empirical evidence which have so far stood up to sceptical challenge.
>
> (Barnes *et al.* 1996: 141)[128]

Although these passages do not indicate unequivocal support for clairvoyance or astrology, they do demonstrate a tolerant (and even cautiously favorable) attitude toward these theories, as well as a failure to comprehend the vast gulf between the established natural sciences and the pseudosciences as regards both methodology and degree of empirical confirmation. As physicist David Mermin noted in his review of the Barnes *et al.* book:

> BBH's gloss on astrology – "the existence of forces and interactions unrecognized by current scientific theory" (BBH, 141) – fails adequately

to convey the truly spectacular degree to which compelling evidence in support of astrology would require a massive radical reconstruction of our current understanding of the world.

(Mermin 1998: 642)

(A similar remark can be made for homeopathic claims, although the reconstruction might be somewhat less radical in this case.) Mermin goes on to note that

> An important motive behind rejecting such claims without any attempt at replication, unmentioned by BBH but clearly recognized by those doing the rejecting, is the gross inefficiency of investing extensive time and resources in an attempt to refute overwhelmingly improbable claims. For similar reasons, one turns down an offer, rendered on the spot, to purchase the Brooklyn Bridge for five dollars, without making a trip to the courthouse to confirm the conjectured non-existence of the claimed deed of ownership.
>
> (ibid.: 642)

Postmodernists on pseudoscience: III

In the work of relativist–constructivist practitioners of "science studies" and "cultural studies of science," one frequent theme is the study of dissident or marginalized communities, such as those of parapsychology or alternative medicine.[129] On the one hand, the methodological (and in some cases also epistemological) relativism that is virtually axiomatic in science-studies circles precludes any rational evaluation of the scientific evidence pertaining to the factual questions under debate.[130] On the other hand, this methodological relativism allows the authors' sympathy for the "marginalized" – or distaste for mainstream science – to determine their intellectual stance.

For instance, cultural-studies exponent Andrew Ross has published an impressionistic ethnography of New Age interventions into science and technology, in which sometimes astute sociological observations are combined with an overarching lack of interest in whether the theories in question are true or even plausible. Ross leads the reader through a panoply of New Age enthusiasms – bioenergetics, crystal healing, magnet therapy, brain machines and channeling, to name only a few – with a wry mixture of sympathy, bemusement, and detachment. Although Ross does not say so explicitly, the reader gets the distinct impression that he is skeptical about many of the New Agers' factual claims; but his explicit criticisms concern only the socio-economic and political aspects of New Age "science" (commercialism, individualism, desire to become part of "respectable" science), not the utter implausibility of the theories.[131] Furthermore, when discussing the intellectual luminaries of the New Age (Karl Pribram, David Bohm, and others), Ross becomes more respectful:

It is from modern brain science, however, that New Agers have drawn the most competent explanatory models for a new cosmology with science as its sustaining core. ... Once the brain's ecology is understood as holographic, the principles of isomorphism and synchronicity, from brain to brain, come into play. Sensory reality appears as a relatively stable representation, but is projected holographically from a point that is, in principle, beyond time and space. If the universe itself becomes a master hologram, all of reality can then be recovered from its smallest portion; each brain incorporates the universe's information. Holism is thereby established at all the implicate levels of experience.

(Ross 1991: 41)

In Ross' view, this paradigm has the advantage that

It not only establishes a permanent, fluid ground for intersubjective communication, but also allows for a more socially equitable overall distribution of energy than the *karmic* universe of retributions and rewards. Just as a formalist might argue that the politics of atom-smashing somehow equates to an attack on the centered Cartesian subject, so holism's proponents see the unified holographic field of perceiver and perceived as a leveling critique of the privileges of subjectivism. Such a field accommodates "mystic experience" not as a contingent or aberrant encounter but as a rational apprehension of the conscious holo-movement of sensory reality.

(ibid.: 42)

(Come again?) In a footnote, Ross cites approvingly Rupert Sheldrake's eccentric notion of "morphogenetic fields ... operating on a subquantum level, linking every pattern in the universe" (ibid.: 253, note 20).[132]

Along similar lines to Ross, but in a more professional manner, anthropologist-sociologist of science David Hess has produced a fascinating book-length ethnography of Spiritism in Brazil, placing it in the context of Brazilian religious syncretism (principally Yoruba and Catholic). Hess provides a series of case studies of what he calls "Spiritist scientific thought" but without once (as far as I can tell) asking whether the doctrines in question merit, on epistemic grounds, to be called "science." Indeed, he explicitly rules that question out of bounds:

I am making no claim that one or another of the discourses discussed here is more or less scientific than any other, nor even that the phenomena labeled "paranormal" have obtained the status of scientific facts; instead, I put in brackets the question of the scientific status of Spiritist thought as "true" or "false," and I use the claims of scientificity (or lack thereof) in order to get at issues of cultural values and ideological meaning.

(Hess 1991: 54–5)

Hess refers in passing to the mainstream medical community's disapproval of Spiritist cures, but only in sociological terms, as "boundary-work" by the orthodoxy to contain heterodox competitors; at no point does he inquire into the objective evidence concerning the efficacy of different therapies, or even acknowledge that the question exists. The same strict methodological relativism governs Hess' subsequent book on New Agers, parapsychologists, and skeptics in the United States (Hess 1993).[133] The net effect of this forced "neutrality" is to give unearned credence to pseudoscience.

Sociologist of science Steve Fuller is more explicit than Ross or Hess in advocating the demotion of science from its position of epistemic hegemony (a programme that he terms the "secularization of science"). Noting the little progress made thus far in this direction by sociologists of science, he says: "[I]t may turn out that more effective vehicles for the secularization of science will be found among the customized knowledges promoted by such New Age movements as homopathic [*sic*] medicine, parapsychology, dianetics, and (*mirabile dictu!*) Creation science" (Fuller 1996: 47; italics in original).

Discussing the controversy over teaching creationism alongside evolution in American public-school science classes, Fuller makes the sensible pedagogical observation that "Given that two thirds of those who believe in evolution also believe that it reflects a divine intelligence, it would seem that such ex cathedra dismissals [of theological ideas] fail to engage the average student's intellectual starting point" (ibid.: 49). But far from taking this as an opportunity to challenge students' prejudices and to teach the critical analysis of evidence, Fuller urges that students' prejudices be comforted wherever possible:

> [F]rom a Creationist standpoint, just because some important findings and perspectives in environmental science were originally developed under the rubric of Darwinian evolution, it does not follow that those findings and perspectives cannot be understood or appropriated without the Darwinian framework. In order to protect students' freedom of inquiry, teachers should try, whenever possible, to show that similar results can be reached holding alternative theoretical presuppositions.
>
> (ibid.: 48–9)

What this suggestion really protects is not students' freedom of inquiry, but rather parents' freedom to insulate their children *from* inquiry.

A few pages later, Fuller predicts that

> As governments continue to let market demand drive science policy ... scientific teams in search of funding will need to adapt their research goals to the interests of potential investors. This, in turn, will bring them closer to the kind of customized knowledge production that is

characteristic of New Age movements: that is, they will gradually lose the universalist gloss of knowledge per se and become knowledge for specific constituencies.

(ibid.: 50)

Fuller's prediction may, alas, come to pass; but he sloughs over the question of whether homeopathy, parapsychology, and dianetics are *really* knowledge (i.e., rationally justified true belief) or merely *purported* knowledge. Advertisers and cynics might not care about the difference, but consumers and rationalists should.

Concluding remarks

Among academic intellectuals whose primary commitment is to postmodernism (broadly defined), only a tiny handful appear to exhibit, at least in public, any significant attraction to pseudoscience. Occasionally, it is true, they make favorable comments about homeopathy, astrology, or parapsychology; but this seems, in most cases, to be simply a calculated attempt to *épater les scientifiques*, not a sincere assertion of their own belief. The confluence of postmodernism with pseudoscience seems, rather, to be strongest among those whose primary commitment is to one or another brand of pseudoscience, be it Hindutva or Therapeutic Touch. For these people, postmodernism supplies a ready-made ideology that they can use opportunistically to ward off the critiques of rationalists.

There is, however, one situation in which postmodernists seem more readily to give unequivocal endorsement of pseudoscience: namely, when the theories in question appear to support their intellectual and/or political goals. For instance, Sandra Harding (1991, 1993, 1994, 1996, 1998) has proposed to remake science along feminist and multicultural lines, asserting that the new science will be more "strongly objective" than existing science.[134] Her uncritical recitation of Afrocentric pseudohistory forms part of an effort to show that "Western" science has unjustly neglected discoveries made by Africans – a thesis that, to the extent that it is true, would provide some support for her philosophical and political project. Clearly, Harding's motivation in endorsing pseudoscience is not any attraction to pseudoscience *per se*, but simply opportunism and intellectual laziness (traits that, alas, are not the monopoly of any academic or political faction). As Gross and Levitt comment, harshly but under the circumstances not unjustifiably:

> In the gospel according to Harding, skepticism is to be reserved exclusively for scientific work done by white males and backed by the methodologies of scientific orthodoxy. "Strong objectivity" turns out to be another name for pathetic gullibility.

(Gross and Levitt 1994: 212)

Likewise, Vandana Shiva's endorsement of traditional Indian pseudoscience is motivated by her political and cultural sympathies, not by an objective analysis of the empirical evidence. These incidents provide at least some confirmation of my fear that postmodernist doctrine leads its adherents to look favorably on those theories that seem to support their political goals, while casting a skeptical gaze on theories that they deem politically pernicious.

Does it matter?

> The concept of "truth" as something dependent upon facts largely outside human control has been one of the ways in which philosophy hitherto has inculcated the necessary element of humility. When this check upon pride is removed, a further step is taken on the road towards a certain kind of madness – the intoxication of power which invaded philosophy with Fichte, and to which modern men, whether philosophers or not, are prone. I am persuaded that this intoxication is the greatest danger of our time, and that any philosophy which, however unintentionally, contributes to it is increasing the danger of vast social disaster.
>
> (Russell 1961a: 782)

Does it matter if some people believe in homeopathy or Therapeutic Touch? Perhaps not a great deal. I personally am irked when the purveyors of quackery (many of whom are now large corporations) succeed in lightening the wallets of the gullible; but in this scam, unlike most consumer frauds, the victim is a willing participant in his own victimization. My libertarian instincts urge a hands-off attitude toward pseudoscientific acts between consenting adults.[135]

Likewise, does it matter if some people – mostly, let's face it, academics – believe that truth is an illusion, that science is merely a species of myth, and that standards for judging rationality and correspondence with reality are thoroughly culture-bound? Once again, perhaps not a great deal: far more pernicious doctrines abound in human society, and anyway, intellectuals' influence on the world outside the ivory tower is much smaller than we frequently flatter ourselves into thinking.

In the preceding two paragraphs I have – as the reader will no doubt have guessed – bent over backwards to be tolerant, perhaps to the extent of obscuring my real views.[136] Thus I am indeed mildly disconcerted by a society in which 50 percent of the adult populace believes in extrasensory perception, 42 percent in haunted houses, 41 percent in possession by the Devil, 36 percent in telepathy, 32 percent in clairvoyance, 28 percent in astrology, 15 percent in channeling, and 45 percent in the literal truth of the creation story of Genesis.[137] But I am far more profoundly worried by a society in which 21–32 percent believe that the Iraqi government under Saddam Hussein was directly involved in the attacks of 11 September 2001, 43–52 percent think that US troops in Iraq have found clear evidence that Saddam Hussein was working closely with al-Qaeda, and 15–34 percent think that US troops have found Iraqi weapons of mass destruction.[138] And if I am concerned about public belief in clairvoyance and the like, it is largely because of my suspicion that credulity in minor matters prepares the mind for credulity in matters of greater import – and, conversely, that the kind of critical thinking useful for distinguishing science from pseudoscience might also be of some use in distinguishing truths in affairs of state from lies.[139] (Not a panacea, mind you, but just *of some use.*)

As historian of science Gerald Holton (2000) has observed, both pseudoscience and postmodernism – and the Romantic rebellion against science and reason that often links them together – become most dangerous when they are conjoined to political movements, such as National Socialism in Germany or Hindu nationalism in India. In the West, it is unlikely that either New Age spiritualism or academic postmodernism will, in the foreseeable future, acquire significant political weight. Christian fundamentalism remains, despite ups and downs, a powerful political force in the United States, but one that has been contained, thus far at least, by a countervailing legal tradition of separation between church and state. In large parts of the developing world, by contrast, profound social and economic dislocations coexist with a strong popular religiosity and weak (or non-existent) traditions of liberalism and secularism. In these circumstances, religiously inspired reactionary modernism is a permanent threat or, in some countries, an ongoing reality.

According to one prominent postmodernist epistemologist (echoing the ideas of dozens of others),

[T]here has never been a science without presuppositions, one that is "objective" and free of values and worldview. ... That Newton's system conquered the world was not the result of its internal truth content and value or of its persuasive power, but rather an aftereffect of the political hegemony that the British acquired in that era and that grew to an Empire.

(Krieck 1942: 9, 13)[140]

This thinker derides the objectivity of science in terms virtually identical to those of the Indian "postcolonial" theorists:

The case is simply this, that an idea born of the Enlightenment – that is, an idea of Western civilization, bearing the marks of a limited period – has set itself up as an absolute and declared itself a criterion applicable to all peoples and at all times. Here we have an example of Western imperialism, a bold assertion of supremacy.

(Krieck 1936: 31; as translated in Holton 2000: 340)

On this basis, he concludes that

> Decisions grounded on a race-based worldview determine the basic form – the principle or elemental phenomenon – upon which a science is founded. ... [A] German can look at and understand Nature only according to his racial character.
>
> (Krieck 1942: 13, 19)[141]

The postmodernist in question is Ernst Krieck, notorious Nazi ideologue and rector of the University of Heidelberg in 1937–38.[142]

I am not, of course, claiming that all postmodernists are Nazis, far from it. I am not even claiming that postmodernist ideas are in some way "proto-Nazi." My claim is, rather, that postmodernism – like most philosophical ideas – has no inherent political coloration at all, and can be used for a variety of purposes. In particular, postmodernism's attack on universalism and objectivity and its defense of "local knowledges" fit particularly well with nationalist ideologies of all stripes. Most contemporary postmodernists are politically progressive intellectuals, sincerely concerned with the fate of the poor and the downtrodden. But ideas have a way of escaping from the intentions of their creators.

Of course, if a theory is supported by cogent reasoning or persuasive empirical evidence, then it is unfair to criticize it on the grounds that it may lead, in some people's hands, to bad consequences; rather, it is the misuse of a valid idea that should be criticized instead. But if a doctrine is based on sloppy reasoning – as I believe postmodernism is[143] – then it is not out of place to observe that it can *also* have pernicious consequences.

Although intellectuals tend to overestimate their impact on the larger culture, it is nevertheless true that the ideas – even the most abstruse ones – taught and debated within universities have, over time, cultural effects beyond academia. For instance, postmodernist theorizing has had real effects "on the ground" in India, and those effects have not been uniformly positive, to put it mildly. Bertrand Russell (in the epigraph to this section) undoubtedly exaggerated when he denounced the perverse social consequences of confusion and subjectivism, but his fears were not entirely unfounded.

In this essay I have given examples of explicit convergence between pseudoscience and postmodernism: cases in which pseudoscientists resorted to postmodernist arguments, or in which postmodernists defended pseudoscience. To be honest, my (admittedly incomplete) research has turned up fewer instances of explicit convergence than I had initially expected to find.

But perhaps the most serious nexus between postmodernism and pseudoscience is one that I have not investigated here at all – one that is less explicit, and harder to pin down, but more insidious. To the extent that postmodernist ideas are widely disseminated in the culture, even in watered-down form, they create a climate in which the incentives promoting the rigorous analysis of evidence are undermined.[144] After all, doing real science is difficult. Why bother investing the time to seriously learn physics, biology, and statistics if it's all, in the end, just a matter of opinion anyway? One paradigm against another, your paradigm against mine. (Or in the more fashionable argot, "one among many truth games.") It's a lot quicker, and more exhilarating as well, to erect a revolutionary system based on verbal manipulation of phrases culled from vulgarizations of popularizations of relativity and quantum physics. Why bother studying David Bohm (1951, 1952) when it's far more exciting, and a hell of a lot easier, to read David Bohm (1980)? Why bother learning about non-commuting operators, when you can get all the quantum mechanics you need from Fritjof Capra?

There are also powerful psychological motivations impelling pseudo-science, which postmodernism reinforces. As Francis Bacon recognized nearly four centuries ago, "man prefers to believe what he wants to be true" (Bacon 2000 [1620]: 44). Logic and empirical science, on the other hand, intrude on human freedom, or at least on our fantasies of it: the universe may or may not turn out to conform to our desires. Indeed, one aspect of the transition from childhood to adulthood involves learning to relinquish pleasant but false beliefs – in Santa Claus, for instance – and, more generally, to distinguish between our desires and reality. But this is a difficult process, and none of us, scientists included, achieves it perfectly.[145] Natural selection equipped the human brain with propensities toward accurate perception and reasoning in those areas of life that were relevant to our ancestors' survival and mating; but there was no selective pressure toward accuracy in cosmology, and there may even have been selective pressure against it.[146] Science is an extremely recent (relative to our species' lifetime) cultural innovation that has allowed humans to overcome some of our innate propensities toward wishful thinking and to harness our intellectual capacities towards ends light-years distant (literally) from life on the African savannah. It is utterly extraordinary how effective that innovation has proved, in a mere 400 years, in generating accurate knowledge of the world, from quarks to quasars; indeed, that success would have to be reckoned a near-miracle if we did not already take it for granted. But the scientific attitude toward the world – the "scientific temper," as our colleagues in India so elegantly put it – is still very much a minority taste, even in the advanced industrialized countries where the technological products of science are ubiquitous. In many ways science cuts against the grain of human psychology, both in its methods and in its results; pseudoscience may well be more "natural" for our species. To maintain a scientific outlook requires a constant intellectual and emotional struggle against wishful, teleological, and anthropomorphic thinking, misjudgments of probability, correlation, and causation, percep-tion of non-existent patterns, and the tendency to seek confirmation rather than refutation of our favorite theories.[147]

Postmodernism did not create pseudoscience, and in most cases does not explicitly promote it. But by weakening the perceived intellectual and moral foundation for scientific thought, postmodernism abets pseudoscience and heightens the "ocean of insanity upon which the little barque of human reason insecurely floats."[148]

Acknowledgments

I would like to thank Jean Bricmont, Norm Levitt, Meera Nanda, and Marina Papa Sokal for many interesting discussions on the issues discussed here; Meera Nanda for making available to me a pre-publication copy of her book as well as many other documents; and Helena Cronin, Richard Evans, Garrett Fagan, Sarah Glazer, Arne Jarrick, Noretta Koertge, Norm Levitt, Meera Nanda, and Marina Papa Sokal for providing comments on drafts of this essay; and Helena Cronin, Richard Dawkins, Richard Evans, Garrett Fagan, Sarah Glazer, Gerald Holton, Arne Jarrick, Noretta Koertge, Norm Levitt, Donald Marcus, Latha Menon, Meera Nanda, Arnold Relman, Wallace Sampson, Gerhard Sonnert, and Perez Zagorin for suggesting references. Of course, none of these people are in any way responsible for what I have written.

I would also like to thank the Interlibrary Loan office at NYU's Bobst Library for efficiently processing my innumerable requests.

Finally, I wish to thank Garrett Fagan for his kind invitation to write this article, and for his tolerance both of my tardiness in producing it and of its unexpected length.

Appendix: religion as pseudoscience

> The attempt to efface the features of the struggle between religion and science is nothing but a hopeless effort to defend religion.
>
> (Sadiq al-'Azm 1982: 116)

Some readers will no doubt be offended by my description of the Pope as "the leader of a major pseudoscientific cult." Others will concede the accuracy of the description but consider it unnecessarily aggressive. I beg to differ on both counts.

Few people would, I presume, take umbrage were I to term Heaven's Gate a "pseudoscientific cult" or call the gods of Olympus a "myth"; these would simply be considered accurate descriptions of the epistemic status of the beliefs in question.[149] But, adherents of Heaven's Gate are few and socially marginal, while believers in the Greek gods are long dead. Judaism, Christianity, Islam, and Hinduism, by contrast, number millions of adherents around the world – hundreds of millions in the case of the latter three – and wield significant (although by no means unchallenged) political, economic, and social power in many countries. As a consequence, honest talk about the epistemic status of the dominant religions (e.g. Christianity in the West) is generally considered bad manners at best, blasphemous at worst. Nevertheless, to include these religions in a discussion of pseudoscience is in no way "aggressive"; it is simply to refuse the double standard that mandates favored treatment for some pseudosciences over others. Indeed, an unbiased count would probably show that Christianity, Islam, and Hinduism are *the most widely practised* pseudosciences in the world today, far above homeopathy or astrology. And in their fundamentalist versions they are the most dangerous as well.

In saying this so openly, I realize that I am in the minority. Even most liberals and agnostics nowadays take a dim view of blunt talk about religion, except to denounce the excesses of fundamentalism. After all, the battles of the eighteenth and nineteenth centuries between the Church and secular liberals were largely resolved in favor of the latter; religion in the West has largely abandoned its pretensions to political influence, except on matters of sexual morality and (in areas of the United States where fundamentalists are strong) education. As a consequence, non-believers have reached a *modus vivendi* with organized religion: you agree to stay out of politics (more or less); we, in turn, will refrain from publicly questioning your theology and from attacking the remnants of your temporal privileges (e.g. state subsidies in Europe, tax exemptions in the United States). Why bother criticizing ideas that are so inoffensive? Indeed, the liberal churches do much social good (e.g. in the civil rights and anti-war movements in the United States, and liberation theology in Latin America) and serve as an ethical counter-weight to the untrammeled power of money.

A similar *modus vivendi* has been reached between the scientific community and the non-fundamentalist churches. The modern scientific world view, if one is to be honest about it, leads naturally to atheism – or at the very least to an innocuous deism or pan-spiritualism that is incompatible with the tenets of all the traditional religions – but few scientists dare to say so publicly.[150,151] Rather, it is religious fundamentalists who make this (valid) accusation about "atheistic science"; scientists, by contrast, generally take pains to reassure the public that science and religion, properly understood, need not come into conflict. This is no doubt shrewd politics, especially in the United States, where the majority of people take their religion quite seriously; some scientists have labored to convince themselves (and the rest of us) that it is intellectually honest as well.[152] But the arguments do not hold water.[153]

Look back at my definition of pseudoscience and ask honestly whether the traditional religions fit:

1. It makes assertions about real or alleged phenomena and/or real or alleged causal relations that mainstream science justifiably considers to be utterly implausible.
2. It attempts to support these assertions through types of argumentation or evidence that fall far short of the logical and evidentiary standards of mainstream science.
3. Most often (though not always), pseudoscience claims to be scientific, and even
3'. claims to relate its assertions to genuine science, particularly cutting-edge scientific discoveries.

4. It involves not a single isolated belief, but rather a complex and logically coherent system that "explains" a wide variety of phenomena (or alleged phenomena).
5. Practitioners undergo an extensive process of training and credentialing.

Items (1), (2), (4), and (5) describe the traditional religions so perfectly that further explanation is hardly needed.[154] Items (3) and (3') are less common in the traditional religions, but are becoming increasingly frequent in recent years among the more sophisticated advocates of religious ideas.[155]

After all, when we say of a pseudoscientific cult – Therapeutic Touch, for instance, or Lacanian psychoanalysis – that it has become "virtually a new religion" or that its adherents "defend its doctrines with a quasi-religious fervor," we mean these comments as epistemic judgments, and we mean them pejoratively. Should doctrines that *admit* to being religions be treated any differently?

Notes

1. Or, rather, postmodernists *profess* to withhold such belief. Whether they actually do so in practice – for example, when they are seriously ill and must decide which type of medicine to follow – is a different question.
2. Let me emphasize that there is no one "right" definition of these (or any) terms. Rather, each author has the obligation to his readers to clarify, to the greatest extent possible, how *he* proposes to use the word.
3. For a good discussion of this point, see Weinberg 1992 (especially chapters II and III).
4. These two situations correspond to historian of science Thomas Kuhn's (1970) notions of "normal science" and "revolutionary science," respectively. Let me stress that while this part of Kuhn's theory is fairly uncontroversial, the same cannot be said for the rest, particularly the alleged "incommensurability of paradigms," which has led many of Kuhn's followers to a full-fledged relativism. For a critique of Kuhn's ideas on incommensurability, see Maudlin (1996) and Sokal and Bricmont (1998: 71–8).
5. See Sokal and Bricmont (1998: chapter 4) and Bricmont and Sokal (2004a) for further details on my conception of science and scientific knowledge. For an excellent introduction to contemporary debates in the philosophy of science, see Brown (2001).
6. Please note the limitation to questions of fact. I intentionally exclude from my purview questions of ethics, aesthetics, ultimate purpose, etc.
7. The allusion to historians and detectives was employed previously by Haack (1993: 137): "there is no reason to think that [science] is in possession of a special method of inquiry unavailable to historians, detectives, and the rest of us." See also Haack (1998: 96–7, 2003: 18, 24, 95, 102 and *passim*).
8. The fact that we all practise science from time to time does not mean that we all practise it equally well, or that we practise it equally well in all areas of our lives. See, for instance, note 145 below.
9. I stress that points (3), (4) and (5) are *optional* aspects of "pseudoscience" in my definition. In particular, while (5) tends to hold for the grand schools of pseudoscience, it may not apply to all pseudosciences. For instance, Garrett Fagan has pointed out to me that pseudoarchaeology is most frequently a solo endeavor, not one in which "schools" are established.
10. Numerous specific examples of pseudoscience are analysed in the books of Gardner (1957), Radner and Radner (1982), Broch (1992), Park (2000), Feder (2002b), and Shermer (2002). Several of these books also contain general discussions of the characteristics of science and

pseudoscience; Radner and Radner (1982: chapter III) and Feder (2002b: chapter 2) are particularly illuminating. Feder (ibid.: chapter 1) also provides a very useful table of references to earlier skeptical analyses of various types of pseudoscience.

11. Regarding Judaism, Christianity, Islam, and Hinduism, I am referring, of course, to the corpus of factual assertions about the natural and human world that are contained in the traditional doctrine of each of these religions (or of each variant thereof). It goes without saying that some practitioners of these religions adhere to the religion primarily for ethical, cultural, social, familial or nostalgic reasons without accepting any significant part of their religion's professed doctrine concerning matters of purported fact. For further discussion of the radical methodological opposition between science and religion, see al-'Azm (1982), Bricmont (1999), Haack (2003: chapter 10) and Kitcher (forthcoming). See also the appendix to this essay.

12. Popper's demarcation criteria are set forth in Popper (1959, 1963). For critiques, see Newton-Smith (1981), Kitcher (1982: 42–50), Laudan (1996: chapter 11) and Sokal and Bricmont (1998: 61–9), among many others.

13. The fact that temperature is a continuum does not imply that the words "hot" and "cold" are meaningless or that there is no difference between boiling water and ice!

14. Since the demise of Popper's attempts to draw a sharp demarcation between genuine science and pseudoscience, philosophers seem largely to have abandoned the task of developing and evaluating criteria for distinguishing the two. This is a shame, because although it may be impossible to draw a sharp demarcation based on universal methodological rules, it may nevertheless be possible to develop criteria that, taken together, can help to locate theories along the continuum illustrated in Figure 12.1 (or, perhaps better, a multidimensional analogue). For example, some scientists have proposed criteria for distinguishing good science from shoddy science (e.g. Langmuir 1989); it seems to me that philosophers and historians of science could play a useful role by carefully analysing the strengths and flaws of these criteria.

15. Noretta Koertge has kindly drawn my attention to an article by Philip Kitcher (1984/ 85) that eloquently makes these same points. Speaking of the gap between genuine sciences such as evolutionary biology and pseudosciences such as "creation science," Kitcher writes (p. 170): "We can manage without a criterion of demarcation. ... The issue is the location of various proposals on a continuum. To put the point briefly: There is excellent science, good science, mediocre science, poor science, [and] dreadful science."

   Susan Haack (2003: 116) takes a similar view: "[R]ather than criticizing work as 'pseudo-scientific,' it is always better to specify what, exactly, is wrong with it: that it is not honest or serious inquiry; that it rests on assumptions for which there is no good evidence, or which are too vague to be susceptible to evidential check; that it uses mathematical symbolism, or perhaps elaborate-looking apparatus, purely decoratively; etc. ... [I]f we want to understand how creationism differs epistemologically from physical cosmology or evolutionary biology, we will do better to focus directly on questions of evidence and warrant, instead of fussing over whether creationism is bad science, or not science at all."

16. Alternatively, postmodernists may concede that statements can be objectively true or false but insist that the criteria for judging whether a belief is *rationally justified* (relative to some specified set of evidence) are thoroughly culture-bound.

17. For further discussion of redefinitions of truth, along with examples and a critique, see Bricmont and Sokal (2004a: section 2.4).

18. For example, Griffin (1988), who advocates an "affirmative postmodernism" based on the "reenchantment of science," explicitly reaffirms that the goal of science is the search for truth, understood as correspondence with reality. He is thus *not* a postmodernist in the sense defined here. (In my opinion, Griffin's program is flawed by a series of gross misunderstandings about the content of modern science, which lead him give undue credence to crazy ideas like telepathy and clairvoyance; but relativism is not one of his sins.)

19. Two qualifications need to be made: First, this statement is offered as part of Collins' introduction to a set of studies (edited by him) employing the relativist approach, and it

constitutes his summary of that approach; he does not *explicitly* endorse this view, although an endorsement seems to be implied by the context. Second, while Collins appears to intend this assertion as an empirical claim about the history of science, it is possible that he intends it neither as an empirical claim nor as a normative principle of epistemology but rather as a methodological injunction to sociologists of science: namely, to act *as if* "the natural world ha[d] a small or non-existent role in the construction of scientific knowledge," in other words to *ignore* ("bracket") whatever role the natural world may in fact play in the construction of scientific knowledge. See Bricmont and Sokal (2001, 2004b) for an argument that this approach is seriously deficient *as methodology* for sociologists of science.

20. For a shrewd meditation on the former question, see Levitt (1999, especially pp. 12–22 and chapter 4). The latter question is indirectly addressed by Burnham (1987) in the context of a fascinating history of the popularization of science in the United States in the nineteenth and twentieth centuries.

    For my own part, I have been struck by the fact that nearly all the pseudoscientific systems to be examined in this essay are based philosophically on *vitalism*: that is, the idea that living beings, and especially *human* beings, are endowed with some special quality ("life energy," *élan vital*, *prana*, *qi*) that transcends the ordinary laws of physics. Mainstream science has rejected vitalism since at least the 1930s, for a plethora of good reasons that have only become stronger with time (see, e.g., Mayr 1982). But these good reasons are understood by only a tiny fraction of the populace, even in the industrialized countries where science is supposedly held in high esteem. Moreover – and perhaps much more importantly – the anti-vitalism characteristic of modern science is deeply unsettling emotionally to most (perhaps all) people, even to those who are not conventionally religious. See again Levitt 1999. Of course, none of these speculations pretends to any scientific rigor; careful empirical investigation by psychologists and sociologists is required.

21. There is an extensive literature on Therapeutic Touch, by both its advocates and its critics. In describing Therapeutic Touch and its alleged theoretical basis, I will draw on the advocates' own explanations wherever possible. See, for example, Krieger 1979, 1981, 1987, 1993, 2002; Borelli and Heidt 1981; Macrae 1988; Kunz 1995: 211–88, 307–26; Cowens and Monte 1996; Wager 1996; Fischer and Johnson 1999; Fontaine 2000: chapter 13; Freeman and Lawlis 2001: chapter 18; and Sayre-Adams and Wright 2001, among many others. For critiques, see Rosa *et al.* 1998 and the literature cited there, as well as the essays in Scheiber and Selby 2000.

22. For a more detailed description of the experiment and its statistical analysis, see Rosa *et al.* (1998). Of course, some aspects of Emily's experimental design can be criticized: for example, the sample sizes were small; there was no documentation of the practitioners' "qualifications" in TT; the immobile palms-up position of the practitioner is atypical of TT practice; controls were arguably inadequate. All of these features could easily be corrected if enough TT practitioners were to volunteer for a new study with a mutually agreed protocol. For some other recent experimental tests of TT, see Scheiber and Selby 2000: chapters 13–22.

23. Supporters and critics of TT are in general agreement as to these basic facts. Among supporters, see, e.g., Krieger 1987: 8, 1993: 5, 187, 2002: 12; Fontaine 2000: 221; Freeman and Lawlis 2001: 493. Among critics, see, e.g., Rosa *et al.* 1998: 1005; Stahlman 2000: 37–9, 47–8; Glazer 2000b: 320. Nevertheless, these figures should be taken with a grain of salt inasmuch as both advocates and detractors of Therapeutic Touch have an interest in exaggerating its incidence, albeit for different reasons.

24. Kolata 1998: A20. If true, this is an astounding figure. Even if the course of study lasts only one week, it amounts to training a new class of thirty-five students each week, year in year out, for a quarter of a century. According to a recent textbook of alternative medicine, "estimates of the total number of persons that have learned therapeutic touch now exceed 85,000" (Freeman and Lawlis 2001: 493).

25. OCLC WorldCat, as of 7 November 2003. Available online at http://newfirstsearch.oclc.org.

26. My account of pseudoscience and postmodernism in nursing is strongly indebted to the pioneering work of health journalist Sarah Glazer (2000a, 2000b). While I have added much new detail and documentation, the basic thread of the story is the one traced by Glazer.

27. Krieger (1979: 4–13, 1981: 138–47) provides a brief history of the development of Therapeutic Touch. See also Stahlman 2000 and Sarner 2002 for more detailed histories, written by critics.

28. Kunz (1991: 5–6) recalls that "Both my mother and grandmother had psychic abilities. ... As for my clairvoyance, I suppose I began to become aware of it and to develop it when I was around six or seven years of age."

   The Theosophical Society is a mystico-religious organization founded in 1875 by celebrated psychic Helena Petrovna Blavatsky together with lawyer Henry Steel Olcott. For a history, see Campbell (1980); additional information can be found in Carlson (1993) and Godwin (1994). Dora Kunz served as president of the American section from 1975 through 1987.

29. Freeman and Lawlis (2001: 495) confirm that "this process does not require that the patient consciously participate, nor is its effect dependent on the patient's belief in the intervention."

30. Of course, many biological processes involve low-level electric and magnetic fields within the body; but these fields decay rapidly outside the body, and in any case they cannot be detected or significantly affected by human hands.

31. See also Krieger 1981: 143.

32. It is true (and obvious) that human beings are open systems, i.e. they interact with the world around them. Everything else in this quotation is nonsense, despite the purportedly scientific language. For what it is worth, "wave phenomena" and "energy" are not synonyms, nor does energy have any "intrinsic rhythmicity." "Electron transfer resonance" is not, to my knowledge, a standard term in either physics or chemistry.

33. Homeopathy was developed by Samuel Hahnemann (1755–1843), and its basic principles remain largely unchanged to this day, despite radical advances in our understanding of physics, chemistry, and biology that thoroughly undermine its alleged scientific basis. Its central tenets are the so-called Law of Similars, or "like cures like" (i.e., the claim that a disease can be cured by small doses of a substance that in larger doses produces symptoms similar to the disease itself); the so-called Law of Potentization (i.e., the claim that homeopathic remedies become *stronger* with each successive dilution, provided that they are shaken ("succussed")); and a vitalist theory of biology, which holds that living beings are endowed with some special quality ("vital force") that transcends the ordinary laws of physics.

   It is important to stress that homeopathy is *not* a species of herbal medicine. Plants contain a wide variety of substances, some of which can be biologically active (with either beneficial or harmful consequences, depending on the situation). Homeopathic remedies, by contrast, are pure water and starch: the alleged "active ingredient" is so highly diluted that in most cases *not a single molecule remains in the final product*.

34. Castro (1999: 280) begins by stating, without any qualifications, that "Homeopathy is an effective and scientific system of healing ... The homeopathic principles constitute a unified hypothesis whose validity is tested empirically: cured patients confirm the hypothesis."

35. For a devastating critique of one of these two studies, devoted to documenting "children's lived experiences of perceiving the human energy field," see Glazer (2000b: 331–2).

36. It goes without saying that the claim of the "anonymous scientist" is nonsense.

37. Malinski *et al.* (1994) is a useful biography of Rogers edited by her disciples, which also contains extensive excerpts from her writings and a series of brief articles "saluting" her contributions to nursing and to science.

38. Not only is Rogers "the 20th-century [Florence] Nightingale" (Fitzpatrick 1994: 322), she is also "a leader in the development of contemporary science" who has "made major

contributions to science at large", extending far beyond nursing (Phillips 1994b: 330, 335). Indeed, Rogerian scholarship "will revolutionize all views of the universe, similar to Einstein's theory of relativity" (Phillips 1997: 18).

39. Reprinted in Malinski *et al*. 1994: 234.
40. Reprinted in Malinski *et al*. 1994: 235.
41. For instance, "energy" and "field" both have precise (not metaphorical!) meanings in physics; but "energy field," a key term in Rogers' writings, is meaningless in physics. Of course, Rogers and her supporters might reply that they are not purporting to give these terms their standard meaning in physics but are instead providing their own definitions. That would be fine in principle; the trouble is that Rogers' purported "definitions" are as meaningless as the terms allegedly being defined. For instance, Rogers says that "Four-dimensionality ... is defined as a nonlinear domain without spatial or temporal attributes." But she nowhere clarifies what she means here by "domain" (much less "domain without spatial or temporal attributes"); moreover, the mathematical adjective "nonlinear" is meaningless in this context. Every one of Rogers' "definitions" suffers from a similarly fatal vagueness. See also Raskin (2000: 34) for a patient dissection of Rogers' pseudoscience.
42. Reprinted in Malinski *et al*. 1994: 235.
43. Reprinted in Malinski *et al*. 1994: 235.
44. Rogers 1990, 1992. A useful overview of the evolution of Rogers' Science of Unitary Human Beings is given by Malinski (1994). See also Malinski 1986: xiii–xix.
45. Reprinted in Malinski *et al*. 1994: 217–18. Please note that Rogers' "equation" is mathematically meaningless. Her use of symbols resembling (to a lay person's eye) a mathematical equation is nothing more than a crass attempt to give her ideas a veneer of "scientificity"; the "equation" in fact adds nothing to its verbal "translation" (which, alas, is also scientifically meaningless).
46. Reprinted in Malinski *et al*. 1994: 230.
47. Reprinted in Malinski *et al*. 1994: 237.
48. See, e.g., Sokal and Bricmont 1998: chapters 2, 3, 9 and 10.
49. Malinski 1986; Barrett 1990; Madrid and Barrett 1994; Madrid 1997. See also Rogers *et al*. 1985; Sarter 1988; Lutjens 1991; Barrett and Malinski 1994.
50. For example, Riehl-Sisca 1989; McQuiston and Webb 1995; Meleis 1997; Fawcett 2000; Young *et al*. 2001; George 2002; Marriner-Tomey and Alligood 2002; Alligood and Marriner-Tomey 2002. It is important to note that Rogers' Science of Unitary Human Beings is by no means the only pseudoscientific theoretical framework that has achieved prominence in the nursing profession. As one advocate of "alternative/complementary modalities" points out,

> there are several nursing theories that incorporate the concept of "human energy field" and "environmental energy field," specifically Rogers' Theory of Unitary Human Beings, Newman's Theory of Expanding Consciousness, and Parse's Theory of Human Becoming. All energy-based modalities are congruent with these theories. While Therapeutic Touch (TT) is a modality developed by and researched by nurses, other energy-based modalities such as Reiki and Healing Touch techniques are widely used by and taught to non-nurses.
>
> (Frisch 2001)

In fact, most of the textbooks cited above also have chapters on Newman's and Parse's theories.
51. Science and Social Science Citation Indexes combined, as of 7 November 2003. Available at http://isi4.isiknowledge.com.
52. Dissertation Abstracts, as of 6 November 2003. Available at http://wwwlib.umi.com/dissertations. It is likely that many masters' dissertations are missing from this database.
53. The full text of the citation is available at http://nursingworld.org/hof/rogeme.htm.
54. See Williams (1985) for a judicious and balanced overview of "holistic nursing."

55. Very similar comments are made by the editor of a recent textbook on "complementary and alternative medicine" (Micozzi 2001: 4).

56. Note also that the allusion to Descartes is highly misguided. If modern science has any characteristic world view, it is surely not Cartesian dualism but rather materialist monism, i.e. "the view that there is essentially only one kind of 'reality,' one kind of material existence, governed by its unique and invariable set of laws or, if you prefer, regularities" and in particular that the mind "must be understood as a physical function of a physical body." Descartes' philosophy is more accurately understood as a dead end in the history of science, "a late, postmedieval attempt to rescue the world of thought from the monism toward which it was apparently heading" (quotations from Levitt 1999: 19). Alas, this clarification is hardly likely to increase the fondness of "holists" for modern science.

57. See Weinberg (1992: chapter III, 1995) for a clear explanation of this point.

58. The first sentence of this quotation is a fairly accurate, although incredibly superficial, summary of certain aspects of special relativity (interchangeability of energy and matter) and quantum mechanics (interconnectedness in a certain limited sense). But to call the universe a "living web" is pure metaphor; and the last two sentences of this quotation are a complete *non sequitur*. It goes without saying that modern physics provides no support whatsoever for the notion of "life force."

59. The author is a Distinguished Professor of Nursing at the University of Colorado Health Sciences Center and former president of the National League for Nursing. For what it's worth, quantum physics does *not* lend any credence whatsoever to the bizarre notions proffered by Watson.

60. Dossey's earliest work (1982: 98–101, 122–34, 146–50, 194–6, 208–9, 233–4) invokes quantum mechanics, as interpreted in the extremely controversial speculations of some physicists, to argue that human consciousness is a fundamental element in the ontology of the universe. In later books he elaborates on this theme, stressing the element of non-locality – a rather technical, very important, but also extremely controversial aspect of quantum physics (see, e.g., Mermin 1993; Maudlin 1994) – from which he draws increasingly exotic conclusions about telepathy and kindred "phenomena": see Dossey 1989: 153–86 and *passim*, 1993: 84–5, 128, 155–6; 1999: 26–7, 68; 2001: 113–14, 189–91, 238–9). At one point, Dossey (1993: 85) observes correctly that quantum-mechanical non-locality *cannot* be used to send messages – thereby demolishing his claimed physical basis for telepathy – but he then goes on to conjecture, bizarrely and erroneously, that "perhaps nonspecific prayer strategies do *not* violate physics' prohibition on sending messages nonlocally" (italics in original). For clearly explained critiques of "quantum medicine" and "quantum parapsychology," see Stalker and Glymour 1985; Gardner 1981.

61. These notions are also incorporated into the *Core Curriculum for Holistic Nursing* developed by the American Holistic Nurses' Association (AHNA) and are enshrined in the practice examination questions designed to help the reader to prepare for the Holistic Nursing Certification (HNC) exam. See Dossey 1997: 7–8, 249. Some parts of this core curriculum are quite bizarre. For example, in the chapter on "energetic healing," among the "knowledge competencies" required of the student are to "Describe two characteristics of an electromagnet," "Discuss the quantum theory of consciousness-created reality," "Compare a Fourier analyzer to the chakra system and L–C circuits to individual chakras," and "Describe one traditional portrayal of an aura" (ibid.: 52).

62. To be sure, double-blinding is not always feasible or effective: the patient may be able to deduce from the drug's side-effects whether he is in the experimental or control group; and for some interventions it may be physically impossible to devise "sham" interventions that maintain the double-blinding. The classic example of the inability to double-blind is the path-breaking study "Is coitus implicated in causing pregnancy? Some preliminary findings."

63. Fontaine (2000: 12) makes the valid observation that medical tests and procedures are not subjected, under current American law, to the same rigorous evaluation that new

drugs are required to undergo. But the proper remedy would be to close this loophole by requiring a higher standard of scientific evidence for all medical interventions, not to extend the loophole by lowering the standard of proof for "alternative" treatments (some of which are indeed drugs). Indeed, most "alternative" treatments are already exempt from regulation, either *de jure* or *de facto*.

64. Even cruder versions of begging the question can be found in the writings of other advocates of "alternative healing practices." For instance:

> The fact that cellular, organ, and whole-organism phenomena, as are reported in mice and people under the influence of *qigong* and other energy healing modalities, have continued to attract patients and practitioners for literally thousands of years, must surely indicate that there is something of untold significance to be rediscovered.
>
> (Jobst 2002: 524)

> Homeopathy is an effective and scientific system of healing. ... The homeopathic principles constitute a knifed hypothesis whose validity is tested empirically: cured patients confirm the hypothesis.
>
> (Castro 1999: 280)

> [O]ur intuitive faculty is nothing other than a source of sound premises about the nature of reality. ... [T]here exists within us a source of direct information about reality that can teach us all we need to know.
>
> (Weil 1998: 151–2; see also vii)

See Beyerstein (1999, 2001) for an incisive analysis of some common errors of reasoning among advocates and users of alternative medicine; and see Relman (1998) for a detailed analysis and critique of the epistemology underlying the writings of Andrew Weil, the self-described "guru of alternative medicine."

65. Similar arguments are offered by many advocates for (or sympathetic analysts of) "complementary and alternative medicine." See, for example, the essays by Cassidy and Watkins in Micozzi (2001) and the essays by Schaffner, Hufford, O'Connor, Wolpe, and Tauber in Callahan (2002).

66. For a summary and critique of Kuhn's ideas on the incommensurability of paradigms, see Maudlin 1996; Sokal and Bricmont 1998: 71–8.

67. Another example of extreme postmodernist relativism is provided in a recent textbook on complementary and alternative medicine: "[A]ll answers are right from within the logic of the model in use. ... From this position, clinicians, researchers, or students ... can avoid becoming mired in determining which method is true because nothing is really true when all realities are constructed" (Cassidy 2001: 21). Similarly, a disciple of Martha Rogers states that "the Rogerian ontology does not distinguish between subjective and objective realities. Furthermore, pandimensionality recognizes multiple, even infinite, realities" (Butcher 1999: 113). Finally, another nursing theorist sympathetic to the "new paradigm" ideas of Rogers and her successors argues that "upon close examination of the ontologies, it is clear that core postmodern ideas, such as constructed realities, the centrality of meaning and interpretation, and valuing the multivocality of discourse, are also central to the new paradigm ontologies" (Cody 2000: 94).

68. Watson's pseudoscientific theories can be found in Watson (1999). See also Watson and Smith (2002), in which Watson's Caring Science and Rogers' Science of Unitary Human Beings are "creatively synthesized" into a new Unitary Caring Science; and see the extensive interview with Watson published by Fawcett (2002).

69. For comparison, see the introduction to the University of Warwick conference devoted to "DeleuzeGuattari and Matter," cited in Levitt (1999: 85–6). Or see Sokal and Bricmont 1998: chapter 9.

70. The Cumulative Index to Nursing and Allied Health Literature (CINAHL) lists 131 articles using the words "postmodernis$" or "poststructural$" ($ = anything) in the title or
abstract. The first of these articles appeared in 1989, but in the period 1989–1994 they
averaged only two per year; starting in 1995 they took off and averaged fourteen per year,
continuing up to the present. Data are as of 10 December 2003. See also the much larger
number of articles cited in the next note. CINAHL is available online at http://
gateway.ovid.com.
71. CINAHL shows a whopping 663 articles that mention Foucault in the title, abstract, or
bibliography/cited references, 531 for Heidegger, 99 for Rorty, and 81 for Derrida.
Nearly all these citations appeared in 1995 or later. Data are as of 10 December 2003.
72. See, e.g., the essays in Omery *et al.* (1995), Kikuchi *et al.* (1996), and Thorne and Hayes
(1997).
73. Glazer 2000b; Thompson 2002; Glazer 2002.
74. See Dzurec (1989: 75) for another example of a postmodernist nursing theorist
commenting favorably on Rogers' Science of Unitary Human Beings.
75. Rogers' grasp of basic physics is perhaps also illustrated by her enthusiastic and wholly
uncritical endorsement of Immanuel Velikovsky's crackpot theories of astronomy (Rogers
1970: 12). For further analysis of Rogers' pseudo-physics, see Glazer (2002: 63) and
Raskin (2000: 34).
76. A preliminary analysis of this last question can be found in Glazer (2000b).
77. Nehru's book was written in April–September 1944 in Ahmadnagar Fort prison, where
he and other leaders of the Indian independence movement had been interned by the
British since mid-1942.
78. Indeed, since the 1960s, a plethora of People's Science Movements have been active
throughout India – numbering well over 100,000 members in total – under the banner
of "science for social revolution," which includes promoting a scientific world view "in
order to demystify the religious legitimations of caste, patriarchy, and other sources of
discrimination based on concepts of purity" (Nanda 2003: 220). For more information on
these movements, see ibid.: 219–22; Isaac *et al.* 1997.
79. Let me stress that my quarrel is only with the second sentence, which asserts the epistemic equality of astrology and modern science. The first sentence may well be an astute
sociological observation (that is an empirical question that I am not competent to assess).
But the following recent comment by Nandy (assuming that he has been accurately
quoted) is worth noting: "'Astrology hardly has any influence among the illiterate and
poor in rural India,' said a sociologist, Asish [*sic*] Nandy. 'It's the urban educated, grap-
pling with an increasingly complex and uncertain reality, who are in its thrall'" (Rahman
2003).
80. Suffice it to say that, like much postmodernist discussion of science, these claims are
based on simplistic readings of controversial works in the philosophy of science (notably
Kuhn and Feyerabend), combined with cavalier leaps of (il)logic about subtle issues like
the role of epistemic and non-epistemic values in science, the theory-ladenness of observation, the epistemic status of scientific knowledge, the multiple aspects of reductionism,
and the conceptual and socio-economic relations between science and technology. For
more detailed critiques of postmodernist and "postcolonial" claims in the philosophy of
science, see Nanda 2003: chapters 5 and 6; Sokal and Bricmont 1998: chapter 4; Haack
1998, 2003; Brown 2001.
81. This theme can also be found in some Western authors, beginning with Carolyn
Merchant (1980), albeit most often in a less extreme form.
82. See also Alvares (1992: 64) for a similar statement.
83. Unfortunately, Shiva rides roughshod over the crucial distinctions between different
notions of reductionism. For a clear discussion of these different notions, see Weinberg
1992: chapter III, 1995.
84. See also Shiva 1989: chapter 2.

85. See also the essay by Nandy and Visvanathan (1990), which is a paean to Theosophy, vitalist biology, and Ayurvedic medicine as allegedly prescient critiques of modern scientific medicine ("a politically powerful knowledge system which shows immediate practical results in some areas but is intellectually, socially, and morally disorienting" (p. 181)). In lauding "cognitive resistance to the gross appetite of modern science" (p. 175), Nandy and Visvanathan go so far as to approvingly quote Gandhi: "to study European medicine is to deepen our slavery" (p. 174).

86. In the first year of the plan's operation, "the UGC selected 19 universities for providing exclusive teaching and training in the subject leading to undergraduate, postgraduate and doctoral degrees. During the financial year 2001–02, an amount of Rs. 2.71 crore [= 27.1 million rupees ≈ $600,000] was paid to 17 universities for setting up of these departments" (Government of India, Department of Education 2003: 132). Although this sum is modest, it is nearly double what was spent in the same year to upgrade/modernize the computer centers at fifty-nine Indian universities (ibid.: 145).

87. See, e.g., Ramachandran (2001), Balaram (2001), and Jayaraman (2001a, 2001b), among many others. In particular, Jayaraman (2001a) provides a detailed explanation of why astrology is a pseudoscience.

88. See Menon and Rajalakshmi (1998), Panikkar (2001), Bidwai (2001), and Menon (2002) on the rewriting of history textbooks; Ramachadran (2001), citing the UGC guidelines, on *vastu shastra* and Vedic mathematics; Government of India, Department of Education (2003: 134–5) on yogic science; and Nanda (2003: 73, 75–6) generally. See also Dani *et al.* (2001) for a scathing critique of "Vedic mathematics", signed by over a hundred Indian mathematicians, scientists, and other academics, and Patnaik (2001) for a probing critique of the BJP's educational policies.

89. Another central aspect of Hindu nationalist ideology – not discussed here, for lack of competence on my part – is the tendentious rewriting of the early history and archaeology of South Asia. For a detailed analysis, see Chapter 9 by Michael Witzel.

90. See, for instance, Frawley (1990: 117): "In the Vedic system knowledge is defined as both higher and lower or superior and inferior (para and apara). The lower or inferior knowledge consists of the knowledge of the outer world. ... All science is a form of the lower knowledge, as it is based on measurement and mathematics and the information which comes to us through the senses."

91. This excerpt comes from a lecture on "The Vedanta" delivered in Lahore on 12 November 1897.

92. For details of Kak's calculations, see Kak (1994) and Feuerstein *et al.* (1995: 201–8); and for a critique, see Plofker (1996), Witzel (2001a: §28), and Nanda (2003: 112–14).

93. Subhash Kak provides a foreword in which he lauds Roy's "audacious reinterpretation of [the] Vedic system of knowledge' (Roy 1998: xv) and concludes: "Roy's book is a bold, new way of looking at Vedic physics. Since he is a pioneer, this is not the place to quibble with the details of his story. We celebrate the new path he has hewn through the bush of old scholarship. It is the task of future researchers to further sharpen and modify the ideas of Roy" (ibid.: xviii).

94. Subhash Kak, in his foreword to Roy's book, says this explicitly: "knowing oneself one can know the world!" (ibid.: xvi).

95. As evidence for the claim that the human being is a mirror image of the cosmos, the authors adduce the following: "the Ayurvedic savants made the astonishing discovery that the number of bones in the human body equals the number of days in the year. They arrived at this number by counting the 308 bones of the newborn, 32 teeth, and 20 nails" (p. 197). Even more astonishing, it seems to me, is the discovery, by this method, that the year has exactly 308 + 32 + 20 = 360 days, not 365.25636 (sidereal orbit) as modern astronomers have hitherto naively believed. Feuerstein *et al.* also explain that the theory of correspondences and equivalences underlies the development of other important sciences, notably astrology (p. 211) and Ayurvedic medicine (pp. 212–16).

354   *Alan D. Sokal*

96. The author is editor of *The Astrological Magazine*. This article appeared in *The Organiser*, an English-language publication of the Rashtriya Swayamsevak Sangh (RSS), the main radical Hindu-nationalist organization.
97. The author is a prominent foreign sympathizer of Hindutva.
98. It goes without saying that the scientific method involves amassing data or doing experiments to *test* a theory (or various competing theories), not to *prove* it! Indeed, some philosophers (e.g. Popper) have argued that the essence of the scientific method is the attempt to *falsify* theories. Frawley attempts to justify his final rather extraordinary claim by arguing that "as Einstein noted, it is the theory that determines what the facts are and where to look for them" (p. 20). But this is a vulgarization of Einstein's view. It is indubitably true that *some* theoretical presuppositions are needed to translate raw sensory data into presumed facts about the world, but these theoretical presuppositions need not (and ought not!) include *the particular theory under test*; furthermore, these presuppositions can themselves be subjected, at least in part, to independent experimental tests where needed. For a brief discussion of what the theory-ladenness of observation does and does not entail, see, e.g., Sokal and Bricmont (1998: 64–7).
99. In the idiosyncratic process of inventing scientific theories, all methods are in principle admissible – deduction, induction, analogy, intuition, and even hallucination – and the only real criterion is pragmatic. On the other hand, the justification of theories must be rational; otherwise, we would simply not be doing science.
100. The authors of this 950-page tome are candid about their goals:

> [We] are members of the Bhaktivedanta Institute, a branch of the International Society for Krishna Consciousness that studies the relationship between modern science and the world view expressed in the Vedic literature. This institute was founded by our spiritual master, His Divine Grace A. C. Bhaktivedanta Swami Prabhupāda. ... From the Vedic literature, we derive the idea that the human race is of great antiquity. ... [W]e expressed the Vedic idea in the form of a theory that various humanlike and apelike beings have coexisted for a long time.
>
> (Cremo and Thompson 1993: xxxvi)

Seven hundred and fifty pages later, they conclude that, indeed, "anatomically modern humans have coexisted with other primates for tens of millions of years" (p. 750). Nanda (2003: 119) comments that

> So far, this United States-based Vedic anti-Darwinism has not made significant inroads in India. Darwinism is not much of an issue in India, as it has never been able to displace the traditional Hindu cosmology in the first place. Creationism in India takes the form of giving a scientific gloss to the Hindu view of transmigration, karma, and cyclical time.

101. "We have won through to the recognition that there is only one science – that the laws of science do not change relative to our varying opinions or beliefs, cultures, or customs. ... Similarly, there is only one Truth, one Reality, to be discovered by humanity. There is not a distinct God, or Truth, for each of the world's religions, any more than there is a different Sun or Moon for astronomers of various nations" (Feuerstein *et al.* 1995: 278). Note also that Elst (2001: 8) decries postmodernism and claims to "restore objectivity."
102. See, e.g., Mukhyananda (1997: chapter 5) for a detailed statement. See also Frawley (1990: 20–3) and Feuerstein *et al.* (1995: 217–28, 272–85), among many others.
103. By the same "logic," David Beckham's and my ways of playing football are not only compatible but essentially identical, because both of us endeavor to score goals.
104. Hardcore poststructuralists are particularly assiduous in avoiding any whiff of essentialism, but neo-Gandhians and eco-feminists are more ambiguous. An extreme example of neo-Gandhian essentialism is provided in an essay by Ashis Nandy and Shiv

Visvanathan (1990: 158), who quote approvingly an author who writes: "to put women to do men's work is as foolish as to set Beethoven or a Wagner to do engine driving."

105. See Nanda (2003: 156–7) for a more detailed discussion.

106. Among Western supporters, Sandra Harding (1996: 21–2) is typical in urging the coexistence of "many, different, and in some respects conflicting representations of nature"; she insists that this does not lead to relativism but rather to "a borderlands epistemology that values the distinctive understandings of nature that different cultures have resources to generate." She does not explain the criteria by which these distinctive understandings are to be reconciled when they conflict, as she admits they will.

107. Meera Nanda, personal communication to the author, 15 January 2004.

108. For a detailed discussion of this principle of "epistemic charity," see Nanda (2003: chapter 5).

109. In the Western science-studies literature, assertions of this kind go back at least to Carolyn Merchant (1980).

110. See Nanda (2003: 95–103) for further discussion. As Nanda (2004) observes, "Most of the claims of superiority of 'holism' are unsubstantiated. On closer examination, they end up affirming pseudo-sciences involving disembodied spirit acting on matter through entirely unspecified mechanisms."

111. Meera Nanda, personal communication to the author, 14 January 2004.

112. *The Bible Code* (Drosnin 1997) was on the *New York Times* best-seller list (for non-fiction!) for thirteen weeks in the period June–September 1997, at one point reaching #3. The original claims about the encoding of future events in the book of Genesis can be found in Witztum *et al.* (1994). For a careful refutation, see McKay *et al.* (1999); see also the introduction by Kass (1999).

113. Nearly four centuries ago, Francis Bacon observed that

> Men fall in love with particular pieces of knowledge and thoughts: either because they believe themselves to be their authors and inventors; or because they have put a great deal of labour into them, and have got very used to them.

And again:

> Once a man's understanding has settled on something (either because it is an accepted belief or because it pleases him), it draws everything else also to support and agree with it. And if it encounters a larger number of more powerful countervailing examples, it either fails to notice them, or disregards them, or makes fine distinctions to dismiss and reject them, and all this with much dangerous prejudice, to preserve the authority of its first conceptions.

See Bacon 2000 [1620]: 46 (Aphorism 54) and 43 (Aphorism 46). Luckily, the social organization of the modern scientific community – which in most cases allows for reasonably open debate, in which even the ideas of great scientists can be challenged – ensures that the scientific community *as a whole* is more objective than any of its individual members. For further discussion of this point, see Haack (1998: 97–9, 104–9).

114. This view was notably promulgated by Carolyn Merchant (1980) and has since become the conventional wisdom not only among radical environmentalists but also among many feminists. For similar views, see Easlea (1981), Shiva (1989), and Plumwood (1993, 2002), among many others.

115. The currently available evidence is inconclusive as to whether the Palaeolithic extinctions of large mammals in the Americas and Australia were caused by human hunting, by climatic and environmental changes, or by some combination of the two (see, e.g., Bogucki 1999: 102–4). I thank Arne Jarrick for drawing my attention to this issue.

116. Some relevant essays are collected in Jenkins (1997). Among the vast literature on postmodernism in historiography, Evans (1997) and Zagorin (1999) give particularly illuminating and judicious analyses; both of them also provide extensive references to

earlier commentary. See also the reply to Zagorin by Jenkins (2000), and the rejoinder by Zagorin (2000).

The books by Appleby *et al.* (1994) and Windschuttle (1997) are also of considerable interest, although they suffer, in my view, from curiously complementary flaws. Appleby *et al.* are unfortunately somewhat superficial and confused in their treatment of the epistemology of science (chapter 5), which leads them to concede too much to weak critiques of science; they are consequently too soft on postmodernism (though they do begin and end their book by arguing strongly for the importance of truth in historical research). Windschuttle's discussion of the philosophy of science (chapter 7) is more detailed and solid, but it ultimately founders on his untenable claim that science seeks (and in some cases attains) not just well-founded objective knowledge but *certainty*. As a result, he gives short shrift to some legitimate ideas (e.g. moderate versions of the theory-ladenness of observation) that cast doubt on some traditional philosophies of science (e.g. logical positivism, Popperian falsificationism) but in no way undermine the objectivity of the scientific enterprise. For my own views on these matters, see Sokal and Bricmont (1998: chapter 4) and Bricmont and Sokal (2004a).

117. Particularly fascinating is the monograph of Spitzer (1996), who demonstrates that even hardcore postmodernists (e.g. Derrida) will put aside their declared philosophy and argue on the basis of *facts* (which they accuse their opponents of *distorting* or *misrepresenting*) when issues they consider important are at stake.

There is an extensive literature critically analysing Foucault's histories of madness, medicine, incarceration, and ideas: see, for example, Huppert (1974), Midelfort (1980, 1990, 1994, 1999), Megill (1987), Porter (1987, 1990), Gordon (1990), Scull (1990, 1992), Gutting (1994a, 1994b), and Jones and Porter (1994) for a variety of viewpoints.

Several chapters of Windschuttle (1997) are devoted to detailed analyses of case studies of postmodernist-oriented history, often to devastating effect (at least as regards the history of the Pacific). See also Hobsbawm (1990), Spiegel (2000), and Jarrick (2003) for analyses of specific instances of postmodernist-influenced historical work.

118. Feminist postmodernist Kelly Oliver (1989: 146) has explicitly advocated this sort of politicization of science:

> in order to be revolutionary, feminist theory cannot claim to describe what exists, or, "natural facts." Rather, feminist theories should be political tools, strategies for overcoming oppression in specific concrete situations. The goal, then, of feminist theory, should be to develop *strategic* theories – not true theories, not false theories, but strategic theories [italics in original].

But even if we put aside the obvious scientific and moral objections to this version of postmodernist doctrine, we are still left with the perennial problem of self-refutation: how can one know whether or not a theory is "strategic" except by asking whether it is *truly, objectively* efficacious in promoting one's declared political goals? The problems of truth and objectivity cannot be evaded so easily.

119. For further discussion of this point, along with examples from the science-studies literature, see Bricmont and Sokal (2000: 376–7).

120. For a sober (but ultimately caustic) evaluation of von Däniken's theories on ancient extraterrestrial visitors, see Feder (2002b: chapter 9).

121. Among the genuine facts are an eyewitness account of a Caesarean section in Uganda, at a time (1879) when successful Caesarean sections in Europe were still rare (Davies 1959); and a 2,000-year tradition of steel-making in Tanzania (Schmidt and Avery 1978; but see also Rehder 1986 and Avery and Schmidt 1986).

122. In a subsequent article, Harding moves the alleged discoveries back more than a thousand years: "Many of the observations that Galileo's telescope made possible were known to the Dogon peoples of West Africa more than 1,500 years earlier: either they had invented some sort of telescope, or they had extraordinary eyesight" (1994: 309).

123.For a refutation, see Ortiz de Montellano (1996: 566 and 570, note 32).
124.Shiva (1989: 58); Mies and Shiva (1993: chapter 11). It goes without saying that ancient traditions and modern indigenous beliefs should not be assumed, *a priori*, to be pure superstition; some of them may indeed constitute perfectly valid – indeed, perfectly *scientific* – knowledge of the local ecosystem. I merely insist that all the relevant empirical evidence needs to be weighed rationally, without prejudice or romanticism.
125.The chapter from which this quotation comes was written by Shiva.
126.See Dasgupta (1999) for a biography of J.C. Bose; and see Jitatmananda (1991) for a celebration of Bose's theories by a partisan of Vedanta.
127.Bizarrely, in this list of "rejected or marginal sciences," Aronowitz also includes "ecological and evolutionary biology" – a fact that would surely be news to most biologists.
128.Here they are referring to data collected by Michel Gauquelin in support of the astrological theory that there is a so-called "Mars effect" affecting the destiny of sports champions. See Benski *et al.* (1996) for a critical and detailed factual examination of this "Mars effect."
129.For some early examples, see the essays collected in Nowotny and Rose (1979) and Wallis (1979).
130.It is very important to distinguish between methodological relativism and various forms of philosophical relativism. Roughly speaking, methodological relativism is the precept that "the sociologist or historian should act as though the beliefs about reality of any competing groups being investigated are not caused by reality itself," while epistemological relativism is the claim that "one social group's way of justifying its knowledge is [always] as good as another's," and ontological relativism is the claim that "reality itself is different" for different social groups (Collins 2001: 184; see also Bricmont and Sokal 2001: 244, note 4). In the 1980s, statements implying epistemological relativism were fairly common in the science-studies literature; but nowadays most sociologists of science stress that they advocate only methodological relativism, not ontological or epistemological relativism. However, what they fail to do is to give a cogent argument in favor of methodological relativism; the appropriateness of a relativist methodology for sociologists of knowledge is largely taken for granted. By contrast, Bricmont and I (2001, 2004b) have argued that methodological relativism is unjustifiable *unless* one adheres to some form of philosophical relativism. For a detailed debate of this issue, see the various essays collected in Labinger and Collins (2001).
131.On Ross' approach, see especially Ross (1991: 8–9, 27–8). To his credit, Ross does address the question of scientific accuracy at least in passing (p. 29): "I do not believe that New Age culture has produced anything like a more consistently accurate account of the world than rationalist science."
132.However, it should be noted that Ross also makes an astute and cogent criticism of Fritjof Capra's *The Tao of Physics*:

> For those who want scientists to make their work more accountable to the nonexpert, Capra's analogy [between physicists and Zen students] is, in every respect, a step in the wrong direction. Far from demystifying the work of science, it elevates the scientific vocation beyond the status it already enjoys as a secularized Western priesthood. Ordinary language and everyday rationality are revealed as inadequate, archaic, and therefore redundant media of communication. When the words of the physicist begin to sound like a koan, the aim of explicating science in the vernacular to a nonexpert audience has been abandoned.

(ibid.: 44)

133.At one point, Hess does let his relativism slip: he admits that "the skeptically minded *rightly* reject the scientific solidity of much New Age discourse and practice" (Hess 1993: 175; italics added). But this is a rare lapse.
    It is worth noting that, despite his methodological relativism, Hess makes what is in my view a sensible psychological/sociological observation:

A large number of sincere people are exploring alternative approaches to questions of personal meaning, spirituality, healing, and paranormal experience in general. To the skeptic, their quest *may* [my italics] ultimately rest on a delusion, but debunking is hardly likely to be an effective rhetorical device for their rationalist project of getting the Other to recognize what appears to the skeptic as mistaken or magical thinking. Instead, if skeptics were to understand the world more from the perspective of their Others, then their attempts to educate and enlighten them might be more successful.

(ibid.: 158–9)

134. The idea that increasing the cultural and gender diversity of the scientific profession could, *in some cases* and *to some extent*, lead to more objective science (in addition to being a worthy social goal in its own right) ought not be rejected out of hand; in my view, it has some validity, most obviously in the social sciences and areas closely related to them (e.g. primatology) but conceivably also elsewhere. On the other hand, it also seems to me that the relevance of these considerations to the bulk of the natural sciences has been vastly overrated by some feminist and multiculturalist theorists. For moderate views on this question, see, e.g., Wylie (1992) and Brown (2001: 89, 184–7, 201–5).

135. A far more serious ethical question is raised when *children* are endangered on account of their parents' pseudoscientific beliefs (often but not always religiously based). In this case, I have no hesitation in insisting that the state impose the scientifically indicated best treatment, and if necessary undertake criminal prosecution for child abuse (or, in cases of avoidable death, negligent manslaughter) against recalcitrant parents and their accomplices. For a preliminary quantitative investigation of the incidence of this type of child abuse in the United States, resulting in the death of the child, see Asser and Swan (1998). For related statistical information concerning preventable illness short of death, see Salmon *et al*. (1999) and Feikin *et al*. (2000). Concerning the ethical and legal issues, see American Academy of Pediatrics (1997), Dwyer (2000), and Merrick (2003).

136. For instance, I have not mentioned the real danger when people with curable illnesses are diverted from effective treatments. And I have been worried enough about the harmful cultural effects of postmodernism to co-author a book criticizing it (Sokal and Bricmont 1998).

137. All data are from Gallup polls taken in the United States in 2001. Concerning "ESP or extrasensory perception," 50 percent "believe in," 20 percent "are not sure about," and 27 percent "don't believe in" (the remainder have "no opinion"). "That houses can be haunted": 42–16–41. "That people on Earth are sometimes possessed by the devil": 41–16–41. "Telepathy, or communication between minds without using the traditional five senses": 36–26–35. "Clairvoyance, or the power of the mind to know the past and predict the future": 32–23–45. "Astrology, or the position of the stars and planets can affect people's lives:" 28–18–52. "Channeling, or allowing a 'spirit-being' to temporarily assume control of a human body during a trance": 15–21–62. See Gallup (2002: 136–8).

Concerning creationism, the exact question was: "Which of the following statements comes closest to your views on the origin and development of human beings – human beings have developed over millions of years from less advanced forms of life, but God guided this process; human beings have developed over millions of years from less advanced forms of life, but God had no part in this process; or God created human beings pretty much in their present form at one time within the last 10,000 years or so?" The results were 37 percent developed with God, 12 percent developed without God, and 45 percent God created in present form (the remainder have "no opinion"). These results have been essentially stable for at least the past twenty years. See ibid. (52–4). A Gallup poll from 1982 also gave breakdowns by sex, race, education, region, age, income, religion, and community size. Differences by sex, race, region, income, and (surprisingly) religion were rather small (perhaps because evangelical Protestants and liberal Protestants were lumped together). By far the largest difference was by education: only 24 percent of college graduates supported creationism, compared with 49 percent of high-school graduates and 52 percent of those with a grade-school education. See Gallup (1983: 208–14).

138.Kull *et al.* (2003: 3–5, 2004: 3–5), reporting results of a series of PIPA/Knowledge Networks polls taken in the United States between February 2003 and March 2004.

Concerning Iraq and September 11, respondents were offered four choices: "Iraq was directly involved in carrying out the September 11th attacks"; "Iraq gave substantial support to al-Qaeda, but was not involved in the September 11th attacks"; "A few al-Qaeda individuals visited Iraq or had contact with Iraqi officials"; "There was no connection at all." The results averaged 21, 35, 30, and 8 percent, respectively, and have been quite stable (plus or minus only a few percent) over the whole period from February 2003 to March 2004. In an August 2003 *Washington Post* poll, respondents were asked: "How likely is it that Saddam Hussein was personally involved in the September 11th attacks?" 32 percent answered "very likely," 37 percent "somewhat likely," 12 percent "not very likely," and 3 percent "not at all likely."

Concerning Saddam Hussein and al-Qaeda, respondents were asked: "Is it your impression that the U.S. has or has not found clear evidence in Iraq that Saddam Hussein was working closely with the al-Qaeda terrorist organization?" Between June 2003 and March 2004, the results have varied in a narrow band from 43 to 52 percent yes, averaging to 48 percent.

Concerning weapons of mass destruction, respondents were asked: "Since the war with Iraq ended, is it your impression that the U.S. has or has not found Iraqi weapons of mass destruction?" The results have shown a gradual decline over time, from 34 percent in May 2003 to 15 percent in March 2004.

N.B.: I am writing this in August 2004. I do not exclude the possibility that U.S. troops might at some future date discover weapons of mass destruction in Iraq. But that could not retrospectively legitimate the belief that U.S. troops have *already* found such weapons.

139.The degree of validity (if any) of this conjecture is an empirical question that merits careful investigation by psychologists, sociologists, and educational researchers.

140.I thank Gerald Holton and Gerhard Sonnert for translating this quotation and the next two.

141.Ironically, a nearly identical assertion is made by Afrocentrist author Hunter Havelin Adams III (1983a: 32): "[S]cience cannot always spring from a universal or culturally independent base. It must be consistent with the essentials of its people's 'common sense.'" Alas, postmodernism makes strange bedfellows.

142.Gerhard Sonnert and Gerald Holton have kindly provided me with the following brief biography of Krieck:

> Ernst Krieck (1882–1946) was a fierce ideologist and voluble writer, Nazi since the early 1920s, but originally a teacher in a primary school (*Volksschule*). On 1 April 1934 he was appointed to the chair of Pedagogy and Philosophy at the University of Heidelberg; his subsequent rise was, at first, irresistible. In mid-1935, upon the dismissal of the philosopher Ernst Hoffmann, Krieck became co-head of the Philosophical Seminar, together with Karl Jaspers. On 30 September 1937, Jaspers was pushed out as having "Jewish connections," leaving Krieck as the sole head. Concurrently, in January 1937, Krieck was made rector (= president) of the University of Heidelberg. He remained as rector only until 1 October 1938, having submitted his resignation because his views on anthropology had annoyed Alfred Rosenberg. Krieck remained in the chair of Pedagogy and Philosophy, and wrote numerous books on National Socialist education.

143.The degree of validity of postmodernist ideas is, of course, a vast issue that goes far beyond the scope of this essay. It becomes particularly thorny because of the great diversity of ideas that go under the name of "postmodernism" (even within my rather restrictive definition). Some of my views on these matters can be found in Sokal and

360 Alan D. Sokal

Bricmont (1998, especially chapters 4 and 12) and Bricmont and Sokal (2004a). See also Haack (1998, 2003), Brown (2001), and Nanda (2003) for cogent critiques of postmodernist philosophical doctrines.

144. For an entertaining account of the proliferation of various types of woolly thinking in modern public life, see Wheen (2004).

145. For example, it is embarrassing nowadays to read what some eminent British scientists were writing in the 1930s about the new socialist commonwealth then being constructed under Stalin. Clearly, these authors' powerful and legitimate desires for a more just society overrode their trained scientific skepticism.

146. See Miller (2000: 262–5, 420–5) for the intriguing (although insufficiently fleshed-out) suggestion that the human propensity for creative but not necessarily factually accurate ideologies – as exemplified by the near-universality of religion in human society – may arise, at least in part, from sexual selection. See also Boyer (2001) and Atran (2002) for detailed analyses of religion through the lens of evolutionary psychology. I thank Helena Cronin for very interesting discussions on this issue.

147. Ideas similar to those in the preceding two paragraphs have been put forth by Levitt (1999, especially chapters 2, 4, and 14) and Wolpert (1993: chapter 1). Please note that there is no contradiction between this emphasis on the *psychological* impediments to accurate reasoning and the contention that, as a *logical* matter, the scientific method is nothing more or less than the deepest (to date) refinement of the rational attitude in everyday life (Sokal and Bricmont 1998: 56 *et seq.*; Bricmont and Sokal 2004a).

148. The phrase is due to Bertrand Russell (1961b: 531), who was speaking of nationalist and religious passions.

149. For those who may not remember: Heaven's Gate was a group, based in southern California, who believed that a spaceship traveling behind (or alongside) the comet Hale–Bopp would transport their liberated souls to heaven; thirty-nine members committed suicide in March 1997. For a history, see Daniels (1999, chapter 12); and for a fascinating "inside" ethnography, written before the mass suicide, see Balch (1995).

150. Some prominent exceptions are Dawkins (1987, 2003), Weinberg (1992), Levitt (1999), and Bricmont (1999).

151. The empirical data on scientists' religious beliefs are mixed. A recent survey shows that approximately 39 percent of U.S. scientists believe in "a God to whom one may pray in expectation of receiving an answer," while 45 percent disbelieve and 15 percent have no definite opinion (Larson and Witham 1997). On the other hand, among members of the National Academy of Sciences, belief dropped to 7 percent, with 72 percent disbelieving and 21 percent agnostic (Larson and Witham 1998). See also Iannaccone *et al.* (1998) and Brown (2003) for different viewpoints on the available evidence.

152. Most such arguments come, of course, from believers: see, for example, Barbour (1990), Peacocke (1990), and Polkinghorne (1991). A theologically more modest version is offered by physicist Freeman Dyson (2000), who describes himself as "a practicing Christian but not a believing Christian" (Dyson 2002: 6). A different argument in favor of the compatibility of science and religion – the so-called "non-overlapping magisteria" (NOMA) – comes from palaeontologist Stephen Jay Gould (1999), who calls himself an "agnostic" (p. 8) but who could perhaps more accurately be described as "an atheist bending over backwards far beyond the call of duty or sense" (Dawkins 2003: 252, note 89).

153. See Bricmont (1999) for a brief but devastating critique of four variants of the idea that science and religion are compatible; and see Dawkins (2003: 146–51) for a briefer but equally devastating critique of several of these variants. See also Kitcher (forthcoming) for a more detailed account of the multifaceted incompatibility between science and religion.

154. Well, I *thought* that this point was so obvious that no further explanation was needed! But since some readers of an early draft of this essay requested elaboration of points (1) and (2), let me try to provide it briefly.

Examples of (1) include alleged "miracles" of all types – both the ancient miracles recounted in the holy books and those purportedly occurring in modern life – and more generally, all the interventions by God(s), saints, angels, and sundry supernatural beings (e.g. in response to prayer) that, by definition, involve suspension or temporary modification of the ordinary laws of physics and biology.

Examples of (2) include alleged eye-witness observations taken at face value without being subjected to the critical scrutiny that is routinely practised by historians, jurors, and indeed all human beings in our daily lives; alleged historical accounts taken at face value without being subjected to the cross-checking of evidence that is routinely practised by historians and archaeologists; and alleged accounts of miracle cures, healing by prayer, etc. taken at face value without being subjected to the statistical tests routinely employed by medical researchers and epidemiologists.

155. Particularly noteworthy in this regard are the activities of the John Templeton Foundation, which makes grants (over a hundred each year) to promote

> work in which both science and religion are taken seriously in the quest to more fully understand reality. What can research tell us about God, about the nature of divine action in the world, about meaning and purpose? What spiritual insight can be gained from the way in which science unveils aspects of nature and of human creativity?

Special attention is given to subsidizing college courses in Science and Religion, which are diverse in detail but uniformly aimed at showing that science and religion are compatible (see Wertheim 1995 for a report by a supporter). In addition, the Foundation awards an annual Templeton Prize for Progress Toward Research or Discoveries about Spiritual Realities, valued at slightly over $1 million, which according to a Foundation press release "is the world's largest monetary annual award given to an individual":

> [T]his award is intended to encourage the concepts that resources and manpower are needed to accelerate progress in spiritual discoveries, which can help humans to learn over 100 fold more about divinity. . . . The Prize is intended to help people see the infinity of the Universal Spirit still creating the galaxies and all living things and the variety of ways in which the Creator is revealing himself to different people.

Recent recipients include physicist (and Anglican priest/theologian) John Polkinghorne, biochemist (and Anglican priest/theologian) Arthur Peacocke, and physicists Ian Barbour, Paul Davies and Freeman Dyson. (Quotations and information come from Templeton Foundation (2003).)

For a detailed statement of the Templeton credo, see Templeton and Herrmann (1989). For critiques of the Templeton Foundation's activities by scientists and others sharing a scientific world view, see Krauss (1999), MacIlwain (2000) and Brown (2000). For an amusing (but perfectly cogent) critique of the Templeton Foundation's wishy-washy theology from the perspective of Christian fundamentalism, see Grigg (2002) and Herrmann (2002).

Playing a similar (but possibly less lavish) role in the French-speaking world is the Université Interdisciplinaire de Paris (UIP), which is not in fact a university but an association that organizes conferences on science and religion and publishes a journal, *Convergences*. For further information on the UIP, along with a sharp critique, see Dubessy and Lecointre (2001).

13. Concluding observations

Garrett G. Fagan

If this book has demonstrated anything at all, it is that pseudoarchaeology and its allies in the pseudosciences represent an insidious cultural phenomenon. While professionals tend to scoff and dismiss, it would be more in their interest to understand and resist. In the hope of furthering such an effort, I bring together here those key points that strike me as particularly salient from the foregoing chapters. Other readers may draw their own conclusions.

First, pseudoarchaeology is not to be understood in isolation. It is related to the wider phenomenon of pseudohistory (see Chapters 9 and 11), and both pseudoarchaeology and pseudohistory are part of a broader pattern of pseudoscience (see Chapters 2 and 12). The principles and practices of pseudoarchaeology (as charted in the Introduction and Chapters 1 and 2) sit on the other side of a vast abyss from intellectually honest inquiry. Pseudoarchaeology therefore cannot be considered a real "alternative" to archaeology or viewed as a storehouse of good ideas in waiting, to echo Flemming in Chapter 2. Even as it dons the mantle of scholarship, it remains the very antithesis of rational analysis. In reality, it is a clearing-house for any number of magical, mythical, irrational, or more sinister motifs. While these motifs may be popular and psychologically appealing, that does not make them valid. Pseudoarchaeology is exactly what the moniker captures: a travesty and a sham.

Second, pseudoarchaeology is not restricted to fringe fantasies about pyramid-building extraterrestrials, antediluvian sunken civilizations, or entrepreneurial survivors of catastrophe bringing the light of high culture to the four corners of the globe. Chapters 7–9 pointedly illustrate the manner in which nationalistic impulses can demand that the past be rewritten to conform to predetermined agendas. There is nothing inevitable about this process, insofar as nations do not necessarily engage in the fantastical revision of their history (although some might disagree; see Kohl and Fawcett 1995), but when given free rein, a guiding nationalist ideology embeds an essential dishonesty at the heart of historical investigation: it requires that potentially productive avenues of inquiry be closed off as politically (or religiously or ideologically) unconscionable while others be favored solely on the basis of their alignment with the preferred agenda. Such attitudes fertilize the pseudoarchaeological weed.

In the past, European colonialists could not countenance that native "savages" had built impressive monuments without pale-skinned instructors to help them out. So it is disconcerting, even in books published today, to find talk of white, bearded "Viracochas" bringing the gift of civilization to the gormless natives of ancient Peru (to take but one example).[1] On the other side of the coin, modern jingoistic movements in postcolonial contexts often require that the national achievement remain "pure" and uncontaminated by "foreign" influences. Both phenomena afford glimpses at an ugly face of pseudoarchaeology, one that serves ethnocentric or even openly racist agendas (see Chapters 7, 9, and 12).[2] None of this is to claim that purveyors of pseudoarchaeology are inherently racist, but they may be unwitting vessels for messages with distinctly unattractive resonance. It is pertinent here that pseudoarchaeology is an outlet for ideas drawn from outdated scholarship, proposals that were originally formulated in different times, under less tolerant socio-cultural systems. In rehashing discredited ideas for the contemporary public, pseudoarchaeological screeds risk smuggling into the modern forum certain sets of assumptions best left in the past.

A good example of such assumptions is hyperdiffusionism, which is part of the furniture in most pseudoarchaeological scenarios. It is particularly prominent in those promoted by nationalist programs, since the favored nation can be presented as the crucible of regional high achievement, or worse, of global civilization. The supposition here is that only one nation or people originated great things, which then diffused to the less creative populations. The direction of the alleged hyperdiffusion is irrelevant; the initial assumption is what matters. Thus the Egyptians actually got their pyramids from the Greeks, or vice versa (see Chapter 8); Hindu India is the font of all worthwhile culture (see Chapter 9); or, perhaps less aggressively, the Celts conveniently provide Europeans with a shared ancestry at a time when the continent is seeking greater integration (see Chapter 7). Other movements naturally spring to mind, such as Afrocentrism, the contention that white Europeans "stole" their culture from black Africans – as if culture were some unitary commodity that can be packaged and pilfered by one people at the expense of another. (Acculturation is in fact far more complex than that, and it is never completely unidirectional.) Another example is the notion of a prehistoric, matriarchal, and egalitarian paradise presided over by a Mother Goddess, which was subsequently overthrown by hierarchical and patriarchal societies worshiping male deities. (But why should the gender of a deity reflect anything about how a society functions?) While we may empathize with the desire of the marginalized to have their voices heard in the halls of history, it is surely very much in their interests that the content of their claims be valid and verifiable rather than dubious or demonstrably false. The truth is surely preferable to the snake-oil promises of ideological myth-making, whether it be nationalistic, or ethnic-, race- or gender-oriented, and no matter how temporarily uplifting or edifying the myth may seem. All peoples have contributed to the vast tapestry of the human experience; to assign to only one the role of sole designer and weaver is pure hubris.

Third, the public appeal of pseudoarchaeology is a multifaceted cultural and psychological phenomenon. A variety of cognitive styles and sociological processes are at work in driving some intellectually curious persons into the arms of the pseudohistorical gurus (see Chapters 2–4). Individual differences certainly play a central role, in that pseudoscientific scenarios will tend to appeal to fantasy-prone personalities and to those who adopt a suspicious stance with regard to the "establishment," usually conceived in monolithic terms. Conspiratorial thinking is often rife among people like this, who can readily convince themselves that they are the true skeptics and questioners, that they alone have the inside track, while lamenting that everyone else is hoodwinked by the ivory tower and its dark-suited backers in government. But the problem far outstrips such individual outlooks. Wider cultural trends – distrust of science and reason as a whole, heightened public religiosity, rising fundamentalism, to name a few – influence the attitudes of many who are not necessarily fantasy-prone conspiracy theorists (see Chapter 11). Another facet of the problem is the long-recognized public relations problem of "liberal science," broadly defined. Rational scholarship of the sort conducted by university scholars of all stripes is too often seen by the public as elitist, coldly arrogant, and utterly convinced of its own omniscience. There appears, then, to be a nexus of psychological and socio-cultural factors that renders the field of public perception fertile ground for conmen, charlatans, and the purveyors of nonsense. Only some of these factors have been explored here; more work needs to be done on this important issue.

Fourth, the complicity of professional archaeologists in the promulgation of pseudoarchaeology, even if largely unintentional, is better acknowledged than denied. I am not thinking here of the less than glorious past of the discipline, when frankly racist ideas were embraced in accordance with the tenor of the times. Rather, as Webster (Chapter 6) shows and Jordan (Chapter 5) implies, when it suits their cause, professionals today are not slow to exploit the "mysteries" and "wonders" and "treasures" of ancient cultures. Whether they do so for the public in front of the cameras or in print to impress potential funders, such actions play directly into the hands of the mystery-mongers and cranks who populate the pseudoarchaeological zoo. The public comes to expect archaeology to be all about spectacularly rich, history-altering discoveries, unsolved mysteries, and the promise of ancient wisdom – precisely the obsessions of the fringe. In fact, everyday archaeology is far more mundane than this, and often the most interesting and far-reaching conclusions are drawn from the drabbest of sources. For instance, hugely important inferences have been made about the onset of a sedentary lifestyle in the Levant by a team working at Abu Hureyra in Syria.

Examination of 12,000-year-old cereal grains from the site suggested that drought forced hunter-gatherers to start planting grain-yielding grasses to fend off starvation. If this is right, agriculture may have been an accident, a byproduct of urgency (Harris and Hillman 1989; Moore *et al.* 2000). A further inference is that the emergence of civilization in the Levant, itself dependent on agriculture, was not some step on a ladder of inevitable progress but an unintended consequence of a series of contingencies. It is an intriguing possibility.

But how many people on the street have ever heard of Abu Hureyra or, indeed, appreciate the importance of palaeobotany (or palaeozoology) to an understanding of prehistory? Ways must be found to make such fascinating discoveries suffuse into the public consciousness. Chris Hale (Chapter 10) gives us the key: narrative. We do not need Indiana Jones battling natives and Nazis to make archaeology good stuff for the general public. If material is presented in such a way that a gripping tale is told, in which the chain of archaeological reasoning is in effect a character in the plot, discoveries like those at Abu Hureyra can be presented as compelling narrative. This can be done well without cheapening, let alone bastardizing, either the products or the process of rational analysis. Good examples are at hand, even on television (Fagan 2003). In the printed realm, effective popularizers of archaeology are in some ways the front-line forces against irrational "alternative" archaeology. They present stimulating ideas founded on solid evidence and sound reasoning to the general public in synthesized and distilled form. They ought to be encouraged and supported by the profession – too often they are looked at askance – in order to further their efforts and to spread as widely as possible reliable rather than fantastical information.

Fifth, and finally, it seems clear that commitment to pseudoscience (including pseudoarchaeology) is essentially a political rather than an intellectual act. This crucial fact is what binds together the disparate forms of pseudoarchaeology and pseudoscience surveyed in the preceding chapters. For nationalists, co-religionists, and fellow ideologues, political cohesiveness comes naturally and can readily reinforce (and be reinforced by) pseudoarchaeological speculations. A sturdy sense of victimhood facilitates the process. The fundamentally *political* allegiance of believers to truly fringe constructions of the past means that no amount of argument over facts, evidence, or method is likely to dent the resolve of the committed (although fence-sitters might be swayed). Their political allegiance to the visionary underdog of their choice has been vaccinated against reasoned critique by the conviction that academics are untrustworthy dogmatists, priestly inquisitors of a Church of Science and/or conspirators seeking to hide the dreadful truth about the past from the public. In the nationalist and ideological arenas, critics can be even more readily dismissed by sloganeering: they are "unpatriotic," "neo-colonialist," "Marxist," "racist" – whatever label applies. By thus shifting the argument from the rational and evidentiary plane to the political, promulgators of pseudoscience immunize their claims against serious scrutiny. Argument rages over a critic's alleged motives; the claims themselves stand unexamined.

I myself have experienced first-hand and repeatedly in discussion groups on the Internet how this process plays out. I provide only one example. In February 2004, my 20,000-word critique of Robert Schoch's book *Voyages of the Pyramid Builders* (2003) was posted at the *In the Hall of Ma'at* website. The *first* reaction of Professor Schoch's webmaster, Steve LeMaster, was a single paragraph of seventy-two words in which he alleged that my review (1) stemmed from dogmatic closed-mindedness, (2) spearheaded an inquisition, and (3) was motivated by book sale envy. In other words, the reaction was wholly and completely political. Not a word was addressed to any of the substantive points raised in the review about Schoch's highly implausible scenario for ancient history founded on serious misrepresentations, factual errors, and crude methods. LeMaster, rather, was playing to the peanut gallery, and task number one was to get the politics sorted out. In reactions to my review posted on "alternative" websites, true believers duly rehashed the familiar themes *ad nauseam* – I was closed-minded, self-serving, fearful for my job, envious, a member of the academic club or cabal, and so on. Anything was discussed except substance. John Anthony West subsequently posted what he claimed to be a more considered response, but in the first paragraphs he set about the issue of my motives and liberally salted his text with the *ad hominem* puerilities one expects from this source.[3]

On other occasions, I have witnessed campaigns of personal vilification orchestrated against critics by the gurus themselves, using all the political tricks in the book to play to their enthralled followers. The level of sheer cheapness reached in these campaigns defies analysis. As a last resort, threats of legal action for supposed "defamation of character" can be leveled against those with the temerity to question the open-minded seekers after hidden mysteries. A not dissimilar process is revealed in the reaction of "alternative" writers Graham Hancock and Robert Bauval to the BBC *Horizon* program critical of their ideas (see Chapter 10). Again and again, their actions and reactions are political and have nothing to say about history, archaeology, or honest methods of inquiry. This is hardly surprising, since the chief objective of pseudoarchaeological spin is to energize the political base. Since their cases are so terribly weak and open to criticism, it is far easier for them to shoot the messenger than deal with the message.

In all this, the believers usually cheer one another on. It may have to be accepted, however reluctantly, that the most committed have to be abandoned to the clutching mud of the pseudoscientific swamp. But the situation is not entirely hopeless. Feder (Chapter 3) shows us that undergraduate students, at least, are not powerfully devoted to pseudoarchaeological fantasies. And as Reece documents in her personal memoir (Chapter 4), if the gurus can be goaded into showing their true colors, if their followers can awaken to their question-dodging, evidence-evading tactics, some, but by no means all, may find themselves questioning the basis for their allegiance. For the allegiance has to be broken before the hard data can be allowed in. To be sure, it takes an act of courage to admit to having been hoodwinked. The door thus opened can be stepped through – or slammed shut and bolted tight. That choice ultimately lies in the hands of the devotee. The primary role of professionals in this process may be to do what they do best – ask the hard questions, probe, and expose. Critique, after all, is the heart and soul of true scholarship.

Notes

1. "Our route took us through the towns of Puccarini and Laha [in Peru], populated by stolid Aymara Indians who walked slowly in the narrow cobbled streets and sat placidly in the little sunlit plazas. Were these people the descendants of the builders of Tihuanaco, as the scholars insisted? Or were the legends right? Had the ancient city been the work of foreigners with godlike powers who had settled here, long ages ago?" (Hancock 1995: 71).

2. It is highly instructive – and supremely ironic – that modern "native" nationalisms should employ investigative methods analogous to those of their erstwhile colonial oppressors. The methods of pseudoarchaeology are useful to propagandists, regardless of their specific agendas.

3. My review of Schoch 2003 is here: http://www.thehallofmaat.com/article79.html. LeMaster's reaction ran as follows: "Fascinating how science, which is about asking questions, following the data where it leads, not discarding that data out of hand, no matter if said evidence flies in the face of possibly upsetting any reigning paradigms, has been redefined here at, what was at one time an open forum, to the Inquisition. I also noticed that *Public Bathing in Rome* [sic] hasn't changed too much in Amazon.com rankings, is the real issue here [sic]?"; it can be read online at http://www.thehallofmaat.com/ post187440.html. West's reaction is available at http://www.thehallofmaat.com/ post191498.html.

Bibliography

Note: original publication dates for older works are cited in square brackets. Works of pseudo-archaeology are often published and republished in different places by different publishing houses; page numbers may therefore diverge from those cited in the text.

Abrams, E. (1994) *How the Maya Built their World*. Austin: University of Texas Press.

Abu el-Haj, N. (2001) *Facts on the Ground: Archaeological Practice and Territorial Self-fashioning in Israeli Society*. Chicago: University of Chicago Press.

Achar, B.N. (1999) "On exploring the Vedic sky with modern computer software." *Electronic Journal of Vedic Studies* 5-2. Available at http://users.primushost.com/~india/ejvs/issues.html.

—(2003) "The date of Mahabharatha war based on simulation using Planetarium software." Paper presented at International Colloquium on the date of the Kurukshetra War, based on astronomical data, held in Bangalore on 5–6 January 2003. Available at http://www.hindunet.org/saraswati/colloquium/colloquium01.htm and http://www.hindunet.org/saraswati colloquium/narahari01.htm.

Ackermann, J. (1970) *Hitler als Ideologe*. Göttingen: Musterschmidt.

Adams, H.H., III (1983a) "African observers of the universe: the Sirius question," in I. van Sertima (ed.), *Blacks in Science: Ancient and Modern*. New Brunswick, NJ: Transaction Books.

—(1983b) "New light on the Dogon and Sirius," in I. van Sertima (ed.), *Blacks in Science: Ancient and Modern*. New Brunswick, NJ: Transaction Books.

Aiyar, S.R. (1922–23, reprinted 1975) *Dravidian Theories*. Chennai: Madras Law Journal Office.

al-'Azm, S. (1982) "A criticism of religious thought," in J.J. Donohue and J.L. Esposito (eds), *Islam in Transition: Muslim Perspectives*. Oxford: Oxford University Press; excerpted and translated from *Naqd al-Fikr al-Dini* (A criticism of religious thought), Beirut: Dar al-Tali'ah, 1969.

Alekseev, G.V., Kondratov, A.M. and Volchok, B.Y. (1969) *Soviet Studies on Harappan Script*, translated by H. Chandra Pande, edited by H. Field and E.M. Laird, Coconut Grove: Field Research Projects.

Allchin, B. and Allchin, F.R. (1982) *The Rise of Civilization in India and Pakistan*. Cambridge: Cambridge University Press.

Allchin, F.R. (1995) *The Archaeology of Early Historic South Asia: The Emergence of Cities and States*. Cambridge: Cambridge University Press.

Allen, S.H. (1999) *Finding the Walls of Troy: Frank Calvert and Heinrich Schliemann at Hisarlik*. Berkeley: University of California Press.

Alligood, M.R. and Marriner-Tomey, A. (2002) *Nursing Theory: Utilization and Application*, 2nd edn. St Louis: Mosby.

Alvares, C. (1988) "Science, colonialism and violence: a Luddite view," in A. Nandy (ed.), *Science, Hegemony and Violence: A Requiem for Modernity*. Tokyo: United Nations University and Delhi: Oxford University Press.

—(1992) *Science, Development and Violence: The Revolt against Modernity*. Delhi: Oxford University Press.

American Academy of Pediatrics, Committee on Bioethics (Frader, J.E. *et al.*) (1997) "Religious objections to medical care." *Pediatrics* 99(2): 279–81.

Anderson, B. (1983) *Imagined Communities: Reflections on the Origin and Spread of Nationalism*. London: Verso.

Andrews, G. (1975) *Maya Cities: Placemaking and Urbanization*. Norman: University of Oklahoma Press.

Anthony, D. (1995) "Horse, wagon and chariot: Indo-European languages and archaeology." *Antiquity* 69: 554–65.

Anthony, D. and Brown, D.R. (2000) "Neolithic horse exploitation in the Eurasian steppes: diet, ritual and riding." *Antiquity* 74: 75–86.

Anttila, R. (1989) *Historical and Comparative Linguistics*. Amsterdam and Philadelphia: John Benjamins.

Appleby, J.O., Hunt, L.A. and Jacob, M.C. (1994) *Telling the Truth about History*. New York: W.W. Norton.

Aravaanan, K.P. (1980) *Anthropological Studies on the Dravido-Africans*. Chennai: Tamil Kootam.

Armillas, P. (1951) "Mesoamerican fortifications." *Antiquity* 25: 77–86.

Arnold, B. (1990) "The past as propaganda: totalitarian archaeology in Nazi Germany." *Antiquity* 64(244): 464–78.

—(1992) "The past as propaganda: how Hitler's archaeologists distorted European prehistory to justify racist and territorial goals." *Archaeology*, July/August: 30–7.

—(1998) "The power of the past: nationalism and archaeology in 20th century Germany." *Archaeologia Polona* 35/36: 237–53.

—(1999) "The contested past." *Anthropology Today* 15(4): 1–4.

—(2002) "Justifying genocide: the supporting role of archaeology in 'ethnic cleansing'," in A. Hinton (ed.), *Annihilating Difference: The Anthropology of Genocide*. Berkeley: University of California Press.

—(2004) "Dealing with the devil: the Faustian bargain of archaeology under dictatorship," in M. Galaty (ed.), *Archaeology Under Dictatorship*, New York: Kluwer.

Aronowitz, S. (1988) *Science as Power: Discourse and Ideology in Modern Society*. Minneapolis: University of Minnesota Press.

—(1996) "The politics of the science wars." *Social Text*, 46–7: 177–97; reprinted in A. Ross (ed.), *Science Wars*. Durham, NC: Duke University Press.

Asser, S.M. and Swan, R. (1998) "Child fatalities from religion-motivated medical neglect." *Pediatrics* 101(4): 625–9.

Assmann, J. (2000) *Weisheit und Mysterium: Das Bild der Griechen von Ägypte*. Munich: C.H. Beck.

Atkinson, J.A., Banks, I. and O'Sullivan, J. (eds) (1996) *Nationalism and Archaeology: Scottish Archaeological Forum*. Glasgow: Cruithne Press.

Atran, S. (2002) *In Gods We Trust: The Evolutionary Landscape of Religion*. New York: Oxford University Press.

Aveni, A. (1990) *The Lines of Nazca*. Philadelphia: American Philosophical Society.

Avery, D.H. and Schmidt, P.R. (1986) "The use of preheated air in ancient and recent African iron smelting furnaces: a reply to Rehder." *Journal of Field Archaeology* 13: 354–7.

Bacon, F. (2000 [1620]) *The New Organon*, edited by L. Jardine and M. Silverthorne. Cambridge: Cambridge University Press.

Bahcall, J. (1990) "The solar-neutrino problem." *Scientific American*, May: 54–61.

Bainbridge, W.S. (1978) "Chariots of the gullible." *The Skeptical Inquirer: The Zetetic* 3(2): 33–48.

Baines, J. (1996) "The aims and methods of *Black Athena*," in M.R. Lefkowitz and G.M. Rogers (eds), *Black Athena Revisited*. Chapel Hill: University of North Carolina Press.

Bala, S. (2004) "Year of Mahabharata." *The Pioneer*, 26 February. Available at http://www.dailypioneer.com/archives2/default12.asp?main_variable = OPED&file_name = opd1%2Etxt&counter_img = 1&phy_path_it = %5C%5C1u%5Cdailypioneer%5Carchives 2%5Cfeb2604.

Balaram, P. (2001) "The astrology fallout." *Current Science* (India) 80(9): 1085–6.

Balch, R.W. (1995) "Waiting for the ships: disillusionment and the revitalization of faith in Bo and Peep's UFO cult," in J.R. Lewis (ed.) *The Gods Have Landed: New Religions from Other Worlds*. Albany: State University of New York Press.

Bamshad, M. *et al.* (1998) "Female gene flow stratifies Hindu castes." *Nature* 395: 651–2.

—(2001) "Genetic evidence on the origins of Indian caste populations." *Genome Research* 11: 994–1004.

Barber, R. (1995) *Blue Guide to Greece*. New York: W.W. Norton.

Barbour, I.G. (1990) *Religion in an Age of Science*. San Francisco: Harper & Row.

Barker, G. and Grant, A. (1999) *Companion Encyclopedia of Archaeology*. London: Routledge.

Barker, P. (1994) *Techniques of Archaeological Investigation*, 3rd edn. London: Batsford.

Barnes, B. and Bloor, D. (1981) "Relativism, rationalism and the sociology of knowledge," in M. Hollis and S. Lukes (eds), *Rationality and Relativism*. Oxford: Basil Blackwell.

Barnes, B., Bloor, D. and Henry, J. (1996) *Scientific Knowledge: A Sociological Analysis*. Chicago: University of Chicago Press.

Barrett, E.A.M. (ed.) (1990) *Visions of Rogers' Science-Based Nursing*. New York: National League for Nursing.

Barrett, E.A.M. and Malinski, V.M. (eds) (1994) *Martha E. Rogers: 80 Years of Excellence*. New York: Society of Rogerian Scholars Press.

Barta, T. (1998) "Film Nazis: the Great Escape," in T. Barta (ed.), *Screening the Past: Film and the Representation of History*. New York: Praeger.

—(ed.) (1998) *Screening the Past: Film and the Representation of History*. New York: Praeger.

Basu, A. *et al.* (2003) "Ethnic India: a genomic view, with special reference to peopling and structure." *Genome Research* 13: 2277–90.

Bauval, R.G. (1989) "A master-plan for the three pyramids of Giza based on the configuration of the three stars of the belt of Orion." *Discussions in Egyptology* 13: 7–18.

—(2000) "Open letter." Graham Hancock Message Board, online posting. Available at http://www.grahamhancock.com/phorum/read.php?f = 1&i = 2068&t = 2068.

Bauval, R.G. and Gilbert, A. (1994) *The Orion Mystery: Unlocking the Secrets of the Pyramids*. London: Arrow Books.

Becker, M. (1979) "Priests, peasants, and ceremonial centers: the intellectual history of a model," in N. Hammond and G.R. Willey (eds), *Maya Archaeology and Ethnohistory*. Austin: University of Texas Press.

—(1984) *Theories of Ancient Maya Social Structure*. Occasional Publications in Anthropology no. 53, Museum of Anthropology, Greeley: University of Northern Colorado.

Beekes, R.S.P. (1995) *Comparative Indo-European Linguistics: An Introduction*. Amsterdam/Philadelphia: J. Benjamins.

Belchem, J. (2000) "The little Manx nation: antiquarianism, ethnic identity, and home rule politics in the Isle of Man, 1880–1918." *Journal of British Studies* 39(2): 217–40.

Benedict, J. (2003) *No Bone Unturned*. New York: HarperCollins.

Benski, C. *et al*. (1996) *The Mars Effect: A French Test of over 1,000 Sports Champions*. Amherst, NY: Prometheus Books.

Ben-Yehuda, N. (1995) *The Masada Myth: Collective Memory and Mythmaking in Israel*. Madison: University of Wisconsin Press.

Berger, R.L. (1990) "Nazi science – the Dachau hypothermia experiments." *New England Journal of Medicine* 322: 1435–40.

Bergunder, M. (2002) "Umkämpfte Vergangenheit. Anti-brahmanische und hindu-nationalistische Rekonstruktionen der frühen indischen Religionsgeschichte," in M. Bergunder and R.P. Das (eds), *"Arier" und "Draviden." Konstruktion der Vergangenheit als Grundlage für Selbst- und Fremdwahrnehmungen Südasiens*. Halle: Verlag der Frankeschen Stiftungen zu Halle.

Bergunder, M. and Das, R.P. (eds) (2002) *"Arier" und "Draviden." Konstruktion der Vergangenheit als Grundlage für Selbst- und Fremdwahrnehmungen Südasiens*. Halle: Verlag der Frankeschen Stiftungen zu Halle.

Bernal, M. (1987, 1991) *Black Athena: The Afroasiatic Roots of Classical Civilization*, Vols 1 and 2. New Brunswick, NJ: Rutgers University Press.

—(2001) *Black Athena Writes Back: Martin Bernal Responds to his Critics*, edited by David Chioni Moore. Durham, NC: Duke University Press.

Beyerstein, B.L. (1999) "Social and judgmental biases that make inert treatments seem to work." *Scientific Review of Alternative Medicine*, 3(2): 20–33.

—(2001) "Alternative medicine and common errors of reasoning." *Academic Medicine* 76(3): 230–7.

Bharatiya Vidya Bhavan: see Majumdar 1951.

Bidwai, P. (2001) "Hindutva ire." *Frontline* (India) 18(25), 8 December.

Binford, L. (1977) "General introduction." in L. Binford (ed.), *For Theory Building in Archaeology*. New York: Academic Press.

Bishop, J.P., Koenig, H.D. and Stenger, V. (2004) "Retroactive prayer: lots of history, not much mystery, and no science." *British Journal of Medicine*, 329: 1444–6

Black, S.L. (1990) "Field methods and methodologies in lowland Maya archaeology." PhD dissertation, Harvard University.

Blavatsky, H.P. (1888 [1971]) *The Secret Doctrine: The Synthesis of Science, Religion and Philosophy*, 6th edn, 6 vols. Chennai: Theosophical Publishing House.

—(1931) *Isis Unveiled*. Los Angeles: Theosophy.

Boese, A. (2002) *The Museum of Hoaxes*. New York: Dutton.

Bogucki, P. (1999) *The Origins of Human Society*. Malden, UK: Basil Blackwell.

Bohm, D. (1951) *Quantum Theory*. New York: Prentice Hall.

—(1952) "A suggested interpretation of the quantum theory in terms of 'hidden' variables, I and II." *Physical Review* 85: 166–79 and 180–93.

—(1980) *Wholeness and the Implicate Order*. London: Routledge & Kegan Paul.

Borelli, M.D. and Heidt, P. (eds) (1981) *Therapeutic Touch: A Book of Readings*. New York: Springer.

Bowman, M. (2002) "Contemporary Celtic spirituality," in J. Pearson (ed.), *Belief Beyond Boundaries: Wicca, Celtic Spirituality and the New Age*. Milton Keynes: Open University Press.

Boyer, P. (2001) *Religion Explained: The Evolutionary Origins of Religious Thought*. New York: Basic Books.

Brainerd, G. (1954) *The Maya Civilization*. Los Angeles: Los Angeles Southwest Museum.

Breckenridge, C.A. and van der Veer, P. (eds) (1993) *Orientalism and the Postcolonial Predicament: Perspectives on South Asia*. Philadelphia: University of Pennsylvania Press.

Brennan, P. (1999) "Homeopathic remedies in prenatal care." *Journal of Nurse-Midwifery* 44(3): 291–9.

Bricmont, J. (1999) "Science et religion: l'irréductible antagonisme," in A. Pickels and J. Sojcher (eds), *Où va Dieu?* Revue de l'Université de Bruxelles, Editions Complexe; reprinted in *Agone* 23 (2000): 131–51; and in J. Dubessy and G. Lecointre (eds), *Intrusions spiritualistes et impostures: intellectuelles en sciences*. Paris: Editions Syllepse (2001).

Bricmont, J. and Sokal, A.D. (2000) "Authors' response [to David Turnbull, Henry Krips, Val Dusek and Steve Fuller]." *Metascience* 9(3): 372–95.

—(2001) "Science and sociology of science: beyond war and peace," in J. Labinger and H. Collins (eds), *The One Culture? A Conversation about Science*. Chicago: University of Chicago Press.

—(2004a) "Defense of a modest scientific realism." in M. Carrier, J. Roggenhofer, G. Küppers and P. Blanchard (eds), *Knowledge and the World: Challenges beyond the Science Wars*. Berlin/Heidelberg: Springer.

—(2004b) "Reply to Gabriel Stolzenberg." *Social Studies of Science* 34(1): 107–13.

Broch, H. (1992) *Au Coeur de l'extraordinaire*. Bordeaux: L'Horizon Chimérique.

Bronkhorst, J. and Deshpande, M. (eds) (1999) *Aryan and Non-Aryan in South Asia: Evidence, Interpretation and Ideology*. Cambridge, Mass.: Harvard Oriental Series, Opera Minora, Vol. 3.

Brown, C.M. (2003) "The conflict between religion and science in light of the patterns of religious belief among scientists." *Zygon* 38(3): 603–32.

Brown, H.A. (1966) *Cataclysms of the Earth*. New York: Twayne.

Brown, J.R. (2000) "Privatizing the university: the new tragedy of the commons." *Science* 290: 1701–2.

—(2001) *Who Rules in Science? An Opinionated Guide to the Wars*. Cambridge, Mass.: Harvard University Press.

Brunhouse, R.L. (1971) *Sylvanus G. Morley and the World of the Ancient Maya*. Norman: University of Oklahoma Press.

Bryant, E.F. (1999) "Linguistic substrata and the indigenous Aryan debate," in J. Bronkhorst and M. Deshpande (eds), *Aryan and Non-Aryan in South Asia: Evidence, Interpretation and Ideology*. Cambridge, Mass.: Harvard Oriental Series, Opera Minora, Vol. 3.

—(2001) *The Quest for the Origins of Vedic Culture: The Indo-Aryan Migration Debate*. Oxford: Oxford University Press.

—(2002) "Disput um die Vergangenheit. Indoarische Ursprünge und moderner nationalistischer Diskurs," in M. Bergunder and R.P. Das (eds), *"Arier" und "Draviden." Konstruktion der Vergangenheit als Grundlage für Selbst- und Fremdwahrnehmungen Südasiens*. Halle: Verlag der Frankeschen Stiftungen zu Halle.

Burle, A. (1999) *Great Stone Circles: Fables, Fictions, Facts*. New Haven, Conn.: Yale University Press.

Burnham, J.C. (1987) *How Superstition Won and Science Lost: Popularizing Science and Health in the United States*. New Brunswick, NJ: Rutgers University Press.

Butcher, H.K. (1999) "Rogerian ethics: an ethical inquiry into Rogers's life and science." *Nursing Science Quarterly* 12(2): 111–18.

Callahan, D. (ed.) (2002) *The Role of Complementary and Alternative Medicine: Accommodating Pluralism*. Washington: Georgetown University Press.

Campbell, B.F. (1980) *Ancient Wisdom Revived: A History of the Theosophical Movement*. Berkeley: University of California Press.

Capra, F. (1975) *The Tao of Physics: An Exploration of the Parallels between Modern Physics and Eastern Mysticism*. Berkeley: Shambhala.

Carew, M. (2003) *Tara and the Ark of the Covenant: A Search for the Ark of the Covenant by British Israelites on the Hill of Tara*. Dublin: RIA/Discovery Programme.

Carlson, M. (1993) *"No Religion Higher than Truth"*: A *History of the Theosophical Movement in Russia, 1875–1922*. Princeton, NJ: Princeton University Press.

Carr, E.H. (1961) *What Is History?* New York: Vintage Books.

Cassidy, C.M. (2001) "Social and cultural context of complementary and alternative medicine systems," in M.S. Micozzi (ed.), *Fundamentals of Complementary and Alternative Medicine*, 2nd edn. Philadelphia: Churchill Livingstone.

Castro, M. (1999) "Homeopathy: a theoretical framework and clinical application." *Journal of Nurse-Midwifery* 44(3): 280–90.

Cavalli-Sforza, L.L. and Cavalli-Sforza, F. (1995) *The Great Human Diasporas: The History of Diversity and Evolution*. Reading, Mass.: Helix Books.

Cavalli-Sforza, L.L., Menozzi, P. and Piazza, A. (1994) *The History and Geography of Human Genes*. Princeton, NJ: Princeton University Press.

Cayce, E.E. (1997) *Mysteries of Atlantis Revisited*. New York: St Martin's Paperbacks.

Chakrabarti, D.P. (1997) *Colonial Indology: Sociopolitics of the Ancient Indian Past*. New Delhi: Munshiram Manoharlal.

Chantraine, P. (1984) *Dictionnaire étymologique de la langue Grécque*. Paris: Klincksieck.

Chatters, J. (2001) *Ancient Encounters: Kennewick Man and the First Americans*. New York: Simon & Schuster.

Chattopadhyaya, B. (1998) *Representing the Other? Sanskrit Sources and the Muslims*. New Delhi: Manohar.

Chengappa, R. (2002) "The lost civilisation." *India Today*, 11 February: 80–90.

Childress, D.H. (1988) *Lost Cities of Ancient Lemuria and the Pacific*. Stelle, Ill.: Adventures Unlimited Press.

Chippindale, C. (1983) *Stonehenge Complete*. London: Thames & Hudson.

Chomsky, N. (1972) *Problems of Knowledge and Freedom*. London: Fontana/Collins.

Choudhury, P. (1990) *Indian Origin of the Chinese Nation: A Challenging, Unconventional Theory of the Origin of the Chinese*. Calcutta: Dasgupta and Co.

——(1993) *The Aryans: A Modern Myth. Part I: A Story of a Treacherous Theory that Concerns Every Indian. A book that offers many things to think anew*. New Delhi: Eastern Publishers' Distributor.

Churchward, J. (1931) *Atlantis Rising: The Lost Continent of Mu*. New York: Ives Washburn.

Cody, W.K. (2000) "Paradigm shift or paradigm drift? A meditation on commitment and transcendence." *Nursing Science Quarterly* 13(2): 93–102.

Coe, M. (1956) "The funerary temple among the Classic Maya." *Southwestern Journal of Anthropology* 12: 387–94.

——(1957) "The Khmer settlement pattern: a possible analogy with that of the Maya." *American Antiquity* 22(4): 409–10.

——(1999) *Breaking the Maya Code*, revised edn. London: Thames & Hudson.

Coe, W. (1967) *Tikal: A Handbook of the Ancient Maya Ruins*. Philadelphia: University Museum, University of Pennsylvania.

Cole, J.R. (1979) "Incriptionmania, hyperdiffusionism and the public: fallout from a 1977 meeting." *Man in the Northeast* 17: 27–53.

——(1980) "Cult archaeology and unscientific method and theory." in M.B. Schiffer (ed.), *Advances in Archaeological Method and Theory*, Vol. 3. New York: Academic Press.

——(1982) "Western Massachusetts' 'monk's caves'; 1979 University of Massachusetts field research." *Man in the Northeast* 24: 37–70.

Coleman, J. (1996) "Did Egypt shape the glory that was Greece?" in M.R. Lefkowitz and G.M. Rogers (eds), *Black Athena Revisited*, Chapel Hill: University of North Carolina Press.

Collins, H. (1981) "Stages in the empirical programme of relativism." *Social Studies of Science* 11: 3–10.

—(2001) "One more round with relativism." in J. Labinger and H. Collins (eds), *The One Culture? A Conversation about Science*. Chicago: University of Chicago Press.

Collis, J. (1996) "Celts and politics," in P. Graves-Brown, S. Jones, and C. Gamble (eds), *Cultural Identity and Archaeology: The Construction of European Communities*. London: Routledge.

Cordaux R. *et al.* (2004) "Independent origins of Indian caste and tribal paternal lineages." *Current Biology* 14(3): 231–5.

Corlett, C. (2003) "Coveting the Ark," review of M. Carew's *Tara and the Ark of the Covenant: A Search for the Ark of the Covenant by British Israelites on the Hill of Tara*." *Archaeology Ireland* 17(2): 42.

Cotterell, M. (1997) *The Supergods*. London: HarperCollins.

—(1999) *The Tutankhamun Prophecies*. London: Headline.

—(2003) *The Terracotta Warriors: Secret Codes of the Emperor's Army*. London: Headline.

Cotterell, M. and Gilbert, A. (1995) *The Mayan Prophecies*. Shaftesbury: Element.

Covarrubias, M. (1957) *Indian Art of Mexico and Central America*. New York: Knopf.

Cowens, D. and Monte, T. (1996) *A Gift for Healing: How to Use Therapeutic Touch*. New York: Crown Trade Paperbacks.

Cremo, M.A. and Thompson, R.L. (1993) *Forbidden Archeology: The Hidden History of the Human Race*. San Diego: Bhaktivedanta Institute.

Crooke, E. (2000) *Politics, Archaeology and the Creation of a National Museum in Ireland: An Expression of National Life*. Dublin: Irish Academic Press.

Cunliffe, B., Davies, W. and Renfrew, C. (eds) (2002) *Archaeology: The Widening Debate*. Oxford: Oxford University Press.

Dani, S.G. *et al.* (2001) "Neither Vedic nor mathematics." Available at http://www.sacw.net /DC/CommunalismCollection/ArticlesArchive/NoVedic.html.

Daniel, G.E. (1979) "The forgotten milestones and blind alleys of the past." *Royal Anthropological Society News* 33: 3–6.

—(1981) *A Short History of Archaeology*. London: Thames & Hudson.

Daniels, T. (ed.) (1999) *A Doomsday Reader: Prophets, Predictors, and Hucksters of Salvation*. New York: New York University Press.

Danino, M. (1996) *The Invasion That Never Was / Song of Humanity by Sujata Nahar*. Delhi: Mother's Institute of Research and Mysore.

Darvill, T. (2002) *The Concise Oxford Dictionary of Archaeology*. Oxford: Oxford University Press.

Dasgupta, S. (1999) *Jagadis Chandra Bose and the Indian Response to Western Science*. New Delhi: Oxford University Press.

David, L. (2002) "Satellite search underway for Noah's ark." Available at http://www. space.com/scienceastronomy/ark_hunt_020830.html.

Davidson, D. (1932) *The Great Pyramid, Its Divine Message*. London: Williams and Norgate.

Davies, J.N.P. (1959) "The development of 'scientific' medicine in the African kingdom of Bunyoro-Kitara." *Medical History* 3: 47–57.

Davis, T.W. (2004) *Shifting Sands: The Rise and Fall of Biblical Archaeology*. Oxford: Oxford University Press.

Dawkins, R. (1987) *The Blind Watchmaker: Why the Evidence of Evolution Reveals a Universe without Design*. New York: W.W. Norton.

—(1998) *Unweaving the Rainbow: Science, Delusion, and the Appetite for Wonder*. London: Penguin Books.

—(2003) *A Devil's Chaplain*. London: Weidenfeld and Nicolson.

Dayanand Sarasvati (1915) *The Light of Truth* (English translation of *Satyarthapraka*, 1882). Allahabad.

Dean, J. (1998) *Aliens in America: Conspiracy Cultures from Outer Space to Cyberspace*. Ithaca, NY: Cornell University Press.

[Delhi Historians' Group] (2001) *Communalism of Education: The History Textbooks Controversy*. New Delhi: Delhi Historians' Group, Jawaharlal Nehru University.

Demarest, A., Rice, P, and Rice, D.S. (eds) (2004) *The Terminal Classic in the Maya Lowlands*. Boulder: University of Colorado Press.

Demeritt, D. (1994) "Ecology, objectivity and critique in writings on nature and human societies." *Journal of Historical Geography* 20(1): 22–37.

Denton, G.H., Prentice, M.L. and Burkle, L.H. (1991) "Cainozoic history of the Antarctic ice sheet," in R.T. Tingey (ed.), *The Geology of Antarctica*. Oxford: Clarendon Press.

Deo, S.B. and Kamath, S. (1989) *The Aryan Invasion: A Myth*. Nagpur: Baba Saheb Apte Smarak Samiti.

—(1993) *The Aryan Problem: Papers Presented at the Seminar on the Aryan Problem Held at Bangalore in July 1991*. Pune: Bharatiya Itihasa Sankalana Samiti.

de Santillana, G. and von Dechend, H. (1969) *Hamlet's Mill*. Boston: Nonpareil Books.

Dhavalikar, M.K. (1997) *Indian Protohistory*. New Delhi: Books and Books.

Diamond, J.M. (1997) *Guns, Germs and Steel: The Fates of Human Societies*. New York: W.W. Norton.

Diaz Santana, B. (2002) *Los celtas en Galicia: arqueología y política en la creación de la identidad gallega*. Noia A Coruña: Toxosoutos.

Diaz-Andreu, M. (1996) "Constructing identities through culture: the past in the forging of Europe," in P. Graves-Brown, S. Jones and C. Gamble (eds) *Cultural Identity and Archaeology: The Construction of European Communities*. London: Routledge.

Diaz-Andreu, M. and Champion, T. (eds) (1995) *Nationalism and Archaeology in Europe*. London: UCL Press.

Dietler, M. (1994) "Our ancestors the Gauls: archaeology, ethnic nationalism, and the manipulation of Celtic identity in modern Europe." *American Anthropologist* 96(3): 384–605.

—(1998) "A tale of three sites: the monumentalization of Celtic oppida and the politics of collective memory and identity." *World Archaeology* 30: 72–89.

Dillehay, T. (1992) "Widening the socio-economic foundations of Andean civilization: prototypes of early monumental architecture." *Andean Past* 3: 55–65.

Diop, C.A. (1974) *The African Origin of Civilization: Myth or Reality?* Chicago: Lawrence Hill.

Donnelly, I. (1970 [1882]) *Atlantis: The Antediluvian World*. London: Sidgwick & Jackson.

Dossey, B.M. (ed.) (1997) *Core Curriculum for Holistic Nursing*. Gaithersburg: Aspen Publishers.

Dossey, B.M. and Guzzetta, C.E. (2000) "Holistic nursing practice," in B.M. Dossey, L. Keegan and C.E. Guzzetta (eds), *Holistic Nursing: a Handbook for Practice*, 3rd edn. Gaithersburg: Aspen Publishers.

Dossey, B.M., Keegan, L. and Guzzetta, C.E. (2000) *Holistic Nursing: A Handbook for Practice*, 3rd edn. Gaithersburg: Aspen Publishers.

Dossey, L. (1982) *Space, Time & Medicine*. Boston: Shambhala.

—(1989) *Recovering the Soul: A Scientific and Spiritual Search*. New York: Bantam Books.

—(1993) *Healing Words: The Power of Prayer and the Practice of Medicine*. San Francisco: HarperSanFrancisco.

—(1999) *Reinventing Medicine: Beyond Mind–Body to a New Era of Healing*. San Francisco: HarperSanFrancisco.

—(2001) *Healing Beyond the Body: Medicine and the Infinite Reach of the Mind.* Boston: Shambhala.

Dove, D. and Johnson, P. (1999) "Oral evening primrose oil: its effect on length of pregnancy and selected intrapartum outcomes in low-risk nulliparous women." *Journal of Nurse-Midwifery* 44(3): 320–4.

Downey, G.L. and Rogers, J.D. (1995) "On the politics of theorizing in a postmodern academy." *American Anthropologist* 97(2): 269–81.

Drew, C.B. (2001) *Apostles of Disunion.* Charlottesville: University Press of Virginia.

Drosnin, M. (1997) *The Bible Code.* New York: Simon & Schuster.

Dubessy, J. and Lecointre, G. (eds) (2001) *Intrusions spiritualistes et impostures intellectuelles en sciences.* Paris: Editions Syllepse.

Dufkova, M. and Pecirka, J. (1970) "Excavations of farms and farmhouses in the Chora of Chersonesos in the Crimea." *Eirene* 8: 123–74.

Duncan, D.E. (1998) *Calendar.* New York: Avon Books.

Dwyer, J.G. (2000) "Spiritual treatment exemptions to child medical neglect laws: what we outsiders should think." *Notre Dame Law Review* 76(1): 147–77.

Dyson, G. (1997) *Darwin among the Machines.* London: Penguin Books.

—(2000) "Science and religion can co-exist peacefully." *The Independent* (London), 23 March.

—(2002) "Science & religion: no ends in sight." *New York Review of Books* 49(5): 4–6 (28 March).

Dzurec, L.C. (1989) "The necessity for and evolution of multiple paradigms for nursing research: a poststructuralist perspective." *Advances in Nursing Science* 11(4): 69–77.

Easlea, B. (1981) *Science and Sexual Oppression: Patriarchy's Confrontation with Women and Nature.* London: Weidenfeld & Nicolson.

Eco, U. (2000) *Kant and the Platypus: Essays on Language and Cognition.* London: Vintage Books.

Edelstein, T.J. (1992) *Imagining an Irish Past: The Celtic Revival 1840–1940.* Chicago: Museum of Art/University of Chicago Press.

Edgar, M. (1924) *The Great Pyramid.* Glasgow: Bone and Hulley.

Ehret, C. (1988) "Language change and the material correlates of language and ethnic shift." *Antiquity* 62: 564–74.

Elfenbein, J.H. (1987) "A periplous of the 'Brahui problem'." *Studia Iranica* 16: 215–33.

Ellis, J.S. (1998) "Reconciling the Celt: British Nationality, Empire, and the 1911 investiture of the Prince of Wales." *Journal of British Studies* 37(4): 391–418.

Elst, K. (1999) *Update on the Aryan Invasion Debate.* Delhi: Aditya Prakashan.

—(2001) *Decolonizing the Hindu Mind: Ideological Development of Hindu Revivalism.* New Delhi: Rupa and Co.

Emeneau, M.B. (1956) "India as a linguistic area." *Language* 32: 3–16.

Erdosy, G. (ed.) (1995) *The Indo-Aryans of Ancient South Asia.* Berlin: de Gruyter.

Evans, C. (1973) *Cults of Unreason.* London: Harrap.

Evans, R. (1997) *In Defence of History.* London: Granta Books.

Fagan, G.G. (2002), "Alternative archaeology," in M. Shermer (ed.), *The Skeptic Encyclopedia of Pseudoscience,* 2 vols. Santa Barbara: ABC-CLIO.

—(2003) "Far-out television." *Archaeology* 56.3 (May/June): 46–50; reprinted in S. Pinker (ed.), *The Best American Science and Nature Writing 2004.* Boston: Houghton Mifflin (2004).

Fagan, G.G. and Hale, C. (2001) "The new Atlantis and the dangers of pseudohistory." *Skeptic* 9: 78–87.

Fairservis, W.A. (1992) *The Harappan Civilization and its Writing: a Model for the Decipherment of the Indus Script.* New Delhi: Oxford University Press.

Farmer, S. (2001) "Three problems in Indology approached from comparative perspectives: textual layering, the dates of the Vedas, and the Harappan 'writing' question." Available at http://www.fas.harvard.edu/~sanskrit/RoundTableSchedule01.html.

—(2002) "New proofs of the non-linguistic nature of the Indus valley inscriptions." Available at http://www.fas.harvard.edu/~sanskrit/RoundTableSchedule.html.

—(2003) "Five cases of 'dubious writing' in Indus inscriptions: parallels with the Vinca symbols and Cretan hieroglyphic seals." Available at http://www.fas.harvard.edu/~sanskrit/RoundTableSchedule03.html.

—(2004) {various updates on the Indus signs} Available at http://www.safarmer.com/downloads.

Fauvelle-Aymar, F.-X. (2000) "Cheikh Anta Diop, ou l'africaniste malgré lui," in F.-X. Fauvelle-Aymar, J.-P. Chrétien and C.-H. Perrot (eds), *Afrocentrismes*. Paris: Karthala.

Fawcett, J. (2000) *Analysis and Evaluation of Contemporary Nursing Knowledge: Nursing Models and Theories*. Philadelphia: F.A. Davis.

—(2002) "The nurse theorists: 21st-century updates – Jean Watson." *Nursing Science Quarterly* 15(3): 214–19.

Feder, K.L. (1984) "Irrationality and archaeology." *American Antiquity* 49(3): 525–41.

—(1985/86) "The challenges of pseudoscience." *The Journal of College Science Teaching* 15(3): 180–6.

—(1987) "Cult archaeology and creationism: a coordinated research project," in F.B. Harrold and R.A. Eve (eds), *Cult Archaeology and Creationism: Understanding Pseudoscientific Beliefs about the Past*. Iowa City: University of Iowa Press.

—(1995) "Ten years after: surveying misconceptions about the human past," *CRM* 18(3): 10–14.

—(1998) "Perceptions of the past: survey results – how students perceive the past." *General Anthropology* 4(2): 8–12.

—(2002a) "Atlantis in fantasyland: a Mickey Mouse documentary about the Lost Continent." *Skeptic* 9(3): 11–12.

—(2002b) *Frauds, Myths, and Mysteries: Science and Pseudoscience in Archaeology*, 4th edn. Mountain View: Mayfield/McGraw-Hill.

Fedick, S.L. (ed.) (1996) *The Managed Mosaic*. Salt Lake City: University of Utah Press.

Feikin, D.R. *et al.* (2000) "Individual and community risks of measles and pertussis associated with personal exemptions to immunization." *Journal of the American Medical Association* 284(24): 3145–50.

Feldman, R. (1980) "Aspero, Peru: architecture, subsistence economy and other artifacts of a preceramic maritime chiefdom." PhD dissertation, Harvard University.

Ferguson, N. (2003) *Empire: The Rise and Demise of the British World Order and the Lessons for Global Power*. New York: Basic Books.

Fernández-Armesto, F. (1997) *Truth: A History*. New York: St Martin's Press.

Feuerstein, G., Kak, S. and Frawley, D. (1995) *In Search of the Cradle of Civilization: New Light on Ancient India*. Wheaton, Ill.: Quest Books.

Fischer, S. and Johnson, P.G. (1999) "Therapeutic touch: a viable link to midwifery practice." *Journal of Nurse-Midwifery* 44(3): 300–9.

Fitzpatrick, A.P. (1996) "'Celtic' Iron Age Europe: the theoretical basis," in P. Graves-Brown, S. Jones and C. Gamble (eds), *Cultural Identity and Archaeology: The Construction of European Communities*. London: Routledge.

Fitzpatrick, J.J. (1994) "Rogers' contribution to the development of nursing as a science," in V.M. Malinski, E.A.M. Barrett and J.R. Phillips (eds), *Martha E. Rogers: Her Life and Her Work*. Philadelphia: F.A. Davis.

Fitzpatrick, M. (2004) *MMR and Autism*. London, Routledge.

Flem-Ath, R. (1995) *When the Sky Fell: In Search of Atlantis*. London: Weidenfeld & Nicolson.

Flemming, N.C. (1978) "Holocene eustatic changes and coastal tectonics in the north-east Mediterranean: implications for models of crustal consumption." *Philosophical Transactions of the Royal Society* 289: 405–58.

—(1998) "Archaeological evidence for vertical tectonic movement on the continental shelf during the Palaeolithic, Neolithic and Bronze Age periods," in I.S. Stewart and C. Vita-Finzi (eds), *Coastal Tectonics*. London: Special Publications of the Geological Society.

Flemming, N.C. and Webb, C.O. (1986) "Tectonic and eustatic coastal changes during the last 10,000 years derived from archaeological data." *Zeitschrift für Geomorphologie* Suppl. Bd 62: 1–29.

Fontaine, K.L. (2000) *Healing Practices: Alternative Therapies for Nursing*. Upper Saddle River, NJ: Prentice Hall.

Foucault, M. (1977) *Discipline and Punish: The Birth of the Prison*, translated by A. Sheridan. New York: Pantheon Books.

—(1978) *The History of Sexuality*, translated by R. Hurley. New York: Pantheon Books.

—(1988) *Madness and Civilization: A History of Insanity in the Age of Reason*, translated by R. Howard. New York: Vintage Books.

Fracchia, H.M. (1985) "The Peloponnesian pyramids reconsidered." *American Journal of Archaeology* 89: 683–9.

Frantz, A. and Roebuck, C. (1941) "Blockhouses in the Argolid: notes on the excavation." *Hesperia* 10(2): 109–12.

Frawley, D. (1990) *From the River of Heaven: Hindu and Vedic Knowledge for the Modern Age*. Salt Lake City: Passage Press.

—(1994) *The Myth of the Aryan Invasion of India*. New Delhi: Voice of India.

—(1995) *Arise Arjuna: Hinduism and the Modern World*. New Delhi: Voice of India.

—(1998) *Awaken Bharata: A Call for India's Rebirth*. New Delhi: Voice of India.

Frazer, J.G. (1913) *Pausanias's Description of Greece*. London: Macmillan.

Freeman, D.S. (1935) *R. E. Lee: A Biography*, 4 vols. New York: Charles Scribner's Sons.

Freeman, L.W. and Lawlis, G.F. (2001) *Mosby's Complementary & Alternative Medicine: A Research-based Approach*. St Louis: Mosby.

Frisch, N.C. (2001) "Nursing as a context for alternative/complementary modalities." *Online Journal of Issues in Nursing*, vol. 6(2) (31 May). Available at http://www.nursingworld.org/ojin/topic15/tpc15 2.htm.

Frischauer, W. (1953) *Himmler: The Evil Genius of the Third Reich*. Boston: Beacon Press.

Fuller, S. (1996) "Does science put an end to history, or history to science? Or, why being pro-science is harder than you think," in A. Ross (ed.), *Science Wars*. Durham, NC: Duke University Press.

Galaty, M. (ed.) (2004) *Archaeology Under Dictatorship*. New York: Kluwer.

Gallup, G.H., Jr (1983) *The Gallup Poll: Public Opinion 1982*. Wilmington, Del.: Scholarly Resources.

—(2002) *The Gallup Poll: Public Opinion 2001*. Wilmington, Del.: Scholarly Resources.

Gann, T. (1925) *Mystery Cities*. London: Duckworth.

Gann, T. and Thompson, J.E.S. (1931) *The History of the Maya*. New York: Charles Scribner's Sons.

Gardiner, Sir A. (1961) *Egypt of the Pharaohs*. Oxford: Oxford University Press.

Gardner, M. (1957) *Fads and Fallacies in the Name of Science*. New York: Dover Publications.

—(1981) "Parapsychology and quantum mechanics," in G.O. Abell and B. Singer (eds) *Science and the Paranormal: Probing the Existence of the Supernatural*. New York: Charles Scribner's Sons; reprinted in P. Kurtz (ed.), *A Skeptic's Handbook of Parapsychology*. Buffalo, NY: Prometheus Books (1985).

Gathercole, P. and Lowenthal, D. (eds) (1989) *The Politics of the Past: One World Archaeology 12*. London: Routledge.

Gautier, F. (1996) *Rewriting Indian History*. New Delhi: Vikas Publishing House.

Geake, J. and Cooper, P. (2003) "Cognitive neuroscience: implications for education." *Westminster Studies in Education* 26.1: 7–20.

Geary, P.J. (2002) *The Myth of Nations: The Medieval Origins of Europe.* Princeton, NJ: Princeton University Press.

Gell-Mann, M. (1994) *The Quark and the Jaguar: Adventures in the Simple and the Complex.* London: Abacus, Little, Brown.

George, J.B. (2002) *Nursing Theories: The Base for Professional Nursing Practice,* 5th edn. Upper Saddle River, NJ: Prentice Hall.

Gergen, K.J. (1988) "Feminist critique of science and the challenge of social epistemology," in M.M. Gergen (ed.), *Feminist Thought and the Structure of Knowledge.* New York: New York University Press.

Ghosh, B.K. (1951) "The Aryan problem," in R.C. Majumdar (ed.), *History of the Indian People: The Vedic Age.* Mumbai: Bharatiya Vidya Bhavan.

Gimbutas, M. (1991) *The Civilization of the Goddess: The World of Old Europe.* New York: Harper.

Glazer, S. (2000a) "Postmodern nursing." *The Public Interest* 140: 3–16.

—(2000b) "Therapeutic touch and postmodernism in nursing," in S. Gorenstein (ed.), *Research in Science and Technology Studies: Gender and Work (Knowledge and Society,* vol. 12). Stamford, Conn.: JAI Press; reprinted in *Nursing Philosophy* 2 (2001): 196–212.

—(2002) "Response to critique of 'Therapeutic touch and postmodernism in nursing'," *Nursing Philosophy* 3: 63–5.

Godwin, J. (1994) *The Theosophical Enlightenment.* Albany: State University of New York Press.

Golwalkar, M.S. (1939) *We, or the Nationhood Redefined.* Nagpur: Bharat Prakashan.

González Reimann, L. (2002) *The Mahabharata and the Yugas: India's Great Epic Poem and the Hindu System of World Ages.* New York: Peter Lang.

Gordon, C. (1990) "*Histoire de la folie*: an unknown book by Michel Foucault." *History of the Human Sciences* 3(1): 3–26.

Gould, S.J. (1999) *Rocks of Ages: Science and Religion in the Fullness of Life.* New York: Ballantine.

—(2002) *I Have Landed.* London: Jonathan Cape.

Government of India, Department of Education (2001) "Guidelines for setting up departments of Vedic astrology in universities under the purview of University Grants Commission." Available at http://www.education.nic.in/htmlweb/circulars/astrologycurriculum.htm.

—(2003) *Annual Report 2002–2003.* Available at http://www.education.nic.in/htmlweb/annual report03/ar en 03 cont.htm.

Graves-Brown, P., Jones, S. and Gamble, C. (eds) (1996) *Cultural Identity and Archaeology: The Construction of European Communities.* London: Routledge.

Greene, B. (1999) *The Elegant Universe.* London: Jonathan Cape.

Greener, L. (1966) *The Discovery of Egypt.* London: Cassell.

Grieder, T., Bueno, A.M., Smith, C.E. Jr and Malina, R.M. (1988) *La Galgada, Peru: A Preceramic Culture in Transition.* Austin: University of Texas Press.

Griffin, D.R. (1988) "Introduction: the reenchantment of science," in D.R. Griffin (ed.) *The Reenchantment of Science: Postmodern Proposals.* Albany: State University of New York Press.

Grigg, R. (2002) "Evangelical colleges paid to teach evolution." *Answers in Genesis,* available at http://www.answersingenesis.org/docs2002/0806templeton.asp.

Gross, P.R. and Forrest, B.C. (2003) *Creationism's Trojan Horse: The Wedge of Intelligent Design.* New York: Oxford University Press.

Gross, P.R. and Levitt, N. (1994; 2nd edn 1998) *Higher Superstition: The Academic Left and Its Quarrels with Science.* Baltimore: Johns Hopkins University Press.

Gross, P.R., Levitt, N. and Lewis, M.W. (eds) (1996) *The Flight from Science and Reason*. Annals of the New York Academy of Sciences, Vol. 775, New York: New York Academy of Sciences.

Gupta, S.P. (1996) *The Indus–Sarasvati Civilization: Origins, Problems and Issues*. Delhi: Pratibha Prakashan.

Gutting, G. (1994a) "Foucault and the history of madness," in G. Gutting (ed.), *The Cambridge Companion to Foucault*. Cambridge: Cambridge University Press.

——(1994b) "Michel Foucault's *Phänomenologie des Krankengeistes*," in M.S. Micale and R. Porter (eds), *Discovering the History of Psychiatry*. Oxford: Oxford University Press.

Gwyn Griffiths, J. (1970) *Plutarch's De Iside et Osiride*. Cardiff: University of Wales.

Haack, S. (1993) *Evidence and Inquiry: Towards Reconstruction in Epistemology*. Oxford: Basil Blackwell.

——(1997) "Concern for truth: what it means, why it matters," in P. Gross, N. Levitt and M. Lewis (eds), *The Flight from Science and Reason*. Baltimore: Johns Hopkins University Press.

——(1998) *Manifesto of a Passionate Moderate: Unfashionable Essays*. Chicago: University of Chicago Press.

——(2003) *Defending Science – Within Reason: Between Scientism and Cynicism*. Amherst, NY: Prometheus Books.

Haksar, P.N., Ramanna, R., Bhargava, P.M. *et al.* (1981) "A statement on scientific temper." *Mainstream* (New Delhi), 25 July: 6–10.

Hale, C. (2003) *Himmler's Crusade: The True Story of the Nazi Expedition into Tibet*. London: Bantam Books.

Hall, M. (2000) *Archaeology and the Modern World: Colonial Transcripts in South Africa and the Chesapeake*. London: Routledge.

Hall, N.F. and Hall, L.K.B. (1986) "Is the war between science and religion over?" *The Humanist*, May/June: 26.

Halle, U. (2002) *"Die Externsteine sind bis auf weiteres germanisch!" Prähistorische Archäologie im Dritten Reich*. Bielefeld: Verlag für Regionalgeschichte.

Halle, U. and Schmidt, M. (1999) "'Es handelt sich nicht um Affinitäten von Archäologen zum Nationalsozialismus – das ist der Nationalsozialismus,' Bericht über die Internationale Tagung 'Die Mittel- und Osteuropäische Ur- und Frühgeschihctsforschung in den Jahren 1933–1945'." *Archäologische Informationen* 22(1): 41–52.

Hallote, R.S. and Joffe, A.H. (2002) "The politics of Israeli archaeology: between 'nationalism' and 'science' in the age of the Second Republic." *Israel Studies* 7(3): 84–121.

Hamilakis, Y. (2002) *The Labyrinth Revisited: Rethinking "Minoan" Archaeology*. Oxford: Oxbow Books.

Hammond, N. (1975) *Lubaantun: A Classic Maya Realm*. Cambridge, Mass.: Monographs of the Peabody Museum, no. 2.

——(1997a) "Did the early Greeks simply copy the pyramids of Egypt?" *The Times* (London), 1 August: 18.

——(1997b) "New chronicle of ancient sunlight dates Grecian age." *The Times* (London) 19 November: 24

Hancock, G. (1995) *Fingerprints of the Gods*. New York: Doubleday.

——(1998a) *Heaven's Mirror: Quest for the Lost Civilization*. London: Michael Joseph.

——(1998b) *Mars Mystery: The Secret Connection between Earth and the Red Planet*. New York: Three Rivers [R. Bauval and J. Grigsby are cited as co-authors in UK version].

——(2001) *Fingerprints of the Gods*. London: Heinemann (unaltered reissue of original 1995 text with new introduction and appendices).

——(2002a) *Underworld: Flooded Kingdoms of the Ice Age*. London: Michael Joseph; published in the USA as *Underworld: The Mysterious Origins of Civilization*. New York: Crown.

—(2002b), *Underworld*. Available at http://www.grahamhancock.com/underworld/cambay1 .php?p = 1 and http://www.grahamhancock.com/underworld/cambay3.php?p = 1.

—(2002c) "Online introduction to *Underworld*: from *Fingerprints of the Gods* to *Underworld*." Available at http://www.grahamhancock.com/underworld/underworld1.php.

Hancock, G. and Bauval, R. (1996) *The Message of the Sphinx: A Quest for the Hidden Legacy of Mankind*. New York: Crown; published in the UK as *Keeper of Genesis: A Quest for the Hidden Legacy of Mankind*. London: Heinemann.

—(2004) *Talisman: Sacred Cities, Secret Faith*. London: Element Books.

Haniotis, J. D. (1971) *Chios Island*. Athens: John D. Haniotis.

Hapgood, C.H. (1958) *Earth's Shifting Crust: A Key to Some Basic Problems of Earth Science*. New York: Pantheon Books.

—(1966) *Maps of the Ancient Sea Kings: Evidence of Advanced Civilization in the Ice Age*. Philadelphia: Chilton Books.

—(1970) *The Path of the Pole*. Philadelphia: Chilton Books.

Haraway, D. (1990) *Primate Visions*. London: Routledge.

Harder, H. (2003) "Populärversionen des Ariertums in Indien um die Wende zum 20. Jahrhundert," in M. Bergunder and R.P. Das (eds), *"Arier" und "Draviden." Konstruktion der Vergangenheit als Grundlage für Selbst- und Fremdwahrnehmungen Südasiens*. Halle: Verlag der Frankeschen Stiftungen zu Halle.

Harding, S. (1991) *Whose Science? Whose Knowledge? Thinking from Women's Lives*. Ithaca, NY: Cornell University Press.

—(1993) "Introduction: Eurocentric scientific illiteracy – a challenge for the world community," in S. Harding (ed.), *The "Racial" Economy of Science: Toward a Democratic Future*. Bloomington: Indiana University Press.

—(1994) "Is science multicultural? Challenges, resources, opportunities, uncertainties." *Configurations* 2(2): 301–30.

—(1996) "Science is 'good to think with'." *Social Text* 46–7: 16–26; reprinted in A. Ross (ed.) *Science Wars*. Durham, NC: Duke University Press.

—(1998) *Is Science Multicultural? Postcolonialisms, Feminisms, and Epistemologies*. Bloomington: Indiana University Press.

Hardy, D.A, Keller, J., Galanopoulos, V.P., Flemming, N.C. and Druitt, T.H. (eds) (1990) *Thera and the Aegean World III*, Vol. 2: *Earth Sciences*. London: Thera Foundation.

Härke, H. (ed.) (2000) *Archaeology, Ideology and Society: The German Experience*. Frankfurt: Peter Lang.

Harris, D.R. and Hillman, G. (eds) (1989) *Foraging and Farming: The Evolution of Plant Exploitation*. London: Unwin Hyman.

Harrison, P. (1999) *The Lords of Tikal*. London: Thames & Hudson.

Harrison, P. and Turner, B.L., II (eds) (1978) *Pre-Hispanic Maya Agriculture*. Albuquerque: University of New Mexico Press.

Harrold, F.B. and Eve, R.A. (1986) "Noah's ark and ancient astronauts: pseudoscientific beliefs about the past among a sample of college students." *The Skeptical Inquirer* 11(1): 61–75.

—(1987), "Patterns of creationist belief among college students," in F.B. Harrold and R.A Eve (eds), *Cult Archaeology and Creationism: Understanding Pseudoscientific Beliefs about the Past*. Iowa City: University of Iowa Press.

—(eds) (1987) *Cult Archaeology and Creationism: Understanding Pseudoscientific Beliefs about the Past*. Iowa City: University of Iowa Press.

Hartley, L.P. (1958) *The Go-Between*. New York: Penguin Books.

Haßmann, H. (2002a) "Archaeology in the Third Reich," in H. Härke (ed.), *Archaeology, Ideology and Society: The German Experience*. Frankfurt: Peter Lang.

—(2002b) "Archäologie und Jugend im 'Dritten Reich': Ur- und Frühgeschichte als Mittel der politisch-ideologischen Indoktrination von Kindern und Jugendlichen," in A. Leube (ed.), *Prähistorie und Nationalsozialismus: die mittel- und osteuropäische Frühgeschichtsforschung in den Jahren 1933–45*. Heidelberg: Synchron.

Hatziioannou, P. (1994) "I piramides stin Ellada." *Davlos* 156: 9214–34.

Hawass, Z. (1997) "Tombs of the pyramid builders." *Archaeology* 50(1): 39–43.

Hawass, Z. and Lehner, M. (1997) "Builders of the pyramids." *Archaeology* 50(1): 31–8.

Hay, C.L., Linton, R.L., Lothrop, S.K., Shapiro, H. and Vaillant, G.C. (eds) (1940) *The Maya and Their Neighbors*. New York: Appleton-Century.

Hayles, N.K. (1992) "Gender encoding in fluid mechanics: masculine channels and feminine flows." *Differences: A Journal of Feminist Cultural Studies* 4(2): 16–44.

Heinrich, P.V. (2002) "Artifacts or geofacts? Alternative interpretations of items from the Gulf of Cambay." Available at http://www.intersurf.com/~chalcedony/geofact.shtml.

Herf, J. (1984) *Reactionary Modernism: Technology, Culture, and Politics in Weimar and the Third Reich*. Cambridge: Cambridge University Press.

Herrmann, R.A. (2002) "The theological foundations of the John Templeton Foundation." Available at http://www.serve.com/herrmann/tphilo.htm.

Herz-Fischler, R. (2000) *The Shape of the Great Pyramid*. Waterloo: Wilfrid Laurier University Press.

Hess, D.J. (1991) *Spirits and Scientists: Ideology, Spiritism, and Brazilian Culture*. University Park: Pennsylvania State University Press.

—(1993) *Science in the New Age: The Paranormal, Its Defenders and Debunkers, and American Culture*. Madison: University of Wisconsin Press.

Hobsbawm, E. (1990) "Escaped slaves of the forest." *New York Review of Books* 37(19): 46–8; reprinted in E. Hobsbawm, *On History* (London: Weidenfeld & Nicolson, 1997), chapter 15, under the title "Postmodernism in the forest."

—(1993) "The new threat to history." *New York Review of Books* 40(21): 62–4; reprinted in E. Hobsbawm, *On History* (London: Weidenfeld & Nicolson (1997), chapter 1, under the title "Outside and inside history."

—(1997) *On History*. London: Weidenfeld & Nicolson.

Hock, H.H. (1986) *Principles of Historical Linguistics*. Berlin: Mouton de Gruyter.

—(1999) "Out of India? The Linguistic Evidence," in J. Bronkhorst and M. Deshpande (eds), *Aryan and Non-Aryan in South Asia: Evidence, Interpretation and Ideology*. Cambridge, Mass.: Harvard Oriental Series, Opera Minora, Vol. 3.

—(2002) "Wem gehört die Vergangenheit?" in M. Bergunder and R.P. Das (eds), *"Arier" und "Draviden." Konstruktion der Vergangenheit als Grundlage für Selbst- und Fremdwahrnehmungen Südasiens*. Halle: Verlag der Frankeschen Stiftungen zu Halle.

Hodder, I. (1987) *The Archaeology of Contextual Meanings*. Cambridge: Cambridge University Press.

—(1992) *Theory and Practice in Archaeology*. London: Routledge.

—(1999) *The Archaeological Process: An Introduction*. Oxford: Basil Blackwell.

Hodder, I. and Hutson, S. (2003) *Reading the Past: Current Approaches to Interpretation in Archaeology*, 3rd edn. Cambridge: Cambridge University Press.

Hodder, I., Shanks, M., Alexandri, A., Buchli, V., Carman, J., Last, J. and Lucas, G. (1995) *Interpreting Archaeology: Finding Meaning in the Past*. London: Routledge.

Hoenigswald, H.M. and Woodard, R.D. (2004) "Indo-European," in R.D. Woodard (ed.), *The Cambridge Encyclopedia of the World's Ancient Languages*. Cambridge: Cambridge University Press.

Höhne, H. (1967) *Der Orden unter dem Totenkopf: die Geschichte der SS*. Gütersloh: S. Mohn.

Holton, G. (2000) "The rise of postmodernisms and the 'end of science'." *Journal of the History of Ideas* 61(2): 327–41; a slightly different version of this article was also published in C. Véliz (ed.), *Post-Modernisms: Origins, Consequences, Reconsiderations.* Boston: Boston University, University Professors (2002).

Hornung, E. (2001) *The Secret Lore of Egypt: Its Impact on the West,* translated by David Lorton. Ithaca, NY: Cornell University Press.

Houston, S., Chinchilla, O.M. and Stuart D. (eds) (2001) *The Decipherment of Ancient Maya Writing.* Norman: University of Oklahoma Press.

Howe, S. (1998) *Afrocentrism: Mythical Pasts and Imagined Homes.* London: Verso.

Hume, D. (1993 [1777]) *An Enquiry Concerning Human Understanding.* Indianapolis: Hackett.

Huppert, G. (1974) "*Divinatio et Eruditio*: thoughts on Foucault." *History and Theory* 13: 191–207.

Hüser, K. (1987) *Wewelsburg 1933 bis 1945: Kult- und Terrorstätte der SS.* Paderborn: Verlag Bonifatius-Druckerei.

Hutchinson, J. (1987) *The Dynamics of Cultural Nationalism: The Gaelic Revival and the Creation of the Irish Nation State.* London: Allen & Unwin.

—(2001) "Archaeology and the Irish rediscovery of the Celtic past." In special issue, "Nationalism and archaeology," of *Nations and Nationalism* 7(4): 505–19.

Iannaccone, L., Stark, R. and Finke, R. (1998) "Rationality and the 'religious mind'." *Economic Inquiry* 36: 373–89.

Ignatieff, M. (1993) *Blood and Belonging: Journeys into the New Nationalism.* New York: Farrar, Straus and Giroux.

In the Hall of Ma'at: weighing the evidence for alternative history. Available at http://www.thehallofmaat.com.

Inden, R. (1990) *Imagining India.* Oxford: Basil Blackwell; reprinted, Bloomington: Indiana University Press (2000).

Inomata, T. and Houston, S. (eds) (2001) *Royal Courts of the Classic Maya.* Boulder, Colo.: Westview Press.

Isaac, T.M.T., Franke, R.W. and Parameswaran, M.P. (1997) "From anti-feudalism to sustainable development: the Kerala peoples science movement." *Bulletin of Concerned Asian Scholars* 29(3): 34–44.

Jaffrelot, C. (1996) *The Hindu Nationalist Movement and Indian Politics 1920 to 1990s.* London: C. Hurst.

James, G.G.M. (1954) *Stolen Legacy.* New York: Philosophical Library.

James, S. (1999) *The Atlantic Celts: Ancient People or Modern Invention?* London: British Museum Press.

Jarrick, A. (2003) "The soap of truth is slippery, but it exists." *Axess* (Stockholm) no. 5. Available at http://www.axess.se.

Jasanoff, J. (1997) "Stolen legacy? The evidence from language," in A. Ross and A. Lea (eds), *Were the Achievements of Ancient Greece Borrowed from Africa?* Washington: Society for the Preservation of the Greek Heritage.

Jasanoff, J. and Nussbaum, A. (1996) "Word games," in M.R. Lefkowitz and G. M. Rogers (eds), *Black Athena Revisited.* Chapel Hill: University of North Carolina Press.

Jayaraman, T. (2001a) "Vedic astrology and all that." *Frontline* (India) 18(10).

—(2001b) "A judicial blow." *Frontline* (India) 18(12).

Jenkins, K. (ed.) (1997) *The Postmodern History Reader.* London: Routledge.

—(2000) "A postmodern reply to Perez Zagorin." *History and Theory* 39: 181–200.

Jha, N. (1996) *Vedic Glossary on Indus Seals.* Benares: Ganga Kaveri Publishing House.

Jitatmananda, S. (1991) *Holistic Science and Vedanta.* Mumbai: Bharatiya Vidya Bhavan.

Jobst, K.A. (2002) "Passionate curiosity: from thoughts to cures through energy's myriad forms." *Journal of Alternative and Complementary Medicine* 8(5): 523–5.

Johanson, D.C. and Edey, M.A. (1981) *Lucy: The Beginnings of Humankind*. London: Paladin.

John Paul II (1998) *Encyclical Letter "Fides et Ratio" of the Supreme Pontiff. John Paul II to the Bishops of the Catholic Church on the Relationship between Faith and Reason*. Washington: United States Catholic Conference.

Johnson, S. (2001) *Emergence*. London: Allen Lane.

Jones, C. and Porter, R. (eds) (1994) *Reassessing Foucault: Power, Medicine and the Body*. London: Routledge.

Jones, S. (1997) *The Archaeology of Ethnicity: Constructing Identities in the Past and Present*. London: Routledge.

Jordan, P. (1998) *Riddles of the Sphinx*. Stroud, UK: Sutton Publishing.

—(2001) *The Atlantis Syndrome*. Stroud, UK: Sutton Publishing.

Kak, S. (1994) *The Astronomical Code of the Rigveda*. New Delhi: Aditya Prakashan; reprinted, New Delhi: Munshiram Manoharlal Publishers (2000).

Kalyanaraman, S. (2000) *Sarasvati*. Bangalore: Babasaheb (Umakant Keshav) Apte Smarak Samiti.

Kaplan, D. (1963) "Men, monuments, and political systems." *Southwestern Journal of Anthropology* 19: 397–410.

Karashima, N. (1984) *South Indian History and Society: Studies from Inscriptions, A.D. 850–1800*. Delhi: Oxford University Press.

—(2001) *History and Society in South India: The Cholas to Vijayanagar*. Oxford: Oxford University Press.

—(2002) *A Concordance of Nayakas: The Vijayanagar Inscriptions in South India*. Delhi: Oxford University Press.

Kass, R.E. (1999) "Introduction to 'Solving the Bible Code puzzle' by Brendan McKay, Dror Bar-Natan, Maya Bar-Hillel and Gil Kalai." *Statistical Science* 14(2): 149.

Kater, M. (1974) *Das "Ahnenerbe" der SS 1935–1945: ein Beitrag zur Kulturpolitik des Dritten Reiches*. Studien zur Zeitgeschichte/Institut für Zeitgeschichte. Stuttgart: Deutsche Verlags-Anstalt.

Kathiroli, S. *et al.* (2002) "A new archaeological find in the Gulf of Cambay, Gujarat." *Journal Geological Society of India* 60: 419–28.

Katsiadramis, V. (1994) "Ta panarchaia piramidioeidi ktismata tou ellinikou kai tou Ligouriou Argous." *Davlos* 156: 9214–36.

—(1996) "Itan mnimeio i Piramida Argous kai mia paidariodis apopsi archaiologou." *Davlos* 179: 10873–81.

Kazanas, N. (2002) "Indigenous Indoaryans and the Rigveda." *Journal of Indo-European Studies* 30: 275–334.

Kazamiakis, K.N. (2003) "Pirgos Ayias Marinas Keas." *Athemion* 10: 24–7.

Kelley, J.H. and Hanen, M.P. (1988) *Archaeology and the Methodology of Science*. Albuquerque: University of New Mexico Press.

Kennedy, K.A.R. (1995) "Have Aryans been identified in the prehistoric skeletal record from South Asia? Biological anthropology and concepts of ancient races," in G. Erdosy (ed.), *The Indo-Aryans of Ancient South Asia*. Berlin: de Gruyter.

—(2000) *God-apes and Fossil Men: Paleoanthropology of South Asia*. Ann Arbor: University of Michigan Press.

Kenoyer, J.M. (1995) "Interaction systems, specialised crafts and culture change: the Indus valley tradition and the Indo-Gangetic tradition in South Asia," in G. Erdosy (ed.), *The Indo-Aryans of Ancient South Asia*. Berlin: de Gruyter.

—(1998) *Ancient Cities of the Indus Valley Civilization*. Oxford: Oxford University Press/American Institute of Pakistan Studies.

Kidd, C. (1994) "Gaelic antiquity and national identity in Enlightenment Ireland and Scotland." *The English Historical Review* 109(434): 1197–214.

Kidder, A.V. (1950) "Introduction," in *Uaxactun, Guatemala: Excavations of 1931–37*, by A.L. Smith. Washington: Carnegie Institution of Washington Pub. 588.

Kidder, A.V., Jennings, J.D. and Shook, E.M. (1946) *Excavations at Kaminaljuyu, Guatemala*. Washington: Carnegie Institution of Washington Pub. 561.

Kikuchi, J.F., Simmons, H. and Romyn, D. (eds) (1996) *Truth in Nursing Inquiry*. Thousand Oaks, Calif.: Sage.

Kirfel, W. (1927) *Das Purana Pancalaksana*. Bonn: K. Schroeder.

Kirschvink, J., Ripperdan, R.L. and Evans, D.A. (1997) "Evidence for a large-scale reorganization of early Cambrian continental masses by inertial interchange true polar wander." *Science* 277: 541–5.

Kitcher, P. (1982) *Abusing Science: The Case against Creationism*. Cambridge, Mass.: MIT Press.

—(1984/85) "Good science, bad science, dreadful science, and pseudoscience." *Journal of College Science Teaching* 14 (December/January): 168–73.

—(forthcoming) "The many-sided conflict between science and religion." *Blackwell Companion to the Philosophy of Religion*. Oxford: Basil Blackwell.

Kivisild, T. *et al.* (1999) "Deep common ancestry of Indian and western-Eurasian mitochondrial DNA lineages." *Current Biology* 9: 1331–4.

—(2003) "The genetic heritage of the earliest settlers persists both in Indian tribal and caste populations." *The American Journal of Human Genetics* 72: 313–32.

Klostermaier, K. (1997) "Preface," in N.S. Rajaram and D. Frawley (eds), *Vedic Aryans and the Origins of Civilization: A Literary and Scientific Perspective*, 2nd edn. New Delhi: Voice of India.

—(1998a) *A Short Introduction to Hinduism*. Oxford: Oneworld.

—(1998b) "Questioning the Aryan invasion theory and revising ancient Indian history." *ISKCON Communications Journal*, 6(1): 1–7.

—(2000) *Hinduism: A Short History*. Oxford: Oneworld.

Knorozov, Y.V. and Volchok, B.Y. (1973) *Proto-Indica*, translated by H. Chandra and edited by Pande H. Field. Miami: Field Research Projects.

Knorozov, Y.V., Albedil, M.F. and Volchok, B.Y. (1981) *Proto-Indica, 1979: Report on the Investigation of the Proto-Indian Texts*. Moscow: Nauka Publishing House.

Kohl, P.L. and Fawcett, C. (eds) (1995) *Nationalism, Politics and the Practice of Archaeology*. Cambridge: Cambridge University Press.

Kolata, A.L. (1993) *The Tiwanaku: Portrait of an Andean Civilization*. Oxford: Basil Blackwell.

—(1996a) *Valley of the Spirits: A Journey into the Lost Realm of the Ancient Aymara*. New York: John Wiley & Sons.

—(1996b) *Tiwanaku and Its Hinterland*, Vol. 1: *Archaeology and Palaeoecology of an Andean Civilization*. Washington: Smithsonian Institution Press.

Kolata, G. (1998) "A child's paper poses a medical challenge." *New York Times*, 1 April: A1 and A20.

Kosok, P. (1965) *Life, Land and Water in Ancient Peru*. New York: Long Island University Press.

Koubalakis, P.L. (1996a) "Tarachi prokaloun oi Ellinikes piramides." *Davlos* 171: 10354.

—(1996b) "Tarachi stous kilous tou Diethnous Exousiasmou prokaloun oi panarchaaies Ellinikes piramides." *Davlos* 172: 10417–20.

Koutoulas, D. (1994) "Ergo tis 3is khilietias pro Khristou kai archaioteri ton Aigiptiakon." *Davlos* 156: 9233.

—(2001) "Amphion: i klimatikoti pyramida ton Thebon." *Ellinki Agogi*, 4/57: 18–23.

Krauss, L.M. (1999) "An article of faith: science and religion don't mix." *Chronicle of Higher Education* 46(14): A88.

Krieck, E. (1936) "Die Objektivität der Wissenschaft als Problem," in B. Rust and E. Krieck (eds), *Das Nationalsozialistische Deutschland und die Wissenschaft*. Hamburg: Hanseatische Verlagsanstalt.

—(1942) *Natur und Naturwissenschaft*. Leipzig: Quelle and Meyer.

Krieger, D. (1979) *The Therapeutic Touch: How to Use Your Hands to Help or to Heal*. Englewood Cliffs, NJ: Prentice Hall; reprinted New York: Simon & Schuster (1992).

—(1981) *Foundations for Holistic Health Nursing Practices: The Renaissance Nurse*. Philadelphia: Lippincott.

—(1987) *Living the Therapeutic Touch: Healing as a Lifestyle*. New York: Dodd, Mead.

—(1993) *Accepting your Power to Heal: The Personal Practice of Therapeutic Touch*. Santa Fe, NM: Bear and Co.

—(2002) *Therapeutic Touch as Transpersonal Healing*. New York: Lantern Books.

Krishna, N. (2002) "Marine archaeology and the study of the past." Available at http://www.newindpress.com/Sunday/sundayitems.asp?id = SEC20020817100019&eTitle = Columns&rLink = 0.

Krishnakumar, A. (2003) "Pioneering power research." *Frontline*, vol. 20, issue 22. Available at http://www.flonnet.com/fl2022/stories/20031107004410800.htm.

Krov, K.N. (1999) "Review of Barbara Geraghty, *Homeopathy for Midwives*." *Journal of Nurse-Midwifery* 44(3): 334–5.

Krupp, E. (2003) "Astronomical integrity at Giza." Available at http://www.antiquityofman.com/Krupp_refutes_Bauval_and_Roy.html.

Kuhn, T. (1970, 3rd edn 1996) *The Structure of Scientific Revolutions*, 2nd edn. Chicago: University of Chicago Press.

—(1977) *The Essential Tension*. Chicago: University of Chicago Press.

Kuhnen, H.-P. (ed.) (2002) *Propaganda. Macht. Geschichte: Archäologie an Rhein und Mosel im Dienst des Nationalsozialismus*. Trier: Rheinisches Landesmuseum.

Kuiper, F.B.J. (1955) "Rigvedic loan-words," in O. Spies (ed.), *Studia Indologica. Festschrift für Willibald Kirfel zur Vollendung seines 70. Lebensjahres*. Bonn: Orientalisches Seminar.

—(1991) *Aryans in the Rigveda*. Amsterdam/Atlanta: Rodopi.

—(2000) "A bilingual Râi," in A. Hintze and E. Tichy (eds), *Anusantatyai. Fs. für Johanna Narten zum 70. Geburtstag*. Dettelbach: J.H. Roell.

Kulke, H. and Rothermund, D. (1998a) *A History of India*, 3rd edn. London: Routledge.

—(1998b) *Geschichte Indiens: von der Induskultur bis heute. 2., verbesserte und aktualisierte Auflage*. Munich: C.H. Beck.

Kull, S. *et al.* (2003) "Misperceptions, the media and the Iraq war." PIPA/Knowledge Networks Poll, Program on International Policy Attitudes (PIPA), 2 October 2003. Available at http://www.pipa.org.

—(2004) "US public beliefs on Iraq and the presidential election." PIPA/Knowledge Networks Poll, Program on International Policy Attitudes (PIPA), 22 April 2004. Available at http://www.pipa.org.

Kunz, D. (1991) *The Personal Aura*. Wheaton, Ill.: Quest Books.

—(ed.) (1995) *Spiritual Healing*. Wheaton, Ill.: Quest Books.

Labinger, J. and Collins, H. (eds) (2001) *The One Culture? A Conversation about Science*. Chicago: University of Chicago Press.

Lal, B.B. (1997) *The Earliest Civilization of South Asia: Rise, Maturity and Decline*. New Delhi: Aryan Books International.

—(2002a) *The Sarasvati Flows On: The Continuity of Indian Culture*. New Delhi: Aryan Books International.

—(2002b) "The homeland of Indo-European languages and culture: some thoughts." Paper presented at a seminar organized by the Indian Council for Historical Research on the same theme in Delhi, 7–9 January 2002. Available at http://www.geocities.com/ifihhome /articles/bbl001.html.

—(2003) "Why perpetuate myths? A fresh look at ancient Indian history." Lecture given at the National Council of Educational Research and Training (NCERT), New Delhi. Available at http://www.geocities.com/ifihhome/articles/bbl002.html.

Lamberg-Karlovsky, C.C. (1997/98) "Colonialism, nationalism, ethnicity, and archaeology." Part 1: *The Review of Archaeology* 18(2): 1–14; Part 2: *The Review of Archaeology* 19(1): 35–47.

—(2002) "Language and archaeology: the Indo-Iranians." *Current Anthropology* 43: 63–88.

Landa, D. (1941 [*c*. 1570]) *Relacion de las Cosas de Yucatán*. annotated and edited by A. Tozzer. Cambridge, Mass.: Papers of the Peabody Museum of Archaeology and Ethnology, vol. 18.

Lang, T. (1997) "Review of S. Smiles *The Image of Antiquity: Ancient Britain and the Romantic Imagination*." *American Historical Review* 102(1): 104–5.

Langmuir, I. (1989) "Pathological science." *Physics Today* 42(10): 36–48.

Larson, E.J. and Witham, L. (1997) "Scientists are still keeping the faith." *Nature*, 386: 435–6.

—(1998) "Leading scientists still reject God." *Nature*, 394: 313.

Laudan, L. (1990) *Science and Relativism*. Chicago: University of Chicago Press.

—(1996) *Beyond Positivism and Relativism: Theory, Method, and Evidence*. Boulder, Colo.: Westview Press.

Lawrence, A.W. (1979) *Greek Aims in Fortification*. Oxford: Clarendon Press.

Lazos, C. (1995) *Pyramides Stin Ellada*. Athens: Aiolos.

Le Plongeon, A. (1896) *Queen Móo and the Egyptian Sphinx*. Published privately by the author.

Lech, J. (1998) "Between captivity and freedom: Polish archaeology in the 20th century." *Archaeologia Polona* 35–36: 255–85.

Lefkowitz, M. (1996) "Ancient history, modern myths," in M.R. Lefkowitz and G.M. Rogers (eds), *Black Athena Revisited*. Chapel Hill: University of North Carolina Press.

—(1997) *Not Out of Africa: How Afrocentrism Became an Excuse to Teach Myth as History*. New York: Basic Books.

Legon, J.A.R. (1995) "The Orion correlation and air-shaft theories." *Discussions in Egyptology* 33: 45–56.

Lehner, M. (1997) *The Complete Pyramids*. London: Thames & Hudson.

Leibovici, L. (2001) "Effects of remote, retroactive intercessory prayer on outcomes in patients with bloodstream infection: randomized controlled trial." *British Medical Journal* 323: 1450–1.

Lemaire, A. (2003) "James ossuary: a fake?" *Biblical Archaeology Review*, November/December. Available at http://www.bib-arch.org/bswbOOossuary_IAAreport.html.

Lemesurier, P. (1987) *The Great Pyramid: Your Personal Guide*. Shaftesbury: Element Books.

Leube, A. (ed.) (2002) *Prähistorie und Nationalsozialismus: die mittel- und osteuropäische Ur- und Frügeschichtsforschung in den Jahren 1933–1945*. Heidelberg: Synchron.

Levitt, N. (1998) "Why professors believe weird things." *Skeptic* 6(3): 28–35.

—(1999) *Prometheus Bedeviled: Science and the Contradictions of Contemporary Culture*. New Brunswick, NJ: Rutgers University Press.

Lewis, M.W. (1996) "Radical environmental philosophy and the assault on reason," in P.R. Gross, N. Levitt and M.W. Lewis (eds), *The Flight from Science and Reason*. New York: New York Academy of Sciences.

Lipner, J. (1992) "On 'Hindutva' and a 'Hindu-Catholic,' with a moral for our times." *Hindu-Christian Studies Bulletin* 5: 1–8.

Liritzis, I.G. (1998) *To Misterio Ton Ellinikon Pyramidoeidon*. Athens: Academia Delphikon Meleton.

Liritzis, I., Guibert, P., Foti, F. and Schvoerer, M. (1997) "The temple of Apollo (Delphi) strengthens novel thermoluminescence dating method." *Geoarchaeology* 5(12): 479–96.

Lloyd, A.B. (1975) *Herodotus Book II: Introduction*. Leiden: E.J. Brill.

—(1976) *Herodotus Book II: Commentary 1–98*. Leiden: E.J. Brill.

Lockyer, Sir N. (1894) *The Dawn of Astronomy*. London: Macmillan.

Lord, A.B. (1991) *Epic Singers and Oral Tradition*. Ithaca, NY: Cornell University Press.

Lord, L.E. (1938) "The 'pyramids' of Argolis." *Hesperia* 7(4): 481–527.

—(1941) "Blockhouses in the Argolid." *Hesperia* 10(2): 93–109.

Lubotsky, A. (2001) "The Indo-Iranian substratum," in C. Carpelan, A. Parpola and P. Koskikallio (eds), *Early Contacts between Uralic and Indo-European: Linguistic and Archaeological Considerations*. Helsinki: Suomalais-Ugrilainen Seura.

Lurz, R. (1975) *Die Heidelberger Thingstätte: die Thingbewegung im Dritten Reich – Kunst als Mittel politischer Propaganda*. Heidelberg: Schutzgemeinschaft Heiligenberg.

Lutjens, L.R.J. (1991) *Martha Rogers: The Science of Unitary Human Beings*. Newbury Park, Calif.: Sage.

Macauly, D. (1979) *Motel of the Mysteries*. New York: Houghton Mifflin.

MacGillivray, J.A. (2000) *Minotaur: Sir Arthur Evans and the Archaeology of the Minoan Myth*. New York: Hill & Wang.

MacIlwain, C. (2000) "AAAS members fret over links with theological foundation." *Nature* 403: 819.

MacKay, T.S. (1976) "Phalara," in R. Stillwell, W.L. MacDonald and M.H. McAllister (eds), *The Princeton Encyclopedia of Classical Sites*. Princeton, NJ: Princeton University Press.

Macrae, J. (1988) *Therapeutic Touch: A Practical Guide*. New York: Knopf.

Madhivanan, R. (2002) *Language Archaeology: A Journey towards the Parent Language of the World*. Chennai: Tamil Etymological Project.

Madrid, M. (ed.) (1997) *Patterns of Rogerian Knowing*. New York: National League for Nursing Press.

Madrid, M. and Barrett, E.A.M. (eds) (1994) *Rogers' Scientific Art of Nursing Practice*. New York: National League for Nursing Press.

Mahadevan, I. (2002) "Aryan or Dravidian or neither? A study of recent attempts to decipher the Indus script (1995–2000)." *Electronic Journal of Vedic Studies* 8-1: 3–21. Available at http://users.primushost.com/~india/ejvs/issues.html.

Majumdar, R.C. (ed.) (1951) *History of the Indian People: The Vedic Age*. Mumbai: Bharatiya Vidya Bhavan.

Malek, J. (1994) "Orion and the Giza pyramids." *Discussions in Egyptology* 30: 101–14.

Malinski, V.M. (ed.) (1986) *Explorations on Martha Rogers' Science of Unitary Human Beings*. Norwalk, Conn.: Appleton-Century-Crofts.

—(1994) "Highlights in the evolution of nursing science: emergence of the science of unitary human beings," in V.M. Malinski, E.A.M. Barrett and J.R. Phillips (eds), *Martha E. Rogers: Her Life and Her Work*. Philadelphia: F.A. Davis.

Malinski, V.M., Barrett, E.A.M. and Phillips, J.R. (eds) (1994) *Martha E. Rogers: Her Life and Her Work*. Philadelphia: F.A. Davis.

Manchel, F. (1995) "A reel witness: Steven Spielberg's representation of the Holocaust in *Schindler's List*." *Journal of Modern History* 67(1): 83–100.

Marriner-Tomey, A. and Alligood, M.R. (2002) *Nursing Theorists and Their Work*, 5th edn. St Louis: Mosby.

Martin, S. (2001) "Under a deadly star: warfare among the classic Maya," in N. Grube (ed.), *Maya: Divine Kings of the Rain Forest.* Cologne: Könemann Verlagesellschaft.

Martin, S. and Grube, N. (2000) *Chronicle of the Maya Kings and Queens.* London: Thames & Hudson.

Mason, J.A. (1938) "Observations on the present status and problems of Middle American archaeology, part II." *American Antiquity* 3: 300–17.

Mathivanan, R. (1995) *Indus Script among Dravidian Speakers.* Coimbatore: Rukmani Offset Press.

Matton, R. (1966) *Mycènes et l'Argolide Antique.* Athens: Institut Français d'Athènes.

Maudlin, T. (1994) *Quantum Non-Locality and Relativity: Metaphysical Intimations of Modern Physics.* Oxford: Basil Blackwell.

—(1996) "Kuhn édenté: incommensurabilité et choix entre théories" (original title: "Kuhn defanged: incommensurability and theory-choice"), translated by Jean-Pierre Deschepper and Michel Ghins. *Revue philosophique de Louvain* 94: 428–46.

Mayr, E. (1982) *The Growth of Biological Thought: Diversity, Evolution, and Inheritance.* Cambridge, Mass.: Belknap Press.

Mazhar, M.A. (1982) *Sanskrit Traced to Arabic.* Faisalabad: Sheikh Aziz Ahmad.

McAllister, M.H. (1976) "Kenchreai," in R. Stillwell, W.L. MacDonald and M.H. McAllister (eds), *The Princeton Encyclopedia of Classical Sites.* Princeton, NJ: Princeton University Press.

McArthur, C. (1998) "*Braveheart* and the Scottish aesthetic dementia," in T. Barta (ed.), *Screening the Past: Film and the Representation of History.* Westport, Conn.: Praeger.

McDonald, M. (1989) *"We Are Not French!" Language, Culture and Identity in Brittany.* London: Routledge.

McFarlin, B.L., Gibson, M.H., O'Rear, J. and Harman, P. (1999) "A national survey of herbal preparation use by nurse-midwives for labor stimulation: review of the literature and recommendations for practice." *Journal of Nurse-Midwifery* 44(3): 205–16.

McIntosh, G.C. (2000). *The Piri Reis Map of 1513.* Athens: University of Georgia Press.

McKay, B., Bar-Natan, D., Bar-Hillel, M. and Kalai, G. (1999) "Solving the Bible Code puzzle." *Statistical Science* 14(2): 150–73.

McKee, R (1999) *Story.* London: Methuen.

McKie, R. (2003) "'Prophet' opens theme park for our alien heritage." *The Observer*, 16 March.

McQuiston, C.M. and Webb, A.A. (1995) *Foundations of Nursing Theory: Contributions of 12 Key Theorists.* Thousand Oaks, Calif.: Sage.

Meades, J. (1994) "The devil's work." *The Times Magazine*, 29 October: 36–44.

Meadow, R. (ed.) (1991) *Harappa Excavations 1986–1990: A Multidisciplinary Approach to Third Millennium Urbanism.* Madison, Wis.: Prehistory Press.

—(1998) "Pre- and proto-historic agricultural and pastoral transformations in northwestern South Asia." *Review of Archaeology* 19: 12–21.

—(2002) "A note on the horse in pre- and proto-historic South Asia: a comment on Kazanas." *Journal of Indo-European Studies* 30: 389–94.

Meadow, R. and Patel, A. (1997) "A comment on: horse remains from Surkodata by Sándor Bökönyi." *South Asian Studies* 13: 308–15.

Meek, D.E. (2002) "The faith of the fringe: perspectives and issues in 'Celtic Christianity'," in J. Pearson (ed.), *Belief Beyond Boundaries: Wicca, Celtic Spirituality and the New Age.* Milton Keynes: Open University Press.

Meggers, B.J. (1954) "Environmental limitation on the development of culture." *American Anthropologist* 56: 801–24.

Megill, A. (1987) "The reception of Foucault by historians." *Journal of the History of Ideas* 48(1): 117–41.

Mehdi, S.Q. *et al.* (1999) "The origins of Pakistani populations: evidence from Y chromosome markers," in S. Papiha, R. Deka and R. Chakraborty (eds), *Genomic Diversity: Applications in Human Population Genetics*. New York: Kluwer/Plenum.

Meleis, A.I. (1997) *Theoretical Nursing: Development and Progress*, 3rd edn. Philadelphia: Lippincott.

Menon, P. (2002) "Mis-oriented textbooks." *Frontline* (India) 19(17).

Menon, P. and Rajalakshmi, T.K. (1998) "Doctoring textbooks." *Frontline* (India) 15(23).

Menzies, G. (2002) *1421: The Year China Discovered the World*. New York: Bantam Books.

Merchant, C. (1980) *The Death of Nature: Women, Ecology, and the Scientific Revolution*. San Francisco: Harper & Row.

—(1992) *Radical Ecology: The Search for a Livable World*. New York: Routledge.

Mermin, N.D. (1993) "Hidden variables and the two theorems of John Bell." *Reviews of Modern Physics* 65: 803–15.

—(1998) "Abandoning preconceptions: reply to Bloor and Barnes." *Social Studies of Science* 28: 641–7.

Merrick, J.C. (2003) "Spiritual healing, sick kids and the law: inequities in the American healthcare system." *American Journal of Law and Medicine* 29(2/3): 269–99.

Meskell, L. (ed.) (1998) *Archaeology Under Fire: Nationalism, Heritage and Politics in the Eastern Mediterranean and Middle East*. London: Routledge.

Michaels, A. (2003) *Hinduism: Past and Present*, translated by B. Harshav. Princeton, NJ: Princeton University Press.

Micozzi, M.S. (ed.) (2001) *Fundamentals of Complementary and Alternative Medicine*, 2nd edn, Philadelphia: Churchill Livingstone.

Midelfort, H.C.E. (1980) "Madness and civilization in early modern Europe: a reappraisal of Michel Foucault," in B.C. Malament (ed.), *After the Reformation: Essays in Honor of J.H. Hexter*. Philadelphia: University of Pennsylvania Press.

—(1990) "Comment on Colin Gordon." *History of the Human Sciences* 3(1): 41–5.

—(1994) *Mad Princes of Renaissance Germany*. Charlottesville: University of Virginia Press.

—(1999) *A History of Madness in Sixteenth-Century Germany*. Stanford, Calif.: Stanford University Press.

Mies, M. and Shiva, V. (1993) *Ecofeminism*. London: Zed Books.

Miller, G. (2000) *The Mating Mind: How Sexual Choice Shaped the Evolution of Human Nature*. London: William Heinemann.

Misra, S.S. (1992) *The Aryan Problem: A Linguistic Approach*. New Delhi: Munshiram Manoharlal.

—(1999) *The Date of the Rigveda and the Aryan Migration: Fresh Linguistic Evidence*. Pune: University of Pune.

Montserrat, D. (2001). *Akhenaten: History, Fantasy and Ancient Egypt*. London: Routledge.

Moore, A.M.T., Hillman, G. and Legge, A.J. (2000) *Village on the Euphrates: From Foraging to Farming at Abu Hureyra*. Oxford: Oxford University Press.

Morley, S.G. (1915) *An Introduction to the Study of the Maya Hieroglyphs*. Washington: Bureau of American Ethnology, Bulletin 57.

—(1920) *The Inscriptions at Copán*. Washington: Carnegie Institution of Washington Pub. 219.

—(1940) "Maya epigraphy," in C.L. Hay, R.L. Linton, S.K Lothrop, H. Shapiro and G.C. Vaillant. (eds), *The Maya and Their Neighbors*. New York: Appleton-Century.

—(1946) *The Ancient Maya*. Stanford, Calif.: Stanford University Press.

Morris, S. (1996) "The legacy of Black Athena," in M.R. Lefkowitz and G.M. Rogers (eds), *Black Athena Revisited*. Chapel Hill: University of North Carolina Press.

Moseley, M.E. (1992) "Maritime foundations and multilinear evolution: retrospect and prospect." *Andean Past* 3: 5–42.

—(2001) *The Incas and their Ancestors: The Archaeology of Peru*, revised edn. London: Thames & Hudson.

Mughal, M.R. (1997) *Ancient Cholistan: Archaeology and Architecture*. Rawalpindi: Ferozsons.

Mukhyananda, S. (1997) *Vedanta in the Context of Modern Science: A Comparative Study.* Mumbai: Bharatiya Vidya Bhavan.

Munn, M.H. (1982) "Watchtowers, blockhouses, and farmsteads." *American Journal of Archaeology* 86: 278.

—(1983) "Studies on the territorial defenses of fourth-century Athens." PhD dissertation, University of Pennsylvania.

Murphy, P.A., Kronenberg, F. and Wade, C. (1999) "Complementary and alternative medicine in women's health: developing a research agenda." *Journal of Nurse-Midwifery* 44(3): 192–204.

Murtha, T. (2002) "Land and labor: Classic Maya terraced agriculture at Caracol, Belize." PhD dissertation, Pennsylvania State University.

Nanda, M. (1997) "The science wars in India." *Dissent* 44(1): 78–83.

—(2002) *Breaking the Spell of Dharma and Other Essays.* New Delhi: Three Essays.

—(2003) *Prophets Facing Backward: Postmodern Critiques of Science and Hindu Nationalism in India.* New Brunswick, NJ: Rutgers University Press.

—(2004) "Postmodernism, Hindu nationalism and 'Vedic science'," part 2. *Frontline* (India) 21(1).

Nandy, A. (1981) "Counter-statement on humanistic temper." *Mainstream* (New Delhi), 10 October: 16–18.

—(1987a) *Traditions, Tyranny and Utopias: Essays in the Politics of Awareness.* Delhi: Oxford University Press.

—(1987b) "Cultural frames for social transformation: a credo." *Alternatives* (Boulder, Colo.) 12: 113–23; reprinted in B. Parekh and T. Pantham (eds) *Political Discourse: Explorations in Indian and Western Political Thought.* New Delhi: Sage (1987).

—(ed.) (1988) *Science, Hegemony and Violence: A Requiem for Modernity.* Delhi: Oxford University Press.

Nandy, A. and Visvanathan, S. (1990) "Modern medicine and its non-modern critics: a study in discourse," in F.A. Marglin and S.A. Marglin (eds), *Dominating Knowledge: Development, Culture, and Resistance.* Oxford: Clarendon Press; reprinted in S. Visvanathan (ed.), *A Carnival for Science: Essays on Science, Technology and Development.* Delhi: Oxford University Press (1997).

National Institute of Ocean Technology (NIOT, 2002–04) *Marine Archaeology in the Gulf of Khambayat.* Available at http://www.niot.res.in/m3/arch.

Nehru, J. (1946) *The Discovery of India.* New York: John Day.

Nelson, M.R. (2002) "The mummy's curse: historical cohort study." *British Medical Journal* 325(1): 482–4.

Nesselrath, H.-G. (2002) *Plato und die Erfindung von Atlantis (Lectio Teubneriana XI).* Munich: K.G. Saur.

Newton-Smith, W.H. (1981) *The Rationality of Science.* London: Routledge & Kegan Paul.

Nickell, J. (2003) "Bone (box) of contention: the James ossuary." *Skeptical Inquirer* 27. Available at http://www.csicop.org/si/2003-03/bonebox.html.

Nolan, A.T. (1991) *Lee Considered: Robert E. Lee and Civil War History.* Chapel Hill: University of North Carolina Press.

Nowotny, H. and Rose, H. (eds) (1979) *Counter-Movements in the Sciences.* Dordrecht: D. Reidel.

Ober, J. (1985) *Fortress Attica: Defense of the Athenian Land Frontier, 404–322 B.C.* Leiden: E.J. Brill.

Oberhammer, G. (1983) *Inklusivismus: eine indische Denkform*. Vienna: Institut für Indologie der Universität Wien.

Oestigaard, T. (2002) *Political Archaeology and Holy Nationalism: The Struggle for Palestine's Past*. London: Pluto Press.

Oliver, K. (1989) "Keller's gender/science system: is the philosophy of science to science as science is to nature?" *Hypatia* 3(3): 137–48.

Olshansky, B. and Dossey, L. (2003) "Retroactive prayer: a preposterous hypothesis?" *British Medical Journal* 327: 1465–8.

Olson, S. (2001) "The genetic archaeology of race." *Atlantic Monthly* 287(4). Available at http://www.theatlantic.com/issues/2001/04/olson-p1.htm.

Omery, A., Kasper, C.E. and Page, G.G. (eds) (1995) *In Search of Nursing Science*. Thousand Oaks, Calif.: Sage.

Ortiz de Montellano, B.R. (1996) "Afrocentric pseudoscience: the miseducation of African Americans," in P.R. Gross, N. Levitt and M.W. Lewis (eds), *The Flight from Science and Reason*. New York: New York Academy of Sciences.

Owens, M.T. (2003) "The Lost Cause in retreat." *Claremont Review of Books*. Available at http://www.claremont.org/writings/crb/summer2003/owens.html.

Pal, Y., Sahai, B., Sood, R.K. and Agrawal, D.P. (1984) "Remote sensing of the 'lost' Sarasvati River," in B.B. Lal and S.P. Gupta (eds), *Frontiers of the Indus Civilisation*. Delhi: Books and Books.

Palmer, R.E. (1977) "Postmodernity and hermeneutics." *Boundary 2*, 5(2): 363–94.

Pande, G.C. (ed.) (1999) *The Dawn of Indian Civilization (up to 600 BC)*. Delhi: Munshi Ram Manoharlal (Project of History of Indian Science, Philosophy and Culture, Centre for Studies in Civilizations).

Panikkar, K.N. (2001) "Outsider as enemy: the politics of rewriting history in India." *Frontline* (India) 18(1).

Park, R.L. (2000) *Voodoo Science: The Road from Foolishness to Fraud*. Oxford: Oxford University Press.

Parpola, A. (1994) *Deciphering the Indus Script*. Cambridge: Cambridge University Press.

Parpola, A. and Koskenniemi, S. (1969) *Decipherment of the Proto-Dravidian Inscriptions of the Indus Civilization: A First Announcement*. Copenhagen: Scandinavian Institute of Asian Studies.

Parry, J. and Keith, R.G. (eds) (1984) *New Iberian World*. New York: Times Books.

Parry, M. (1930–32) *Studies in the Epic Technique of Oral Verse-Making* [n.p.].

Pathak, A. and Verma, N.K. (1993) *Echoes of Indus Valley*. Patna: Janaki Prakashan.

Patnaik, P. (2001) "The assault on reason." *Frontline* (India) 18(18).

Peacocke, A. (1990) *Theology for a Scientific Age: Being and Becoming – Natural and Divine*. Oxford: Basil Blackwell.

Pendlebury, J.D.S. (1930) *Aegyptiaca: A Catalogue of Egyptian Objects in the Aegean Area*. Cambridge: Cambridge University Press.

Penrose, R. (1991) *The Emperor's New Mind: Concerning Computers, Minds, and the Laws of Physics*. Oxford: Oxford University Press.

Petrie, Sir W.F. (1883) *The Pyramids and Temples of Gizeh*. London: Field and Tuer.

Phillips, J.R. (1994a) "Foreword," in V.M. Malinski, E.A.M. Barrett and J.R. Phillips (eds), *Martha E. Rogers: Her Life and Her Work*. Philadelphia: F.A. Davis.

—(1994b) "Rogers' contribution to science at large," in V.M. Malinski, E.A.M. Barrett and J.R. Phillips (eds), *Martha E. Rogers: Her Life and Her Work*. Philadelphia: F.A. Davis.

—(1997) "Evolution of the science of unitary human beings," in M. Madrid (ed.), *Patterns of Rogerian Knowing*. New York: National League for Nursing Press.

Piazzi Smyth, C. (1864) *Our Inheritance in the Great Pyramid*. London: A. Straham and Co.

Pickering, A. (1984) *Constructing Quarks: A Sociological History of Particle Physics*. Chicago: University of Chicago Press.

Pikoulas, G.A. (1996) "Oi 'piramides' tis Argolidas." *Archaiologia* 59: 60–3.

Pinker, S. (1994) *The Language Instinct: The New Science of Language and Mind*. London: Allen Lane.

Pinnick, C. (1998) "What's wrong with the Strong Programme's case study of the 'Hobbes-Boyle' dispute?" in N. Koertge (ed.), *A House Built on Sand*. Oxford: Oxford University Press.

Piteros, C. (1998) "Oi 'Piramide' tis Argolidas." *Praktika tou E' Diethnous Synedriou Peloponnisiakon Spoudon (Argos–Navplion 6–10 Septembriou 1995)* 3: 343–94.

Pitts, M. and Roberts, M. (1997) *Fairweather Eden: Life in Britain Half a Million Years Ago*. London: Century.

Plato (1992) *Theaetetus*, translated by B. Williams. Indianapolis: Hackett.

Plofker, K. (1996) "Review of S. Kak, *The Astronomical Code of the Rigveda*." *Centaurus: International Magazine of the History of Science and Technology* 38: 362–4.

—(2000) "How to interpret astronomical references in Vedic texts?" *Electronic Journal of Vedic Studies* 6-2. Available at http://users.primushost.com/~india/ejvs/issues.html.

Plumwood, V. (1993) *Feminism and the Mastery of Nature*. London: Routledge.

—(2002) *Environmental Culture: The Ecological Crisis of Reason*. London: Routledge.

Poe, R. (1997) *Black Spark, White Fire*. Rocklin: Prima Publishing.

Pohl, M. and Bloom, P. (1996) "Prehistoric Maya farming in the wetlands of Belize," in S.L. Fedick (ed.), *The Managed Mosaic*. Salt Lake City: University of Utah Press.

Polkinghorne, J. (1991) *Reason and Reality: The Relationship between Science and Theology*. Philadelphia: Trinity Press International.

Pollock, H.E.D. (1965) "Architecture of the Maya lowlands," in G. Willey (ed.), *Handbook of Middle American Indians*, Vol. 2. Austin: University of Texas Press.

Popper, K.R. (1959) *The Logic of Scientific Discovery*. London: Hutchinson.

—(1963; 5th edn 1989) *Conjectures and Refutations: The Growth of Scientific Knowledge*. London: Routledge & Kegan Paul.

Porter, J. (1866) *The Scottish Chiefs*. Philadelphia: J.B. Lippincott.

Porter, R. (1987) *Mind-forg'd Manacles: A History of Madness in England from the Restoration to the Regency*. Cambridge Mass.: Harvard University Press.

—(1990) "Foucault's great confinement." *History of the Human Sciences* 3(1): 47–53.

Possehl, G. L. (1996) *Indus Age: The Writing System*. Philadelphia: University of Pennsylvania Press.

—(1999) *Indus Age: The Beginnings*. Philadelphia: University of Pennsylvania Press.

—(2002) *The Indus Civilization: A Contemporary Perspective*. Walnut Creek: Altamira Press.

Powell, A.B. and Frankenstein, M. (eds) (1997) *Ethnomathematics: Challenging Eurocentrism in Mathematics Education*. Albany: State University of New York Press.

Powell, E. (2004) "Theme park of the gods?" *Archaeology* 57(1): 62–7.

Prakash, G. (1999) *Another Reason: Science and the Imagination of Modern India*. Princeton, NJ: Princeton University Press.

Preucel, R.W. and Hodder, I. (1996) *Contemporary Archaeology in Theory*. Oxford: Basil Blackwell.

Pritchett, W.K. (1980) *Studies in Ancient Greek Topography*, Part III (*Roads*). Berkeley: University of California Press.

Proctor, R.A. (1883) *The Great Pyramid: Observatory, Tomb and Temple*. London: Chatto & Windus.

Proskouriakoff, T. (1960) "Historical implications of a pattern of dates at Piedras Negras, Guatemala." *American Anthropologist* 25: 454–75.

Puleston, D. and Callender, D.W., Jr (1967) "Defensive earthworks at Tikal." *Expedition* 9: 40–8.

Radner, D. and Radner, M. (1982) *Science and Unreason*. Belmont, NY: Wadsworth.

Rahman, M. (2003) "Matches, hatches and dispatches are all made in heaven for India's millions." *The Guardian*, 29 November.

Rahn, O. (1933) *Kreuzzug gegen den Gral*. Freiburg: Urban Verlag.

Raisler, J. (1999) "Editorial: complementary and alternative healing in midwifery care." *Journal of Nurse-Midwifery* 44(3): 189–91.

Rajaram, N.S. (1993) *The Aryan Invasion of India: The Myth and the Truth*. New Delhi: Voice of India.

—(1995) *The Politics of History*. New Delhi: Voice of India.

—(1998) *A Hindu View of the World: Essays in the Intellectual Kshatriya Tradition*. New Delhi: Voice of India.

—(2000) "Jha sent the photo . . . I have not computer enhanced it," interview with N.S. Rajaram. *Frontline* 17(23). Available at http://www.frontlineonnet.com/fl1723/17231220.htm.

Rajaram, N.S. and Frawley, D. (1997) *Vedic Aryans and the Origins of Civilization: A Literary and Scientific Perspective*, 2nd edn. New Delhi: Voice of India.

Rajaram, N.S. and Jha, N. (2000) *Deciphering the Indus Script: Methodology, Readings, Interpretations*. Delhi: Aditya Prakashan.

Ramachandran, R. (2001) "Degrees of pseudo-science." *Frontline* (India) 18(7).

Raman, V.V. (2002) "Science and the spiritual vision: a Hindu perspective." *Zygon* 37(1): 83–94; also in C.N. Matthews, M.E. Tucker and P.J. Hefner (eds), *When Worlds Converge: What Science and Religion Tell Us about the Story of the Universe and Our Place in It*. Chicago: Open Court (2002).

Rands, R. (1952) "Some evidences of warfare in Classic Maya art." PhD dissertation, Columbia University.

Rao, S.R. (1981) *Dawn and Devolution of the Indus Civilization*. Delhi: Aditya Prakashan.

—(1982) *The Decipherment of the Indus Script*. Mumbai: Asia Publishing House.

—(1999) *The Lost City of Dvaraka*. New Delhi: Aditya Prakashan.

Raskin, J. (2000) "Rogerian nursing theory: a humbug in the halls of higher learning." *Skeptical Inquirer* 24(5) (September/October): 31–5.

Ratnagar, S. (1981) *Encounters: The Westerly Trade of the Harappa Civilization*. Oxford: Oxford University Press.

—(1999) "Does archaeology hold the answers?" in J. Bronkhorst and M. Deshpande (eds), *Aryan and Non-Aryan in South Asia: Evidence, Interpretation and Ideology*. Cambridge, Mass.: Harvard Oriental Series, Opera Minora, Vol. 3.

Rau, W. (1957) *Staat und Gesellschaft im alten Indien nach den Brahmana-Texten dargestellt*. Wiesbaden: Otto Harrassowitz.

—(1971) "Weben und Flechten im vedischen Indien." *Akademie der Wissenschaften zu Mainz: Abhandlungen der Geistes- und Sozialwissenschaftlichen Klasse 1970* 11: 649–82.

—(1974) "Metalle und Metallgeräte im vedischen Indien." *Akademie der Wissenschaften zu Mainz, Abhandlungen der Geistes- und Sozialwissenschaftlichen Klasse 1973* 8: 1–70.

—(1976) "The meaning of *pur* in Vedic literature." *Abhandlungen der Marburger Gelehrten Gesellschaft* III/1: 1–16.

—(1983) "Zur vedischen Altertumskunde." *Akademie der Wissenschaften zu Mainz, Abhandlungen der Geistes- und Sozialwissenschaftlichen Klasse 1983* 1: 1–16.

Rauch, J. (2003) "Will Frankenfood save the planet?" *Atlantic Monthly* 292(3): 103–8.

Ravenscroft, T. (1973) *The Spear of Destiny: The Occult Power behind the Spear which Pierced the Side of Christ*. New York: Putnam.

Reardon, C. (1997) *Pickett's Charge in History and Memory*. Chapel Hill: University of North Carolina Press.

Rehder, J.E. (1986) "Use of preheated air in primitive furnaces: comment on views of Avery and Schmidt." *Journal of Field Archaeology* 13: 351–3.

Reid, D. (2002) *Whose Pharaohs? Archaeology, Museums and Egyptian National Identity from Napoleon to World War I*. Berkeley: University of California Press.

Relman, A.S. (1998) "A trip to Stonesville: Andrew Weil, the boom in alternative medicine, and the retreat from science." *The New Republic* 219(24) (14 December): 28–37.

Renfrew, C. (1972) *The Emergence of Civilization: The Cyclades and the Aegean in the Third Millennium B.C.* London: Methuen.

—(1989) "Comments on 'Archaeology into the 1990s'." *Norwegian Archaeological Review* 22: 33–41.

Renfrew, C. and Bahn, P. (2000) *Archaeology, Theories Methods and Practice*, 3rd edn. London: Thames & Hudson.

Richardson, S.C. (1999) "A study of student beliefs in popular archaeological claims." MA dissertation, University of Southampton.

Riehl-Sisca, J.P. (1989) *Conceptual Models for Nursing Practice*, 3rd edn. Norwalk: Appleton and Lange.

Rivet, P. (1960) *Maya Cities*. New York: Putnam.

Rogers, M.E. (1970) *An Introduction to the Theoretical Basis of Nursing*. Philadelphia: F.A. Davis.

—(1980) "Nursing: a science of unitary man," in J.P. Riehl and C. Roy (eds), *Conceptual Models for Nursing Practice*, 2nd edn. New York: Appleton-Century-Crofts; reprinted in V.M. Malinski, E.A.M. Barrett and J.R. Phillips (eds), *Martha E. Rogers: Her Life and Her Work*. Philadelphia: F.A. Davis (1994).

—(1986) "Science of unitary human beings," in V.M. Malinski (ed.), *Explorations on Martha Rogers' Science of Unitary Human Beings*. Norwalk: Appleton-Century-Crofts; reprinted in V.M. Malinski, E.A.M. Barrett and J.R. Phillips (eds), *Martha E. Rogers: Her Life and Her Work*. Philadelphia: F.A. Davis (1994).

—(1990) "Nursing: science of unitary, irreducible, human beings: update 1990," in E.A.M. Barrett (ed.), *Visions of Rogers' Science-Based Nursing*. New York: National League for Nursing; reprinted in V.M. Malinski, E.A.M. Barrett and J.R. Phillips (eds), *Martha E. Rogers: Her Life and Her Work*. Philadelphia: F.A. Davis (1994).

—(1992) "Nursing science and the space age." *Nursing Science Quarterly* 5(1): 27–34; reprinted in V.M. Malinski, E.A.M. Barrett and J.R. Phillips (eds), *Martha E. Rogers: Her Life and Her Work*. Philadelphia: F.A. Davis (1994).

Rogers, M.E., Malinski, V.M. and Young, A.A. (eds) (1985) *Examining the Cultural Implications of Martha E. Rogers' Science of Unitary Human Beings*. Lecompton: Wood–Kekahbah Associates.

Roland, A. (1988) *In Search of Self in India and Japan: Toward a Cross-cultural Psychology*. Princeton, NJ: Princeton University Press.

Rosa, L., Rosa, E., Sarner, L. and Barrett, S. (1998) "A close look at therapeutic touch." *Journal of the American Medical Association* 279(13): 1005–10.

Rosenberg, A. (1982) *The Myth of the Twentieth Century: An Evaluation of the Spiritual–Intellectual Confrontations of our Age*. Torrance: Noontide Press [translation of 1935 German original].

Roskams, S. (2001) *Excavation*. Cambridge: Cambridge University Press.

Ross, A. (1991) *Strange Weather: Culture, Science, and Technology in the Age of Limits*. London: Verso.

—(ed.) (1996) *Science Wars*. Durham, NC: Duke University Press.

Roy, R.R.M. (1998) *Vedic Physics: Scientific Origins of Hinduism*, with a foreword by Subhash Kak. Toronto: Golden Egg Publishing; lengthy excerpts from this book are available at http://www.goldeneggpublishing.com.

Russell, B. (1961a) *History of Western Philosophy*, 2nd edn. London: George Allen & Unwin; reprinted, Routledge (1991).

—(1961b) *The Basic Writings of Bertrand Russell, 1903–1959*, edited by R.E. Egner and L.E. Denonn. New York: Simon & Schuster.

Rutherford, A. (1957) *Outline of Pyramidology*. London: Institute of Pyramidology.

Ruz, L.A. (1950) "The likeness of Sylvanus Griswold Morley," in A.O. Andersen (ed.), *Morleyana*. Santa Fe, NM: School of American Research.

—(1973) *El Templo de las Inscripciones*. Mexico City: Instituto Nacional de Antropologia e Historia.

Ryan, W. and Pitman, W. (1997) *Noah's Flood: The New Scientific Discoveries about the Event that Changed History*. New York: Simon & Schuster.

Sabbagh, K. (2002) *Dr Riemann's Zeros: The Greatest Problem in Mathematics*. London: Atlantic Books.

Sagan, C. (1996) *The Demon-Haunted World: Science as a Candle in the Dark*. London: Hodder.

Sakovich, A. (2002), "Counting the stones: how many blocks comprise Khufu's pyramid?" *KMT* 13.3: 53–7.

Salmon, D.A. *et al.* (1999) "Health consequences of religious and philosophical exemptions from immunization laws: individual and societal risk of measles." *Journal of the American Medical Association* 281(1): 47–53.

Sanders, W.T. and Webster, D. (1988) "The Mesoamerican urban tradition." *American Anthropologist* 90: 521–46.

Sandweiss, D. and Moseley, M. (2001) "Amplifying the importance of new research in Peru." *Science* 294: 1651–3.

Sarner, L. (2002) "Therapeutic touch," in M. Shermer (ed.), *The Skeptic Encyclopedia of Pseudoscience*. Santa Barbara, Calif.: ABC–CLIO.

Sarter, B. (1988) *The Stream of Becoming: A Study of Martha Rogers's Theory*. New York: National League for Nursing.

Satterthwaite, L., Jr (1935) "Palace structures J-2 and J-6, with notes on structures J-6-2nd and other buried structures in court 1." *Piedras Negras Preliminary Papers*, no. 3. Philadelphia: University Museum.

Savarkar, V.N. (1949) *Hindu Rashtra Darshan: A Collection of the Presidential Speeches Delivered from the Hindu Mahasabha Platform by V. D. Savarkar*. Mumbai: Khare.

—(1969) *Hindutva*. Mumbai: n.p.; reprinted, New Delhi: Bharti Sahitya Sadan (1989).

Sayre-Adams, J. and Wright, S.G. (2001) *The Theory and Practice of Therapeutic Touch*. Edinburgh: Churchill Livingstone.

Scheiber, B. and Selby, C. (eds) (2000) *Therapeutic Touch*. Amherst, Mass.: Prometheus Books.

Schmidt, P. and Avery, D.H. (1978) "Complex iron smelting and prehistoric culture in Tanzania." *Science* 201: 1085–9.

Schmitz, T. (1999) "Ex Africa Lux? Black Athena and the debate about Afrocentrism in the US," in S. Conermann (ed.), *Mythen Geschichten, Identitäen: Der Kampf Um die Vergangenheit (Asien und Africa Band 2)*. Hamburg: E.B. Verlag.

Schoch, R.M. with McNally, R.A. (1999) *Voices of the Rocks: A Scientist Looks at Catastrophes and Ancient Civilizations*. New York: Harmony.

—(2003) *Voyages of the Pyramid Builders: The True Origins of the Pyramids from Lost Egypt to Ancient America*. New York: Tarcher/Putnam.

Schwaller de Lubicz, R. (1998 [1958]) *The Temple of Man: Apet of the South at Luxor*, 2 vols, translated by D. and R. Lawlor. Rochester, Vt: Inner Traditions.

Schwarzschild, B. (2002) "Direct measurement of the sun's total neutrino output confirms flavor metamorphosis." *Physics Today* (July): 13–15.

Scientific American (2001) "A demon-haunted world: belief in the paranormal." (September): 21.

Scranton, R.L. (1938) "The pottery from the Pyramids." *Hesperia* 7(4): 528–38.

Scull, A.T. (1990) "Michel Foucault's history of madness." *History of the Human Sciences* 3(1): 57–67.

—(1992) "A failure to communicate? On the reception of Foucault's *Histoire de la Folie* by Anglo-American historians." in A. Still and I. Velody (eds), *Rewriting the History of Madness*. London: Routledge.

Semino, O. (2000) "The genetic legacy of Paleolithic *Homo sapiens sapiens* in extant Europeans: a Y chromosome perspective." *Science,* 290: 1155–9.

Sergent, B. (1997) *Génèse de l'Inde*. Paris: Bibliothèque scientifique Payot.

Sethna, K.D. (1980) *The Problem of Aryan Origins: From an Indian Point of View*. Calcutta: S. and S. Publishers.

—(1981) *Karpasa in Prehistoric India: A Chronological and Cultural Clue*. New Delhi: Biblia Impex.

—(1989) *Ancient India in a New Light*. New Delhi: Aditya Prakashan.

—(1992) *The Problem of Aryan Origins: From an Indian Point of View*, 2nd extensively enlarged edition with 5 supplements. New Delhi: Aditya Prakashan.

—(2000) *Problems of Ancient India*. New Delhi: Aditya Prakashan.

Shaara, M. (1974) *The Killer Angels*. New York: McKay.

Shady-Solis, R. (1997) *La Ciudad Sagrada de Caral – Supe en los albores de la Civilizacion en el Peru*. Lima: Universidad Nacional Mayor de San Marcos.

Shaffer, J.G. (1984) "The Indo-Aryan invasions: cultural myth and archaeological reality," in J. R. Lukas (ed.), *The People of South Asia: The Biological Anthropology of India, Pakistan and Nepal*. New York: Plenum.

Shaffer, J.G. and Lichtenstein, D.A. (1995) "The concepts of 'cultural tradition" and 'paleoethnicity" in South Asian archaeology," in G. Erdosy (ed.), *The Indo-Aryans of Ancient South Asia*. Berlin: de Gruyter.

—(1999) "Migration, philology and South Asian archaeology," in J. Bronkhorst and M. Deshpande (eds), *Aryan and Non-Aryan in South Asia: Evidence, Interpretation and Ideology*. Cambridge, Mass.: Harvard Oriental Series, Opera Minora, Vol. 3.

Shanks, H. and Witherington, B., II (2003) *The Brother of Jesus: The Dramatic Story and Meaning of the First Archaeological Link to Jesus and his Family*. San Francisco: Harper.

Shanks, M. and Hodder, I. (1995) "Processual, postprocessual and interpretive archaeologies." in I. Hodder *et al.* (eds), *Interpreting Archaeology: Finding Meaning in the Past*. London: Routledge.

Shapin, S. and Schaffer, S. (1989) *Leviathan and the Air-Pump*. Princeton, NJ: Princeton University Press.

Shaw, I. and Nicholson, P. (1995) *The Dictionary of Ancient Egypt*. London: British Museum Press.

Shermer, M. (1997, revised edn 2002) *Why People Believe Weird Things: Pseudoscience, Superstition, and Other Confusions of Our Time*. New York: W.H. Freeman.

Shirer, W. (1981) *The Rise and Fall of the Third Reich: A History of Nazi Germany*. New York: Touchstone.

Shiva, V. (1988) "Reductionist science as epistemological violence," in A. Nandy (ed.), *Science, Hegemony and Violence: A Requiem for Modernity*. Delhi: Oxford University Press.

—(1989) *Staying Alive: Women, Ecology and Development*. London: Zed Books.

Shore, C. (1996) "Imagining the new Europe: identity and heritage in European Community discourse," in P. Graves-Brown, S. Jones and C. Gamble (eds), *Cultural Identity and Archaeology: The Construction of European Communities*. London: Routledge.

Silberman, N. (1982) *Digging for God and Country: Exploration, Archaeology and the Secret Struggle for the Holy Land, 1799–1917*. New York: Knopf.

—(1989) *Between Past and Present: Archaeology, Ideology and Nationalism in the Modern Middle East*. New York: Anchor.

Silverman, N.A. and Goren, Y. (2003) "Faking biblical history." *Archaeology* 56(5): 20–9.

Simpson, R.H. (1965) *A Gazeteer and Atlas of Mycenaean Sites*. Bulletin of the Institute of Classical Studies Supplement, Vol. 16. London: University of London.

Singh, B. (1995) *The Vedic Harappans*. New Delhi: Aditya Prakashan.

Sklar, B. (1977) *The Nazis and the Occult*. New York: Dorset.

Smiles, S. (1994) *The Image of Antiquity: Ancient Britain and the Romantic Imagination*. New Haven, Conn.: Yale University Press.

Smith, A.L. (1950) *Uaxactún, Guatemala: Excavations of 1931–37*. Washington: Carnegie Institution of Washington Pub. 588.

Smith. R. (2003) "When you're in a hole . . . ." *The Guardian*, 16 June.

Smyth, C.P. (1864) *Our Inheritance in the Great Pyramid*. London: A. Straham and Co.

—(1867) *Life and Work at the Great Pyramid*. Edinburgh: Edmonton and Douglas.

Sokal, A.D. and Bricmont, J. (1998) *Fashionable Nonsense: Postmodern Intellectuals' Abuse of Science*. New York: Picador; published in the UK as *Intellectual Impostures: Postmodern Philosophers' Abuse of Science*. London: Profile Books (1998); originally published in French as *Impostures intellectuelles*. Paris: Odile Jacob (1997).

—(2003) *Intellectual Impostures: Postmodern Philosophers' Abuse of Science*, 2nd edn. London: Profile.

Southworth, F.C. (1979) "Lexical evidence for early contacts between Indo-Aryan and Dravidian," in M.M. Deshpande and P.E. Hook.(eds), *Aryan and Non-Aryan in India*. Ann Arbor, Mich.: Center for South and Southeast Asian Studies.

—(1990) "The reconstruction of prehistoric South Asian language contact," in E.H. Bendix (ed.), *The Uses of Linguistics*. New York: New York Academy of Sciences.

—(1995) "Reconstructing social context from language: Indo-Aryan and Dravidian prehistory," in G. Erdosy (ed.), *The Indo-Aryans of Ancient South Asia*. Berlin: de Gruyter.

—(forthcoming) "Dravidian place names in Maharashtra." *International Journal of Dravidian Linguistics*.

Spence, J.L.T.C. (1926) *The History of Atlantis*. New York: Bell Publishing.

Spennemann, D. (1996) "Current attitudes of parks management and ecotourism students II: popular opinions about the past." Report no. 7 (unpublished). Copies available from School of Environmental and Information Sciences, Charles Stuart University, Albury, NSW, Australia.

Spiegel, G.M. (2000) "Épater les médiévistes." *History and Theory* 39: 243–50.

Spinden, H. (1975 [1912]) *A Study of Maya Art*. New York: Dover.

Spindler, K. (1994) *The Man in the Ice*. London: Weidenfeld & Nicolson.

Spitzer, A.B. (1996) *Historical Truth and Lies about the Past: Reflections on Dewey, Dreyfus, de Man, and Reagan*. Chapel Hill: University of North Carolina Press.

Spivak, G.C. (1988) "Subaltern studies: deconstructing historiography," in R. Guha and G.C. Spivak (eds), *Selected Subaltern Studies*. New York: Oxford University Press.

Sprague de Camp, L. (1963) *The Ancient Engineers*. New York: Doubleday.

—(1970) *Lost Continents: The Atlantis Theme in History and Literature*. New York: Dover.

Srinivas, M.N. (1952) *Religion and Society among the Coorgs of South India*. Oxford: Clarendon Press.

—(1988) *The Role of Sanskritization and Other Essays*. Oxford: Oxford University Press.

Stahlman, J. (2000) "A brief history of therapeutic touch," in B. Scheiber and C. Selby (eds), *Therapeutic Touch*. Amherst, Mass.: Prometheus Books.

Stalker, D. and Glymour, C. (1985) "Quantum medicine," in D. Stalker and C. Glymour (eds), *Examining Holistic Medicine*. Buffalo, NY: Prometheus Books.

Steibing, W.H. (1984) *Ancient Astronauts, Cosmic Collisions, and Other Popular Theories about Man's Past.* Amherst, Mass.: Prometheus Books.

Stein, B. (1985) *Peasant State and Society in Medieval South India.* Oxford: Oxford University Press.

—(1998) *A History of India.* Malden, Mass.: Blackwell.

Stephens, J.L. (1949) *Incidents of Travel in Central America, Chiapas, and Yucatán.* New Brunswick, NJ: Rutgers University Press.

Steuer, H. (ed.) (2001) *"Eine hervorragend nationale Wissenschaft": Deutsche Prähistoriker zwischen 1900 und 1995.* Berlin: de Gruyter.

Stevenson, C. and Beech, I. (2001) "Paradigms lost, paradigms regained: defending nursing against a single reading of postmodernism." *Nursing Philosophy* 2: 143–50.

Steward, J. (1949) "Culture causality and law: a trial formulation of the development of early civilizations." *American Anthropologist* 51: 1–27.

—(1955) *Theory of Culture Change.* Urbana: University of Illinois Press.

Stone, M. (1976). *When God Was a Woman.* New York: Harcourt Brace Jovanovich.

Szemerényi, O. (1996) *Introduction to Indo-European Linguistics*, 5th edn. Oxford: Clarendon Press.

Talageri, S. (1993) *Aryan Invasion Theory and Indian Nationalism.* New Delhi: Voice of India; reprinted, New Delhi: Aditya Prakashan.

—(2000) *Rigveda: A Historical Analysis.* New Delhi: Aditya Prakashan.

Taylor, J. (1864) *The Great Pyramid: Why Was It Built? And Who Built It?* London: Longmans, Green.

Taylor, W. (1948) *A Study of Archaeology.* Memoir Series of the American Anthropological Association, no. 69, Menasha, Wis.

Templeton Foundation (2003) websites of the John Templeton Foundation. Available at http://www.templeton.org and http://www.templetonprize.org.

Templeton, J.M. and Herrmann, R.L. (1989) *The God Who Would be Known: Revelations of the Divine in Contemporary Science.* San Francisco: Harper & Row.

Termer, F. (1951) "The density of population in the southern and northern Maya empires as an archaeological and geographical problem," in S. Tax (ed.), *The Civilizations of the Ancient Americas.* Chicago: University of Chicago Press.

Thapar, R. (1966) *A History of India,* Vol. 1. Harmondsworth, UK: Penguin Books.

—(1968) "Presidential address." *Proceedings of the Indian History Congress.* Indian History Congress, 31st session, Delhi: n.p.

—(1989) "Which of us are Aryans?" *Seminar* 364: 14–18.

—(1992) "The perennial Aryans." *Seminar* 400: 2–24.

—(1996) "The theory of Aryan race in India: history of politics." *Social Scientist* 24: 3–29.

—(2002) *Early India: From the origins to AD* 1300. Berkeley: University of California Press.

—(2004) *Somanatha: The Many Voices of a History.* New Delhi: Viking Penguin.

The Hindu (2002) "Oldest settlement discovered off Gujarat coast?" 17 January. Available at http://www.hinduonnet.com/thehindu/2002/01/17/stories/2002011701200600.htm.

—(2004) "Solution to many scientific problems hidden in Veda: Joshi." 4 April. Available at http://www.hinduonnet.com/thehindu/holnus/002200404031801.htm.

Theocaris, P. and Veis, G. (1995) "Ai piramides tis Argolidos, i chronologisis kai i simasia ton." *Praktika tis acadimias Athinon* (Proceedings of the Athens Academy) 70: 209–41.

Theocaris, P., Liritzis, I. and Galloway, R. (1997) "Dating of two Hellenic pyramids by a novel application of thermoluminescence." *Journal of Archaeological Science* 24(5): 399–405.

Thomas, D.H. and Colley, S. (2001) *Skull Wars: Kennewick Man, Archaeology, and the Battle for Native Identity.* New York: Basic Books.

401

Bibliography

Thompson, E.H. (1892) "The ancient structures of Yucatán not communal dwellings." *Proceedings of the American Antiquarian Society* 8: 262–9.

Thompson, J.E.S. (1927) *The Civilization of the Mayas*. Chicago: Field Museum of Natural History.

——(1942) *The Civilization of the Mayas*. Chicago: Field Museum of Natural History

——(1954) *The Rise and Fall of Maya Civilization*. Norman: University of Oklahoma Press.

Thompson, J.L. (2002) "Which postmodernism? A critical response to 'Therapeutic touch and postmodernism in nursing'." *Nursing Philosophy* 3: 58–62.

Thorne, S.E. and Hayes, V.E. (eds) (1997) *Nursing Praxis: Knowledge and Action*. Thousand Oaks, Calif.: Sage.

Tilak, B.G. (1903) *The Arctic Home in the Vedas: Being also a New Key to the Interpretation of Many Vedic Texts and Legends*. Pune: Kesari; Mumbai: Ramchandra Govind and Son.

Tomlinson, R.A. (1972) *Argos and the Argolid*. Ithaca, NY: Cornell University Press.

Tompkins, P. (1971) *Secrets of the Great Pyramid*. Harmondsworth, UK: Penguin Books.

Tozzer, A.M. (1911) *A Preliminary Study of the Prehistoric Ruins of Tikal, Guatemala*. Cambridge, Mass.: Peabody Museum of Archaeology and Ethnology Memoir 5:2.

Traill, D.A. (1993) *Excavating Schliemann: Collected Papers on Schliemann*. Atlanta: Scholars Press.

——(1995) *Schliemann of Troy: Treasure and Deceit*, 2nd edn. New York: St Martin's Press.

Trigger, B. (1993) *Early Civilizations: Ancient Egypt in Context*. Cairo: American University in Cairo Press.

Tripathi, D.N. (1988) *Archaeology and Tradition*. New Delhi: Ramanand Vidya Bhavan.

——(2002) review of B.B. Lal, *The Sarasvati Flows On: The Continuity of Indian Culture*. New Delhi: Aryan Books International; in *Summerhill. IIAS Review*, Indian Institute of Advanced Research, Simla. vol. VIII, no. 1. Online. Available at http://www.iias-library.org/IIAS%20Review%20Summer%202002/mainpage.htm.

Tritle, L. (1996) "Black Athena: vision or dream of Greek origins?" in M.R. Lefkowitz and G.M. Rogers (eds), *Black Athena Revisited*. Chapel Hill: University of North Carolina Press.

Trulock, A.R. (1992) *In the Hands of Providence: Joshua L. Chamberlain and the American Civil War*. Chapel Hill: University of North Carolina Press.

Tyson, N. deGrasse (2002) "Hollywood nights." *Natural History* (June): 26–31.

Underhill, P.A. (2000) "Y chromosome sequence variation and the history of human populations." *Nature Genetics* 26: 358–61.

van der Veer, P. (1994) *Religious Nationalism: Hindus and Muslims in India*. Berkeley: University of California Press.

van Sertima, I. (ed.) (1983) *Blacks in Science: Ancient and Modern*. New Brunswick, NJ: Transaction Books.

Vasudev, G.D. (2001) "Vedic astrology and pseudo-scientific criticism." *The Organiser* (India), 10 June; reprinted in *The Astrological Magazine* (India), June 2001.

Vats, M.S. (1940) *Excavations at Harappa*. Delhi: Manager of Publications, Government of India.

Veit, U. (1989) "Ethnic concepts in German prehistory: a case study on the relationship between cultural identity and archaeological objectivity," in S.J. Shennan (ed.), *Archaeological Approaches to Cultural Identity*, One World Archaeology 10. London: Unwin Hyman.

——(2002) "Gustaf Kossinna and his concept of a national archaeology," in H. Härke (ed.), *Archaeology, Ideology and Society: The German Experience*. Frankfurt: Peter Lang.

Velikovsky, I. (1950) *Worlds in Collision*. Garden City, NY: Doubleday.

——(1952) *Ages in Chaos*. Garden City, NY: Doubleday.

Venkataraman, R. (2004) "Revamp of education system." *The Hindu*, 27 January, open page. Available at http://www.hindu.com/op/2004/01/27/stories/2004012700671600.htm.

Verner, M. (1997) *The Pyramids*, translated by S. Rendall. New York: Grove Press.

Vivekananda, S. (1970 [1907]) *The Complete Works of Swami Vivekananda*, 8 vols. Calcutta: Advaita Ashrama.

von Däniken, E. (1968a) *Chariots of the Gods? Unsolved Mysteries of the Past*. New York: Berkeley Books.

—(1968b) *In Search of the Gods*. New York: Avenel.

—(1970) *Return to the Stars: Evidence for the Impossible*. London: Corgi Books.

—(1971) *Gods from Outer Space: Return to the Stars, or Evidence for the Impossible*. New York: Putnam.

—(1973a) *The Gold of the Gods*. New York: Putnam.

—(1973b) *In Search of Ancient Gods: My Pictorial Evidence for the Impossible*. London: Book Club Associates.

—(1976) *Miracles of the Gods: A New Look at the Supernatural*. New York: Delacorte Press.

—(1977) *According to the Evidence: My Proof of Man's Extraterrestrial Origins*. London: Souvenir.

—(1996) *The Eyes of the Sphinx: The Newest Evidence of Extraterrestrial Contact in Ancient Egypt*. New York: Berkeley Books.

—(1998a) *Arrival of the Gods: Revealing the Alien Landing Sites of Nazca*. Boston: Element.

—(1998b) *Return of the Gods: Evidence of Extraterrestrial Visitations*. Boston: Element.

—(2000) *Odyssey of the Gods: The Alien History of Ancient Greece*. New York: HarperCollins.

von Stietencron, H. (1989) "Hinduism: on the proper use of a deceptive term," in G. Sontheimer and H. Kulke (eds), *Hinduism Reconsidered*. New Delhi: Manohar Publications.

Wager, S. (1996) *A Doctor's Guide to Therapeutic Touch*. New York: Berkeley Books.

Walker, J. (2002) "Hayden White's *Metahistory*." Available at http://www.stanford.edu/~skij/white.html.

Wall, J. (2002) "Going Orion in a circle." Available at *www.thehallofmaat.com/article16.html*.

Wallis, R. (ed.) (1979) *On the Margins of Science: The Social Construction of Rejected Knowledge*. Sociological Review Monograph 27, Keele, UK: University of Keele.

Waradpande, N.R. (1993) "Fact and fictions about the Aryans," in S.B. Deo and S. Kamath (eds), *The Aryan Problem: Papers Presented at the Seminar on the Aryan Problem Held at Bangalore in July 1991*. Pune: Bharatiya Itihasa Sankalana Samiti.

Warring States Project, "Antiquity frenzy." Available at http://www.umass.edu/wsp/methodology/antiquity/index.html.

Watson, J. (1995) "Postmodernism and knowledge development in nursing." *Nursing Science Quarterly* 8(2): 60–4.

—(1999) *Postmodern Nursing and Beyond*. Edinburgh: Churchill Livingstone.

Watson, J. and Smith, M.C. (2002) "Caring science and the science of unitary human beings: a trans-theoretical discourse for nursing knowledge development." *Journal of Advanced Nursing* 37(5): 452–61.

Wauchope, R. (1965) *They Found the Buried Cities*. Norman: University of Oklahoma Press.

—(1973) *Lost Tribes and Sunken Continents*. Chicago: University of Chicago Press.

Webster, D. (1976) *Defensive Earthworks at Becán, Campeche, Mexico: Implications for Maya Warfare*. New Orleans: Middle American Research Institute Pub. 41.

—(ed.) (1989) *The House of the Bacabs*, Studies in Precolumbian Art and Archaeology no. 29. Washington: Dumbarton Oaks.

—(2000) "The not so peaceful civilization: a review of Maya war." *Journal of World Prehistory* 14(1): 65–117.

—(2001) "Spatial dimensions of Maya courtly life: problems and issues," in T. Inomata and S. Houston (eds), *Royal Courts of the Maya*, Vol. 1. Boulder, Colo.: Westview Press.

—(2002) *The Fall of the Ancient Maya*. London: Thames & Hudson.

Webster, D., Freter, A. and Gonlin, N. (2002) *Copán: The Rise and Fall of an Ancient Maya Center*. Fort Worth: Harcourt Brace.

Weeks, K. (1998) *The Lost Tomb*. New York: William Morrow.

Weil, A. (1998) *The Natural Mind: An Investigation of Drugs and the Higher Consciousness*, revised edn. Boston: Houghton Mifflin.

Weinberg, S. (1992) *Dreams of a Final Theory*. New York: Pantheon.

—(1995) "Reductionism redux." *New York Review of Books* 42(15) (5 October): 39–42.

Wells, P. (1999) *The Barbarians Speak: How the Conquered Peoples Shaped Roman Europe*. Princeton, NJ: Princeton University Press.

—(2003) *The Battle that Stopped Rome: Emperor Augustus, Arminius and the Slaughter of the Legions in the Teutoburg Forest*. New York: W.W. Norton.

Wertheim, M. (1995) "The John Templeton Foundation model courses in science and religion." *Zygon* 30: 491–500.

West, J.A. (1973) *The Case for Astrology*. New York: Viking Press.

—(1993) *Serpent in the Sky: The High Wisdom of Ancient Egypt*, 2nd edn. Wheaton: Quest Books.

West, M.L. (1978) *Hesiod, Works and Days*. Oxford: Clarendon Press.

Wheeler, R.E.M. (1966) *Civilizations of the Indus Valley and Beyond*. London: Thames & Hudson.

Wheen, F. (2004) *How Mumbo-Jumbo Conquered the World*. London: Fourth Estate.

White, H.V. (1973) *Metahistory: The Historical Imagination in Nineteenth-century Europe*. Baltimore: Johns Hopkins University Press.

Whitley, D.S. (1998) *Reader in Archaeological Theory: Post-processual and Cognitive Approaches*. London: Routledge.

Widmer, T. (2003) "Die Kelten: Unsere Vorfahren." *Facts: Das Schweizerische Nachrichtenmagazin* (23 January): 100–6.

Willey, G. (1956) "Problems concerning prehistoric settlement patterns in the Maya lowlands," in G. Willey (ed.), *Prehistoric Settlement Patterns in the New World*. New York: Wenner–Gren Foundation for Anthropological Research.

Willey, G. and Hammond, N. (1979) "Introduction," in N. Hammond and G. Willey (eds), *Maya Archaeology and Ethnohistory*. Austin: University of Texas Press.

Willey, G.R. and Philips, P. (1958) *Method and Theory in American Archaeology*. Chicago: University of Chicago Press.

Williams, B. (2002) *Truth and Truthfulness*. Princeton: Princeton University Press.

Williams, S. (1991) *Fantastic Archaeology: The Wild Side of North American Prehistory*. Philadelphia: University of Pennsylvania Press.

Williams, S.M. (1985) "Holistic nursing," in D. Stalker and C. Glymour (eds), *Examining Holistic Medicine*. Buffalo, NY: Prometheus Books.

Wilson, I. (2002) *Before the Flood*. New York: St Martin's Press.

Wilson, J.A. (1951) *The Burden of Egypt*. Chicago: University of Chicago Press.

Windschuttle, K. (1997) *The Killing of History: How Literary Critics and Social Theorists Are Murdering Our Past*. New York: Free Press.

Witzel, M. (1979) *On Magical Thought in the Veda*. Leiden: Universitaire Press.

—(1984) "Sur le chemin du ciel." *Bulletin des Études Indiennes* 2: 213–79.

—(1987) "On the origin of the literary device of the 'frame story' in old Indian literature," in H. Falk (ed.), *Hinduismus und Buddhismus, Festschrift für U. Schneider*. Freiburg: Hedwig Falk.

—(1989) "Tracing the Vedic dialects," in C. Caillat (ed.), *Dialectes dans les littératures indo-aryennes*. Paris: Edition-diffusion de Brocard.

—(1991) "On Indian historical writing: the case of the Vamsavalis." *Journal of the Japanese Association for South Asian Studies* 2: 1–57.

—(1995) "Early Indian history: linguistic and textual parameters" and "Rgvedic history: poets, chieftains and polities," in G. Erdosy (ed.), *The Indo-Aryans of Ancient South Asia*. Berlin: de Gruyter.

—(1997) "The development of the Vedic canon and its schools: the social and political milieu," in M. Witzel (ed.), *Inside the Texts, Beyond the Texts: New Approaches to the Study of the Vedas*. Cambridge, Mass.: Harvard Oriental Series, Opera Minora, Vol. 2.

—(1999a) "Substrate languages in Old Indo-Aryan (Rgvedic, middle and late Vedic)." *Electronic Journal of Vedic Studies* 5-1: 1–67. Available at http://users.primushost.com/~india/ejvs/issues.html.

—(1999b) "Early sources for South Asian substrate languages." *Mother Tongue* (extra number): 1–70.

—(1999c) "Aryan and non-Aryan names in Vedic India. Data for the linguistic situation, *c.* 1900–500 B.C.," in J. Bronkhorst and M. Deshpande (eds), *Aryan and Non-Aryan in South Asia: Evidence, Interpretation and Ideology*. Cambridge, Mass.: Harvard Oriental Series, Opera Minora, Vol. 3.

—(1999d) "The Pleiades and the Bears, viewed from inside the Vedic texts." *Electronic Journal of Vedic Studies* 5-2. Available at http://users.primushost.com/~india/ejvs/issues.html.

—(2000) "The home of the Aryans," in A. Hintze and E. Tichy (eds), *Anusantatyai: Festschrift für Johanna Narten zum 70. Geburtstag*. Dettelbach: J.H. Roell.

—(2001a) "Autochthonous Aryans? The evidence from old Indian and Iranian texts." *Electronic Journal of Vedic Studies* 7-3: 1–93. Available at http://users.primushost.com/~india/ejvs/issues.html.

—(2001b) "Westward ho! The incredible wanderlust of the Rgvedic tribes exposed by S. Talageri (Saavadhaanapattra no. 2): a review of Shrikant G. Talageri, *The Rigveda: A Historical Analysis*." *Electronic Journal of Vedic Studies* 7-2: 1–29. Available at http://users.primushost.com/~india/ejvs/issues.html.

—(2003a) *Das alte Indien*. Munich: C.H. Beck.

—(2003b) "Ein Fremdling im Rgveda." *Journal of Indo-European Studies* 31: 107–85.

—(2003c) *Linguistic Evidence for Cultural Exchange in Prehistoric Western Central Asia*. Philadelphia: Sino-Platonic Papers 129.

—(forthcoming) "The Rgvedic religious system and its Central Asian and Hindukush antecedents," in A. Griffiths and J.E.M. Houben (eds), *The Vedas: Texts, Language and Ritual*. Groningen: Forsten.

Witzel, M. and Farmer, S. (2000a) "Horseplay in Harappa: the Indus valley decipherment hoax." *Frontline* (India) 13 (October). Available at http://www.frontlineonnet.com/fl1720/fl172000.htm.

—(2000b) "New evidence on the 'Piltdown horse' hoax." *Frontline* (India) (November). Available at http://www.frontlineonnet.com/fl1723/17231260.htm.

Witztum, D., Rips, E. and Rosenberg, Y. (1994) "Equidistant letter sequences in the book of Genesis." *Statistical Science* 9(3): 429–38.

Wolpert, L. (1993) *The Unnatural Nature of Science*. Cambridge, Mass.: Harvard University Press.

Wylie, A. (1992) "The interplay of evidential constraints and political interests: recent archaeological research on gender." *American Antiquity* 57(1): 15–35.

—(2002) *Thinking from Things: Essays in the Philosophy of Archaeology*. Berkeley: University of California Press.

Young, A., Taylor, S.G. and Renpenning, K.M. (2001) *Connections: Nursing Research, Theory, and Practice*. St Louis: Mosby.

Zagorin, P. (1999) "History, the referent, and narrative: reflections on postmodernism now." *History and Theory* 38: 1–24.

—(2000) "Rejoinder to a postmodernist." *History and Theory* 39: 201–9.

Zechenter, E. (1988) "Subsistence strategies in the Supe valley." PhD dissertation, UCLA.

Zimmer, S. (2003) "The easy way to truth: 'heaven does not lie'." *Journal of Indo-European Studies* 30: 401–10.

Index

Related titles from Routledge

Archaeology Coursebook, 2nd Edition
An Introduction to Study Skills, Topics and Methods
Jim Grant, Sam Gorin and Neil Fleming

This fully updated and revised new edition of the bestselling title *The Archaeology Coursebook*, is a guide for students studying archaeology for the first time. Including new methods and case studies in this second edition, it provides pre-university students and teachers, as well as undergraduates and enthusiasts, with the skills and technical concepts necessary to grasp the subject.

Specially designed to assist learning it:

- introduces the most commonly examined archaeological methods, concepts, and themes, and provides the necessary skills to understand them
- explains how to interpret the material students may meet in examinations and how to succeed with different types of assignments and exam questions
- supports study with case studies, key sites, key terms, tasks and skills development
- illustrates concepts and commentary with over 200 photos and drawings of excavation sites, methodology and processes, tools and equipment
- contains new material on British pre-history and the Roman Empire; new case studies, methods, examples, boxes, photographs and diagrams; as well as updates on examination changes for pre-university students.

A book no archaeology student should be without.

Hb: 0-415-36076-5
Pb: 0-415-36077-3

Available at all good bookshops
For ordering and further information please visit:
www.routledge.com

Related titles from Routledge

Archaeology: An Introduction
Fourth Edition
Kevin Greene

'The best one-stop introduction to archaeology.'
Mick Aston, University of Bristol, Time Team

This substantially updated fourth edition of the highly popular, and comprehensive *Archaeology: An Introduction* is aimed at all beginners in the subject. In a lucid and accessible style Kevin Greene takes the reader on a journey which covers history, techniques and the latest theories. He explains the discovery and excavation of sites, outlines major dating methods, gives clear explanations of scientific techniques, and examines current theories and controversies.

This fourth edition constitutes the most extensive reshaping of the text to date. New features include:

- A completely new user-friendly text design with initial chapter overviews and final conclusions, key references for each chapter section, an annotated guide to further reading, a glossary, refreshed illustrations, case studies and examples, bibliography and full index
- A new companion website built for this edition providing hyper-links from contents list to individual chapter summaries which in turn link to key websites and other material
- An important new chapter on current theory emphasizing the rich-ness of sources of analogy or interpretation available today.

Archaeology: An Introduction will interest students and teachers at pre-university and undergraduate level as well as enthusiastic general readers of archaeology. The stimulating coverage of the history, methods, science and theory of archaeology make this a book which has a life both within and beyond the academy.

Hb: 0-415-23354-2
Pb: 0-415-23355-0

Available at all good bookshops
For ordering and further information please visit:
www.routledge.com